Douglas and Rosamond
with best wishes
Bridget

This Master Firebrand

This Master Firebrand

A LIFE OF CHARLES MORDAUNT
3RD EARL OF PETERBOROUGH
1658–1735

Bridget Cameron

MICHAEL RUSSELL

First published in Great Britain 2009
by Michael Russell (Publishing) Ltd
Wilby Hall, Wilby, Nowich NR16 2JP

Typeset in Sabon by Waveney Typesetters
Wymondham, Norfolk
Printed by the MPG Books Group
in the UK

For JTC with love and thanks

Contents

Foreword

The portrait of a bewigged and armoured figure hanging on my grand-mother's dining-room wall was pointed out to me in childhood as 'the third Earl of Peterborough, one of Queen Anne's generals'. This relatively modest claim contrasts with that on the memorial to his daughter, Henrietta Duchess of Gordon, in Elgin Cathedral, 'Charles Mordaunt, Earl of Peterborough and Monmouth, who conquered Spain'. To be Commander-in-Chief of an expeditionary force which made a remarkable capture of Barcelona and thereafter had some success in the kingdom of Valencia hardly amounted to the conquest of Spain but Peterborough's exploits and adventures were legendary in his own lifetime. These adventures reached a wider public with the appearance in 1728 of the first edition of *The Memoirs of Captain Carleton,* a work now considered to have been written by Defoe, probably based on original memoirs. This book introduced Peterborough to later admirers such as Sir Walter Scott and Dr Johnson. But the earl always had his critics. His admirers overdid their praise but equally his detractors went too far in the attempt to demolish his reputation. From the material now available, it is possible to gain a more balanced view. In telling the story of Peterborough's life, I have had access to family papers which have helped to bring out of the shadows his first wife, Carey Fraser. I have also paid more attention to his later diplomatic career in its official and unofficial capacities.

This biography has been a long journey and many of those who helped me along the way may have forgotten they ever did so. I am grateful to the staffs of all the libraries and record offices where I have worked but would like to record particular thanks to the British Library, the Public Record Office, the Kent Archives Office, the Northamptonshire Record Office, the Österreichisches Staatsarchiv and Kriegsarchiv in Vienna and to Sr Verrié and Sra Carmen Gomez of the Museo de la Ciudad, Barcelona. My main research base was the National Library of Scotland where I enjoyed many years of readership; I very much appreciate the help and encouragement I received from the staff then and also more recently. I am grateful to Major Peter

Sturgis for having allowed me to visit Dauntsey Park many years ago. I received help with translation from Mrs Jean de Vink, Dr Edwin Ten Dam and the late Mrs Birgit George. My relatives have helped with some of the illustrations and Lord Langford kindly photographed his portrait of Anastasia Countess of Peterborough for me. Finally, my husband has been a constant companion on the journey; for his help, encouragement and loyalty to the project I am truly grateful.

Edinburgh 2008   BRIDGET CAMERON

Note on Dates

During the period of Peterborough's life, Britain still used the Old Style or Julian Calendar whereas the New Style or Gregorian Calendar was in use in Continental Europe. In the seventeenth century there was a difference of ten days, in the eighteenth century eleven days. Generally dates in Britain are given in Old Style and on the Continent in New Style. Sometimes for clarity both dates are given. Also in Old Style, the New Year began on 25 March, which explains the occasional occurrence of dates such as January 1710/11.

Note on Dates

One

To be born a child of Royalist conspirators in the early months of 1658 was to enter an uncertain and dangerous world. A brief glimmer of expectation had been fanned by the January visit of the exiled King Charles II's emissary, the Marquess of Ormond, who had come to coordinate plans for a rising to take place in March in conjunction with an invasion from across the Channel. John Mordaunt, an active Royalist conspirator, was in frequent touch with Ormond during his visit. He was engaged in recruiting forces for the rising in Surrey and Sussex while, in the midst of the excitement, his wife was expecting their first child in a matter of weeks. A self-confident individual, Mordaunt asked Ormond to find out whether the King would honour them by standing godfather to the expected baby. Charles Mordaunt duly entered this busy world at Berkshire House in London in mid-February. As was the custom, his christening followed very soon after the birth, before there had been any reply from the royal godparent. A proxy stood in for the monarch and John Mordaunt boldly added a reminder of his request to Ormond at the conclusion of his next despatch. Three months later, in very different circumstances, the answer came: 'The King thanks his gossip and has a great mind to see his godson.'

In the event the plans for March came to nothing. The invasion had to be postponed as the English fleet had effectively blockaded the Channel. Government intelligence had been aware that something was afoot. Mordaunt was one of those who fell under suspicion and he was called before the Protector to be questioned about Ormond's visit. He denied any involvement and was discharged but subsequently one of his associates, John Stapley, made a confession implicating both him and others. Mordaunt was arrested and soon found himself in the Tower awaiting trial. His wife voluntarily shared part of his imprisonment, leaving their son to the care of his grandmother, the Dowager Countess of Peterborough.[1]

John Mordaunt, the second son of the first Earl of Peterborough, initially involved himself in the Royalist cause when he joined his elder brother Henry, the second earl, in Lord Holland's rising in 1648. When this venture collapsed, both brothers escaped safely to the Low Countries. Henry suffered the sequestration of his family lands but the penalty did not affect the considerable jointure property of his mother the dowager countess, a staunch Parliamentarian, who supported her younger son from this source. By 1652 John had returned to England and a few years later he began his courtship of his mother's cousin, Elizabeth Carey, whom he married in May 1657. Elizabeth had also spent time in Holland as her stepfather, Sir Edward Herbert, was Attorney-General to the exiled court. She was a friend of the family of Elizabeth Queen of Bohemia, with whom she later corresponded, and her portrait was painted by the talented Princess Louise Palatine.[2]*

John Mordaunt had returned to political activity before his marriage and about a year before Ormond's visit with the intention of raising four or five hundred horse. From that time he maintained regular contact with Royalist agents. After his arrest in May 1658, a special High Court was set up to try him along with Sir Henry Slingsby and Dr Hewet on a charge of treason.

Before the trial took place, the baby Charles Mordaunt made his first recorded public appearance. On his grandmother's instructions, he was taken to the Tower to receive his father's last blessing. When the prisoner was marched out into the Court of Guard, a small group with the child were waiting to meet him. The prisoner removed his hat and solemnly blessed his son, making a poignant speech in which he asked that the child should be educated in his father's principles and religion. He continued that 'though hereafter he came to that end which he was going to, he could not chuse but die happily and nobly'. This little ceremony was said to have profoundly moved even 'the most barbarous'.

Mordaunt's case was heard on 1 and 2 June. The panel of judges consisted of forty members, some of whom had to be persuaded to sit. Mrs Mordaunt, her mother-in-law and their friends were active in trying to raise as much support as possible. The three witnesses called against Mordaunt were John Stapley, his brother Anthony and Captain Mallory. Mallory managed to escape from prison through the connivance of Mordaunt's friends and servants and was not recaptured until after the trial. Anthony Stapley's evidence proved useless and John's lame and uncorroborated. During the trial, one of the judges, Colonel Pride, was taken ill and obliged to leave the court before the

*Elizabeth Carey was painted as Pomona with Prince George of Denmark as Vertumnus. The painting is now at Castle Ward.

vote took place. Mrs Mordaunt saw in this the providence of God. In the event, the bench was equally divided. The President, John Lisle, made his casting vote in Mordaunt's favour, acknowledging some obligation to Lady Peterborough.

But release was only momentary. Annoyed at the outcome of the trial, Cromwell had Mordaunt re-arrested under his military powers. However further attempts to obtain more information from him were unsuccessful and one of his examiners described him as 'a confident resolved cavalier'. He was released on 10 June and surprised his family at Berkshire House by walking in while they were at supper.[3]

After lying low for a few months, Mordaunt renewed his offers of service to the King himself in November 1658. Numerous letters during the ensuing winter bear witness both to his own ceaseless activity as an agent and his wife's loyal support. The Mordaunts received their reward in the spring. In a graceful gesture, the King wrote to Mrs Mordaunt on 21 March 1659 NS thanking her for her service and enclosing a blank warrant for a viscountcy 'to borrow [bestow] upon the person you think fittest to oblige as an earnest of my kindness to you both'.[4]

Mordaunt now received a commission from the King called the Great Trust which was intended to coordinate Royalist activity in England towards a general rising in July 1659. The Trust had thirteen members, of whom five belonged to the Sealed Knot, hitherto the main organisation of conspiracy. It had particular powers to contact persons on the Parliamentary side and one of its members, Lord Willoughby of Parham, was of that persuasion. When the time came, a number of betrayals and a degree of uncertainty caused the rising to be postponed. Only Sir George Booth and his supporters rose in Cheshire, gaining the whole county and part of Lancashire before they were dispersed by a body of troops who took three weeks to reach them. Followed later by his wife, Mordaunt escaped to France and remained abroad for six months. His children, Charles and John, were left to the care of their grandmother, Lady Peterborough, whose estates were now sequestered as her support of her son had become too obvious to be overlooked.

As events moved towards the restoration of the monarchy, Mordaunt worked steadily for the support of the City of London where he had always maintained contacts. His negotiations with the City and his winning over of important Presbyterian peers were his main contributions to the outcome of restoration by agreement rather than force.[5]

On the return of the King, Mordaunt was under no illusion that the rewards for services rendered would be open-handed. He was able to obtain a one third share of a lease of the Newcastle coal farm. This was a profitable concern: by 1679 the income on his share amounted to around £3,000 per annum. Later he was appointed Governor of Windsor Castle and also Lord Lieutenant of Surrey. After the Restoration the Mordaunt family lived at the Villa Carey at Parsons Green, Fulham, a property Lady Mordaunt had inherited from her father, Thomas Carey, who had married Margaret, the daughter of Sir Thomas Smith of Fulham. Here the Mordaunts raised their family of eleven children. Mordaunt was a keen horticulturalist and the gardens were extensive. His method of building 'a neat and useful hot-bed' was acknowledged by John Evelyn, a family friend, in his address to the Royal Society entitled 'A Philosophical Discourse of Earth'. The twenty acres of enclosed ground and the additional forty-four acres of copyhold land included a productive market garden.[6]

By the time Lord Mordaunt had surrendered his governorship to Prince Rupert in September 1668, his son Charles had begun his formal education at Westminster School. Although enrolled among former pupils, there is no record of the date of his arrival nor of whether he was a King's Scholar like his younger brother, Harry. In March 1674 he went up to Christ Church, Oxford. At the beginning of his university career, his mother prayed that his soul might be beautified and that he might be given 'the holiness of David and the wisdom of Solomon'. Neither of these attributes was particularly noticeable in his later life. Like many young men of his background, he never graduated nor is it recorded when he ceased his studies.[7]

In the spring of 1675 the Mordaunts were trying to negotiate a marriage between their son Charles and Lady Bridget Osborne, the daughter of the Earl of Danby. The earl had been instrumental in obtaining for Mordaunt an extension of the lease of the Newcastle coal farm. It would have been an advantageous match both politically and financially. Lady Bridget's portion of £6,000 would have paid off the encumbrances of the Parsons Green property, and in return the young couple would receive Reigate Priory (which had belonged to the Countess of Peterborough) for their maintenance and her jointure. Nothing came of this project.* It may have been affected by Lord Mordaunt's death, after a short illness, on 5 June 1675. Lady Mordaunt faced

*Lady Bridget Osborne married the Earl of Plymouth in September 1678. G. E. C(ockayne), *The Complete Peerage* vol. x, p. 560.

widowhood with a large family, another child expected in December and an encumbered estate. The heir, Charles, inherited the viscountcy at the early age of seventeen.

Leaving Oxford, young Lord Mordaunt went to Paris in February 1676 to finish his education. It was a common procedure in those days for a young nobleman to join an establishment such as Monsieur Foubert's (Protestant) Academy to learn the arts of horsemanship and fencing as well as the social graces. John Evelyn wrote to his saintly friend Mrs Godolphin, already in Paris, 'to have some eye over him'. This unwelcome restraint proved ineffective. The young lord conducted a very public affair with Mistress Moll Kirke;* gossipmongers said they were married but this information turned out to be false. On his return in April 1677 he brought with him from his Paris days a fluency in French which he maintained for the rest of his life.[8]

In May 1677 Mordaunt began his seagoing career. His mother recorded his departure in her diary and although there is a strong tradition that his first expedition took place three years previously, the absence of any diary entry and of concrete supporting evidence suggests that the tradition is untrue. There was already a sailor in the family, Mordaunt's step-uncle, Captain Arthur Herbert, now in command of the *Rupert*. Mordaunt probably sailed with Sir John Narborough for the Straits, joining Herbert's ship when she joined the Straits fleet in November. If Mordaunt remained with the *Rupert*, he would have been present at the encounter in April 1678 with an Algerine man-of-war. In the fighting which ensued, many men were killed and Captain Herbert was wounded, losing the sight of one eye. On the approach of another English ship, the Algerine surrendered. Mordaunt returned to England the next month on board the *Leopard* which was escorting the Straits merchant fleet. Also in the convoy was the Algerine prize, renamed the *Tiger*.

By September Mordaunt had volunteered for a further period of naval service and this time joined the *Bristol* at Portsmouth for his passage out to the Straits. The Revd Henry Teonge was the chaplain on board the *Bristol* and the pages of his diary provide the first glimpse of Charles Mordaunt as an individual. A gentleman volunteer of his rank travelled with four servants and enjoyed the privacy of his own cabin. When the *Bristol* had been at sea for about a week, Mr Teonge was

---

*Moll Kirke was the daughter of George Kirke, Groom of the Bedchamber and Keeper of Whitehall Palace. She married Sir Thomas Vernon in May 1677.

taken ill. Unfortunately his indisposition occurred on a Saturday, 2 November, and appeared likely to affect his Sunday duties. The following day

> the Lord Mordaunt, taking occasion by my not being very well, would have preached, and asked the Captain's leave last night, and to that intent sat up until four in the morning to compose his speech, and intended to have Mr Norwood to sing the Psalm. All this I myself heard in agitation; and, resolving to prevent him, I got up in the morning before I should have done had I had respect to my own health, and came into the great cabin, where I found the zealous Lord with our Captain, whom I did so handle in a smart and short discourse that he went out of the cabin in great wrath. In the afternoon he set one of the carpenter's crew to work about his cabin; and I, being acquainted with it, did by my Captain's order discharge the workman, and he left working; at which the Reverend Lord was so vexed that he borrowed a hammer, and busied himself all that day in nailing up his hangings; but, being done on the Sabbath day, and also when there was no necessity, I hope the work will not be long-lived. From that day he loved neither me nor the Captain.

Mr Teonge's vigorous reaction to Mordaunt's proposal suggests that he had already encountered and disapproved of his religious views. Although reared by devout parents and a Presbyterian grandmother, Mordaunt was not known for much piety in his later life but he was always tolerant of other denominations; religious bigotry was simply not a part of his character.

The *Bristol* reached Cadiz on 22 November and later Mordaunt transferred to his uncle's ship. Herbert was now acting locally as Vice-Admiral of the Straits fleet. The naval life gave Mordaunt the stimulus, excitement and involvement that he always sought. There is no reason to suppose that he did other than remain with the Straits fleet until some time during the winter of 1679–80. When Narborough returned in June 1679, Herbert was left in command. Mordaunt is not recorded as having been present at his mother's funeral in May, nor was he summoned to attend Charles II's fourth Parliament in October although he had attained his majority the previous February. This suggests absence abroad.

By the time he returned to England, the country had survived the Popish Plot and the Exclusion Crisis. The Duke of Monmouth, an immensely popular figure, had returned from exile in Holland while the Duke of York had gone to Scotland as King's Commissioner. Mordaunt, like most of his friends, moved in Court circles. In February 1680 he took part in a duel as second to the Earl of Plymouth. At this time seconds also fought and it was Mordaunt's misfortune to be the only party who was 'shrewdly but not mortally' wounded by his opponent, Lord Cavendish. The quarrel arose over some idle words spoken in the Park by an 'orringe wench' who liked to amuse herself by causing trouble.[9]

Apart from duelling, another way of passing the time was to make up to the Maids of Honour and in Mordaunt's case to Mistress Carey Fraser. In late May 1680 Mrs Fraser was obliged to leave the Court because she was discovered to be pregnant; it was being said that her marriage to Lord Mordaunt would take place shortly, 'my lord seeming to own something of a contract'. Dorothy Countess of Sunderland, a Mordaunt family friend, wrote to her brother, Henry Sidney, Ambassador at The Hague: 'Mrs Fraser has taken her leave at the Court, in order, they say, to being owned my Lady Mordaunt, though yet he denies it, but she and her friends do not; so two deplorable things to two of our prime young lords have happened, his marriage and my Lord Shrewsbury's eye, which is out...'

Whether the marriage took place then or whether, as some biographers have presumed, it took place two years previously, it was in social terms 'deplorable' in comparison to the ambitious union planned for Mordaunt by his parents five years earlier. Carey Fraser came of good family but she brought no property. However it is reasonable to suppose that she was not exactly dowerless. Her father, Sir Alexander Fraser, was Principal Physician to the King and came of an old Scottish family with its roots in the county of Kincardine. Her mother, who had been a wealthy widow at the time of her marriage, was Mary Carey, the fourth daughter of Sir Ferdinando Carey and a second cousin of Elizabeth, Viscountess Mordaunt. Sir Alexander had been awarded a baronetcy by Charles II in acknowledgement of his services to himself and his father. Carey's mother was his second wife and, with the wealth she brought, he had been able to buy back the family lands of Durris.

At the time of her marriage Carey Fraser was about twenty-one years old. Because of her father's employment, her childhood had been spent in the proximity of the Court. Her mother had been appointed a Woman of the Bedchamber and Dresser to the Queen in 1662. Carey herself became a member of the Royal Household in 1674 as a Maid of

Honour to the Queen. Contemporary notices suggest that she was beautiful, vivacious, rather extravagant and ambitious. Her dress for the Queen's Birthday in 1676 caused some comment, as it was said to have cost £300. It was an ensemble of embroidered black velvet, trimmed with ermine and gold lace. Lady Chaworth found herself unable to admire it but wrote of the wearer, 'her face and shape must be aproved by everybody...'[10]

The new Viscountess Mordaunt was pleased with her lot. On her side, she claimed that this love affair led to happiness. In 1707 the bride of 1680 wrote to her husband: 'My dear Life, you once mayd me happy; and 'tis you alone can preserve mee so, by believing I cane die much easier than ever cease loving you...' The partnership thus formed lasted twenty-nine years. It was cemented by a genuine affection and interdependence which survived infidelities and the vicissitudes of fortune.

The couple were well matched in temperament and had much in common, including their friends. Carey was politically alert and supported her husband enthusiastically. In private, she was free with her advice and scolded him when he did not follow it. She gave birth to five children: John was born later in 1680 (he was elected to Parliament in 1701), Henrietta (usually called Harriet) in 1682 and Henry in 1683. There were then two sons, Thomas (1684) and George (1685), neither of whom survived their first year.[11]

If the new Viscountess Mordaunt found happiness, she was soon left to enjoy it by herself. Within two weeks of the dust raised over his marriage, Mordaunt had enlisted to join a relief force going out to Tangier to assist the besieged garrison there. He accompanied his friend the Earl of Plymouth and other young noblemen. Such a venture promised action but it also offered escape. Lady Sunderland certainly thought so; his 'being married few do doubt,' she wrote, 'and that he repents it and is ashamed.'

The expedition under the overall command of the Earl of Mulgrave arrived at Tangier on 2 July. It had left just too soon to hear that a four-month-long truce had been arranged and that there would be no prospect of action before September. In the light of this the commander and some others preferred to return home, but Mordaunt and Plymouth stayed behind, filling in the time sailing with Vice-Admiral Herbert in search of pirates.

Soon after the truce expired on 15 September Mordaunt joined a reconnaissance party sent to inspect forts which had been recently in enemy hands. When found to be deserted, the forts were garrisoned by a detachment of 500 men under the command of Colonel Sackville. Mordaunt, Plymouth and others joined the garrison. This military activity provoked an attack by the Moors. In the ensuing action which lasted several days, the young lords were in the forefront and behaved with bravery to the point of rashness.

During this expedition the Earl of Plymouth contracted a 'violent flux' from which he suffered for almost a month before dying at Tangier on 17 October. It was a sad conclusion. Sir Palmes Fairborne wrote to the Secretary of State: 'My Lord Mordaunt, who comes along with the body of his friend, deserves his Maty's and Your Hon.'s kind reception, having shown on all occasions both on horseback and on foot actions of courage suitable to the family from whence he comes...' With this kind commendation, Mordaunt reached Cadiz on 5 November. There Lord Plymouth's body was transferred to the *Foresight* which left for England on 15 November. It was a sobering homecoming in December for Mordaunt and a prelude to acknowledging the responsibilities of a father and a peer of the realm.[12]

Two

Mordaunt's political career began in December 1680 when he took his seat in the House of Lords in place of his father. His royal godfather was present as he took the oaths and subscribed the declaration necessitated by the Test Act. From his first days in Parliament he ranged himself with the Country party, soon to be known as Whigs, under their leader, the Earl of Shaftesbury. This was no revolt or departure: the late Lord Mordaunt had been allied with Shaftesbury, as were many former Royalists who had been disappointed with their rewards after the Restoration. Charles Mordaunt was taking his place among his father's political associates. It is not known when his political interests were first kindled but in this company he would have learned the principles of constitutional government; almost certainly his friendship with John Locke dated from these days.[1]

With Shaftesbury and others, Mordaunt signed the petition against the calling of Parliament at Oxford instead of London, but when the petition was unsuccessful he went there in a party surrounding the Duke of Monmouth which was accommodated in Balliol College. The Oxford Parliament was of short duration. From one of the few letters which survive from this period in Mordaunt's life, it appears that he already felt himself part of the opposition and was looking round for new areas of employment. He wrote to his uncle, Admiral Herbert:

> I am called one of the discontented and factious, but am glad to be sure you are of my mind in this; there is no tye but honour and gratitude. I am sure you, as little as anybody, can bear ill-usage and contempt, and since I never could deserve a good word from the King, nor ever had any obligation from White Hall, whatsoever your thoughts are you will allow me the liberty of mine, and not confound as some do betwixt public and privat concerns...[2]

Mordaunt had not outgrown a fondness for idle pranks and involving himself with other people's quarrels. His penchant for breaking windows was a futile activity, a symptom of the problem that there were not enough serious calls on his time. To one who in middle age was noted for ceaseless activity, enforced idleness in the full vigour of youth must have been frustrating in the extreme. There was not even the routine attendance at Parliament to occupy the winter, since the King showed a marked disinclination to continue the sitting of any Parliament called.

Since no 'obligation from White Hall' could be expected, Mordaunt took steps to find employment elsewhere. Before the sitting of the Oxford Parliament, he had made a very significant move. On 23 February 1681 the Earl of Sunderland wrote to his young uncle, Henry Sidney, English Ambassador to the United Provinces: 'My Lord Mordaunt has desired me to write to you to recommend him to the Prince of Orange as a young man very desirous to serve him, if he thought him capable of it. I told him I would do it, and it could not but be well taken, but that I thought the first employment that fell his Highness might already be engaged to dispose of...' In May Sidney was able to report that the Prince was willing to have Mordaunt 'if he comes to Court'.

It is tempting to suggest that Mordaunt's request was shrewdly far-sighted. It was certainly prudent to offer one's services to the husband of the Princess who stood second in succession to the throne. The right of the Princess of Orange had been discussed frequently by the Exclusionists, as ways were canvassed of by-passing the Duke of York's succession. To some, the Prince of Orange himself was a suitable candidate.

Personal advantage would have been uppermost in Mordaunt's mind. Public service was the only way for a nobleman to achieve advancement and further honours, particularly in the tangible forms of land and wealth – unless he could acquire these through marriage. Another pressing consideration was the opportunity for activity in a fresh field. Many young Englishmen entered military service in Holland, particularly in one of the six British regiments in the Dutch service which were responsible to the States General.

However it may not have been military service that Mordaunt had in mind. In June of that year it was revealed that he had acquired a ship at Deptford. It was not a yacht; it bore all the appearance of a frigate. Rumour was rife as to the ship's origin and particularly her purpose. It was believed that Mordaunt had acquired her from the executors of the rich East India merchant Sir William Courteen, and that she was to be used for reprisals against the Dutch. Given Mordaunt's recent overtures, this purpose seems unlikely. The Spanish Ambassador complained to the King that he had heard that the ship was designed for the Elector of

Brandenburg's service. Other rumours suggested she might be sailed to the Straits.

In the event, his lordship was summoned to Whitehall to give an account of himself and his ship. His bland explanation, that a vessel of fifty guns and three hundred men enabled one to sail without the necessity of a convoy for protection against pirates, was not enough to allay suspicion. An embargo was placed on the ship; for weeks she remained at Woolwich, ready to sail.[3]

During July 1681 William of Orange paid a brief visit to Whitehall. In view of his earlier contacts, it would have been surprising if Mordaunt had failed to pay his respects. One may speculate also whether such a meeting had any bearing on Mordaunt's decision to make his peace with Whitehall and wait upon the King. On 29 August, having duly 'submitted himself and kissed the King's hands', he then talked to His Majesty in his closet for almost two hours and was said to have made 'great discoveries'. The embargo on his ship was lifted.

Whether or not Mordaunt made a voyage at this juncture (he was at Newmarket in October), the new ship, which was named the *Loyall Mordaunt* and emblazoned with the Mordaunt arms, received royal approval in person on 10 November. Accompanied by several courtiers, the King dined on board while the ship lay at anchor in Long Reach. Mordaunt was always an affable and charming host, at ease with all ranks. The entertainment offered was obviously enjoyable, as the King arrived three hours late for a meeting with the Treasury Lords.[4]

It is not known how much sailing Mordaunt managed to do with his man-of-war. He was probably at sea in the Channel shortly after the royal visit but his original schemes may have been abandoned after his reconciliation with the Court. The ownership of such a vessel was an expensive hobby. Certainly there were problems over payment of the crew's wages. In 1683 the ship was bought by the Admiralty and subsequently listed as 'H.M.S. Mordaunt, fourth rate'.*[5]

Now in the sunshine of royal favour, there was speculation that Mordaunt might become a Commissioner of the Admiralty. This proved unfounded. But he did make use of the royal favour to beg for the same state of grace for his friend the Duke of Monmouth. Catching the King 'accidently in his closet', he pleaded Monmouth's cause until midnight, in two hours of hard talking, but without success.

---

*A model of the *Loyall Mordaunt* may usually be seen in the National Maritime Museum, Greenwich. Under war conditions, her maximum complement was 230 men and 46 guns.

Since the Court was now a welcoming place, it was time for a very belated debut. In December 1681 it was noted: 'Lord Mordaunt has brought out as well as owned his lady.' Lady Mordaunt had lost her father earlier in the year and was now expecting her second child, Harriet, who was born in April.[6]

Mordaunt was also engaged in important family business at this time. After his mother's death in 1679, her trustees found themselves attempting to administer a bankrupt estate; it was not possible to satisfy the daughters' portions let alone the many legacies. Perhaps in anticipation of this, Lady Mordaunt had left directions in her will that the Parsons Green property should be sold. A possible sale in April 1680 fell through, but in October 1681 Mordaunt offered to provide £2,000 to cover his brothers' and sisters' portions if the trustees would settle on him outright Parsons Green and his mother's share of the Newcastle coal farm. During the Michaelmas term of 1681, Mordaunt sold Reigate Priory and its lands to John Parsons, a London brewer who later became Lord Mayor. In March 1682 the Lord Chancellor ordered the trustees to make over to Mordaunt all his mother's real and personal estate, subject only to certain annuities, in return for the payment of all debts, portions and legacies remaining unpaid from her estate. Hence Mordaunt obtained the property which would be his main residence for most of his life and where, like his father before him, his love of horticulture would find its chief outlet.[7]

Mordaunt's presence in the party which surrounded the Duke of Monmouth involved him in the furore which followed the attack on Thomas Thynne of Longleat on 12 February 1682. 'Tom of Ten Thousand' was returning from the Park when three armed men rode up at the corner of Pall Mall and St Albans Street and fired into the carriage, mortally wounding him. Sir John Reresby, a justice of the peace, was called, search warrants issued and a hue and cry ensued in which both the Duke of Monmouth, a close friend of Thynne who had left the carriage moments before the attack, and Lord Mordaunt took part. Arrests were eventually made of three men who proved to be the servants of Count Königsmarck, a Swedish adventurer.

The previous year Königsmarck had been one of the suitors for the hand of Lady Ogle, the teenage widow and Percy heiress. However the Countess of Northumberland had other plans for her granddaughter: Lady Ogle was to be married secretly to Thomas Thynne of Longleat. The bride was not a willing party to the contract and defected within hours of the ceremony. Königsmarck, it seemed, was now taking the revenge of a disappointed suitor.

The Count was arrested at Gravesend but at the subsequent trial his servants were sentenced to death while he was acquitted of all involvement. Thynne's friends felt that justice had not been done. Lord Cavendish, always keen for a fight, with Mordaunt as his second, sent a challenge to Königsmarck in Flanders. Unfortunately the reply was opened and the authorities alerted. Both lords were called before the Deputy Earl Marshal and asked to give their word that they would not prosecute the matter. Later the ports were stopped and a writ issued preventing them leaving and obliging them each to give security of £1,000.[8]

There is no evidence that Mordaunt was involved in any of the plans of insurrection subsequently concocted by the Earl of Shaftesbury, nor that he accompanied Monmouth to Cheshire on the progress which led to the duke's arrest as a disturber of the peace. Nor is it clear whether or not he ever broke his new-found easy relationship with the Court; on the contrary, one author considered that he may have been the 'friend at Court' who warned Shaftesbury of his imminent arrest in November 1682, thus enabling him to escape abroad.

In June 1683 the Rye House Plot, a plan to assassinate the King and the Duke of York, was uncovered. Subsequently several leading Whigs were arrested and tried. Lord Russell was executed in July and, in the same month, the Earl of Essex committed suicide in prison. Algernon Sidney was also arrested but was not tried and executed until December.

There is no record that Mordaunt was in any way involved in the Plot and no suggestion to that effect made by anyone except himself. If the aged memory of Henrietta, Countess of Suffolk, may be relied upon, she recalled in 1761 that she had either read in the memoirs of the Earl of Peterborough, or the earl had told her, that he had been very much involved as a young man with Lord Russell and Algernon Sidney. Having picked up some letters which had been discarded from the Duchess of Portsmouth's apartments as waste paper, he became aware that one of his Whig associates was passing information to the Court. Through the good offices of a maid, he concealed himself in the duchess's apartments in order to observe who visited her. Lord Howard of Escrick turned out to be one of her callers. Lord Howard was implicated in the Plot and later turned evidence. Mordaunt then retired to the country until the storm had died down.

In September 1683 Mordaunt applied for, and was granted, a pass to travel to Holland in the company of another Whig, Sir Rowland

Gwynne. John Locke was another of the same political persuasion who felt it wise to make a more discreet departure earlier in the same month. It is probable that Mordaunt returned to England before Sidney's execution on 7 December. There is a tradition that he accompanied his friend on the day of his death but this is not substantiated by contemporary accounts. Lady Suffolk recalled that Mordaunt and Henry Sidney sat up part of the night with Algernon before his execution.

The interest Mordaunt showed in republicanism at the time of the Revolution of 1688 may have been derived from Sidney's influence. The death of Shaftesbury the previous January and the punitive effects of the uncovering of the Plot left the Whig party in disarray. It was confidently reported in March 1684 that Mordaunt was expected to be at the opening of the Spanish Campaign in Flanders but further details do not appear. The record remains silent on his movements for the rest of the reign.[9]

When Charles II died on 6 February 1685, his brother James succeeded him without incident or dispute. The new King called a Parliament which met on 19 May. Mordaunt put in an irregular attendance. He remained aloof from Monmouth's rising in June: only two Whig peers, Lord Grey and Lord Delamere, were involved. Affecting only the West Country and Cheshire, the rebellion was easily crushed by the available army units assisted by the militia but it strained the military resources of the country to their limits. It was not surprising that the King's speech to Parliament in November 1685 should stress the importance of the improvement and increase of the permanent armed forces both for defence and the prevention of insurrections. Both during the emergency and afterwards, the King had employed several Catholic officers who were legally able to serve for only three months before submitting to the Test. It was noted with concern that James had no intention of parting with good men who had served him well.

When unease over the increase of a standing army was voiced in the Lords, the House was informed that it was out of order to criticise a King's speech for which thanks had already been tendered. This view met with opposition from various peers and the Bishop of London, Henry Compton, moved that a day be appointed to consider the King's speech. He was supported by the Marquess of Halifax, the Earl of Sunderland and also Lord Mordaunt in a maiden speech in which 'he spake handsomely'. The motion was carried and the speech put down for a debate which never took place as the King, displeased at the turn of events, prorogued Parliament.[10]

[15]

Described by a contemporary biographer of James II as 'always of a turbulent and factious spirit and incapable of doing good', Mordaunt appeared to have no difficulty in obtaining a pass to travel abroad in August 1686 and spent the next two months in Holland. His wife's aunt, Simona Carey, had married the English Ambassador to the United Provinces, Bevil Skelton, and the contact was useful.

Mordaunt made the most of his time in Holland. He visited the Prince of Orange at Het Loo, and there met and befriended various members of the Prince's court, including Hans Willem Bentinck. On his return he began to correspond with Bentinck at least as 'brothers gardeners', although too much talk of plants and flowers would make 'les pénétrants' look for a mystery. It was quite common at this time to use such terminology, or often that of trade, as a blind for political information. Mordaunt also visited Utrecht, a favourite haunt of Whig refugees and where John Locke was staying at the time. He also became acquainted with Benjamin Furly, a Quaker merchant living in Rotterdam. Meanwhile at the Court in England, letters were being discussed which told of Mordaunt's treatment as an honoured guest by William, who spent long hours in conversation with him. Judging by his behaviour in the last Parliament, it was suggested that he was treating with William on behalf of the opposition.[11]

Gilbert Burnet stated in his *History* that Mordaunt was the first of the English nobility to cross openly to see the Prince of Orange. He wrote that it was in 1686 that Mordaunt pressed the Prince 'to undertake the business of England... he represented the matter as so easy, that this appeared too romantical to the Prince to build upon it.' The Prince promised to watch the situation, to take action if the King changed the established religion, tried to deny the Princess's right of succession or raise forged plots in order to destroy his friends. Beyond this, the Prince allowed Mordaunt to talk. Burnet gave a character-study of Mordaunt: 'He was a man of much heat, many notions, and full of discourse; he was brave and generous; but he had not true judgement; his thoughts were crude and indigested; and his secrets were soon known.'

Mordaunt's return to England on 12 October, after a rough crossing of three days, was followed by tales of his activities in Holland. Among groups of political exiles it was not unheard of for some members to use their inside knowledge to inform against others for the purpose of financial gain. Later that month a story was current in London that an Englishman living in Utrecht had laid information on oath before Bevil

Skelton regarding Mordaunt's activities, claiming to know him well. Mordaunt confronted the informant incognito, heard the story repeated to his face and then revealed his identity. Having mistaken his man, the embarrassed informant withdrew his allegations. By November the story had lost nothing in the telling and a fuller, more detailed and perhaps embroidered version appeared. Whatever the truth of the matter, it indicated that Mordaunt's conversations with the Prince of Orange were the subject of talk and speculation in Holland as well as at home.[12]

If Mordaunt had been asking the Prince to intervene with an armed force at this particular time, his judgement was at fault. There was insufficient cause and the build-up of support for William, both in the United Provinces and in England, had yet to take place. Why should Mordaunt ask now for William's intervention? A clue to his thinking may be found in part of his maiden speech in the House of Lords. There he referred to the existence of a standing army, partly officered by Catholics who could not be continued in their employment without a change in the law. To keep an army in being, while there was no war either within or without, was to establish arbitrary government, the concept of which was abhorrent to Englishmen. Mordaunt sought William's support against the establishment of such a government.

The summer of 1686 had seen a court decision supporting the King's dispensing power in the case of Sir Edward Hales. In June a military camp had been set up on Hounslow Heath and this was regarded with grave suspicion. The Ecclesiastical Commission had been established to reform spiritual abuses; also Henry Compton, Bishop of London, had been suspended for failing to punish a clergyman in his diocese who preached an anti-Catholic sermon. To the imaginative Protestant, these moves smacked of absolutism and a threat to the established religion. The Protestant interest was in need of a head.[13]

During the winter of 1686–7 the King continued to press for the repeal of the penal laws against Catholics and the Test Act. The methods he used involved private conversations in his closet with peers and members of Parliament. Those who did not agree with his views, or come round to his way of thinking, were dismissed from their employments and their places filled by Catholics. Those who were approached by the King knew that they stood to lose if they did not comply. In an unexpected move, Admiral Herbert, Mordaunt's step-uncle, stood out against the King and was dismissed from his post in March 1687. Herbert had owed his position and advancement entirely to James.

Mordaunt wrote: 'Mon oncle Herbert a surpris tout le monde; cett un parent gagné pour moy; il y a longtemps que je ne luy avois point parlé, mais nous somme bon amys, et la conduite de la Cour a son égard a fait un très bon effet...'

In November 1686 William Penn the Quaker was sent over to The Hague to persuade William of the necessity of his support for religious toleration but William maintained that the repeal of the Test Act was a matter for Parliament and would not interfere. Mordaunt, along with several others, kept up a correspondence with The Hague during this winter, although communications were infrequent because of the necessity to exercise discretion.

In February 1687 William of Orange sent over Everard van Weede van Dijkvelt on a mission to James II, in part at least to assure him of his committed views regarding the Test Act. Dijkvelt's other unofficial remit was to test opinion among the nobility. The true purpose of the visit, which lasted three months, was a matter for general speculation. The envoy entertained generously, particularly 'those that the Court thinks worst affected'. His meetings with Mordaunt and his associates were of necessity kept secret. He returned to Holland in June, taking with him his impressions of the political situation.[14]

In July 1687 Mordaunt was given further official permission to travel abroad and was back and forth to Holland, this time accompanied by his wife. On 2 August he entered into a partnership with twelve other individuals 'for the raising a joint stock of £6,400 for an undertaking to the West Indies'. Mordaunt himself subscribed for twelve shares, investing £2,400 in the venture. The next largest shareholder was Sir Dalby Thomas with six shares. The rest of the partners had either one or two shares each. It appears that Mordaunt had interested the Prince of Orange in the project and his large share may have reflected the Prince's involvement. It seemed that the purpose of the venture was to look for treasure on a Spanish wreck which had lain for forty-two years off the island of Hispaniola. Previous expeditions had proved worthwhile and the wreck was still thought to be a fruitful source. At the end of August Sir John Narborough set sail on board the *Foresight* for this fishing-ground. His departure, with the prospect of competition, prompted a cautious letter from Mordaunt to William on 4 September OS.

Sir, if as to that particular affair I had the honour to give your Highness an account of, (and that you were pleased frankly to engage in) my expectations are so far diminished, that I think myself obliged to own I am become very doubtful of the success of it, and for that reason must rather dissuade from, than persuade to the expense those for whom I have, and ought to have the last respect, and whose interest I would manage with a tenderness, equal to my desire of serving them, yet I think myself sufficiently recompensed for any private disappointment by the prospect of public affairs, and the hopes I have your Highness' interest increases every day more and more in strength, and do not doubt will grow stronger even by the endeavours of the court to weaken it and be past being shaken by their tricks or by their power...I flatter myself I shall not be long absent from Loo, my old passport stands good still, (my dear Roman Catholic friends not being able to quit their greedy hopes, but persisting in their desires to me, and entreating me every hour to proceed in this affair, though I fear, not with good reason of their side...)

This letter has been taken to refer to Mordaunt's withdrawal of his invitation to William to undertake 'the business of England', but read in the context of the West Indian expedition this seems unlikely. In April William had told Pensionary Fagel about Mordaunt's proposal and it was planned to use a small squadron of Dutch ships. Mordaunt's 'Catholic friends' presumably had a financial interest in the expedition, but their encouragement may reflect an extra motive, the removal of this troublemaker from the scene for a time. Almost on receipt of this letter, William wrote to Bentinck indicating that he was prepared to risk the plan if Job de Wildt, the Secretary to the Admiralty, was in favour of it. In November, two months late, great quantities of provisions and baggage were loaded on board ship at Amsterdam. The three vessels were joined by a man-of-war and when a contrary wind turned in early December the squadron was on its way.[15]

Shortly after Mordaunt's departure, the *Endeavour* was sent to warn Narborough of the coming competition. The West Indies were unprepared for the arrival of the Dutch squadron. The Governor of the Leeward Islands, Sir Nathaniel Johnson, was taken by surprise when three ships sailed by on 2 February and anchored in the old roadstead at St Christopher's. He kept the island on the alert under arms all night, until a message from Lord Mordaunt the following day indicated peaceable intentions and made a request for wood and water. Mordaunt also stated his intentions regarding the wreck which he considered available to any who might come. Opposition would, if necessary, be countered by force.

It was thought at the time that this treasure-hunt was a blind for another motive. The motive has never emerged; as a search for treasure, the expedition was a total failure. Narborough courteously invited some of Mordaunt's officials to view the wreck but they were inexperienced, ill-equipped and the sea rough, so they saw little. Mordaunt then sailed to the Bay of Samara, where he had a friendly encounter with Captain Wright of the *Assistance* and a yacht belonging to the Governor of Jamaica, the Duke of Albemarle. After April, no one heard any more about him and it was presumed he had sailed for home. That William had sent him to find out Narborough's views on the loyalty of the Navy or to test the loyalty of the West Indian colonies is a possibility which cannot be ruled out.[16]

Three

Mordaunt had returned to England from the West Indian expedition by mid-July 1688 and soon crossed to Holland with his wife and family. By this time William had decided that he would invade England later in the year, provided that he received an invitation to do so with definite promises of support. Following the trial of the seven bishops and the birth of the Prince of Wales, the invitation was duly forthcoming and signed in a prearranged code by the Earls of Devonshire, Danby and Shrewsbury, Lord Lumley, Henry Compton Bishop of London, Edward Russell and Henry Sidney. In July Admiral Herbert, disguised as an ordinary seaman, crossed to Holland with the invitation in his pocket.[1]

Meanwhile James II had steadily refused to believe that William was preparing to invade England, despite repeated warnings from the French, but in September he announced that an invasion was expected and recalled the recently issued writs for a new Parliament.

At the end of September William published a declaration of his reasons for invasion. Drafts of this document were shown to various people. John Wildman, the Republican pamphleteer, criticised it and offered alterations which were supported by Lord Mordaunt and the Earl of Macclesfield. This was the first time, but by no means the last, that Mordaunt's name was linked with that of Wildman. This old Cromwellian soldier wished to fix the blame for the public grievance against the Crown in England squarely on the shoulders of the government in the reign of Charles II. He defended James's use of his prerogative, an unlikely attitude for a man of republican views, and this made Burnet suspect that he had an ulterior motive. Wildman's version of the declaration would have antagonised the Church of England and his old enemies, the Anglican Tories, and would have given the invasion a specifically Whig colour. This was a divisiveness which William was particularly anxious to avoid. An acceptable compromise was eventually reached. The final document blamed James's evil counsellors for the troubles and claimed that William's invasion was intended to ensure the election of a free parliament, a cause which would unite all parties. The compromise appeared to satisfy Mordaunt and Macclesfield, who had threatened to abandon the enterprise if their views were not accepted. Mordaunt at this time appeared a radical Whig; William and many others were inclined to suspect him of republican tendencies.[2]

It was not possible for William to embark on any foreign undertaking while a French army remained near the Low Countries threatening invasion. On 17/27 September, Louis XIV diverted his army to attack Philippsburg on the Rhine, believing that William would never set out so late in the season. With this danger out of the way, William could now sail for England. The first departure on 20 October OS met with violent storms in which some ships were damaged and horses lost. The fleet was ordered back to port for repairs but set out again on 1 November. In England all references to the forthcoming invasion included Mordaunt's name in the list of those leading the expedition, along with Henry Sidney, Admiral Herbert and the Earls of Wiltshire and Macclesfield. In fact Admiral Herbert had overall command under William with the rank of Lieutenant Admiral-General.

The fleet, which consisted of about 400 vessels, had set out for the second time in a northerly direction but a brisk wind soon developed which caused the ships to alter course for the English Channel. The same wind hindered the English fleet, at present in the Gunfleet, from emerging from behind the sandbanks to intercept them. William's fleet was blown steadily on down Channel past the Isle of Wight until the wind slackened and veered to allow the ships to sail easily into Torbay, one of the safe landings of the West Country. Bells rang out in celebration on 5 November as William came ashore. It was the anniversary of the discovery of the Gunpowder Plot.[3]

William's army consisted of approximately 15,000 foot and 3,000 horse. It contained many nationalities, both Catholic and Protestant, and some were mercenaries. Most of the foot were British or Dutch and included the six regiments of the Anglo-Dutch brigade.[4]

Contemporary accounts pay attention to the persons of note, and often notoriety, who accompanied the Prince and whose names were familiar to the public ear. Many had left England or Scotland in the previous ten years for reasons of safety, banishment or discontent, and their return was of more than usual interest. They have been described as including among them 'enough disreputable types to disturb any decently run kingdom that did not happen to agree with them - disgruntled peers, redundant MPs, proclaimed traitors, escaped spies, fugitive rebels, suspected republicans, renegade officers and mischievous divines'. The name of the Viscount Mordaunt appears early in most accounts, together with those of the Earls of Shrewsbury, Macclesfield and Wiltshire, Sir Robert Peyton, Dr Burnet, Sir William Waller, William Harbord, Robert Ferguson, William Carstares, Edward Russell and Henry Sidney.[5]

The army began to move in the direction of Exeter on 6 November. Lord Mordaunt and Dr Burnet were in the van when it reached the city two days later. They found that the gates had been shut on the orders of the magistrates. Mordaunt ordered that they be opened, with the penalty of death for non-compliance. The threat was effective. The Bishop of Exeter had left on hearing of William's approach and the Dean hurried away from the Deanery, thus leaving vacant accommodation for the reception of the Prince. Mordaunt demanded and obtained the release of one Hicks, who had brought the news of the Prince's landing. William and his troops remained at Exeter until 21 November. Meanwhile James had ordered his army to move towards Salisbury Plain to check William's advance.[6]

William had brought with him equipment and arms for many more men than were already under his command; he eventually granted seven commissions to form regiments. The first three commissions issued were given to Viscount Mordaunt, Sir Robert Peyton and Sir John Guise. These colonels were all particular in their choice of men and their regiments took shape slowly. There was no lack of volunteers. On 10 November the first commissions to officers in Mordaunt's regiment were handed out. At this time he only had nine captains out of the eventual total of thirteen and these included his brother, Lewis, and Robert, the son of Sir Philip Monckton. (The rest of the commissions, to make up the full complement, were not dated until 31 December.) Mordaunt was quick to note that other foot regiments were able to form only six or eight companies out of twelve. Bentinck considered his selectivity gave hopes of a very fine regiment.

Although busy with his regiment, Mordaunt was always as near as possible to the hub of activity and was known widely as a member of the Privy Council which advised the Prince and met daily. The other members of this Council were the Earls of Shrewsbury, Macclesfield, Abingdon and Wiltshire, Viscount Colchester, Lord Cornbury, the Hon. Edward Russell (son of the Earl of Bedford), Henry Sidney, Thomas Wharton, Sir John Hotham, Edward Russell, William Harbord and William Jephson. Shrewsbury, Henry Sidney and Edward Russell were three of the 'Immortal Seven' signatories of the invitation to William. All the Council members were Whigs, with the exception of the Earl of Abingdon and Lord Cornbury. Abingdon had joined William at Exeter, arriving on 14 November, and contributed a large sum (£30,000) to his cause.[7]

Although local interest had been cautious and limited at first, a good number of West Country gentry had now joined the Prince. At Exeter, Sir Edward Seymour suggested to William that his supporters should sign an Association, a promise to defend his life and cause, which would bind them together with a community of purpose; otherwise they would be 'as a rope of sand'. Signature of the Association became a test of good faith towards the cause. Also at Exeter, William received encouraging news that Lord Delamere had risen in his support in Cheshire and the Earls of Danby and Devonshire had been active around Nottingham. He was nonetheless disappointed at the absence of large numbers of defecting royal troops; on the other hand, volunteers were so numerous that he had to put a stop to recruitment.[8]

James left London on 17 November to join his army. A council was held to decide whether the troops should advance or withdraw. The decision for the latter movement seemed to trigger defections including that of Lord Churchill, the Duke of Grafton and Colonel Berkeley who were followed soon afterwards by Prince George of Denmark and others. The King returned to London when the van of the Prince's army approached Salisbury and on 27 November summoned a Great Council of peers temporal and spiritual who happened to be in town. About forty lords appeared and, in the emergency of the moment, were free in their advice. 'Many bold and home Things were s'd before him wch he heard wth some uneasiness.' The peers urged the calling of a Parliament. They advised that commissioners should be sent to treat with the Prince of Orange, without whose cooperation no Parliament could assemble to the satisfaction of everyone. The King took time to consider but eventually agreed to these requests. The Marquess of Halifax, the Earl of Nottingham and Lord Godolphin were appointed commissioners to go to the Prince. Instructions were given for writs to be issued for a Parliament to be summoned on 15 January. In addition, the King offered a general pardon to those who had taken arms against him.

William was staying at Berwick St Leonard's when he issued passes to the King's commissioners. He also received the Dutch Ambassador from London who was able to tell him what was happening in the capital. The Earl of Clarendon arrived and was able to answer William's questions about the council of peers. He assured him that, if he adhered to his Declaration, most people were of the opinion that 'he might hope to see a happy settlement'.[9]

On 4 December William moved in towards Salisbury then crossed the Plain, reaching Hungerford on 7 December. Here he received the King's Commissioners in the presence of all the peers in his entourage. The Commissioners were asked to put the King's proposals in a written statement and when this was presented it contained for the most part a list of conditions to be met to allow a free Parliament to assemble.

William summoned a council of lords and gentlemen, 'all the persons of any quality save those of the Scotch or Irish nation', to consider the proposals, while he himself retired to Littlecote. With the Earl of Oxford reluctantly in the chair, those assembled began to discuss methods of ensuring that the meeting of Parliament was both free and safe. Gradually it became clear that many of those present did not want this Parliament to meet at all and would prefer that the writs issued should be superseded. After much discussion, the council produced its own list of proposals to be sent to the King, including a clause about the supersession of the writs. When William saw the proposals, he accepted them all except the clause about the writs which he wanted removed. There was further debate but William remained adamant. 'We may drive away the King,' he said, 'but perhaps we may not know how easily to come by a Parliament.' After another debate in William's presence, the clause was finally struck out.

William's requests and proposals were not alarming nor unexpected and avoided all mention of controversial matters. He demanded the dismissal from public positions of Papists and others not qualified by law, the recall of proclamations issued against his followers and himself, the release of any who had been arrested for assisting him and the conveyance into safe hands of the Tower of London, Tilbury and Portsmouth. If the King wished to remain in London for the calling of Parliament, William would be there too with a similar number of guards. Otherwise each might remain an equal distance away from the capital at a place of the King's choice. Both armies should remain thirty miles away from London and no more foreigners (e.g. Irish) were to be admitted to the forces. Finally, and prudently, William and his army were to be maintained at the public expense until the meeting of Parliament.[10]

Letters already sent to the King by his Commissioners, before they had heard William's answers, had done little to reassure him. Even before he received the answers, James seemed to have given up hope of a reasonable solution and to have made up his mind to leave the country. On 9 December he sent the Queen and his son away to France in the charge of the Comte de Lauzun. The next day he cancelled and burned the writs for the general election and secretly prepared for his own departure. That evening William's proposals reached him. It was too late; the King merely remarked that he would answer them in the morning. Late that night, with Sir Edward Hales and Ralph Sheldon, he quietly left the Palace on the first stage of his journey to join his wife. Crossing to Vauxhall, James dropped the Great Seal into the river. It was found by a fisherman the following May 'over against the lime killnes'.[11]

When the news of the King's flight reached William, he was at Abingdon on his way to Oxford. He immediately changed course and made for Wallingford on the road to London.

The peers who had gathered in London in response to the King's summons, constituted themselves into a sort of provisional government. They met at the Guildhall for reasons of security and so that they could take the necessary steps to maintain calm in the City in the face of renewed anti-Catholic disturbance. Both they and the City of London sent messages to William which reached him at Henley on 16 December. The peers sent a copy of a Declaration they had issued, on the King's having withdrawn himself, in which they resolved to approach the Prince of Orange and undertook to support his endeavours for the calling of a free Parliament. In order to preserve peace and security, they proposed to disarm Papists and secure Jesuit priests.

William seemed unimpressed with the Declaration. It was noted that he gave a much warmer reception to a letter from the Lord Mayor and Corporation which was couched in a more laudatory vein; the letter concluded by issuing an invitation to the Prince 'to repaire to this City, where your Highnesse will be received with universall joy and satisfaction'.

While representatives of the peers and the City were delivering their messages, the vanguard of William's army was entering London with the Duke of Grafton and Viscount Mordaunt. The duke was under orders to take two battalions to Tilbury and to hand the place over to the care of the City of London as stated in William's conditions. The following morning Grafton approached the Lords' council to obtain orders for barges to transport his men to Tilbury. Riding past Somerset House, he narrowly escaped injury from a bullet fired by a soldier on horseback who was instantly shot by one of Grafton's men. It was not clear at the time whether this was a genuine assassination attempt or a drunken gesture and the duke made little of the incident. Presumably still accompanied by Mordaunt, he returned on 15 December to William who was now at Windsor.[12]

Grafton brought unwelcome news from the peers in London. While attempting to escape to France, James had been arrested by some fishermen who were unwilling to release him. The peers had sent an escort of Guards and some of James's personal servants to him and he was on his way back to London. The provisional government now melted away, feeling that it was no longer required. Accompanied by his Horse Guards, the King arrived at Whitehall on the afternoon of Sunday 16 December. That evening he held a privy council and attended mass in his chapel. Many Catholics and others flocked to Whitehall to greet him. James sent a message to William inviting him to a meeting at Whitehall. He chose as his envoy the Earl of Feversham whom William promptly arrested. William had been angered by Feversham's disbandment of the army and the manner in which it had been carried out. The arrest was made as much in response to that as to James's unexpected return to the capital. It was also an indication to the King that it was no longer possible for them to meet in a spirit of friendship. The action was intended to alarm him and in this it was successful.[13]

The Prince of Orange had arranged to leave Windsor and go to Syon House on Monday 17 December. That morning he called together all the peers who were at Windsor and asked them to decide what should be done now that the King was at Whitehall. The Prince was not present during the discussion and Halifax acted as chairman. It took some time to reach a decision. When William reappeared, he was told that the discussion had been very free and so he 'enjoined secrecy'.

Clarendon recorded some of the debate in his diary but he was late in arriving and only heard that part of the meeting which took place after a decision had been reached. Halifax himself made some notes. Apparently only twelve peers, including Clarendon, attended. Lord Delamere proposed that the King should leave Whitehall and be lodged in the Tower, a motion seconded by Mordaunt with the support of the Earls of Macclesfield and Stamford. However the Duke of Grafton spoke against the motion, as did the Earl of Shrewsbury and Lord Churchill. A general consensus emerged that perhaps a lodging in the Tower was rather harsh treatment but that the King should go to more neutral ground than one of his own palaces. Ham was considered a suitable venue and the Prince approved this choice. Mordaunt recorded the decision in writing.

William sent Halifax, Delamere and Shrewsbury with the message to the King; the decision had been taken by the peers and they should carry it. The delegation arrived late at Whitehall and delivered their message. As they were about to leave, they were called back to be told that the King would prefer to go to Rochester rather than Ham. When told, William raised no objection. At 11 am on Tuesday 18 December the King went downstream by barge, this time attended by Dutch Guards. His choice of Rochester had indicated that again flight was in his mind and William wanted nothing to hinder it.[14]

Later that afternoon the Prince arrived at St James's. Huge crowds had gathered to greet him and many were disappointed when he entered the palace quietly by a back way. The soldiers accompanying the Prince were amazed at their welcome. Orange women handed out their fruit to them as they passed. In the evening bells rang out all over the city and bonfires were lit. There was a great crush at St James's. John Evelyn managed to catch a glimpse of the Prince and met various friends who had come over with him. Clarendon could not get near, 'the crowd was so great'.

Despite all the rejoicing and perhaps also from a feeling of relief, people took time to think of the King and the manner of his departure with a degree of compassion. In this volatile period it was wise that the Prince had ensured that his own Dutch troops, and not the English regiments, were given the guard duties and kept the peace.[15]

Most of the peers who arrived in the Queen's Presence Chamber the next day had been called but some had stayed away and others appeared unbidden. The Prince attended initially and explained that the purpose of the meeting was for them to advise him on how best to carry out the aim of his Declaration, namely the calling of a free Parliament. The peers were left by themselves to discuss the matter and went about it with obvious uncertainty. It was suggested that the Declaration be read and this was done. It was then moved that the Prince should be thanked for it and for calling them together and that they should then adjourn. Another speaker felt that the urgency of the matter would admit of no adjournment but that the presence of learned counsel might be of service. Halifax was in favour of thanking the Prince for his Declaration but warned that returning thanks for calling them together might prejudice their birthright. Some peers preferred to meet in the House of Lords as they were unsure of the legality of meeting elsewhere. Lord Delamere wished the Prince to be thanked for his Declaration and thought they should undertake to stand by him with their lives and fortunes 'towards attaining those ends'. This found some support but Halifax was unhappy about 'lives and fortunes'. Mordaunt now entered the debate, speaking in favour of the former motion that no notice should be taken to the Prince of the lords' meeting for they met of right. He believed that something indeed should be said in the vein of 'lives and fortunes', but proposed that the lords should sign the Association which had been drawn up at Exeter. He also moved that all Roman Catholics should leave town.

In conclusion, it was resolved to reassemble at the House of Lords the next morning with learned counsel in attendance. In the meantime the Association was read and, after some debate, eleven lords voluntarily added their signatures. Some were of a loyalist persuasion and had not previously been numbered among William's supporters. When the Prince reappeared, he was thanked for his Declaration and for 'the vigour and conduct he hath shewn in the prosecution of the same'.[16]

When the lords assembled at Westminster the following day (Saturday, 22 December), they considered first Mordaunt's second motion, the removal of Papists from the city. After much discussion, orders were given similar to those issued in the reign of Charles II. Consideration of the harder question of how to obtain a free Parliament was adjourned until Monday.

Meanwhile at Rochester where his guard was kept deliberately light, James was aware of what was afoot in the capital and may have heard rumours of the peers' discussions at Windsor. He told Lord Ailesbury that he would be put in the Tower if he stayed in England. On 22 December the Duke of Berwick arrived at Rochester with some blank passports. There was no need for further delay. Early next morning the King slipped away quietly to begin his journey to France. He arrived there on Christmas Day to an assured welcome.[17]

Four

On 22 December 1688 the Earl of Clarendon, after much waiting around, was at last successful in obtaining an audience of the Prince. The meeting was entirely private and the Prince asked for Clarendon's views on what should be his next move. 'The Prince heard me with great patience; and very calmly said (when I expected he would make me some answer): "My Lord, the King is gone from Rochester." "Whither, Sir?" said I. "I know not," replied the Prince, "he went away about one or two this morning." I was struck to the heart; and, without saying one word, I made my leg, and went home as fast as I could.'

Many more were as shaken as Clarendon, who likened the event to an earthquake. However, the news of the King's departure led to less restraint in the lords' discussions when they met on Monday 24 December. Initially there were some questions regarding the King's destination and manner of departure. Mordaunt had no doubts that inquiring into this was a waste of time. That the lords were meeting in this manner showed that the King was absent 'either in power, or otherwise, and therefore not to be applied to'. Further debate followed, achieving little, leaving the matter unresolved.

After some preliminary discussion as to whether or not there had been a demise of the government in law, it was considered whether any of the writs prepared for the calling of the next Parliament could be used. Apparently only sixteen of these had been issued. The Earl of Devonshire then read a paper signed by the Prince of Orange which summoned all those who had sat in the Parliament of Charles II. He moved that a way might be found for the choice of representatives for the cities, counties and boroughs. Clarendon proposed as an expedient that the sixteen writs should bring in about 180 members who, as a body, could ask that further writs be issued. Mordaunt objected to the use of the King's writs, as those elected thereby would be under the Oath of Allegiance and this would detract from their freedom; 'the freedom of a Parliament is the chief thing.'

The Earl of Nottingham was the first to mention the idea of a Convention rather than a Parliament, thus removing the problem of oaths.

A Convention had been held once before when Prince John had acted as Regent without the King's commission, while Richard I was in prison abroad. However there could be a difficulty if the Convention was in the King's name, as it was 'owning the King who hath forsaken the Kingdom'. Lord Nottingham proposed that the Prince be asked to take upon himself the office of Regent. Lord Mordaunt then said that the Prince had done all he could to act according to his Declaration towards the calling of a free Parliament but that the King had made it impossible by withdrawing himself. He could have added, but may not have known, that the King actively tried to prevent the calling of a Parliament, by destroying the unissued writs and taking away the Great Seal.

Two addresses to the Prince were therefore prepared and then approved at a meeting of seventy-six peers on the afternoon of Christmas Day. The first asked the Prince to send letters to 'the Lords Spiritual and Temporal being Protestants' and to the counties, universities, cities, boroughs and Cinque Ports. Those other than the peers were to be asked to choose persons to represent them 'as are of right to be sent to Parliament'; such representatives were to appear at Westminster on 22 January. The second address asked the Prince to take upon himself 'the administration of publick affairs' until the meeting of the Convention on 22 January. Three days later the Prince indicated his acceptance.*[1]

While the elections were taking place, the Convention Parliament was being anticipated with a variety of hopes. Lady Mordaunt, still in The Hague, wrote to John Locke on 21/31 January, reflecting on events. She had been ill for a fortnight but the condition had cleared the day before 'with violence as all great things do but kings; ours went out like a farthing candle, and has given us by this Convention an occasion, not of amending the government, but of melting it down and make [sic] all new; which makes me wish you there to give them a right scheme of government...'† Whether these views reflected those of her husband is a matter of probability but not certainty. Lady Mordaunt was a woman of independent mind. Her husband was a radical Whig but not such a violent one as Lord Delamere. Mordaunt's support of a motion to send a crowned king to the Tower was enough to confirm a suspicion in William's mind that he was at heart a Republican.

*An assembly of commoners, consisting of the remaining members from Charles II's Parliament, the Lord Mayor and Court of Aldermen and some fifty representatives from the Common Council of London, having been summoned to meet by William, issued a similar petition on 26 December.
†Spelling modernised.

Early in 1689 a correspondence began between Lady Mordaunt and John Locke. If she is the lady referred to in a letter from Locke to Edward Clarke (18/28 January), she made a visit to Rotterdam specially to seek his acquaintance. This may have been at her husband's suggestion, as Locke was already known to Mordaunt who later asked him to take care of his wife on her journey to England. Locke returned the visit and described the lady as an 'extraordinary fine woman'. A close friendship developed and Locke's heartfelt admiration of Lady Mordaunt lasted until his death. This admiration appeared undiminished by her eccentric and extraordinary spelling and punctuation of English (she was more accurate in writing French). It is hard to believe that this was not an affectation as she seemed aware of it: 'i kno my falts are so crose [gross]in wryting.'

In London, Mordaunt had a long conference with the Prince on 29 December of which the practical result was another batch of commissions in his regiment. As would later emerge, he was maintaining links with Whigs in the City and, in the spirit of uncertainty, mutterings were heard about the opportunities there were for Commonwealth's men.[2]

The Convention Parliament assembled on 22 January 1689. The House of Commons held a majority of moderate Whigs whereas in the Lords political sympathies had produced a majority of Tories. Quite a large proportion of members of the House of Commons (183) had been elected for the first time and about 200 had sat in the Parliament of 1685. However neither House seemed over-enthusiastic about tackling the State of the Nation or melting down the government. A debate on the subject in the Commons was postponed to 28 January. On that day a resolution was passed, and ordered to be sent up to the Lords, in the following terms: 'That King James II, having endeavoured to subvert the constitution of the kingdom, by breaking the original contract between king and people; and by the advice of Jesuits and other wicked persons having violated the fundamental laws; and having withdrawn himself out of this kingdom; has abdicated the government; and that the throne is thereby vacant.'[3]

With a Tory majority in the Lords, the constitutional question would not find so ready a solution there or such agreement as was found in the Commons. On 29 January, while the Lower House moved on to consider the Heads of Grievances and the foundation for a new monarchy (which would take shape ultimately in the Declaration of Right), the Lords addressed themselves to the Commons' resolution in committee. A proposal by the Earl of Rochester that a Regency might solve the problem was defeated on a vote. After some debate, the peers decided to amend the Commons' resolution by using the word 'deserted' instead of 'abdicated'.

On 31 January a proposal that the Prince and Princess of Orange should be declared King and Queen was defeated. The question whether the throne was vacant was decided in the negative, Mordaunt being one of several peers who entered their dissent. The debate on this occasion had been undertaken with 'great warmth and smartness'.

On 4 February the question of the vacancy was again put and defeated by the very narrow majority of one. Again Mordaunt was among the thirty-nine peers who registered their dissent. The situation had almost reached stalemate and William had begun to lose patience. He let it be known privately, probably at a small gathering of peers on 3 February, that if he was not offered the crown he would return to Holland. Some people had thought that the Princess Mary, as the next Protestant heir, should reign alone. She informed Dr Burnet that it was her wish to reign jointly with her husband. This cleared the air; on 6 February the Lords voted to agree with the word 'abdicated' as used in the Commons' resolution. Some party work had gone in to the bringing up of 'backwoodsmen' for the vote. The Earl of Lincoln and the Bishop of Durham voted with the 'Contents' and for the first time in this debate. There also appeared Lord Astley and Lord Howard of Escrick. Lord Lincoln had the reputation of being a little weak in intellect. Clarendon felt he confirmed this when he declared 'he came to do whatever my Lord Shrewsbury and Lord Mordaunt would have him...' Some peers who had previously opposed the motion now voted in favour but others absented themselves.[4]

Having solved the problem of the vacancy of the crown, it was not a matter of difficulty to pass a resolution that the Prince and Princess of Orange be declared King and Queen. At this time the Princess was in Holland, waiting to sail for England with the first fair wind.

Mordaunt had already written to John Locke in January, asking him to act as escort to his wife on her journey home. As Locke assured a friend, this request could not be refused as the task also afforded him personal pleasure; it also ensured the opportunity of travelling in safety. Lady Mordaunt herself had been making preparations for a new reign. She had been accustomed to courts and wrote to Dijkvelt in January asking for his assistance in obtaining for her a post as lady-in-waiting in the household of the Princess of Orange.[5]

[33]

On 8 February Mordaunt was one of the peers asked to report on the free conference held two days previously with the Commons. He also took part in the conference on the Lords' amendments to the Heads of Grievances compiled by the Commons, a document which eventually emerged as the Declaration of Right. On 12 February a declaration was issued by both Houses of Parliament of the intention to offer the crown to both William and Mary as joint sovereigns but with the executive power vested in William alone.[6]

It was appropriate that the Princess of Orange should arrive the same day at Greenwich and be welcomed at Whitehall in the afternoon. After a slight delay because of adverse weather, the *Mary* yacht, with the Princess on board, had set sail for England on 10/20 February. Lady Mordaunt and John Locke made the journey from Brill on board the *Isabella*.

The day following (13 February), the lords went in a body to pay their respects to the Prince and Princess at Whitehall. The Declaration of Right was read and the crown was offered to William and Mary by the Marquess of Halifax. William accepted on behalf of them both and undertook to preserve the religion, laws and liberties of England. Much has been read into the order of proceedings in the Banqueting Hall. The Declaration was read first and the offer then made. It is known that William was not in favour of any kind of contract with the people and opposed to any conditions being attached to the offer of the crown. His views were not necessarily shared by his new subjects, many of whom now strongly believed in the theory of contract. The Declaration, so firmly read before the sovereigns whether they approved of it or not, became the foundation for a new constitutional monarchy, later to be formalised in the Bill of Rights.[7]

When the list of William's Privy Council was published, Viscount Mordaunt's name appeared among the thirty-two members. The Council largely consisted of Whig sympathisers but, as far as Court and government appointments were concerned, William strove to balance parties and interests. He had a natural inclination to favour the Tories but most of the active support he had received had come from the Whigs and therefore it was not surprising that they had their expectations of high office. Halifax declined a secretaryship and was made Lord Privy Seal; he felt that he was blamed by the disgruntled, including Mordaunt, for what had gone wrong. The Earl of Danby, a long-term supporter of William and a signatory of the invitation, was made Lord President of the Council; it was believed that he had hoped to be made

Lord Treasurer. The Secretaries of State were the Earl of Nottingham, a Tory who had been one of the negotiators at Hungerford, and the Earl of Shrewsbury, a Whig and long-standing supporter who had also signed the invitation. At twenty-eight years of age, Shrewsbury was considered rather young for the job. No lawyer could be found who was of sufficient seniority and experience to be Lord Chancellor and so the Great Seal was put in commission.

As early as 16 February 1689 it was rumoured that the Treasury would be put in commission and that Mordaunt would be First Lord. The official announcement came on 6 April and the commissions passed the Great Seal three days later. Joined with Mordaunt in the commission were Lord Delamere, Lord Godolphin, Sir Henry Capell and Richard Hampden. Lord Delamere, a fiery Whig soon to be created Earl of Warrington, developed an animosity for Mordaunt which became mutual. Lord Godolphin was a Tory and had been a Treasury commissioner since 1686. He was the only experienced member of the commission and had been brought in, according to Burnet, 'to the great grief of the other two, who soon saw that the King considered him more than them both. For, as he understood Treasury business well, so his calm and cold way suited the King's temper.' These peers were joined by Sir Henry Capell, a Whig and a brother of the Earl of Essex, and Richard Hampden, a long-serving Member of Parliament, at present representing Wendover. Hampden was also chairman of the Commons' Committees of Supply and of Ways and Means. A staunch Presbyterian, he was much respected and claimed to be the only English politician whose advice William sought on religious matters. Lord Delamere became Chancellor of the Exchequer and William Jephson the secretary.[8]

To many people Mordaunt's appointment was a strange one. Sir John Reresby doubted the wisdom or the suitability of it, considering that Mordaunt 'never saw £100 together of his own money'. Mordaunt, on the other hand, had a complete confidence in his own capabilities and considered himself able to 'understand the business of it [the Treasury] as well as Lord Godolphin in a fortnight'. He also thought he should have sat alone. As a Treasury Lord, he 'was generous, and gave the inferior places freely; but sought out the men who were most noted for republican principles for them all...'

William himself had great doubts about Mordaunt; he feared not so much his inability but his immaturity and openness to the influence of others. William had a phobia about people who held republican (or commonwealth) principles and believed that Mordaunt and his friends in the City were of this persuasion. The King muttered to Halifax about 'this jackanapes on horseback'; he may have been referring to the commission Mordaunt received on 5 March to form a volunteer regiment of horse from the City of London. A similar comment to that of the King appeared about a year later in a political poem entitled 'The Nine' in a verse said to describe Mordaunt:

> Next, Painter, draw a Jackanapes of State,
> A Monkey turn'd into a Magistrate;
> A saucy Wight born up with Heat and Noise,
> Fit onely for a Ringleader of Boyes,
> To untile Neighbor's Houses, and to play
> Such uncouth Gambols on a Holiday;
> Strange! That such a young Government shou'd doat
> So as to let a Whirlwind steer the Boat.

When Mordaunt was not out of town on other business, he was a faithful and regular attender at Treasury meetings. The salary for this post amounted to £1,600 per annum.[9]

Also this month, Mordaunt began to attend meetings of the Lords' Committee on the Affairs of Ireland, and the Committee on Trade and Plantations. There was also a flurry of interest in the work of the close committee on the circumstances of the death of the Earl of Essex, of which Mordaunt was a member. It was alleged that one Holland, who had been formerly a butler in the household of the Earl of Sunderland, had confessed to the murder of Lord Essex on promise of a pardon. Mordaunt set various people to watch for Holland so that he could be apprehended for questioning. He was eventually arrested in Essex Street on Mordaunt's orders on 25 February. On 22 May the committee ceased meeting and sent in a report of its findings. It was reconstituted the following November, with the same membership.

The Treasury, his committees and his other interests gave Mordaunt the reputation of being a quick mover, always darting from one place to another. His activity attracted sufficient notice to appear in a poem in 1690 entitled 'The Modern Lampooners':

> How does he do to distribute his hours,
> Some to the Court, and some to the City,
> Some to the State, and some to Love's powers,
> Some to be vain, and some to be witty?

This was a period, rare at this time in his life, when Mordaunt had enough regular occupation to satisfy and utilise his considerable energy of mind and body. On 23 February he was appointed a Gentleman of the Bedchamber to the King. This was a coveted position of some prestige and carried an annual salary of £1,000.* In March he was appointed Lord Lieutenant of Northamptonshire, a position previously held by his uncle, the Earl of Peterborough.[10]

In the general distribution of employments, Mordaunt did not forget his friends. He was able to convey to John Locke the King's offer of the post of Ambassador to the Elector of Brandenburg. Locke was deeply appreciative of the gesture but, despite his anxiety to serve the King, he felt it impossible to accept the assignment on grounds of his poor health. William subsequently offered Locke another ambassadorial post, this time to the Emperor at Vienna. Locke declined again, remaining firm in his decision to remain at home. Later he did accept a post which was undemanding but lacked the value and prestige of the others. He became a Commissioner for Appeals in Excise, an occupation which only required very infrequent attendance.[11]

As the Coronation approached, more honours were distributed. Among new creations in the peerage, Mordaunt received an earldom under a warrant dated 28 March. The warrant named the title as the earldom of Chichester. It is not known why Mordaunt made the choice of this title but it seems that he subsequently withdrew it. At the King's request, the Keepers of the Great Seal were instructed to ensure that the date of the grant was noted, so that Mordaunt would not lose his place in the order of precedence by the delay in his choice of title.

When the new warrant was issued on 9 April, it was revealed that Mordaunt had decided to take the title of Earl of Monmouth. There was much speculation on the reason for his choice. Those who had been friends of the late Duke of Monmouth (and Mordaunt had been among them) were inclined to take exception to it. The King thought that Mordaunt hoped that he might ultimately receive a dukedom of the same, thinking in this way 'to have the inheritance of his [the duke's] popularity'. William's enemies, such as the Earl of Dartmouth, were happy to think that the King would take pleasure in doing something ill-natured like this to prevent any restoration of the title to the Duke's children. At this time William was in fact taking care to avoid

*The salary was frequently in arrears. There were ten Gentlemen in addition to Grooms of the Bedchamber, esquires and others. William, Earl of Portland was appointed Groom of the Stole with a salary of £500 per quarter.

being too lenient towards the Duchess of Monmouth precisely to prevent anyone from having a reason to say that he had actually approved of Monmouth's rebellion. Dartmouth also believed that Mordaunt had been 'put upon' to ask for the earldom of Monmouth.

Mordaunt's own reasons are not recorded. However, the last earldom of Monmouth had been held in his mother's family, the Careys, and had become extinct on the death of his great-uncle and godfather, Henry Carey, the second earl. There could have been sentimental and family reasons for its revival. The suggestion that Mordaunt aimed for a dukedom of the same name failed to take into consideration another fact. At almost any time he stood to inherit the senior earldom of Peterborough from his infirm uncle, at present imprisoned in the Tower. In the event, this older title was the one he carried for the greater part of his long life.[12]

The Coronation ceremony took place on 11 April in Westminster Abbey. In the procession from Westminster Hall, the regalia, two of everything, were carried before the joint sovereigns. William and Mary walked side by side under a large canopy held over them by the Barons of the Cinque Ports. The King's train was carried by the Groom of the Stole, the Earl of Portland, and four pages. Behind the King walked the Earl of Monmouth, Gentleman of the Bedchamber in attendance, accompanied by two Grooms. At 4 pm the joint sovereigns were crowned. They swore to govern 'according to the statutes in Parliament agreed on', a significant re-wording of the old oath. Another innovation was the presentation of the Bible, 'the most valuable thing that this world affords', immediately after the crowning. All the changes in the ceremony were supervised and directed by the Bishop of London, Dr Compton.* Lady Rachel Russell wrote: 'Those that saw this and the last Coronation tell me this was much finer and in better order; and, if the number of the ladyes were fewer, yet their attendance was with more application near the Queen all the time, and with more chearful faces by a great deal...'[13]

---

*The same order, with only one or two minor changes, was still in use at the coronation of Elizabeth II in 1953.

Five

Two days after the Coronation the Earl of Monmouth was formally introduced to the House of Lords in his new degree. He sat first as a Lord Commissioner of the Treasury on 10 April. Treasury days varied from seventeen to twenty-five in a month and Monmouth generally attended most of them. He also appeared in the Lords regularly except when absent on other affairs or at court.[1]

On 10 May 1689 Monmouth was named as one of nine Commissioners appointed to 'reform abuses in the Army'. The Commission was headed by Frederick Duke of Schomberg, whose chairmanship was largely nominal as he was overall commander of all the forces in Britain, both indigenous and foreign. There were two other peers, the Earl of Devonshire (the Lord Steward) and Viscount Lumley. From the House of Commons, the Commission was joined by Thomas Wharton (Comptroller of the Household) and William Harbord. To these were added three army officers, Major General Sir John Lanier, Major General Percy Kirke and Colonel Charles Trelawney.

The purpose of the Commission was to investigate claims that many officers had been returning false musters and pocketing the money saved. It was generally believed that there were little enough funds available for the forces; that such funds should be misspent in this way was a matter requiring urgent correction. Already there had been trouble in various parts of the country: in Berwick-on-Tweed in December soldiers had claimed free quarters because of lack of pay. In January it was announced that all arrears of pay would be met immediately.

Evidence of disaffection in the Army was another problem. In March there was a mutiny by half the regiment of Royal Scots at Ipswich. As a result, some other regiments, including Monmouth's foot, sent loyal addresses to William. The mutiny was treated leniently by the standards of the time. The cause of it turned out to be a resistance to the prospect of being shipped to join the forces in the Low Countries rather than an objection to the regime.

Since the Dutch had declared war on France in February 1689, William intimated to Parliament on 7 May his intention to make a similar declaration on behalf of England. The Army Commission was charged with the task of finding out the quality and content of the forces which could be utilised in this war. The commissioners undertook to visit the regiments in their quarters and inquire into the number, quality and fitness of the men. If they found that soldiers were living in free quarters, they were instructed to deduct sums from the soldiers' pay to compensate the householders. They were also to ask those living in the neighbourhood of any regiment whether they had seen or heard any signs of disaffection. They were to inquire into musters and check that the calculation of off-reckonings was being made correctly and according to the rules. In cases of false musters or of disaffection, the commissioners had powers to disband.[2]

The three peers received leave of absence from the House of Lords on 22 May and began their tour of inspection a few days later. On their way north they dined at Burghley. Travelling by Hull and York, they had reached Newcastle by 9 June. There, having inspected Lord Delamere's regiment among others, Monmouth wrote to John Locke:

> Mr Locke, I must begin with a description of Lord Delamere's army; it wanted nothing to be a complete regiment but clothes, boots, arms, horses, men and officers: there never was anything so scandalous as that the King should have paid near 9000 pounds already to that rout of fellows, that have been more disorderly than any, never having all the while but one captain with them...

This regiment had been raised by Delamere in Cheshire and marched to join William on his arrival. Even allowing for Monmouth's personal antipathy to Delamere, the account makes sad reading.

By this time the commissioners had visited several regiments and had covered the ground fast. Some felt like a pause for a day or two. Monmouth and Wharton decided to visit Scotland and some relatives there. In the end, only Wharton set off for Edinburgh while Monmouth went to Berwick to examine some regiments, returning the next day.

It was not in Monmouth's character to be idle and he never seemed to suffer from fatigue. He told Locke, rather sententiously, 'att least no reproach shall lye at my door, for I can bragg that pleasure when I am engaged in businesse, never made me goe on hower out of my way.' The commissioners continued their tour by way of Hexham to Carlisle and Penrith. They then went by Kendal, Lancaster, Preston and Warrington to Chester. Next visiting Shrewsbury and Stafford, they parted from each other at Northampton. By 25 June Monmouth had returned to London.

Over all, the Commission achieved very little. It displaced several officers for false musters, a common practice, and a very few for disaffection. Its movements had been well publicised; there had been no sudden descent at an unexpected moment to find a regiment in disarray and undermanned. Advance warning meant that at least temporary steps could be taken to remedy deficiencies. As far as disaffection was concerned, it was no longer a major issue. By this time, those who believed their allegiance lay elsewhere had already left the Army.[3]

After this summer journey Monmouth returned to the duties of the Treasury Board. The Lords Commissioners sat throughout the summer, although only on eight days in July.* Constant attendance, by at least a quorum, was essential to the running of the administration. The Treasury was responsible for the issue of money to all departments of the government. Each department had its own estimates and budget but it was impossible to hand out an annual, or even twice-yearly, lump sum as the funds were simply not available. In practice, money was issued almost on a weekly basis, and there had to be continual discussion on the rival claims of different departments to whatever funds were available. There was much paperwork; there were claims for money and also for property, offices and other matters often quite trivial. In every case, statements had to be read, questions asked, discussion held on the merits and a decision taken. The Treasury also had control of direct taxation and an overseeing responsibility for indirect taxation such as Customs and Excise. It was also responsible for the raising of loans on expected income, a vital part of the money supply. Of William's Treasury Lords, only one, Lord Godolphin, really knew the work and was an expert in this field. Monmouth himself had useful links with the City but he had a poor reputation for managing his own finances, let alone those of anyone else.[4]

In conversations held with Halifax this year, the King expressed a negative opinion of the efforts of the new Earl of Monmouth. William found him disobliging, if not actually disobedient, and rather overbearing. He thought his wife ruled him: the Countess of Monmouth and John Hampden 'contrived and my Ld executed'.

John Hampden was the son of Richard Hampden, one of the

---

*The Commissioners sat on twenty-three days in August, sometimes both morning and afternoon. The busiest month was November when they sat on twenty-five days.

Treasury Lords. He was a grandson of his namesake of ship-money fame, and he and his father alternated in the representation of Wendover or Buckinghamshire in the House of Commons. Generally known as 'young Hampden' to distinguish him from his father, John was an extreme Whig and a freethinker but was prone to depression. Arrested after the Rye House Plot on the evidence of only one witness, he was tried for a misdemeanour and fined £40,000. Unable to pay the fine, he had two of his estates confiscated. After Monmouth's rebellion, another witness was found and this time he was tried for high treason and confessed to knowledge of the plot but not of the assassination. He paid £6,000 to secure a pardon, which was granted. Although eventually accepted back into the Whig fold, William believed him to be unstable and later declined to give him a diplomatic post at The Hague. Hampden subsequently refused the offer of a post in Spain. At this time his name was often linked with that of the Countess of Monmouth. He was described as 'a great beau, dresses and powders, courts Lady Monmouth and a far greater'. Hampden believed wrongly that Halifax was his enemy and he often found himself opposed to his father in Parliament. He was said to be possessed of considerable intellectual gifts.[5]

Halifax now believed that William's opinion of Monmouth was so low that it could never recover. The King was adamant that Monmouth should never become a Secretary of State but his place in the Treasury entitled him to membership of the Cabinet. His fear of republicanism appeared again; Monmouth and his City friends, he thought, were surely 'commonwealthsmen' and the new regiment of horse raised in the City was bound to include them. There had already been comment that some of the officers in this regiment might not be able to take the Test for religious reasons, because of the stipulation that the sacrament must be received according to the Anglican rite. The City regiment was completed in July and the King reluctantly accepted the colonelcy. He thought the post an 'inconvenient thing' but something he could not well refuse. Monmouth was the lieutenant-colonel and the major and six captains were drawn from the City. The regiment numbered 400 men, but when the King saw it in August he thought it made rather a 'small appearance'.[6]

A government representing a new regime must be aware that supporters of the previous order may be seeking ways to overturn it. From time to time Monmouth and others heard reports of disaffected talk from people who wished to inform on their friends and acquaintances. Sometimes the talk was merely the indiscretion of those who had drunk too freely but rumours of plots had to be checked and a guard maintained.

An incident of this type occurred in July 1689. Late one evening a well-horsed stranger arrived at Parsons Green with an urgent letter for the Earl of Monmouth who was not at home. The letter contained a warning that an attempt would be made on the King's life at Hampton Court the next evening, which was a Sunday. Under a pretext of ensuring her safety, the Queen would be hurried away to the Isle of Wight, where the Governor was said to be sympathetic, and then shipped to France. To create a diversion, cities and suburbs would be set on fire 'in forty places'.

In the morning Monmouth took the matter to the King, who ordered the arrest of Sir Tamworth Reresby, the only conspirator actually named in the letter. Extra precautions were taken at Hampton Court and a watch was ordered for Richmond Park, where the conspirators were believed to have a rendezvous. Monmouth then sent the letter to the Earl of Shrewsbury, the Secretary of State, with the suggestion that he should alert the Lord Mayor so that he might 'take some care towards the security of the city, for the least accident, should it be known that we had such advertisements, would lay very heavy upon us...' He presumed it would be thought proper to send 'some very intelligent and honest man to the Isle of Wight' to keep an eye open for strangers. In the event, it proved a false alarm; the worst that occurred was the consternation caused in the city by all soldiers being called to arms and a double watch being set.[7]

Sometimes Monmouth had the task of interviewing Jacobites, or proscribed persons, who had been arrested. One such was Nathaniel Hooke, who had been chaplain to the Duke of Monmouth and probably known to the earl in that capacity. In the course of their summer tour, the Army commissioners had come up with Hooke at Penrith, where he was in prison; he had been arrested at Whitehaven as he came off a ship from Ireland. The commissioners entertained him with much wine and conviviality and endeavoured unsuccessfully to persuade him to abandon King James's interests. Later Monmouth visited him in the Tower and spoke with him in private. Hooke's suspected treasonable practices cannot have amounted to much; he appeared before the King in August and was later released.[*][8]

*Hooke lived to serve with distinction in the French army and hold high rank. He was seen at Versailles in 1715 by Dr George Clarke, 'in good credit'.

In August 1689 Monmouth's contact with the City was revealed in an unusual incident. At this time, a Bill to encourage the wearing of woollens for six months in the year was before Parliament. The silk weavers believed that it would be a disaster for their livelihood if this Bill became law. While it was being considered in the House of Lords, the Bailiffs, Wardens and Assistants of the Companies of Weavers at London and Canterbury sent a petition to the House asking that their grievances be heard. The petition was brought to Westminster by a crowd of several thousand weavers and their wives. The Lords read the petition but sent a message that they would consider their objections and do justice accordingly, if the crowds went home.

This reply angered their leader, Captain Tom, and the atmosphere became agitated and unpleasant. At this point three Parliamentarians who were held in esteem by the leaders of the protest, the Earl of Monmouth, Dr Edward Fowler and Thomas Firmin, addressed the mob. They gave them 'good words', assuring them that their petition was very reasonable but they did not in any way commend their manner of presenting it. Later, two members of the House of Lords emerged to reassure the weavers that nothing would be done to their detriment. Soon afterwards the crowds began to make their way home. Guards were placed around Westminster but no further disturbance took place.[9]

At the Lord Mayor's Show on 29 October, Monmouth appeared at the head of his London Regiment of Horse which had been appointed as the guard for the King and Queen. From a balcony in Cheapside, Their Majesties witnessed a pageant entitled 'London's Great Jubilee'. Celebrating the Glorious Revolution, the pageant showed a decidedly Whig bias but it was a sumptuous performance and was greeted with acclaim. At a banquet at Guildhall the Lord Mayor, Sir Thomas Pilkington, entertained the King and Queen, the foreign ambassadors and members of both Houses of Parliament. Sir John Knatchbull recalled attending a similar occasion in 1660 but this time 'the entertainment was great and as orderly as the thing would admit'. Seeing Lord Monmouth with his regiment, perhaps some recalled his father, Viscount Mordaunt, at the head of a troop of Spanish merchants clad in black velvet. It is likely that Monmouth inherited many of his connections in the City from his father.[10]

The Treasury Commissioners were responsible for raising loans for public funding, should the need arise. In the autumn of 1689 they approached the City of London for such a loan. Some of the City Whigs were not prepared to agree to this at once. Although many were willing to give tokens of loyalty and support to the King, they would not do so until the King showed similar qualities to them, by dismissing from his employment those who had been in control of the public funds in the previous reign. The situation was at an impasse, as the King was unlikely to give way to the wishes of extreme Whigs whom he distrusted. As Parliament had voted £300,000 towards the payment of the armed forces, a loan was now a matter of urgency as the money could not be found solely from the revenue.[11]

On Wednesday 18 December Lord Monmouth invited to dinner his friend Charles Duncombe, a goldsmith of considerable wealth, Stephen Evance, the banker, and others. He persuaded them to raise a loan on the revenue of £300,000 and suggested 'how very kindly it would be taken, if they would doe it before Saturday'. They agreed to pay down £140,000 by then and to pay off the rest in other ways. When the Treasury Commissioners met at Kensington that evening, Monmouth was able to tell the King that the problem was solved for the time being. The King told him that he 'had done him so great a service that he must be counted highly ungratefull if ever he did forget it'. The King may not have been quite so gratified when the earl cheerfully replied that the money 'was raised generally by some that were counted disaffected to his Government, and friends to a Common Wealth, for it was mostly Fanaticks and Wiggs money'*.[12]

During the autumn of 1689 Monmouth's name appears for the first time in connection with affairs in Scotland. The Scottish Convention Parliament contained a strong opposition party known as 'the Club'. This party had been formed to push through Parliament a list of grievances which it was felt would not otherwise be addressed. The Privy Council in Scotland contained people who strongly ressembled 'the country's old oppressors'. Parliament was not so much against James II, as aware that he was no longer in power; it had no difficulty in resolving that he had 'forfeited' the throne. The Claim of Right subsequently drawn up had in it a strong contractual element; it was looked upon by many as embodying the conditions on which William accepted the throne of Scotland.

A representation from the three estates went to London to offer the Crown to William. One of them, Sir James Montgomery of Skelmorlie,

*This example may serve to counter the suggestion that the City was reluctant to make loans to a Treasury Commission headed by Monmouth, see C. Clay, *Public Finance and Public Wealth: The Career of Sir Stephen Fox* (Oxford, 1978), p. 233.

who represented the shires, was a highly gifted politician. He claimed to be a Whig and he was considered an equal in debate to Sir John Dalrymple of Stair. An avowed enemy to the royal prerogative, he was seen by some as an obvious candidate for the office of Secretary of State under the new regime. In the event, the Earl of Melville received this appointment. It is not known how much Sir James had considered this office his own, but on being offered the post of Lord Justice Clerk, he declined it. This man was designed, for political if not personal reasons, to be the leader of the opposition in the new Parliament.

The grievances listed for discussion by Parliament all reflected the desire for parliamentary rather than royal government. One, which sought the establishment of Presbyterianism, was an obvious meeting-point between the King and Parliament, so this request was held in abeyance until the others had been satisfied.

The opposition, 'the Club', fought well in the summer session of 1689. Tired of the strife, the King's Commissioner, the Duke of Hamilton, adjourned Parliament in August. The Club was not to be put off or thwarted; it decided to organise an address to the King, asking him to ratify acts voted by the Parliament. Having acquired seventy-two signatures to the address, Skelmorlie and his party set off for London. Sir James was officially accompanied by the Earl of Annandale and Lord Ross, but other members also made their own way south. On arrival in London, they heard a rumour that the King was about to appoint new Lords of Session. The use of the royal prerogative to appoint judges, who could be used as instruments of oppression by the Crown, was one of the grievances which had been under discussion. Finding the King at Newmarket, Lord Annandale asked for an audience which was refused. Undaunted, the party approached the Earl of Portland and voiced their concern over the naming of the judges. As a result the naming was postponed.

When the Court returned from Newmarket on 10 October, Monmouth was now in attendance on the King and it became known that William was prepared to receive the address brought from Scotland. This was duly presented by Lord Annandale. The King agreed to many of the matters contained in the address but he never relinquished the power to appoint judges.

While the commissioners and their supporters were in London, some Williamite politicians took the opportunity to try to win them over, and were in many cases successful. Increasingly, Sir James Montgomery found his support ebbing away and he himself treated by the Court as some sort of wrongdoer. Clearly *persona non grata* for a number of reasons, he found a sympathetic listener in Monmouth to whom he unburdened himself of his problems. Initially hurt by his treatment, Sir James was now angry and wanted any information laid against him submitted to public examination. Monmouth spent two hours with the King pleading Sir James's cause and was successful in persuading him that he had been misinformed. He then performed the same good office for Montgomery with the Earl of Portland. However the treatment which Montgomery received from the Court was instrumental in turning a gifted opposition leader into a secret Jacobite plotter.[13]

On 8 February 1690 the Marquess of Halifax resigned the post of Lord Privy Seal. Monmouth was among the mainly extreme Whigs who had formed an opposition to Halifax. They doubted the sincerity of his support of the new regime, given that he had been one of those chosen by James II to treat with William at the Hungerford conference. Knowing that William relied on Halifax's advice, they believed that this senior statesman was blocking appointments which might have been given to Whigs.

The previous November a House of Lords Committee had been formed by the Duke of Bolton (formerly Marquess of Winchester) to discover who had been the 'Advisers and Prosecutors of the Murders of Lord Russell, Colonel Sydney, Sir Thomas Armstrong, and others' and to inquire into other matters. This was a gambit inspired by Lord Montagu and the Earl of Monmouth in order to embarrass Halifax. The committee eventually consisted of thirty-five peers with a later addition of seventeen including the Lord Privy Seal himself. Monmouth busied himself with canvassing peers to form an opposition to Halifax but they were unsuccessful in pushing through the accusations of involvement made against him.[14]

The conversations which the King and Halifax were in the habit of holding ceased on a regular basis after his resignation but they did discuss who might succeed him as Lord Privy Seal. The King's general dissatisfaction with Monmouth, and what to do about him, were recurring themes in the conversations. One solution considered was to offer him the place of Lord Privy Seal: 'kick him up stayres,' Halifax recorded. It would not have been a compliment to offer this post to Monmouth after his place in the Treasury. To be Lord Privy Seal was a ministerially superior position but very much less profitable.*

*The office was put in commission.

Monmouth had expressed a wish to accompany the King to Ireland in the expedition being planned for the spring of 1690. William was disinclined to take him, believing he might find him troublesome, but there was always the chance that he might be more so at home. In February it seemed that Monmouth was no longer so keen to go. The campaign in Ireland in the late summer and early autumn of 1689 had been a disaster. The spring expedition, with the presence of William himself, was intended to remedy the situation.

Before leaving, the King was intent on making changes in the Treasury Commission. He thought he could dispense with Lord Delamere and compensate him with a gift of money. It was rumoured in early February that Monmouth was about to lose his Treasury position; a bystander recorded that this would be 'a clear Shiboleth, for there is no man hath done more for his Maty'. Part of the difficulty lay in the fact that it was important that the Treasury Commissioners themselves should be persons of substance who could lend money or were in ready contact with those who would. There had also been complaints that the existing commission was said to consist mainly of Whigs and dissenters and that not enough money was reaching the Church of England.[15]

On 17 March 1690 all but one of the Treasury Commissioners received letters from the King informing them that their attendance was no longer required. Monmouth, Lord Delamere, Lord Godolphin and Sir Henry Capell found themselves replaced by Sir John Lowther, Sir Stephen Fox and Thomas Pelham. Only Richard Hampden remained, with the office of Chancellor of the Exchequer.[16]

Six

Monmouth seemed undaunted by his loss of place and continued to play an active part in the House of Lords, speaking vigorously in debates. The Earls of Shrewsbury and Devonshire had sufficient confidence in him to leave their proxies in his charge when they went to Newmarket in May. In April he had been appointed one of four commissioners given the task of inspecting the new Lieutenancy of the City of London and making a report*.[1]

At this time Monmouth was looking for advice on the appointment of a tutor for his eldest son, John Viscount Mordaunt. The boy was now about nine years of age and it appears that he did not follow his father to Westminster School. As his health gave reason for concern later, possibly his parents thought him delicate and preferred to have him educated at home. In his search for a suitable mentor, Monmouth consulted both Isaac Newton and John Locke. Newton was slow to make any recommendation. Locke disagreed with Monmouth's wish to engage a 'thorough scholar' and gave the earl his views in a letter which embodied some of the ideas later expressed in *Some Thoughts concerning Education*.

Locke himself stayed at Parsons Green for two months in the early summer and may well have taken steps to guide the boy's curriculum. He had been asked to approach Monmouth on behalf of Isaac Newton, whose friends were looking for a post for him as he had failed to obtain a seat in Parliament in the election of February 1690.† Efforts made on Newton's behalf were unsuccessful until much later but he considered himself obliged to Lord and Lady Monmouth for this and other services.[2]

In June Monmouth received a grant of land from the Crown. The royal warrant gave to 'Charles earl of Monmouth and to his heirs for ever (in consideration of many faithful and acceptable services)' the

---

*The suggestion that Monmouth also received a pension at this time is supported only by a statement in a letter from a Jacobite agent dated 8/18 April 1690 and may have been purely speculative. It is referred to by Macaulay in his *History*, vol. ii, p. 146n.
†The post may have been that of Comptroller of the Mint.

manor of Dauntsey in Wiltshire and all other lands which had been forfeited to the Crown from the estate of the late Sir John Danvers. Monmouth was fortunate in obtaining this grant; although he had requested it, his uncle, the Earl of Torrington, was another interested party.

From early records the manor of Dauntsey had been part of a gift of land from King Ethelwulf to Malmesbury Abbey in 850. At the Restoration it had long been the property of the Danvers family. However Sir John Danvers, who died in 1655, had been a regicide and all property that he had owned was forfeited to the Crown. Sir John's son, another John, had been a minor at the time of his father's death. As heir of entail, he was still waiting for the court hearing of a writ of error which he had taken out when James II, as Duke of York, had obtained a judgment in ejectment against him.*

In 1662 Charles II had granted the forfeited Danvers lands to his brother, James Duke of York. In 1685 James, now King, made over the same estates to Queen Mary's jointure trustees. In the reign of William and Mary it was believed that such lands had reverted to the Crown but there was some uncertainty. The wording of the grant to Monmouth attempted to block all loopholes:

> The present grant is to date from the decease of the said late Queen or from any sooner determination of the said trust estate [the Queen's jointure trust], and if the said trust estate be not valid in law then to hold from date hereof...the King herein covenanting to make further effectual grant of the premises if they hereafter come to vest in the Crown by any Act of Parliament or otherwise, and to assent to any Act of Parliament for confirming the premises to said Earl and his heirs.

According to a survey taken at the beginning of the year, the manor consisted of 3,400 acres. The present rental amounted to £1,096 per annum but it was noted that the improved annual value was £2,689. The grant to Monmouth was made at an annual rent of £300 to the Crown, a sum the earl soon allowed to fall into arrears.³

William left for Ireland on 4 June. Two days beforehand he presented to the Queen the nine Privy Councillors whom he had appointed as her special advisers during his absence. It had taken him

*John Danvers and Lord Monmouth were distant cousins. His great-grandfather, Silvester Danvers, had married Elizabeth Mordaunt, daughter of the first Baron Mordaunt of Turvey.

some time to decide finally that Monmouth should be of their number. The other members were the Marquess of Carmarthen (the Lord President), the Earl of Devonshire (Lord High Steward), the Earl of Dorset (Lord Chamberlain), the Earl of Pembroke, the Earl of Nottingham (Secretary of State for the Northern Department), the Earl of Marlborough, Sir John Lowther (First Treasury Commissioner) and Edward (now Admiral) Russell. The original list had numbered only six councillors; Monmouth, Marlborough and Russell were added later.[4]

The Queen was in nominal charge of the government but she was expected to look to her special Council of Nine for guidance and advice. The Council met regularly on Tuesdays and Saturdays; out of the thirty-four recorded meetings in 1690 the Queen was present at twenty-three. Mary took her responsibilities very seriously; she was over-anxious to do what William would approve of and to avoid errors and pitfalls. She rarely took a decision unless the matter was of immediate importance and postponed anything which might reasonably be left to William's return. Of her councillors, four were Whig and five were Tory and in general her opinion of them was poor. She was aware of Jacobite plotting and unsure of whom to trust. She was very careful about those in whom she confided.[5]

Mary recorded her opinion of Monmouth in her memoirs: 'Lord Monmouth is mad, and his wife who is mader, governs him...' The Countess of Monmouth was one of the noblewomen who were in regular attendance on the Queen. As such, she was painted by Sir Godfrey Kneller sometime in 1690. This portrait was one in a series commissioned by the Queen for Hampton Court and is the only full-length portrait known of the countess. A tall elegant woman, she is depicted beside a statue of Minerva. Kneller also painted a small oval portrait of the earl about this time*.[6]

In the seventeenth and eighteenth centuries satirical verse took the place of the popular comment on political affairs now found in various branches of the media. In June 1690 a poem entitled 'The Nine' appeared. A verse was devoted to each of the Queen's nine councillors, and the description of Monmouth has been already quoted. Lord Mulgrave may have been the author but the poem was published anonymously. Soon afterwards another poem, 'The Female Nine', turned public attention to the wives. It was believed to have been written by

---

*The portrait of the countess still hangs at Hampton Court. The earl's portrait is at Marble Hill.

Monmouth himself, or at least made to look like his work by a more cunning satirist. Lady Monmouth is described as follows:

> The tall one with an humble mien
> Comes next to wait upon the Queen.
> There goes about the town a rumor
> For want of key* she's out of humor.
> The bauble hangs by Derby's side
> Which does provoke her natural pride,
> Which some conceive to be exceeding:
> Well, 'tis corrected by her breeding...

Later still, 'An Excellent New Ballad' purported to describe how Lady Monmouth's indignation at the portrait of her husband in 'The Nine' made her urge him to write 'The Female Nine' in response. It was said that she told him 'I'll furnish the sense, if you'll tag it with rhymes.'

> Her spouse, fired at this, screamed aloud and cried forth,
> And fetching his dead-doing pen in his wrath,
> He worked off his piece with such art of the pen,
> That he aimed at the ladies, but wounded the men,
> And laboured so hard
> The doors were all barred,
> And none was admitted but trusty Blanchard,†
> 'Twas writ in such haste, you're desired to dispense
> With the want of true grammar, good English or sense.

The Queen believed that Monmouth was 'deeply engaged in Scotland and not much to be trusted, yet must know all...' Her information is likely to have come from Bishop Burnet who, after two conversations with Monmouth, thought the earl was involved in a plot being directed by Sir James Montgomery aimed at forming an alliance in Scotland between the 'Club' opposition and the Jacobites. This alliance would effectively control a majority in the Scottish Parliament which would deny William supply and render his government impossible. It was then intended to ask James to return at the invitation of Parliament. Montgomery had not only been in contact with leading Whigs in England, but also with the exiled court through Neville Payne and Robert Ferguson. His Whig contacts besides Monmouth included the Duke of

*The key was the badge of office of the Mistress of the Robes.
†Blanchard was Monmouth's steward.

Bolton and John Wildman, the Postmaster. Now that they had managed to rid themselves of Halifax, Montgomery urged the Whigs to oppose the King by attacking people such as his friend Bentinck, the Earl of Portland. In the earlier of his two conversations with Burnet, Monmouth had given him some idea of the way in which men's minds were working but the bishop had dismissed the matter as part of 'the ramble of discourse'. On the second occasion Monmouth 'set forth the reasons for it with much advantage, and those against it very faintly'. It was this which made Burnet believe he was already involved in the plot.

We should constantly bear in mind that at this time (June 1690) William's tenure of the government of England and Scotland was by no means the sure and certain thing which hindsight would have us believe. His position was greatly strengthened by his victory over the Jacobite forces at the Boyne in July. Until that decisive outcome, there was room for a 'fire insurance policy' among those who, like Monmouth, were men on the make and anxious about their future.[7]

Monmouth told the Marquess of Carmarthen that the King had given him permission to keep an eye on Scottish affairs, asking him to acquire intelligence from there for his service and to try to prevent anything occurring to his disservice. His brother-in-law, Sir Peter Fraser, had gone to Scotland in January followed by a warning from the Earl of Shrewsbury to the King's Commissioner that a strict eye should be kept on his actions. Provided he did not consider Monmouth one of the 'ill men' whom the administration employed, Fraser could have been a source of information. Hitherto the Jacobite view of Monmouth had been that he was an 'unreconcilable' enemy of King James. Carmarthen, a friend whom Monmouth respected, believed that the earl had become involved, possibly with altruistic motives, and had been 'privy to more of the Scotch designs than he now wishes he had known'. Monmouth's actions at the time of the arrest of Robert Fergu-son, now a Jacobite, further supported this view. Having handed a 'treasonable letter' to Monmouth who took it to the King, Ferguson was then arrested and his papers searched, although he was later released on lack of evidence.

John Wildman, another of Monmouth's friends, was certainly believed to be involved in the Scottish plot. His control of the mail gave him illicit access to information. He was said to be adept at opening the seals on letters, mastering or taking a copy of the contents and then resealing them. At one point in late June no one but Monmouth appeared to be receiving letters from Scotland and Wildman's tricks were suspected. At the time of Ferguson's arrest, it was noticed that Wildman found it necessary to spend some time burning his own papers. A frequent visitor to Ferguson's lodgings, he hovered around while they were searched. Monmouth also called several times; both he and Wildman seemed concerned at what might be found.

Carmarthen thought Wildman a most unsuitable person to have control of the Post Office; not even the Queen's letters were sacrosanct from his meddling. His influence and contact with Monmouth seemed bound to lead the earl into trouble.[8]

Soon after William's departure for Ireland, the Council of Nine had its attention drawn to the 'lemon letters'. These were addressed to a Mr Coutenay of Amsterdam (presumably a French agent) and were interlined in white ink 'with the best intelligence which can be given of Your Majesty's councils and affairs'. Monmouth had reported a correspondence of this kind two months previously but the letters which Wildman now intercepted and passed to the Council were coming at regular intervals. Carmarthen believed them to be a sham; they were either intended to point out the unreliability of some member of the council who was revealing secrets or to demonstrate Wildman's great efficiency at the Post Office. Needless to say, all members of Council speculated on which of their number was the culprit; some of them, including the Queen, were inclined to point to Monmouth.

In the meantime, more details of the Scottish plot were being revealed and some Jacobites were arrested. One of them, Crone, who had been taken up in March and put in the Tower, was now in Newgate. On 19 June Monmouth and the Earl of Lincoln spent some time trying to persuade Crone to make a full confession and name those involved in the plot. On 25 June it was believed that he was ready to make a confession and Monmouth and Nottingham went to hear it. Crone directed them where to find certain papers but only named Montgomery as a conspirator, having conveniently forgotten the names of two others.

Monmouth alone seemed to have contact with Scotland. He produced the information that the Marquess of Atholl, the Earl of Arran and the Earl of Annandale had absconded, perhaps with the intention of leading an insurrection.* The fact that no one else had received any news was blamed once again on Wildman's activities.[9]

---

*The Marquess of Atholl had gone to Glenalmond to drink goatsmilk for his health; Lord Annandale had repaired to Bath also in search of health and 'to be out of the way in quiet'. Leven and Melville Papers, Answers of Lord Ross to Questions p. 454.

Meanwhile William was in Ireland at the head of a strong force of 35,000 men of whom only around half could call themselves British. James, confronting him, had command of a mainly Irish and French army, only slightly smaller in numbers. At home, the anxieties of the Queen and her Cabinet Council focused on the nearer prospect of a French attack on the Fleet in the Channel. In June the Fleet, which consisted of Dutch as well as English ships, lay off the Isle of Wight under the command of Arthur Herbert, Earl of Torrington. Numbering twenty-eight sail, it was not as strong as had been hoped. Many ships were still refitting at Portsmouth and the force was further weakened by the absence of one squadron on escort duty to Mediterranean merchantmen and another stationed in the Irish Sea.

On 13 June a French fleet, numbering around seventy-five ships of the line under the command of Admiral Tourville, sailed from Brest and made its way up the Channel. While off Torbay, Tourville received reports of the position and numerical strength of the Allied Fleet and resolved to attack if possible. As the French moved up Channel, Torrington sailed gradually eastwards, aiming for the Gunfleet and to protect the mouth of the Thames. He had received an exaggerated account of the size of the French fleet and wanted to avoid a fight, at least for the time being, considering it folly to sacrifice unnecessarily a good working fleet to grossly superior numbers. However the reports of the French fleet which reached the Cabinet Council had by contrast underestimated its strength and this led to an awkward discrepancy in the views of shore and sea command.

With a rising sense of crisis, it was felt that Torrington must at all costs stand and fight but how to get him to do this was not easy. Feelings were strong in the Council. The Earl of Nottingham told the Queen of their concern; the Earl of Devonshire had proposed that someone be joined in commission with Torrington but others had thought this was not possible. Monmouth offered to take one of the Commissioners of the Navy whom the King had once considered for the command and the two of them should go on board Torrington's ship as volunteers, taking with them a commission in case Torrington should be killed. The Queen demurred at this; she did not believe that the King would ever grant such a commission but told Nottingham that Monmouth should be thanked for his offer. 'I added', she wrote to William, 'that I could not think it proper that he, being one of the 9 you had named, should be sent away, upon which he [Lord Nottingham] laughed and said, that was the greatest compliment I could make him, to say I could not use his arms, having need of his counsell. I suppose', the Queen added, 'they are not very good friends, but I said it really as I meant...'

Even in a time of national emergency, there were factions and opposing interests in the Council of which the Queen was becoming increasingly aware. She knew that if she allowed Monmouth to go (and of all of them she felt he could well be spared), she was quite certain that Carmarthen would then find some reason to send away Admiral Russell. Mary had found Russell helpful and had sought his advice over the lemon letters. Carmarthen, Nottingham and Marlborough had already told her that they were sure the letters were the work of Wildman, as Monmouth spoke to him freely.[10]

On 20 June the Council received a letter from Torrington in which he stated that he declined to fight under the present circumstances. This caused consternation. Carmarthen proposed that Russell be sent to the Fleet. The Queen was not in favour of this move and did not think that anything should be done to 'provoke' Torrington. She found widespread agreement in the Council where a 'pretty sharp letter' was composed but later softened. For some reason Monmouth was not at this Council but he arrived that evening at Nottingham's office where he found several lords sitting up late, discussing the emergency. Hearing the latest developments, he at once offered to go to Portsmouth. If he could be given a captain's commission, he would fit out the best ship there and join Torrington; 'being in a great passion', he swore that he would not come back if they did not fight.

At Monmouth's urgent request, and with the approval of the other lords present, Nottingham went at once to the Queen, despite the fact that she had already retired for the night. She questioned him closely regarding the number of lords present in his office and, realising that they represented two-thirds of her Council and thus would have carried any vote, she agreed to the request although finding it somewhat irregular. It occurred to her also that Monmouth's absence might test his responsibility for the lemon letters, still coming regularly. As if to prompt her concern, another lemon letter came the next day; it reported matters discussed late the previous evening.

Monmouth arrived at Council next day having found a Major Bourne in the City to carry the commission of Captain so that his own involvement could remain a secret if the ship was not ready in time. Nottingham later sent him a commission for his own use if necessary and asked for news of the Fleet. To Torrington, Nottingham wrote that

Monmouth had 'very generously offered his service' and was hoping to fit out a ship and join the Fleet.[11]

On 29 June, while Monmouth arrived in Portsmouth, the Queen in Council decided that Torrington must be ordered to attack the French fleet rather than withdraw any further eastward than the South Foreland. Should he disobey these orders, Russell should have a commission and go at once to Dover so that he could take command if necessary.

It did not take Monmouth long to ascertain the state of affairs in Portsmouth. From all the reports he could obtain, it appeared that Torrington had used the prevailing easterly wind to continue to move towards the Gunfleet. Since it was known that the full complement of Dutch ships had joined, it was believed locally that orders from above must have prevented an engagement. Some broadsides had been heard from the south-east on 27 June but, as they ceased immediately, they were presumed to be from scouts.

Monmouth wrote to Nottingham as requested. His hope of getting a ship was frustrated. Those lying in dock were not in the state of readiness that had been reported – 'not one of them hath a cable abord but what they ride by, and not ten men to be had in all this harbord.' They were only fit to replace returning disabled ships. With little prospect of action, Monmouth decided to return to London.

While Monmouth returned to town and Russell travelled to Dover, action did take place off Beachy Head on the morning of 30 June. The Dutch attacked first; most of the fighting which ensued was between Dutch and French vessels. Torrington engaged at once but then managed to keep out of range. This enabled the French to approach nearer to the Dutch ships who bore the brunt of the action. By midday, the Allied Fleet was again withdrawing to the east. As the wind dropped, an increasing space formed between the opponents. Torrington took advantage of the ebb tide and cast anchor so that the distance between the lines gradually increased. Action was not resumed; although the French maintained a pursuit, this was ineffective after darkness fell. Torrington continued to withdraw to the Thames. The engagement proved a humiliating Allied defeat. The Dutch were justifiably annoyed at the damage inflicted on their ships and at an apparent lack of support from the English.*

With the Channel now under French control, it was logical to expect an invasion. The usual restrictions against Papists were announced and

*The Dutch lost four ships and the English only one.

known Jacobite sympathisers (such as the Earl of Clarendon and Lord Dartmouth) were arrested. Enemies within (there was grave suspicion of Jacobitism in the Fleet) were as much feared as enemies without. The national emergency brought about a closing of ranks.

On 3 July it was decided in Council that Torrington should be relieved of his command and that two members of Council should be sent to the Fleet. The Queen was given no help with her choice and so she selected the Earl of Devonshire and the Earl of Pembroke. She could see that Carmarthen and Monmouth were displeased. However Monmouth had begged to be excused on the grounds of his relationship to Torrington. The trouble lay deeper; in reality Monmouth believed that the command should be given to him. However Sir John Ashby received it temporarily as a reward for good behaviour.

The Queen spoke to the dissatisfied earl after Council and told him that she 'knew it was not fit for him to go to sea, who was a seaman, without having the command'. Monmouth made little of this, 'he was content with anything as he said', but he understood that the King had once thought of sending him to command and therefore considered he might expect it. The Queen thought to herself that she had never heard William express such an idea and had reservations about it.

In fact the Queen had regretted Monmouth's rapid return from Portsmouth. In his absence, the lemon letters had ceased, but Wildman passed this off as 'the people were gone'. Later the letters started again. In the Queen's mind the link was established, as it seemed to be in the minds of others. As it was, she was very agitated over the state of affairs and Monmouth did not make her lot any easier by constantly reminding her of the dangers. She wished to send 'some person of quality' to the States of Holland to express her resentment of Torrington's conduct and also to ask for more ships. Monmouth offered to go. The Queen was sorely tempted to accept his offer but she sent William Harbord instead.[12]

By 6 July Devonshire and Pembroke had returned from the Fleet, which they had found off Deal. They reported that the English officers were unanimous in their decision that action could not be resumed against the enemy and that they were resolved to continue towards the Thames. The urgent question of the command reasserted itself, as there was a strong sentiment that Torrington should be removed. The news of the victory at the Boyne had arrived but scarcely seemed to lift the prevailing mood. Monmouth again pressed the Queen for the naval command. She could see that all discussion in Council was doomed to failure as long as this uncertainty continued. She informed him that she would not 'undertake to pitch upon anybody' but would write to the King in Ireland to know his pleasure. She ordered that the matter should not be raised in Council and that names should be given to her to be passed on to the King.

At this time of crisis Monmouth continued to claim the Queen's ear. He told her one morning how ill-served the country was by the present administration. 'Things went thus ill...certainly by the faults of those who were in trust; that it was a melancholy thing to the nation to see themselves so thrown away.' 'To speak plain,' he said to her '...do you not see how all you do is known, that what is said one day in the cabinet council is wrote next day to France...' He then went on to suggest that the lemon letters emanated from Nottingham's office, not from the Secretary himself but from one of the others, perhaps William Blathwayt. The Queen thought this mere sniping. When Monmouth began to speak of ill administration, she countered strongly that she saw no reason why the King should not choose his own ministers. They had driven away Halifax, they were trying the same tactics on Carmarthen and it appeared they were beginning to treat Nottingham in the same way. Was the King always to be controlled in his choice? For herself, she would not tolerate it. In recounting the story to her husband, Mary thought she might have overstepped the mark in speaking so freely. In fact, her spirited response forced Monmouth to adopt a milder tone. Although indeed he had been opposed to Halifax, he had tried to support Carmarthen as he believed him 'firm to our interest'. Fortunately for the Queen, they were called to Council before the earl could expand his views on how the nation could be satisfied.

The Earl of Nottingham was now the sole Secretary of State and Mary was obliged to take his advice in default of any other. It was unfortunate that Shrewsbury had resigned as the other Secretary at the beginning of June; William originally thought that he would be the member of the Council of Nine on whom Mary could mainly rely. Nottingham's advice at the time of the Battle of Beachy Head has since been considered wrong. It has been described as a classic example of the statesman interfering with the local commander. Other seamen thought that Torrington was right to try to avoid a battle; being at sea, the admiral was in a better position to assess the strength of the enemy. Torrington was suspended from his charge, arrested and sent to the Tower. In December he was court-martialled and acquitted. The Navy expressed great joy at his acquittal but he was never employed again.[13]

Seven

With the French fleet still in the Channel, the possibility of invasion was a present fear and the muster of troops continued. However the defence of the country was proving expensive and the administration was extremely short of funds. Monmouth and some of his City Whig contacts thought that the situation could be used to their advantage. On 14 July he approached the Queen with the offer of a loan of £200,000 from the City, provided that she would agree to dissolve the Tory-dominated Parliament. The Queen firmly turned this down; even if the entire Council agreed, she would not consent to such a proposition without the King's opinion. If those were the only terms upon which the City would lend, she could not borrow. Later a delegation from the Council which included Monmouth, together with the Treasury lords, went to the City to ask for a loan of £100,000. The City undertook to do its best to provide the money. Some City Whigs wished to obstruct the loan but most realised that to do so might favour the King's enemies.[1]

Monmouth was undaunted after his conversation with the Queen on 14 July and continued to come and tell her 'many extraordinary things'. He put in a good word for the Earl of Shrewsbury, whom he believed to be now regretting his resignation and anxious to be of service again, and wondered if there was a way of restoring him. The Queen asked if he had any proposal to make, but the earl assured her that he had no commission to do so. Only two days previously Shrewsbury had written to Carmarthen offering himself for the naval command if he could be linked with two seamen. Monmouth's inquiry may have been speculative; on the other hand, if he had heard of Shrewsbury's offer, he may have been attempting to sound out the Queen's intentions in a matter which concerned him personally.

The Queen consulted Admiral Russell about the naval appointment and he advised her to form a commission of three. Russell himself suggested the Earl of Shrewsbury or the Earl of Pembroke, but advised against the choice of the Duke of Grafton and particularly Monmouth. Carmarthen had already advised Monmouth not to ask for the position alone, as no one man was suitable. 'T'other [Monmouth] pretended to thank him, but in a passion begg'd not to be named as one who would go in commission.' The Council later approved the choice of Sir Richard Haddock and Sir John Ashby with a third to be chosen by the King. During the discussion, Monmouth alone remained silent. The choice turned out to be unacceptable to the Admiralty who would have preferred Russell alone but he steadily declined the appointment. Eventually the Council chose Killigrew, Ashby and Haddock. After some heated argument, it emerged that Haddock was the man to whom the Admiralty had an insuperable objection, and the matter was resolved by selecting a commission of two.[2]

In the last days of July 1690 invasion fever was rife. On 28 July there was a rumour that the French had landed. In fact they had done no more than set fire to the village of Teignmouth and some shipping there as they made their way back to Brest. Forces on land were nevertheless in a constant state of alert; Monmouth, for instance, could be seen at Hackney, exercising with six troops of the City Royal Regiment. When the French were known to have reached Brest on 12 August, the danger was over for the time being.[3]

At this stage those who had participated in the Scottish plot now felt that the time had come to mend fences. Montgomery, much in the style that Monmouth had foretold, tried to rectify his position. He approached the Earl of Melville with an offer to 'tell all', provided that there was an undertaking on Melville's part that he would not be cited in evidence against anyone else. Montgomery inferred darkly that various leading members of the English court might be named. He offered to go to London to reveal all he knew to the Queen for the considerable price of a complete pardon, should he fulfil his part of the condition. Melville felt that the risk was worth taking but pointed out to the Queen that to imprison or fine Montgomery would be counter-productive, as he had only a small estate. Later the Queen developed doubts about Montgomery's intentions when she discovered that he had been in London for a week without making any attempt to get an audience.[4]

When the Queen eventually saw Montgomery in early September, much of what he was to tell her she already knew. He pleaded illness and the mislaying of an important letter for his delay in approaching her. He continually asked for secrecy about what he might say, which the Queen thought unnecessary since he had already informed Commissioner Melville and the Earl of Monmouth. The earl appeared to have been made a confidante of Montgomery, but he had a shrewd opinion of his character. Sir William Lockhart thought Montgomery a man who would promise anything while his luck was low but in better days would unhesitatingly repudiate friendships and promises.

This conspiracy faded from the scene after William's return from Ireland. Annandale and Ross received pardons, but none was given to Montgomery, who felt it expedient to leave the country.

Following the victory of the Boyne, William followed up his success by laying siege to Limerick, one of the main Jacobite bases in Ireland. James had withdrawn further south with his army and before July was over he was safely back in France. The siege of Limerick was protracted, and hindered by the loss of William's siege train which had been blown up by the opposing force. William raised the siege at the end of August and returned to England, as heavy rain had made the campaign virtually impossible.

In September a detachment of troops under the Earl of Marlborough sailed to Ireland to attempt the capture of Cork and Kinsale; among them were 200 men from the Earl of Monmouth's Regiment of Foot. After landing, Marlborough was soon joined by the Duke of Württemburg with 5,000 men. Cork submitted after only two days' siege and at once the earl turned his attention to Kinsale. The Old Fort was taken on 2 October, but the New Fort, under a determined and courageous governor, held out for a fortnight longer. Marlborough lost 250 men during the siege, one of them a younger brother of Monmouth, Osmond Mordaunt. Strategically, Marlborough's success in this corner of south-east Ireland was of considerable importance in the control of the country as a whole and in preventing the arrival of assistance from France.[6]

In early September the Countess of Monmouth was in Bath. On the evening of Sunday 7 September Monmouth had left London to visit his wife when news reached him that the King had landed in England. He at once changed course and went to meet him. On Monday at noon they met north of Marlborough and Monmouth was given a very gracious reception.[7]

In December 1690 the King was making plans to go to Holland in the New Year. Once again the Queen would look to a Council of Nine for advice and assistance but there were changes in its membership. The Earl of Monmouth and Sir John Lowther lost their places to Prince George of Denmark and Lord Godolphin. Clearly the Queen found Monmouth unreliable and she was uncomfortable in his company. William had the same experience and was also increasingly unhappy with extreme Whigs. On the record of the past year, it was not surprising that Monmouth was excluded from the inner circle, given his taste for intrigue and his obvious association with the production of the lemon letters. Any remaining hope he may have had of the Secretaryship of State, left vacant since June, was finally removed by the appointment of Henry Sidney, one of the 'Seven'.[8]

As Monmouth accompanied the King to Holland as a member of his suite in attendance, his absence from the Nine was made less obvious. The royal party left Gravesend on 16 January 1691 in poor weather. It was the King's first return to his own country since his departure in the dramatic autumn of 1688 and he was understandably impatient to reach Holland. After three days at sea in bad visibility, he received news from a passing fishing-boat that they were in fact close to land. He therefore elected to abandon the yacht and put the company ashore in boats. He himself transferred to an open boat and was joined by the Duke of Ormonde, the Earls of Devonshire, Dorset, Portland and Monmouth, together with Hendrik van Ouwerkerk and Frederick van Zuylestein. They expected to reach land in a couple of hours but a sea fog enveloped them, land was nowhere visible and they soon lost sight of the ships. To add to the discomfort and danger of the journey, they were surrounded by large ice floes so it was decided not to attempt to make further progress during the hours of darkness. Next morning they found themselves off Goeree where they landed to find warmth and nourishment. After putting to sea again, they landed at Maasluis at 2 pm, having been at sea in an open boat for fourteen hours.

Travelling by road towards The Hague, the King was greeted at Honselersdijk by a deputation from the States and was given a civic welcome in The Hague on 21/31 January. He had come there to attend a conference of Heads of State and politicians, a wide representation of those who found themselves in alliance against the French. A congress had been in session for some time but this was now a conference of leaders from whom much was expected. It was hoped that the outcome would be a firm commitment of forces to the alliance. After a forceful opening speech, William contrived not only to get the members to confer urgently with one another but also to make the necessary commitment. In terms of diplomacy it was a greater success than many a victory of arms. Having achieved this, William withdrew to Het Loo, his favourite hunting-seat, for rest and recuperation.[9]

Monmouth had taken trouble to contact old friends while at The Hague. One of these was Benjamin Furly, the Quaker merchant in

Rotterdam, whom he planned to visit. Furly also corresponded fairly regularly with John Locke. By the end of February Monmouth and others were waiting for a suitable wind to take them home. Conditions at last changed on 8/18 March, while he was visiting Furly. At once there was a rush to get goods on board. Monmouth overheard Furly giving instructions to the captain of the vessel to take care of a new bag specially constructed by Mrs Furly for the carriage of books. As the bag contained literature for John Locke, the earl had it placed in his own cabin for safety.

Next day Furly was at the Exchange when an express came from Monmouth at the Briel. A further delay had occurred because the escort vessel was short of crew, despite the fact that the ship had been fully manned a few days previously. Monmouth asked Furly to complain urgently at the Admiralty. Short of reprimanding the captain, nothing could be done until another ship could provide some men. On 10/20 March it was believed that a ship expected 'every hour' would fill the need, but there was also a rumour that the yachts had already left in company with some privateers. Furly was writing to Locke describing the crisis when 'behold my Lord at the doore, and coming upstairs'. Some time later Furly resumed his letter: 'I have now been up and down with him [my Lord] to get an order for that friggot but find an order sent to the other assigning him [the captain] people in their service upon their ships, and commanding him to sea, upon his peril, tomorrow morning; so my Lord is just now about 10 at night gone down in an open boat rowing, it being a dead calm, having bought a blanket to lap himself in. I wish him safe over...' He arrived in England with the earls of Dorset and Derby on 14/24 March.[10]

The following month Monmouth was involved in a dramatic event at Whitehall Palace. On 9 April 1691 a disastrous fire broke out during the night and destroyed about two-thirds of the apartments in the Stone Gallery, where the earl, as a Gentleman of the Bedchamber, had lodgings. An accident with a candle started the blaze in a set of rooms being prepared for the Princess Anne's young son, the Duke of Gloucester. A maid attempted to detach a candle from the pound in which they were supplied by burning instead of cutting a candle off and managed to set fire to all the wicks. She had hurried away before the flames were properly extinguished and a conflagration resulted. The fire spread rapidly to the neighbouring apartments which were occupied by the Earl of Devonshire, Heer van Ouwerkerk, Heer van Zuylestein and Monmouth. According to Lady Elphinstone, Monmouth was not one to lose his head in a crisis. 'He behaved like what he is a brave hero, for without any concern of his particular losses, he commanded [them] to blow up his own lodgings; there was some others that did not behave so well for they took more care to save their goods than the king's house...' Explosives were used more than once before the fire was brought under control. In the end, only part of Monmouth's lodgings was destroyed but he and his wife lost much in the way of goods and furnishings. In July rebuilding began and the lodgings, which overlooked the privy garden, were repaired.[11]

The King returned to England only briefly in April. One of the few occasions he attended was a great dinner at the house of Lord Montagu at which Monmouth was also present. A considerable stir in the political world was the reappearance of Robert Spencer, Earl of Sunderland. Now a practising Protestant, he took the oaths and subscribed the declaration at a brief meeting of Parliament on 28 April. As a chief minister to James II, when he had deemed it prudent to espouse Catholicism, Sunderland had remained unpardoned. Having escaped to Holland in 1688, he was allowed to return a year later but lived in retirement at Althorp. His reappearance in the House of Lords began a slow process of reinstatement and return to influence. He did not resume sitting regularly in the Lords until November 1692 but long before that he began to give William advice privately. Monmouth did not accompany the King when he returned to Holland but, with many others, he attended the consecration of Doctor John Tillotson as Archbishop of Canterbury on 31 May at the church of St Mary-le-Bow.[12]

Lord and Lady Monmouth spent part of the summer of 1691 in Wiltshire. Monmouth wrote to Locke at the end of July from Court saying that he and his wife planned to leave London for Bath in a day or two but would be happy to delay their journey to suit his convenience. He added that 'my Damsell [Lady Monmouth] hopes the watters will entice the watter Drinker...' Locke had been staying at Oates with Lady Masham. His journal records that he reached Dauntsey on 8 August, presumably in company with his host. Dauntsey was within easy reach of Bath, but not so near as to obviate the use of lodgings for a course of water-drinking and the party moved there later in the month.

Later that autumn, while still in London, Locke called on the Monmouths at Parsons Green and left us a brief glimpse of his friends in a domestic setting. On his arrival, he found the earl busy in the garden 'but (he) promised to carry me to town with him whither he was going to dinner. This put off all talk with him then, he telling me he would call me in my Lady's chamber, whither I went to make her my visit. When my Lord came they both agreed I must stay and dine with my Lady, so I was left...' The gardens at Parsons Green maintained a reputation for beauty and variety throughout the earl's occupation, although there were some periods of neglect.[13]

The winter of 1691-2 was marked for Monmouth by a series of litigations which involved him personally. The first of these concerned the manor of Dauntsey. The legal point in question went back to a very much earlier period in the estate's history. As has been noted earlier, Dauntsey had for many years been the property of the Danvers family. The present representative, John Danvers, was the son of the regicide, Sir John Danvers, who had died in 1655 leaving his heir still in his minority. In 1661 the Act of Pains and Penalties deprived Sir John Danvers retrospectively of all 'the lands, tenements and hereditaments' which he owned on 25 March 1646 or at any time since. The lands having been thus forfeited to the Crown, Charles II granted the manor to his brother James Duke of York in September 1662. The Duke of York then granted a lease of the manor to Edmund Wayte for a period of years which in 1691 was still unexpired. In May 1674 John Danvers, as heir of entail, in his turn granted a lease to Richard Browne. He did so on the grounds that it was impossible to forfeit an entailed estate as the owner had no power of alienation and could only dispose of a life-interest.

Wayte managed to eject Browne from the manor, claiming previous possession. Browne contested Wayte's claim in the Court of King's Bench, which found for Wayte; a subsequent case in the Court of Exchequer reached the same conclusion. A unique feature of the case was that it was the first time that the effect of the penalty for treason on an entailed estate had been tried in a court of law.

In the autumn of 1691 the case reached the House of Lords. By now, it had become a matter of considerable political importance. Should the House of Lords overturn the previous decisions, not only would the Earl of Monmouth have lost a good estate but, more importantly, the Crown might find itself being called upon to repay to Danvers the accumulated rent of thirty years.(The rental in 1690 was £1,096 per annum.) The case of Browne v. Wayte was in reality John Danvers v. The King or, more popularly, 'the great cause between the Earl of Monmouth and Mr Danvers'.

Edmund Wayte had died before the appeal to the Court of Exchequer had taken place in 1689. He was now represented by his executor,

Ayliffe Wayte. It would appear that the Waytes had accepted the grant to Monmouth as one of the effects of the Revolution, as there is no indication that they disputed his occupation of the estate when he paid a brief visit there the previous summer.

The case appeared before the Lords on 23 November. Counsel were heard for both sides and the judges were called upon to give their opinions. The majority of the judicial bench held that the general words in the Act of Pains and Penalties covered all the estate of which a man was in possession in his lifetime, and that this included any entailed estates. Only two judges gave dissenting opinions.

There was much canvassing of the peers' opinions. Blanchard, Monmouth's steward, was continually at the door of the Chamber in order to take a report to Lady Monmouth each day. He approached many lords to find out how they would vote, as a strong opposition to the Crown was building up under the powerful leadership of Carmarthen and Halifax. Some peers had axes to grind regarding such estates but others were ambivalent or frankly embarrassed, having interests on both sides.

The judges gave further opinions on 30 November. There was subsequently a long debate followed by a vote. The Crown case had strong support led by the two Secretaries of State and including Portland, Rochester, Shrewsbury, Montagu, Marlborough and Godolphin. Seventy-eight peers were in the Chamber to cast their votes when the question was put. The outcome was evenly divided, with thirty-nine votes on each side. Thus the judgment of the lower courts was upheld, there being no remedy for the petitioner when the division is equal.

It was a close thing and just how close was revealed by many stories circulating later. One factor that may have saved the day for the Crown was the powerful pleading of the Earl of Nottingham, whose cogent reasoning of the legitimate forfeiture of the estate won some support. Monmouth himself, realising the outcome might be close, asked if he might use his own vote as it was for the King's interest. He was told there was no need but in fact he did so. Interested parties on the other side, such as the Earl of Abingdon, also used theirs.

Monmouth showed himself a generous winner. He declared that he would give John Danvers £300 per annum for the rest of his life. As the earl allowed the rent reserved to the Crown (a similar amount) to fall into arrears in 1694, he may well have carried this out.[14]

Another litigation was of a different nature and arose from a mare's nest of complications regarding a matter which the earl may have taken up in the first instance through a desire for profit but perhaps also with a degree of misplaced generosity.

On 17 December 1691 a petition was read in the House of Lords in the name of Mrs Mary Wallwyn, a widow. She had a son, Fulke, who was described as an idiot. Fulke was the tenant for life of an estate of £400 per annum in Herefordshire and he lived with his mother at Hellens, Much Marcle. On 7 December 1689 the Earl of Monmouth had obtained a grant of the custody of the idiot boy and, on 11 April 1690, a second grant of wardship founding on the first. In these grants the earl had covenanted to pay Mrs Wallwyn £200 per annum for her maintenance and that of her son out of the income of the estate, the remainder of which would be paid to the earl. In her petition Mrs Wallwyn claimed that she had received only £100 of the sum due to her since the earl took possession of the estate and, when the earl's agents came to take possession and receive rents and arrears, no provision was made for her. Consequently she and her tenants refused to pay further rents or attorn to the earl. When Monmouth tried to acquire an Order of Assistance from the Lords Commissioners of the Great Seal, he was told that the case was one of 'great compassion' and Mrs Wallwyn should receive what had been ordered. Mrs Wallwyn claimed that the earl had declined a hearing and that she was unable to proceed against him in the lower courts because of his privilege. She further made the surprising claim that the earl had entered Hellens by force, put her sons-in-law under restraint, seized her son and carried him away. The earl had then forced her tenants to pay rents and arrears. She now prayed the Lords that she might be allowed the provision made for her in the original patent.

This interesting scene having been set, the earl's answer was awaited with curiosity. It came on 21 December. First, Monmouth claimed that he had always been ready to answer in the inferior courts, had never insisted on his privilege but was ready to waive it. He related that he had agreed that the idiot should remain in his mother's keeping, although he was under no compulsion to do so, and that she should be supplied with £200 out of the estate. In June 1690 his agents had gone to the estate, peaceably taken possession and received the attornment of all the tenants save that of Hellens. The agents took up about £90 in rent. In the following September, Mrs Wallwyn 'obstructed Respondent in the further receipt of rent', and forcibly repossessed the estate. The earl further stated that, in June of the present year, one Rawlins paid £40 in rent to his agent and subsequently had his cattle distrained for failure to pay rent to Mrs Wallwyn. In August, having received information with proof that it was no longer advisable for the idiot to remain in the care of his mother, the earl went in person to Hellens to remove the boy. He sent a servant ahead to warn them of his approach and that he came to take possession. Whereupon Mrs Wallwyn's son-in-law, John Noble, and some others 'with blunderbusses and other weapons' threw the servant out. A pistol having been fired at him as he approached, the earl then removed the idiot by force. On this visit Monmouth received over £100 in rents from the tenants, gave Mrs Wallwyn £100 and discharged the tenants from liability for the rents they had already paid to her. The earl's defence for not paying Mrs Wallwyn all she had expected was simply that she had obstructed the collection of the rents out of which the money should have been paid.

Both petition and answer were referred by the House of Lords to the Committee of Privileges, before which body counsel would be heard and witnesses examined. Meantime, 'the idiot occasions much talk,' Robert Pawling told Locke. Whatever his motives, Monmouth had become embroiled in a family dispute of some complication.

Mary Wallwyn had borne her husband, John, two daughters and two sons. Sadly both sons proved mentally deficient. In 1684 John Wallwyn obtained a patent from the Crown giving the custody of his two sons and the administration of the estate to his wife in the event of his death, so that she might be financially independent and thus better able to pay his debts. As this patent was granted 'during pleasure', it was necessary to make a second application on the death of Charles II and another patent was duly granted by James II. The process was then repeated on the accession of William and Mary. By this time John Wallwyn had died and so had one of his sons, leaving Fulke heir to the estate. When Mrs Wallwyn applied for the patent, it was granted; but before it could be issued, the Earl of Monmouth also made application for it. He did so at the request of Fulke's impoverished uncle, Richard Wallwyn, who was next heir to the estate. The Lords Commissioners of the Great Seal refused Monmouth's application but their decision was overridden by a warrant from the King, giving custody to Monmouth. Mrs Wallwyn then tried to get Monmouth's grant cancelled. She wrote to the Secretary of State, the Earl of Nottingham, and offered to pay Richard Wallwyn £40 or £50 per annum out of the estate. She was unsuccessful; the earl's grant was reissued on 5 April and incorporated the financial provisions for Mrs Wallwyn and her son.

There is no explanation given why Richard Wallwyn had been passed over by his brother as guardian for the two sons. Speculation suggests a quarrel, or the unexplained reason for Richard's poverty, which might have been caused by fecklessness or inability, thus rendering him an unsuitable administrator. As a near male relative, he was an obvious choice. In any event, the courts considered this a very singular case of 'the greatest calamity', because the custody and wardship had not been granted to a relative.[15]

In June 1690, after the first rent collection had been undertaken by Monmouth and the sum of £90 gathered, the earl paid part of the sum to Richard Wallwyn but none to Mrs Wallwyn. This may have prompted Mrs Wallwyn's vigorous attempt to prevent the earl's collection of the next payment of rent and to re-enter possession. A Colonel Babb, who had lived with Richard Wallwyn, gave evidence before the Committee of Privileges that the earl had planned to pay Richard an annual sum of £120 out of the estate. This and the payment to Mrs Wallwyn would leave little over from the annual income.

Richard had little time to enjoy his slight improvement in fortune as he died well before the time of Mary Wallwyn's petition in December 1691. On Fulke's death the estate would now be inherited by his sister Margaret, the wife of John Noble. Monmouth wished to remove the boy from Hellens in August 1691 because he had heard, and could prove, that Mrs Wallwyn and John Noble had entered into 'agreements' concerning the estate. Also the boy had been diagnosed as suffering from a 'convulsive distemper'.

On 4 January 1691/92, counsel and witnesses were heard by the Committee of Privileges. Evidence was led regarding instances of obstruction by Mrs Wallwyn and members of her family of the earl's management of the estate and accounts were given of his visit to Hellens in August 1691.

In June 1690 all but one of the tenants of Fulke Wallwyn's estate attorned to the earl's agent, Mr Penington, in the presence of Mrs Wallwyn. The only exception was the tenant of Hellens, Mrs Wallwyn's other son-in-law, John Shepheard. The agent met with no difficulty and some rent was collected. However, as has already been noted, no part of this rent reached Mrs Wallwyn. Later, in July or August, the widow paid a visit to London; it was after her return that she began to order the tenants to ignore the earl's agents and pay their rent to her. Evidence regarding her actions had been collected, presumably at Monmouth's request, by means of sworn statements made before a magistrate at

Hereford in September 1690, and these statements were read to the Committee. One incident related to the attempt by the son of a deceased tenant to deliver up the property to the earl's agent. The son received verbal abuse from Mrs Wallwyn and her daughter and was offered physical violence by Noble and Shepheard. He managed to escape through a back door, prudently taking the key. On another occasion, a tenant had his cattle and sheep seized as a punishment for paying rent to the earl. There were other incidents of interference.[16]

The earl's agents were careful to collect evidence of obstruction soon after the incidents occurred. These acts of defiance on the part of Mrs Wallwyn led to a visit from the earl himself on 11 August. Monmouth sent ahead a servant, William Ferris, to warn the household at Hellens that he was on his way to take possession. Ferris found the door open and announced his message. Noble threatened him with a gun, which Ferris managed to remove from him as the earl approached. Monmouth was armed with a pistol, as were the four or five servants who accompanied him. From the various accounts given, it is clear that the show of resistance was quite sufficient to ignite the earl's temper, which he proceeded to lose resoundingly. Noble and Shepheard were placed under armed guard, while the earl stormed up the stairs to look for the idiot. Frances Shepheard had given birth to a child a few days previously. Hearing a commotion on the stairs, she went out from her room with her sister, Margaret Noble, to find several men coming up with pistols in their hands. She boldly asked the leader for his identity, and being told 'the Earl of Monmouth', she said, ''Tis much to your Lordship's honour if you make my seven children motherless, for I am a dead woman.' She turned away into her room, but not before she had seen the earl take hold of her sister and drag her along 'in a great passion, bidding her tell him where the idiot was'. Frightened, the sister indicated the room; the earl kicked the door open, went in and took the boy. Frances Shepheard heard the earl say 'he was resolved to take the house, or else he would have brought his regiment and blown it up'.

After this incident, and after Monmouth had got what he came for, the atmosphere calmed. The earl remained in the neighbourhood for two days; rents were paid in to a certain extent and the earl gave £100 to Mrs Wallwyn. Those tenants who had already paid rent to her under compulsion were not asked to pay again, contrary to their expectations. Frances Shepheard stated that the earl 'spoke kindly to the family' before he left, and made promises which the vicar urged her to comply with. Her son, to whom she had recently given birth, was named

Charles. This was not a family name and suggests that the earl stood sponsor to the baby at his christening, which may have taken place before he left. One of the earl's servants deponed that Monmouth gave Mrs Shepheard's child three guineas each day he was there. John Shepheard, who had expected to be thrown out with his wife and seven children, was told that the earl was offering him a captaincy in his regiment and so 'between hope and fear' he attorned tenant on 13 August. Mrs Wallwyn quite willingly set off for Bath in the earl's carriage, accompanied by her son.

Monmouth, still determined that the idiot would be better away from his family, eventually appeared to shake off Mrs Wallwyn. She later complained that she had only seen her son once, at Parsons Green. Her demands for the arrears of her money continued and received an increasingly brusque response until her petition to the House of Lords took place. On 8 January 1691/92 it was reported that Monmouth was prepared to meet the Solicitor-General, Sir John Somers, and Sir Thomas Powys, Mrs Wallwyn's counsel, to try to compose the matter. On 11 January Sir John conveyed to Mrs Wallwyn's counsel some proposals from the earl.[17]

The last recorded papers in this case were read before the Committee of Privileges on 19 February. They were a draft agreement between the earl and Mrs Wallwyn. In the agreement, the earl undertook to pay the arrears of £500 due to her and also £200 per annum in half-yearly payments, as under the original arrangement. He agreed that the idiot should live with his mother, provided that they resided at some place within a specific distance from London (yet to be arranged) 'so as he shall not be under the power of any of his heirs-at-law', and where he and his mother would be maintained at the earl's expense. Arrangements were also made for the financial support of Mrs Wallwyn out of the estate, in the event of the idiot's death and the termination of the wardship. John Locke was upset by the case. 'It vexes me cruelly,' he wrote, 'I mean the whole business, I always saw inconvenience in it, and did what I could.' Nothing further is heard of the matter. The idiot died later that year at twenty years of age. The wardship seemed a great trouble, lasting only too short a time; little of value can have accrued to Monmouth from it.[18]

Eight

The early months of 1692 were marked by a period of intensely cold weather. The frost broke on 13 February after weeks of heavy snow, frozen rivers and disrupted mails. The Thames had been passable on ice in more than one place and it was impossible for the transport vessels to move until the ice cleared. Abroad, the conditions postponed preparations for the forthcoming campaign.

Great plans had been made for the campaigning season of 1692. The rebuilding programme undertaken in the Fleet after Beachy Head had produced a navy which might reasonably be considered superior to that of the French and which also had highly efficient fire power. For the summer, William had planned a descent on France at either Brest or St Malo. The French planned an invasion of England in support of King James with the intention of weakening the Allied strength on the Flanders front to French advantage.

William left for Holland on 4 March, earlier than usual, while gunners and bombardiers could be seen in practice on Blackheath. At the beginning of April there was a heady atmosphere of optimism. Lady Monmouth told Locke that no one spoke of anything but descents and everyone was dreaming about conquest and artillery trains. She urged him to leave Oates and Lady Masham and pay her a visit at Parsons Green; she was in need of some rational thought in the midst of so much excitement. 'You and your Lady', she told him 'are Virgil's shepherds, fitter for the state than country, thinking there what I wish our councils executed here…' If not brought to herself, she was afraid she might commit some extravagance such as taking a house in Paris for next winter instead of staying at Parsons Green. Even her husband had been infected by her mood and had promised to make no plans for next year.[1]

Despite the optimism, preparations for the descent, under the overall command of the Duke of Leinster, went ahead but slowly. In early April William suspected that the French military build-up on the coast of Brittany, attended by King James in person, could be intended for an invasion of the Channel Islands. Monmouth's regiment of foot had been on garrison duty in Guernsey and Jersey for the past year. On 6

April all officers were ordered to return at once to their commands and the regiment was sent extra supplies including trench tents. A squadron of twelve ships under the command of Rear-Admiral Carter was appointed to cruise in the area. Monmouth himself was sent to take command in Guernsey during the absence of the Governor, Lord Hatton. Lord Jermyn was sent to Jersey.[2]

Before leaving, Monmouth told Nottingham that he did not think a squadron would prevent a French invasion of the Channel Islands and recommended that a second regiment be sent to Guernsey. The Duke of Leinster agreed with this view and in order not to delay the squadron, Carter was ordered to take on board Colonel Purcell's regiment. Unimpressed by Leinster's command and the slow speed of arrangements for the descent, Monmouth left London for Portsmouth on the evening of 18 April, taking with him four of his watermen and twenty-one French reformed officers who were to command the Guernsey militia. The word was that he had laid a wager in one of the coffee houses, £40 to £10, that the French would make a descent on England before the English landed in France.[3]

As Monmouth left London, it was becoming increasingly clear that the French descent was intended for the coast of England and not the Channel Islands. Soon afterwards instructions were received by Rear-Admiral Carter cancelling the embarkation of Colonel Purcell's regiment. Unfortunately the men were all on board and it took another two days to reverse the process. Monmouth's own departure was held up first by contrary winds and then by Carter's wish that the *Charles* galley, on which Monmouth was to sail, should take up one hundred soldiers. During the delay, a privateer owned by Lord Danby brought in a French vessel which she had captured off Guernsey. The Frenchman had been carrying naval stores and had taken up a pilot at Havre de Grace. They were able to report that there was a concentration of troops on the coast of France and what appeared to be landing-craft ('flattbottom boats') among the shipping there but no expectation of invasion among the islanders. Monmouth felt extremely frustrated by the delay; had they been at sea sooner, they might have met the 'eighteen great ships' seen by the privateer off Guernsey the previous Sunday.

Before sending the master of the French ship and his pilot to be questioned by the Earl of Nottingham, Monmouth used his good command of French to interrogate the pilot regarding the quantity, type and content of the shipping at Havre de Grace. The pilot gave the common report that King James was in Normandy and that troop preparations were general along the coast to deter an English landing. However the provision of large quantities of hay in Normandy and the stores put on board ship suggested an attempt against England. From a recent letter from Nottingham, Monmouth knew that this was now the general belief. He noticed, however, that the Secretary did not suggest that he should alter his plans for Guernsey accordingly. 'You must give me leave to observe I am reckon'd to be of no use but where I can be of none,' he wrote. 'Since your aprehensions for the islands are over, and that you suspect other designs, to be sent to two hundred men is a very extraordinary employment found out for me, but my Lord assure your self if his orders prevent not the Admiral giving me a ship, which I have sent to desire of him, the first moment there is a possibility I am gone.'[4]

Adverse weather conditions continued to delay the departure of Carter's squadron. As there was no real prospect of leaving before it, Monmouth filled in time by continuing to gather information from shipping. Then a request from the Lieutenant Governor to Nottingham for a strict order to keep all officers at their posts gave the earl an opportunity to unburden himself to the Secretary of State regarding an army matter which had caused him annoyance and disgust. At the embarkation of Purcell's regiment, Monmouth had noticed that six captains were away recruiting although the regiment had mustered complete only six weeks previously. The arrival of Hastings's regiment, with only three captains present, pointed up the situation. In Monmouth's view, the cause of the trouble was the scandalous sale of commissions by the colonels to the highest bidders. There was no question of suitability of character. The commission went to the man who could offer the most money. This prevented good officers, who hoped to rise in the regiment 'by their service and diligence', from receiving the just rewards of their labours.

Monmouth had discovered this in the short time in which he himself had been among them as a colonel. He had been told that there were two coffee-houses in London which were used for what was none other than commission-broking, and no attempt was made to make a secret of it. 'These unjust partialities,' he told Nottingham, 'and for money, have offended my conscience, and att this rate the King of France might secure att a cheape expence [a] good number of friends in our army.' Monmouth's complaint and the incidents which gave rise to it resulted in a summons to all colonels of regiments then in London to appear before the Queen at a Cabinet Council. They were ordered to return to their regiments and give an account of all absent officers.[5]

On 24 April Monmouth left Portsmouth for Spithead on board Lord Danby's galley and crossed to Guernsey. Carter's squadron left soon afterwards but experienced bad weather on their crossing and reached Guernsey road on 27 April. Carter had intended to continue next day for the coast of France and St Malo but Monmouth insisted that he should first leave them some 'sea victuals', having already discovered that there was not enough food on the island to withstand a week's siege. Carter proceeded to offload 3,500 lb of bread and 1,810 pieces of beef and pork; with a little careful husbandry and some local supplement, he considered this should keep 500 men for a fortnight.

A ship from Jersey brought pilots for the Fleet and also four French prisoners taken up as suspected spies. Monmouth and Carter examined the prisoners on oath and sent depositions to Nottingham. Evidence gathered showed clearly that Havre de Grace was the French rendezvous and that no shipping remained at St Malo. There seemed little point in proceeding there.[6]

Guernsey was not after all required to withstand a siege. The island appeared to be no longer in the centre of the action. There was little for Monmouth to do but examine the condition of the island and send reports home. By 21 May he was back in London, claiming that the island was sufficiently provided for. He brought with him news of an imminent naval engagement as the French and English fleets were facing one another off the Isle of Wight.

In fact the Battle of La Hogue had commenced on the morning of Thursday 19 May. By this date the Dutch fleet had joined the English ships. An attempt by the Dutch and English to encircle the French failed when the wind dropped. In the middle of the day a duel between the two flagships commenced and other ships were gradually drawn in. Around 4 pm a fog settled in, concluding the action. When the fog cleared, the French could be seen in retreat towards the west, their ships dispersed in many directions. The action took place off Barfleur. On 23 May Admiral Rooke entered the bay of La Hougue* and set fire to several French ships sheltered there.[7]

The Earl of Danby was not the only nobleman to own, in whole or in part, a merchant ship for profit. As a privateer, the ship might be commandeered for naval service in time of war as she would normally have an armed capability. Monmouth himself was part owner of a yacht of Dutch extraction called the *Soest Dijk* or *South Dyke*. Lighter and faster

*The correct original spelling, though the battle is recorded as 'La Hogue'.

than a galley, this yacht had a royal commission during the war, although she was still manned and victualled at the owners' expense. Sent on an errand to warn the Fleet that the French were off the coast of England, the yacht encountered, and later took as prize, a French vessel, the *Prince William*, 'laden with French wines and brandies, and other goods of the growth of France'. As the yacht was in Her Majesty's employment at the time, Monmouth and his co-owners were disappointed to find that they could not consider the prize conclusively theirs. Consequently on 3 June they petitioned the Queen that they might be granted the vessel 'with all her lading'. The Treasury lords advised Her Majesty that it was in her discretion whether she made the grant or not. Happily for the owners, their petition was successful.[8]

Meanwhile King William was in Flanders, keeping one eye on the situation in the Channel and the French intentions towards England. The French opened the campaigning season in May by laying siege to Namur and William moved by stages in that direction. By 29 May/8 June he had reached Lincent; from there he moved to a position on the River Mehaigne where he confronted the French army under the command of the Duc de Luxembourg.

The passage of troops across the Channel was held up by stormy weather. Monmouth was more fortunate when he travelled to Rotterdam with his wife in early June. Benjamin Furly was delighted to meet the couple on the Exchange one day. They were accompanied by Lady Monmouth's aunt, Lady Wentworth. From there Monmouth went to William's camp at Ramillies, where he arrived on 7/17 June.

The reason for Monmouth's visit to the army was probably for a tour of duty in attendance on the King, as he remained in Flanders for about a month. On 22 June NS, the army moved again, to Sombreffe, and two days later to Mellet. Here, on 3 July, William heard of the capitulation of Namur. In an attempt at retaliation, he despatched a force to attack Mons. The force was intercepted by some French troops who had been alerted by a spy in the suite of the Elector of Bavaria and the attempt was abandoned. At Mellet the camp was so surrounded by French patrols that it was impossible for troops to move except in large numbers, so William was obliged to move to Genappe. Here the army remained until the necessity of finding a new forage area caused a move to Halle on 31 July. By this time Monmouth was back in London with no fresh news; he had left the camp before the latest despatches and had taken time to visit Furly again on his homeward journey.[9]

The Monmouths took their son, Lord Mordaunt, to Bath in early

September as he had been ill. The weather was fine and the earthquake which shook London on 6 September was much less severe in the west. As usual they encouraged John Locke to join them. He declined but sent the boy a book which, according to his father, Johnny read 'a thousand times'.*10

After a disastrous summer campaign the King arrived in England on 20 October. The defeat at Steenkirk in late July had done nothing for morale and later raised questions, perhaps unjustly, about foreign commanders of British troops.

In a break from Parliamentary attendance in November, Monmouth wrote again to Locke who had not yet availed himself of the earl's invitation to stay.

> I am afraid of mentioning Parson's-green to you for I find you would be importuned, if so near, to come to town, and our innocent air would be accused of the ill effects of London smoke. If your acquaintances would make you visits, and expect no returns, I would do all in my power to tempt you to a lady, who would take all possible care of you: she has prepared you a very warm room…for as your physician you must refuse none of her prescriptions; and she will not allow you to come up but in a glass coach. This is no compliment; and you can gain no admittance unless my coach brings you, which I can send without the least inconvenience…

If Locke decided to stay in the country, Monmouth offered to send him news letters about the political scene.

> Our revolving Government always affords us something new every three or four months; but what would be most new and strange would be to see it do anything that were really for its interest; there seems a propensity towards something like it; I fear their sullen and duller heads will not allow it. Mons. Blanquet tells us the King is grown in love with Englishmen and Whigs; it is true he talks and smiles with us, but Messrs. Semour and Trevor come up the back stairs.

The Common Council of the City of London had moved a petition against the Earl of Nottingham, a Tory, claiming he had interfered in City elections, 'yet the Court have taken all possible pains to prevent

*The book described the 'caracter of the little steeds'.

the petition against him and my good Lord Mayor, to set it aside, broke up the court so abruptly, as my Lord Sidney the Irish Parliament.' Monmouth concluded his letter cheerfully: 'I will engage no further in politics, for being sick, am going, by way of physic, to eat a good supper, and drink your health in a glass or two of my reviving wine.'[11]

Criticisms of the conduct of the summer's campaign were voiced in the Commons in November. Lord Monmouth's brother, Henry Mordaunt, who had been returned as a member for Brackley in January, vehemently complained about almost everyone in the government. A captain in a cavalry regiment, Mordaunt had served under William in the last campaign in Flanders. He spoke for many when he complained of the command of English troops being given to foreigners. By the end of November the peers had also passed a resolution against the appointment of foreign generals over British troops. However Monmouth was one of eighteen peers who protested when the House turned down a proposal that a joint committee should be set up with the House of Commons to consider the advice to be given to the King about this matter.[12]

It was a busy winter for legislation. A Place Bill intended to prohibit office-holders from sitting in the Lower House successfully passed through the Commons in December but ran into trouble on its appearance in the Lords. In January it was rejected at the third reading by only two votes. Afterwards, Monmouth was one of a small group of peers who entered a protest without reasons given. It was generally believed that he had given his support to the Bill as a frustrated Whig but as a Gentleman of the Bedchamber he was also an office-holder under the Crown. He was seen looking dejected as he left.[13]

In January 1693 Monmouth took a marked interest in the trial of Lord Mohun held in Westminster Hall. It was a difficult case. Charles Lord Mohun and Captain Richard Hill had attempted to abduct an actress, Anne Bracegirdle. In the course of this attempt William Mountford was stabbed and killed by Hill who then absconded, leaving Lord Mohun to face an arrest from which he was later released on bail. Mohun had been charged with the crime but many questions were asked of the judges regarding the criminal responsibility of someone who was present when a crime was committed but was not necessarily a party to it. Each peer was entitled to put questions to the judges on his own behalf, with the approval of the House. Two questions were marked as having been put by Monmouth. Judgment was pronounced on the fourth day of the trial. By a majority of 64 votes to 14, Lord

Mohun was found not guilty. Monmouth and Shrewsbury both voted with the minority.

Monmouth attended the rest of the parliamentary session with reasonable frequency. He was named as a member of a variety of committees on bills whose purposes ranged from preventing abuses committed by traders in butter and cheese or the importation of foreign hair buttons to the regaining and encouraging the Greenland trade.[14]

Before leaving for Holland on 4 April, the King made two new Whig appointments: Sir John Trenchard, an exclusionist, became Secretary of State for the Northern Department and Sir John Somers was appointed Lord Keeper. This increase in Whig influence pleased Monmouth and prompted a letter to John Locke.

> Mr Locke, shall we pretend more that nothing shall surprise us? and have you heard of our late Whiggish promotion without admiration? I cannot but confess I rather wish we had our Whiggish laws; but, however, I think there must be some consequence, not so much of our joy, as of the ill humour of the Tories, which is so apparent, and so great, that I am resolved to enjoy the satisfaction it gives me, and not lose the few moments of mirth offered us by a too nice examination. The new Secretary treads the stage with quite another air than our friend; the poor Lord Keeper looks as if he wanted the comfort of his friends; but the other thinks he may depend on his own parts and the ability of Mr Bridgman. Whether to congratulate with your friends, or to see the silly looks of the enemy, I suppose you will give us one week in town. There is a little philosophical apartment quite finished in the garden that expects you, and if you will let me know when you will come, it will not be the least inconvenience to me to send my coach twenty miles out of town to meet you, and may make your journey more easy, and if you would make me so, pray, Mr Locke, be less ceremonious to your affectionate servant...[15]

The summer campaign of 1693 was generally unsuccessful for the confederates. William's army awaited developments near Brussels. The stalemate of the early months resolved itself into the Battle of Neerwinden or Landen on 29 July NS. William's army was outnumbered from the start and the defeat which followed was not surprising. Later in the summer the French added to their success by besieging Charleroi, which surrendered after thirty-two days.

When Parliament reassembled in November, there were many questions to be asked about the war and its attendant huge cost but a major concern was the loss of the Smyrna convoy. An Anglo-Dutch fleet of 400 merchantmen sailed on 30 May OS, unaware that the French fleet had left Brest and was sailing ahead of them for the Portuguese coast. Off Lagos the French attacked, dispersing the merchantmen of which 100 were destroyed. The loss was computed at around £1 million, the Levant Company alone losing £600,000. One result of the disaster was the renewal of calls for the presence of an Anglo-Dutch fleet in the Mediterranean.[16]

In 1693 various methods were used to try to raise funds for the conduct of the war. Finances were at a seriously low ebb and a move was made to encourage public subscription through loans, lotteries, tontines and increased taxation. For some time public money had been subscribed through various 'aid' funds. In 1689 Monmouth, while a Treasury Commissioner, had subscribed £950 on 17 April and £2,000 on 27 May to aid the King. Interest, initially paid at 6%, was later increased to 7%.

An example of the absence of liquid cash at this time can be seen in the payment of salaries to Gentlemen of the Bedchamber. These officials received a salary of £1,000 per annum, normally paid quarterly. Increasingly, payment fell into arrears. In his capacity as a Gentleman of the Bedchamber, Monmouth was issued with a money warrant on 28 October 1690 for £750, which represented three quarters' salary to 29 September. The following May (1691), a further warrant was issued for £250 for the Christmas quarter of 1690. However, it appeared that the previous warrant had not been fully paid and was to be completed by loans made by Monmouth on the duties on East India goods. Some quarterly payments became too difficult to manage. On 18 April 1692 a Treasury order was made to pay Monmouth £1,000, his entire salary for 1691. This was done by five payments of £200 made between 14 July and 18 August. In July 1693 a similar warrant was issued for the salary for 1692, and on 4 July the Secretary to the Treasury was instructed to pay the Gentlemen of the Bedchamber out of loans made by them or their appointees. This pattern was followed for several years.[17]

In November 1693 the Triennial Parliaments Bill made an early reappearance in the House of Lords. It had first passed through Parliament in January but had been vetoed by the King. This time its chief sponsor was Monmouth, who made it clear that the Bill was an identical measure to that which had appeared the previous winter. That a prominent peer should be encumbered with the introduction of a Bill which had already been rejected twice did not pass unnoticed. The policy of frequent Parliaments was dear to the Whig party. Just how dear was shown by the Earl of Shrewsbury when he made the King's consent to the Bill's passage through Parliament a condition of his acceptance of the Secretaryship which William had offered him. William would not agree to the condition so Shrewsbury retired to the country to avoid further persuasion.

The Bill passed its first and second readings in the Lords but at the Committee stage there was much debate about annual Parliaments, although little was altered. Monmouth took part in the discussion but seemed 'not so zealous as last session'. At the third reading an interpretative proviso relating to the protection of the prerogative was introduced by the Earl of Devonshire. After much debate the proviso was adopted, as it was supported by all those who were against the Bill as well as by some others. Monmouth was disgusted by this. The Bill passed its third reading, to come to grief at a later date in the House of Commons.[18]

Monmouth was not only lacking in zeal this session, he was discontented and out of sorts. A friend of his at Court who corresponded with Dijkvelt had been concerned about his attitude for some time. It seemed that the earl believed he had genuine grievances. He took it personally that his brother, Henry, a captain in Lumley's regiment, had not yet received a colonelcy. Concerned about the Triennial Parliaments Bill, he had been annoyed at the clause, mentioned above, which had been introduced at the last moment and passed; he was also angry with peers like Lord Mulgrave who had experienced a change of heart over the Bill during the last year. He considered himself to be in the wrong place; certainly he could see William appoint Whigs to positions and yet appear to have no use for him. The friend begged him not to throw away his advantages and make matters worse by giving up his places. He should consider his family and what the King had done for it. 'Je scay', Dijkvelt's correspondent concluded, 'que des esprits mal intentionnez le poussent contre son propre interest sous prétexte d'amitié.'

Monmouth appeared to have been thinking of giving up his places in protest but his purpose is not clear. Were the evil spirits extreme Republican Whigs or a different variety 'over the water', such as Sir James Montgomery of Skelmorlie? By Christmas a rumour was circulating that Monmouth was to be 'discarded'.[19]

In January 1693/94 little occurred to fuel this rumour but on Sunday 4 February the Earl of Portland was sent to inform Monmouth that he was dismissed from his employment in the Bedchamber and from the colonelcy of his regiment. It was also indicated that he would not be summoned to attend meetings of the Privy Council. All the contemporary notices of this event use the words 'dismissed' or 'removed'; there is no suggestion of resignation. It was presumed that this action was intended as a reprimand for bringing in the Triennial Parliaments Bill.

At almost the same time Captain Henry Mordaunt relinquished his command in Lumley's regiment and was replaced by the Earl of Warwick. Monmouth's regiment was still on garrison duty in the Channel Islands. It was not until 25 April that the announcement was made of the appointment of Henry Mordaunt as colonel, the commission being granted with his brother's consent. In the meantime Monmouth lost no time in petitioning for any back payments and monies due to him as colonel.*[20]

There was nothing in Monmouth's demeanour to indicate regret or shame at the removal of his places. He appeared the next day in the House of Lords as usual and was involved in committee work, at least ostensibly, in the normal way. On 27 February news reached London from Cadiz that HMS *Mordaunt*, the fourth-rate which had once belonged to Monmouth and still bore his arms, had been lost on a rock near Cuba. On the West Indian station, she had been acting as convoy to some merchantmen heading for Jamaica and had left them at the west end of Cuba on 21 November. She then ran aground off the Colorados 'through the obstinacy of her pilot' and began to sink. The company did their best to make rafts from the masts and yards but found that the boats could not tow them. However, all those on board were successfully landed on the island of Buena Vista, twelve miles from the ship. From there they reached the mainland of Cuba where they were able to buy provisions and find fresh water. The captain returned to England on board the merchant fleet and most of the ship's company were on their way home in March.[21]

Whether it is mere coincidence or more significant, Monmouth attended Parliament on only one occasion between 27 February and 15 March and on the latter date only in response to a summons. During the month of March Shrewsbury accepted the seals as Secretary for the

*On 23 March he gained a warrant for £3,117.3s.7d.

Northern Department. The reasons for his acceptance are not known but it is considered likely that he had received some assurance from William regarding the Triennial Parliaments Bill. In April there were more new appointments, many involving Whigs; among elevations in the peerage, Shrewsbury received a dukedom.[22]

Nine

Before the prorogation of Parliament on 25 April 1694 and the King's departure for the summer campaign, the Tonnage Bill moved on its controversial way through Parliament. Its provisions included the granting of the proceeds of taxes on shipping and liquor to supply interest at 8% to the subscribers to a perpetual loan of £1.2 million. This Bill made provision for the foundation of what eventually became the Bank of England. Although there was no real opposition in the Lords to the idea of the loan, which was vital to the war effort, there was much concern over the concept of the bank as a privileged corporation with its own managers in charge of such a considerable fund. It was unheard of for such a sum to be held outside government control.

At the committee stage in the Lords on 23 April a lengthy debate ensued. Monmouth joined Halifax, Nottingham and Rochester in opposing the establishment of the bank. They argued that such a fund in the hands of a private corporation would be a disadvantage to the King and would create a monopoly of public credit. Considering that the scheme received criticism as a Whig republican idea, it is strange to find Monmouth on the opposing side and suggests that his opposition was motivated by an anti-government stance. In the event, the opposition was overcome by persuasion, in particular that of Lord President Carmarthen; as the matter closely affected supply and could give rise to controversy with the Commons if opposed, it was important that there should be no delays at this stage. So the Bill passed without amendment. Monmouth did not register an objection to the bank clause.[1]

William left for Holland on 7 May, irritated that the long session of Parliament had delayed the start of the summer campaign and had thus given an advantage to the enemy. Monmouth was left with less to do than usual but he was not entirely in the backwoods. In June he was appointed one of the Privy Councillors to sit as a Commissioner for Prizes during the present war. It also appeared that he had made other arrangements to provide against future disappointments and reverses.

In July Secretary Trenchard and his department uncovered a Jacobite plot in Lancashire and several arrests were made. Riots took place in

Northamptonshire but it was not clear at first whether these had any political implications. On 15 July NS the King wrote to Shrewsbury:

> With respect to the riots in Northamptonshire, I recollect that not long ago I was informed that Lord Monmouth had made his peace at St Germains. Not knowing what to believe, you must try to discover, if possible, whether he, who is lord lieutenant of the county, has fomented or interfered in those riots; and you will please to give me your opinion, whether that employment should not be given to another person...

Shrewsbury's reply was calm and generous to Monmouth.

> I can give no answer to what your Majesty is pleased to inquire concerning my Lord Monmouth's making his peace at St Germain's. It is natural for a man that is very ill on one side, to desire not to be so on the other; but I dare say, let him have made what advances are possible of that kind, if he could find his account under your majesty's government, it is what he would prefer much before any such alteration; and at this time he appears in so much a better temper to act anything for your majesty's service than you can believe, that I should not think it at all advisable to turn him out of his lieutenancy; and for his having anything to do in that disturbance at Northampton, I dare engage he knew no more than an accidental tumult of the rabble, occasioned by their seeing corn sold in quantities out of the town, and is now quiet, without any interposition, but that of the magistrates alone.

William seemed more concerned at Monmouth's possible involvement with riots than by his contacts with St Germain's. The latter he treated with equanimity and even uninterest, only too well aware that many of his courtiers and statesmen were in the same position. Monmouth's uncle, the Earl of Peterborough, provided a sure route of approach to the exiled court and there were no doubt other routes. Shrewsbury himself was embarrassed by close Jacobite relatives, his mother and his two aunts. His own involvement has never been proved, but there was room for misunderstanding and question. When suspicion was later cast on him publicly, Shrewsbury tried hard and unsuccessfully to retire from government service.

Monmouth's slight involvement with Jacobitism was of a 'fire insurance' variety. Like all his contemporaries, including William, he believed that the previous regime could still be restored. James might yet return with the right timing and sufficient help from France. Monmouth's true attitude had been summarised correctly by Shrewsbury; he would much prefer to serve under King William. The Jacobites themselves never considered Monmouth a serious supporter, rather the reverse.[2]

One of the earliest measures to be considered when the Parliamentary session began on 12 November was the Triennial Bill on yet another appearance. This time it was introduced in the House of Commons by Robert Harley after consultation with Shrewsbury. The measure received its first reading in the Lords on 14 December and passed through to receive the Royal Assent on 22 December. On its passage through the Lords there had been no division and no amendment but some discussion had arisen at the committee stage over the question whether the Bill applied to the existing Parliament. The Commons had held that it did and that the present Parliament must terminate in 1696. Monmouth supported the earlier date of 1695 but did not press the point when it became clear that a delay might cause the Bill to be lost.[3]

A tragedy overshadowed the Court at Christmas. After a week's illness, the Queen died on 28 December. Her disease was originally diagnosed as measles but proved to be a severe strain of smallpox. On 27 December, when her recovery seemed unlikely, the Privy Council met to consider whether her death would cause an automatic dissolution of Parliament as at the demise of a reigning monarch. It was agreed in Council that, since the administrative power was vested in the King, there would be no need to call for elections.[4]

Monmouth maintained a frequent attendance in Parliament this session. On 25 January 1694/5, the House of Lords was in committee over the state of the nation. Nottingham made a speech in which he was strongly critical of the administration. He covered many subjects, the government during the King's absence, the conduct of investigations into the Lancashire plot, naval affairs, the bank and the coinage. He was supported by Rochester, Monmouth and Halifax. The House resolved to deal only with the state of the Fleet and a debate took place on 1 March. The address subsequently presented to the King, and which Monmouth had helped to prepare, stressed the importance of maintaining the fleet in the Mediterranean as well as increasing the force so that the coasts could be guarded at home as well as in the West Indies.[5]

If Monmouth had been relegated to the backwoods, it was not long before his exile was ended. 'By his behaviour this session', it was reported, he had 'restored himself to his Majesty's favour'. On 24 March he was summoned to take his place in the Privy Council. He was informed that his place in the Bedchamber had not been disposed of and that he might come into waiting at his next turn. Despite his absence from duty, he received the full year's salary. Inevitably his restoration attracted comment and there were those who believed that the grave illness of Sir John Trenchard might eventually bring a Secretaryship into his hands.[6]

In May both Houses concerned themselves with allegations against certain people of bribery to promote interests in Parliament. In the House of Lords the investigation centred on the person of the Marquess of Normanby (formerly Earl Mulgrave) and his connection with a company which was attempting to acquire a patent to put convex glass lamps in the streets of London.

A man called Hutchison was at the head of the convex glass project. He had authorised Arthur Moore to make over to Roman Russell a twelfth share of thirty-two parts in the company as consideration for promoting Hutchison's interests in Parliament. Roman Russell was the Marquess of Normanby's steward. In evidence led before the House on 1 April, it appeared that Russell had been expected to approach various lords but in fact had only spoken to his master. Subsequently Normanby had been heard to inform interested persons during the passage of the Orphans Bill that, unless they came to an agreement with Hutchison, the Bill would not pass.

Ever since his sponsorship of the Triennial Bill, Monmouth had held a grudge against Normanby for his behaviour on that occasion. Consequently he became one of the most eager to penetrate and expose the marquess's involvement in this case. He claimed to know someone who could shed light on the business and seemed 'resolved to stick upon my Lord Normanby's skirts'. Should he fail to have Normanby censured by a vote, he undertook to have a protestation minuted so that the affair would be on record for ever. The person to whom Monmouth looked for further information may have been Sir Robert Clayton.

Monmouth revealed that recently Normanby had been granted a lease by the City of London of eleven acres of land lying behind Clarendon House. A Lords' Committee examined Sir Robert Clayton and Mr Maurice, both Members of the House of Commons. The House having considered both the examinations and the evidence laid before it, the question was put whether there was any ground for censure of the Marquess of Normanby in the matter of the convex lights or the lease from the City of London. The question was resolved in the negative by only four votes. On the face of it, Normanby was a fortunate man. Monmouth and six other lords signed reasons for their dissent.

Monmouth had hoped that Normanby would be sent to the Tower for bringing dishonour on the House. When told that the marquess had used words in committee disrespectful of the House which could lead to such a censure if complained of, Monmouth shrugged that off as a measure which was a mere formality and hoped that a better reason would be found. Normanby, for his part, was sick of Monmouth's hounding and complained in one of his speeches in the House that the earl 'had in all the prosecution not treated him like a gentleman'. Monmouth was quick to respond that he was prepared to give him the satisfaction of a gentleman outside the House.

In the general wave of investigations, Monmouth was also involved in the examination of Sir Thomas Cook, the Governor of the East India Company which had been accused of producing some of the bribes. The prorogation of Parliament on 3 May put an end to any further activity.[7]

Before the King left for Holland on 12 May 1695, mindful of the revelations of recent months and the operation of the Triennial Parliaments Act, he informed three of his ministers of his intention to dissolve Parliament. No official announcement was made but Monmouth spread it about that the King had spoken of his intention before he left.

One other commitment was brought to fruition before the King's departure. It had been Queen Mary's hope that the ruined part of Greenwich Palace could be rebuilt as a hospital for seamen. This wish gave birth to the Royal Naval Hospital, designed by Sir Christopher Wren and incorporating the Queen's House of Inigo Jones. A commission was formed to set this work in motion in memory of the Queen, and on 9 May it had its first meeting at Guildhall. The Duke of Shrewsbury and the Earls of Dorset, Pembroke and Monmouth were among the commissioners. Wren was already heavily engaged with work at Hampton Court and on St Paul's Cathedral, and the project at Greenwich was not completed until 1702. Monmouth would have appreciated the value of such an undertaking, not least for its importance for the state of the Navy in which he maintained a continuing interest.*[8]

*His signature can be seen on the document normally on show in the Painted Hall.

The summer campaign of 1695 concluded with triumph and rejoicing over the recapture of Namur. Invested by Allied troops on 28 June OS, the fort capitulated on 26 August. Knowing that such a success would be beneficial to the Whig interest in the forthcoming election and of importance to the conduct of the war in future, Shrewsbury urged the King to leave the campaign at that, in case any further undertaking might not meet with the same success.

The proclamation dissolving Parliament was issued on 11 October, the day after the King's return from Holland. Already Monmouth had been active in the City in connection with the forthcoming elections, and he and the Earl of Sunderland were held responsible for ensuring that Monmouth's brother, Harry Mordaunt, was chosen again as a candidate for Brackley.[9]

On his return, the King was greeted with a greater outburst of popular feeling than he had ever previously experienced. This new attitude of optimism and goodwill may have encouraged him to spend some of the time before the meeting of the new Parliament on a royal progress through the East Midlands. Beginning at Newmarket, the King travelled across to Northamptonshire where he stayed with the Earl of Sunderland at Althorp and spent several days hunting and receiving hospitality from neighbouring hosts. From Althorp he made day visits to Boughton and Castle Ashby. He then travelled to Lincoln by way of Stamford and Grantham.

At Belton the King was lavishly entertained by Sir John Brownlow. Monmouth was among the large number of noblemen accompanying him, and the party also included numerous servants as well as guards. In order to provide for the entertainment of such a gathering, Sir John had killed 'twelve fat oxen and sixty sheep'. A contemporary account records that 'the King was exceeding merry there, and drank very freely, which was the occasion that when he came to Lincoln, he could eat nothing but a mess of milk.' This was unfortunate as the Lincoln host, Mr Dorell, had laid on another splendid feast which cost him 'above five hundred pound'.

Whether or not the coachmen in the royal service were treated equally well is not known. For some reason or other the royal coach which was carrying Monmouth and Mr Capell overturned somewhere between Grantham and Lincoln and the earl was very much bruised. Monmouth's injuries were sufficiently severe to make him forgo the journey to Welbeck and he was left behind at Lincoln to recover, later returning directly to London.[10]

When the new Parliament assembled at Westminster on 22 November 1695, the King's speech referred to current concerns including the state of the coinage (there was more clipped money in circulation than milled coins) and the conditions of trade. Monmouth was a member of a committee which drew up an address to the King on 4 December, asking him to proclaim that no clipped money should pass in any payment. He also took an interest in the affairs of the East India Company which had complained that it was experiencing considerable losses because its fleet was not receiving sufficient protection from the Navy. The coast of Ireland appeared to harbour a large number of privateers who were quick to prey on a passing merchant fleet. The Company was also concerned about an Act passed by the Scottish Parliament which appeared to set up a possibly competitive organisation.[11]

These concerns required the oversight of a new and efficient Commission or Board of Trade. By December the King had been persuaded by his ministers that such a Commission was needed, Somers had drawn up a list and the name of John Locke appeared on it. However the Commons decided that they would propose such a body and select the members themselves. There is evidence that the Whig ministry was also behind the Commons' project and it was discussed at a meeting of the Privy Council in November. Matters became confused when the King indicated that the Commons' project was trespassing on his prerogative.

On 12 December Monmouth wrote to Locke to give, as he explained,

some ease to my ill-humour...I was some days ago extremely pleased when the King was brought to so reasonable a resolution as to determine upon a council of trade, where some great men were to assist but where others, with salaries of a thousand pounds a year, were to be fixed as the constant labourers. Mr Locke being to be of the number, made me have a better opinion of the thing, and comforted me for our last disappointment upon your subject: but, according to our accustomed wisdom and prudence, when all things had been a good while adjusted, the patent ready for the seal, and some very able and honest men provided for your companions, it was impossible to get the King to sign it; but delaying it from day to day, the Parliament this day fell upon it, and are going to form such a commission to be nominated by themselves. Our great managers, surprised, were forced to run up to some in our House, others to go to Kensington, so that at last the Secretary informs the House at the latter end of the debate (and much consultation), that the King had just formed such a commission, with all that could be said to prevent their further proceeding; but they all looked upon it as a trick, and all they could do was to put it to a vote for an adjournment, which, in a full House, after great exertions, they carried but by eleven: this is the effect of our gravity and prudence; what the event will be I know not, but for the little I am able I shall endeavour Mr Locke may be the choice of the House, as well as the King's; if it take that course, if the ill weather prevent you not, it were not improper you were in town...

On 17 December Somers wrote to Locke asking if he was willing to be named in the Commission and Locke came up to town to signify his acceptance. The Parliamentary Board duly went through the Commons and was passed by only one vote. The measure was set aside during the crisis surrounding the discovery of the Assassination Plot in February but a royal commission passed the seals in May 1696.*12

The Trials for Treason Bill received the Royal Assent on 21 January 1696. This enacted certain provisions regarding defence in a trial for treason and also laid down that no one could be convicted of treason without the evidence of at least two witnesses. The Whigs had long wished that a measure of this sort should appear in the statute books. Their thinking reflected the long-held grievances over the trials of such party icons as Algernon Sidney, who had been found guilty of treason on the evidence of a single witness. This Act came into force while several trials of Jacobite conspirators were being held.

During the winter of 1695–6 contingency plans were laid between James II in France and Jacobites in England for a French invasion of England to occur simultaneously with a Jacobite insurrection there. As early as December the usual informative underground was producing reports of French invasion plans. As the reports increased, the Council recalled Admiral Rooke and the Mediterranean squadron on 26 January.

In February 1696 the Duke of Berwick was sent on a secret mission to England to check the temperature of English Jacobites and to assure

---

*The 'great men' were the Earls of Tankerville and Bridgwater; William Blathwayt, Sir Philip Meadows, John Pollexfen, Abraham Hill and John Methuen might be described as 'able and honest' and, together with John Locke, formed the Commission.

them of French sincerity. Also Sir George Barclay was commissioned by James to recruit Jacobite troops who would be commanded by Sir John Fenwick. Whatever recruitment took place, Barclay and Fenwick soon involved themselves in extra-curricular activities in the shape of a plot to assassinate King William at Turnham Green. The plot foundered in a way common to such arrangements – two of the conspirators talked. In the event, all the conspirators were arrested except for Fenwick who went into hiding and Barclay who managed to escape to France.[13]

On 24 February the King informed Parliament of the discovery of the plot and its association with a French invasion and also revealed that many arrests had already been made. The reaction in both Houses reflected dismay, indignation and an upsurge of support for William. The next day the Commons approved that an Association should be formed in which they recognised William as their 'rightful and lawful' sovereign, and pledged themselves to be revenged against his enemies in the event of his death by violence.

On 26 February the Association was proposed in the House of Lords by Monmouth supported by the Earl of Tankerville. Monmouth spoke for over two hours and the debate, described as 'regular and very fine', lasted until 11 pm. The peers had much more trouble with 'rightful and lawful' King and the statement eventually produced was far more anti-Jacobite than that in the Commons. Should the King die in an untimely and violent manner, the peers undertook to 'freely and unanimously oblige ourselves to unite, associate, and stand by each other, in revenging the same...' The Duke of Leeds was responsible for finding a more acceptable formula than 'rightful and lawful'. On 27 February the House was called and eighty-one peers signed the Association. Nineteen refused to do so.[14]

The whole experience of the Assassination Plot and its aftermath strengthened the position of William and the Whig government. Subsequently it was required of all office-holders that they sign the Association, and this greatly reduced the possibility of Jacobite influence. Legislation was hurried through to provide for the continuation of the sitting of Parliament for six months in the event of the sudden demise of the sovereign. Support was also forthcoming from unusual quarters. On 8 April Monmouth introduced into the royal presence a representation of Quakers bearing a loyal address which they had drawn up, along similar lines to the Association.[15]

The parliamentary session closed on 27 April, leaving the Whigs in a strong position; more advancement was expected for them at the

expense of Tory office-holders. Monmouth, who had been openly critical of the management of the Fleet off Dunkirk in March, was now
offered the post of First Commissioner of the Admiralty. In some quarters he was considered eminently suitable for the job. His naval experience had been undertaken in the Mediterranean and the West Indies
and he was known and liked by all the merchants, which augured well
for the arrangement of convoys. Monmouth later related that the King
had told him that all was not well with the Fleet, and that he was
needed 'to bring things into a better posture'. Nevertheless, he declined
the offer; all the plans for the summer had been already made and
anything that went wrong would be laid at his door. In truth, he might
have given a different answer if his predecessor and old rival, Admiral
Russell, had not been asked to remain on the Commission.[16]

Ten

There is little information about Monmouth's activity during the summer of 1696 except that he was kept waiting for a consignment of two hogsheads of prize wine from Guernsey which was impounded by the Customs Commissioners. But one evening in September he was returning to Parsons Green when his coach was held up by a party of five or six footpads near Chelsea. Shots were fired which attracted the attention of the guards at Chelsea College. When the guards approached, the footpads dispersed. Monmouth was unharmed and appeared to be in possession of most of his property but later he complained to the Lords Justices about the behaviour of the guards. An inquiry by the court of general officers proved inconclusive. A report was made to the Lords Justices and James Vernon, Shrewsbury's secretary, was instructed to show it to Monmouth. Vernon noticed that the guards' account of the incident did not entirely tally with that given by the earl.

Little more was heard of this for some time. Two men, Ulysses Brown and John Davis, were arrested for the robbery. Davis remained in Newgate while Brown was released with a promise of pardon having revealed the names of his accomplices who belonged to a better class of footpad than was usual. The party had consisted of mainly Jacobite officers and others who had fallen on hard times. Their purpose seemed either a straightforward robbery for profit or to inconvenience someone against whom they bore a grudge, such as Lord Cutts. Monmouth happened to be on the road that night; the robbers mistook their man, both in identity and as a source of rich pickings.

Monmouth seemed to dwell on this incident. At the beginning of October he told Vernon that it had been 'more than a design to rob him'. Late in December he complained to Sir William Trumbull that he had been receiving letters through the post 'wherein people offer to discover how he came to be set upon by Chelsea College, and some other designs'. Later he talked of putting a notice in the *Gazette* about it and taking steps to prevent Davis from leaving Newgate.[1]

In January 1697 Ulysses Brown, the apparent leader of the enterprise, felt obliged by a twinge of conscience or a lack of funds to reveal his side of the story. His was a hard luck tale. The son of an Irish gentleman, he began a career at the Middle Temple with an allowance from his father. His circumstances changed when his father's estates were forfeited and he lost that means of support. Since then he had learnt to pick up money where and when he could and 'lived by play, sharping, and a little on the highway'.

On 22 January 1697 Vernon was approached by Sir John Talbot who had heard Brown's story from a mutual friend, also called Talbot. Sir John trusted his friend sufficiently to have already acquainted the Lord Keeper with what he came to tell Vernon. Sir John told Brown's account of the hold-up at Chelsea when they had removed from Monmouth his hat, sword, periwig, a ring he was wearing and six shillings which was all the money he had in his pocket. 'My Lord, making them a compliment that by their behaviour they looked like gentlemen, and to take that course only out of necessity, therefore desired to know how he might place ten guineas upon them.' This mild reaction induced the men to return all his property to him but the earl generously declined the return of the six shillings. When the guard from the College approached, discharging firearms, the robbers told Monmouth that they would be obliged to injure him if he did not call out that they were merely friends. This the earl did and then drove on.

Brown took Monmouth at his word and called on him at Parsons Green, rather to the earl's surprise. He was given a few guineas but afterwards they met quite often. Later Monmouth asked Brown whether he would be prepared to declare, if required, that the attack at Chelsea had been an attempt to kidnap him and remove him to France where he was to be kept a prisoner until exchanged for the Earl of Ailesbury. Brown understood that the leaders of this attempt included, rather surprisingly, the earl's brother-in-law, Sir Peter Fraser. Brown claimed to have received subsequently instructions in writing from Monmouth, he had written letters at the earl's dictation and sent them to various public persons such as the Lord Keeper. The project was also known to Davis, a prisoner in Newgate.

Brown had now taken against the scheming and was anxious to make a clean breast of the matter. He chose to do so at a time when a particular piece of ill fortune had befallen Monmouth, for which it is necessary to return to the previous autumn.[2]

Having managed to evade capture after the failure of the Assassination Plot, Sir John Fenwick remained at large until 11 June when he was arrested at New Romney. Sent first to the Tower and then to Newgate, his trial was fixed for 13 July. At once he and his wife, Lady Mary, bent all their energies to get a postponement. Sir John offered to make a full confession in return for a pardon, adding the condition that he should not be asked to give evidence. The trial was duly postponed until the next session. In August Sir John produced three pages of writing in which he said nothing of his accomplices but tried to incriminate Godolphin, Shrewsbury, Marlborough and Russell. None of the revelations was news to the King.

The contents of Fenwick's paper were not made public and were known to very few. By the end of September the trial had still not taken place and rumours abounded as to who had been named in the paper. Symon Harcourt overheard a conversation in a coffee-house which suggested that Monmouth's name was among them and that the information came from Lady Mary Fenwick. Monmouth reacted with vociferous indignation.

When the King returned from Holland in October, a policy meeting was arranged in his presence with Lord Somers (the Lord Keeper), the Earl of Sunderland and Admiral Edward Russell as Shrewsbury was still in the country. After much discussion, it was decided that Fenwick should appear before the King in the presence of the chief members of the government and judiciary.

Before this could happen, Monmouth and other Whigs used Fenwick's rumoured allegations to threaten the position of Godolphin, a Tory, as First Commissioner of the Treasury. Monmouth undertook this with too much zeal and many, including the King, tried to restrain him. In the event, Godolphin offered his resignation at the end of October, which was accepted – rather to his disappointment.[3]

When Sir John Fenwick was brought before the King for interrogation on 2 November, he had the confidence of knowing that, of the two prosecution witnesses, one had escaped to France and the evidence of a single witness was insufficient for a prosecution under the Treasons Act. Consequently he was unforthcoming and stuck firmly to his papers.

The Council decided that, despite the impossibility of gaining a conviction in a trial, the whole matter must be given an opportunity for public condemnation. But the Whigs had another card up their sleeve. On 6 November the subject was raised in the House of Commons by Edward Russell. There had been much gathering of support for Shrewsbury in the Lower House and there were few dissenting voices when Sir John Fenwick's papers were voted false and scandalous. However a subsequent motion, that a Bill of Attainder should be proceeded with against Sir John, met with far more opposition and was passed with a majority of 179 votes to 61. The measure was to have a rough ride through Parliament.[4]

Monmouth had been in touch with a spy, Matthew Smith, who had supplied Shrewsbury with information about Jacobites in the past. Shrewsbury had found him often inefficient and inaccurate and now considered him a waste of money. Unfortunately Smith had warned of the Assassination Plot and the threat of a French invasion, had been rewarded in a small way but not believed. He had received no acclaim. Aggrieved, he began to build on the idea that Shrewsbury might have deliberately disbelieved him. He approached Monmouth hoping to find a friend at Court and asked him to speak to the other Secretary of State, Sir William Trumbull, on his behalf. He compiled his writings and papers into a book to present to the King. Mischievously, Monmouth told Somers that he was having trouble in preventing Smith from revealing his allegations to members of the House of Commons when they were discussing Fenwick's paper. Somers thought that this was beyond an acceptable line of conduct and took the opportunity to give Monmouth a taste of plain speaking. He pointed out the dangers of such an action, that there was a view of Fenwick's paper 'that he and every Whig is as much concerned in it, and as open to an accusation, as the persons who are named'. The earl was 'much startled'.[5]

The Bill of Attainder had an awkward passage through the Commons as many members felt it was an inappropriate measure in the circumstances. It passed its third reading on 21 November. Meanwhile preparations were being made for the passage of the Bill in the House of Lords. Somers was uncertain how Monmouth would behave, particularly after his dealings with Smith, but was reassured to find him entirely accommodating. As one of the chief Whig spokesmen in the House, Monmouth's active support was of importance. He wanted to know how the King considered the measure and was told that it had his full support. In late November Monmouth was observed spending an hour and a half in deep conversation with the Tory Earl of Nottingham in the Court of Requests and Westminster Hall. He told Blanchard later that 'Lord Nottingham was persuading him to be against the Bill, and he was endeavouring to convert him to be for it.'[6]

On 1 December the Bill of Attainder had its first reading in the Lords under the management of the Earl of Tankerville. Afterwards Sir John Fenwick was brought to the Bar and questioned. He declined to acknowledge his paper, make any confession or answer any questions, but repeatedly asked that his counsel might be heard. Eventually the House agreed to hear counsel on 8 December. During the questioning it was noted that Monmouth was 'pretty easy and favourable to the prisoner, and to give him all encouragement to have made out the accusations in his paper; but when he found him resolved to do nothing of the kind, seemed to show a good deal of zeal against him afterward…'[7]

In the event, the hearing was postponed to 15 December, as Fenwick's counsel claimed that his witnesses were not ready. Meanwhile a paper entitled 'Advice to Sir John Fenwick' was in circulation and its authorship was being ascribed to Monmouth.*

Basically it encouraged Sir John to make a full confession and substantiate claims made in his former papers. Fenwick's counsel and solicitors declined to use the proposals, being 'concerned only in the management of his defence'.[8]

On 15 December 1696 evidence was led and witnesses examined. This continued for the next two days, concluding with the summing up for both sides. On 18 December Sir John was called and given an opportunity to speak. He did so briefly and made no attempt at confession or excuse. There followed a long debate until late at night when the Bill passed its second reading with a majority of 73 Content against 55 Not Content. The Earls of Tankerville and Monmouth were among the Bill's leading protagonists and they were supported also by the Bishop of Salisbury, Lord Haversham, Lord Cornwallis, Lord Wharton and others.

On 22 December the Lords were again engaged on Fenwick's business. Sir John had petitioned the House that he might be heard before the third reading and he was duly called in but he did little more than attempt to justify his position and dissociate himself from any involvement in the Assassination Plot or the proposed invasion. Before he withdrew, the Earl of Carlisle asked that he might be questioned as to whether he had received 'any directions, by writing or message, from any person, how he should behave himself at his trial, either at the House of Commons or this House'. Sir John replied that he had only received advice from counsel as allowed. Sir John then withdrew but Carlisle wished his question repeated in a slightly altered form: 'Whether he did not receive directions in writing, either from one of this

*The paper, as given in HMC *Buccleuch* MSS vol. ii, p. 426, is a shortened and altered version of one of three papers later produced in evidence.

House or of the House of Commons, how to govern himself at his trial?' Sir John was called in again and Carlisle's revised question put to him. He replied that he had not received directions in writing while at the Bar of this House. On being asked if he had before, he admitted that he had been told something to his advantage and he named the author of the advice as the Earl of Monmouth. Further questions revealed that the advice had been given in a paper received by Lady Mary Fenwick from the Duchess of Norfolk, and that this had occurred while the Bill was before the House of Commons. Monmouth disclaimed giving such a paper and asked for it to be produced. He did agree that some relatives of his had asked his opinion of the best course that Sir John could follow, and he had told them that Fenwick should make 'a frank and open confession of all he knew'. If anything else had been put in a paper, the earl claimed it was an invention.

Monmouth then asked that the Duchess of Norfolk should attend the House and Carlisle asked for Lady Mary Fenwick and Mrs Lawson. In the meantime Sir John was asked further questions regarding his information but feeling he lacked security against incriminating himself in other courts, and despite assurances from the King and the House, he refused to be drawn. The Bill was ordered to be read the third time the following day.

After being called in, Lady Mary Fenwick revealed that she had in fact three papers, two were copies but one was the original. She reluctantly admitted that she had received them from the Duchess of Norfolk. After the receipt of one paper, she had been given to understand that the Earl of Monmouth was willing to meet Sir Thomas Powys, Sir John's counsel, but this meeting did not take place as Sir Thomas was too busy.[9]

Of the three papers eventually read to the House, the third was the shortest. It did indeed urge Sir John that the best method to stop the Bill passing in the House of Lords 'is frankly owning and endeavouring to prove there the confession made to the King'. By making good his confession, Sir John would succeed in disproving the allegations in the Bill that his paper was false and scandalous and only submitted to obtain a delay. The first two papers went into some detail about proof. The first recommended that questions should be asked of the Earls of Portland and Romney about intelligence brought to them regarding correspondence between King James and 'great men in the government'. The King should be asked to lay before the House the reasons why the Earl of Marlborough was suddenly deprived of his places and sent to the Tower. The Duke of Norfolk should be asked about information given him by Matthew Smith regarding correspondence between ministers in the government and King James. Captain Smith could also give some information on this and on some letters of the Duke of Shrewsbury. Also the King might be asked to lay before the House letters which had come to his hands from King James and his Queen in France to Lord Godolphin. The second paper elaborated on the first and included a suggestion that the 'manner and time' of the resignations from office of Shrewsbury and Russell should be looked into.

The papers were very badly read by a clerk so that few people were very sure of their exact contents. One clear fact was that Monmouth had urged Fenwick to use Smith and his letters to help to prove his paper. The first two papers read to the House were copies but their contents were new to most hearers. Only the short original paper had previously been in circulation.[10]

The following day, 23 December, debate on the Bill was resumed and lasted six hours. When the question was put, the Bill was carried by a majority of only seven. Forty-one peers signed a written and reasoned dissent. Their main objections were to the admissibility of some of the evidence and that the machinery of a bill of attainder had been used at all against 'so inconsiderable a man, as to the endangering the peace of the government'. It had been the use of a sledgehammer to crack a nut.

The Bill having passed, the House turned its attention to the Earl of Monmouth. At 6 pm the Duchess of Norfolk attended and spent an hour under examination on oath regarding the papers she was understood to have passed to Lady Mary Fenwick. Asked whether she could identify the papers as those she had passed to Lady Mary, she was vague in her reply but after a little pressing she did acknowledge that she had received two or three papers from Lord Monmouth to give to Lady Mary. Her interest in the matter was solely to assist a friend in trouble. She had approached Monmouth for advice only after having obtained for him a letter from Lady Mary assuring him that he was not named in Fenwick's paper.

In the course of the examination Monmouth had a chance to question the duchess himself. 'In the heat of doing it, it was thought that he discomposed the concert between them, if there were any.' The duchess did not think that any of the papers she had passed had been written in the earl's hand; she was confident that, if any were, it was not in his normal writing. In answer to the earl's question, she confirmed that her first meeting with him had been in connection with satisfying him that he was not named by Sir John. She also agreed that the earl's advice to Sir John had been to be 'ingenuous in his confession'. During the questioning, Wharton thought that Monmouth behaved 'with more disturbance of mind, than I thought he could have been capable of'.

After the duchess had withdrawn, Monmouth reiterated his reasons for contacting her in the first place. He said his advice was given only for the discovery of the truth. People were ascribing to him a collection of things from others that were not his actions. Lord Wharton summed up the day: 'He [Monmouth] was so confused in what he said, and it was so late, and the House so weary, that it was hard to make head or tail of what he said; and so that matter rests...' The business was adjourned until 7 January 1696/97.[11]

During the parliamentary recess Monmouth behaved as if he knew himself to be in a tight corner and was unsure of the way out. At first he was indignant at the aspersions cast on him and seemed to think his cousin, the duchess, was the main culprit. Then he became a 'disturbed and distempered man'. As a Privy Councillor, he obtained an audience of the King and talked for an hour and a half. He also spent some time with Lord Chief Justice Holt and Sir William Trumbull and mentioned the Chelsea College incident as a possible plot against his person. He approached Sunderland with the intention of making friendly overtures towards Shrewsbury and Russell, despite the fact that he had been cheerfully prepared to assist in substantiating allegations against them in the House of Lords. Somers thought that there was little to fear from him now as his slight gesture with the white flag seemed to indicate that he was aware of the dangers.[12]

The House of Lords resumed on 7 January and spent some time hearing evidence about the papers believed to have come from Monmouth. The Bill having passed and Monmouth's overt hostility to Sir John noted, the Fenwick support group were unrestricted in what they were now prepared to say. Lady Mary Fenwick, her cousin Mrs Lawson and the Duchess of Norfolk all gave evidence and a companion of Lady Mary's, Mrs Symonds, testified to copying two of the letters.

Lady Mary's evidence related that while her husband's case was before the House of Commons she had received a message from the Duchess of Norfolk that a 'great lord (who is a privy councillor)' had been with her and had offered to give advice on how Sir John could save his life and honour. Lady Mary was interested but indisposed and she sent Mrs Lawson to the duchess with instructions to ask for this advice. Subsequently the duchess visited Lady Mary, bringing with her a paper containing various heads of advice for use in Sir John's defence which she insisted should be copied (Mrs Symonds obliged) and she took away the original.

After examining the paper, Lady Mary felt that there were certain parts of it which were not entirely suitable for use by counsel and other parts whose purpose she could not understand. Being still unwell, she sent Mrs Lawson again to the duchess to ask for clarification and a paper suitable for the use of counsel. This time it was the duchess who was unwell and in her bedchamber, a room from which, in the best style of nobleman's residences, there was more than one exit. While the ladies were talking, the duchess was informed that the Earl of Monmouth had called. Mrs Lawson, 'being undressed', had no wish to meet the earl and left the room by another door. From her place of concealment, she claimed she was able to hear very well the conversation between Monmouth and the duchess. After the earl had left, she emerged from her refuge, obtained the clarification she had come for and told the duchess that she had overheard what was being said.

When Mrs Lawson returned to Lady Mary, she found the Earl of Carlisle also present. As she related what she had learnt, Lady Mary asked the earl to write it down. Next morning the useful Mrs Symonds made a copy of the earl's paper and the original was burnt. The same day the duchess came and confirmed all that Mrs Lawson had said.

In addition, Lady Mary now produced a fourth paper which she claimed the duchess had said had been dictated by the Earl of Monmouth. It had arrived after counsel had seen the paper which was eventually prepared for him. It said:

> The Party is of opinion, with the counsel, that Sir John must never speak, not only till the House has assured his own words shall not hurt himself; but till he has the promise of the House likewise, that they will warmly assist him in what shall be necessary towards discovering the truth. As to what is mentioned, of his not being engaged in a confession; it is apprehended it is meant, his not being forced to be an evidence, which he may insist of, as he thinks fit.[13]

As Lady Mary had provided a considerable amount of hearsay evidence regarding the conversation overheard, Mrs Lawson's evidence was mostly taken up with this episode. From her place of concealment, Mrs Lawson said she heard the earl state to the duchess that Sir John

Fenwick would be either fated or mad to refuse to follow the directions he had sent him, and that he would save his life and honour; also, the Bill before the House of Commons would certainly be thrown out. The duchess had asked whether, if the Bill were thrown out, Sir John would not be at risk of being tried at common law. The earl did not think it would matter if he were, 'for he [Monmouth] would answer for his life there, as well as in the other place; for he had an interest in those sort of people.' Then the earl said 'that the King used Sir John Fenwick basely by sending his papers to the parliament as false and scandalous, when, by Almighty God, he knew it all before to be true' and he listed the examples which had been read to the House from the first paper laid before them, by which it was evident that the King had knowledge of the correspondence with King James. Mrs Lawson could not remember if she had repeated what Monmouth had said of the King to the duchess then but that they had spoken of it since.

When the duchess was examined, she said she could not testify to the papers shown her as she had never been able to read them, they were so badly written. However she agreed that she had only ever received papers from the Earl of Monmouth and, at his request, they had been sent as soon as possible to Lady Mary Fenwick. The earl was with her sometimes twice a day for three weeks. He believed that Sir John was unkindly used everywhere but when she had asked him, if he thought so, why was he against him, he replied that he had his reasons. She had heard Monmouth say that, to his knowledge, the King had known all the matter already as indeed had several of the peers.

The duchess confirmed that her meetings with Monmouth stemmed from his desire to find out whether he was named in Fenwick's paper and had not occurred before. She had been unable to arrange a meeting between Lady Mary and the earl but he had been willing to meet Sir John's counsel. She stated that Mrs Lawson had told her that she had overheard the conversation between herself and the earl and added 'Mrs Lawson so punctually repeated to me what my lord had said, that she must have heard him speak it.'

The duchess also stated that the paper which Lady Mary had given in that day was in her own writing and was a copy of a paper written by Monmouth. She was questioned again regarding what Monmouth had spoken of the King, whether she had told it all. The duchess replied that 'my Lord Monmouth seemed to blame the King; and thought His Majesty had done hardly by Sir John Fenwick in exposing his papers. My Lord expressed himself with a little heat, as if it had been unjust;

but I remember not the particular expressions, but my Lord spoke in a little passion.'[14]

The House adjourned the sitting to Saturday 9 January when there was a recapitulation of the evidence heard before Christmas; the three papers handed in by Lady Mary on 22 December were read again and the Earl of Carlisle gave evidence concerning the paper he wrote at Mrs Lawson's dictation. Monmouth was reminded that he could now speak in his own defence and he was then heard on the depositions and papers. He spoke for at least two hours and at the end 'there was a pretty long silence after he had done'.

Monmouth's first line of attack was to question the credibility of the witnesses. Much of what they had offered had been hearsay and therefore normally inadmissible. The duchess had claimed that she knew nothing of the papers and was merely a form of carrier; then she admitted that she had copied something of Monmouth's, although she had declined to meddle in the matter, and this paper had been only recently produced by Lady Mary. Two of the ladies were Catholics and 'inclined to stretch as far as possible to serve that interest'. One, Lady Mary, 'a person of busy temper, to bring things to her end', was in a position of dependence on Sir John as his wife and Mrs Lawson was receiving an annuity of £100 from him while he lived. Their claim, that Monmouth had spoken disrespectfully of the King for making the papers public, was quite inconsistent with his pressure to have things brought to light by Sir John's full and ingenuous confession. Had the earl been guilty, it must surely have been madness to put himself so much into the power of these people by such conversations and then irritate them so greatly by becoming one of the most active managers of the Bill of Attainder in the House of Lords. Monmouth hoped that such hearsay and contradictory evidence would not be held against one who had served the government with so much zeal and was £20,000 the poorer in its service, having made no substantial gains from his offices or been able to build fine houses as some had, his own being almost ready to fall down.

Monmouth then gave an explanation of the ruse which he claimed had been used to get him involved. He believed that the duchess and Lady Mary had deliberately spread the rumour that he was named in Sir John's paper, and he could prove that the information could be traced to Lady Mary. The duchess had made several attempts to call on him before he was prepared to see her. She gave as her reasons her regret that their families had kept such a distance between them and her concern that he might be upset by the current rumours which she knew were untrue and could obtain a letter from Sir John confirming this. Monmouth said he did not wish to enter into any kind of correspondence with Sir John but he accepted the offer of a similar letter from Lady Mary as a sort of insurance against being charged. The duchess had then introduced the subject of Sir John's plight, how he had been persuaded to make a confession and now the House of Commons had brought a Bill of Attainder, although Sir John could prove his allegations with the assistance of Captain Smith and others.* The duchess had then asked the earl's advice and he gave his opinion that Sir John should make a 'true and ingenuous discovery of all he knew'.

Monmouth claimed that everything else laid on him by these witnesses was based on malice and he stressed again the poor quality of the evidence. He then said that the first three papers were indeed scandalous but only admitted the authorship of the fourth. He concluded his speech by professing his continued zeal for the King's service and his reliance on the Lords to do him justice.

Vernon was surprised that the earl admitted so much in acknowledging the fourth paper. 'He looks upon this as the least criminal, and thought a seeming ingenuity here would have gained him belief in denying the rest.' After the silence which greeted the conclusion of the speech, the House of Lords went into debate. Later it resolved that 'those three papers do contain in them matter of a scandalous nature; and that the contrivance of them is a high crime and misdemeanour.'[15]

Before the House rose at 11 pm, the first of Monmouth's witnesses, Councillor John Robins, a lawyer, gave evidence of how he heard that Monmouth was named in Fenwick's paper from his friend Symon Harcourt.

The next day, Sunday 10 January 1696/7, Monmouth seemed to be trying in every way to avoid the censure which would be his lot if the other papers were judged to be his. The King refused to intervene on his behalf; he listened to the earl in private for an hour and a half, then said 'Very well, my lord' and nothing more. The earl busied himself in marshalling his witnesses. On 11 January Smith was examined about his letters but nothing of much value emerged. On 13 January eleven witnesses were heard on Monmouth's behalf. The earl's aim appeared to be to discredit the duchess's evidence but, at the end of the day, the witnesses merely showed that the lady was fond of rather underhand

*The earl stressed in his speech that it was the duchess who first introduced the name of Captain Smith.

intrigues and perhaps mildly involved in the Jacobite cause. In addition to this, Symon Harcourt was produced to testify to what he had over-heard in a coffee house regarding those named in Sir John Fenwick's paper.[16]

Monmouth had still a few friends in the House and most of them met at the home of the Duke of Bolton on the evening of 14 January to see if they could find any means by which he could be brought off. The next day the House met for the last time on this business. Monmouth made little use of his evidence; it seemed that many minds were already made up and there was little he could say in mitigation. All the papers and notes of evidence were read through again, which took around two hours. Monmouth then spoke for another hour in his own defence. Once again he stressed the untrustworthiness of the witnesses against him and the unlikelihood of his ever having spoken disrespectful words of the King. He hoped that if any charge were to be laid against him, he would be informed of the nature of it and allowed to answer it before judges. He withdrew and the debate commenced.

The Duke of Leeds, the Earls of Rochester, Nottingham and Marl-borough and Lord Godolphin were keen that the House should resolve that Monmouth was the sole contriver of the papers. Together with the Duke of Bolton, Monmouth's supporters appeared to include the Earls of Oxford, Stamford, Sandwich, Macclesfield and Warrington and Lords Haversham, Delawarr and Abergavenny. Lord Oxford was the most extreme in his support and moved for an acquittal as the evidence against him came from discreditable witnesses. However the Duke of Bolton, Lord Haversham and others believed that he had behaved with some indiscretion and deserved the censure of the House but nothing more. Some of those who believed that he had been the sole contriver wished to have him barred from sitting and voting in the House for the rest of his life.

If the Court appeared to have given Monmouth up, the King had not done so entirely. Dr Burnet, the Bishop of Salisbury, was asked privately by William to do all he could to 'soften his censure'. When the Bishop came to speak, he said that although Monmouth could not be excused for being the author of those papers, the House should take into consid-eration the eminent services he had done for this government in the past and 'that he set the revolution first on foot, and was a great promoter of it'. Burnet then moved that Monmouth should be sent to the Tower. It was then argued that one could not send a man to the Tower only for having spoken indiscreetly as some suggested. If such faults were worthy of imprisonment, many would be found under restraint. Lord Wharton eventually provided a formula which was generally accepted; words had been spoken improperly regarding the person of the King. This fault was agreed to merit such a punishment.

After a long debate, in which the earl's friends were mostly cautious enough to join with peers of a moderate opinion, a resolution was reached which was approved by the vast majority of a well-filled House. Somers said later that he had never known a question put with so few negatives. Monmouth's wrongdoing was lightly defined and this was largely the result of the hard efforts of his friends.

The House resolved

> That it doth appear to this House, by the depositions taken in this House, that Charles, earl of Monmouth hath had such a share and part in the contrivance of the papers delivered to the House by the Lady Mary Fenwick, that for that offence, and for the undutiful words which were sworn before this House to be spoken by him of the King, that the said Charles, earl of Monmouth shall be committed prisoner to His Majesty's Tower of London, there to remain during His Majesty's pleasure, and the pleasure of the House.[17]

Eleven

Monmouth was now lodged in the Tower but no one seemed to expect him to stay there long. Soon he was seeking Somers's help to obtain the King's leave to petition the House for his release. The Earl of Sunderland was one of his earliest visitors. However, Portland's call on 19 January 1696/7 was probably made to warn him that the King intended to strike his name out of the Council Book at the next meeting. Monmouth had not expected this and was disturbed by the news as he thought he had convinced the King of his innocence of what had been represented as disrespectful behaviour. So little had he succeeded that Portland was sent again, on 25 January, this time to tell him that the King intended to dispose of his place in the Bedchamber.[1]

During Monmouth's imprisonment Sir John Fenwick was executed at the Tower on 28 January. Another fellow prisoner was a more distinguished Jacobite, the Earl of Ailesbury, whose memoirs, although written with the recollection of old age (and he lived until 1741), leave some interesting impressions of Monmouth. Among the contemporary accounts Ailesbury alone suggests that Monmouth and his cousin, the Duchess of Norfolk, were in love with each other, which may have accounted for the daily meetings the previous October. It would appear that their fondness did not survive the Fenwick case. Ailesbury had no doubts that Monmouth was deeply involved over the letters and thought that, if the duchess had been rather less 'squeamish' in her evidence and had told all she knew, 'that Lord had been fined so deep that he could never have paid it, and must have suffered imprisonment until he had'.

Years later, when Ailesbury was permanently resident in Brussels, Monmouth (then Earl of Peterborough) called on him. The two gentlemen sat in the garden 'in an arbour to free us from the sun'. Ailesbury recalled that Monmouth began:

'My Lord, do you remember that I was in the Tower in the same time with you?' I said only 'Aye', but I thought within myself the causes were far different... This Lord was full of matter by starts, and said, 'My Lord, you and I were never of one opinion in the house,' I answered, 'Nor I believe we never shall be.' Said he, 'You act always on a principle,' I could have answered, 'And you not...'[2]

During this period of Monmouth's imprisonment, the moment arrived when Ulysses Brown, the gentleman-footpad, made revelations about his dealings with Monmouth. Having heard the story, Lord Keeper Somers and James Vernon agreed that Brown should be examined but when summoned for this purpose he failed to appear.

Somers informed Monmouth in advance of Brown's forthcoming examination and the earl's reply showed 'a good deal of confusion and mistrust of what he [Brown] had to discover'. Monmouth told Brown to leave the country or he would prosecute him but Somers tried to assure him that the risk of being arrested at Monmouth's request was not great; if there was a chance of the earl's release, it would be better to have made his disclosures before that occurred. Vernon thought that Brown's information could be a useful insurance against any further 'pranks' that Monmouth might think of in the future.

During the month of February Monmouth considered a further petition for his release. He had occupied his time by writing what he saw as a justification of his conduct, apparently convinced of his own innocence and now certain of the identity of the person who had advised the duchess. This document, being circulated by his friends, varied little from his defence in Parliament but also pondered the reasons why the Lords had treated him so roughly despite his innocence. He blamed this on the fact that he had always believed in plain speaking, praising those who deserved it but also openly blaming others. This made him enemies who had joined with the Fenwick party to tarnish his reputation.[3]

Meanwhile, in trying to acquire a pass to go abroad, Brown had been arrested as a Proclamation man (his name had once appeared in a proclamation in connection with a crime or crimes). On 18 February he was still in close confinement and unexamined. Vernon hoped that the examination was not being put off out of consideration for Monmouth, but the following day Brown was examined at Somers's house by the panel already chosen and it transpired that his evidence could hurt no one but Monmouth. He remained in custody until May 1697 when he was released on bail and was discharged at the King's Bench on 23 June. For some time to come he would recur as a nuisance, only tolerated because of his possible use against Monmouth.[4]

Towards the end of March, Monmouth finally decided to petition the House of Lords for his release. The Duke of Devonshire, the Earl of Sunderland and other friends were active on his behalf and on 30 March the House was informed that the King had given the necessary permission and was willing that he should be granted his liberty. His petition was read and he gave as his reasons his long imprisonment, a current indisposition and affairs which needed his attention. It was said that he had postponed his petition because of the supplication involved; presumably he hoped that one day his freedom would be given without petition. His illness, said to be an attack of gravel with a swelling in his side, overcame his reluctance. The Lords made an order for his release but he was not well enough to take advantage of it for two days.

Before Monmouth left the Tower, it was announced that his Bedchamber place would be given to Lord Clifford and the Earl of Montagu would receive the lord-lieutenancy of Northamptonshire. These appointments came as a clear reminder that release and rein-statement were not the same thing; there was no automatic return to the good graces of the sovereign. 'The earl of Monmouth is now a free man,' commented Vernon. 'If he can be a quiet one, it will be better for himself and his neighbours...'[5]

During the month of March there was some concern over the health of Monmouth's uncle, the Earl of Peterborough. Now in his seventy-seventh year, he had recently suffered several fits of ague and on 23 March he was considered still dangerously ill. However the old earl was made of tough material and made a slow but steady recovery. The news that he was out of danger and on the mend coincided more or less with Monmouth's release from prison. Being notoriously short of funds and standing to inherit the earldom and part of his uncle's estate, Monmouth appeared to have been dealt another blow by his uncle's recovery. It was said that, had the death occurred, it would have been concealed until quarter day had passed.[6]

Monmouth made one of his first public appearances at the house of the Earl of Sunderland, a figure whose activities were at the centre of political interest. The following day, 7 April 1697, he took his place in the House of Lords and found himself part of a committee formed to consider a Bill regarding the Bridlington Piers. He only attended twice more before Parliament was prorogued on 16 April. No one knew what he would do next. No one believed him when he spoke in May of embracing a bucolic existence in the country, following the plough while his wife was a dairywoman. However he did receive a warrant for his salary to Christmas 1696 as a Gentleman of the Bedchamber.

In June Matthew Smith published the letters of information he had sent to Shrewsbury in a book entitled *Memoirs of Secret Service*. As it contained no reference to either Mr Secretary Trumbull or to Monmouth, it was presumed that one or other of them had assisted in putting the material together, for both had helped Smith in the past.[7]

The Earl of Peterborough's recovery from illness proved after all to be only temporary and he died at Drayton on 19 June. His daughter, the Duchess of Norfolk, was present at her father's deathbed for filial reasons and also to ensure possession of her inheritance. The earldom passed to Monmouth as the next heir but it was accompanied by only a part of the property which had been owned by the second earl; the remainder, including Drayton, was left to the duchess.

Monmouth was said to have received an increase in fortune of £4,000 per annum with the title, but it was soon known that he intended to try to acquire the entire property. His claim was based on a trust deed made by his grandfather, the first earl, in 1641 by which, as heir in tail male, he stood to inherit the whole estate. Later in the year the new Earl of Peterborough brought an action in the Court of Chancery against the duchess 'for a discovery and proof of her title, and delivery of the deeds'.*

Whether or not Lord Peterborough mourned his uncle is not known. Relationships in the family had once been cordial. There is evidence in Thomas Weston's account book that the second earl kept an avuncular eye on the health and welfare of his brother's family. As Viscount Mordaunt, the third earl named his daughter Henrietta after his uncle and her portrait at Drayton, as a little girl with a pet dog, suggests a special affinity.[8]

A new identity as Earl of Peterborough might have cleared away the faults of the Earl of Monmouth but nothing suggests that such a change of heart took place. However an inheritance of any size brings with it at least some business to keep the recipient occupied initially. In mid-August Lord and Lady Peterborough left London for Dauntsey where they remained for several weeks. Soon after his arrival, the earl wrote to

---

*The lands and property which passed with the earldom, and were not in contention, were the old Mordaunt property of Turvey in Bedfordshire, with the manors of Carlton, Chellington and Stagsden in the same county and Sudborough in Northamptonshire. V. C. H. Bedfordshire, vol. iii, pp. 51, 55, 96, 109–10; V. C. H. Northamptonshire, vol. iii, p. 243; N. R. O. MSS Y2 ff. 1464–8.

John Locke in a relaxed and cheerful style which indicated that at least this friendship was in good repair.

> Mr Lock, you know the impatience Country Gentlemen have for News; we are here as Found of a Gazette as the Sparks are of their mistresses with you. We lay waggers of Ponty and nevill and Conti and Saxe, to passe away the Time, instead of playing att pickett.* pray give us a letter now and then to decide who has won; this request is made you not only by myself, but by some other of your humble friends PETERBOROW

John Locke had been busy all summer as a Commissioner of Trade, but he replied to Peterborough's letter promptly on 17 August and his pains were acknowledged by his 'most affectionate servant' on 4 September.

> Mr Locke, We all return you thanks for your charitable Correspondence but the Lady is a little out of humour since your last, having long agoe settled the peace with the restitution of Strasbourgh, and Luxembourgh and Lorraine, and sunk and destroyed all or most of Ponti squadron, not considering the generous Knight-Errantry of our Admiralls, who scorn to beat their Ennemies with odds, nine to Five being shamefull Advantage...†[9]

Soon after this Peterborough was back in town. Ulysses Brown was still in the wings, occasionally emerging for funds. He was now hoping to gain some support by threatening to go to the Lords Justices to reveal the services he had done in bringing Peterborough's practices to attention. Some felt that he should be allowed to do so if he wished. His story was well enough known and it had some little benefit in keeping Peterborough 'in awe'.[10]

In November 1697 the Lords Justices issued a proclamation to arrest the Duke of Berwick and other Jacobites who were rumoured to be about town. This proclamation was triggered by evidence brought to the Earl of Romney by a Frenchman called Morin who kept a shop in

---

*Baron de Pointis had sailed from France in April with ten ships. Followed by Admiral John Neville with six English and four Dutch ships, he had crossed the Atlantic and captured Cartagena in May. The Prince de Conti and the Elector of Saxony were rival claimants for the crown of Poland.
†The peace of Ryswick was not signed till 20 September. At an engagement in May, Neville was said to have twenty-two ships against Pointis's ten. Luttrell, vol. iv, p. 262; Locke, *Corr.* vol. vi, p. 185.

Cranbourne Alley. When a gentleman visited the shop one afternoon, Morin was struck by a familiarity which he could not place. Later he decided that the man had been the Duke of Berwick, a proscribed person, and felt obliged to report the matter. Morin was examined and his evidence noted. After the proclamation, a general search was made, without success, and the whole business became rather ludicrous when, other witnesses having been traced, it was found that the customer had been the Earl of Peterborough.

Morin's evidence, like a clip from an old newsreel, brings the earl momentarily to life:

> That on Sat. last about 3pm a tall handsome man came into his shop, muffled up in a cloak, with an old fair peruke on, and bought a hat and a pair of stockings of his daughter, for which he paid 16s. He pulled out a handful of guineas and changed one of them... He came into the shop on foot, and went away in a chair. One Clark, passing by as he was in the chair, made him a low bow, which he returned with a nod.

Ailesbury remembered Peterborough as 'the same stature and size of the Duke of Berwick, both most thin in shape and face and by accent English'.[11]

In April 1697 the Earl of Sunderland had emerged from the shadows to take the post of Lord Chamberlain. Together with Shrewsbury and Somers (now Lord Chancellor), he was one of those on whom the King chiefly relied and who had great influence over appointments. It was a difficult political climate. Sunderland was falling under the suspicion of the Whig Junto and some others who feared that, once the Peace was concluded, other hands from another party would be given places. He was believed to have been in touch with Tories such as Marlborough, Rochester and Godolphin. To placate rumours, Montagu, a member of the Junto, was made a Cabinet Councillor.

As the King's adviser, Sunderland's aim was to form a government of moderates and to reconcile opposing political factions. It was known that he hoped before long to bridge the gap which existed between Peterborough on the one side and Shrewsbury and Russell (now Earl of Orford) on the other. Orford was sceptical about his chances but Sunderland managed to extract from Peterborough the promise of some sort of truce. Sunderland's approaches to men such as Rochester were all similarly motivated; it was unfortunate that his past history made many people look on his efforts with distrust.

With the reassembly of Parliament for the new session, the murmuring against Sunderland began. He attracted negative comment in a variety of contexts, gradually fuelling the rumour that a team of members, led by Lord Norris, would make an all-out attack in the House of Commons on 23 December. Long before this, Sunderland had become alarmed. On 5 December he went to the King and tendered his resignation, which William refused to accept. Instead the King tried unsuccessfully to get some of the Whigs to support him; but the only one who would do so was Peterborough.

Sunderland had appeared to be Peterborough's only friend in the days of his imprisonment. Peterborough was now reciprocating Sunderland's good offices. No one was surprised that he should involve himself in the conflict, should it arise. 'These are fit waters for one of the Earl of Peterborow's humour to fish in.' In the event, the attack never materialised before Parliament adjourned for the Christmas recess. Sunderland, however, was taking no further chances. On 26 December he again tendered his resignation to the King and again it was refused. On his way out, Sunderland left his keys with Vernon who presumed that the King had accepted them. When this was found not to be the case, the King sent the keys after him but he refused to take them back.

The reasons for Sunderland's seemingly precipitate departure were widely canvassed. Peterborough and his Commons associates may have overstressed the dangers threatened in an attempt to win Sunderland over to their side. Their treatment did not have the effect they anticipated. Certainly Sunderland seemed exasperated with the Whigs and found them an impossible party to please. He unburdened himself to Vernon one day, bursting out that 'there was no rack like to what he suffered by being ground as he had been between Lord Monmouth and Lord Wharton'.

Vernon, now a Secretary of State, was not the only person to wonder at the Sunderland-Peterborough friendship, but at least he had the opportunity to ask questions about it. Sunderland claimed that he maintained it entirely for the benefit of Shrewsbury and Orford, hoping to gain by it some sort of reconciliation. The fact that the friendship caused some people to doubt Sunderland's sincerity towards Shrewsbury caused the earl distress and some amazement. If he could be so misrepresented, he considered it was time for him to retire.

Sunderland startled Vernon with his views on how Peterborough should be treated. He believed he would behave better if he could be made 'easier in his fortune, which was very low'. A pension of £2,000 per annum and restoration to his place in the Council were the things he thought he should have. Vernon said: 'I did not know anybody would grudge it him, if they would make him Vizir, that he might be great and at a distance, but I thought bringing him into the Council might be joining men together sooner than they were ripe for it...' Sunderland thought Peterborough would never be at ease while any mark of disgrace remained. He thought about telling the King this but later on seemed to change his mind.

Sunderland's view of Peterborough contained much truth. His belief that he had been misjudged over the letters in the Fenwick case still rankled; he had a way of harking back to the episode which at times gave the impression that he would like to reopen the matter in the House of Lords. However by this time he had already launched into the first of many court cases to recover Drayton.[12]

After the Treaty of Ryswick in 1697, the Peace between France and England was marked by the resumption of formal diplomatic relations between the two countries. William III sent the Earl of Portland as ambassador to the Court of France and Louis XIV reciprocated with Marshal Tallard, a figure of equal stature and experience, as his representative in London. At the end of March 1698, Tallard reported to Louis the presence of 'strong cabals' in Parliament against the Court, that in the Lords being headed by the Duke of Leeds and the Earls of Rochester, Nottingham and Peterborough. Once again, Peterborough is mentioned in association with Tories in opposition.

The Whigs were gratified by the departure of Sunderland and also the subsequent fall from grace of one of his tools in the House of Commons. Charles Duncombe was an immensely wealthy goldsmith in the City of London who was sitting at this time in the House of Commons as a Tory member for Downton in Wiltshire. A friend of Sunderland, he had for long been one of Peterborough's city associates and was said to have 'a faculty of helping those that have money to dispose of it, and those who have none, to borrow...' Duncombe and others had attacked Charles Montagu, the Chancellor of the Exchequer, in the House of Commons for malpractice in his department. This produced a backlash of accusations against Duncombe and two others of irregularities in dealings with exchequer bills. A Bill of Pains and Penalties against Charles Duncombe for falsely endorsing exchequer bills was brought in the House of Commons and had its first reading in the Lords on 4 March 1698. Tory peers spoke against the Bill and were joined in their opposition by two Whigs, the Duke of Bolton and the Earl of Peterborough, who were concerned that the prerogative of the Lords in judicial matters was being challenged here by the House of Commons. They felt that the charge would have been more suitably brought in a court of law; it was certainly too light for an impeachment. Peterborough was appointed a manager for a conference with the Commons on the subject. At the second reading, on 15 March, Rochester and Peterborough both spoke warmly and at length against the Bill, which was lost at committee stage by one voice.[13]

Peterborough's interest in trade was a by-product of his contacts with the City of London. This interest could be seen in action on 9 June 1698 when a Bill concerning the trade with Africa was being debated in a committee of the whole House of Lords. This Bill, which had already passed rapidly through the House of Commons, concerned the Royal African Company which had held a monopoly of trade to the Guinea Coast since receiving a charter from James II. Correctly, the Company had assumed that their charter might not hold good under a change of sovereign and for some time they had been attempting to acquire a new grant.

During the debate the Lords expressed concern over the position of free traders in relation to the Company. Peterborough left the chamber and called together a group of four gentlemen of the African Company and four free traders. He asked the members of the Company what, if any, 'protection and relief' they would give to the persons and goods of free traders to the African coast. The Company members replied that they would feel obliged, and undertook, not only to protect the free traders but also to give them the freedom of the forts and castles in their possession for their use and for their goods; the free traders would only be required to pay a 'small consideration' for the privilege. When the free traders pointed out that there was no penalty on the African Company should they fail to keep their promise, the Company replied that 'in case they did not perform what they then told his lordship, the free traders would then have just reason to complain and they to be ashamed'. The agreement was immediately recorded in writing and signed by the free traders. Its conditions were embodied in the charter subsequently granted to the Royal African Company.[14]

There were often opportunities for ill-feeling and misunderstanding between the two Houses of Parliament as had occurred over Duncombe. Peterborough became involved in discussions with the Commons on a matter of procedure over the impeachment of John

Goudet and other merchants who had traded illegally during the war. He was also a member of the Committee which drew up heads for the discussion, and of another which was required to search for precedents in the Journals of the House of Lords. Once again Peterborough and the Earl of Rochester were noted as being 'very stiff upon the prerogative of the Peers'.[15]

On 5 July 1698 Parliament was prorogued and subsequently dissolved for the first time under the requirements of the Triennial Act. Peterborough's name is mentioned once more before the dissolution, as one of the dissenting peers when a Bill to form a new East India Company was passed by the Lords.[16]

Writs were issued for the election of a new Parliament immediately after the close of the session and before the King left for Holland. Electioneering activity had been noticed as early as January but the main campaign took place in July. In August all the results were gathered and duly published. In popular opinion the parties were divided on a Court or Country footing rather than as Whigs and Tories. According to a contemporary analysis, the Court party retained the majority it had held before but only about 64% of the old members were returned. A similar proportion was returned in the Country interest. It was a matter for speculation whether the Whig Junto would be able to retain its hold.

In August William III entered into the final stages of negotiation with the French over settling the matter of the Spanish inheritance. The task was made urgent by the Spanish king's poor state of health. Should he die, hostilities could break out over the disposal of his kingdom. William considered that the terms agreed with the French, regarding the amicable partition of the Spanish dominions, were the best obtainable and the First Partition Treaty was eventually signed on 11 October 1698. Under this Treaty, Spain, the Indies, the Netherlands and Sardinia would be bestowed on a child claimant, the Electoral Prince of Bavaria. Naples, Sicily, Guipuzcoa, Finale and the Tuscan *presidii* would go to the Dauphin and the duchy of Milan to the Archduke Charles, second son of the Emperor of Austria.

Subsequently the King of Spain made a will, leaving the whole of his dominions to the Electoral Prince and thereby indicating Spanish disapproval of partition. At this point the totally unlooked-for occurred: the King of Spain's health improved, giving him two more years of life, but the young Bavarian prince died on 6 February 1699.[17]

Records are generally silent on Peterborough's activities during that whole summer and autumn of 1698. In the early part of the summer he wrote twice to Sunderland about a servant he had previously employed and in October he wrote again to say that he was in the neighbourhood and might visit him at Althorp. He also claimed that 'he avoided company, was a philosopher, and very easy in his own concerns'. No visit was received but Sunderland heard that he had been seen about Drayton.

Although not wealthy by many standards, Peterborough had enough property to look after. In addition to his house and grounds at Parsons Green and his estate at Dauntsey in Wiltshire, his accession to his uncle's title added the ancestral lands of Turvey and other manors in Bedfordshire, as well as some property in Northamptonshire adjoining Drayton. Residence at Turvey Old Hall would have given him a reasonable journey to his other manors in that area.

Sunderland also mentioned a 'business' to which Peterborough had referred and which Sunderland thought he would be mad to revive. It is not clear what this was but no action appears to have been taken. It may have been just one of numerous passing references to previous troubles with which the earl liked to alarm his friends.

At about this time an agent reported to Louis XIV on the state of affairs in England and told him that the Duke of Leeds, the Earl of Peterborough and others 'are able to form a pretty powerful party in Parliament, and this will certainly be done'. He considered them to have 'no less talent and boldness than the principal actors of the preceding reigns'.[18]

On 8 February 1699 a debate in the Lords on the King's speech revealed some considerable support for allowing the King to retain his Dutch Guards, which the Commons had wished to be sent home. But there was also vigorous opposition. Gibert Burnet, Bishop of Salisbury, argued in favour of their retention. He was a little disconcerted when the Marquess of Normanby quoted a passage from the Bishop's *History of the Reformation in England* where he had recorded with approval that there were no foreign troops maintained here in those days. The bishop justified himself by explaining that he had his reasons for writing this but before he had a chance to expand on them, Peterborough interrupted to ask if he was thus admitting to the whole House that he was a bad historian. Despite jibes, the resolution to retain the Guards was carried. Peterborough was among the thirty-seven peers who entered their dissent.[19]

During the winter season of 1698–9 there was a brief reappearance of Ulysses Brown. From time to time he had been supplied with sums of money from the Secretary of State's office to keep him away but this proved ineffectual. Vernon found that his word was unreliable and so the money ceased. Irritated, Brown contrived to gain access to Peterborough again, through the good offices of Dr Chamberlain, the Whig obstetrician. By March Vernon had heard that 'of late they have shaken him off'.[20]

Peterborough at last appeared to show interest in coming in from the wilderness of distrust and caution to which his own actions had exiled him. The previous winter he had asked Secretary Vernon for an interview, proposing a rendezvous at Somerset House in the rooms of a lady unknown to Vernon, which caused the Secretary to postpone accepting the invitation. In August 1699 Vernon felt he could go to the house of a Mr Clement near Chelsea. The conversation on the morning of 16 August lasted three hours and ranged over a variety of topics.

Vernon found it useful to learn from the earl himself that he had shaken off all contact with Ulysses Brown. Soon after Peterborough was sent to the Tower, he discovered that Brown was a rogue. Vernon was able to assure him that all Brown's letters to Shrewsbury had been passed to him; Brown had only been kept in reserve while Peterborough was believed to be engaged in ruining other people's reputations, 'a defensive weapon taken up against those that use offensive arms'. If Peterborough wished to live in peace, the remedy was in his own hands.

Aware that Vernon was close to Shrewsbury, Peterborough was dismissive about Matthew Smith. He claimed that the motives he had for keeping Smith's papers were not to hold them against the duke with the intention of harming him but merely for discussion with him later. It had been the Duchess of Norfolk's idea, not his, to name Smith in Fenwick's trial. He had not expected Smith's book to be printed and never advised it.

It was clear that Peterborough wished 'to live well' with Shrewsbury whom he said he had always held in esteem. But there had always been a lack of rapport between the two men, even in Revolution days. Peterborough had often confided in Shrewsbury but never felt that the trust was returned. Shrewsbury on the other hand generally found Peterborough incomprehensible and once said: 'When I neither see him nor hear him I understand him as well as when I do both.'

Peterborough cited only one instance when the duke seemed to trust him – but only when he had already made it clear that he was aware of the secret. It was in 1694, when Shrewsbury had been persuaded to take up office again as Secretary of State. This always required persuasion but there was a story current at the time that he had been compelled to take up the seals on orders from the Jacobite Court. Peterborough (then Earl of Monmouth) went with many others to congratulate the new Secretary but stayed behind for a private word. They

fell into discourse...about the reasons for his [Shrewsbury's] coming into employment again, which Lord Peterborough said was a great surprise to many people, and to himself in particular. The Duke answered that if he could furnish him with a good reason for his coming in he would oblige him, for he knew of none, whereupon L[ord] Pet[erborough] replied that he having been let into the secret of some messages, letters, and discourses that had passed between the Duke, Sir James Montgomery and others, he comprehended the reason for his taking an employment, and on that account excused him and no other; the Duke then laying his hands upon L[ord] Pet[erborough]'s arms saying, There is nothing so strange but that it may come to pass; one would hardly have expected that Sir James Montgomery should be able to make a Secretary to K[ing] William.

Shrewsbury's biographer observes that Peterborough failed to note the sarcasm. For one generally so quick-witted, this seems a little odd. The earl appeared to take the remark at its face value. At least he claimed he never told the King nor made political capital out of it. If he believed that Shrewsbury was there to be of use to St Germains, he was not alone in this; Marlborough was of the same opinion.

On yet another subject, Peterborough believed that the Whig party had been ungrateful to Sunderland who, at the time of this conversation, was attempting to pull strings to form a moderate government in which it was hoped that Shrewsbury would be a key figure. Vernon had heard that Sunderland had some sort of job for Peterborough but the earl laughed this off and told him that he 'talked like a courtier'. Sunderland may well have been the moving spirit behind Peterborough's attempt to mend his fences. He had told him that he must oppose him as long as he did not work with the party. Peterborough was not offended by this but appreciated its frankness.

In the course of this long conversation the Secretary realised that he was talking to a man who had become almost paranoid about people laying schemes to ruin him. Peterborough felt himself generally ill used, he was constantly on his guard and for three years had recorded in a 'table book' where he went and to whom he spoke. Even acts of kindness were misconstrued. Shrewsbury had played a part in acquiring the office of Treasurer of the Ordnance for Peterborough's brother, Colonel Harry Mordaunt. Peterborough considered this no sort of compliment to himself: 'his brother was one that would cut his throat if they would have him, and he had not come near him these two years.'

Vernon put in a few words of advice which the earl took in good part. He told him that 'it was in his own power to make himself and others more at quiet, if he would take but half the pains to show a peaceable temper that he does to show a restless one'. Vernon was sure that the root cause of the trouble was money. 'All this finding of fault and teasing of people is only to procure himself a good pension.' No one might feel at all inclined to give him anything but it was useful to know that his complaisance and good behaviour could be purchased.

For Peterborough, financial problems never seemed to be far away. It may not have been symptomatic of his other properties, but a report from the Surveyor-General in the summer of 1699 showed that the rent due to the Crown from the estate of Dauntsey was eight and a half years in arrears; the earl owed the Crown £2,550. To busy himself with his estates and the management of his financial affairs would have been a useful but perhaps unattractive commitment. One reason for the 'finding of fault and the teasing of people' could have been that a mischievous, creative and energetic mind was seriously underoccupied.[21]

Twelve

When Parliament reassembled on 16 November 1699, the Duke of Shrewsbury had accepted the White Staff of the Lord Chamberlain. He withdrew to the country later in the month for health reasons but he had other problems too; one of them was the reappearance of Matthew Smith. This persistent agent was about to publish another book. Having been sent a copy in advance of publication, James Vernon thought that Peterborough's hand showed more strongly in it than he had at first suspected it might. He was disgusted to be given evidence that Dr Chamberlain, together with Peterborough, had 'managed' Smith all along and knew about the publication date. After Peterborough's protestations that summer, Vernon dismissed them all as 'a parcel of rogues'.

On 7 December the House of Lords resolved that Smith should be attached for publishing *Remarks on the Duke of Shrewsbury's Letter to the House of Lords re Captain Smith*, 'by Matthew Smith of the Inner Temple'. Peterborough was present in the House and had told Lord Jersey beforehand that he wondered that Smith should publish this, 'that if he had any hand in advising him he should have gone another way to work'. When the matter was brought forward, he moved that the letter should be compared with what had been printed in the Journal of the House of Lords as he believed there was some discrepancy, in that some words had been omitted. This motion was looked on by others as a further indication of his involvement. If this was the bomb that Peterborough had spoken of throwing, Vernon thought it had turned out 'very ineffectual'. To add to the confusion, Peterborough protested at Smith's being attached, despite the fact that he had seconded the motion for the attachment, as at present there was no proof that the book emanated from Smith.

Four days later at the Bar of the House, Smith acknowledged the book to be his. Peterborough strongly supported a call for it to be read. While this was done, it was noted with some surprise that the earl spent most of the time conversing with the Lord Chancellor 'in a careless manner' so that, at the conclusion, he had not heard half of it and asked

for the book to be read again. The House had no time for such inatten-
tion and proceeded to re-commit Smith for a breach of privilege in
printing part of their proceedings. On 15 December the House resolved
that the book was a false and scandalous libel, reflecting on the honour
of the Duke of Shrewsbury, which should be burnt by the common
hangman and Smith conveyed to the Gatehouse prison.

There was a rumour current at the time that Smith's book was not
written in his style but in that of someone of more educated tastes
with a flair for writing and lucid argument. Many thought that
Peterborough was behind it somewhere; other suspects were the Duke
of Leeds or some discontented Tories. Shrewsbury believed the blame
lay at Peterborough's door and remained mystified by the reason for
his malice. Vernon discovered later that Peterborough believed that he
had been sent to the Tower on Shrewsbury's account, despite the fact
that both Marlborough and Godolphin had been implicated by
Fenwick's letters. He was also envious of Shrewsbury's positions, no
matter how reluctantly held, and may have believed that all of them
might have been his had things worked otherwise. Some people
harbour grudges long after others have forgotten the incidents which
gave rise to them.[1]

Early in 1700 the affairs of Scotland were under consideration in the
House of Lords. Having been prevented from trading in competition
with the East India Company, the Company of Scotland had looked for
fresh areas where they would have fewer rivals and where it might be
possible to develop a trading station and colonise. In 1698 an expedition had set out to Darien on the isthmus of Panama, an area in fact
annexed to Spanish territory. The venture seemed doomed to failure,
particularly from disease and mismanagement. Two more expeditions
set out later but these were threatened by Spanish interests. Also,
William III had sent orders to English colonists to give no assistance to
the Scots.

These expeditions had been a determined effort to improve the
financial situation in a country which had experienced a series of bad
harvests. They had involved a huge subscription of private capital and,
because of their failure, many people now faced financial ruin. It was
unfortunate that William's foreign policy, which involved placating
Spain in order to balance the power of France, finally crushed what
may at best have been a forlorn hope.

Early in 1700 a pamphlet entitled *An Enquiry into the Causes of the
Miscarriage of the Scots Colony at Darien* was published in Glasgow. In

England, it was considered insolent and scurrilous. It defended the project and said some hard things about the English government. For some time there had been a plan to bring the pamphlet to the notice of the Commons, but it was thought that Scottish agents had managed to prevent this. Peterborough introduced it in the Lords during a debate. He read some extracts and then opened his theme stating that the pamphlet 'was writ passionately, and in the language of persons that smarted under great losses; yet, they do throughout the book aim at what may properly relieve them viz. their being admitted to an union with England.' He pointed out the convenience of this and its use in achieving future tranquillity. There were two young princes, he reminded the peers, who might find themselves in competition for the Crown; 'if one of them, as has been usual, would change his religion for a kingdom, it is not unlikely he would put himself under the education of the Kirk; in which case perhaps, they would prefer him to one brought up in episcopacy, though it were by a Scotch bishop...'*

In conclusion, the earl moved for a Union with Scotland. After some debate it was resolved to take the matter into consideration on 16 January.

Peterborough's motion gave rise to speculation regarding his motive. In the Earl of Argyll's opinion, the King intended to have such a motion made and the Cabinet Council had been told of it. Before any action had been taken, Peterborough heard of it and decided to put the Court in an awkward position by taking the wind out of their sails. Although Argyll knew that Peterborough had professed a regard for the Scots nation on more than one occasion in the past, he was afraid that his action now might 'ruin the success of the project'. Viscount Seafield thought that the motion would have done better coming from the government.

Five days after Peterborough's motion, there was a heated debate on the same subject in the Commons. Mr Montagu was reported as saying that a lord in another place had moved for a Union 'certainly only in jest, for in truth it was only a jest'. Peterborough was so annoyed that he sent him a challenge.[2]

In the Lords at this time, support for a Union was both lukewarm and qualified. The King was genuinely in favour, but nothing was effectively carried out, despite constant royal reminders. However, the

*Peterborough alluded to Gilbert Burnet, Bishop of Salisbury, who was then Preceptor to the young Duke of Gloucester. A motion for his removal from this post had been rejected in the House of Commons the previous month.

House did discuss the situation at Darien. Because of trading difficulties between the two kingdoms, the King asked again that some way of uniting them should be found; he had first asked this soon after his accession.

On 13 February the House took the matter of Union into consideration and a Bill was prepared to appoint Commissioners to treat about it. The subsequent Bill passed its first and second readings, but vanished at Committee stage and never reached the Statute Book. There were two more unsuccessful attempts at legislation before the end of the reign.[3]

On 16 February 1700 the Duke of Norfolk's petition was debated in the House of Lords. For the second time, the duke was attempting to obtain a divorce from his duchess 'to enable him to marry again, he having certain proof of his wife's living in adultery with Sir John Germaine'. Despite having been active in defeating the previous attempt, Peterborough now sponsored the petition with enthusiasm. Speculation was rife as to his motive. Some thought that the duke might choose another Mordaunt as his second wife, namely Peterborough's daughter, Lady Henrietta. Others thought that the earl aimed to ensure that the duchess would feel obliged to convey Drayton to him. He seemed too occupied with the business to have time for anything else.

The Norfolk case aroused much interest and was heard over several days. It was well advanced by the time Vernon next met Peterborough. It was a chance meeting on 24 February 1700 at the Earl of Jersey's front door. Vernon had just stepped into a chair to make his departure when another stopped alongside. It contained Peterborough who said he would take that opportunity of speaking to him, 'and kept me there, tête à tête, near one hour in the view of all persons that passed by'. The conversation ranged over the usual topics and was only interrupted by the arrival of other visitors.

Later Vernon recounted the meeting to Somers. The Lord Chancellor had enemies of his own and, although he agreed that Peterborough was 'a very ill man', he thought that there were others as bad. Vernon believed that Peterborough was restrained by his lack of justification; once clear of any blame, he would be up to mischief again. Vernon's character of the earl is the blackest ever written; he thought him malicious, mad, terrible, faithless and of an equivalent greed. 'He wants money and would leap at it; but he has no moderation in anything, and I question whether the King would be willing to satisfy his cravings,' he wrote.[4]

The Norfolk divorce case passed through the Lords, reached the Commons, and received the Royal Assent on 11 April 1700. The duke never remarried and died the following year. The duchess, 'now bare Lady Mary Mordaunt again, from being the first Dutchess of England', never relinquished the use of her title and, after her husband's death, married Sir John Germaine.[5]

The Parliamentary session came to an end on 11 April after several days of difficult relations between the two Houses. The Commons had passed a Bill for granting aid to the Crown through the sale of Irish forfeited estates which they sent up to the Lords tacked to the Land Tax Bill. In the Lords, the Bill met with many objections. The crisis deepened when the Lords' amendments were repeatedly rejected by the Commons and no solution was found in conferences. Eventually the opposition weakened when the King let it be known that he was prepared to see the Bill pass. Enough bad blood had been raised in the course of the proceedings to make the King prorogue Parliament immediately after the Bill became law, and without the courtesy of the customary speech. Peterborough's only recorded contribution to the debate was his analogy of the situation to the case of a man who was obliged to marry a rich wife even although she was known to be a baggage.[6]

In February 1700 a second Partition Treaty had been signed, following the death of the Electoral Prince. The terms of the Treaty were not publicly known until after William's departure for Holland in July. The Treaty, which had been signed by the Earls of Portland and Jersey, provided that the Archduke Charles of Austria should inherit the share of the Spanish dominions which had been apportioned to the Electoral Prince. France would receive Naples, Sicily, Tuscany and the Duchy of Lorraine if the duke was prepared to exchange it for Milan.

In October 1700 Carlos II of Spain died. In order to avoid partition, he had left a will which provided that his entire inheritance should pass to the Duke of Anjou, the grandson of Louis XIV. Failing the Duke of Anjou, it was devised on his brother, the Duke of Berry, failing whom the Archduke Charles of Austria and then the Duke of Savoy.

When William returned to England at the end of October, he heard that Louis XIV had decided to accept the will in breach of the Partition Treaty. Because of the sanctity attached to inheritance and dying wishes, a large number of people believed that the French king had taken the right decision. However, such a decision could mean the possibility of war in the future. For England at least, an Act of Succession must be passed. In William's eyes all these problems merited consideration by a new Parliament. A dissolution was announced on 19 December.[7]

The King's administration had steadily acquired a Tory complexion. Sir Charles Hedges had been appointed to the vacant Secretaryship in November. The next month Rochester was appointed Lord Lieutenant of Ireland and Godolphin First Lord of the Treasury. In Parliament the two parties took different views of the international situation. The Tories hoped that our interests could be safeguarded by peaceful methods, whereas the Whigs were prepared to countenance a war if that was shown to be necessary.

In his opening speech to Parliament on 11 February 1701, the King referred first to the sad death of the young Duke of Gloucester and the necessity of settling the succession. Then he moved on to the situation in Europe following the death of Carlos II, the importance of retaining a strong fleet and the clearing up of all remaining debts.

In the debate on the speech the following day, Peterborough was a leading speaker in favour of a war with France – so that the bishops would not wear cardinals' hats, as he believed that a peace would enable King James to be restored. His vigour in debate inevitably earned him a place on the committee formed to draw up an address in return for the King's speech, and he was also given the task of reporting the committee's efforts to the House. Having received some additions, the address was then recommitted for alterations as it had been decided to invite the Commons to concur in it. It thanked the King for his concern and care for the succession in the Protestant line. It asked that all treaties made by the King and any other prince 'since the late war' might be laid before the House, and also asked the King to 'enter into Alliance with all those Princes and States willing to unite for the preservation of the balance of Europe'.

At a conference on 17 February the Commons returned the address, having agreed on their own vote to the King. Subsequently, a debate was held on a Jacobite letter received by the King and sent to Parliament. The letter purported to come from Lord Melfort and revealed that Louis XIV was considering supporting another Jacobite invasion. The letter may have been a deliberate plant but its effect was to encourage the Lords to add another paragraph to their address, urging 'the speedy setting out of the Fleet'.[8]

By this time Peterborough had been reinstated as Lord Lieutenant of Northamptonshire and had chosen as one of his deputies his brother Harry, which suggested a thaw in family relationships.

When the treaties which they had requested and the papers which had formed the preceding negotiations had been delivered and read to the House of Lords on 14 March, a criticism was voiced in a subsequent debate that the King had not taken proper advice before concluding the Partition Treaty. Peterborough was a member of a committee appointed to draw up an address asking that in future there might be consultation with the Privy Council and Parliament.

In the debate on the address on 18 March it was revealed through Portland that the King had consulted English ministers before concluding the Treaty but in fact he had not followed their advice. Also it was noted that 'verbal orders and instructions' had not been considered by any of the Councils. Regarding the apparent violation of the Treaty by Louis XIV in accepting the King of Spain's will, the peers recommended that the King should 'proceed with such caution as may carry with it a real security'. It was decided not to ask the Commons to concur in this address.[9]

However the Lower House had its own concern over the Partition Treaty. On 1 April the members intimated their intention to impeach Portland for his part in its implementation. After questioning Vernon, it became clear that more information could be uncovered. The Tories set off on the trail of Somers. Further questioning revealed the existence of the First Partition Treaty and the fact that Somers had affixed the Great Seal to a commission in which the names of the negotiators had been left blank. It became obvious how much had occurred, unknown to the legislators; their ignorance was no longer palatable or acceptable. On 15 April the Commons conveyed to the Lords their intention to impeach Somers, Orford and Halifax. By May there had been weeks of arguments between the Houses over impeachment procedure and relations became soured and bitter. On 9 May, articles against the Earl of Orford eventually appeared.

On 10 May the urgency of the international situation broke in. The Lords discussed a request for aid from the Dutch who believed that a French invasion was imminent. The previous day the Commons had promised supply so that the King's allies could be supported. The Lords produced an address (which Peterborough reported from committee) urging the King to make good all the articles previously entered into with our allies and also to make 'a strict League, Offensive and Defensive' with them. A further clause referred to alliances with the Emperor. This request formed the earliest foundation of what became known as the Grand Alliance.[10]

In the midst of all this activity, the Bill of Succession moved on its untroubled course through the process of legislation and received the

Royal Assent on 12 June. It named the Princess Sophia, Electress of Hanover, as the next Protestant heir after the Princess Anne and among other provisions it disqualified from the succession heirs who were Roman Catholics.[11]

After several reminders, the Commons sent up articles of impeachment against Somers on 19 May. More delays followed. The Lords' committee on procedure in impeachments reported twice and afterwards the House decided not to discuss procedure with the Commons. Peterborough, an unfailing advocate for good relations between the Houses, and twenty other peers registered their dissent on the grounds that to act against the existing precedent (a joint committee) would at the present time constitute 'a great obstacle'. The Lords then chose a date for Somers's trial which the Commons considered was acting in an arbitrary fashion. The Lords then retaliated for the Commons' delays by sitting on supply bills.

The Lords stuck to their decision not to consult the Commons and Somers's trial was fixed for Monday 17 June. In Westminster Hall on the appointed day, the articles were read but no member of the House of Commons appeared to conduct a prosecution. The Lords voted to acquit Somers by a majority; Peterborough was among the thirty-two peers who voted for a conviction.

On 20 June the Commons announced that they were now ready to go to the trial, provided that the 'necessary preliminaries' were adjusted by a joint committee. They offended the Lords by ascribing delays in supply to those who tried to make divisions between the Houses while seeking indemnity for their crimes.[12]

On 23 June the Lords fought back. They passed a resolution that the vote in the Commons on 20 June regarding delays contained 'most unjust reflections on the honour and justice of the House of Peers' and was an attempt to cover 'their affected and unreasonable delays in prosecuting the impeached lords'. The final paragraph of the resolution read: 'Also resolved That whatever ill consequences may arise, from the so long deferring the supplies for this year's service, are to be attributed to the fatal counsel of putting off the Meeting of a Parliament so long, and to the unnecessary delays of the House of Commons.' To this last paragraph, only one peer recorded a reasoned signed dissent:

> Because, though I humbly conceive it is evident to all Englishmen, that nothing could be more fatal to the interest of Europe, to the interest of the Protestant Religion, and the safety of England than

the so long delay of the meeting of a Parliament after the death of the King of Spain: yet I cannot agree to the latter part of this vote, which lays imputations of unnecessary delays to this House of Commons. PETERBOROW.

The same day the House of Lords proceeded to Westminster Hall for the trial and subsequent acquittal of Lord Orford. On 24 June the Lords dismissed the impeachments of the Earl of Portland and Lord Halifax before lifting the stop on the supply bills.[13]

Before the session ended, one final attempt was made to address the matter of a Union with Scotland. A committee of nine whose members were chosen by voting consisted of the Dukes of Somerset, Newcastle and Bolton, the Earls of Carlisle, Peterborough, Scarbrough and Tankerville, Lord Wharton and Lord Somers. They or any three of them were to consider a Union between England and Scotland and to meet when, where and as often as they pleased. The prorogation postponed any further meetings and later the dissolution of Parliament was announced.

During the lifespan of this brief but active Parliament, the foundations of ministerial responsibility towards Parliament had been securely laid. The Grand Alliance, giving rise to Britain's involvement in the European political scene, and the Act of Succession providing for the future inheritance of the Crown, were of immense significance for the years that lay ahead.[14]

Throughout the summer the inevitability of the outbreak of hostilities was in the forefront of most minds. The Whigs were keen that William should call an election to find a new Parliament which would be supportive of the coming war. Numerous pamphlets were being published, encouraging a stand against France. An impetus was given to the whole process by the death of James II on 5 September. Louis XIV, in a moment of regal sympathy and solidarity, pledged to support the young Prince of Wales and acknowledged him publicly as King. The Grand Alliance between William III, the Emperor and the United Provinces was signed on 27 August/7 September 1701.[15]

Whig pressure on the King to call an election increased. The death of James II gave rise to speculation as to whether the Tories' Jacobite sympathies might make them an unreliable support in wartime. The Whigs also believed that a dissolution by choice at the present time might give them a better return than one by force at a later date. In September the King consulted Lord Somers, who proved in favour of an immediate dissolution and gave a reasoned opinion. On 11 November 1701 William announced the dissolution to his Privy Council.

It seemed clear, at least from the tone of popular pamphlets, that the country was expecting a war and prepared to support one. The new Parliament gathered for the first time on 30 December 1701. Each party believed they held the majority; in fact they were fairly evenly divided. The determination of the Whigs in the elections had managed to remove a certain Tory Jacobite element but it left a party with a strong hard core, able to maintain itself.

Whig enthusiasm left in its wake one or two disputed elections. On 14 January 1701/2 some burgesses of Malmesbury petitioned the House of Commons in the belief that corrupt practices had been used to ensure the election of their two members, Edward Paunceford and Sir Charles Hedges (Secretary of State at the time), and they accused an attorney, William Ady. Investigations revealed that Ady had not endeavoured to bring about the election of Paunceford and Hedges but that of an entirely different candidate, Daniel Park (sometimes described as Colonel Park). Also associated with the election of Park was one Gould, the schoolmaster at Dauntsey on the estate of the Earl of Peterborough and within his sphere of influence. Park and Gould were summoned to attend a sitting of the House on 29 January.

On the day appointed Ady appeared with a sum of money and a bank bill for £200 which he claimed had been given him by Park. After hearing counsel and witnesses, the House then resolved that Paunceford and Hedges had been duly elected to serve as members for the borough of Malmesbury; the petition from the burgesses was considered 'scandalous, false, and vexatious', and the burgesses who brought it were to be taken into custody.

Counsel for Daniel Park was then called in and heard. The House found Park guilty of bribery and corruption and he was ordered to be taken into custody and prosecuted by the Attorney-General.* Mr Gould, the schoolmaster, was found guilty of corrupt practices and also taken into custody.

During the course of evidence, the name of the Earl of Peterborough had been mentioned. After the resolutions on Park and Gould, a debate developed regarding the earl's part in the business. Peterborough had

*Park later went to Flanders as a volunteer, became an aide-de-camp to Marlborough and entered history as the man who brought the good news of Blenheim to Queen Anne. He was later rewarded by being made Governor of the Leeward Islands.

been in attendance in the Lords that day and asked to be admitted and heard. The Commons agreed 'and the door being opened, his Lordship came in; and came up to the Bar, where a chair was set for him a little within the Bar, on the left hand as he came up; whereupon his Lordship reposed himself a little while, covered; and then stood up, uncovered; and was heard.' Before he withdrew, Peterborough left with the House a letter from Samuel Powell. At this point a motion was made for an adjournment but it was defeated. The question was then put 'that Charles Earl of Peterborough is guilty of many indirect practices, in endeavouring to procure Daniel Park Esq. to be elected a Burgess to serve in this present Parliament for the Borough of Malmesbury'. There followed a debate on the question, another motion to adjourn was defeated, the question was then put, and resolved in the affirmative. The House rose at midnight.

The determination with which the Commons pursued the matter to its conclusion illustrated the importance with which they regarded any action infringing their fundamental rights. Committed Whigs like the Earl of Shaftesbury rejoiced that Peterborough had been treated this way by 'his new friends the Tories'. This was his reward for joining them last year in the impeachments of his 'brother Whigs. The experience was salutary; as Shaftesbury predicted, 'this fixes him ours.'[16]

On 31 December 1701 the King made a speech to both Houses which referred to his resentment at Louis XIV's acknowledgement of 'the pretended Prince of Wales' as King of England. With his grandson on the throne of Spain, the French king was in effect in control of the Spanish monarchy, a state of affairs which must inevitably affect our trade, peace and safety. Because of this situation William had concluded several alliances, shortly to be laid before Parliament. 'The eyes of all Europe', he continued, 'are upon this Parliament, all matters are at a stand until your resolutions are known', and he urged them to take hold of this opportunity. To maintain the balance of power, it would be necessary to keep a great strength at sea and to provide a land force proportional to those of the allies. He asked for Parliament's support in granting supply for these purposes.

Perhaps the most dramatic and deeply felt speech of William's reign received a rapid response from both Houses, at least to its earlier part. On 2 January 1701/2, the Lords considered the speech in committee and drew up an address in reply. Peterborough reported the address from committee and it was agreed as it was read, paragraph by paragraph. The Lords pledged their support in 'the great work (which seems reserved for you) the reducing the exorbitant power of France and maintaining the balance of Europe'.

However, the great work was not destined to be William's, and on 4 January his successor in it, the Earl of Marlborough, performed the task of laying before the House several treaties which he had entered into at The Hague the previous year. His negotiations had covered not only the alliance with the Emperor and the United Provinces and its provisions to control the power of France but also the arrangement of troop quotas from each power. There was no difficulty in acquiring the Commons' agreement to the troop quotas and their prompt granting of the required supply.

From the terms of the Treaty of Grand Alliance, it was clear that the power of France must be controlled and opposed in a wider field than that of Europe. In the Spanish West Indies, trading interests must be protected. There were opportunities of seafaring acquisitions, a prospect which always appealed to the blue-water policy of the Tory party.

Within days of the Treaties being laid before the House, it was rumoured that Peterborough would receive a commission as Captain-General of all the forces in the West Indies and go there in command of 8,000 men. Such an expedition was not discussed with any certainty until July, and even then in strict secrecy. This early rumour was a sign that life might change for Peterborough in the future. As had happened for Marlborough, the summons to leave the backwoods of uncertainty and unemployment was on its way and the opportunity was about to appear of being entrusted with a task which would utilise constructively the energy and ingenuity hitherto spent on mischief and intrigue. Someone had found a way by which, in Vernon's words, he might be 'great and at a distance'.

There was little time left to run in the reign of William III. Echoing a national mood for war, Parliament was occupied in February in providing the ways and means of granting the supply already voted. However there was less consensus over a Bill for the abjuration of James III which had a more difficult passage through Parliament.

On 21 February 1701/2, while riding in Richmond Park, the King suffered a fall from his horse which resulted in the inconvenience of a broken collar-bone. His health improved after his fall until he caught a chill which developed into fever. With his poor lungs, it was not long before his doctors believed that the illness might prove fatal and they warned the Cabinet on 6 March. In this time of anxiety both Houses

[134]

were in regular attendance at Westminster. They heard the Royal Assent to two bills given by commission on Saturday 7 March and then, unusually for a Sunday, gathered again the following day in expectation of news. They were not kept waiting long. During the morning the Earl of Manchester came with a message to the Houses from the Queen's Majesty in Council. King William had died at 8 am. Queen Anne's 'sunshine day' had begun.[17]

Thirteen

Queen Anne was the first reigning sovereign to inherit a sitting Parliament. Under the provisions of the 1696 statute, Parliament was not automatically dissolved on the King's death but continued to meet and do business. The peers and members of the House of Commons, who had gathered at Westminster for news on 8 March, were still in session for another two months, thus enabling the plans for the war to proceed without loss of impetus.

It was a matter of course, as it would have been of choice, that the Earl of Marlborough should be at the new Queen's right hand. He and his wife, together with Lord Godolphin, had been part of the close-knit circle around the Princess Anne at the Cockpit in less fortunate times. It was part of the policy of the new reign to make clear to all that William's treaty obligations would be honoured. The plans already laid led to the declaration of war against France and Spain by England, Scotland, the Emperor and the United Provinces on 4/15 May 1702.

There were different manifestations of the mood for war. At the time of the proclamation of hostilities, a new translation of the Orations of Demosthenes was undertaken by five gentlemen under the direction of Lord Somers. It was considered a suitable exercise, given that the danger from the power of Louis XIV resembled that of Philip of Macedon against Athens. Those who took part were Lord Peterborough, Lord Lansdowne, Dr Samuel Garth (the Whig physician), Colonel Stanhope and Mr Topham. Peterborough's contribution was a translation of the *First Olynthiac*. It was a surprising collaboration in view of his support of Somers's impeachment the previous year.[1]

In June Peterborough was confirmed in his appointment as Lord Lieutenant of Northamptonshire under the new monarch. In July the appointment of Governor of Jamaica and the overall command of the forces there was under discussion. It is not clear at what point his name was first considered, as there were other candidates in the field, but on 27 July Marlborough asked Godolphin whether Peterborough could be used as he knew he 'had had it long in his head'.

When it became obvious that the forces in the West Indies must be strengthened, the possibility that the situation might produce the naval command he had long coveted must have occurred to Peterborough – he had been to those parts before. A small squadron was normally kept on the West Indian station, at present under Admiral Benbow. In January a French squadron, under the command of Admiral Francois Louis Rousselet de Châteaurenault, had arrived to await the outbreak of war. Its appearance had caused consternation as it greatly outnumbered the English ships. By the time the news of the formal declaration of hostilities had reached the West Indies, the French squadron had moved away towards Cuba; most of its complement subsequently left the area as escort to the Spanish treasure fleet. In October this same squadron was attacked and destroyed in the safe haven of Vigo bay on the coast of Spain by an Anglo-Dutch fleet under Sir George Rooke on its way home after a dismally unsuccessful attempt against Cadiz.

Peterborough was appointed Governor of Jamaica in the early days of October 1702. Preparations for the departure of the expedition moved on rapidly in the hope of being ready to leave at the end of November but it was not until Christmas that Peterborough was able to say that they expected to leave by the first easterly wind.[2]

After the announcement of such an appointment, Peterborough inevitably received requests from various people that their friends or protégés might find employment in the Governor's suite or somewhere under his auspices. Some requests were channelled through Locke and not all were successful, but Peterborough did manage to find a place for a destitute bookbinder promoted by Lady Calverley. He did not forget his own friends. Writing to Benjamin Furly in Rotterdam to acquire supplies for his equipage, Peterborough asked if he had anyone he wished to recommend for employment. Furly gave the matter some thought and, hearing that Simon Clement was to go as secretary to the Governor, he suggested his son, Arent, who, as a close friend of Locke, had a double recommendation. Later he was less keen for Arent to go, as Clement's appointment was not after all a certainty and Peterborough controlled only naval and military posts.[3]

Everyone embarking on this expedition was aware that the most threatening enemies might prove to be the climate and disease rather than the French. Because of this, Peterborough produced £300 of his own money to provide necessary medicines 'without which it were barbarous to send troops into such climates' when he found that the official supply was being held up for want of ready money. A down payment of £100 speeded up the delivery and the earl was later reimbursed.

John Locke, at Oates in Essex, was frustrated by poor health ('my troublesome ear, my breathless lungs') from coming up to town to take his leave of Peterborough. 'Yet I know not what I could do were I in London,' he wrote, 'but intrude upon his Lordship unseasonably amidst a croud of business...' Instead he pestered his cousin Peter King with letters and messages for the earl. He was pathetically anxious to be of some service to Peterborough in his absence – 'it would make me put some value upon the little remainder of my life.'

It was with a touching degree of joy and excitement that Locke greeted the news that, despite the 'croud of business', Peterborough intended to travel into Essex to take leave of his old friend. The meeting was arranged for 11 am on Friday 20 November, at the Crown, 'the best Inne in Epping'. The early hour was appointed to take advantage of daylight for travelling, 'the days being now short and the ways durty'. The visit was a great success, particularly as Lady Peterborough came too. However despite detailed directions, the visitors went several miles out of their way in Epping Forest, which Locke ascribed to Peter King's failure to escort them.[4]

Meanwhile, in the West Indies, another friend was awaiting Peterborough's arrival with anticipation and some anxiety. The Governor of the Leeward Islands, Christopher Codrington, was the son of an extremely wealthy planter who had been his predecessor in the post of governor. Sent home for his education at an English school, Christopher had gone up to Christ Church, Oxford, in 1685. In 1689 he was honoured with the award of a probationer-fellowship at All Souls. While there, he began to gather from all over Europe the famous collection of rare books for which he is now chiefly remembered. Away from Oxford, Codrington followed a military career but he was also a poet and a friend of Joseph Addison, Richard Steele and Charles Boyle. He returned to the West Indies in 1693 as a volunteer in Colonel Goodwin's regiment but later went back to England to obtain his M.A. degree. Shortly afterwards he enlisted for the campaign in Flanders under King William and fought the next two campaigns. At the end of the war Codrington spent some time in London; it may be that it was at this time that he developed a friendship with Peterborough, possibly through another Fellow of All Souls, Doctor Samuel Garth. He bought the family property of Dodington Park in Gloucestershire from a cousin and appeared to have enlisted Peterborough's assistance in planning the garden. However in November 1702 he asked for more assistance. 'I doubt my Lord has executed but little there,' he wrote, 'his designs were too large to be finisht..'

Now Codrington was concerned about plans of action in the West Indies. The enemy was well prepared and entrenched and it could be difficult to make a surprise attack.

> Yet such a fleet with such a man at the head of it must not come into the Indys for nothing, and I shall not fail to tell my Lord he had better lose fifteen hundred men sword in hand than twice as many with fevers and fluxes...My Lord is brave and determined - he will push and will be followed...Miracles are sometimes done by bravery, and we must exert all we have. I have but one life to lose and my Friend and Country deserve it...[5]

Peterborough exerted himself with vigour and enthusiasm in the preparations for the expedition, sometimes in areas where his interest was not wanted. In October he had noticed twenty-four brass guns which had been captured and placed in the Tower. These he thought would be of use on board HMS *Boyne*. The Queen's approval was obtained and the request passed to the Prince's Council. The reply indicated that the *Boyne* was already adequately gunned, that these guns were not suitable for the sea service and that there would be trouble in transporting them out and recovering the original; but if it was the Queen's pleasure...

As the date approached for departure, and only the wind and the arrival of the Dutch were awaited, the lack of medicines was not the only problem that the earl had to face. Much of the ordnance which had gone with the Duke of Ormonde to the Mediterranean was being transferred to this expedition but, in many cases, reduced in quantity. The exercise was intended for a major surprise attack; a lack of obvious equipment such as shot would look like a bad excuse if the expedition failed. To hurry matters on, the earl wrote to Marlborough, explaining his need for various items, such as an additional fourth part of the horse harness 'because we shall find some little sort of horses used to the Sugar mills that will draw, and some for Draggons [Dragoons] and ease our men where hard labour is so fatall'. All the sandbags had been removed, 'a triffling expense but [these] must be had since one of the places the government have an eye upon is all upon the rock.'

There was also a shortage of manpower at various levels and for different reasons. On 4 January Peterborough inquired of Hezekiah Marshall, the Commissary of Provisions, how many assistants he had and was told 'only one clerk'. The ensuing lecture on the probable activity in his department caused the Commissary to write to Nottingham begging for more help, together with a boat for six or eight oars with oarsmen.

Increasingly Peterborough was made to feel that no one wanted to go on this expedition 'but those that must go or hang'. On 3 January, with the arrival of the Dutch expected at any time, he told Nottingham of his difficulties. The physician had declined to serve because he had been offered only half the pay received by his colleague on board Benbow's fleet. The chaplain, Mr Friend, was ill 'or sick of the voyage'. Peterborough had heard of no general officers preparing to go; he had tried to attract Lord Portmore, but 'there is an irresolute and fond Lady in the case'. He assured Nottingham that

> no alterations…no coolness in others hath abated my zeal and steadinesse, but, my Lord, you would have an ill opinion of mee if you could think me so mistaken as to believe myself all-sufficient…It is a fatal circumstance in our Constitution that men engaged, and under characters that oblidge their duty, that such must be courted and entreated. It is not in my power to mend these absurdities, but it is so well known that troops must have officers to command them, that I think I may conclude the necessary measures will be taken.

He also expressed concern regarding how much support he might expect to receive when at the other side of the Atlantic, when so little was given when he was here to ask for it. To Marlborough, Peterborough could be more frank. 'My Lord, I think they are all madd.' Even James Stanhope had been with him that morning to say that his father had commanded him not to go to the West Indies. 'Of all mankind I think I am the only one not willing to desert..'[6]

The continuing non-appearance of the Dutch forces was a major worry. On 8 January Peterborough wrote to Pensionary Heinsius and voiced the concern of the Queen and her ministers that the last fair wind had not brought their fleet and troops. He had heard a rumour that the Dutch thought that it was already too late to embark on such an expedition but in reality he felt it could be accomplished in four or five weeks. In fact, Marlborough and Heinsius were in agreement that it was now too late in the season to attempt such a major project in the West Indies, 'a very great misfortune the greatest part of our men being already there'. Heinsius explained that the ships had been delayed and perhaps an expedition to Portugal was more important, but they must return to Holland before the end of June.

On 13 January Peterborough assured Marlborough that, as soon as the Dutch arrived, he would be ready to leave at an hour's notice. If the expedition could leave before the end of the month, there might still be three months of service available. If at this stage 'other services' were preferred, the disappointment would be severe; men had already been deployed to the West Indies and twenty-four good ships were waiting for their complement of Dutch troops.

On the afternoon of 14 January six Dutch men-of-war with troops on board, together with twenty-eight merchantmen, arrived at Portsmouth. Peterborough had received orders to join the fleet on 16 January and his equipage and servants were already there. On the day the Dutch arrived, Peterborough was sent for to 'the place of wisdome'. He was asked

> whether I could not effect with three thousand men what I was to have effected with above double the number. I modestly confest myself no worker of miracles, and being told that the States had desired the Dutch Squadron and land Forces might be employ'd upon other services...I likewise desired that they would excuse my going if the season were past, when I was sure the force would not answer what the world expected from her majesty's Arms and the preparations so long talk'd off...

He was also aware that the 3,000 men on whom he must rely would have been in service against the French in the islands for four months before he could reach them. With the accidents of action and the ravages of disease, they were unlikely to muster such a number by then.

According to Peterborough's own account, his refusal to go was not accepted and his requests to be sent his commissions, patents and instructions were met with orders from the Cabinet Council reproaching him for not being on board and requiring instant information on his time of embarkation. In a few days it was settled that the Dutch ships and regiments would not go to the Indies. Later some ships did leave for Jamaica with transports, stores and more soldiers. Once the dust had settled, Peterborough wrote to Locke: 'Our American Expedition is Fallen as a mushroom rises in a night...' Locke would not be surprised to know that he 'refus'd to goe to the other world Loaded with empty titles and deprived of Force...'

In view of the failure of the Dutch to provide their agreed quota of troops, a surprise attack on the French in the West Indies had become impracticable. In the event of such a postponement or impossibility, Peterborough had already asked if he might delay his departure until later in the year, as he had neglected family business in the interests of public concerns. He considered rightly that civil matters could be handled efficiently by the Lieutenant-Governor of Jamaica, Colonel Handayside, and that Colonel Codrington, the Governor of the Leeward Islands, could undertake all military matters.

In the end Peterborough never attended his governorship. In 1704 Colonel Handayside was given the full appointment. Later, the earl would claim that his commission, as Commander-in-chief of all the forces in the Americas and West Indies, had cost him the sum of £5,000. He had also spent some £200 on patents and commissions but when these were returned to the office he was not reimbursed. At least he was paid for the medicines; also the government accepted the bill for £600 of freight charges on his goods loaded on HMS *Resolution* for the voyage. Peterborough came to wish that the West Indian expedition had been only a dream and not 'a severe reality'. The only thing he was able to do for the West Indies this season was to introduce a Bill in the House of Lords for the preservation of trade there and the encouragement of privateers.[7]

During the winter of 1702–3 domestic affairs in Parliament were dominated by the passage of the Occasional Conformity Bill, which originated in the House of Commons. It was sponsored by the High Tories, in particular by a promising new member, Henry St John (later Viscount Bolingbroke). The purpose of the Bill was to impose steep fines on Dissenters who qualified for public office in accordance with the Test Act of 1673 by receiving Anglican communion but thereafter reverted to non-conformist worship. Fines were fixed at £100 and later paid to the informer. The Queen supported the Bill for religious reasons and for the protection of the services of the Church from improper use, despite the fact that her husband himself was an Occasional Conformer. Public opinion had been inflamed by the preaching of Dr Sacheverell at Oxford and the Church as a whole supported the outcry. The Tories also saw the Bill as a means to attack Whig influence in both the national, parliamentary and municipal scenes, most dissenters being of the Whig persuasion.

The Bill passed through all stages in the House of Commons. In the House of Lords opposition was skilfully managed by the Whigs, whose object was not so much to oppose the Bill but to alter it into unacceptability. An attempt was made to thrash out the problems in a conference between the Houses. Five Tories, including Henry St John, were sent up by the Commons whereas the Lords supplied five Whigs, the Duke of Devonshire, the Earl of Peterborough, the Bishop of Salisbury, the Earl of Halifax and Lord Somers. The conference began on the day on which Peterborough should have sailed for Jamaica. It failed to resolve the differences and the Bill was subsequently lost.

This political grouping shows Peterborough back in the Whig party and working alongside Somers. In November 1702 Shaftesbury recorded that Peterborough had thrown himself for the last two years 'so eagerly into the Tory interest, and prosecuted both the impeachments and all those other fatal, obstructive and unjust measures with so much violence. He has now smarted for it, having been barbarously treated by that party he went over to, who sacrificed him last year in the House of Commons...My lord is now come back to his original friends and principles, and those sores are all healed up...'[8]

A sore of another kind had not healed up; this was Peterborough's continuing litigation against his cousin, the former Duchess of Norfolk. On 16 December 1702 the Court of Chancery dismissed the earl's case and on 23 December he brought a petition and appeal to the House of Lords. On 22 January 1702/3 the Lords upheld the decision of the Court of Chancery. The Appellant's case had been signed by his counsel, Mr James Sloane and Mr John Chesshyre. On 20 January the case was heard in the Lords and there appeared for the Appellant rather different artillery in the shape of Sir Simon Harcourt and Mr Cowper (later Lord Chancellor). Serjeant Hooper, appearing for the duchess, remarked audibly that 'the Earl's Cause had quite another face at the Bar from what it had in the Paper: which Remark wrought wonders in the Countenance of Mr Sloan, who was one of the By-standers, the rest laughing aloud or smileing abundantly.' On this happy note the hearing commenced and lasted five hours.[9]

Soon after the accession of Queen Anne, the Earl and Countess of Peterborough began to court the friendship of the Earl of Marlborough and his countess, as many letters in the Blenheim MSS bear witness. From the viewpoint of political advancement this was a wise move, but the Peterboroughs were considering the possibility of a closer tie. They hoped that the Marlboroughs might consent to the marriage of Viscount Mordaunt to their youngest daughter, Lady Mary Churchill. Peterborough had obtained the services of the Earl of Sunderland, his old friend and ally, to promote the match, and was flattered when he accepted the task with 'zeal and pleasure' although living in retirement at Althorp. Peterborough visited Sunderland on 8 September to find that his friend had died only a few moments before his arrival. With this death he lost both a moderating influence and a source of encouragement.

Despite many attentions, the Countess of Marlborough turned down Peterborough's suit on behalf of his son but in such a way that made the earl acknowledge that she had the art of 'obliding with a deniall'. The following year Marlborough congratulated his wife on 'disengaging yourself from that proposal, for I have heard that he is what they call a raskell, which never can make a good husband...'

In December 1702 Marlborough was rewarded for his services with a dukedom. The following February he and his wife suffered the loss of their only son, the Marquess of Blandford, from smallpox. Before the duke left belatedly for the front in early March, Peterborough sent him a carefully phrased letter of condolence and later wrote to the duchess from Dauntsey, expressing sympathy and encouragement.[10]

Parliament did not sit between February and November in 1703. After the collapse of the American expedition, Peterborough had told Locke that he would return to his 'farm' and he and his wife were still at Dauntsey in August. Their second son, Harry, now twenty years of age, had taken up a career in the Navy. Meanwhile Lord Mordaunt, despite rascally behaviour, obtained a captaincy in the Earl of Romney's regiment, the First Foot Guards, on 30 November 1703.[11]

Also in November, another Occasional Conformity Bill was presented to Parliament. Although this Bill contained reduced penalties, it lacked the support of the ministry and also the Queen, who thought it badly timed. It was defeated in the Lords after its first reading. Peterborough spoke in the debate in response to a speech from the Archbishop of York. The Bill was a nationally divisive measure. Many clergy were genuinely concerned at the threat to the Church should the Bill fail. In writing to Dr Jonathan Swift, Peterborough said that 'if he had the least suspicion the rejecting this Bill would hurt the Church, or do kindness to the Dissenters, he would lose his right hand rather than speak against it'.[12]

In October 1702 John Locke had felt that his health was failing and that he was 'upon the brink of another world', but a year later it had in fact improved, particularly his hearing. Mindful of the passage of time, he commissioned Peter King to have a gold tumbler worth £50 made as a present for the Countess of Peterborough. The gift was graciously received. 'She told me long stories of her bringing you over from Holland,' King wrote, 'and your obliging her with a ramble in an open calesh for 150 miles, and at last she told me that for your sake she would study to do me any kindness that lay in her power.' A few days later King met the earl who, he told Locke, 'in his jocular way, thinks that he has a reason to suspect an intimacy between you and his Lady, if he were not sure that you follow the rules of true philosophy'.

Lady Peterborough had promised to visit Locke at Oates and she and her husband managed to do so briefly for one hour in mid-December (probably the 13th). She received another present in March 1704, a specially bound set of the plays of Molière, but there were no more visits before Locke died in October of the same year.[13]

In 1703 the Allied fortunes in Europe were virtually at their worst. The campaign of that season had seen the fall of Bonn, Huy and Limburg but Marlborough's 'great design' of gaining Antwerp and Ostend had failed and the Dutch had refused him permission to force the Lines of Brabant. There had been a Whig outcry against Marlborough and Godolphin, calling for their resignation. Marlborough in fact agreed to act as commander-in-chief under a royal Captain-General; the Elector of Hanover had been suggested as a suitable candidate. Vienna, the capital of the Empire, was threatened on the one side by a strong French and Bavarian army on the Danube and on the east side by the Hungarian revolt which the French were doing their best to encourage.

There was some good news. After strenuous efforts by the English Ambassador, John Methuen, the Portuguese were eventually persuaded to join the Alliance. Portugal's attachment to France and Spain had been threatened by the blockade to her trade as a neutral. Encouraged by the strength of the British Fleet, its success at Vigo Bay and the manner in which it appeared to sail unchallenged round her coasts, Portugal decided to throw in her lot with the Allies. However her entrance into the Alliance was not made without conditions.

Under the First Methuen Treaty signed in May 1703, it was agreed at Portugal's request that the Allied candidate for the throne of Spain, the Archduke Charles of Austria, should come to Portugal accompanied by an armed force of English and Dutch troops. Together with the Portuguese army, this force would enter Spain from the Portuguese border. The presence of the Archduke was the guarantee that the Allies would not abandon Portugal should things turn against them on this front. The Second Methuen Treaty, signed in December, was entirely concerned with trade. In return for a market for English wool, Portuguese wines would be imported by England at one third less duty than that paid on French wines.

The consequences of these treaties were far-reaching. At last a harbour had been obtained which could support the British Fleet on Mediterranean service. Its value would be demonstrated the following year after the capture of Gibraltar, an acquisition which could scarcely have been retained without such background support. However this advantage had to be weighed against the fact that another front had opened up in the war. As the years passed, increasing numbers of troops were needed in the Peninsula; this was a continuous drain on Allied resources. The presence of the Allied candidate for the Spanish dominions with the army in Portugal changed the emphasis of the war from partition of the Empire to obtaining the whole of it for the Archduke Charles. This commitment involved troops which could have been put to good use by Marlborough on the main front and its existence was one important reason for the lengthy continuation of the war. The cry 'No Peace without Spain' was to postpone the conclusion of the conflict.[14]

On the Allied side another gain was made when Victor Amadeus, the Duke of Savoy, entered into an alliance with the Emperor in 1703. The Duke had a highly developed instinct for self-preservation in its widest sense. That his territory of Savoy-Piedmont should survive intact was his life's work and his obsession, no matter how frequently this meant changing both sides and friends. On whichever side he currently found himself, he was almost always also in touch with the other, hoping for concessions, bargaining to retrieve forfeited property or looking for chances of territorial expansion. Since 1696 he had been officially the ally of France. Twice over he had linked the House of Savoy to the House of Bourbon. His elder daughter, Marie-Adelaide, had married the Duke of Burgundy and the younger, Marie-Louise, the Bourbon King of Spain, Philip V.

Victor Amadeus had hoped that Louis XIV might have assisted him in attacking Milan. Such assistance had in fact been promised in the agreement with France made in 1696 but, in the general pacification, this promise was not renewed. Victor Amadeus himself had a claim to the throne of Spain through his great-grandmother, a daughter of Philip II. However he received no compensation nor were his rights mentioned in the First Partition Treaty. The suggestion made by Louis XIV, that the Duke should be given Milan as compensation, was considered derisory by William III, an abandoned ally. In the discussions which preceded the Second Partition Treaty, the Duke's rights were at least recognised but the terms given on which he would surrender Savoy to France, in exchange for Naples and Sicily, were unacceptable to him. In the event, the Treaty awarded Milan to the Duke of Lorraine but to Victor Amadeus should Lorraine refuse it. A common dislike of the terms of the Treaty brought the Duke of Savoy and the Emperor briefly in touch again but their rival claims to Milan always proved a stumbling-block in negotiations.

At the time of the death of Carlos II of Spain, Louis XIV had been continuing to try to improve the terms of the Second Partition Treaty, particularly in regard to the claims of the Duke of Savoy, as he was aware that the Duke was moving in sympathy towards the Emperor. However Milan declared at once for Philip V on his accession and Victor Amadeus found himself awkwardly placed in the centre of the sphere of Bourbon influence. Initially Marshal Tessé was sent to propose a military alliance by which the Duke would hold the title of Supreme Commander of the Savoy and Bourbon armies in Italy. The alliance was cemented by the marriage of Marie-Louise of Savoy to Philip V and by subsidies to increase the Savoy army. In the ensuing two years Victor Amadeus found that Piedmont was used increasingly as the highway by which French troops passed to Milan, Naples and Sicily. Also he himself was no longer courted and humoured by the French king but treated as little more than a vassal.

In May 1701 an Imperial army under the command of Prince Eugène was sent into Italy and gained a victory at Chiari in September. In 1702 Philip V took command of the Bourbon army and Victor Amadeus remained in Turin. Imperial fortunes dwindled this year and the Bourbons regained much of their lost ground. Because of the worsening position, the Emperor, later assisted by England and Holland, attempted to gain the support of Victor Amadeus and subsequently added offers of territorial gain in Lombardy. In 1703 the Bourbon domination of Northern Italy continued. Louis was aware of Victor Amadeus's contacts with the Emperor and not unprepared for his defection in August. At about the same time the English government was of the same opinion and accredited an envoy, Richard Hill, to Turin.

On orders from Louis XIV in early September, Vendôme captured 4,500 of the best Savoyard troops at San Benedetto. This action forced the Duke's hand and a draft treaty with the Emperor was drawn up.

Finally signed in November, the Treaty transferred to Savoy some territory in Northern Italy held by the Empire and also 25,000 Imperial troops who would help to establish an Alpine barrier towards the Dauphiné. The agreement was to be underwritten by England and Holland, from whom the Emperor agreed to obtain subsidies.

It was a lonely and dangerous undertaking to turn against France in this way. However, to the south lay Nice, Villefranche and the Mediterranean, where direct contact could be maintained with the English Fleet. From the north, an Imperial army under Staremberg made forced marches to reach Piedmont in January before Vendôme had made a move.

In 1703, on the wider map of Europe, there was now a base for the English Fleet at Lisbon and an ally in Savoy-Piedmont. Once again there was a possibility that French Protestants might rise in the Cévennes and join with Allied forces. A decisive attack on Toulon could ruin the French fleet and draw away forces from the Rhine and Vienna. Plans which had been originally conceived by William III were being newly considered by Marlborough.[15]

In the autumn of 1703 the Archduke Charles, now proclaimed Charles III of Spain, left Vienna on his way to Lisbon. Travelling by way of The Hague and then England, he visited Queen Anne at Windsor on 29 December and finally set out for Lisbon on 12 February 1703/4 on board a ship of Sir George Rooke's squadron, the *Royal Catherine*. He was accompanied by a group of Viennese courtiers, including his former tutor, Anton Florian, the Prince of Liechtenstein.

The Anglo-Dutch fleet then assembled numbered 188 ships including transports and carried a force of around 10,000 men. On arrival in Portugal, this force was joined by 20,000 Portuguese infantry. A grand council then decided that it would be wiser to conduct a defensive campaign on land, in view of the very much larger French and Spanish force moving towards the Portuguese border under the command of the Duke of Berwick.[16]

Soon after their arrival Sir George Rooke received mainly secret instructions from London that the fleet should conduct an offensive campaign at sea in the Mediterranean. Accompanied by Prince George of Hesse-Darmstadt, a former Governor of Catalonia who could act as a liaison officer with the Spaniards, Rooke set sail in early May and landed 2,000 marines at Barcelona. As no local support was forthcoming, the troops were re-embarked and the fleet sailed towards the French coast.

The French Brest fleet passed the mouth of the Tagus on 22 May NS on its way to Toulon. Having sighted it on 7 June, Rooke made a determined effort to intercept it but the French had the benefit of the wind, slipped past and reached Toulon in safety the next day.

On 27 June NS Rooke's fleet joined with that of Sir Cloudesley Shovell off Lagos which gave the Allied Fleet a superiority in strength over the French. Such a reinforcement might make possible another attempt on Cadiz and instructions from London and Lisbon urged this. Rooke, however, was averse to the idea as he felt he had an insufficient force to man a formal siege without reinforcements. The idea was abandoned and instead it was decided to attack Gibraltar.

A notable fort commanding the Straits, Gibraltar had been eyed acquisitively, as of strategic importance, since the days of Cromwell. It has been called the key to the Mediterranean. Although at this time its harbour was small and unsuitable for a war fleet, it was of supreme importance as a haven for a trading fleet. The garrison was not large and, in common with most of Spain, the fortifications were in a poor state of repair.

The Fleet blockaded the harbour at Gibraltar on 21 July/1 August. Two days later Byng's squadron opened fire on the fort and after a full day of bombardment the garrison capitulated on 4 August NS. Marching out two days later, they were replaced by British troops with Prince George of Hesse-Darmstadt as governor. Gibraltar retained a British garrison throughout the war and became the only British acquisition at the end of it.

Despite the failure of the Spanish authorities to maintain their forts, the loss of Gibraltar caused them consternation. The French Fleet put out rapidly from Toulon in an attempt to retake it. The subsequent naval engagement with the Allied Fleet off Málaga on 13/24 August was the only major sea battle of the whole war. Indecisive at the time, although hard fought on both sides, the engagement could only be considered an Allied victory by virtue of the withdrawal of the French Fleet to Toulon after the first day. Although the Allied Fleet was numerically superior, it was in poor condition compared to the French and had a serious shortage of ammunition after the bombardment of Gibraltar; to be obliged to fight for a second day could have courted disaster.[17]

In May 1704, in a letter to Marlborough, Peterborough revealed that he was in correspondence with the Emperor's Ambassador to the Court of St James, Count Wratislaw, who had been enthusiastic in his praise of what Marlborough was doing for the Allied cause. Serving under

Marlborough was Lord Mordaunt, who had already entered into negotiations with the duke towards obtaining his own regiment. On 6 July,
from his camp near Donauwörth, Marlborough acknowledged Peterborough's letter, a task which he would have accomplished sooner 'if it
had not been for the hurry of a long march, which ended in an action,
whereof I cannot doubt but you have had the particulars from my Lord
Mordaunt, who had so good a share in it...' Mordaunt had
commanded a volunteer force of fifty grenadiers as a 'forlorn hope'
which had captured the fort of the Schellenberg at Donauwörth. He
and only ten of his volunteers survived this brave venture.[18]

The summer campaign culminated in the Battle of Blenheim, or
Höchstädt as it was then known, on 2/13 August. This Allied victory
turned the tide of the war and sealed Marlborough's reputation as a
military commander. It gave a much-needed boost to the war effort in
England and as a result more support for the pro-war party developed.
It was a hard-fought battle with many casualties; among the wounded
was Lord Mordaunt, with a shattered left arm.

Subsequently Mordaunt obtained the command of the Regiment of
Scots Fusiliers. He was making a good recovery from his wound and
Marlborough hoped that his appointment would contribute to it. The
news of his son's progress reached Peterborough later than it might, as
he was away on a 'little expedition for Curiosity into Wales'. His
acknowledgement of Marlborough's letter showed a keen awareness of
the value of this victory over the power of France 'and those protected
by itt'. He also identified correctly the secret of Marlborough's skill.
'We have fought well sometimes, but we have never thought so well in
military matters these many ages...'[19]

By the time Lord Mordaunt had returned to London in December in
the duke's suite, Parliament had reassembled in a mood of national
pride. The Tory majority in the Commons preferred to celebrate Sir
George Rooke and Málaga whereas the Whigs in the Lords spoke of
Blenheim with scarcely a mention of the sea battle. The general feeling
was expressed when the Commons unanimously passed an increase in
the naval and military estimates for the following year. Over nine
million pounds was voted without trouble.

In November 1704 a new Occasional Conformity Bill had been
introduced in the Commons. Having passed through the Lower House,
it was rejected by the Lords. During the debate on 15 December 1704,
Peterborough spoke against it. In reply to a statement by the Archbishop of Canterbury that he was in support of as much of the Bill as

concerned the Church, Peterborough welcomed the acknowledgement that the Bill had both an ecclesiastical and a political part, and he hoped that all the peers 'who in their conscience were satisfied...that the Bill was framed to serve a temporal as well as a spiritual end, would vote against it'. Lord Winchelsea, supporting the Bill, warned the House rather imperiously that later they might be forced by the Commons to pass the measure. Peterborough accused him of bullying the House. Winchelsea replied warmly in the negative; 'he was neither for bullying nor would he be bullyed.' A whispered challenge was overheard by the Earl of Abingdon and the House enjoined peace on the two peers.[20]

Earlier in the month, on 6 December, there had been a debate in the Lords on the affairs of Scotland. The Godolphin ministry had found itself in trouble after advising the Queen to give her assent to the Act of Security passed by the Scottish Parliament in defiance of England. Its main provision was that, on the death of Queen Anne, the Scottish Parliament would choose as her successor a person who was of the royal line and also a Protestant. However this successor would not be the same person as the successor to the English throne, unless England agreed to certain conditions regarding the government of Scotland and the freedom of her trade. Earlier in the year the Queen had given offices in Scotland to members of the Squadrone Volante party, who were allied to the English Whigs. They had undertaken to try to get round this unpalatable Act and ensure the Hanoverian succession. Unfortunately the Squadrone was unable to modify the terms of the Act as the party did not command a working majority in Parliament. Should the assent not be given, Scotland's ultimatum was the refusal of supply and the threat of insurrection and rebellion during the ensuing winter. Against the background of affairs in Europe, and before the news of Blenheim had reached England, the Godolphin ministry bent before the storm.

Called to account for their actions, the ministry appeared to be in deep trouble, particularly when the altered European picture was taken into consideration. During the debate the Whigs treated the ministry with restraint. It was said that it was fitting that the Queen should resist their advice. Peterborough contributed that the Queen already had to resist the power of France, the folly of Austria, the selfishness of the Dutch and the ignorance of the Portuguese, let alone factions and disorders at home. All of these she had resisted and would continue to do so, 'but he should be sorry to have her accustomed to resist Parliament'. Criticism was voiced of the Scottish Secretary, Mr Johnstone, who had been in office during the past two sessions. His friends appealed to Peterborough, among others, to vindicate his conduct but the earl remained silent. Lord Halifax believed that the Act of Security was only a symptom of the disease not the trouble itself; the country had always been uneasy since the miscarriage at Darien. Peterborough believed that the way to put things right was to cancel the wrong by new legislation and ultimately it was resolved to do so. 'Scotland', he stated, 'was long since observed to be our little sister, and she will squawl till something's given her...' The legislation which followed was given the name of the Aliens Act. If the Crown of Scotland was not settled by Christmas 1705, all Scots would subsequently be considered as aliens. However the Act also empowered the Queen to appoint commissioners to treat for a union between the two countries.[21]

Fourteen

During the winter of 1704–5 plans were being laid for a new expedition to the Mediterranean. Prince George of Hesse-Darmstadt, writing to Peterborough on 20 February from a still-besieged Gibraltar, had heard of the plans and hoped that the earl would do all that he could to obtain the command of the expedition. In Portuguese and Austrian circles, it was thought that Prince George himself would be a suitable candidate for the command, if indeed it were not given to the young Archduke Charles.[1]

George of Hesse-Darmstadt had seen much military service. Born a Lutheran, he had served under William III at the Battle of the Boyne but later converted to Roman Catholicism in order to obtain a commission in the Imperial Army. His conversion disqualified him from holding the command of British troops. In 1695, he was sent to Spain with three German regiments in support of the Spanish army. He took part in the siege of Barcelona in 1697 and a year later was made Viceroy of Catalonia, a post he held until 1701. He always kept in touch with the Catalans, with whom he had been immensely popular and whose messages of readiness and support encouraged the attempt on the coast of Spain in 1705. Prince George was now an Imperial field marshal; he had taken part in the Cadiz expedition and since then had been Governor of Gibraltar. Since October 1704 the Rock had been under siege from the landward side by a Franco-Spanish army commanded by Marshal Tessé.[2]

Peterborough's appointment as General and Commander-in-Chief of the Forces accompanying the Fleet was announced on 31 March 1705, two days after his readmission to the Privy Council. The reasons for his appointment have always been a source of speculation. There were no doubt still those who wished him to be great and at a distance. Ostensibly the Queen reposed 'particular trust and confidence' in his 'prudence, courage and loyalty', but the choice may have owed more to the fact that the Duchess of Marlborough did so too. In May 1704 Peterborough had assured the duke that he was happy to accept all favours that the Queen intended him but he made no reference to their nature, no doubt on grounds of confidentiality. In a letter to the duchess Peterborough referred to a recent conversation with the Lord Treasurer which had convinced him of her good opinion which would create the same in others. He told her he was 'so deeply touched with itt, as to be affected with a kind of melancoly...' and if others agreed, he was ready to comply. On 2 March 1704/5 he could tell the duchess that he had now received the Queen's commands 'in relation to what I first heard of from yourself'.

Peterborough often referred to the duchess as if she were the guardian angel of the expedition and had it under her protection. In 1706 he was to write: 'I hope you are of opinion I have done all in my power to justifye your favour to me.' The Duke of Marlborough must have approved the appointment but his views are not recorded. In later years, the Earl of Ailesbury discussed the expedition with the duke and wondered at the choice of Peterborough, whom he described as a person of 'great talents if his head had been more composed. A stout brave man he certainly was but had never been in any service of consequence.' The duke had maintained a diplomatic silence.[3]

Sir Rowland Gwynne, the British resident in Hanover and an old friend from Revolution days, considered Peterborough had 'too much fire, to have a judgement and prudence equal to it' but his training as a seaman under his uncle, the Earl of Torrington, was in his favour and his friendship with the Hanoverian family could be useful. However Johann Philipp Hoffmann, one of the Imperial ministers in London, expressed concern at the earl's apparent lack of war experience on land and at sea and misgivings about his restless character.

Both Hoffmann and Count Gallas, the Imperial ambassador, would have preferred the command to have been given to Prince George of Hesse-Darmstadt, who was disqualified by his Catholicism. However there was also a strong feeling in Parliament against the holding of commissions by foreigners, although many already did so, including the Duke of Schomberg and the Earl of Galway. Hoffmann canvassed the possibility of Prince George having the actual if not the nominal command and told the Prince that Peterborough would not cavil at being under his orders when the expedition arrived in Catalonia, provided he did not interfere with the conduct of the troops. Despite his misgivings about the appointment, he was impressed with the enthusiasm and vigour which the earl showed in preparing for the expedition and noted that he appeared to favour a descent in Catalonia.

Marlborough himself hoped that the expedition might achieve the capture of Toulon. This was a major strategic aim; other activities in Catalonia were merely a diversion. The naval authorities considered Toulon a difficult, if not impossible, assignment. Marlborough told the Comte de Briançon, the Savoyard envoy, in confidence, that the Duke of Savoy would have to provide an officer to command such an attempt, as even Peterborough, 'quoique homme d'esprit et d'une valeur distinguée', had no experience of war on land and there was no officer under him who could carry such a responsibility.[4]

Peterborough also received the commission of Admiral of the Fleet jointly with Sir Cloudesley Shovell for the duration of the expedition. This joint appointment was an attempt to obviate some of the difficulties which had arisen during the Cadiz venture. The sea and land commands had then been divided between Sir George Rooke and the Duke of Ormonde. Their experience had shown that it was essential in any expedition where the land forces were dependent on the fleet both for transport and back-up support on land that there should be coordination and agreement in command.

As preparations for the expedition moved steadily forward, Peterborough also made provisions for his own support and sent servants to Holland to acquire various goods more cheaply obtainable there. He required 'tea, chocolate, rum, claret, Rhenish, Burgundy, and some eatables.... pickled herrings, and sturgeons, and stock fish', also 'some little wearing things, as lace, and some sort of linen...'

The flagship of the Grand Fleet bound for Lisbon in the early summer of 1705 was the *Britannia*, a first rate. Prince George of Denmark gave orders that the cabin should be fitted out according to Peterborough's requirements, as had been done for the Duke of Ormonde. His requirements were precise: the partition between the living and sleeping quarters was to be taken down and in its place installed 'a little rail and bannister across the cabin and of both sides the bed'. The rail, about three feet high, should be finely wrought and gilded to match his bed and chairs, and adorned at intervals with carved ornaments such as caskets with fruit and flowers.[5]

The British forces on board the Grand Fleet were expected to number 5,000 men. In addition, the Dutch were supplying 2,400 men. Marlborough envisaged a force of 7,000 effective men, although the full complement of each regiment would bring the number to a higher total. The regiments mustered consisted of Colonel Southwell's (6th), Colonel Elliot's and Colonel Hans Hamilton's (34th) from England, and from Ireland Colonel Lord Charlemont's (36th), Brigadier Gorges's and Colonel John Caulfield's. They were all regiments of foot. On board the Dutch ships the States General were supplying four regiments under the command of Major-General van Schratenbach with Brigadier St Amand. There were no horse or dragoons among the descent troops. The artillery train was very small for a force of this size and relied heavily on assistance from the Fleet.

Marlborough thought that the expedition was very well provided for but that the government was paying too much for it. He was critical of some of the expenses that the Cabinet Council had made. Peterborough had persuaded them to allow ordnance stores which had not been included in the Parliamentary estimates, a proceeding which Marlborough had forbidden; Godolphin did not think half of them would be needed. By 8 May the stores and ordnance were all on board. Three 'close waggons' had conveyed Peterborough's personal baggage to Portsmouth, ready for embarkation.[6]

When Sir Cloudesley Shovell arrived on 13 May, fifty ships had assembled off Spithead with only two of the full complement, one of which was the *Ranelagh*, still undergoing repairs at Portsmouth. Since a favourable wind was prevailing, the Queen ordered the Fleet to sail and the two ships to follow later.

Peterborough's commission was dated 15 May. In accordance with the provision of the Test Acts, the earl received communion on Sunday 20 May and took the oaths in Westminster Hall the following morning. He then 'rid post in the night to loose no moment of Time' and arrived at Portsmouth at 9 am on 22 May. That afternoon he went on board the Admiral's flagship, the *Britannia*, with the gilded cabin, and sailed to St Helens. Two days later and still with a favourable wind, he was 'out of danger of being oblidged to come backwards towards England'.[7]

By 28 May the Fleet had reached Ushant where it lay for two days waiting for a report from Sir George Byng's squadron on the strength of the French fleet in Brest. There were worries over the number of French ships in that harbour as the Fleet lacked the Dutch complement which had already sailed for Lisbon escorting merchantmen and transports and which would have provided additional strength. However, off Ushant the Fleet was unexpectedly joined by three Dutch ships from Zeeland. An expedition to 'look into Brest harbour' reported the presence of only fourteen men-of-war. Twelve ships were detached under Sir John Jennings's command to cruise off Ushant with Sir George Byng's squadron and watch for the movement of the French fleet.[8]

The progress of the Fleet to Lisbon was now held up by southerly winds at gale force. On 6 June, impatient of delays and slow progress, Peterborough transferred from the *Britannia* to the faster *Ranelagh*, which made good time to Lisbon and reached anchorage in the river on 9/20 June. Three days later the Grand Fleet also arrived, having bene-fited from a favourable change in the wind. The Dutch fleet had arrived one week previously. This huge anchorage also accommodated Sir John Leake's squadron which had put in for repairs and supplies.[9]

On the Portuguese frontier, after an ineffectual and indeterminate spring campaign, the Allied army had separated into summer quarters. At Lisbon the English ambassador, John Methuen, was endeavouring to persuade the Portuguese to make a definite commitment for the autumn campaign, particularly with regard to an attack on Cadiz. In this task, he gladly recruited the energies of Peterborough.

Another source of operational difficulty in Portugal was the divided command. Each national unit had its own commander: the Earl of Galway commanded the English, General Fagel the Dutch and the Conde de Corzana (a Spaniard) the Portuguese. Some kind of unifying overall command was necessary and it had been Methuen's aim to try to obtain this for Galway.

A danger arising from the lack of military activity on the borders of Portugal was the freedom this gave to the French army to reinforce any part of Spain which might be threatened by the forces on board the Grand Fleet. Another problem was the difficulty caused by the poor state of health of the King of Portugal. Pedro II was a dying man; owing to the youth of his heir, the Prince of Brazil, the regency was in the hands of the King's sister, Catherine, the Queen-Dowager of Great Britain, known to the Portuguese as Doña Catalina de Braganza.

After the arrival of the Grand Fleet, a council of war was called by the Archduke Charles, whom the Allies referred to as the King of Spain, in order to concert a plan of action. All the generals and ministers were called together, including Prince George of Hesse-Darmstadt from Gibraltar.

The instructions which had been issued to Peterborough and Shovell early in May were in two sets: one was intended for public knowledge while the other was to remain secret, even from the King of Portugal, until the point of execution. The secret instructions concerned the proj-ect so greatly prized and planned for by the Duke of Marlborough, namely the descent on Toulon. The Savoyard envoy in London, Briançon, had informed the Cabinet that the Duke of Savoy was able to support such an operation this year. In early April the envoy had attended a conference with Marlborough and Godolphin at which he was told that they were prepared to mount an expedition against Toulon, if the Duke of Savoy thought it practicable. Briançon replied that the Duke's assistance would only be possible if affairs in Italy altered. The general impression received by the Cabinet in London was that the Duke's support would be forthcoming and so the secret instructions, dated 7 May, were based on his agreement to take part. Also in May Peterborough had begun what was to become a frequent correspondence with the Duke of Savoy. In this letter, he referred to 'a great and glorious design upon Toulon'. He was cognisant of the plans and was setting his heart on the project, ignorant of the fact that Marlborough did not think him suitable for the conduct of such an enterprise.*

The secret instructions clearly stated that, given assurances by the Secretaries of State, the Duke of Savoy or the British envoy in Turin, Richard Hill, that the Duke was willing and able to cooperate, Peterborough and Shovell were to apply themselves 'to the execution of that service preferably to any other to be performed in the Mediterranean'. After all, it was not so very far from Barcelona and an attempt there could be used as a blind.[10]

Barcelona was more than a blind. The public instructions issued on 1 May, which as far as the world knew were the only instructions, were concerned broadly with an attempt against Spain. Peterborough and Shovell, with the forces on board the Fleet, were to proceed initially to Lisbon and join Sir John Leake and his winter squadron. Thereafter action against Spain would be decided by a council of war. Before such action took place, a friendly manifesto would be circulated among the coastal towns in the area. It would be issued in Peterborough's name and would urge the Spaniards to acknowledge their lawful sovereign, Charles III. The manifesto would also explain that the presence of Her Majesty's Fleet on their coasts was in support of the claims of the House of Austria and not to gain territory for Her Majesty. Those who supported the Austrian cause were promised protection but responsibility for any damage inflicted on those who opposed it was disclaimed.

In their deliberations, the joint admirals were asked that 'special efforts be made to get possession of Barcelona and Cadiz'. In fact, the

---

*Briançon's letter of 7 April to the Duke of Savoy was intercepted by the French. This may account for the fortifying of the approaches to Nice and Villefranche that were being busily undertaken in June 'as if expecting a visit from Lord Peterborough'. Hill *Corr.* vol. ii, p. 556.

French and Spanish forces besieging Gibraltar had now moved to defend and fortify Cadiz. As it was considered more practical to leave Cadiz to the return journey, the admirals were instructed to proceed first to Catalonia. However 'if any opportunity arises whereby the Duke of Savoy may be assisted or relieved, they are particularly required to act accordingly'.

The special efforts against Barcelona had been instigated by representatives of the Catalan gentry. One of these, Don Antonio Paguera y Aymerich, had written to the Queen asking that a larger force might be sent to Catalonia this year. Mitford Crowe, formerly resident in Barcelona, was then sent to Genoa to meet Catalan agents and in June 1705 signed a treaty whose main provisions were that Great Britain would promise to land 8,000 infantry and 2,000 cavalry and arms and ammunition to equip 12,000 Catalans. The Catalans on their side agreed to provide 6,000 regular troops, ready to join the Allied forces. Of particular importance was the guarantee, undertaken by the British government, that Charles III would promise to uphold the Catalan laws. In March the Earl of Galway had been told by Catalan contacts that 6,000 men were already assembled in the mountains of Vich. In Gibraltar the Prince of Hesse had also received reports of preparations but remained sceptical of their efficacy; he was more impressed by the preparations the Spaniards were making to defend Barcelona.[11]

On his arrival in Lisbon, Peterborough received a letter from the Secretary of State telling him that the Duke of Savoy was in no condition to assist with a descent on Toulon. This letter, couched in a difficult cypher, was a bitter disappointment. Having broken the unwelcome news, it did not contain any guidance on what subsequent action should therefore be taken. Later an encouraging letter arrived from Mitford Crowe, who was making progress in his talks with Catalan envoys at Genoa. From Turin, Richard Hill stressed that, although the Duke of Savoy was unable to help with troops until the French left Nice, their departure would no doubt be accelerated if the Fleet appeared off that coast. The Duke of Savoy himself sent a warm invitation to bring the Fleet to Italy, assuring Peterborough that the Queen was sending specific instructions to that end.

In the face of conflicting directions and advice, Peterborough had only Sir Cloudesley Shovell with whom to discuss the secret instructions and whether or not their conditions were fulfilled. It was possible that the secret plans might yet be undertaken and therefore a decision to move the Fleet and troops to Catalonia, or perhaps even Naples, would be sending them in the right direction. Peterborough knew that the Italian project would find favour with both naval and military, as they were all anxious to go somewhere away from the Portuguese. He was nonetheless concerned by the lack of specific advice from home but noted in the letters received by Galway, Methuen and himself the English government's apparent leaning towards Catalonia. He himself would have preferred an attempt against Cadiz. However no one in Lisbon seemed to favour Catalonia. The Dutch envoy, Francis Schonenberg, could scarcely be prevented from protesting against it in council; even Prince George, who still had contacts there, no longer supported it.

The Prince was aware of the care needed to avoid false steps or mistakes. Suspicions or discoveries by the Spanish authorities could lead to arrests and punitive action which in turn could ruin the support on which the Allies were relying. It was difficult to deal with the Catalans who were not rich and quite unused to having any kind of levy put upon them. In early June Prince George had sent a memorial to King Charles in which, for various good reasons, he discarded both Cadiz and Barcelona as objectives in favour of a landing near Alicante while the Fleet were off Catalonia.

At a Grand Council called by the King on 20 June NS, the Almirante of Castile, a distinguished Spanish nobleman who had made a spectacular defection to Portugal three years earlier, opposed with persuasive arguments an idea put forward by Galway that there should be a descent in Provence or Catalonia. The Almirante, supported by the Conde de Corzana, assured the Council that no Castilian would accept a king who came through Aragon; instead he recommended an attempt on Cadiz. He was bitterly disappointed that the young king was not in favour of his views and soon afterwards he retired to the country where he later died.

A second council was held after the arrival of Prince George of Hesse-Darmstadt from Gibraltar on 6/17 July. Despite his misgivings but because he knew that both the English government and the Imperial Court were in favour of it, the Prince proposed that the expedition should proceed to Barcelona. The majority, which included the King, the Prince of Liechtenstein and both Galway and Peterborough, backed the proposal and the decision was taken.

The initial relations between the young King of Spain and Peterborough were extremely cordial. Soon after the earl's arrival, the King took advantage of his friendly ear to pour out the evils of his situation. He had recently lost his father and was anxious to prove his worth in the role which had been set up for him. Receiving no financial support from the Imperial Court, Charles was dependent on the hospitality of the Allies and on his allowance from the Queen. He was unable to live in the kind of state to which he was accustomed. His public appearances were limited to religious festivals; etiquette forbade his appearing at other events in the absence of the King of Portugal whose illness prevented his attendance. He was thus unable to be present at the last campaign. It must have proved a welcome diversion to be invited, with the young Prince of Brazil, to review the Grand Fleet from on board the admirals' flagship.

Peterborough was impressed by the young man, who was full of zeal, piety and an anxiety to do something for the cause, even if it were only to hold a commission in the Queen's forces. They discussed together the possibility of taking the Fleet to Naples and the advantages that would accrue with the gain of that part of the Spanish Empire. The King expressed an eagerness to accompany such an expedition. Peterborough was struck instantly by the benefits of such a presence, giving greater weight and importance to the venture and a higher chance of success. Later he casually mentioned to Ambassador Methuen that he wondered that no one had thought of taking the King on special expeditions. Methuen replied that they had and that he did have powers to make such an offer, should it be thought advisable. After consultations between the ambassadors, the offer was made and gladly accepted. Later Peterborough recalled: 'The wonder is how I could prevail to engage an Austrian Prince to such an attempt; I made it plain to Liechtenstein he should be Vice-roy of Naples, to the Prince of Hesse he should be Vice-roy of Catalonia, and to the King he should never be nothing but by embracing this opportunity…' The Portuguese did not approve; they felt that they were losing the King from their front and also from their sphere of influence. It was stressed that the offer had been made at the King's request and in the Queen's name.

To lessen the cost of transporting the King of Spain and his suite, the royal guest would be entertained at Peterborough's table. The expense, the earl assured Godolphin, would be 'considerable but shall be managed with a frugality…that shall not be displeasing to you'. The only misgiving felt by the Allies was their responsibility for the King's personal safety.

Peterborough was quick to acknowledge the unselfishness, as he described it, of both Methuen and Galway at this juncture. Methuen, who would also feel the full brunt of any Portuguese displeasure, persuaded the King of Portugal to give King Charles part of a cargo of silver from South America expected at Lisbon and managed to borrow money for him on the expectation. Galway offered two of his regiments of dragoons and, together with Fagel, arranged for two of Peterborough's rather raw regiments of foot to be exchanged for seasoned and experienced troops presently stationed at Gibraltar.[12]

It took some time to embark Raby's and Conyngham's dragoons as well as a regiment of Spanish Guards belonging to the King. The artillery train was loaded on board under the eye of the newly-appointed colonel, John Richards*, a Catholic who held a temporary commission from Peterborough. The delays were irksome to the earl, who was sensitive about suggestions from ministers at home that he was being unduly dilatory in leaving Lisbon. In fact he had taken a dislike to the place and was working all day, and indeed all night, to speed up their departure.

On this expedition Peterborough had obtained the services of Arent Furly, the son of his friend Benjamin in Rotterdam, as his secretary; both Furly and John Methuen bore witness to the earl's unflagging energy. Methuen thought that Peterborough was an excellent choice as commander and admired his methods with the Portuguese. 'Beside the life, spirit and resolution which indeed I expected, there appears in him a great temper [and] calmness which seem the effects of a strong judgement.' Furly was amazed at how little the earl was affected by the excessive heat of the climate. To Colonel Hans Hamilton, Peterborough appeared 'teeming with vast projects' and in daily conferences with Galway and the grandees. This was the honeymoon period in Peterborough's command. He acted with restraint and diplomacy, yet with great vigour and zeal. His more indiscreet reflections were restricted to letters and the dual command operated harmoniously.[13]

The Grand Fleet had already sailed early in July to cruise off Cape Spartel and prevent a junction of the French fleets. Peterborough's departure was further delayed by the late appearance of the victualling ships who did not arrive until 25 July. By that time the King of Spain and his suite were installed aboard the *Ranelagh* and ready to depart. Among those accompanying the King were the Prince of Liechtenstein, his former governor and a person of considerable influence, Count

---

*John Richards held a commission as Superior Officer of Artillery to the King of Portugal and was seconded from the Portuguese Army at the Queen's request. He was highly regarded by Marlborough.

Zinzerling, his principal secretary, Count Uhlfeldt and Count Zinzen-dorf. On 28 July, escorted by the eleven remaining warships and flying the Union flag to indicate the presence of the Joint Admiral and Commander-in-chief, the *Ranelagh* set sail down the Lisbon river on her way to Gibraltar, saluted by the forts as she passed.[14]

On 31 July the Grand Fleet was sighted near Cape Spartel. Since the Fleet had sailed before the second council, a message was sent to Sir Cloudesley Shovell informing him of the decision to go to Catalonia, since the Portuguese would not support any attempt on Cadiz, and asking him to proceed at once through the Straits. The admiral called a council of war which decided unanimously to assist in the descent. Some of the transport ships and merchantmen which had come with the *Ranelagh* now attached themselves to the Grand Fleet, while she and her attendant ships made straight for Gibraltar, arriving there on 2 August.

Here the sea was so calm that the King and his party were rowed ashore in boats in order to view the fortifications. On 3 August Caulfield's and Elliot's regiments were disembarked. In their place came on board a combined battalion of First and Coldstream Guards and the regiments of Barrymore (13th), Donegal (35th) and Mountjoy, as well as several companies of marines.

Prince George of Hesse-Darmstadt and his brother Henry now joined the expedition, leaving Brigadier Shrimpton as Governor of Gibraltar. Morale was high. The King was well, Peterborough was busy and both were appreciative of the able assistance given them by Paul Methuen, the Ambassador's son. 'Amongst ourselves,' Peterborough wrote, 'God be thanked, there is health, unanimity and good humour.'[15]

Fifteen

On 5 August 1705 NS, sufficient breeze having risen during the day, Peterborough gave the order for departure at 5 pm and the Grand Fleet was rejoined the next day off Cape Málaga. Here the King and Peterborough moved their quarters from the *Ranelagh* to the *Britannia*. On 9 August the Fleet was off Alicante. Letters were sent ashore to the magistrates of the town but their reply was not auspicious; the King's letter remained unopened, Peterborough's was returned and they also declined to supply provisions.

The next day the Fleet anchored in Altea Bay having come from Gibraltar in four days, a journey which could take four weeks. This excellent progress compensated for earlier delays. The reception at Altea was more favourable. A large number of country people brought provisions and came on board the *Britannia* to kiss the King's hand. A small river provided a supply of fresh water. However the governor of the town kept a low profile, some troops in a nearby fort vanished and no one of local importance came forward in welcome.[1]

The Fleet remained at Altea for five days. Here it was joined by the *Lyme* frigate from Genoa, bringing letters from Hill and Crowe. Also on board were Don Antonio de Paguera y Aymerich, the Catalan gentleman who had been Crowe's main contact over the treaty, and two officers from the Duke of Savoy.

For some reason the Prince of Hesse now revived his old plan of making a landing at Alicante or Valencia and marching from there to Madrid. There was a good supply of horses in this area and the support of the country people at Altea seemed a favourable omen. However the King remained loyal to the Barcelona project and nothing would move him. He was completely satisfied by the assurances of support expressed by the Catalans. At a council of both English and Dutch flag officers on board the *Britannia* on 2/13 August, it was resolved that, since the King wished to be conveyed to Barcelona, they would sail at the first opportunity and land the troops. Peterborough could do no other than give this wish his support as it was entirely in accordance with his instructions. No junction with the Duke of Savoy had been envisaged except in the case of Toulon or after all attempts at a siege on the coast of Spain had been concluded or abandoned.

Nevertheless Peterborough still retained a strong desire to help the Duke of Savoy. His disappointment, first incurred by Hill's letters received at Lisbon, was compounded by conversations with the Savoyard officers. They told him and anyone else who would listen that, had the Fleet gone straight to Nice and Villefranche, with the addition of Prince Eugène's forces now near Milan to those of the Duke, the French could have been expelled from Italy. As Peterborough explained to Godolphin, it could have been done with the money they already had, and Milan and Naples would have been gained for the King of Spain. After Barcelona, Peterborough had already in mind going straight to Madrid but he knew it to be an impossible task without more money – £200,000 was necessary to finance a march of eighteen days. The idea of such a march was known in the Fleet at this time as a real possibility; in the atmosphere of high morale, it seemed appropriate to try to take the enemy by surprise.

Peterborough was disappointed with Don Antonio de Paguera. The son of a Catalan nobleman well known to Mitford Crowe, Don Antonio had spent a large part of the past year in Vienna and Genoa on behalf of the Catalans and he now seemed out of touch with the situation in Catalonia. The Prince of Hesse also had contacts. From these, the large number of regular troops said to be mustered at Cardona turned out to be non-existent but there were still a great many people who were prepared to enlist. There was more confident information about a gathering of supporters around Vich, awaiting the arrival of the Fleet. However Don Antonio did bring with him a copy of the Treaty signed by Mitford Crowe on 10 June, a forceful reminder of the obligations entered into and the pledge which now had to be honoured.

Peterborough was still apprehensive of the venture in Catalonia as he had been concerned by the lack of influential support at Altea despite the interest from the country people. He was hopeful that it might yet be possible to go on to Italy afterwards but time was running short; the Dutch ships were under orders to return home in early September.[2]

When the Fleet departed from Altea on 5/16 August, the coordination of local support was left in the hands of Don Francisco Garcia de Avila. Favourable news had come from Denia, so a small number of ships were detached from the Fleet to appear before that town and Colonel Juan Bautista Basset y Ramos was put ashore to explain the purpose of their arrival. Since the town was already surrounded by armed peasants and more were known to be on their way from Altea under Don Francisco Garcia, it was not surprising that the citizens declared for King Charles and the Governor surrendered. Some Spanish troops were put ashore to form a garrison, and powder and stores were landed to put the town in a position of defence.

Colonel Basset was a Valencian by birth and the son of a sculptor. He had left Spain in order to take up a career in the Imperial Army where he served with some distinction. He is said to have gained the admiration and friendship of the Archduke Charles. He was with the Prince of Hesse at Gibraltar in 1704 and joined this expedition in the Prince's company in July. With considerable military experience in the Milanese wars and also against the Turks in Hungary, he could be considered a very suitable candidate to take responsibility for raising support in Valencia.[3]

As the Fleet left Altea, the *Devonshire*, together with the *Fowey* and the *Roebuck*, was detached to sail on to Barcelona for information. On board was the Prince of Hesse who hoped to make contact at Mataró with the leaders of the rising at Vich. He also wished to arrange some form of military cover to protect the landing of the troops at Barcelona. It was essential to make contact soon with the local support who were said to be almost despairing of the Fleet's arrival. On 9/20 August the *Devonshire* came up to report that the garrison at Barcelona, believed to be 4,000 strong, had recently been reinforced by 400 Neapolitans commanded by the Duke of Popoli. On sighting the English ships, the reinforcements had been obliged to land at Mataró. Subsequently the *Devonshire* gave chase to a *settia* and the two galleys which had brought the reinforcements and took two prisoners off the *settia*. The small squadron then anchored off Mataró on 10/21 August.[4]

The main Fleet was not far behind. On 9/20 August Peterborough and 'four persons of note' went on board the *Fubbs* yacht which stood close in to Vilanova while the boat went ashore with a flag of truce. The magistrates asked for three days for consideration. Nearby Sitges returned a 'saucy answer'. The despatch of a small frigate and a detachment of foot produced a more amenable response. Another coastal town declined to capitulate and would give no supplies without directions from Barcelona.

On 11/22 August the Fleet reached Barcelona and anchored three miles to the east of the city. From there they could see smoke rising from burning fields as parties from the city set fire to the forage on the

Governor's orders. This turned out to be less of a disaster than it looked; there was sufficient left. A council of war was held immediately and the King made a persuasive speech urging that the troops be put ashore as soon as possible. It was decided to attempt to land. Peterborough went on board the *Lyme* frigate in order to look for a good area but a strong levant wind blew up which made the sea so rough that a landing then was clearly impossible.[5]

The following day (12/23 August) the order was given to land the foot soldiers although the sea was still fairly high. At 10 am the first longboats made their way ashore. A point had been chosen about five miles to the east of the city, between there and Badalona and near the River Besóz. Many country people were attracted by the spectacle. Some just watched while others went into the water to assist the boats and even carried some of the officers on their shoulders. However there was no sign of the regular troops promised to cover the landing nor of the Prince of Hesse; he 'unluckily was gone a chasing some galleys with my Ld Dursley in the Devonshire' but he arrived later in the afternoon.

After five hours fifteen battalions had been put ashore and a camp set up. During the day a steady trickle of Miquelets armed with rifles and pistols came in to the army. These soldiers were country militia who knew little of military discipline and formal manoeuvres but were adept at what later became known as guerrilla warfare. Those who came brought no officers or persons of importance in command of them. Colonel Richards, in charge of the ordnance, did not find this lack unduly depressing and thought the reactions of Peterborough and other senior officers exaggerated, 'for one might read in their faces the end of the expedition'. The Catalan historian Feliú de la Peña records that immediately after the arrival of the Fleet the Jurados of Mataró hastened to pay homage to King Charles. He carefully enumerates all seven of them; they included two of his relatives.

As the Fleet passed the city of Barcelona, there seemed little opposition from the garrison and no attempt was made to oppose a landing. The Governor of the city, Don Francisco de Velasco, was in a difficult position. He was aware that there was considerable sympathy within the city for the invading force. He had punished severely anyone found guilty of treasonable activities; he had also offered passports to any who wished to leave the city before any siege commenced so that he could rely on those who remained. He had failed in an attempt to recruit forces for the garrison from Catalonia, hence the necessity for the Neapolitans. It was believed that many of his gunners had already left the city and many would desert in an attack on the invaders.[6]

On the second day of the landings, Peterborough came ashore while the King watched the operations from the *Fubbs* yacht. The order was given to march and set up camp about a mile from the city. Some of the forces moved a little nearer but still the only response from the garrison was an occasional shot at the sentinels. The position which the army was now taking up was suitable for siege operations, should they be undertaken. Only some of the horse were put ashore as Peterborough seemed unwilling to land the dragoons in their entirety while so little support was being shown. However the awaited arrival of Don Francisco Ponch from Vich with 1,200 Miquelets altered the situation and on 14/25 August most of the dragoons came ashore.

The camp stretched from within half a mile of the seashore as far as San Anton de Palomar and St Martin's with a river on its right flank. Colonel de St Pierre of Raby's Dragoons recorded that a party of dragoons also kept a post near 'a cross that parted the Road', probably the Croix Couvert which marked a large crossroads on the west side of the city. The Miquelets posted themselves all round the city by convents and country houses, preventing any provisions or supplies from getting in. The numerous Catalans who arrived from time to time to assist were reluctant to form a regular force without cash payment, a characteristic which Crowe had already mentioned. Peterborough issued an advertisement for paid assistance and persuaded the flag officers to meet the expense from the Fleet's short allowance money.[7]

No decision had as yet been taken regarding the next move. On 16/27 August a council of war of land officers at which the King was present was held on board the *Britannia* to decide whether or not a siege was practicable. The officers agreed that a siege was unwise because of the strength of the garrison and the small size of the forces with the Fleet. A formal investment was impossible, given the numbers in the army and the nature of the ground which was 'for the most part, a bog'. The engineers had thought it feasible to prepare a battery of fifty-two guns against the curtain for the purpose of making a breach and launching an assault, even although this would be done under the fire of three bastions. Any attempt of this kind would necessitate assistance from outside the army, such as from the seamen and countrymen. The general officers did not think it necessary to make a desperate attempt as there were other important services in their instructions which they could perform, such as assisting the Duke of Savoy, but they offered to march towards Valencia, taking what towns they could on the way. The King, anxious for a siege, persuaded them to make a 'tentation' on the town before they left. Later the same day a council of flag officers agreed to support the actions of the land officers.

With hindsight, Colonel Richards thought that this was a way of involving the forces gradually in what they could not do at once; he distrusted the tactics of the King and his advisers. Peterborough assured him that the 'tentation' would amount to little more than a false sea attack or a few bombs thrown into the town.[8]

On 17/28 August, encouraged by his Austrian court, the King came ashore. This move was unpopular with the 'wise men'; it was another small step taken towards commitment. The event could scarcely be missed by the town as it was marked by a gun salute from the Fleet. With the dragoons drawn up and the army under arms, large numbers of country people watched as the King proceeded to his quarters near the camp at St Martin's.

Already differences of opinion in the command and among the highest ranks were beginning to crack the harmony of Altea. Since his arrival at Lisbon, Peterborough had never been in favour of attacking Barcelona and his misgivings had been confirmed by the lack of local support. Prince George of Hesse-Darmstadt was also initially against an attack but was being swayed by Austrian influences from his original judgement. The King wanted the attack and was strongly supported by his Austrian court, whose disruptive influence was now beginning to make itself felt. Chief among the court was the Prince of Liechtenstein who still maintained a considerable hold over the opinions of his former pupil. The general officers usually followed Peterborough's opinion. The naval officers were becoming restive under the joint command and felt that land councils were being used to move the Fleet away from the King of Spain's cause, which they believed they had been specifically sent to assist. This view was particularly marked when, at a council of flag officers on 19/30 August, Peterborough asked them whether they would be prepared to transport the forces to Italy since the land officers were unanimously of the opinion that an attempt on Barcelona was impossible. The flag officers considered their instructions and concluded that they had been ordered to attempt other places on the coast of Spain should Catalan support prove insufficient and only leave for Italy if troops could be spared. Therefore, having landed troops at Barcelona, they resolved to make an attempt in Spain irrespective of the hazard.

The decision pleased the Austrian Court at whose instance, so it was said, the navy had landed ten heavy cannon for the 'tentation'. In the meantime some seamen had come ashore to help to dig trenches. As preparations for the tentation went forward, Richards was also instructed to make his artillery field train ready for a march.[9]

On 20/31 August, at a council held by the King and attended by his ministers, Peterborough and Paul Methuen, the earl again put forward his plan for a march in the direction of Valencia. He offered this as the only solution, as he was unable to conduct a siege in direct opposition to the unanimous opinion of a council of war. In a letter to Richard Hill, Peterborough had already explained his view that this march was the way forward and the surest method of placing King Charles on the throne of Spain. Such a move would even affect affairs in Italy, as an army heading in the opposite direction and 'increasing like a snowball' would draw troops from Provence against it. He was aware of the 7,000 French troops in Andalucia but if they moved they would abandon the frontiers of Portugal. The Allies would have an advantage of twenty days over those approaching from Roussillon.

The plan outlined to the King involved an initial march to Tarragona where the garrison was known to be weak. Having taken this town and if no difficulties presented themselves, they could proceed to Tortosa. From there the King and the infantry could be transported by the Fleet to winter quarters in Valencia where there was little opposition and a plentiful supply of horses. Meanwhile the dragoons would proceed overland.

At the council Prince George of Hesse-Darmstadt strongly supported the plan as entirely in accordance with his own views but Liechtenstein, equally strongly, opposed it. The King, however, agreed to it and plans were accordingly set forward. The next day, the influence of Liechtenstein having been at work, the plans were set aside and the siege was revived.

The change of decision was intimated to Peterborough in a letter from the Prince of Hesse. Disappointed by this loss of support, 'My Ld was nettled to the quick at it', and sent Colonel Richards to find out what lay behind the decision. Richards had some sympathy for the Prince, who explained with diffidence that 'the King had rebuked him for his forwardness in approving of the march and that my Ld might do what he pleased'. He believed that the Prince had been constrained to write this letter probably by Liechtenstein whose 'most horrible ayres' in council were causing dissension between the Army and the Court.

As relationships deteriorated, Richards feared for the outcome of the expedition. He found himself increasingly used as a go-between by Peterborough and the Prince of Hesse. With his responsibility for the artillery, he was also under pressure from many sides. He himself believed that a siege was feasible and that a breach could be made; this was considered obstructive by those who did not share his opinion. While siege preparations were going forward, his refusal to commit himself over the positioning of the great guns was also considered obstructive; in fact he was unable to reveal his plans as he was simultaneously preparing the field train for a march.[10]

On 1 September NS there was increased activity among the country people who came in with numerous carts laden with fascines for the intended siege. The next day Peterborough called a further council of general officers, this time at the quarters of Major-General Schratenbach. Once again, as the King was still pressing for a siege, he put to them the proposed attack on the breach. The outcome of the council was a negative vote by everyone except the earl himself, who declared in favour of a siege. He gave as his reason the King's earnest desire for it. That day the King wrote to Peterborough asking him to consider a tentation of eighteen days before the city, before proceeding to Italy.

Early the next morning, 3 September, Peterborough rode out with the Prince of Hesse and Richards to inspect both the ways and the town on that side. Later in the day the *Swallow's Prize* arrived from England, bringing letters from Godolphin. These letters urged the expedition to go to the assistance of the Duke of Savoy should Barcelona prove impracticable.

As the King had asked particularly for the support of the admirals for the tentation, Peterborough called a council of war of flag officers on 24 August/4 September. Referring to both the King's letter regarding the eighteen-day tentation and Godolphin's letter about Savoy, he asked them whether they would be prepared to assist the army in a shore enterprise after the eighteen days' tentation and whether there would still be time to go to Italy if the troops re-embarked within a week. The officers resolved that they were willing to give the support of the Fleet for a siege or assist in a shore enterprise to Tarragona or Valencia and would re-embark the troops should a siege prove impossible. However, if the troops wished to be taken to Italy, they must re-embark within a week as the Dutch were under orders to return home on 20 September/1 October. It was a choice of one or the other. Peterborough's personal wish to assist Savoy was only confirmed by Godolphin's letter. The earl had, however, just voted in favour of a siege.

Colonel de St Pierre of the Royal, or Raby's, Dragoons kept a military journal of these times. He noted that 157 gentlemen, including some knights of Malta, had now joined the King's troops. In a conversation with the King himself, he found that he was not at all discouraged by the level of local support (the Miquelets under arms now numbered some 3,000 men) but he was irked by 'the dilatoriness of the general officers'. St Pierre felt that the indecisive attitude towards the siege was losing valuable time. Between the Austrians and the army officers there was increasing hostility. It was to the naval officers that the Court looked for its main support. On the other hand, the Army believed that the Court had encouraged the Fleet to put difficulties in the way of going to assist the Duke of Savoy. It was an uneasy situation. Those who envisaged the avoidance of problems between Army and Navy by giving Peterborough a joint command could not have foreseen a third and formidable source of contention in the shape of the Austrian courtiers.[11]

The King now made an emotional appeal in person to each of the general officers for their support, but this appeared to have little effect. A council held in Peterborough's quarters on 25 August/5 September broke up after midnight with a majority vote against the tentation. The majority consisted of the Major Generals Conyngham and Schratenbach, Brigadier Gorges, Colonel Hans Hamilton, Colonel Wills, the Earl of Donegal and Viscount Shannon. Their opinion was that the eighteen days' tentation was a waste of time and troops and was virtually a formal siege. It made a good retreat impracticable and obviated any other attempts elsewhere. Peterborough was still in favour of it and he was joined in the minority by Brigadier de St Amant and Brigadier James Stanhope.

The following day, 26 August/6 September, a further council, perhaps 'teased on every side', remarkably produced a unanimous vote in favour of undertaking the siege but with the proviso that there should be 5,000 men available each day for the trenches. Such a condition incorporated a request for the use of 1,000 Miquelets and 1,500 seamen. It cannot have been on this occasion that the irascible Prince of Liechtenstein threw a stool at Mr Furly's head 'for having brought him the resolutions of a councell of war wch he did not like'.

Peterborough himself was at this time the subject of much criticism. He appeared to St Pierre as a man who could not make up his mind.

But he could not act against the opinion of a council of war and was therefore blamed for the delays. Vice-Admiral Leake believed he was trying to persuade the Fleet to assist the Duke of Savoy instead of the King of Spain. The earl found himself now at the lowest ebb of self-confidence. He was certain that his instructions for Italy were clear and insistent and regularly confirmed; the instructions for Barcelona were always a contingency and an alternative to other places such as Cadiz or even Valencia. The impasse in which he found himself prompted a letter to the King of Spain in which he suggested that the way forward might be for the King to appoint Prince George of Hesse his Grand Vicar and captain general, a commission superior to Peterborough's own in Spanish territory and which would give the earl a reason for following the Prince's orders. There is no firm evidence that such an appointment was ever made but Peterborough felt at present unfit for the command, perplexed and dazed.[12]

The conclusion of the last council had not been reached without reluctance. Colonel Richards found himself the Army whipping-boy for the decision, as he was known to have always considered the siege a practical possibility. He was obliged to state his views in writing. By his own reconnaissance, he had already identified a part of the curtain, between the second and third bastions, where a breach could be made. Both the Prince of Hesse and Colonel Petit, the chief engineer, had agreed with this.

Richards believed that it was a matter of honour to make any possible attempt. Assistance had been assured from the country people who would suffer if they were abandoned at this stage. He was nonetheless only too aware of how vulnerable the army would be if this assistance was removed, as it might be on the approach of reinforcements for the garrison from either Madrid or France. The support of the Fleet, necessary for a rapid re-embarkation, could be removed by adverse weather conditions. Any quick departure would necessitate the abandonment of the siege train and the stores of war. Finally, lack of success could ruin a fine body of men. At present the garrison of Barcelona was believed to contain between 5,000 and 7,000 men and 800 horse; the army of the Allies consisted of 8,000 men and 1,000 horse.[13]

The decision taken at the Council of War of general officers on 6 September NS was conveyed to the naval officers by Brigadier Stanhope the following day; he also requested a supply of 1,500 men each day to work on the trenches. It was noted by the flag officers that Peterborough himself did not attend, 'not thinking fit to afford us his company'. It cannot have relieved the earl's spirits to have received that morning from Lisbon further letters from the government at home urging assistance for the Duke of Savoy. In a note attached to the minute of the naval council of war, Peterborough's reasons for non-attendance were given. He preferred to leave them to their own conclusions on the matter before them. His own opinion was that they could not afford to give the extra men, and the letters he had received that morning from England inclined him to pass on to Italy. The flag officers ignored this opinion and resolved to increase their shore commitment to 2,500 men. This figure included the marines already ashore as well as an extra 600 men supplied by the Dutch ships. All the ships were now reduced to their middle complement.

Peterborough also sent a request to the King and the Prince of Hesse to release 1,000 Miquelets per day to work on the trenches. The Catalan leaders were unhappy at this; they could not provide men who would be obliged to work under possible fire and they considered only regular troops should be exposed in this way.

Later that day, at a council of general officers, Peterborough communicated the contents of the letters received earlier from the Secretary of State and the Lord Treasurer. All agreed that it was necessary to comply with their requests and go as soon as possible to Italy.[14]

The next morning, 8 September, Peterborough went on board the Fleet. In the afternoon, accompanied by Paul Methuen, he had an audience of the King and tried unsuccessfully to persuade him to come with them to Italy. Methuen made translations of the English letters for the King's benefit. The King later explained to Methuen that he felt it a matter of honour and conscience not to abandon the people who had declared for him; he intended to remain with them even if the Army and Fleet went away. He wrote through the Prince of Hesse to Sir Cloudesley Shovell in a similar vein and the Prince besought the admiral to think of some way out of the impasse, 'that his Majesty may not be the sacrifice of Fools and Knaves'. At the first news of a change of plan, the Prince of Hesse had written separately to the admiral asking him to land the guns that had already been agreed so as to make any new arrangements more difficult. At a council of general officers that evening, the decision was confirmed to abandon any idea of a tentation and embark for Italy.[15]

In preparation for such a move, orders were given the next day (9 September) for the re-embarkation of the sick and wounded. Peterborough sent Captain Desborow with the *Fubbs* yacht to Mataró for a supply of wine. Having heard the decision of the previous night's council, the King wrote to Peterborough, reiterating his decision to stay at all costs. Meanwhile Hesse wrote again to Shovell asking for his support. He suggested a way forward might be to persuade Peterborough to revive the plan of the march to Tarragona already approved in principle at a council of war on 27 August. In a conference with Peterborough, Hesse persuaded him to remain; the plans for the march were relaid.

Peterborough's position was indeed awkward. Paul Methuen had some sympathy for him and was sure that the Court was using this pretext of the march in order to allow the expiry of the time during which the Fleet could go to Italy. By 11 September it would be too late. There is evidence that Peterborough was uncomfortable with his authority to make such a decision as the original plan, although approved in a council of war, had been superseded by several other decisions. A letter from the Prince of Hesse on 9 September referred to Peterborough's request for a letter of indemnity from the King, which could be used as a defence against the charge of failing to follow at all times the decision of a council of war. The King felt that such a letter was unnecessary as Peterborough's instructions from home asked him to make the King 'easy by all means'.[16]

On 10 September the general officers again resolved to embark the troops on account of the insufficiency of land forces. At this council no mention was made of the march. The King had written to Peterborough formally accepting his offer and had asked him to make the necessary arrangements. Plans were going forward in private but there was a strong rumour in the army that a decision to march had been taken. The following day (11 September), Peterborough, accompanied by the Prince of Hesse and Colonel Richards, asked the Fleet for their assistance for the march. This was granted; the flag officers also made the expected decision that it was now too late in the year for an expedition to Italy.

On 12 September the King asked that Captain Norris of the *Britannia* might be sent ashore to explain the plans for the attempt on Barcelona from the sea. The King had previously requested that the Fleet before its departure might throw some shells into the city, cannonade the place where the galleys were kept and then summon the city. He also hoped that the Fleet might make an attempt on the Balearic Islands on their way to Tarragona. The same day, 300 marines were ordered to embark for Tarragona in a squadron under the command of Captain Cavendish.[17]

It had been a long and busy day on 12 September. In the course of it Hesse wrote to Shovell complaining that his time had been much taken up, 'being so tormented by my good Lord that I had no moment for myself left to satisfy all his demands'. Peterborough had sent for Richards early and told him of intelligence he had received from some deserters from the citadel of Montjuich, a fort which guarded the south-west corner of the city. The deserters claimed that this fort was in a poor state of defence. Richards was sent to the Prince of Hesse to arrange a time to discuss this information. At the subsequent conference, the plans for the attack on Montjuich were laid. Only Hesse, Peterborough and Richards were present at this conference. Richards's account is emphatic that, at this time, no fourth person knew of the plans. It was decided particularly that the King should not be informed yet 'for fear of the Windy gentm. that are about him'. Peterborough promised that, if they were successful in capturing the fort, he would undertake to lay a formal siege to the city. Richards noted with relief and approval the cordial relations which now appeared between the two leaders, as there had been a time when they only seemed prepared to communicate at all through him. Later an unnamed officer came to look for Hesse but found that the Prince and the earl 'had gone away together'.[18]

Sixteen

Ever since the first accounts of this expedition to Spain were made public, there has been controversy about who actually originated the plan to attack Montjuich. The success of the attempt eventually resulted in the capture of Barcelona itself. In *An Account of the Earl of Peterborow's Conduct in Spain* (1707), Dr Freind, who had been the earl's physician during the campaign, claimed that the idea had been conceived by Peterborough alone and that he had directed its execution. Freind's stance was deliberately adulatory and set out to vindicate Peterborough's conduct which had been called in question after his return.

An earlier printed account appeared in volume IV of Abel Boyer's *Annals of the Reign of Queen Anne*, first published in 1706. This particular volume (3 May 1706) was dedicated to the Earl of Peterborough and Monmouth, 'a person of eminent and uncontested merit'. The author considered the dedication appropriate as, in the fourth year of the reign, Peterborough's 'actions and successes make the greatest figure in it, and to whose courage, resolution, conduct, indefatigable industry, disinterestedness and affability, this nation, and indeed all Europe, is not only indebted for the conquest and preservation of a large part of Spain but likewise for the near prospect of restoring that entire monarchy to the House of Austria...' Such a eulogy, not without political bias, was one of the foundations of what became known as the 'Peterborough tradition'. Nonetheless, from the accounts available to him, the author wrote that the Prince of Hesse 'whose honour and credit were most at stake, as chief adviser and promoter of the expedition, proposed to Peterborough as a thing most expedient and very feasible to take the citadel and castle of Montjuich by surprize'.

Soon after the publication of Dr Freind's account a counterblast appeared entitled *Remarks upon Dr Freind's Account of the Earl of Peterborow's Conduct in Spain*. Here an anonymous author, who claimed to have served with the Prince of Hesse in Ireland and at Gibraltar and to have been present at Montjuich, asserted that the Prince had proposed the plan of a 'surprisal' to Peterborough to help him out of his difficult position. The plan had been proposed before but always rejected. This time the earl had realised that if it succeeded he would gain the glory; if it failed the Prince of Hesse would get the blame. In support of his contention, the author printed an account of the expedition to Barcelona purporting to have been written to the King of Portugal by his ambassador to the King of Spain, the Conde de Assumar. It contends that when councils of war had decided that an attempt on Barcelona was impossible and that other measures should be taken, 'the Prince of Hesse, being of a contrary opinion, proposed to the Earl of Peterborow to take the citadel and castle of Montjuick by surprize, which would be a means to reduce the city of Barcelona with the greater ease...'

It was a reasonable presumption that the idea was more likely to have come from the Prince because he knew the land so well. It was not the first time it had occurred to him, but by June 1705 he had received information that the fortifications at Montjuich had been repaired and the citadel was now less vulnerable. Any suggestion that the idea had been mooted at councils of war at Barcelona was later denied by Brigadier Hans Hamilton, one of the land officers who attended. He testified in the House of Lords that he had never heard an attack on Montjuich mentioned by the Prince of Hesse or anyone else until the troops were on their way there. Paul Methuen in retrospect thought it 'very strange that the Prince of Hesse, who certainly ought to have known this town better than any man in the world, should let so much time pass without thinking of this project'.

Among the extant primary sources there is only one account from someone close to decision-making and in the confidence of a commander. The late G. M. Trevelyan considered that the evidence in the accounts left by Colonel John Richards pointed conclusively to the fact that the originator of the plan to attack Montjuich was the Earl of Peterborough. Richards kept a diary.* In October 1705 he described the events in a letter to his brother-in-law, Joseph Craggs, and later he composed a 'Memorial of the Expedition to Barcelona in 1705'. Although he always gave honour where it was due, Richards was not an admirer of Peterborough. His account of affairs in Spain on his return to England in 1706 contributed to the decision that Peterborough be recalled.

*Stowe MSS 467. In September 1705 the diary dates are one day out as Richards forgot that August has thirty-one days. He corrected the error at a later date.

Richards makes it quite clear:

Notwithstanding the former resolution of a march, My Ld Peterborow, being informed by several deserters of the ill state of Monjuich, the citadel of Barcelona, he proposed to me the surprisal of it this night by scalade, and afterwards to the Prince, who approving thereof a detachment of 400 grenadiers and 600 musketeers were ordered to the rendezvous at 4 o'clock at the Prince's quarters, where I likewise sent the necessary ammunition and scaling ladders. The secret was communicated to no living creature, not so much as to the King...

Colonel de St Pierre records much the same story.

My Lord's thoughts having been at work all night upon the necessity of undertaking something, and upon what some deserters that were come out of Montjoug [sic] the day before had told him of the condition of the place, he resolved to attempt to surprise it, and went early the next morning to propose it to the Prince of Hesse, who readily consented to it.

There is little direct evidence available from Spanish sources. The Catalan writer Castellví would have known many of the participants who supported King Charles at this time. Later he compiled his *Narraciones*, a history of the period in several volumes. He claimed to have been told the background to the attempt on Montjuich by Dr Marcus Folkier whose informant was the Prince of Hesse himself. Castellví says that Prince George had been encouraged to revive his idea of an attack in the light of information emerging from the citadel. He enlisted the support of Admiral Shovell who promised the assistance of sailors and marines. He also undertook to speak to Peterborough. In order to concert plans, Prince George went on board the admiral's flagship early one morning and Peterborough joined him there. There were problems caused by Peterborough's instructions and the decisions of his councils of war, so Prince George offered himself as acting commander-in-chief because of his knowledge of the country, the Catalan people and their language. He was aware that the success of the operation depended on the troops under Peterborough's command and was happy for the credit to be ascribed to the earl. It was essential to maintain complete secrecy about this arrangement. Castellví's informant concluded that the King, Prince George and the Admiral had planned the enterprise and Peterborough agreed.

If plans to attack Montjuich had been discussed before this but after the arrival at Barcelona, the secret must have been well kept by all parties concerned. It appears possible that it had been canvassed and perhaps discarded as impracticable but that the King and Admiral Shovell had been aware of its possibilities. It is tempting to look for clues in existing correspondence.

On 31 August NS, at a council held by the King, Peterborough offered a march to Valencia as the only solution. This had already been approved in principle by his council of war on 27 August. Prince George gave his support and the King agreed. The following day Peterborough was enraged by a letter from Prince George saying that the plan had been set aside. On 2 September, because the King still wanted a siege, a proposal for an attack on the breach was made to the council of war, all of whom, except Peterborough, voted against it. Following this, the King asked that there might be a tentation of eighteen days before the troops moved on to Italy. The next morning, 3 September, Richards's diary records that he was in attendance when the Prince of Hesse and the Earl of Peterborough rode out very early in the morning 'about a league off…to reconnoitre the ways as well as the town on that side…' Later that day the King wrote to Peterborough, 'J'ai songé à la marche proposée comme le Prince de Hesse vous a marqué et m'y était résolu de vous accompagner…' It is possible that this referred to the march to Valencia just declined but it is also possible that the Prince had taken the opportunity during the reconnaissance to point out to Peterborough, unheard by Richards, the way which could be taken to surprise Montjuich under the guise of a march to Valencia. If the Prince had reported to the King that Peterborough's interest had been engaged, the letter quoted could have been the acknowledgement.

In a letter to Prince George of 9 September, the day on which the Prince had persuaded Peterborough to revive the idea of the march to Tarragona, the earl wrote:

> …Vous scavez que [de] quelques mesures que nous prenons la marche est le premier pas. Ne perdez point un seul moment pour le préparatif, une heure est précieuse. J'espère qu'il y a des grands événements en resource, au moins nous périssons avec plaisir pourvue que nous ayons les espérances d'estre utile. Mais il faut que tout soit fini avec la dernière certitude, autrement je ne veux pas perdre l'occasion de passer en Italie…

There is again no certainty of the allusion but it seems to refer to an event of more moment, danger and urgency than a march to Tarragona, even though such a march might eventually lead to Madrid.

Without firmer evidence from more than one source and given the impressions received, it seems that the Montjuich plan had been on the Prince of Hesse's mind for some while, as a contingency which could be used in the right circumstances. It is probable that, at some time, he had explained it to Peterborough and the King and also to Sir Cloudesley Shovell to ensure the provision of sea support. All realised that surprise would be of the essence and therefore it was not even mentioned to Richards nor raised in a council of war. Peterborough alone was in a position to give the orders to deploy the land forces on whom the expedition depended. When the deserters came from Barcelona with certain information of the state of Montjuich, he realised that there was a chance of success. Plans for the covering march were already in place. He sent for Richards.

Peterborough himself has left little information which can throw light on this period of decision-making. Paul Methuen recorded that the earl did not see fit to write to either England or Lisbon between the arrival at Barcelona and 10 October.* When he did eventually write to Godolphin, he deliberately left the King of Spain to record an account of the action at Barcelona. At the end of October, in a letter to Richard Hill, Peterborough does look back.

> It's true our successes here have been beyond hopes and expectations, but not by the measures of those that kept us here, who would have lost our little Army, render'd those mixt attempts of sea and land contemptible, wch I am sure will prove of the consequence I pretended when rightly managed, for so vain and mad an attempt as the Prince of Hesse always insisted upon could have ended in nothing but ruine, so ignorant he was (tho he had been long in the place) of the proper way of attacking itt (how desperate soever itt might seem) the only way that could succeed was the attack of Monjui, which I undertook without the knowledge of the King of Spain, any of his ministers, of the Prince of Hesse, or any of our own Officers, for I was weary of doing nothing, and of Councills of War, the copy of two of which I send you.

In this statement Peterborough claims that he took upon himself the responsibility for taking the decision to attack Montjuich, a decision

---

*But he did write on 9/20 September.

taken without consultation with anyone else. He does not claim to have been the originator of the idea. The 'vain and mad attempt as the Prince of Hesse always insisted upon' was an attack from the sea side. Having taken the decision, he summoned Richards.

As commander-in-chief of the Allied forces, Peterborough alone had the responsibility of giving the orders which committed the Queen's troops to action. This responsibility he took with great seriousness and had very much at heart. There is a story told in the journal of Colonel de St Pierre of a conversation between Peterborough and an officer whom St Pierre describes as being below the rank of those who attend councils of war. It is possible that the officer was St Pierre himself but it could also have been his brother-in-law, Lieutenant Peter Renouard, also of the Royal Dragoons, who for a time was Peterborough's aide-de-camp. The circumstances of this incident are entirely in keeping with the earl's character as he was known for his ease and affability with all ranks.

St Pierre relates that the officer was summoned to Peterborough's quarters because the earl knew him to be one of those who believed that Barcelona could be taken, given the goodwill of the country people and of those within the town itself. Peterborough kept the officer with him until about eleven o'clock at night. Then, dismissing his secretary and his valet, he sat down on the bed in his shirtsleeves and proceeded to unburden himself to his visitor.

The problem was, the earl explained, that he was bound by his instructions from the Queen to undertake only what should be agreed in a council of war. Following such advice, a landing had been made at Barcelona despite the fact that they had been originally on their way to Savoy where the Duke was hard pressed and liable to enter into a peace treaty if not relieved. Landing here had pleased the King and it had been hoped that the country people would rise in his support. It was also hoped that the Marquis d'Arconchel would come from Aragon with 1,200 horse and 6,000 foot but this had not occurred. The country people came in but also went away again. The King's court were very keen for a siege but the general officers would not consent. 'To do it myself,' the earl said, 'it is against my instructions, and if I miscarry, I do not know how to answer it.'

The officer replied that the earl had landed on the advice of his officers but he had put out a declaration in the Queen's name, inviting the people to take up arms and promising them her assistance in maintaining their rights and privileges. The people had taken up arms (about 3,000 were in semi-regular service) and now they were to be left to their enemies' mercy. How was this to be accounted for to the Queen?

Peterborough denied that the army was about to abandon the country by marching to Tarragona. The officer pointed out that the march had that appearance as the army might very well be embarked there. He boldly considered any plan to go to Madrid from Tarragona impossible as they lacked the provisions for so long a march. The only way open was to attempt the town. Although the garrison had thrown up a work at the place where the attack was originally proposed, they were not obliged to attack there. A better place could be found between the New Gate and St Antony's Gate on a long curtain only flanked at intervals with some small round towers; some houses and convents not far away could be used initially as billets.

Peterborough approved of the plan as he recognised the place. He sent the officer away with instructions to find the Prince of Hesse in the morning and tell him about it. When the officer went to the Prince, he found that Peterborough had been there before him and that they had gone away together.[1]

During all the debating some deserters had moved from the Allied camp into Barcelona. Here they informed the Governor, Don Francisco de Velasco, of the rumoured march. At the prospect of being relieved from the danger of attack, the governor commandeered all the wine from the religious houses in Barcelona in order to celebrate this eventuality. On 13 September he was told the march was a certainty although it was noted that the Allies still asked for large quantities of supplies from the country people, as if their stay was assured.

It was vital to the success of the 'surprisal' that the march to Tarragona was seen to be the next move. Richards had to prepare in secrecy a field train suitable for attacking a fort, with scaling ladders for the assault. On the morning of 13 September orders were given for a detachment of 1,000 foot and 300 dragoons to prepare to march. Captain Desborow of the *Fubbs* yacht, returned from Mataró, came ashore to find 'My Lord' (as Peterborough was known to everyone) and was interested to observe some troops lined up outside the earl's quarters. Their commander, Viscount Charlemont, had no idea where they were to go or for what purpose. They were seen to move away soon after noon by Arent Furly, who believed that they were to take possession of a pass to be used by the army next day. Peterborough gave Hesse a formal intimation of the arranged departure of the ships bound for Tarragona that evening and also told him that he was giving orders for the march 'avec la dernière diligence'.

The rendezvous for departure was at 4 pm at the Prince's quarters at San Martín. Here Richards had already sent the equipment needed for the expedition. Before the departure, Hesse sent an aide-de-camp to the King telling him of their true mission. This brought a hastily written answer expressing his great pleasure that they were undertaking what he had asked for. Hesse wrote also to Admiral Shovell, Captain Norris having been allowed into the secret, as he was expected to make contingency arrangements for the landing of marines to the west of the town the next morning.

> I heard just now [the Prince wrote] that Captain Cavendish is to sail [to Tarragona] immediately, according as the King of Spain should have desired it, according to the letter your honour hath writ to the Earl of Peterborow, but I having not been with the King today, and some particular service being resolved, as Captain Norris will tell you when he comes back, I take the liberty to desire of you the favour, if possible, to stop Captain Cavendish's proceeding till to morrow morning; Captain Norris will inform you more at large about the matter in question. My Lord Peterborow desires me to write these lines, and hope that this night's business will make us all easie.[2]

The first detachment of 1,000 foot set off from San Martín at 6 pm. The expedition was accompanied by both Peterborough and the Prince of Hesse and also 300 dragoons under the command of Brigadier Stanhope. Brigadier Gorges and a second detachment of 1,000 men left at midnight. The troops embarked on what proved to be a night's march with no halts made. The route taken was circuitous, passing below the mountains by the Capucin convent of Gracia and then towards Sarriá.

The advance detachment reached the plain below the hill of Montjuich around 3 am. At this point much time was lost on the approach to the fort; the hillside was steep, the force had been divided into three parties and each of them was misled by its guides. Two hundred men went astray during the night march; it was daybreak before a maximum of 800 tired and thirsty men found themselves in a position to begin the assault.

The fort itself covered a rectangular area on the top of Montjuich. The uppermost work was the castle or 'dungeon'. Situated at the southeastern corner, the castle was the strongest part and well fortified. At the west end were two bastions which overlooked the ditch and a covered way. At the south-western corner there was a small ravelin surmounted by two cannon which guarded the entrance to the ditch. The outworks proved to be in a poor condition, although there were signs of repair work in progress. One of the bastions had been partly restored but the other side was still open.

The garrison was believed to consist of 300 men of whom 100 were Miquelets. These latter were on guard on the hillside and fired on the Allied approach. This gave the alarm to both the garrison and the town. Colonel Southwell in command of the Grenadiers led the first attack, entering the works by a small sally-port and easily taking the ravelin with the two cannon at the mouth of the ditch. They found many of the garrison in the covered way, encamped in their tents and with cooking pots on the fire. The resistance to the attack was not determined; very soon the grenadiers gained control of all the outworks, driving the garrison into the castle. The zeal of the attacking forces pushed them on as far as the ditch of the castle itself. Here they were checked, as the scaling ladders proved too short to gain the walls. Also the attackers were very vulnerable to gunfire from the ramparts above. As further progress appeared impossible, they withdrew from the ditch and took up positions in the outworks. Firing now ceased for a while.

In the meantime the shots on the hill had alarmed the town and a party of cavalry could be seen leaving the gate and bringing up on pillion about 300 infantry reinforcements for the castle.* On their arrival, they encountered the flank of 300 Allied troops under Colonel Allen who had been advancing on the gate of the castle through the outworks. They surrounded Colonel Allen's men and took over 200 prisoners, the rest escaping to one of the bastions. The arrival of reinforcements put fresh heart into the garrison. Seeing that the Allies had retired from the ditch and had abandoned the advanced posts, the garrison began to shout 'Viva Carlos Tercero' and sallied as if to surrender. The Allies at once returned to their forward positions and were fired on more vigorously than ever, losing several men in this encounter.

Because of the difficulties of the approach to the fort, Peterborough and Hesse, who had each been with separate parties, did not reach the outworks until after the initial action by Colonel Southwell's grenadiers and the withdrawal of the garrison to the castle. It was the Prince's first

*Later a criticism was made of the Allied attack that a small force placed earlier on the line of communication could have prevented such a relief. HMC *House of Lords* MSS, vol. vii, p. 510—11.

consideration that steps should be taken, belatedly as it turned out, to cut the lines of communication between the castle and the town. Peterborough was concerned about the position of the second detachment of troops under Brigadier Gorges, which by now had entered the plain below the hill and would be about to commence its ascent. He had stationed Brigadier Stanhope with the dragoons near a road junction called the Croix Couvert, so as to protect the advancing foot soldiers from any sortie from the town. To protect the second detachment on their ascent, he ordered Colonel Killigrew to take up a position half way up the hill with 200 dragoons, who were subsequently to dismount and follow the infantry to the attack. Aware of further movements from the town and afraid that an attempt might be made to cut off the second detachment on their way up the hill, Peterborough rode off to obtain a good view of the ground between the town and the castle. Seeing a considerable movement of troops from the town, he ordered the second detachment to face about and resume their original positions, with the 200 dragoons moving at a full trot to sustain them.

Meanwhile the Prince of Hesse had led a party to attempt to cut the communication with the town. He proceeded by way of the main ditch of the fort, where he and his men could be clearly seen from the ramparts of the castle. They were consequently subjected to some brisk fire. The Prince was struck on the right thigh near an old wound. Although he went on for some distance bravely encouraging his men, he eventually fell and was carried off to a little house nearby. Here he died soon afterwards, the wound having severed an artery. Colonel Richards later expressed amazement that the Prince had chosen this route for his mission; had he moved on the outside of the glacis, his party could have reached their destination almost unobserved.

By this time morale was very low among those still maintaining positions in the outworks. By Richards's calculation, the force was reduced to about half the original number of men. Many had been taken prisoner, the fatigue of the march was taking its toll, some had gone to look for water and there was a lack of ammunition. There were about 200 Miquelets in the Allied force at Montjuich and these proved their worth. Brigadier Viscount Charlemont had positioned some on the counterscarp and, as they still had ammunition, they could effectively prevent any sortie from the castle. However the forces posted in the outworks had heard the rumour that troops from the town were coming to cut then off; they may have seen the second detachment below facing about and marching back and believed they were being abandoned. Lord

Charlemont, who was in command, was unable to prevent the gradual development of panic; what had begun as an orderly withdrawal became a most unseemly retreat. Colonel Southwell and Colonel Richards were in the rear of the retreat and had some difficulty in bringing off the wounded and what remained of the ammunition.

Before the retreating forces had left the covered way, Peterborough returned from his reconnaissance. On hearing of the death of the Prince of Hesse, some witnesses observed that the earl appeared irresolute for a time but his knowledge of the true state of affairs, and the spirited remonstrances of a Spanish volunteer known as the Wild Baron, enabled him to recover himself and tell the men roundly that they were safer in the works than out of them. There was no way in which Peterborough was prepared to accept that these posts were untenable and he was not alone in his view. By the time he had fully realised what had taken place, he was extremely angry; 'the horriblest passion that ever man was seen in' checked the rising hysteria. In Colonel Richards's words, the earl 'with a great deal of bravery and resolution, led us back again to the posts which we had quitted; I must confess I then thought it very rash, for the enemy was plainly seen to sally from the town in order to cut between us and home.'

In fact the enemy changed their plan because, on questioning the prisoners who were being then sent down from the castle, they learnt that both the Prince and the Earl of Peterborough were with the troops in person. Hearing this, they turned back 'for they never would believe that such persons would come so slightly accompanied; so that this action of My Lord Peterborow had all the good success imaginable and without any flattery entitled us to all that followed.'

Peterborough's personal presence, anger and fearlessness had saved the situation in a tight corner. He had been in a place of danger; both his aides-de-camp were wounded. It is probable that the Prince of Hesse could have rallied the men but he had fallen and was dying. Lord Charlemont had failed to keep the forces in the works and it is unlikely that he could have persuaded them back again. As it was, the earl contrived to keep them at their posts until they were relieved in due course by the reinforcements who were now free to come up, the danger of interception having passed. The presence of the commander-in-chief also restrained the garrison from making any further sallies.[3]

The capture of Montjuich, during which around 120 men were killed or wounded, was a remarkable achievement for a comparatively small force, after a night march lasting thirteen hours. The position of the forces was further consolidated by the spirited action of the Miquelets in capturing the small fort of San Beltran which contained two cannon. This fort guarded the approach to Montjuich on the town side; its capture cut the communication between the two places and prevented any further relief of the garrison who were now confined to the castle. The Allies were now in control of the fort after only two hours' action.

Colonel Richards was sent back to the camp in haste to make urgent arrangements about ammunition and provisions and he took with him the news of the engagement to the King and the Admiral. About 10 am supplies were on their way to the fort. Peterborough himself reached the camp in the early afternoon. Later seven ships of the Fleet landed marines near Montjuich.

The death of the Prince of Hesse was a major blow to the Austrian cause. The Prince had been deeply loved and respected, not to say venerated, by the Catalans and he would have modified the rather brusque attitude of the Austrian courtiers towards the King's Spanish subjects. Later the King inherited some of the feeling expressed towards Prince George but at present he was a young man with little experience of the Spanish character.

There has been much discussion over which leader had the overall command of the Montjuich expedition. As with the plan's conception, there have been those who considered that the Prince of Hesse was in command and not the Earl of Peterborough. In theory Peterborough was in command of the Allied troops while the Prince had command of the Miquelets in the service of the King. In practice, and for practical reasons, it appears to have been more of a joint command. It is not conclusive proof that the entire rank and file of the army considered the Prince of Hesse to be their leader because one anonymous Royal Dragoon seemed to think so. Conversely, a field officer, Colonel Ambrose Edgeworth, gave evidence later to the House of Lords that 'it was the opinion of all the camp...that the Prince of Hesse went thither [i.e. to Montjuich] as a volunteer'. As a leader the Prince fell rather short of the mark. He was considered a vital member of the expedition because of his knowledge of the terrain and the fortifications. From this belief arose Richards's astonishment that the Prince undertook the useful manoeuvre of attempting to reach the line of communication between Montjuich and the town 'the only wrong way'. In retrospect, criticism was laid at the Prince's door for not placing men on this line sooner and for the mistaken roads in the dark.

In Peterborough's own accounts of the action, there is the suggestion of a joint venture and he gives praise to the men who took part. On 9/20 September he wrote to his wife:

I can now give you hopes of our taking Barcelona which, if effected, I can modestly say such an attempt was never made with such a handful of men; we have taken the castle of Montjuick with sword in hand, that resisted thirty thousand men for three months, in three dayes; there was five hundred men in itt; we march'd with a thousand men thirteen howers, and with scaling ladders took a place upon a rock much stronger than Porthmouth, and had but eight hundred men, two having lost us in the night; this enterprise, which some people would reckon impossible or rash, will save many thousand men's lives; I was forced to lead them on with the Prince of Hesse who was killed; I skaped without hurt tho both my aid de camps were much wounded; I had rather you should heare of this action from others then myself...

To the Duke of Savoy Peterborough wrote that he had been obliged to attack Montjuich from necessity, which was the sole justification. 'Le Prince de Hesse a été obligé d'attaquer en personne avec moi pour pouvoir porter les soldats après treize heures démarche à une telle entreprise...'

At an inquiry some years later into the conduct of Brigadier Viscount Charlemont, it was stated in evidence that at Montjuich Charlemont had no orders but to follow the Prince and was doing so when the Prince fell. The fact that such orders must have been given by Peterborough indicates the Prince's position, that of a distinguished leader and colleague whose local knowledge was relied on. Peterborough was in overall command and, as he well knew, answerable for the outcome.[4]

The Commander-in-Chief ensured that all due ceremony was paid to the remains of the Prince of Hesse. The body lay in state in a convent which Peterborough hired for the purpose and numerous Catalans crowded there to pay their last respects. It was subsequently interred but all traces of the grave have long since disappeared. The heart was embalmed and placed in a casket. It was later sent home to Darmstadt in February 1706 in the care of an officer whose ship was obliged to put ashore on the coast of France, having been chased by a privateer. Both the officer and the casket were taken prisoner by the French near St Malo and remained in custody until 1711; they were then released in exchange for twenty-one French naval officers.[5]

Seventeen

On 15 September 1705 NS Colonel Richards moved his field train from the camp at San Martín to a place near where the Navy were landing stores and ammunition under Montjuich. The ships attracted some firing from the town but the following evening they were able to retaliate, beginning a series of night attacks with firebombs. Meanwhile two seven-inch mortars had been carried up into a striking position and on 16 September these also began to fire. Plans were being made for the attack on the town itself. Peterborough, with Richards and Colonel Petit the Chief Engineer, reconnoitred part of the town perimeter and Stanhope's brigade moved its camp to ground below Montjuich.

On 17 September the firing party against Montjuich managed to drop a bomb into a quantity of gunpowder stored within the castle. The resulting explosion was sufficient to destroy a large part of the castle wall; it also killed the governor, the Marqués di Caraccioli, and some of his officers. The remainder of the garrison surrendered immediately, thus giving the Allied troops control of the entire fort.[1]

The decision was taken to attempt to breach the walls of the town at their weakest point, between the gate of San Antonio and the Bastión del Rey. The Allied forces broke ground on 19 September, unhindered by the enemy, and work began on the batteries immediately. On 23 September a small battery of eight guns and three mortars began to fire. On the previous day some naval gunners had taken up position. It was noticed that they fired all their pieces at once, as in a broadside. A great battery of thirty guns opened four days later and on 29 September a breach was made.

The rapidity and efficiency with which the attack was pressed was a testimony to the cooperation of the Fleet. The army was very dependent on naval supplies of artillery, ammunition and stores as well as gunners and carpenters for the batteries. Although bad weather often interfered with this supply, about 800 seamen came ashore to assist in the attack.

Being responsible for the ordnance, Colonel Richards was acutely sensitive about the shortcomings of the field train. They were in no way his fault, as the present undertaking did not appear to have been fore-seen by those who planned for the expedition. His own staff (a drunken lot, according to Peterborough) consisted of a master-gunner, an adju-tant, four corporals and ten gunners. Despite the shortcomings, it was a matter for justifiable pride that he had fifty-eight guns in battery in only eight days after breaking ground. In the course of the siege Richards received seventy-four pieces of artillery from the Fleet together with ammunition.[2]

The setting up of the batteries was a slow and laborious process. Once landed from the boats, artillery had to be dragged up a steep slope. Mounted on ship's carriages, the guns had to be dismounted and replaced several times before they were in position.

The assistance of the Miquelets and country people increased after the capture of Montjuich but it tended to be spasmodic. They brought in supplies, fascines and carts for ammunition and this assistance had to be paid for in ready money. Once firing began from the batteries and was answered from the town, the country people would drop their loads on the road rather than approach too close to the scene of opera-tions. Sometimes they 'slipt away in ye darck'. Their support was important however: the whole venture would have been impossible if the Miquelets had opposed the Allies by using the same guerrilla tactics as were to prove so effective against the French army the following year. The Miquelets who had enlisted into a more formal body of support had already proved their worth.

After the capture of Montjuich Brigadier Stanhope's brigade had moved into a new camp between Montjuich and Sarriá on 5/16 September. Peterborough set up his quarters at the rear of it two days later. Subsequently the King and his court moved to the Capucin convent at Sarriá. Part of the army still remained at the original camp to guard it, thus reducing the number of men available for the attack but providing a necessary defence against the ever-present possibility of the arrival of French troops coming to relieve Barcelona. This section of the army remained there until capitulation terms were being discussed, when they were relieved by a force of 2,000 Miquelets.[3]

On 8/19 September the *Neptune* galley arrived from Leghorn with dispatches from the Duke of Savoy for Peterborough. The following day Furly recorded that 'my Lord was very much indisposed'. The nature of the indisposition is not known but Peterborough used the day of seclusion to write letters home to his wife and the Lord Treasurer giving the first official news of the taking of Montjuich.

The tone of his letter to Godolphin reflects his indisposition and the news from Savoy.

> The uneasiness, the fatigues, the difficulties I have mett with are inexpressible [he began]. If I have had the least satisfaction it has been in this, that I am certain I shall have your aprobation. I can now say her Majesty's arms will gaine no disrepute under my command; but indeed, my Lord, my heart has been sett upon doing essential services. I was not in pain to gett a reputation myself, but I would have eased the nation of taxes, your Lordship of your cares, which, I confesse, I think might have been done if not crossed by accidents and practises, which I cannot now complain off, tho' I am very full, having received letters last night from the D of Savoy and Mr Hill which make me feare the Duke may be forced to terms when he finds himself disapointed of our assistance, the onely thing he tells mee he depends upon for his relief. I confesse, my Lord, no successe can make amends, in my poor opinion, for...the balance turned against us in Italy. These have ever been my thoughts; to prevent this would have been my particular care...

Peterborough then explained how, not by his wish but from necessity, 'the turn of the expedition has been submitted to sea politicks' and described the difficulties he had experienced with the Navy. He was aware of the good qualities of some of the sea officers but most, he thought, had poor judgement and were positive in their opinions.

> Sir Cloudesly Shovell is a man possest of many good qualityes; those things in which we have differ'd I cannot reproach him for; he has had grounds for his opinions; I can only say I thought and should have acted otherwise if it had been in my power. He is brave, if I may say, to a fault, and in matters he does not understand thinkes yt whatever is directed him must be begun, and when begun must be carryed on, what accidents soever occur or what soever improbabilityes come in the way. He stickes close to what he calls orders, and will conceive no latitude in such instructions that I think were calculated for the greatest. He is a man under that rough case of the greatest good nature, and easily imposed upon that way but, my Lord, he is entirely governed by one Norris, Capt. of the Britannia, a man of whom I can say no good, and will not now speak ill of...and this gentleman, who

thinks himself fitt to govern the world, has been meddling in all things, and by accidents and circumstances has been prevailing in many matters much to my dissatisfaction...

Peterborough believed that no gain in Spain could compensate for the possible loss of the Duke of Savoy to the Alliance. He was resentful against those who had forced his hand in Barcelona. In his view, Norris had used his influence with Shovell to confirm the Admiral in his opinion that Hill's letter in June cancelled the Toulon project for ever. The Prince of Hesse was determined to engage the Allies in Spain at all costs 'and neither had nor was capable of having large thoughts as to the good of the whole'.

For his army Peterborough had nothing but praise, particularly for his officers,

> many of which are of as good judgements and understanding as any men in the world; their behaviour will sufficiently speak for them; what they have done will hardly be believed, and there is nothing that men can doe that I doe not believe them capable off; and if we take Barcelona, which I doe not now think impossible, it will make up a part in the history of Her Maty's reign that I am confident she will be very pleased with, and the taking Monjuick, one of the strongest places in the world....will att least save the troops from the discredit some would have thrown upon them, perhaps only for having better understandings if not even better intentions than themselves...My Lord, I undertook a task too bigg for one man; it was occationed by a too much good will; I have been often allmost oppressed with the weight of it...Our affaire is brought at Barcelona to this passe- it must prove the most amazing action perhaps that ever was heard off, or we must suffer extremly in itt. But I am no ways answerable for the bad and believe I cannot wholy be excluded from the good successe when your Lordship and the world are aprized of all particulars...

The next day, 10/21 September, the *Neptune* set sail for England carrying letters, narratives, minutes of councils of war and particulars in the care of a 'gentleman that will explain them'. It was three weeks before she reached her destination.[4]

On 30 September NS the Fleet decided to postpone its departure and remain before Barcelona, assisting in the siege. Dispositions were made also for a winter squadron as the rest of the Fleet would be obliged to return home sooner or later, as there were neither provisions obtainable nor a port in which to refit.

As firing continued against the breach and the St Antony and King's bastions, more guns were brought into action. On 3 October a further small battery was set up, so that there were now four in all. The same day a bomb landed behind the breach, blew up some grenades stored in the subterranean works there and caused confusion in the town. The citizens believed that an attack was imminent. Peterborough sent a trumpet to summon the town, stating that he had now seventy guns in position against it on land and also the assistance of the Fleet on the sea side. He proposed that they might wish to discuss terms of capitulation with Brigadier Stanhope, who was able to conduct negotiations in Spanish. After a long delay, the trumpet returned with Velasco's agreement to an exchange of hostages. Early the next morning, Stanhope entered the town while a Milanese gentleman, Major General the Conte de la Ribera, arrived at the camp.[5]

Discussions over the articles of capitulation lasted until 6 October when copies were signed and exchanged by Peterborough and Velasco. At the Governor's suggestion, the terms were similar to those given by the French in 1696. Some of Velasco's more extreme demands were avoided as were 'the strangest articles ever man heard' for treating the garrison as prisoners of war which the Prince of Liechtenstein wished to insert. By the terms of the capitulation the Puerta del Angel and its bastion were put into the hands of the Allies immediately, the gate itself remaining closed and only the wicket open. The garrison were to march out with colours flying four days later. On the morning of 9 October the Allied army took possession of the gate and Peterborough moved his quarters to a house nearby.

There was now a steady trickle of deserters reaching the army camp from the town. More importantly, a number of places in Catalonia had declared for King Charles, among them Tortosa, Solsona, Urgel and Lérida. Rosas, Gerona and Tarragona were the only places of strength left. Tarragona was expected to surrender soon; some ships had summoned the town, and a detachment of troops had been sent by land to reduce it. On 13 October came the welcome news that Gerona had fallen to the Miquelets.

Although it was some time before the news reached him, Peterborough would have been relieved to know that already the success at Barcelona was removing some of the pressure from the Duke of Savoy. Hill was able to report that part of the artillery which La Feuillade had intended for the siege of Turin had been withdrawn, three battalions of foot had been returned to France and three regiments of horse and dragoons had been sent to join Vendôme. By 12 October it seemed as if the activity in Catalonia had removed the danger for several months.[6]

By the morning of 14 October the time for the garrison to march out had elapsed. Since no message had come from Stanhope, Peterborough began to fear that Velasco might be going back on the terms of the capitulation. He sent Richards to make preparations for forcing the gate. Before this could be done, a commotion was heard from inside the town. Captain Desborow of the *Fubbs*, coming ashore for instructions, 'heard a great noise in ye town, all ye alarm bells were ringing, the gates shutt, great firing of small arms, and all our boats rowing off with all ye hast they could...' The townspeople, encouraged by the Miquelets, had risen against the garrison.

During his governorship Don Francisco de Velasco had taken various political prisoners. At the cessation of hostilities, the burghers had petitioned unsuccessfully for their release. A rumour spread that it was intended to remove the prisoners along with the garrison. It appeared to be confirmed when, on the morning of 14 October, a party from the garrison marched out of the gate nearest to the Mole in preparation for embarkation. With them was a prisoner who, seeing some of his friends at the gate, called out 'Viva Carlos Tercero', at which his French guard shot him dead. The friends retaliated, shooting the guard and the sentry and taking charge of the gate. The word soon spread and alarm bells were rung in the churches. Many of the garrison were on their way to the rendezvous for departure; they were easily ambushed and cut off in the narrow streets and their baggage carts plundered. Some managed to shut themselves into two bastions. Feliú de la Peña recounts that seventy Neapolitans were disarmed by only three people, one of whom was a woman.

As a result of this confusion, the Puerta del Angel was opened and Peterborough ordered 2,000 of the Queen's troops into the town. Dangerously exposed to stray bullets, he and Brigadier Stanhope rode about endeavouring to pacify the mob. Near the Mole Captain Desborow observed some rough treatment being meted out to French and Neapolitans. He chanced to see 'some persons of quality and several officers' fleeing for their lives and took them on board and treated them 'with all ye civility imaginable I could'. It was some time before order was restored and calm descended on the city. Contrary to their reputation in Spain, the British soldiers made no attempt to plunder the town and maintained an impeccable discipline, saving their enemies from the fury of the citizens, which the King noted with appreciation.

Soon after entering the city, Peterborough had been approached by a terrified lady who asked him to convey her to a place of safety. She was the Duchess of Popoli whose husband had been in command of the Neapolitan soldiers in the garrison. Peterborough at once dismounted and escorted her in person to the gate where her husband, the governor and other senior officers had already gone. The lady's alarm was justified; they were fired at on their way, a bullet passing through the earl's wig. Peterborough then conveyed the whole party to his quarters adjacent to the Puerta del Angel where they were kept under a strong guard for their safety.

The story of the flying Duchess is recorded by Colonel de St Pierre. Another less romantic variant can be found in Boyer's *Annals*. Here the account praises Peterborough for having gone to the place of the greatest confusion and for having such control over his men. 'He exposed his own life to the greatest danger to save those of his enemies; a Miquelet seeing the Duke of Popoli near his Lordship fired at him, but miss'd his mark, and the Bullet went through his Lordship's periwig; which oblig'd him to put that Duke into a house, and set a guard before the door to prevent any further attempt upon his life...'

Later that day Velasco and some of his companions were put on board the *Britannia*. While Peterborough entertained the duke and duchess at his quarters, the story of his gallantry was passed with relish among his officers.[7]

Velasco complained bitterly to Peterborough over the Miquelets' part in the insurrection, which he described as a breach of the capitulation. The earl assured him that he had taken no part in this but, had some of his troops been given leave to enter the city beforehand, such an occasion could have been avoided. He promised to endeavour to arrange restitution of the plundered baggage.*

The day after the insurrection, Peterborough took up lodgings in the house belonging to the Conde de Rosas in the town. Barcelona itself returned rapidly to normality. To avoid what Furly called 'further

---

*In *Le Siècle de Louis XIV* Voltaire tells this story with some inaccurate detail. 'Vous nous trahissez', dit le viceroy à Peterborough; 'nous capitulons avec bonne foi, et voilà vos Anglais, qui sont entrés dans la ville par les remparts. Ils égorgent; ils pillent, et ils violent.' 'Vous vous méprenez,' répondit mylord Peterborough; 'il faut que ce soit des troupes du prince de Darmstadt...Il n'y a qu'un moien de sauver votre ville, c'est de me laisser entrer sur le champ avec mes Anglais...'

inconveniences', the officers of the garrison were housed in Peterborough's quarters outside the gate and the remainder of the garrison were locked up in the arsenal to await embarkation.

The same day, the news of the taking of Montjuich reached London by the *Neptune* galley. It was learnt from a Dutch source that Barcelona had since surrendered. Lady Peterborough was at Dauntsey and did not receive her husband's letter until two days later.

On 16 October part of the Allied army marched into Barcelona. The soldiers found themselves housed in barracks, a considerable relief after the storms and heavy rain of the previous days. The bad weather had made it impossible to embark the garrison, a task not completed until 18 October. With the army in the town, Charles was proclaimed King and on the same day came the news of the surrender of Tarragona.

The magistrates of Barcelona, aware of the reputation of the British soldier as a heretic and a sacker of churches, inquired of Lord Peterborough where he wished to make arrangements for divine worship. He informed them that 'wherever he had his quarters, he had conveniency enough for himself and his attendants to worship God; and as for the rest of the army, that they should strictly follow the rules of war, and perform divine service among themselves, without giving any disturbance or offence to any body.'[8]

Since so many (about 3,000) of the enemy troops in Barcelona had come over to King Charles, only 1,450 were finally embarked on 18 October to land eventually at Almeria or Málaga. In the end they were not allowed to transport the cannon or mortars which had been permitted under the capitulation.

On 12/23 October Sir Cloudesley Shovell and the main fleet sailed for home. The previous evening Lord Peterborough went on board *Britannia* to take leave of his co-admiral and was saluted with twenty-one guns at his going ashore. For the benefit of the army, the Fleet left behind 1,800 barrels of powder, 8 brass guns and a quantity of 3lb shot. Six ships had been detached for the Catalonia service. Brigadier Stanhope, Viscount Shannon and Captain Norris left for home on board the *Canterbury* which left separately the day after the Fleet. They had Peterborough's orders to take official reports of the siege and the present state of affairs in both verbal and written forms.

Sir John Leake's squadron was under orders to return to Lisbon for refitting and to be on stand-by for the Mediterranean, should the need arise during the winter. On 14/25 October the squadron weighed anchor and stood off Barcelona. Some of the ships were carrying the former garrison. Don Francisco de Velasco had been moved from the *Britannia*, with Peterborough's servants in attendance, and was now on board the *Hampton Court*. The Duke and Duchess of Popoli were on board the *Grafton*, having had a good proportion of their belongings restored to them. On board the *Fubbs* yacht, with Captain Desborow in attendance, Peterborough went that evening to bid farewell to the squadron. He visited each ship in turn; it was midnight, Desborow noted, before they left the *Grafton*. There was very little wind, so they went ashore by barge.[9]

Eighteen

The King made his formal entry into Barcelona on 7 November NS. He was met by a deputation at the Covered Cross and escorted to the St Antony Gate by a guard of cavalry. Leading citizens were waiting to greet him and the Earl of Peterborough offered him the keys of the city on a silver plate. Holding a canopy over the King, the citizens took the reins of his horse and led him through the gate. The procession moved through the city, which was *en fête* and elaborately decorated, to a level area near the church of San Francisco where a dais had been erected. Here the King took an oath to maintain the privileges of Catalonia and the islands. A procession of the guilds then filed past. Later the King moved on to the Cathedral where a Te Deum was sung, after which a torchlight procession escorted him to the Palace. The day concluded with fireworks and illuminations. There were more processions the following day and a splendid fiesta in the Disputación.[1]

Soon after the capitulation the Allied troops had taken up their quarters in barracks in the town. The citizens had a privilege that they should not be obliged to provide quarter for troops in their houses and this was respected. The accommodation available was limited; it was often in open galleries in convents where there were no beds or heating provided. At an early stage Peterborough had asked for hospital accommodation for the sick and wounded but this was not forthcoming. As a result, fevers and infections spread from the sick to the well; soon 800 men had been lost through illness, a greater number than in the siege itself. 'No ennemy would have destroyed so many men as we have lost by the good wine and the bad quarters,' wrote the commander-in-chief.

Peterborough blamed the Court for not furnishing accommodation or enabling it to be available. 'Never men suffered so much and with so much patience; it goes to my soul,' he told Stanhope.

Peterborough's solution to the problem was to divide the army among garrison towns outside Barcelona. Although this might have a weakening effect in relation to the enemy without, on the borders of Aragon, it was the only defence against the enemy within. This was precisely the opposite to the advice given by Galway and was effected safely because of factors as yet unknown in this area of the war. It was expected that the French troops which had moved away from the Portuguese border after the raising of the siege of Badajos would be sent to Aragon. A request for more troops was made to Louis XIV by the Duke of Anjou but it was greeted with little enthusiasm and no response as Louis was seriously considering peace moves put forward by the Dutch.

The Allied force was therefore safely divided between Gerona, Lérida and Tortosa. On 9 November Lord Charlemont's regiment and two Dutch battalions under the command of Major General Schraten-bach left for Gerona where they improved the fortifications and built a new bastion loyally named after Queen Anne. After 22 November the regiments of Gorges, Palme and Rivers, Conyngham's Dragoons and two marine regiments made their way to Lérida. The Royal Dragoons and Killigrew's regiment left for Tortosa on 2 December, to be followed three weeks later by Lord Donegal's regiment.[2]

Another problem was a shortage of money. All of the funds raised by Peterborough privately or by Methuen in Lisbon had already gone to support the siege. The Dutch regiments had only been provided with six weeks' subsistence in what had proved an unacceptable currency and were now dependent on what Peterborough could provide. The marines had been on the naval establishment, as it had never been envisaged that they would function on land without the presence of the Fleet. Basically, no provision had been made in the event of the forces under Peterborough's command remaining in the Mediterranean beyond the autumn.

It was frustrating that this shortage of money affected the position of the Spanish troops. The 800 cavalry which had deserted from the Barcelona garrison remained an irregular group and still unpaid. Spanish deserters were so numerous that it would have been possible to enlist three infantry regiments of 1,000 men each. Unfortunately the men were starving and consequently many withdrew their services. The Court itself was penniless and attempted to raise money by selling places, often to very unsuitable people. Peterborough sent home urgent requests for immediate supplies. If these did not come soon, Furly thought, they would be about as useful as 'cordialls to the dead'.

Colonel Hamilton, the Quarter-Master General, had been sent to Savoy to explain the position to the Duke and hear his plans for the next campaign. Mitford Crowe had brought the welcome news that La Feuillade had withdrawn from Turin, although the French were now bombarding Nice. On his return with the cleaned ships, it was hoped that Hamilton would bring with him £100,000 which Peterborough had asked Hill to raise in Genoa. With this money the earl would not only be able to support his own troops and keep the field all winter but he would also be able to 'raise and equip 6,000 men for the King in a month's time.'[3]

By now Peterborough's relations with the King's Court were deteriorating. He both liked and admired the King but the opinion he held of his advisers, particularly the Prince of Liechtenstein, was of the lowest and heartily reciprocated. In a letter to Wratislaw, Liechtenstein complained that he maintained friendly relations only at the considerable cost of the patience he had learnt in Portugal. In his view, Peterborough's lack of sense, conduct and experience had failed to make use of the advantage gained over the enemy. This advantage could have been used to obtain Mallorca and Menorca for the King and his control could have spread by now to the borders of Aragon and Valencia. Liechtenstein lamented that the best of Peterborough's officers had gone home with the Fleet. Moreover, he considered it unlikely that any better general would be sent out from England.

It was clear that petty irritations were being inflated out of all proportion. One of these was the matter of communication. It was beyond the purse of the Court to afford a special messenger to go across country with despatches for Vienna. Consequently it depended on the British ships, plying to and from Italy. These ships were at Peterborough's disposal and, in Liechtenstein's opinion, despatches were sent off or held up according to his lordship's whim. Sometimes the King was obliged to write day and night in the greatest haste only to find that his letters had been left behind.

Peterborough's grievances against Liechtenstein were expressed with even richer fluency and colour. He described the prince as weak and sometimes weeping hysterically which disheartened everyone. He was untrustworthy, proud and rapacious for money but what could spell ruin for all was his 'Medling with everything and understanding Nothing'. Peterborough warned the English ministers that money sent out for a particular purpose could be misappropriated. If it was intended to send funds for the supply of the levies, it would be wiser instead to send out the uniforms for the horse and foot ready-made ('yellow of the outside, lined with red').

By mid-November the King had invited Galway to come to Barcelona. The general was not in a position to do so at the time and thought that the King should arrange this matter with Peterborough first. Peterborough himself was expecting to be replaced. Despite all the difficulties with the Court, he believed that he had worked out a *modus vivendi* which would make it easier for his successor. In a letter written in mid-November he claimed that

> there is no man more innocent than I am of ye Love of Command, when Ever any man layes pride to my charge, when Ever I doe any man the least injustice, when Ever I have a favourite without merritt, or for making applications to my self, when Ever I gett anything by the warr, I give the world leave to putt what interpretation they please upon my actions…[there is] no man more willing for this Queen to goe to the Extremitys of the Earth att ye first summons, there is no man has a greater esteem and a more sincere friendship then I have for some in the ministry, yett no man more willing to return to my Garden, Wills coffee house, the court of request, quiet and liberty, but I think nothing can be of greater consequence then for the Government to be provided with a Shield against Spanish pride, and German ignorance…

In his reply Galway took the opportunity to give some advice on military matters to the King, including the suggestion that the breach in the fortifications of Barcelona should be mended. After repeated representations in this connection, Peterborough eventually offered a memorial to the King, on 1/12 November, urging him to put the frontier towns in a state of defence by repairing fortifications and preparing magazines. The breach of Barcelona remained unrepaired.[4]

Despite the success in Catalonia, all those involved in the Allied venture were still concerned that so few Spaniards of rank and influence had come forward with their support and those that had were mainly from the province of Catalonia. Peterborough's view of the situation was to prove in the long run largely true. 'I believe to the last', he wrote to Hedges, 'the great men will be quiet, they have very little interest upon such occasions, the most can be expected from any of them is a sullen retreat from Madrid.'

However by the end of November the Allied cause had been joined by a notable defector who had long been an opponent of the French-run government in Madrid. Peterborough wrote to the English ministry: 'To our great Ill-luck (to add if possible to our Misfortune) we have come among us the Conde de Cifuentes, in a word, the Lord Pembrock of Spain…' This description would reveal all to his readers.

The Conde de Cifuentes was a nobleman from Aragon who had been arrested for treason in 1704. Having made a spectacular escape from prison, he had since moved from place to place in Aragon and had always managed to evade recapture. A popular figure, everywhere he went he incited discontent against the government by assuring people that their ancient liberties could be taken away. In September he had accepted the surrender of Lérida and later joined the Court at Barcelona, bringing with him 2,000 Miquelets. His contribution to the Austrian cause was his influence and interest in Aragon. Cifuentes was himself impoverished. In his colourful past there had been an incident which had rendered him *persona non grata* in Valencia: he had become an enemy of the family of Nebot, now actively involved in the gaining of that kingdom for King Charles. After his arrival at Court, Cifuentes was at once taken into the inner discussions of the King and his advisers. From these discussions Peterborough and Crowe now found themselves excluded.

Generally, the attitude of the Court towards the Catalans gave concern not only to Peterborough but also to the ministry in London. By 23 November OS Stanhope and other officers had reached home with first-hand accounts of the state of affairs in Spain. On 18/29 December Hedges wrote to Peterborough that 'Her Maty has heard that the Germans treat the Catalans with their ordinary hauteur which may create ill blood, if that be true, your Excy cant but have taken notice of it, and her Maty doubts not but you will…use your endeavours to put a stop to a treatment that may have so mischievous a consequence…' The Queen was right to be so concerned. Peterborough and Crowe were aware of England's position under treaty as guarantor of the liberties of the Catalans. Some of these liberties were being withheld by the King until sums of money had been raised, but the Catalans preferred to grant money to the sovereign in response to the *fueros* and not the reverse.

Sometimes the Court appeared to go out of its way to offend the Catalans. The people themselves still held the King in universal affection despite this treatment but were said to have an aversion for his counsellors. Peterborough tried to mitigate the situation and gained popularity in the eyes of the Catalans by his concern for them. For example, Liechtenstein had told the gentlemen from Vich, early supporters, to go home as their services were no longer required. Some of them had been given commissions by the Prince of Hesse who was always careful of his Catalans. Rather than have them sent home dissatisfied, Crowe thought that it might be possible to form a regiment of guards in which they could be invited to take companies. Peterborough implemented this, the situation was saved and offence avoided.

In this uneasy atmosphere the city of Barcelona sent representations to the Parliament asking it to refuse to deal with any money issues until their privileges (called the 'Insiculation of the City Officers') had been granted by the King. Catalans who had received places at Court had been told that their patents would not be renewed unless they assisted the King in raising loans.[5]

Generally the Austrians treated the Catalans with a lack of tact and understanding. This was abundantly clear in the appointment of the Conde de Cifuentes as Viceroy of Valencia soon after the first news of the surrender of that city had reached Barcelona. As a temporary measure and with popular consent, Colonel Basset y Ramos had already installed the Conde de Cardona as acting Viceroy. Cardona seemed an eminently suitable candidate; he even had a relative at the Viennese Court. It was understandable that the King should wish to reward such an important Spaniard as Cifuentes with a post of this standing but he was unacceptable to the Valencians. It looked as if he was being appointed over the heads of more deserving Catalans. Both Peterborough and Crowe made representations to the King over the appointment; in the event Cardona remained Viceroy.

Despite the difficulties and a growing desire for the presence of Galway, the King did appreciate Peterborough's efforts both for himself and for the Catalans and appointed him Captain General of all his armed forces as long as he remained commander of the Queen's troops, with a power of assembly wherever he might go. Peterborough was flattered and gratified by the honour. He was a little unsure of the propriety of accepting it without the Queen's prior approval; guided by Galway's example in Portugal, it seemed expedient to do so and it was 'evidently for the service'. At his own request his commission empowered him to act as Captain General without giving him the title. Arent Furly recorded: 'My Lord Peterborow is infinitely beloved by ye Nobility and Commonalty here; and ye Court seems in some measure sensible of ye Obligation they ow to him...'[6]

After his arrival in London on 23 November/4 December 1705, Brigadier Stanhope reported in person to the Queen in Council. He stressed that the supply of money was the vital ingredient in the support of the armies in Spain at the present time. A report was subsequently prepared for Parliament and presented the following week. It was noted that, in his letter, Lord Peterborough had 'by way of valuing his success mention'd the great Danger of his Undertaking, in that he serv'd a Kingdom where nothing was justified but by success'. It was considered wise to omit this part of the letter while reading it to Parliament as the remark could be calculated to provoke discussion. In fact Parliament responded with vigour to the call for the supply of money but there were others who qualified the success in Spain. Bishop Nicolson encountered a disgruntled officer who clearly believed that the success had been bought at too great a price. The officer spoke of the rashness of Peterborough's conduct which made it unlikely that anyone would wish to serve under him again either on land or sea.

Peterborough had expected Stanhope to make various representations on his behalf to the government. He considered he had been promised the rank of Vice-Admiral of England and urged Stanhope to assist his wife in pressing for this appointment to be made. As he would necessarily be much occupied on land and would therefore have no time for sea affairs, he was afraid that his joint land and sea commission might not be renewed for the next campaign. If this joint appointment was not forthcoming, he wished to be recalled. As a Vice-Admiral, Peterborough hoped he might be given sole command of the Fleet but he was prepared to accept a joint commission but with a separate ship at sea so that he could have a captain senior to Norris, 'that governing coxcomb'. The importance he attached to the sea command reflected not only a personal preference but also his longer view of the campaign. Should he contrive to draw all the French forces towards Catalonia, it was his intention to make a rapid turn and attack Cadiz.

Stanhope had another commission from Peterborough; he was asked to press for a confirmation of his grant of the manor of Dauntsey. It was also believed that Peterborough now intended to bring a legal action against Sir John Germaine for the property of Drayton, as the Duchess of Norfolk had died in November leaving the estate to her husband.

Finance, both the management and the lack of it, was a continuing concern to Lord and Lady Peterborough. In those times a traditional method of improving family fortunes was through marriage and they hoped that at least their elder son would make an advantageous match. It was therefore a matter of deep concern to them when Lord Mordaunt contracted a marriage with Lady Frances Poulett, the daughter of the Duke of Bolton, in September 1705 without his parents' consent. The only objection to the bride appeared to be that she had no dowry. Lady Peterborough found this disappointment particularly hard to bear and several years passed before the earl was reconciled with his son.[7]

When Methuen heard in November of the King of Spain's intention to winter in Barcelona, he began at once to urge the King of Portugal to put his troops back into the field in order to divert any movement of French troops towards Aragon. Tessé's troops had withdrawn towards Madrid but Galway heard that the Duke of Anjou had left, or was about to leave, for Aragon. Moved by the appeals of both Methuen and the King of Spain, the King of Portugal agreed to put some troops in motion by 20 December and to march into Spain if it transpired that the Duke of Anjou had actually gone to Aragon. He was also prepared to send some money for the personal relief of the King of Spain.

The vigorous support promised by the Parliament at home as a result of the reported successes in Spain was mirrored by the activity in Lisbon for the next campaign. By 9 December NS Methuen had drawn bills to the value of 30,000 milroys ready to send to Peterborough. By 16 December the frigate carrying the money and the King of Portugal's contribution was ready to sail. Unfortunately, because of the delayed arrival of Sir John Leake's squadron which took thirteen weeks to reach Lisbon, there was no flag officer present to give the necessary command.

Also in December, Peterborough was told that five regiments were soon to leave England on their way to Catalonia. Already £40,000 had been sent in bills to Lisbon; this would be converted into specie there and brought under convoy with Stanhope. Bills were also being sent to Italy. This supply seemed prompt and efficient but three months would pass before the men, money and equipment could reach their destination.[8]

By the end of December 1705 all the Allied troops were in garrisons in Catalonia. During November Major-General Conyngham had detached 400 men from the Lérida garrison and successfully attacked Fraga containing 2,000 Bourbon troops. The garrison was driven out and 400 taken prisoner. It was not known exactly how many Bourbon troops were in the area as the Allies lacked spies, but Peterborough believed they numbered around 2,500.

In November Peterborough had been keen to accompany the troops bound for Tortosa and use them to try to coordinate what appeared to be considerable local support on the borders of Valencia. At that time the French troops on the Portuguese border had not made any move in the direction of Valencia or Aragon. Peterborough was concerned that an 'unseasonable rising' might bring enemy troops down on Valencia before the Allied army could link up with Austrian sympathisers. He was aware of how much could be done and anxious to be active again. However the Court would not allow him to leave Catalonia meantime, arguing that it was not proper for his consequence to be accompanied by such a small force. Peterborough also considered going to Portugal but he had to content himself with visiting the border garrisons.

In December an expedition to the kingdom of Valencia looked more certain when encouraging news of the capitulation of the city of Valencia reached Barcelona. Plans were made to spare some of the Lérida garrison troops to boost the force accompanying Peterborough. Moving in that direction might be considered a relatively safe operation as the reinforcements from home were expected to arrive on that coast. For everyone's comfort, it was also becoming necessary that Peterborough and the Court, 'the Vienna crew' as he called them, should part company for a time. The King's request that Galway might come to Barcelona was not granted; the general's presence in Portugal was essential if there was any intention of diverting French troops away from Aragon.[9]

The 'unseasonable rising' in Valencia which Peterborough had feared turned out to be an unqualified success. It took place in two distinct areas, in the southern part of the kingdom beginning at Denia and also on the Catalonian border. The peasants in the *huerta* of Valencia were extremely poor and experienced great deprivation. Living mainly on the estates of powerful landlords, they had taken part in a rising in 1693, having looked in vain to the Crown to ameliorate their condition. The rising had been suppressed but discontent remained and was liable to flare up at a suitable opportunity. The arrival of the Allied Fleet in 1705 with an Austrian claimant for the throne brought this opportunity. Supporters of the Archduke Charles, such as Don Juan Basset y Ramos and Don Francisco Garcia, promised the peasants freedom from taxation and feudal obligations. This was sufficient to fan the smouldering discontent into a flame of activity.

At the fall of Denia the land force was largely composed of peasants. Basset was able to use the town as a base from which to raise support from among the country people towards Valencia itself. Government troops soon appeared outside the town and formed a blockade, keeping Basset inside. However, when the news of the Allied capture of Barcelona reached Madrid, most of the troops were withdrawn; only a regiment of Catalan cavalry under Colonel Rafael Nebot was left in the area.

Basset was by no means unhopeful of the state of affairs. He was aware that the kingdom of Valencia had poor defences. In August 1705, having raised a small number of cavalry, the authorities in the city of Valencia had asked the Bourbon king for assistance and were promised 1,800 horse. After the fall of Barcelona, these were diverted to Catalonia, but at least the proposed removal of Nebot's regiment to Catalonia was not carried out. When Tortosa and later Vinaros fell into Allied hands, further representations were made to Madrid and this time Valencia was allowed to retain a cavalry regiment under the command of the Marqués de Pozoblanco.

Meanwhile in Denia there was much patient waiting. Colonel Rafael Nebot, the commander of the cavalry regiment stationed in the neighbourhood, was a member of a Valencian family who were proving their sympathy with the Austrian cause. Colonel Nebot's brother, Don Joseph, took Tarragona for the Allies in October and Basset was certain that the colonel would in time show his hand. By mid-November Peterborough had received an assurance of the colonel's sympathies, making him anxious to go to Valencia. At the end of the month Colonel Nebot had joined Basset, bringing most of his regiment with him.

Events now moved swiftly. The forces under Basset and Nebot, assisted by large numbers of peasants, received the submission of Oliva, Játiva, Gandia and Alcira on their steady northward progress from Denia. On 16 December they were at the gates of Valencia. Although the nobility and officials were Bourbon sympathisers, the magistrates came out in support, arrested the Viceroy and used his keys to admit Basset who was acclaimed by the populace as a local hero. Basset and Nebot entered the city with 200 cavalry, 100 infantry and about 400 peasants.[10]

The Royal Dragoons under Brigadier Killigrew were in garrison at Tortosa from early December. Major John Jones of Barrymore's regiment, a fluent Spanish speaker, had been borrowed by King Charles to lead a force of 700 Valencian militia gathered from Vinaros and other border areas. Jones tried to persuade Killigrew to join him in an attack on Pozoblanco's Horse at Vinaros and Benicarló. Killigrew's orders did not permit him to cross the Ebro so instead he lent Jones a party of 30 Royal Dragoons and 300 Miquelets. With this force Jones captured Traguera and proceeded to summon San Mateo. This activity caused Pozoblanco's Horse to withdraw towards Segorbe and Aragon. After some deliberation, the governor of San Mateo admitted Jones and his soldiers, having gained the impression that they numbered about 2,500 men and were about to lay siege to the town. The governor then vanished and Major Jones was obliged to take charge.

Almost immediately after this Jones received requests for assistance from Castellón de la Plana on the coast and also Morella, a hilltop town guarding a pass into Aragon. He then made a tactical error in going to Castellón on 21 December. Four days later news was received at San Mateo that Bourbon forces were entering Morella on their way there. Jones was summoned to return and some Miquelets from Peñiscola were sent up to Vallivana to secure the pass, only to find that the van of the detachment was already moving down the valley. On 26 December Jones sent his party of Royal Dragoons, under Cornet Herbert, to the Wood of Vallivana in order to attack the enemy forces as they progressed. The Dragoons did attack several times, splitting up the enemy force, some of which fled to Cati. They also captured thirty well-laden sumpter mules.

The following day the Bourbon forces rallied at Cati and moved on San Mateo which was obliged to take steps to defend itself. On 29 December the enemy opened trenches outside the town but they had no cannon and were only able to fire on the town from the trenches or from a convent or other evacuated buildings. Under cover of darkness and a false alarm on the walls, a peasant and a Miquelet were let out of the town by a secret way with letters for Catalonia and Valencia. By 31 December the besieged had begun to run out of ball and the inhabitants provided pewter dishes and pots to be melted down for ammunition. Reinforcements for the enemy were now beginning to arrive from Morella. They were said to number 1,500 horse and 1,000 foot and were under the command of an able and experienced general, Christobal de Moscoso, Conde de las Torres, assisted by an Irishman holding a commission in the French service, Brigadier Daniel O'Mahony.[11]

When the news of Bourbon forces approaching the borders of Valencia reached the Court, the alarm felt gave Peterborough the release for which he had waited so long. Prevented for two months from going to Valencia, the earl was now being sent there with a small force of 900 foot and 170 horse with the promise of another 200 horse to follow. He noted with irony that, not long before, the Court had considered it improper for a person of his consequence to march with a force of only 1,000 foot and 500 horse into a country where there had been no sizeable enemy presence to reckon with. However it was a relief to be offered activity on this scale, with powers to do as he thought fit, after the frustrations of the previous months. Peterborough had felt so excluded from the Court circle that, on Crowe's advice, he had withdrawn to a small country house. The withdrawal made clear to public view that the decisions and policies formulated by the Court were not ones with which the earl could agree. Accompanied by Brigadier Gorges, Peterborough left Barcelona on 30 December.

Halfway to Tortosa an express from the King overtook him. A report had reached the Court that a Bourbon force of 2,000 men under Tilly (in fact it was Las Torres) had been surrounded in the Wood of Vallivana by a large company of country people. The commanding officer at Tortosa had been asked for responsible men to take charge of the operation but he had been unable to supply them without orders. The King now asked Peterborough to give the necessary orders; if the operation was properly managed, it would be impossible for the enemy to escape.

By the time Peterborough reached Tortosa, the appeals of Major Jones and the country people had become so insistent that a council of war had already decided to try to relieve the town. As it was, the garrison at Tortosa had been reinforced recently by the arrival of Mountjoy's, Barrymore's and Donegal's regiments of foot. When Peterborough arrived there on 4 January, the day before the march was due to begin, most of the relief force was already over the Ebro by the bridge of boats. On 6 January they set forward for San Mateo and Peterborough followed a day later.

At his arrival in Tortosa Peterborough had discovered the truth of the situation. There were in fact no troops surrounded in a wood; more importantly, there were no large crowds of country people waiting to be formed into regular troops. Las Torres was making a formal siege of San Mateo with a force considerably larger than anything Peterborough could bring. The report received by the Court had been 'the idle representation of a priest' to a country gentleman near Tarragona who had sent it on to Liechtenstein.

Peterborough's small army on the borders of Valencia consisted of the three regiments of foot together numbering about 1,100 men, 170 Royal Dragoons mounted on horses 'which could not have galoped a league if it had been to save the kingdom of Spain' and 150 newly raised Spanish dragoons, 'sad fellows, without musquets'. They were joined on the way by 500 militia from Vinaros who were considered good men. Peterborough's artillery consisted of precisely four cannon.

On 8 January this force arrived at the walled town of Traguera. The gates of the town were shut after they had all entered. No one was allowed to leave so that no notice of their arrival could reach the enemy. Peterborough now sent two peasants into the area, each carrying identical letters addressed to Major Jones in San Mateo. One peasant, unaware of the content of the letter, was to allow himself to be captured and to reveal the whereabouts of the other who implicitly believed the information in the letter to be true and who had been instructed to hide in a wood. The letters informed Jones that Peterborough and his whole force were on their way to his relief and that he was to prepare to pursue a flying enemy. The forces were carefully detailed; those from Tortosa were in fact the body Peterborough had brought with him. The earl also claimed that he had with him Colonel Wills and 1,000 foot who had come down river from Lérida, another party of 1,000 foot who had come by sea from Vinaros and the regiments of Zinzendorf and Moras. It was stated that the enemy forces would be obliged to march by the plain, as the hills were guarded by 5-6,000 peasants as well as by Nebot's regiment of horse. Jones might soon expect to see the advance guard on the hills.

Before dawn on 9 January Peterborough set out for San Mateo with 150 dragoons (including St Pierre) and 400 foot. They spread themselves out on the surrounding hillside, giving the appearance of a much larger force. Dr Freind described the country as being 'full of little rising grounds and valleys and cover'd with Olive trees, being favourable for such an approach'.* The advance enemy picket withdrew on their approach. When some of the force reached the tops of the hills surrounding the camp, they witnessed a scene of apparent confusion. It looked as if the letter had been translated and believed. On an 'apparition of redcoats', the enemy was striking camp.

San Mateo had withstood the siege strongly. As the Bourbon army had no artillery, their most formidable means of attack was by mining, which was not always successful. They failed to lay a mine near the Barcelona gate on 1 January, and next day 'two resolute inhabitants' emerged from the town and flooded another mine by releasing the water from a large reservoir used for washing. Later, yet another mine rebounded on the engineers and it was believed that about forty of the enemy were killed.

Within the town a severe shortage of ammunition made it necessary to melt down some of the organ pipes for ball, and a shortage of meal

*In 1984 the countryside around San Mateo still answered to this description.

[211]

was avoided by the people resourcefully setting up a horse-mill within the walls.

On 4 January, the day on which Peterborough reached Tortosa, Major Jones firmly refused Brigadier O'Mahony's call to surrender. Two days later a final call from Las Torres was also turned down. On 8 January further troops of horse arrived at the camp and fire was exchanged all day. The next day smoke was observed outside the general's tent and this seemed to be a signal for departure. There was a burst of activity; horsemen galloped about, tents were taken down and baggage loaded. The army moved off, with the foot taken up behind the horse. It was late at night before they were all gone. In their haste they left behind arms and baggage and food. In the morning the deprived garrison had hoped to find plunder but country people had slipped in during the night and removed most of it.

It was presumed by the garrison of San Mateo that this sudden departure had been caused by the approach of Lord Peterborough's troops. However, accounts from the French side do not give any reason for the haste of the departure. Las Torres's own account states that on 7 January he left O'Mahony to continue the siege and moved away towards Valencia. For personal reasons he wished to meet another Bourbon commander, the Duke of Arcos, who he had heard was moving in that direction. On the 9th O'Mahony gave up the siege and followed Las Torres. The official account states that the siege was abandoned as heavy rain had put the mines out of action and they had no artillery. There is no mention of approaching forces or panic.

Nevertheless Peterborough and his troops believed they had moved the enemy on. There is such good evidence from the Allied side of the haste and carelessness of O'Mahony's departure that it seems likely that his plans were accelerated by some untoward event or news. When the Royal Dragoons reached Traguera that night, they heard that the siege had been lifted. They also found that they had been reinforced by 130 dragoons from Zinzendorf's regiment.

Lord Peterborough wrote: 'Thus I had the pleasure to fright the enemy and free myself from the feares that so unreasonable a command had exposed me too... To drive away 1500 horse with two is not the common practice of warr.' However he thought it a false advantage. It would have been better to get to Valencia first and thus prevent a junction of enemy troops. Peterborough was determined to drive out all enemy forces which blocked his way there, by make-believe and subterfuge if necessary. The Campaign of Valencia had begun.[12]

Nineteen

Entering San Mateo on 10 January 1706, Peterborough and his troops were told that Las Torres was losing no time in taking his force to join the Duke of Arcos and making no secret of his destination. Intending to ensure the steady progress of the Bourbon force, Peterborough left San Mateo the following day for Albocácer, keeping to the hills to conceal the number of his troops. He always took trouble to ensure that he was well informed about the movements of the enemy and that they also had news of him. Numerous messengers were sent ahead along the route, ordering quantities of bread and forage to supply a large army. Originally he had hoped to cut through to Valencia ahead of the enemy but his progress to Albocácer was slow because of the need for conceal-ment. His 900 infantry were almost barefoot while the enemy had good horses and were proceeding quickly.[1]

At Albocácer letters from the Court reached Peterborough. The King urged him to support the insurrection in Valencia and gave him full powers to act according to his discretion. He also informed him that Marshal Tessé was entering Catalonia from the Aragon frontier with an army of 6,000 foot and 2,000 horse. In Valencia, Las Torres was awaited by the regiment of Pozoblanco's horse as well as another force of 1,500 foot and 500 horse under Don Francisco de Velasco, the former Viceroy of Catalonia. Through intercepted letters it had been learnt that the Duke of Arcos with 5,000 men was now only five leagues from Valencia.

On 12 January 1706 Peterborough called a council of war of all the general and field officers with him. The council decided unanimously that further progress into Valencia was impossible in view of the general situation. It was decided to march towards the coast to Vinaros and attempt Peñiscola. From here the force could reach Tortosa by sea. If there was a threat from Tessé's army on the Ebro, they would be in a position to go to the King's assistance and yet still be within Valencia. St Pierre and his brother officers noted Peterborough's displeasure and believed he 'was prickt at the positive orders from Court', but what annoyed him was the unwelcome news that the Court had cancelled his promised reinforcement of 600 good foot. Ahumada's regiment had been returned to Lérida because of the threat to the Aragon frontier. To Peterborough, the King's authority to do as he pleased seemed an empty honour without extra forces.

The decision taken by this council of war was the only decision possible in the circumstances but real concerns remained. Valencia, increasingly under pressure from the troops converging upon it, was only garrisoned by Nebot's regiment and Basset's supporters. Peterborough had received urgent letters from Cardona and Basset. His officers believed that he had also been in correspondence with some ladies in Valencia, in particular with the Marquésa de la Casta, a Catalan lady married to a Valencian nobleman. It is probable that to all these people Peterborough had given promises of support which he was anxious not to break. It was also essential for the well-being of his troops to find horses, a commodity in short supply in Catalonia.

At the conclusion of the council Peterborough announced that the army would move the next day to Vinaros but that he himself would make a rapid march with 150 dragoons in the wake of the enemy to Castellón de la Plana to acquire horses and would return in a few days. He intended to make the enemy believe that he was with the van of his army, thus keeping them on the move. By his presence no news of the withdrawal to Vinaros could reach Valencia and cause the city to give up hope. There was consternation among the officers at the commander's decision. 'Wee did what wee could,' St Pierre wrote later to Lord Raby, 'to dissuade him from so dangerous an undertaking, but all in vain, I offered to go with him, he told me; he would not let me goe, que j'estois trop sage pour aller avec luy...'[2]

The next day, 13 January, most of the small army proceeded on its way in the direction of Vinaros. The detachment of dragoons with Peterborough remained behind, together with Barrymore's regiment reduced to half its complement, which was told to proceed to a place about six hours' march from Castellón de la Plana.

For three days Peterborough and the tired dragoons kept up the pretence of being the van of the army. The earl sent fictitious orders flying back and forth across the country, keeping the local people encouraged and in anticipation of further events. He was clearly enjoying this. 'What with orders to one town to bake bread, to an other to bring oats, to an other straw, I drove them [the French] for three days with ye greatest pleasure imaginable, till they joyned a considerable reinforcement neer the walls of Valencia...' He was now in a part of the country where, at Jones's first appearance, the people had indicated loyalty to the Austrian cause.

The Conde de Las Torres had moved steadily in the direction of Valencia with the intention of making his base at Moncada from where he could consider a move against the city of Valencia itself. His records do not suggest an awareness of an enemy dogging his heels but a consciousness that he was moving through hostile territory. He intended to suppress insurrection firmly but justly when he met it. The town of Villareal near Castellón refused to surrender to his troops. Las Torres did not mean to make an immediate attack but fighting broke out after one of his officers was shot from the walls. In the next two hours around 700 people of the town were killed and many others died from wounds. Later an advance party of 400 horse, led by Las Torres himself, was ambushed in a pass on its way towards Valencia. The general decided to withdraw prudently to Moncada.

Dr Freind's account published some of the stories which circulated at this time about the actions of Peterborough's troops. One such related to a hoax practised on the enemy. A small party of dragoons, together with some local spies, were sent off towards the left flank of the enemy force. The spies were used to alert the enemy to the presence of an army which was in a position to cut across and block some of the passes they intended to use on their way to Valencia. Two Bourbon soldiers disguised as country people were sent back with the spies to verify the report. Coming upon the party of fully-equipped dragoons bivouacked nearby, the soldiers believed they had encountered one of the outlying companies of horse. They were captured by the dragoons who later feigned drunkenness so that the spies could assist the disguised soldiers to escape and return to their army. It was believed that this ruse accelerated the pace of the Bourbon army so that it could ensure control of the passes.

Castellón de la Plana, which had shown its loyalty to Major Jones a month previously, gave a warm welcome to Peterborough and his troops. Here, close to the coast, it was easy for the earl to keep in touch with the city of Valencia by sea.[3]

News had reached Peterborough of how the French had treated Villareal and the story lost nothing in the telling. The day after reaching Castellón, he pressed on 'to keep in motion' to the town of Nules where he had heard there was a quantity of good horses. He was dangerously close to the Bourbon army which had only left the place that morning. On his arrival the gates were shut and the walls manned. Despite this hostile reception, he approached boldly with his dragoons and demanded entry, claiming that his army was behind. If he was forced to attack the town, he threatened to treat them worse than the French had done to the people of Villareal. Fortunately for Peterborough, a priest recognised him and his words were believed. The dragoons entered and were ordered 'to go from house to house, and to take nothing but horses'. From this town he acquired seventy good mounts. Before leaving, Peterborough put into the town some loyal and properly equipped country people to help with its defence.

In the region of Castellón de la Plana Peterborough was successful in gathering about 500 horses in all. On 18 January he set out to join the rest of his army at Vinaros. On the way he came up with Barrymore's Foot who had been sent on to Oropesa. He reviewed the regiment and complimented them, wondering whether they would make as fine a body of dragoons. With his love of the unusual and dramatic, Peterborough had concealed the presence of the horses, keeping them at some distance. The foot were ordered to march towards a small hill behind which they found that each man was awaited by a properly equipped mount; the officers were even better supplied. 'In one fortnight's time, they were as good and well-accoutred dragoons as ever served.' From this time the regiment was known as Pearce's Dragoons, as the lieutenant-colonel of the regiment took command. The colonel, Lord Barrymore, received the least advantage; he was sent home to recruit a fresh body of men. Peterborough also made provision for the Royal Dragoons. Seventy of their number were ordered to come to meet him, bringing their equipment on mules. They were remounted on fine Valencian horses. Meanwhile during all this activity Peterborough's secretaries were left in Castellón with instructions to keep writing to Valencia so that the city would believe he was still there.[4]

On 21 January Peterborough rejoined his army at Vinaros and spent the next four days making arrangements to increase his force and finding a way of extracting Nebot's regiment from Valencia. Having been depressed at Albocácer by the news of the cancellation of the reinforcements, he now re-ordered their departure. Hearing of the earl's continual success, the King and his court were now indicating their approval with 'ample paper acknowledgements'. The King wrote that he would send what troops and money he could; a rather poorly equipped regiment was in fact ready to set out. Once he heard that this regiment was across the Ebro, Peterborough took the decision to relieve Valencia, despite the threat on the Aragon frontier.

To remove so many troops from the immediate vicinity of Catalonia at such a time might seem a rash undertaking. Since the reports of Peterborough's successes in Valencia, the Court seemed only too keen to encourage his further activities in that kingdom. They assured him (and he took the assurance with some latitude) that the mountains on the border with Aragon were now impassable with snow and that the country people were in control of all routes.

Having increased his horse to around 1,400 by the inclusion of Nebot's regiment, Peterborough calculated that the enemy forces in Valencia only outnumbered his by about 1,000 horse. He had also assembled a considerable body of country militia. The goodwill of the people was prodigious and made it possible to lay in magazines to support the movement of an army. Peterborough's one great worry was that Marshal Tessé might move into Valencia from Aragon and thus cut off his retreat; if the Court information was accurate, this seemed impossible in the meantime. Another problem was that he had no place in Valencia already provided, or strong enough, to withstand a siege. On the credit side, most of the Bourbon troops in Valencia were Spanish forces and therefore might desert; if they suffered a defeat, he was certain that the French would not get them to fight again. If the Allied troops succeeded in repulsing a Bourbon force in Valencia, Marshal Tessé would be obliged to realise that the Allied army was nearer to Madrid than his own. Peterborough was certain that the most effective relief for Catalonia was by a powerful diversion.

The commander-in-chief was aware of the fact that his behaviour had not always appeared to be that of a general. In his enthusiasm for action, he had taken risks. 'I have done what I could with my head as a generall, but I have been forced all along to dispose of my person as a dragoon, and the more against my will because I am sensible an accident to myself would be some prejudice to ye public att this time...'[5]

The decision had now been taken and the army was on the road. At Alcalá Peterborough wrote to the King on 27 January telling him of his plans. Acknowledging the gracious tone of the King's last letter, he pointed out clearly and firmly how much both he and Mitford Crowe had felt themselves excluded from the King's confidence and council in recent months. Had their advice been taken, the army would now be in a better state to oppose the King's enemies. Had he been allowed to go to Valencia at his first request, the King would not now merely have a viceroy but an actual kingdom. 'With what I have I march strait to Valencia,' he wrote, 'I can take no other measure, leaving the rest to

Providence.' Such plain speaking might have been forgiven and forgotten had the earl's venture ended in death with honour. With success and a long life, it was well remembered.[6]

Later the same day Peterborough and his escort overtook Brigadier Gorges at Villanueva and reached Villafames. Here, the following day, 28 January, the general made his first review of Pearce's Dragoons before moving on to Castellón de la Plana. Nebot's regiment of horse had already arrived. 'Four hundred as good horse as ever I saw', they had slipped out of Valencia by night and travelled along the seashore in order to avoid the pickets at Murviedro.

That evening Peterborough addressed himself to correspondence. Late into the night he sat up writing fifteen pages of folio to Lord Godolphin, giving a complete account to the day of all his movements since he left Barcelona. Repeatedly he harked back to the problems and difficulties caused by the influence of the Prince of Liechtenstein, 'a recorded idiott in every place where ever he came'; perhaps if the Queen suggested it, the Emperor might remove him to some other post. Complaints apart, the letter was full of valuable information gathered from various sources as well as his view of affairs in Valencia. Enclosed with it, Peterborough sent numerous letters and documents illustrative of events. He was still without news or money from England.[7]

The following day, 29 January, Brigadier Gorges reached Castellón with the two regiments of foot, Pearce's Dragoons and the previously countermanded regiment of Ahumada. They rested here for three days before moving on towards Almenara where Peterborough had appointed a general rendezvous. The muster produced a force composed of ten squadrons of horse and dragoons (1,200 men in all) and four battalions of foot (3,000 men). Peterborough could also count on about 3,000 men from the local militia. The artillery still consisted of only four cannon.

Near Valencia the army of the Duke of Arcos numbered 2,500 horse and 3,000 foot. It had moved round from Moncada, north of the city, to a point to the south-west and rather nearer Valencia, at Torrente. Here Arcos succeeded in cutting off the water supply to the city and hindering the movement of provisions from the country. He gave the appearance of being about to invest the city but had no artillery for a formal siege. Desperate letters to Peterborough from the Jurats and the Viceroy of Valencia made clear that the position was difficult and that morale was low. Basset had assured them that the commander-in-chief was on his way, but they were beginning to think this an illusion. Basset himself had made a brave sally against the Bourbon army but had been routed.[8]

In order to reach Valencia, Peterborough's army had to pass by the town of Murviedro (now Sagunto) which guarded an important river crossing. Las Torres had left in garrison Brigadier O'Mahony and his regiment of Irish horse and some Spanish soldiers, as well as a number of sick and wounded. Meantime Las Torres had joined the Duke of Arcos but the two men had some sort of a disagreement and Las Torres returned to Madrid. From Bourbon records there appears to be no reason to suppose that he had been recalled to account for his conduct, as the Allies believed. However he left behind him a less experienced commander.

Las Torres had expected that O'Mahony would be able to intercept any attempt by Peterborough to reach Valencia. O'Mahony found himself too weak to leave the fortified town. On the approach to Murviedro, Peterborough took trouble to make his force appear larger than it was. He utilised rising ground to move troops further round and bordered his militia with infantry and dragoons so that they all appeared regular troops. The four cannon were displayed to advantage.

O'Mahony was sufficiently impressed. When the army appeared outside the walls, he sent an urgent message to the Duke of Arcos, claiming that the place was untenable without an immediate reinforcement of 500 foot. He was aware that he might have to abandon a strategically important place, and also the sick and wounded, but he only had three hours' ammunition. His impression of Peterborough's force was of 'six squadrons dressed in red, two battalions of English with red colours and one with white, as well as the Nebot cavalry and 5000 peasants'. Any delay could result in a march by the enemy round the town, preventing O'Mahony from joining Arcos.

Peterborough sent two officers to the town to demand a surrender. O'Mahony sent out a captain to ascertain that Peterborough was there in person. These preliminaries over, his only option was to agree to the best possible terms available. Suitably escorted, he agreed to meet Peterborough outside the walls of the town and discuss the situation. After 'some private discourse' the two commanders worked out the terms of the capitulation, which the Bourbons later considered very advantageous to themselves.

Peterborough failed in an attempt to win over O'Mahony and his regiment to the Allied cause. However, according to Arent Furly, he used 'a thousand artifices to create a jealousy between Mahoni and ye

Spaniards'. The arrangements eventually made included care of the sick and wounded and the leaving of some cannon in the town. The Bourbon troops would leave at 1 am, to give time for the message to reach Arcos and enable him to move his forces to meet O'Mahony. Although the guards at the river crossing would have been removed, Peterborough undertook not to cross the river before this time.

As the presence of both O'Mahony and Arcos on the plains of Valencia would still prevent the Allies reaching the city, Peterborough was looking for means to make them leave the area. Arent Furly relates that the Duke of Arcos was prepared for stories about O'Mahony by 'pretended deserters from our Camp'. Dr Freind claims that these were two of Zinzendorf's Dragoons. They were told to say that, while concealed in some rocks refreshing themselves with wine, they both saw and overheard the meeting of Peterborough and O'Mahony. They had seen large sums of money change hands and had overheard the promise of a distinguished rank in King Charles's army. Arcos was advised to be suspicious of a message from O'Mahony to meet him with the army near a Carthusian convent above the plains; this was a ruse and his army would be ambushed.

Before agreeing to the conditions, O'Mahony had asked for half an hour in which to discuss them with his officers and the town. At the appointed time he sent out a senior Spanish officer with his agreement to the terms. Peterborough then attempted to win over the Spanish officer but without success. However he did contrive to arouse suspicions in the officer's mind regarding O'Mahony's intentions, and the officer communicated these suspicions to his colleagues on his return.

During the night Peterborough heard the sound of horses neighing and wondered if some troops might be leaving the town ahead of the agreed time. In order to lend a little colour to this, he ordered some troops to go further up the river and indulge in some small arms fire to suggest a skirmish. As was intended, the Spanish officers in the town thought something was afoot. Their concern obliged O'Mahony to write to Peterborough explaining that he was having difficulty with the Spaniards and begging him to adhere to his part of the agreement. Peterborough replied with the offer of sending some of his dragoons across the river for O'Mahony's security and also some officers into the town as hostages for the capitulation. Subsequently, some of Pearce's dragoons crossed a badly swollen river. This manoeuvre only increased the misgivings of the Spanish officers, as Peterborough had intended it should. At midnight some Spanish troops made a hasty departure, their officers going ahead of them to Arcos. The spies having done their work, this movement only confirmed the news to Arcos who decamped his force and moved rapidly towards the mountains. O'Mahony duly left Murviedro at 1 am with 300 of his regiment and found himself obliged to follow the Bourbon army towards the hills. Thus the road to Valencia was left open.

Since O'Mahony's letter to the Duke of Arcos indicated his imminent withdrawal unless immediate succour was sent, Arcos had to accept that his decision not to send support, perhaps in the belief that it could not possibly arrive in time, would mean that the absence of O'Mahony's troops would leave him open to an attack from the Allied army approaching from that direction. The Bourbon view of O'Mahony's actions was that he had removed himself very creditably from a difficult situation and he was subsequently raised to the rank of major-general. Arcos, who had been appointed the Bourbon Viceroy of Valencia, was later recalled.[9]

It took the rest of the night for Peterborough's army to cross the river and enter the town and some horses were drowned while crossing. In Murviedro the Allied force was rather grudgingly received. 'We seemed to be as welcome as water into a new ship,' wrote a Royal Dragoon. Plenty of food and wine made up for the lack of goodwill. A council of war took the decision to proceed to Valencia the next day and Peterborough prepared the army for a possible encounter with the enemy in the plain. While they were at Murviedro, Valencia heard that O'Mahony had gone and that Peterborough and the Allied troops were in truth on their way.[10]

On 4 February 1705/6 the army set out across the plain. There was no sign of the enemy troops, although they were still believed to be in the vicinity. About a mile and a half from the city, Peterborough was met by a party of leading citizens, Deputies of the States, who formed an escort. On arrival, a civic welcome was given to the entire army. The soldiers noted the enthusiasm of the people and the relief and joy expressed all round. The streets were lined, bells rang and salutes were fired. Many noted the surprising sight of a regiment composed of monks, in varying shades of habit, cheerfully discharging their muskets. Peterborough was heard to remark that he had now seen in reality the Church Militant.

At the former governor's house Peterborough was received by the Viceroy, the Conde de Cardona. Later the earl called on the Condesa and also on his correspondent of many months, the Marquésa de la Casta. The day concluded with bonfires and illuminations.

There was no question of the soldiers being directed to billets. They were invited into houses as they passed along the street until every one was provided with a lodging. Even the leading citizens insisted on putting up their quota. As St Pierre reported later to Lord Raby, 'many of yr sergeants have I believe laid in Damask beds'. Never had they been given better quarters.

Valencian observers thought that Peterborough's force numbered about 10,000 men, including Miquelets. In reality the force was much weaker. The Miquelets were quartered on the outskirts of the city and were not very acceptable guests; they supplied themselves with what they required in their accustomed manner.[11]

It was a time of success and euphoria. From Valencia, St Pierre gave Lord Raby this description of his commander-in-chief.

> My Lord Peterborow is certainly one of the extraordinariest men that ever I knew in my life; had he the experience of some generals, few could be equal to him, and none beyond him; when occasion requireth no man applyeth himself more to business than he doeth, on horseback all day, dispatches all night, and that for a considerable time together; no man enters more into the detail of troops than he doeth, and he is the first General that I know, that can make war without men or money, and better withall the troops under his command; the confounded old lame ugly jades that we brought over are now metamorphosed into fine Andalusian horses…

In the privacy of his journal, St Pierre recorded a similar description of Peterborough with the addition of two small criticisms. 'He is very popular and generous, but may be no extraordinary Courtier…it is a pity he is easily diverted from serious business.'[12]

While the soldiers enjoyed their comfortable billets and gave themselves up, as one Valencian historian records, to idleness and drink, Peterborough's first action was to order the release from prison of those who had been arrested for loyalty to the Bourbon king, Philip V. Basset's military governorship had been marked by an excessive severity towards the large population of French merchants in Valencia and towards Bourbon sympathisers. Some had rapidly left the city, whereupon Basset had confiscated their goods. For a long time there had been a strong anti-French feeling in Valencia, which may have accounted in part for Basset's behaviour. Unfortunately, his attitude served to alienate some Valencians who might otherwise have been persuaded to support the Allied cause and it was not in keeping with the tone of the original manifesto.

For Peterborough it was a priority to try to win over leading citizens and members of the nobility. It was noticeable how few members of this social class had come forward to support Charles III. The greater part of the nobility and the ministers of the Audiencia retained their Bourbon loyalty. Peterborough also ensured that order was restored to the city; church bells no longer rang as an alarm or a call to arms but once again as a call to prayer.

It was surprising how much active support was given to Peterborough by a Church which undoubtedly considered him a heretic. Furly recorded that the earl went everywhere accompanied by his Father. As a very religious city, Valencia began to find it irksome to support this army of incomers whose behaviour was not always such as they could approve. The heretical element is regularly referred to by Valencian writers. Protestant services were held for the soldiers privately in houses. In March a gesture made by Peterborough, in sending as a compliment his band of musicians to play in the choir of San Felipe, did not meet with approval; the musicians were Protestant.[13]

Peterborough had taken up residence in a house in the Plaza de Santo Domingo belonging to the Marqués de Villatorcas. From here on 7 February, accompanied by a mounted escort, he drove with the Conde de Cardona to a solemn ceremony at which the Conde took the oaths as Viceroy. Basset, whom Peterborough treated with a degree of coolness, rode behind the carriage.

The same day Peterborough ordered Colonel Wills at Lérida to detach Rivers's regiment to form a garrison at Tortosa of 600 men to be augmented by marines. On the Aragon frontier Marshal Tessé and his army still waited for the moment to move towards Barcelona. A force from the garrison at Lérida had managed to repel 4,000 enemy troops under d'Asfeld near San Estevan and retain the pass, an action in which Major-General Conyngham was killed, the command now falling on Colonel Wills. It was also known that 5,000 Bourbon forces were on the Ebro near Val de Robres and Gandesa. For this reason it had been essential to reinforce the garrison at Tortosa, particularly as the Court at Barcelona had taken no action to do so in the meantime.[14]

While undoubtedly enjoying the easy ambience of Valencia, Peterborough was nevertheless concerned by the city's lack of defence and its inability to withstand any kind of siege. The citizens had done little to arm themselves and had raised only one regiment. Supplies of cannon and ammunition could only reach them by sea. The earl was not so lost to the easy life as to fail to use a network of spies. Information reached him that a Genoese ship carrying sixteen 24-pound cannon with ammunition had been dispatched by the French from Alicante. He sent an express to Captain George Dolman of the *Lyme*, cruising off Altea. On 13 February the *Lyme* captured a vessel originally thought to be an Algereen but proving to be the Genoese. The cargo became a valuable asset to the defences of Valencia.[15]

At this time the enemy forces in the vicinity were centred at Chiva in the foothills of the mountains. An Allied council of war on 14 February decided that their position and strength made any idea of an attack out of the question; the best course was to put the city in a position of defence. Peterborough was always conscious of the strength of a position near the sea and the system of communication, often rapid, which this afforded. He hoped and expected that the reinforcements coming from England would first reach Valencia on their way to Barcelona.

It was at this point that Peterborough's theory that a major diversion would take the pressure off Barcelona was almost realised. The Bourbon king, Philip V, hearing about affairs in Valencia, summoned Marshal Tessé to assist him to march in that direction. Unfortunately, Louis XIV simultaneously ordered Tessé to prepare to move to join the forces coming from Roussillon towards Barcelona for an attempt on the city in March. Louis was aware that reinforcements were on their way to Barcelona from England and Holland; the opportunity of taking Barcelona, with the Archduke Charles still there, must not be lost.

In Valencia Peterborough had still no news from England and had been without information now for four months. The 6/17 February was a date on which to remember absent friends. The earl marked the Queen's Birthday by giving a splendid banquet. Two days later he was greatly disappointed by the defection to the enemy of three more leading citizens – the Conde de Sumacarcel, the Marqués de la Scala and Don Manuel Ferrer.[16]

While at Chiva the Bourbon forces had received a new commander in the shape of the Conde de las Torres, the Duke of Arcos having been recalled. The force was said to number about 4,000 and included 2,000 horse. Peterborough heard that it was soon to be joined by an additional 2,000 men from Castile, 'under the spirituall directions of two Bishops', as well as 400 horse under the newly elevated Major-General

O'Mahony. Aware of the favourable condition of the countryside and the state of the rivers, Peterborough made a night march with a force of 1,200 men and surprised the enemy reinforcements near Fuente la Higuera. The unexpected attack caused confusion and the Allied force was able to take 600 prisoners including 55 officers. The prisoners were taken to Alcira in the charge of Don Rafael Nebot. On 3 March General Basset y Ramos left Valencia with a party of 200 foot and 100 horse to cover Nebot's onward progress in that direction. This bold action on Peterborough's part could only be justified by its success.

Soon afterwards the Bourbon camp moved from Chiva to nearer Carlet south-west of Valencia. The spy system then revealed that the enemy hoped to cut off supplies from reaching Valencia from the south by gaining a vital bridge at Cullera. Peterborough went to reconnoitre the place on 9 March. He alerted the garrison at Alcira who sent a party to Sueca which managed to prevent the enemy manoeuvre with little time to spare.[17]

All this activity, or lack of it, seems on a very small scale when placed in position in the overall design. It could be wondered, and the Bourbons did wonder, why Peterborough had left the Austrian King in Barcelona with such a small force. The King's request for reinforcements, in the face of the steady movement of Tessé's army towards Barcelona in January, was turned down at a council of war in Valencia on 27 February as 'dangerous and impractical'. Peterborough wrote to the King at this time, telling him that the proposals made were impossible and that they indicated the inexperience in warfare of the Conde de Cifuentes. The same old confrontations were evident in this dampening communication. The only hopeful note was the report that a gentleman at Denia had seen four great ships of war which might be British. Eyes were always on the horizon for the arrival of men or money.[18]

Twenty

During the winter of 1705–6 Parliament had received the news from Spain with approbation and also acclamation. The prosecution of the war in the Peninsula was voted the sum of £250,000. The reinforcements promised, and sent in February, numbered 4,170 men. They left in two detachments: the Royal Fusiliers and Colonel Breton's Regiment sailed from Plymouth and the regiments of Lord Mohun, Lord Dungannon and Colonel Toby Caulfield followed later from Ireland. In addition, a squadron under Sir George Byng was sent out to the Peninsula.

On February 8/19 1706 Brigadier Stanhope left London as the newly appointed envoy extraordinary to the King of Spain with special responsibilities regarding trade. Accompanying him was Colonel Richards who had only reached London about a week previously, bringing letters from the King and Peterborough. Confirmed in his commission and with all the ordnance already embarked, Richards was ordered to turn around and accompany the army and artillery back to Spain. Before leaving, he had time to make a full and personal report to Marlborough and Godolphin.

Richards's account of events in Barcelona may not have been too sympathetic to Peterborough. The government had already heard complaints from the Austrian side; the other half of the picture would have revealed the tinder box of Peterborough's dealings with the Court. Richards himself was no stranger to rough treatment from the Austrians, but Peterborough's response lacked diplomacy and it is noticeable that from this time the government at home showed less sympathy for his situation.

The expedition now setting out also included Comte de Noyelles, a Velt-Marchal of the Empire, who was going to join the entourage of the King of Spain on the Emperor's orders, possibly to fill the military gap left by the death of Prince George of Hesse-Darmstadt. Hedges wrote carefully to Peterborough: 'Whatever commission the Count may have, it can give him no command over Her Majesty's troops.' At the same time Peterborough received fresh instructions, as it had not been envisaged originally that he would remain in the Peninsula after the end of the season. Now he was given leave either to remain or return home should he consider it necessary. He had asked that 'a good horse officer' should be sent out and suggested General Wyndham, at present in Portugal. Wyndham accepted but with surprise that Peterborough had chosen him.[1]

On 22 February the Bourbon claimant to the throne of Spain, Philip Duke of Anjou, left Madrid on his way to join Marshal Tessé near Saragossa on the instructions of Louis XIV. There were now only 5,000 troops to guard the capital against any advance from Portugal. Conscious of this weakness, Louis sent to the area a newly created Marshal of France, the Duke of Berwick, to command the forces there.

Having arrived on 11 March, Berwick was well aware that the Allies had a good opportunity now of capturing Madrid. So was Peterborough, who had accordingly sent a request to Sir John Leake to give him early notice of the approach of the reinforcements as with this additional strength, he might well make an attack from Valencia. On 13 March Peterborough wrote a surprising letter to the King of Spain, outlining a plan to be kept utterly secret. The King should utilise some of the clean ships at Peterborough's disposal and go to Portugal. Here he should join the Allied army of 25,000 troops for the spring campaign and in no time he would find himself in Madrid. In the meantime, Peterborough would hold Valencia and Catalonia for him; he suggested Prince Henry of Hesse as a suitable Viceroy of Catalonia.

Two days later, on 16 March, Peterborough sent Don Pedro Moras to the King with a realistic account of affairs in Valencia. While waiting for the King's reply, he both thought and talked about Madrid. On 21 March he sent the first of a series of letters to Sir John Leake, asking him to land the incoming forces and supplies in the kingdom of Valencia. If joined by reinforcements, Peterborough said he was in a good position for a march towards Madrid. The landing should not be made near Valencia itself but higher up the coast near Vinaros and the Alfaques, half way to Barcelona and close to the border with Aragon. A march from there, Peterborough considered, could divert the Bourbon forces about to threaten Barcelona, particularly if there was also some action on the Portuguese border.

The mood in Barcelona was uneasy. Since the end of February a small French squadron under Duquesne had blockaded the harbour. Crowe was concerned about the expected arrival of the ships bringing Colonel Hamilton with much needed funds from Genoa. In the event they were unable to reach the harbour but did manage to land some Catalan gentlemen at Mataró; and, being newly cleaned and swift, they were easily able to outstrip the French and land the money at Tarragona. Hamilton himself reached Valencia on 14 March. On 6 March a fleet of seventeen men-of-war had left Toulon for Barcelona under the command of the Comte de Toulouse. When Peterborough sent his orders to Leake, he was aware that a squadron of twenty sail stood off Barcelona. While the frigates disembarked the men and supplies on the coast, the earl reckoned that Leake's 'great ships' could destroy the French fleet, if they surprised them after a night approach.[2]

The progress of the Bourbon army towards Barcelona was remarkably slow. Philip Duke of Anjou joined Marshal Tessé at Caspe on 14 March and the combined force moved on by way of Cervera and Martorell. The lack of speed was largely accounted for by the extreme caution which Tessé showed towards Peterborough's troops and the Miquelets. The French general tended to overestimate the strength of Peterborough's force and was very nervous of the Miquelets. Certainly the latter made a great nuisance of themselves whenever possible and cut off the passes behind the army so that there was no retreat.

The threat to Barcelona seemed much more immediate to the inhabitants than in fact it was to prove. A second force under the Duc de Noailles was on its way there from Roussillon but this was also delayed. In the city itself there was only a small garrison consisting of one regiment of the Queen's Guards under Colonel Russell, another of the King's Spanish Guards and some local troops. Little had been done during the winter to repair the ravages of the Allied attack the previous year. The breach in the walls had not been closed and no effort had been made to restore the fortifications at Montjuich.

At the first threat of the French approach, Peterborough had ordered Colonel Wills at Lérida to send 4,000 men to Barcelona. This order was countermanded by the King on the advice of his ministers who believed that Lérida would be attacked first. By mid-March, they were proved wrong; it became clear that the armies would make straight for Barcelona. Lérida was not attacked and it was now too late for its garrison to be reached.[3]

On 24 March Count Cassel arrived at Valencia with the King's refusal to entertain Peterborough's plan regarding Portugal and the information that he intended to remain in Barcelona. Peterborough accepted that he would now have to supply assistance for Barcelona so he informed the magistrates of Valencia that he was about to leave for

Catalonia and would take some of the horse. In consternation, the magistrates in their turn wrote to the King for assistance.

A month previously, a council of war had decided that to detach troops from Valencia would be both 'dangerous and impracticable'. Despite this, Peterborough now began to make immediate arrangements to despatch troops, commencing with some Spanish regiments. On 25 March the regiment of Don Pedro Moras set off for Catalonia, followed the next day by part of a Valencian regiment and Nebot's Horse. On 29 March Brigadier Hamilton was sent to join his regiment of foot at Tortosa. With a rapidity that shamed the efforts of the Bourbon army, Hamilton's Foot made an epic march from Tortosa to Barcelona in two days; normally such a journey would have taken a week. They arrived before the city on 2 April, the same day as the two French armies.[4]

Having forwarded some reinforcements for Barcelona, Peterborough continued to write to Leake recommending that he put ashore the new troops and money in Valencia; Altea or Denia would do as well should the former prove difficult. After months of delay, the money sent by Methuen had arrived on board the *Panther* on 23 March, together with very welcome letters. It is hard to imagine how finances had been managed in the meantime but Peterborough maintained that, for a heretic, he had excellent credit among the Spaniards.

A council of war was held on 30 March in response to further orders from the King. The same conclusion was reached, that no detachments should be made from Valencia. To weaken the defences would open the doors to Las Torres.

The same day Peterborough wrote to the Duke of Savoy describing the situation in Catalonia and Valencia as well as what he hoped to achieve on a broader front. With Galway besieging Badajos and moving 18,000 men into Spain towards Madrid, and with Valencia all for the Allied cause, in his view the arrival of the reinforcements could mean that all of Aragon and Murcia would declare for King Charles. Although there were 4,000 men keeping the French back in the passes of Catalonia, the threat to Barcelona was real and the outcome could not be forecast. Peterborough told the Duke that he was on his way there with 600 horse to see if it could be retained. He was aware that there were grave risks involved and these could include the life of the young King. If the King should be killed, he told the Duke grandly, 'je donneray l'Espagne a celuy qui doit l'avoir...' The possibility of the King being taken prisoner would make matters more complicated.

Peterborough's solution in the possible event of the King's death, that the Duke of Savoy should become the Allied candidate for the throne, seemed to him eminently appropriate. Apparently discounting any charge of disloyalty, he felt no need to be secretive about it, and indeed a copy of this letter, attested as such by Arent Furly, was included in despatches to Godolphin. Later Marlborough suggested to the Lord Treasurer that the original letter, or an authentic copy of it, should be acquired from the Duke of Savoy so that it could be produced if necessary to keep Peterborough 'in awe'.[5]

Meanwhile the Bourbon army under Las Torres still lay encamped to the south of Valencia. The Royal Dragoons, now withdrawn from the garrison at Alcira, were billeted to the north of the city. The French camp had been divided into four parts, and in order to take some action against the enemy before leaving Valencia, Peterborough decided to attack one of these sections. He left Valencia at night on 1 April with all the English troops and went as far as Carlet. Unfortunately the enterprise was 'scandalously disappointed' by the actions of a Spanish regiment which panicked and withdrew in confusion on encountering a small party of horse while on a shorter route to the camp. The English troops were within a mile of the French camp before they were also obliged to withdraw.

On 3 April Peterborough sent orders to Colonel Wills at Lérida to take the English and Dutch troops there to Tarragona. Two days later Brigadier Killigrew and Colonel de St Pierre were also ordered to march to Tarragona. The Royal Dragoons and the rest of the horse were then sent on the road to Catalonia, Peterborough himself joining them at Tarragona on 15 April.

On 7 April Peterborough wrote to Leake, forwarding letters to him from the King. The contents of one letter had been made known to the earl. This contained positive orders to Leake to take the fleet, men and money for the King straight to Barcelona without delay. Peterborough told Leake that the King had now reached a state in which it was impossible for him to leave Barcelona 'without the utmost hazard to his Person' and therefore it was of the greatest importance 'that we all endeavour what humanely is possible for the reliefe of that place'.

Peterborough's own orders to Leake predated those of the King and were given on the advice of several councils of war. He was afraid that the King's orders were the 'produce of Land Admiralls'. In Peterborough's view, transport ships could hinder the movement of a fleet which was about to encounter an enemy of uncertain numbers. He understood that the Comte de Toulouse now had twenty-seven ships off Barcelona. In the light of the orders given by the King, Peterborough made no alteration to his own; he merely stated how and why they had been made. It was for Leake to take the decision. However he did enclose a copy of his commission for Leake to look over, in view of the circumstances. He was privately disgusted at the delay in the fleet's arrival; he believed that they had gone 'a galleon-hunting' and indeed some ships had.

On 9 April Peterborough was at Segorbe. Three days later, in the company of Don Rafael Nebot, he embarked on a light vessel at the Grau in order to make rapid progress to the rendezvous at Tarragona. Pearce's Dragoons, the regiments of Donegal and Mountjoy and some local foot were left to guard the city of Valencia.[6]

What was delaying the expected fleet? When Sir John Leake's squadron had reached Lisbon on 16/27 January 1705/6 after a tedious voyage of thirteen weeks, many of the ships were in poor condition. There were no stores or provisions waiting for them and it was some time before they were fit to go to sea again. At the end of February the *Panther* and *Tiger*, newly cleaned, were sent off with Methuen's money for the troops in Catalonia.

At the beginning of March it was decided to put to sea with the ships that were now ready and the remainder could follow later. The news that a Spanish fleet was about to set out from Cadiz for the West Indies was an inducement for an early departure. Hoping that it could be surprised and attacked, and attempting to ensure some secrecy of the fleet's movements, Leake asked the Portuguese authorities to place an embargo on all shipping from leaving the Tagus until his own fleet had sailed. The embargo was granted but it was believed that a few merchantmen had slipped through, some of whom were bound for the Straits. Whether by design or accident, when the fleet attempted to sail on 8 March they found the embargo operated against them and their departure was held up until the next day, the delay giving the Spanish fleet the advantage they needed. When Leake reached Cape St Mary's on 11 March, he heard that the galleons had already sailed. Some ships set off in pursuit but the two Spaniards they captured turned out to have left Cadiz a day behind the main fleet. With such a distance against them and also a contrary wind, the project was abandoned.[7]

On 23 March Leake received the first communication from Peterborough for several months. It was the first of numerous instructions to land the men and money in the kingdom of Valencia. On 30 March the fleet was off Cape Spartel. Three days later Leake received more instructions from Peterborough, this time to land the troops as high along the coast as Vinaros or Alfaques. Another letter received on 4 April contained the additional news that there were now twenty French ships in Barcelona road.

When Leake's fleet anchored at Gibraltar on 9 April, a council of war decided that the situation in Catalonia required their 'speediest and utmost assistance' in preference to all else. However first of all it was necessary to wait for the rest of the fleet to arrive.[8]

After the fleet left Lisbon, a convoy from England under the command of Captain Price arrived in the Tagus on 21 March. It transported two regiments for service in Catalonia and a great quantity of arms, clothing and supplies for the army. Brigadier Stanhope, in his capacity as envoy to the King of Spain, was also on board, as were other officers. Originally only meant to stay two days, Captain Price was ordered to wait for the remaining Dutch ships. The convoy set sail again for Gibraltar on 31 March.

The transport ships were carrying Colonel Breton's regiment and Sir Charles O'Hara's regiment of fusiliers. As well as Brigadier Stanhope, the officers on board included the surprised but compliant General Wyndham who had been replaced in Portugal by Sir Charles O'Hara, and Colonel Pepper who had returned to Lisbon after the raising of the siege of Badajos and was now being used by Methuen to take despatches to Peterborough. The victuallers were carrying shoes, stockings, hats and shirts for 20,000 foot, boots, saddles, pistols and carbines for a great number of horse and also clothing for 6,000 Spaniards.

Stanhope considered that the regiments on board, including 200 Spanish soldiers, were very good. The Irish convoy, expected daily, would be bringing three complete regiments, 900 recruits for the Guards battalion and an extra 300 men. Both Stanhope and Methuen reckoned that the Grand Fleet could reach Peterborough in twenty days.

After the arrival of Captain Price with the transports at Gibraltar on 14 April, Leake was now in command of thirty good men-of-war and some frigates. The following day a council of war of sea officers was held on board the *Ranelagh*, Leake's flagship. It decided that the Allied fleet was not strong enough to attack the French ships gathered off Barcelona. Consequently it was agreed that a small force of ten men-of-war and three frigates should take on board the two regiments and the 200 Spanish soldiers and proceed to disembark them at Altea or Denia. These ships would then return to Gibraltar to await the arrival of the Irish convoy and, more importantly, Sir George Byng's squadron. The removal of the troops from the transports to the men-of-war was begun immediately. While the council was in progress, letters arrived from the King, Peterborough and Cifuentes with the news that Barcelona had been invested by a French army of 15,000. The King had made an unsuccessful attempt to leave the city and had now decided to remain. Barcelona had a garrison of only 1,000 foot and 400 horse.[9]

Colonel Pepper was amazed at the outcome of the council of war. He poured out his indignation to Brigadier Stanhope, believing that this decision could lead to the loss of Barcelona. According to Pepper, Stanhope reasoned with Leake on the subject and another council was called for the following day to which both Stanhope and Wyndham were invited. It had been reported that the French fleet off Barcelona numbered between twenty-two and twenty-seven men-of-war and around fifty smaller vessels. In addition, the Comte de Toulouse was expected to join them with a squadron of thirteen or fourteen ships. At this council, it was resolved to take all the ships to Altea with the troops on board, leaving behind the empty transports and also instructions for Sir George Byng to follow.

On 17 April a third council resolved that if they obtained certain intelligence at Altea that the enemy had no more than twenty-seven ships, they would proceed and give battle. Four ships would be sent ahead along the coast for intelligence. After this spirited decision, adverse winds delayed departure until 24 April.*

On 22 April Leake was ready to sail but another council postponed the departure. The wind had become easterly and some of the ships were so foul that plying to windward could have damaged them. Also news had reached the fleet that a French squadron was on its way to the Mediterranean from the western seaboard of France. To remain where they were until the first reasonable wind would prevent a junction of French fleets and give a good position for receiving intelligence.

Stanhope and Pepper were on board one of the four ships sent ahead to Altea. When they arrived, they could get no news of Barcelona. It proved difficult to get a ship to go to Denia and so Pepper volunteered

*Peterborough later heard of Stanhope's intervention, possibly from Pepper if not Stanhope himself. He commented: 'The raising of the siege of Barcelona and our successes here are the effects of Colonel Stanhope's being aboard the Fleet.' Peterborough to Lord Treasurer, BL Add. MSS 28,057 f. 150.

to go himself by land. Put ashore between there and Denia, he made his way to Valencia where he arrived on 29 April. Before leaving to find Peterborough near Barcelona, he was able to cheer a despondent garrison with the news that the fleet was really on its way.[10]

On 26 April Leake learnt from some Dutch merchantmen that the Irish convoy was not far off. It had in fact left Lisbon the day before the Dutch, had initially made good progress but then took fright at the appearance of what proved to be the returning transports. It was then becalmed for three days.

Leake reached Altea on 29 April to find that the scouts had brought no information. He sent them off to Vinaros and Tortosa while he waited for the Irish convoy. The next day news came that Sir George Byng's squadron had been sighted off Cape de Gata having overtaken the convoy. The same day Brigadier Gorges arrived from Valencia, carrying letters dated 22 April from Peterborough near Barcelona which stated that the French fleet there consisted of eighteen ships, ten frigates and four bomb vessels. The earl recommended that the transport vessels should still be sent to Vinaros or Tortosa but that 1,000 men should be put on board the men-of-war so that they could be thrown into Barcelona. This news was only eight days old. Peterborough considered that Leake's thirty ships should be sufficient to face the French, but, more cautiously, the admiral preferred to wait for Byng. Gorges also reported that Montjuich had been captured by the French who had also regained Alcira and other places in Valencia.

At 10 am the next day, 1 May NS, Sir George Byng with his squadron of thirteen ships sailed into the fleet. It was decided to sail for Tarragona immediately. If news there indicated that the enemy fleet was not superior, they would proceed to give battle. They set sail but in the next two days hard winds from the north blew them back to Altea where they were joined by the Irish convoy on 3 May.[11]

Having made an abortive attempt to leave Barcelona by sea on the night of 1 April and reach Tarragona, the King had resolved to remain in the city. He claimed to have had a vision of the Virgin Mary who commanded him to stay with his faithful Catalans. This decision endeared him to the people, who already admired him for his religious devotion and his conscientious attention to duty. His presence became a great boost to the civic morale. At a later stage in the siege, the people physically prevented him from making another attempt to leave by surrounding the palace.

On 3 April the entire French army was encamped on the plain to the south-west of Barcelona between the Llobregat river and Montjuich. It appeared to number at least 20,000 men and the encampment stretched for five or six miles. It had made an impressive arrival; the separate armies of the Duc d'Anjou with Marshal Tessé and of the Duc de Noailles had accidentally coordinated their appearance for the same day.

Almost immediately a minor attack was made on the outworks of Montjuich. From the city it could be seen that supplies were being put ashore from the French fleet. This became an important lifeline for the army, as any attempt to raise contributions from an unwilling country-side could be attacked or thwarted by the Miquelets who had already, the day after their arrival, made off with 700 sheep and 12 mules in full view of the camp and contrived to beat off the pursuit unaided. On 5 April the French opened trenches at Montjuich but their cannon were not in battery until 12 April. Tessé was irritated by this considerable loss of time.[12]

Philip Duke of Anjou was in residence at Sarriá and was subjected to a Miquelet attack on 6 April. More than 200 men were killed and Philip was obliged to make an ignominious departure through a back door to find a temporary refuge on board the fleet, out of harm's way. Marshal Tessé and the Earl of Peterborough shared a common responsibility: each had to consider the safety of a monarch. Peterborough has been criticised, rightly, for carrying this burden too lightly. Tessé, on the other hand, was very conscious of his accountability to Louis XIV for Philip's safety; he worried about the possible consequences of a combined attack from enemy forces within the city and those without the camp. This anxiety partly accounted for his extreme caution in the conduct of the siege, although Philip himself was only too keen to take part.

On 5 and 6 April the garrison of Barcelona was further increased by the arrival of Lord Donegal, Brigadier de St Amand and four regiments from the Gerona garrison. It was also augmented by some dragoons from Lérida. The garrison now numbered 3,000 regular troops. The French noted the arrival of the reinforcements and moved round to the east so that they now almost surrounded Barcelona and Montjuich. The city could still receive some supplies by sea.

Morale in the city was good and encouraged by the King, who went everywhere. Work progressed steadily on the fortifications. Officers of the garrison on duty were comforted by the signs of activity in the hills. This they took to be the work of Prince Henry of Hesse and the

Miquelets who were based in the mountains of San Jeronimo. Three days after Anjou's escape, Sarriá and the neighbouring houses went up in flames. By 12 April the French had twelve guns mounted on their battery and on the 14th there was vigorous shelling. An English officer in the garrison recorded: 'Now and then (we) fire a small gun upon them, to let them see we are not asleep. We hope the Earl of Peterborough will convince them and us, that he is not so, and that the Prince of Hesse and he will not delay.' In Barcelona they still had no news of Peterborough.

On 15 April Liechtenstein wrote to Wratislaw, describing the position and only partly blaming Peterborough. The earl had understood the plan of conquering Aragon and Castile and to that end had removed all the Allied troops to Valencia without sending a single man to help Barcelona. However, Liechtenstein also blamed decisions in Portugal. The reinforcements promised in January, of troops who were to be replaced by regiments from home, had never arrived and the squadron due to come straight to Barcelona had gone off to the Canaries after galleons. Privately, Liechtenstein believed that Peterborough had a hatred of the Catalans and would not dream of relieving the city were the King not in it. This was his reason for encouraging the King to leave, although the Austrian courtiers had all done so, but the King was not keen to fall again into his lordship's hands, 'obligé de s'accomoder- nolens volens- à son génie bizarre et ses chicannes'. The anger that the King had felt at being accused by Peterborough for only attending to the counsels of the Conde de Cifuentes still rankled. However, it was now rumoured that the earl and his cavalry were in the vicinity.

The attack on Montjuich began in earnest on 16 April. The French had no difficulty in overcoming some raw Spanish troops in the outworks. The Guards and grenadiers put up more opposition but the French held on to the posts they had taken. 'They will no doubt raise a battery', wrote an English officer, 'and consequently oblige us with the greater earnestness to cry out Good Lord come and help us.' A new dimension was added when two bomb vessels began to target the city.

At Montjuich the English and Dutch garrison bore the brunt of the attack. They were on duty at all hours as the Neapolitans and Spaniards were unreliable under fire. By 20 April 'we are now on all sides mauled confoundedly,' the officer recorded. The next day a small boat reached the city bringing some officers from Peterborough and firm news of attempts to relieve the city.[13]

Tessé had been informed from several places that Peterborough had been asked by the Archduke Charles in Barcelona to come to his assistance but that he had refused to leave Valencia. He was not expecting trouble from that direction, having quite enough to contend with in the immediate vicinity. By 16 April his army was attacked not only by 'une infinité de Miquelets' but also 'par la faim, car il ne vient pas un oeuf au Camp'. The army had become entirely dependent on the fleet for victuals and Tessé was quite certain that, should the admiral hear that the Allied fleet was in the Mediterranean, he would put out to sea or even return to Toulon. Tessé understood that the Conde de Cifuentes was in the mountains behind him with a force of 300 horse and between 8,000 and 10,000 Miquelets and that the Prince of Hesse on the Llobregat had another numerous force.

Peterborough had reached Martorell by 18 April, bringing with him 600 horse and also 2,000 foot which he had ordered to join him from Lérida. Here he held a council at which the Prince of Hesse, Marqués Rubi, Don Phelipe Feran, Don Miguel de Alentour y Pinos, Brigadier Wills and Brigadier Palme were present. A plan was concocted whereby the troops would make a descent from the mountains behind Barcelona by a road running down to the plain. The two brigadiers did not think this plan practicable, as the force would have to cross in front of the enemy in order to reach the city. However the troops were moved and the dragoons camped at San Cugat. It was then found that the narrow road intended for the descent had been fortified by the French at the other end with a redoubt and two cannon and so the plan was abandoned. The brigadiers were in favour of gathering together all the army, reinforced by the Miquelets, for a general attack. A muster of Miquelets raised only 1,000 instead of the expected 10,000 so this plan was also discarded.

While encamped in the mountains, some of the marines and foot found themselves so close to the French camp that 'our out-sentinels and theirs could talk together'. The soldiers were kept continually on the move and the Miquelets lit bonfires as if in expectation of some event, to keep the French on the alert. The troops stayed close to the city for ten or twelve days. Peterborough was constantly in action between San Cugat and Mataró. On 24 April he sent off 500 Neapolitan troops in some barks and half-galleys for Barcelona from Mataró. The enemy attacked them as they entered, taking fifty men prisoner, but 400 managed to land. After this, the French took greater care to ensure that neither men nor provisions reached the city by sea.[14]

On the day the Neapolitans reached the city, the French opened trenches in front of Barcelona. After a further fierce attack on Montjuich on the evening of 21 April, the remainder of the garrison had retired to the castle. On 22 April there was a general attempt from the city to dislodge the French from Montjuich but without success. On 24 April the enemy breached the curtain wall of the castle and destroyed part of the tower. The next day the garrison removed as much as possible from the castle, burning what they could not take away, and withdrew into the city. It had taken the French seventeen days to capture Montjuich.[15]

Confronted by this crisis the King made another attempt to leave the city. He was being constantly urged to do so by Peterborough, who managed to maintain a correspondence with him by means of Miquelets who slipped in under cover of darkness. However the people of Barcelona were not going to let their King go. They believed, as did all the Catalans, that as long as the King remained, Peterborough would have to attack the French in order to save him and thus also Barcelona. If the King escaped, Barcelona would be abandoned.

In the city itself, fortification of the breach and the wall facing Montjuich continued. Meanwhile fire bombs dropped from the sea side were still making havoc. Tessé believed he had intercepted a plan to introduce Allied troops from the south-west coastal area into the city. Thereafter the French set up further works to prevent the arrival of any reinforcements by land.

On 28 April Peterborough sent an urgent message to Leake to make his progress as rapid as possible; the fleet must arrive in four or five days to save the city. 'Crowding Sayle Night and Day is our only Refuge; the news of your being near might save all.' He urged that a fast frigate should be sent ahead to flash false lights off Mataró so that a watcher would know that the fleet was coming. Two days later he was sure that the garrison could hold out no more than three days. He stressed the importance of putting men into the town, for which he had boats ready, before pursuing the French. Some of the French fleet appeared to be absent and might have gone for intelligence.

Early that morning, 30 April, despite the vigilance of the enemy, two half-galleys pushed their way through both lines of the French blockading boats. They brought the Prince of Hesse with a guard of sixty marines under the command of Captain Scott. The Prince's mission was a last-ditch attempt to persuade the King to leave and escort him away. The mission failed. However the city welcomed the prince with universal rejoicing; his arrival looked like a good omen and raised spirits that had almost reached the point of despair.[16]

On 2 May Peterborough could send news to the King that the Allied fleet was at Altea; Colonel Pepper had at last found him in the hills. Pepper only stayed a few hours before returning to the coast with Peterborough's letter to Leake of 30 April. He was picked up by the *Fubbs* yacht which had just deposited Captain Stanhope, who was charged with telling Peterborough of the junction of the fleets. This news had been anxiously awaited since Pepper's visit. On receiving it, Peterborough immediately set his forces in motion, quietly and by night, towards the coast. He arrived at Sitges on 4 May and here, with the assistance of Mitford Crowe, he organised some half-galleys and barks to transport his 2,000 men under cover of the fleet to Barcelona. Of the fleet, however, there was no sign. He settled down to wait, during the day on shore and, on the nights of 6 and 7 May, in an open boat at sea.

After the junction of Byng's squadron, the progress of the fleet had been bedevilled firstly by northerly winds then calms and fog. On 3 May the ships were off Cape Martin. Three days later they encountered a complete calm between Tortosa and Tarragona and were obliged to anchor. At Hospitalet Colonel Richards went ashore to look for news and letters from Peterborough and made his way by land to Tarragona. The next day, 7 May, he saw the transport ships come in towards the town and then, to his dismay, back out again.

The *Leopard* had now joined the fleet with Colonel Pepper and a batch of letters. Four of the letters came from Peterborough. One from the King urged Leake to come to Barcelona without loss of time and 'without stopping or disembarking the forces elsewhere, as some other persons may pretend to direct you'. There were no conflicting orders in the letters from the Other Person. Plans to land troops at Tarragona were abandoned and the whole fleet prepared to get in motion for Barcelona and attack the French. Then the fog descended.[17]

A Genoese tartan managed to warn the French of the nearness and size of the Allied fleet. The garrison at Barcelona had expected a desperate assault on the city as soon as news came of the approaching relief but on 5 May observers noticed that the French ships were all unmoored. On the afternoon of the 7th they loosed their foretopsails; some weighed anchor and went out to sea. Tessé had been warned by the Comte de Toulouse that he had orders not to wait for the approaching Allied fleet and that he would sail on 8 May. In fact Toulouse gave the order for departure on the night of 7 May, having discovered just how close the Allied ships were. The Royal Dragoons' sentry in the mountains watched the French guard ships hurrying into the fleet, firing broadsides in warning.

The wind which blew up during the night favoured the French departure and enabled the Allied fleet to proceed at first light in weather which alternated between gales and fog. The *Fubbs* yacht, detailed to make the best of her way to the King, left at 6 am and soon encountered a large number of small boats. These contained Peterborough and his force, embarked and ready for convoy. The earl went on board the first man-of-war that he met which was the *Resolution*. He went on to find Admiral Leake on board the *Ranelagh*, the Union flag was hoisted at once but Leake was not there; after the junction of the fleets, he had returned to his old flagship, the *Prince George*, where at last Peterborough found him. Again the Union flag was hoisted, but Leake kept his own flag flying.

By this time Leake had already detached Sir George Byng's squadron with Sir John Jennings to convoy the little ships from Sitges. Being the first to arrive at Barcelona, they could see the last ships of the French fleet vanishing into the distance. There was no delay in disembarking the troops. The marines and foot from Sitges, as well as Breton's regiment and the Royal Fusiliers, were soon on shore and marched to the breaches in the wall. The King was already on board a ship in the harbour for safety, as it was expected that the breaches would be stormed that night. Their arrival had been opportune and fortuitous.

That afternoon the rest of the fleet came to anchor in Barcelona road. By evening most of the disembarkation had been accomplished. Peterborough struck his flag on the *Prince George* and went ashore.[18]

Twenty-one

Peterborough's action in coming on board the *Prince George* and hoisting his flag as admiral provoked jealousy in naval circles. He was criticised for trying to claim the glory of the relief for himself instead of allowing it to be given to Sir John Leake. Later Peterborough made clear to Godolphin what his intentions had been. 'Could I have got aboard before ye French scouts had made our Fleet, part of our ships had kept out of sight, and the French would have engaged an equall number, and our fresh ships coming on we might have destroyed the whole Squadron.' To the Queen, Peterborough wrote: 'When I spent two nights in a boat att sea to get aboard the fleet, I was in hopes that I might have given your Majesty some good account of the other trust you have been pleased to honour me with. We had a lucky fogg to bring us upon the enemy, but a discreet retreat prevented those flattering hopes.' Apart from saying that in three months he had raised as many sieges, he claimed little glory for himself but gave the honour to Her Majesty's Forces. A remark in the same letter, that 'getting abord your fleet, I had the satisfaction to see the Admirall of France flying before your flaggs', gives an indication of the relish with which he regarded the 'other trust'.

If Peterborough had been asked to choose between the two commands which he had been given, there is no doubt that he would have chosen the sea service. As Queen Mary had realised sixteen years previously, he considered himself a seaman. With a boyish enthusiasm for ships and seafaring, he rose to the challenge of a sea fight. Although joined in his command with Sir Cloudesley Shovell, Peterborough was intensely proud of it. Hoping and expecting to be made a vice-admiral in his own right, he thought this would give him a better relationship with the Navy.

Although hitherto he had considered Leake a better commander than Shovell, Peterborough was unhappy over the conduct of the Navy on this expedition. No one could have helped the weather but he thought it had been a mistake to go galleon-hunting; the Navy was altogether too keen on gain. Leake had resented Peterborough's action in hoisting his flag but he made no comment at the time and admitted very fairly that the earl had made no attempt to take over the command. In any case, the orders had already been given and the French avoided a fight.[1]

The French army had prosecuted the siege of Barcelona with some vigour and had made three or four practicable breaches before Toulouse intimated to Tessé his decision to depart. The news of their fleet setting sail dealt a severe blow to the troops' morale and on 9 May some deserters reported to the city that the French were preparing to leave. The firing still continued but the expected storming never took place. In Barcelona there was now a strong feeling that the French must soon withdraw: they could obtain few provisions besides the flour and meal which had been landed from the ships. As soon as the Miquelets were alerted to the situation, they were quick to attack anyone near the borders of the camp and were believed to have killed about 400 men. Skirmishing continued until 11 May, then the firing almost ceased, a clamour of activity was heard from the camp and a baggage train was seen setting off in an easterly direction. A brigade of horse was sent out of the French camp to chase the Miquelets away. At 10 pm guns were fired from Montjuich as a signal for departure and the huge army began to move off during the night. Around 9 am the next morning there was a total eclipse of the sun. Complete darkness only lasted four minutes but partial effects lasted for about two hours. It was considered a remarkable omen that an eclipse should occur on the departure of an army whose King had taken the sun for his device.[2]

The route of the French army led towards Roussillon, the nearest way to safety and supply. The Allies had made no provision for this so the Miquelets and a party of horse from the city were in a perfect position to harass the French as they wished; but with no disciplined force in pursuit, there was no temptation for the French to desert. Before leaving, Tessé had sent a letter to Peterborough asking for his leniency towards the large number of sick and wounded they were forced to leave behind because of lack of transportation. He asked that a guard might be set on the hospitals to protect the occupants and also sent a doctor, a commissary and a contribution of 1,000 pistoles. Peterborough promised to do his best for the sick and wounded and the French acknowledged that he 'took all possible care to prevent the Miquelets from cutting their throats'.

The messenger had also brought the interesting news that the Duchess of Anjou had left Madrid for Pamplona. This eventually turned out to be false, but it may have been known in the camp that the Duke had ordered her to do so. This news, together with the huge quantity of artillery, stores and meal left behind (if only through their inability to transport it), suggested that the French had more reasons for pulling out than merely the absence of the fleet. They were abandoning stores sufficient to supply 20,000 men for two months.

As soon as possible, a party from the city headed by the Prince of Hesse went to inspect the camp and check the mines which they knew would have been left. The Miquelets were adept at extinguishing fuses and managed to save a large part of the artillery stores which the French had hoped to destroy.[3]

The rumours reaching Barcelona about the movements of the Duchess of Anjou must have caused speculation about the position of the Allied army from Portugal. Galway and the Anglo-Portuguese army had begun their spring campaign by taking Alcántara close to the border with Portugal. They reached Almaraz by the way of Placentia on 4 May while the Duke of Berwick's army moved just ahead of them, steadily withdrawing in the path of their advance. They gave every appearance of making straight for Madrid.

At Almenara the slow but steady progress came to a halt. The Portuguese, nervous at the possibility of a French return from Barcelona, refused to proceed any further without definite news of the siege. On 10 May an express arrived from Peterborough saying that the siege still continued but that the passes to Aragon were all cut off so that the French army could not return that way. This was not sufficient reassurance for the Portuguese who received orders to remain near Placentia. Before the express arrived, Galway had agreed to besiege Ciudad Rodrigo in the meantime.[4]

At Barcelona, with the siege raised and the danger past, there was time to take stock. The Catalans freely admitted that they would have surrendered the next day had the King left them. That Barcelona did not fall could be attributed in part to the tenacity and bravery of the King himself. He had acted as a catalyst among the varied nationalities and personnel of the garrison. When the bombardment was at its worst, he had been constantly circulating, encouraging everyone – soldiers and civilians – in their tasks.

To those who had captured Barcelona the previous autumn, it appeared that incompetence in the command of the French army had contributed to the city's survival. It seemed inconceivable that the French could take seventeen days to capture Montjuich when the Allies had taken only four; the fortifications of the castle had been little improved in the interim, if at all. Given the formidable array of men and equipment brought to bear against the city, command of the siege appeared to have been dilatory and undecided.[5]

After the arrival of the fleet, the King's advisers began to complain that Peterborough should not have left Barcelona so poorly defended and with such a small garrison. Peterborough defended himself by blaming their poor organisation and their contradictory orders. The Catalans had expressed strong feelings regarding the late arrival of the relief and Peterborough had warned Leake that they might take their revenge on the garrison. Liechtenstein criticised the earl for concentrating on trying to get the King out of the city rather than getting the relief forces in. In the mountains there had been sharp words between the Allied officers and the Catalan leaders when the former had refused to agree to an attempt to get reinforcements into the city by land in the face of the whole French army. The Allied army had believed that Peterborough was in favour of such an attempt but all the English and Dutch officers except Colonel de St Pierre opposed it. They would have to rely on strong Miquelet support and this had not always proved dependable in the past. Peterborough then seemed reconciled to the idea that the only practicable way to put large numbers of reinforcements into the city was by sea, under cover of the fleet.

The Comte de Noyelles, a Velt-Marschal of the Empire, had arrived with the fleet and Count Uhlfeldt had been given the rank of Velt-Marschal by the King. It was with no little surprise and considerable pleasure that Peterborough received a intimation from the King that he was so satisfied with his services that he was giving him entire direction of military affairs, 'that no subject of his', Peterborough told Godolphin, 'should have any pretence by any commission not to obey my commands'. It was an unexpected gesture of appreciation. Stanhope felt and hoped that this would be the foundation of a 'perfect good understanding' between the King's officers and the Allied military command. All animosities seemed at least temporarily forgotten; even Liechtenstein recorded a period of friendship with Peterborough.[6]

Meanwhile the French army was proceeding steadily in the direction of Gerona. The garrison there had been much reduced in order to support Barcelona and only consisted of two Dutch regiments, very much below strength. However, it was now possible to release 500 men from Barcelona to augment it. At Valencia the army of the Conde de las

Torres was still in the vicinity, so two more regiments were detached to meet contingencies there.

With the French steadily distancing themselves and with garrisons supplied, it was now possible to contemplate the journey to Madrid. Both Peterborough and Stanhope urged the King to decide which route he wished to take. Peterborough, supported by Stanhope, had had no doubt for some time that the obvious way was by Valencia. This route had some real advantages: the foot soldiers could be transported there by the fleet, which would shorten their journey by a third of the way, the whole distance would be shorter by 200 miles and the only enemy force to be encountered would be Las Torres's army – to which they would be at least equal in number if the troops already in Valencia were included. Also the fleet could remain within reach. The kingdom of Valencia was considered the Promised Land in terms of mules and horses: they were plentiful there and vital to the transportation of an army and an artillery train. The Valencian campaign had taught a valuable lesson on the wear and tear of a march and the relative importance of the dragoon. On the other hand, the route to Madrid through Aragon was more direct. The French would have a long way round to march before they could catch up. The King, encouraged by Liechtenstein, was believed to favour this route, which was also likely to have the support of the Conde de Cifuentes who had interests and influence there.

Whatever the means of making the case for it, on 18 May a grand council of war took the decision to begin the campaign in Valencia. The foot would be transported by sea and the horse would travel overland to a rendezvous near the city of Valencia itself. Such a show of force might encourage Murcia to offer support. Provision was also made for the garrisons of Barcelona, Lérida, Tortosa and especially Gerona. At a further council of land and sea officers on 21 May, the fleet agreed to give its support, to transport the foot to be landed at Altea or Denia and then proceed to Alicante. The King agreed to leave on 8 June, with an escort of 400 horse, while Peterborough went ahead with the fleet.

Paul Methuen believed that Peterborough was longing to get back to Valencia where he had been well treated and where he enjoyed making 'the most considerable figure'. With poor diplomacy, the earl had revealed that he preferred the Valencians to the Catalans. Methuen himself, now on his way to Turin, had already been taken into Peterborough's confidence. 'My Lord's projects are for the most part too vast,' he wrote. 'His desire to do too much, and all things at once, often hinders the success of any. His thoughts are now not only employed in Spain, but his head also runs on settling affairs in Italy…'[7]

On 22 May 1706 the dragoons began their march to Valencia. The foot were to be embarked four days later but before this occurred it became known that the retreating French army had recently received reinforcements. As the purpose of this was not clear, the Allies agreed to send 1,000 Neapolitan troops to Gerona, together with 600 marines whom Peterborough considered too 'tatter'd and ragged' to go to Valencia. Southwell's (Rivers's) regiment was sent to Valencia instead of Lérida. Rather grudgingly, Peterborough was persuaded to hand over £5,000 for the improvement of the fortifications of Gerona; at least the money would be in the capable hands of Brigadier Stanhope, now in command of the garrison.

Before his own departure for Valencia, Peterborough was irritated by a letter from the King of 25 May asking straight questions about provisions for the army in both Barcelona and Valencia. Charles wished to know whether there would be bread for the Queen's troops in Barcelona and his own in Valencia, forage for his cavalry and carriage for the artillery train. Particularly he wanted to know how much money the Queen could advance for his own benefit, as all he received in Catalonia was being used for the maintenance of his troops.

Probably one of the persuasive arguments used by Peterborough to encourage the King towards Valencia was the availability of provisions there. However the King had heard that the country had been laid waste and he needed reassurance on that point. When Peterborough replied, he did so in the broadest terms. There was no need to worry about bread; the King's troops would be the last to go hungry but he had never been able to afford to make magazines in Valencia, as all forage had to be paid for where it could be found. He had tried all ways of raising money on bills without success but he had paid 5,000 pistoles to the receiver for the King's troops for their maintenance on campaign. He was in the process of raising money in Italy, which he hoped would arrive with some German cavalrymen who were now free to come to Spain. He had just signed the contract for the artillery mules. However he refrained from telling the King at this juncture that he foresaw that the provision of both carriage and bread was likely to be a problem.[8]

The supply of money was a continual difficulty and not one with which Peterborough coped very skilfully. He claimed that no one had ever explained to him just what proportion of the £250,000 voted by Parliament was supposed to be devoted to the King's own use. Stanhope eventually provided him with a rough answer. Once a deduction had been made of the expenses of the five regiments, as well as other sums for artillery, ordnance stores and other matters connected with the troops, a sum of £103,000 should remain. This sum was applicable to the King of Spain for his forces, household and incidental expenses. Peterborough asked Godolphin for further information to be given to him in writing as he was horrified by the complexity and responsibility of the task. 'To be charged with this', he wrote, 'is a post more troublesome and hazardous than the command of a Fleet and Army.'

Peterborough made no use of the information supplied by Stanhope when he replied to the King. It seemed to be his policy not to clarify the issue, even if he fully grasped it himself, so that the Court was dependent on him for money. He told Godolphin: 'In a manner we are forced to bribe and menace them into what is of use to the public.' Paul Methuen, for one, thought this a very unwise attitude to adopt. Peterborough gave the impression of holding plenty of funds (although this was not always so), and being unwilling to release them. This encouraged animosity from the Court, who were inclined to believe that he was keeping back funds intended for their use. The money brought to Valencia in March by the *Panther* was still there, as was Mr Mead the Paymaster. Some of that sum had been due for the King. On the other hand, £40,000 brought to Tarragona with Colonel Hamilton had been taken to Barcelona and all used on the expenses of the siege. Peterborough believed it unlikely that any receipts would ever be received for this money and it would be made an extraordinary charge.

The fleet sailed for Valencia on 29 May, transporting 3,000 foot with it. Peterborough was on board the *Somerset* which flew the Union flag. Before leaving, he took the opportunity to send home some letters; being badly bitten by mosquitoes, he was obliged to dictate to Mr Furly. One to Lord Halifax was written in a humorous vein, with the intention of being read out at the next Sunday dinner. The earl told his friend that he was returning to Valencia with impatience 'to try if I can find the way to Madrid during the consternation of the Ennemy, and from thence to London'.[9]

In such propitious circumstances there was a feeling of optimism in the army that the purpose of the expedition was soon to be accomplished. A Royal Dragoon recorded: 'We began to march up the country againe, with much more rejoycing than we did at the first, for both they and we thought we had no more to doe than just to crowne him [the King] and so to have done but we found it otherwise…'

While on the voyage it was decided to land the troops as near as possible to the city because of the continued enemy presence. As the fleet kept encountering calms, Peterborough left the *Somerset* for the *Panther* on 2 June to make better progress but then landed at Buriana the following day and made the rest of the way by land. The fleet anchored off the Grau of Valencia on 4 June and disembarkation began.

As given in the division of forces at 18 May, the total muster of troops at Valencia was intended to comprise 7,200 men. Peterborough believed his force consisted broadly of 2,000 horse and 5,000 foot. On 5 June a computation, regiment by regiment, raised a total of 6,436 foot. Another calculation, signed by Colonel Allnutt and giving dates of departure from Valencia for each regiment, gives a lower figure of 4,337 foot and 800 dragoons; out of that number 600 men were recorded as being in hospital. With the temperatures of the Spanish summer increasing daily, the new recruits in particular found the climate difficult and succumbed easily to sickness. By the middle of the month Peterborough could record that of the two English regiments that had arrived with the fleet, neither had been complete and now two-thirds of them were hospitalised. The three Irish regiments, Caulfield's, Dungannon's and Mohun's, were complete on arrival but half of them were now off sick. These three were now in Valencia together with Gorges's (formerly Donegal's), Mountjoy's, Allen's (formerly Gorges's), Southwell's and Allnutt's regiments, with a regiment of Guards completing the British foot. The horse consisted of the Royal Dragoons, Killigrew's and Pearce's Dragoons, to which were later added, in the course of their stay, Green's Dragoons. In addition a German regiment and Ahumada's regiment were present. Originally this force was to have included a further 1,000 horse and 2,000 foot but the King retained these in Barcelona after Peterborough had left.[10]

While the earl was at sea, the Court took advantage of his absence to send a courier overland to the Paymaster, Mr Mead, to apply for £10,000 of the money which they were sure was due to the King. The courier was unable to obtain more than £5,000, partly because of Peterborough's rapid arrival and also because the money was securely locked up in the castle of Denia.

On his arrival Peterborough discovered that Mead had been given a strict order regarding the disbursement of the funds in his hands. Out of the £250,000 for the maintenance of the forces, the money allotted by Parliament for the King's use was already written off as overpaid. Many of the expenses of the two sieges had been placed against it, as well as the £40,000 brought from Italy that spring and used in the defence of Barcelona. In theory therefore, Peterborough had neither money nor authority to pay the King of Spain's troops in Barcelona, a statement he reiterated in reply to all requests from the Court. In practice, he went to considerable lengths to raise money on bills, giving his own estate as security; there was no way in which he would let the men starve nor would he tolerate them robbing or plundering. He had also received a verbal assurance through Stanhope from the Lord Treasurer that if at any time he was obliged to draw bills for a particular service which offered a chance of success, those bills would be honoured.

It was a hard task to spell out to the King that the Allied ministers, in providing certain sums for his use, had not envisaged that this would be his sole means of support or that so little financial help would emerge from the country which the King had come to liberate. It was also suspected in some quarters in England that the King was being milked by his ministers or by other pleasures, reasons which did not encourage an increase in his maintenance from the public purse.[11]

By 11 June 1706 Brigadier Stanhope had returned to Barcelona in order to accompany the King and Court to Valencia. Far from finding them on the point of departure, he was amazed to discover that a project in Aragon was being planned and that there was a distinct possibility that the plans for Valencia might be altered as a result.

Although only a few thousand troops of the massive French army still remained in Spain, a strong detachment had re-entered Cerdagne, apparently en route for Aragon. In order to strengthen frontier posts, the King had sent the Count de Noyelles to Aragon on a fact-finding mission and two regiments of horse to Lérida to augment the garrison. Among this detachment were 400 horse under the command of Don Pedro Moras. This company had been ordered to escort the King to Valencia and had already begun their journey when they were recalled.

The King then wrote to Peterborough explaining that he had heard that he was held in much affection in Aragon and that Saragossa was on the point of submitting. He asked for the support of both men and money in the event of success. When Stanhope heard this, he reacted firmly. He told the King that Peterborough could not spare men for Aragon nor was it justifiable to withdraw from him troops which he had been promised in a council of war. After this plain speaking, the King backed down and agreed to leave for Valencia on 21 June, this time accompanied by Zinzendorf's regiment.

Peterborough replied to the King as Stanhope had predicted. To open another front of activity could only increase expense in terms of both men and money, and resources were already limited. He could not ask the men, some of whom were already on the sick list, to march through 'burning mountains' to Aragon. He was short of horse and using all endeavours to move things forward towards Madrid. He aimed to take Requena, a strong town guarding a pass on the direct route, where he hoped to make magazines. He had also sent a handful of troops to support the efforts of the fleet against Alicante. Peterborough was not in favour of disturbing the original dispositions and stressed the value of the fleet's support as it had supplies of corn. If the King required troops for Aragon, he could use some of those left in Barcelona and reduce some garrisons. The Allies must hasten towards Madrid by all means available. Unfortunately the earl's letter struck a despondent note at times and stressed the financial difficulties.[12]

The effort to find mules and horses, involving long hours in the searing heat, was clearly taking its toll of Peterborough's energy. As his officers later bore witness, it was a task which he did not depute. As soon as a regiment was mounted and its baggage transport arranged, it was sent on its way. The day after the earl's dispiriting letter to the King (14 June), three more regiments set out on the road to Requena.

On 14 June the King asked Peterborough for clarification about the orders concerning the payment of the troops. He wrote that he intended to leave within eight days and wished the earl to meet him so that they could march together. This prompted Peterborough to send Major-General Richards to the King to explain the accounts. Richards had already persuaded Peterborough to send him home in order to explain their financial situation to the government and attempt to persuade them to vote a greater supply for the campaign. He considered that 'the Establishment sent from home was Imperfect in Divers respects' and that Peterborough's methods only served to increase the muddle. Many bills drawn on the Treasury were not given to the Paymaster to disburse but put into the hands of private officers who felt uneasy at the responsibility. Richards was also dissatisfied with the amount of information that Peterborough was prepared to give him.

Peterborough wrote to the King on 17 June telling him that Richards was on his way and later told Hedges the same. He took longer than expected to prepare his accounts and meanwhile he sent a long letter to Godolphin explaining his expenses. Richards did not leave until 1 July, knowing that by then the King would have left Barcelona.[13]

On 19 June Peterborough's letter to the King was a little less cold and not so despairing. Although still contending with the lack of mules and money and with the increasing heat taking its toll of the unseasoned troops, he had now put half the army on the road and had created 'the finest regiment ever was seen' entirely accoutred except for horses. That day the artillery had left for Requena. The earl asked for the King's further orders in the case of Basset y Ramos whom he had been obliged to arrest for 'horrible proceedings'. News had come that the Duke and Duchess of Anjou had left Madrid, presumably on the approach of the Portuguese army, and Peterborough asked, reasonably, when the King thought of going there.

In the meantime Stanhope reported continuing efforts to encourage the King to set out for Valencia but he was aware of a 'mighty hankering after Aragon'. The King's next letter to Peterborough made no reference to Aragon or other sidetracks but announced his departure date as 23 June; he expected that the earl would have everything ready for his arrival. On 22 June Peterborough's letter to the King complained of increasing heat and difficulties with baggage. He was uncertain about the movements of the Portuguese army; if they had retired from Salamanca, this could leave the French army in a position to move towards Valencia. However Wyndham was now before Requena with four regiments. More cheerfully, he related that two galleys had been captured by the fleet near Cartagena. They carried 60,000 crowns for the garrison at Oran. The earl proposed to send them to Peñiscola from where the money could reach the King at Tortosa.[14]

As promised, the King set out from Barcelona on the afternoon of 23 June. Two days behind his original schedule, he apologised to Stanhope for the delay, explaining that it had been due to gathering his equipage. This was too much for the hard-pressed envoy. 'The Prince of Orange', he told the King, 'entered London in a coach and four, with a cloak-bag behind it.' The devout monarch and his court now felt they had to make a pilgrimage to Montserrat, 'though much out of their way'. Here the King left the jewelled sword given him by Queen Anne as a votive offering at the shrine of the Virgin.

The royal entourage had reached Villafranca by 29 June. The King held a council at which the majority of those present expressed themselves in favour of advancing by Aragon. This view was strenuously opposed by Stanhope and the Portuguese ambassador. Because of their representations, a final decision was postponed until they reached Tarragona. In the meantime it was hoped that positive news of the

Portuguese army might arrive. The reasons which the King and his advisers were prepared to reveal to Stanhope for preferring the Aragon route concerned the difficulties which Peterborough had indicated over the readiness of the troops and the lack of carriage and forage for the army. They adhered to this opinion despite the news that the Duke of Anjou had left Madrid and that Peterborough already had four regiments at Requena.

'If I understand them right,' Stanhope wrote to the earl, 'they do not desire you should carry them to Madrid, and stick not to say they would be very glad you were as fond of going to Italy now as you have been heretofore.' He thought an encouraging letter from Peterborough might help. De Noyelles was already at Lérida; Don Pedro Moras had taken Barbastro and was on his way to Huesca.

The King wrote to Peterborough the same day. He made no reference at all to Aragon. He acknowledged five of the earl's letters, one of the 24th being the latest date. This last letter is untraced; a letter to Stanhope from Peterborough of the same date contained definite news of the Portuguese army at Salamanca with every indication of their advance towards Madrid. Also the earl believed that Cartagena had been taken by the fleet. The King did not include acknowledgement of Peterborough's letter of 19 June but in fact he answered the request in it for instructions regarding the arrested Basset, ordering that he should be sent for trial to Tortosa.*

At Tarragona on 1 July the Court heard that Saragossa had declared for the King. This proved the decisive factor. The King called a council at once and the decision was taken to leave for Saragossa the next day. The suggestion that a visit there would necessarily delay their arrival at Madrid was ignored, as was any idea that this route could expose them to the attack of enemy cavalry. Madrid now appeared to be without a government; the Duchess of Anjou had left the city and it was believed that the Duke would shortly follow her.

On 2 July the King informed Peterborough of his decision and that the greater part of Aragon was now in his hands. He hoped that a gift of money would be forthcoming from the grateful people of that region and believed that they would be able to support both his Court and his troops, unlike the kingdom of Valencia. He asked Peterborough to send troops towards Saragossa and to divert the regiments destined for

*The letter of 19 June was dated 30 June in Gallas's Memorial. This curious point was used later by Peterborough to prove that his letters had been misquoted in the Memorial.[15]

Alicante to Requena. Supplies and equipment for the troops should be sent to Tortosa. His letter seemed to reflect a belief in the imminent arrival of the fleet under Shovell bringing reinforcements.

Writing again the following day, the King gave his ideas for the disposal of the expected reinforcements. He was confident that the Portuguese army at Madrid would be able to protect him on his journey there. Consequently he now felt able to assist the Duke of Savoy by sending him a detachment of troops on board the fleet. The reinforcements would be better used in Spain but the troops at Alicante and Cartagena might go to Savoy. Should troops be no longer needed there, they should be used for the subjection of Mallorca and Menorca.

The Court proceeded on its way towards Lérida and at Reus met with Major-General Richards. The King seemed surprised at Richards's journey to England, of which he disclaimed all knowledge, and asked him to remain with them a few days while he prepared some letters. Richards was equally surprised at the King's decision to go to Saragossa, a route which he thought would take forty or fifty days longer and would increase the journey by 200 miles. He thought the King deaf to all reason and very obstinate.

The Court was afraid that the true reason for Richards's journey home was to defend Peterborough's conduct. Eventually Count Gallas was sent to Queen Anne with a memorial explaining the King's actions. The Court seemed to feel that their conduct might well be questioned by the Allied governments. They behaved coldly towards Richards, believing he would be censorious about them in England. Richards had no intention of trying to justify Peterborough who did not appear to think that his conduct required it. His only wish was to see the establishment in Spain put on a more reasonable footing.

At Las Borjas de Urgel on 7 July the King wrote to Peterborough again with more explanations of why he had chosen his present route. The earl had informed him that in Valencia he was unable to provide him with financial assistance, there were no mules for the baggage, the infantry were in a poor state and there was no provision for the journey. The people of Aragon, on the other hand, were making such overtures of loyalty and fidelity that he felt obliged to go to Saragossa on his way to Madrid. He acknowledged receipt of a letter from Peterborough written only two days earlier in which he had been given news of the surrender of Cartagena and the capitulation of Requena. He had also been told that Peterborough had enabled the troops to set out by raising money on his own credit and that some of his cavalry were as far advanced on the road to Madrid as Alarcón; deserters were passing along the road three or four at a time and the King could ride to his capital 'comme dans une profonde paix'. Charles's wry comment in response was to ask why Peterborough had therefore no news from Galway by this easy road.[16]

Despite this encouraging news, the King's mind was already made up: he was going to Madrid a different way and he was going without Peterborough. He politely suggested to the earl that, since the journey from Valencia to Saragossa was long and difficult, it would be more valuable for him to remain at Valencia to receive the fleet and also organise reinforcements for Savoy and an expedition against the islands.

The King's official reasons for his decision cited Peterborough's inability to give support to both himself and his troops, the condition of the Allied forces and the new-found loyalty of the Aragonese. There were other reasons which affected his views and these emanated largely from his courtiers. The Austrians encouraged and played on the King's antipathy to Peterborough for their own ends. They were short of funds and they believed that money could be found in Aragon. A new source of income would make the King financially independent of Peterborough. Also among the Court there seemed to be a disinclination to go to Madrid at all, as if once there they might lose their influence or positions. At a later date Galway was clearly aware that De Noyelles, as a Velt Marschal, harboured a professional jealousy towards Peterborough and found it irksome to accept the King's appointment of the English general as commander-in-chief.[17]

Twenty-two

On 6 July 1706, the day after Peterborough had written his encouraging letter to the King, the first express from Galway reached Valencia. The courier carried no letters for Peterborough, only for the King, but he was able to report that a previous express had been stopped at Campillo and his letters sent to the Duke of Anjou. The earlier despatches had been for both the King and Peterborough and were said to ask that the King should proceed as soon as possible from Valencia to Madrid as the generals waiting there did not want to enter the city without him.

The Earl of Galway, the Marqués das Minas and the Allied army had left Ciudad Rodrigo on 3 June and reached Salamanca three days later. The Duke of Berwick's army continued to withdraw in front of them. Berwick had recalled the Conde de las Torres from Valencia. On 12 June the Allies' march took them from Salamanca towards Peñaranda in a clear line for Madrid, whereupon Berwick took up defensive positions, retiring his infantry towards Burgos. By 18 June Galway had reached Espinal. From here he despatched a messenger to the King at Barcelona with a verbal message only – a letter might be intercepted, the journey could be hazardous. Galway did not know of the King's intention to travel by Valencia. The messenger reached the Court at Tarragona on 2 July.

Galway received news from Madrid on 21 June that the Duke of Anjou had left the city and that King Charles was on his way there from Requena. It was this report that must have prompted the despatch of the letters with the messenger who fell into the hands of the enemy at Campillo. Galway pressed on towards Madrid, passing by Guadarrama to Las Rosas which he reached on 24 June. Here he received deputies sent out by the nervous city of Madrid. He also received letters dated 29 May telling him that the King was at Barcelona while Peterborough had set out for Valencia. In the belief and hope that the King's army could not now be far away, the Allied army set up camp outside Madrid. Galway, who was exhausted having lost an arm and then coped with serious illness, settled down to wait for Peterborough who he hoped might be given the command of the British troops after the armies came together. To him, it appeared that the country between Madrid and Valencia now lay open. At this crucial time the King had only just set out from Barcelona.[1]

The news that the Allied army from Portugal had reached Madrid was known in Valencia on 29 June and the following day a Te Deum was sung in celebration. On 7 July Peterborough passed on by letter to the admirals the news of the King's decision to travel by Aragon. He also called a council of war for advice on the next step to be taken. He and his senior officers were joined by the Viceroy of Valencia, the Conde de Cardona, the Conde d'Elda, recently arrived from Madrid, and the Conde de Zavillar, newly appointed Viceroy of Mallorca and Menorca. The council reached the unanimous decision that Peterborough should leave as soon as possible with all available troops and march to Madrid to join the army from Portugal. The King should be urged to take a safer and more direct route, possibly by way of Teruel and the northern parts of Valencia, to join the forces at Requena. In reaching this resolution, the council bore in mind Peterborough's duty to attend the King on his journey to Madrid, Queen Anne's expressed wish that troops should be sent as soon as possible to assist the Duke of Savoy, and the possibility that forces now said to be gathering in Andalucia and Murcia might threaten Valencia from that side.

With the council concluded, it was decided to send Colonel Pepper as a special emissary to try out his powers of persuasion on the King. There was a fear, later justified, that unless the King changed his route the army from Portugal would be obliged to move from Madrid in order to cover his approach. Also there were rumours of discontent in the army from Portugal; Madrid had been reached and the King proclaimed but of him and the other army there was not a sign. To add to his comfort and consequence, Pepper was lent Peterborough's coach to carry him the first thirty miles of his journey.[2]

On 8 July Captain Vernon arrived from England with letters and Peterborough's commission as Ambassador Extraordinary to the King of Spain. Peterborough hoped that his appointment as the Queen's representative would oblige the King to consult him, and that it would 'reduce our German Ministers to some bounds'. He was to work with Stanhope to obtain favourable terms from the King for English merchants. The position of an ambassador in the eighteenth century was one of immense prestige and he was expected to maintain a high standard of living. Also on the way to Spain were a new and splendid coach and a service of silver said to weigh 10,000 oz.

Peterborough had also received some money of his own and credit; he decided, as a last resort, to send all the money to the King. The very same day Stanhope was writing to the earl about his suggestion of 'coming post' to see if he could change the King's mind. 'Nothing you can say', Stanhope wrote, 'will signify anything unless you should bring 10,000 pistoles in your cloak-bag.'[3]

Peterborough's prime concern was to get troops to Madrid, but he had to keep in mind other factors which did not make his task any easier. These factors were the number of troops needed to support the fleet at Alicante and along the coast, the expectation of the arrival of the Grand Fleet with Sir Cloudesley Shovell and also the repeated orders to send troops to assist the Duke of Savoy.

All the same, he has been criticised for failing to keep his forces consolidated for the march to Madrid and dispersing them instead to smaller towns. It was justifiable to attack Requena which, in the wrong hands, could impede the road to Madrid. Diversions to Alicante and Cartagena, on the other hand, were not part of the original strategy.

The Grand Council of War held at Barcelona on 21 May had ruled that the fleet would disembark forces at Valencia and then proceed to Alicante. On 8 June this decision was confirmed at Valencia and Brigadier Gorges's regiment left for Alicante in support. Troops dispersed to this part of the coast could easily be embarked for service elsewhere. Soon after the fleet reached Valencia, news came that the enemy troops had withdrawn from the area between Valencia and Alicante. Peterborough believed that a show of force at this stage might cause Alicante to surrender, particularly when it became known that the King was actually on the road to Madrid.

The fleet, consisting of fifty ships, sailed for Alicante on 12 June but soon learnt that the town was likely to put up a resistance. On the other hand, some usually reliable sources reported that Cartagena was ready to declare for King Charles and also that in the port there were two French galleys already loaded with men and money for the garrison of Oran on the North African coast. The fleet therefore decided to change course for Cartagena and return to Alicante later. Two ships encountered next day off Cape Palos proved to be the galleys in question who surrendered immediately. They were found to be carrying the sum of 60,000 crowns. Peterborough's reaction to this windfall was to order that the money should be transported to Tortosa and landed up river for the King. Also the galleys might even be used to secure Peñiscola before it could be known that they had left the French side. He noted that the fleet had not consulted him first before going to Cartagena and thought this rather odd. Because of this diversion, he ordered Gorges's troops to place themselves at Orihuela and Elche, within reasonable reach of Alicante.[4]

The fleet ordered Cartagena's surrender on 23 June and the town complied within a few hours. Four men of war were sent into the harbour and a garrison of 400 marines was put into the town. After a week the fleet sailed to Altea for water, leaving a small squadron under the command of Sir John Jennings. The sailors were by now much affected by sickness. At Altea the fleet heard that the troops sent by Peterborough were approaching Alicante and so proceeded there, arriving on 7 July.

Sir John Leake's demand for Alicante's surrender received such a strong response from Major-General O'Mahony that it became obvious that a formal siege would be necessary, so it was decided to take no further action until the troops came up. It was two weeks before Brigadier Gorges at last appeared with his somewhat reduced force and some militia on whom he placed little reliance; and only when Allnutt's regiment was diverted to Alicante on 28 July could Gorges take the decision to commence a siege. Jennings and the marines from Cartagena were also summoned to lend their assistance. The bombardment of Alicante commenced on 2 August. Two days later the Allied troops gained control of the suburbs. Batteries were then opened up on the town and a breach was made. On 8 August the seamen stormed the breach and opened the town gates to the troops. Meanwhile the garrison withdrew into the castle, an immensely strong fortification which held out until 4 September.[5]

All troop operations in Valencia and Murcia in the summer of 1706 were carried out in the confident expectation that reinforcements would be arriving on board the fleet with Sir Cloudesley Shovell. When these arrived, it would then be easier to take a decision on the feasibility of sending assistance to the Duke of Savoy. The reappearance of the fleet was confidently expected that summer by the King, Peterborough, Stanhope and Leake; it was by no means the figment of one man's imagination. In early June Leake detached three ships to cruise off Cap Martin to watch for it. His anxiety for its arrival was increased by the difficulties which he could see arising between himself and the commander-in-chief.

At the end of June Peterborough learnt that the Dutch squadron had left Holland on 1 May, seemingly a confirmation of their expectations. However, on 7 July Admiral Wassenaar received notice that Shovell's fleet was to be employed in the Bay of Biscay and so would not be with them. A week later similar information reached Peterborough through private sources but with no reliable news about troops. This prompted the earl to mention in a letter to Hedges that, before leaving the coast, he would have liked some certain news of the squadron under Sir Cloudesley Shovell carrying the troops expected by the King. Recent letters from home had made no mention of it at all. Home sources were aware of their expectations, they had been referred to frequently in letters, but found them a mystery. It seems strange that no official attempt had been made to clarify the position.[6]

Throughout the summer Peterborough had received repeated instructions from the Court at St James to send assistance to the Duke of Savoy. His personal inclination to carry these out has never been in doubt but he has been criticised for keeping the Duke's situation constantly in mind as if this had never been part of his instructions.

In the spring of 1706 the Duke of Savoy found himself in a difficult position. Turin itself was under threat from a French army of 45,000 men under the command of the Duc de la Feuillade. It had not been possible to obtain the assistance of Prince Eugène who was facing an equally strong force under Vendôme in the plains of Lombardy. By the end of May La Feuillade had laid formal siege to the city of Turin. The lines of circumvallation were not completed till the end of June and even then a weak part was left. By this time the Duke of Savoy had left the city with around 6,000 cavalry; he then proceeded to dodge capture and harass the French supply lines for the next two months. The Duke's representative in London made repeated pleas for help as each fresh crisis developed, with the result that further instructions were issued to Peterborough and Leake to send assistance if possible.

When the first two sets of instructions were received at Valencia on 7 June, the later set was already seven weeks old. The instructions were that, if at all possible and after the arrival of the fleet under Sir John Leake, three or more regiments should be transported to Savoy. Whether or not the state of affairs would permit of this was left to the judgement of the King and Peterborough. The fleet expressed itself willing to perform the duties of transport and convoy. Peterborough correctly forwarded the instructions for the King's opinion, an action which Leake's biographer interpreted as procrastination and indecision.

The King's reaction to the request showed his reluctance to part with any troops at this juncture; the small number he could afford he felt would be of little assistance to the Duke. Stanhope believed that these instructions had been sent under the presumption that Barcelona had been lost. Peterborough showed surprise that the Queen had asked for the King's judgement in the matter, being sure that it would be impossible to squeeze out of the Court either 'a man or shilling'.[7]

As the siege closed in around Turin, the Duke of Savoy sent appeals for help directly to Peterborough and with increasing frequency. The earl was anxious to respond but felt restricted by his instructions and without sufficient powers to make the decision himself. Left to himself, he might have despatched troops at an early stage despite the necessities of Spain; he believed that a crushing defeat of the Duke's forces in Piedmont would release French troops there for use in Spain. If the Austrian cause was to succeed in Spain, it was vital that the Duke of Savoy should survive. In truth, as Godolphin had foreseen, the Allied forces in Spain were insufficient to make any detachment feasible at this point. The only chance available could be the arrival of fresh troops aboard the fleet. The matter was shelved until such an event should take place.

On 12/23 June, taking into consideration the advance of the army from Portugal towards Madrid, instructions were sent from England for the despatch of five regiments to Savoy. These instructions were overtaken on their journey to Spain by another set, dated 19/30 June, which only asked for three or more regiments. They were accompanied by a letter from Hedges which conveyed a message to Peterborough from the Duke of Savoy. 'His Royal Highness is so sensible of your Excellency's courage and conduct, and the success that still accompanys [sic] your Person wherever you go, whereby you have more than once restored our affaires when under intricate Difficulties, that he has desired you might yourself bring the succours to him, to which Her Majesty has given her consent, but leaves it wholly to your Excellency to go thither or not, as you shall judge it most suitable to Her Majesty's service and your own conveniency.' These instructions reached the fleet on 21 July/1 August. Peterborough was by then on his way to Madrid. He received them eventually at Guadalajara at a most opportune moment and greatly to his convenience.[8]

As the King and his Court reached Saragossa on 15 July, Galway, Das Minas and the Portuguese army were setting up camp at Guadalajara. Having been obliged to leave Madrid because of lack of provisions, they had moved to Alcalá on 11 July and then further north west.

Meanwhile Berwick's army moved ahead of them across the Henares to Atienza. With the armies disposed in this fashion, Galway sent his Quartermaster General, Du Bourgay, to the King urging him to make haste. He had heard a report, which later proved false, that the siege of Turin had been raised and he was anxious that the Allied armies should have joined forces before any more French troops could be released for the Spanish service. Galway also feared desertions from his ranks, as the Portuguese increasingly chafed at the non-appearance of the King. In addition, some of the towns behind them which had declared for King Charles had now reverted to Anjou and were cutting off their lines of supply from Portugal.

Colonel Pepper, Peterborough's emissary, reached the King at Saragossa. His arguments met with some success. On 17 July it was decided to abandon the direct road to Madrid because of the presence of the enemy at Jadraque and the small size of the King's escort. Instead it was proposed to travel through the north part of Valencia by Teruel, where it would be possible for Peterborough to join them with some of his troops. On 19 July Stanhope wrote to Peterborough telling him that the King now wished him to come to Teruel by way of Cuenca, bringing as much strength as he could muster.

However, on 20 July Du Bourgay arrived from Galway and again there was a change of plan. The northern Valencian itinerary was scrapped and a rapid route by Daroca and Molina, to be covered by the Portuguese army, was put in its place. The King planned to leave on 24 July. It was now known that the French army, said to number 9,000 men, was being reinforced daily. The King therefore sent directions to Peterborough to march straight to Guadalajara with no diversions, taking all the cavalry and as much of the foot as possible. Peterborough had received early news of the French reinforcements and this had been one of his reasons for urging the King to take a safer route. The forces now reaching the Duke of Anjou were those which had been used in the siege of Barcelona. Galway believed that the increase indicated that the French were preparing for a battle. Before the King left Saragossa, it was known there that Peterborough was leaving Valencia with 3,000 foot and 1,300 horse and aiming for the upper Tagus.[9]

At Requena General Wyndham was engaged in forwarding regiments on the road to Madrid with as much despatch as a chronic shortage of mules would allow. He also had on his hands the responsibility of two sickly foot regiments. At Mira the regiments of Don Pedro Moras and Ahumada halted and requested an escort of dragoons for the approach to the town of Campillo which Peterborough had warned was in a very disaffected area. It was essential to secure a crossing of the River Cabriel here for the passage of the troops. Shortly afterwards the Royal Dragoons with Colonel de St Pierre and the regiment of Guards followed them.

The last of the regiments of foot (Southwell's) to leave Valencia for Requena set out on 24 July, as well as fifty large wagons to transport stores and equipment for Wyndham. Two days later Killigrew's and Green's dragoons started their journey. At night, in order to avoid the excessive heat, Peterborough himself left the city with his usual escort. The next evening he was followed by the Colonel's troop of Green's dragoons escorting his secretary, Arent Furly, with the earl's papers and some money.*

The departure of the commander-in-chief was noted in Valencia. A week previously a banquet had been held in the convent of Santo Domingo in his honour and that of other dignitaries. Peterborough's musicians had played for the pleasure of the guests. Undoubtedly Valencia had an elegance and style which would not be found on the journey to Madrid.

Could Peterborough have left sooner? He was later accused of enjoying himself in Valencia instead of moving on to join Galway as quickly as possible. Five of his officers, including Captain Duhamel who had been an ADC to Liechtenstein, gave evidence later that in their opinion Peterborough could not have put the army in a condition to march any earlier. They also claimed that he had been indefatigable in his efforts, particularly in the matter of the acquisition of mules, and had undertaken duties 'below the character of a general'. Valencia in the heat and dust of high summer gave Peterborough and others unpleasant eye infections; 'poor Codrington', he told Stanhope, 'is quite blind.' The attentions of mosquitoes were an added inconvenience.

However Peterborough admitted to Stanhope, in a letter written around the time of his departure, that he had been deliberately secretive about his intentions. Not even Stanhope was informed of the decision of the council of war which empowered Peterborough to march to Madrid despite previous instructions. This deception was to prevent the issue of contrary orders from the Court. Piqued to have been told that

*Peterborough had formed Green's dragoons himself. The regiment consisted of 400 men. The earl claimed to have mounted and armed them in five days. The officers were removed from other regiments including the Royal Dragoons, to St Pierre's annoyance. St Pierre to Lord Raby 16 June, BL Add. MSS 31,134 f. 321.

he and his troops were not wanted at Madrid, that the splendid Portuguese army would carry everything and that he might take himself to Savoy or the islands or anywhere, Peterborough was determined to hide his intentions, having already foreseen the situation in which the King and Court would find themselves. His instructions prevented him from making straight towards Galway after the council of war. He kept the troops in a position not too far advanced so as to make it impossible for them to go to Savoy but also near enough to be called upon to assist the King's progress, as they now were.

Keeping forces in readiness for possible use in Italy made them also useless in Spain. Stanhope repeatedly tried to impress this fact on the Court. Shortly before Du Bourgay's arrival with an exact account of the army with Galway, Stanhope and the Portuguese ambassador had narrowly averted clear instructions being sent to Peterborough to ship six regiments immediately for Italy. One fact was unknown to both the King and Peterborough: Galway's army was numerically much smaller than they had anticipated.

The King's orders of 20 July had reached Peterborough before he left Valencia. Before setting out, the general despatched his aide-de-camp, Lieutenant de Roman, to Teruel with 5,000 pistoles for the King, 1,000 for the Portuguese ambassador and 200 each for three Valencian noblemen who had come over to King Charles and might be unprovided for. Peterborough directed his march in the first instance towards Cuenca, so as to be in a position to divert towards Teruel in the event of the absence of the Portuguese army.[10]

Peterborough left for Madrid not only as commander-in-chief but also as Her Majesty's Ambassador to the King of Spain. He was followed by a sizeable baggage train of sixteen wagons carrying his ambassadorial equipage, his plate and also his credentials. He made sharp progress once on the road. Travelling with two regiments of dragoons, he reached Parilla on 1 August at the same time as the regiments of Ahumada and Kolbatz whom he had caught up with on the way. Some of Killigrew's dragoons were badly affected by the heat and remained with Wyndham at Requena. Mr Furly's escort, which left Valencia a day behind the earl, made cautious progress in hostile country, stopping at Requena and then waiting at Campillo for Wyndham and his three battalions of foot.

Peterborough found the country very disaffected. Many bridges had been deliberately destroyed. Large numbers of country people were under arms and prepared to prevent the crossing of the Júcar. Due to the drought, it proved possible to use other crossing points. The country people also sent word to the French army about the considerable baggage train following Peterborough. On 4 August the Duke of Berwick sent a party of 150 horse to intercept it. At Huete on 8 August, soon after Mr Furly and his escort had left the village, the French party captured the baggage which had been left with a guard of 150 foot and 40 dragoons. The French killed seventy men and took the rest prisoner, removing also two pieces of artillery. Peterborough had provided a suitable escort for the baggage and had given directions for a safe road. However orders from the Court to the Spanish major-general in charge of the escort caused them to take a shorter way through the mountains and then abandon the train only six leagues from the camp. The earl claimed later that he had been left with only two horses and two shirts.

Meanwhile, pressing on with only fifty dragoons, Peterborough had reached the King on 5 August. The following day the greater part of two regiments of dragoons arrived and the combined forces joined Galway and the Portuguese army at Guadalajara.[11]

On 28 July the Duke of Berwick had received the last of the reinforcements of troops which had been at Barcelona. Having no knowledge at all of this addition to the enemy force, Galway had proceeded the following day in the direction of Jadraque, with the intention of protecting the King's advance from Saragossa. The Portuguese army encountered what proved to be the rearguard of the French army under the Count de Fiennes. They attacked a bridge over the Henares and were driven back. On 30 July, at Villanueva, the King and Court could hear the sounds of an engagement. Both armies were surprised by the encounter and neither took full advantage of the situation. Deserters gave Galway a true picture of the size of the French army which at first he found unbelievable. As the truth made itself felt, the only action feasible was to hastily decamp by night. The Anglo-Portuguese army withdrew towards Guadalajara, putting the River Henares between themselves and the enemy. With his large force the Duke of Berwick now advanced to Espinosa and Marchamalo. From here he retook Alcalá and sent 800 horse to Madrid where they received an immediate welcome.

When the King and Peterborough reached Guadalajara on 6 August, the army had placed itself in a defensive position on higher ground with the river giving protection in front. Unfortunately, on their advance they had failed to provide an effective rearguard and had consequently lost some provisions and their bread ovens which had been left at

Alcalá. After these events it is hardly surprising that Galway took a poor view of the one and a half regiments of dragoons which were Peterborough's initial contribution to the force. Two days later the two foot regiments arrived, having been delayed by taking the route through the mountains, and also two squadrons of Royal Dragoons and one of Pearce's.[12]

At this point it was calculated that the French army numbered 14–15,000 foot and 6–7,000 horse. With the addition of the forces now coming up with Wyndham, the Allied army expected to match their opponents in foot but would have 1,000 fewer horse. Until this amalgamation was made, the difference between the two armies was not only numerical: the French were well victualled and could obtain forage whereas the Allied army was on low rations, had great difficulty in acquiring supplies, and was consequently in an untenable and vulnerable position. There was a sentiment among the Allied soldiers that death in battle might be preferable to death from hunger, and on this basis they were prepared to fight. Galway was inclined to put the matter to the test but the position which the army had taken up was ruled out as it gave an equal advantage to the enemy.

In a council of war Peterborough stated that he was not in favour of taking the offensive. He was supported in this by a Dutch general who reasoned that 'we had better keep half that we are sure of than hazard losing the whole'. The earl expressed his deep concern for the starving army. Having 6,500 pistoles in his baggage (in the custody of Furly), he offered to spend these on bread and provisions for the army by purchase from local people, provided that orders were given that there was to be no plunder.* His offer was accepted, but a few hours later he received a request through Stanhope from the King's Secretary of State, Zinzerling, that the money might be given to the King 'for services of the last necessity'. Peterborough wrote later: 'I only answered that bread I thought the main point to a starving army.' He said that the King might have the money if he wished but that there was no way that he would agree to the use of plunder instead of trying by a little fair usage to gain some respect and goodwill from this ill-treated country.

Peterborough also turned his mind to the improvement of the army's strategic position. With the use of 3,000 foot and 2,000 horse, he

---

*In the forces under Peterborough's command, plunder was not allowed; the Duke of Marlborough had always maintained this policy. However in the army from Portugal there was no such rule; Mr Furly had already noted with distaste the effects of plunder in the surrounding countryside while on his journey to the camp.

offered to attempt to gain a pass on the river near Alcalá. Here would be a better position for the camp and also it might be possible to cover Madrid and separate it from the enemy. Initially this suggestion was greeted with approval but when Peterborough approached the council to make definite plans, a decision was postponed. Two days later he was told that they simply did not have a day's bread to give him for such an expedition.[13]

Into this atmosphere of frustration and disappointment came a messenger sent by Admiral Leake carrying the Queen's instructions to Peterborough, which had arrived on 1 August. Leake had also received Peterborough's commission as Joint Admiral of the Fleet. These instructions, that at least three regiments be sent to assist the Duke of Savoy who had asked that Peterborough might accompany them, together with the Queen's gracious permission to go if he wished, must have appeared to the earl as a beam of light showing a way of escape. In Italy, among other things, Peterborough could acquire troops and raise money to assist the cause in Spain.

At a council of war on 9 August it did not take much discussion to approve Peterborough's orders from the Queen. It was only necessary to ensure that he would leave sufficient ships to protect the Andalucian coast in his absence. It was hoped that he might be able to take Mallorca and Menorca on his return, so that the fleet could winter at Port Mahon.

Peterborough now made immediate plans to return to the fleet. 'I thought there were Generalls enough in that army,* and found a management that made me conclude I could doe little service there... The King not only consents but himself approves, and the Councell of War, but I doubt not there are those who will find out I was willing to leave an Army where I could not have the absolute command, and willing for that reason to remove troops from Spain where they were so apparently necessary.'

In the atmosphere of disappointment, many people expressed views on what had gone wrong. An officer in Galway's army thought one reason was Peterborough's failure to appear a month before, which he thought he could have done, and now he was returning 'à son cher Valence'. Peterborough thought that Galway's army should have pushed on, instead of waiting at Madrid, and forced the French over the Ebro. On the opposing side, Berwick himself agreed with Peterborough.

---

*He calculated that there were forty people who could claim that rank.

It would have been impossible for his army to have regained the lost ground before his reinforcements came up; the Allied armies could have made their junction unmolested and gained the upper hand.

Peterborough's own officers thought that he was leaving Guadalajara a disappointed man. In Colonel Pepper's view, 'percieving the bent of the stream ran against him, he parted with the King and Lord Galway dissatisfy'd.' Pepper was ordered to accompany the earl and failed in an attempt to evade the responsibility. St Pierre thought that Peterborough had been thwarted of the supreme command and had gone away 'in a distaste'.[14]

While the Allied armies were approaching Madrid, the absolute command had been a problem pondered by many minds. Galway had no doubts. He had striven nobly to keep the Portuguese army pointing forwards and he had built up a successful working relationship with the Marqués das Minas. In his view Peterborough was now the man for the job. On that basis Galway offered him his command on his arrival at Guadalajara. However, the Marqués das Minas was not prepared to make the same offer and, as in practice Galway had deferred to Das Minas as the commander of the larger part of the combined force, Peterborough declined.

While at Saragossa the King had foreseen problems with the command and indicated to Godolphin that he intended to terminate the commission he had given Peterborough to avoid causing difficulties with Das Minas; Peterborough's commission gave him a very just claim to be considered overall commander but there had been too many problems. Although the King wished to honour the Queen's appointment, he hoped that she might choose someone else, if it was indeed necessary to have an envoy in addition to Stanhope. It had been hoped that the ambassadorial status given to Peterborough would solve many problems; it seemed only to be about to aggravate them.

At home in England, the government were in no doubt that Galway held a senior commission to that of Peterborough. Some advice on the matter was despatched on 23 July/3 August, rather too late to be of any practical value. The Queen wished to make it clear that the order of precedence given by her commissions could not be altered by a commission given by another sovereign. It transpired much later that Peterborough himself believed that he did hold a senior commission to Galway, namely that given for the Jamaican expedition. This had cost him dear and apparently he thought it was still valid.

Whether Peterborough really wanted the overall command is not entirely clear. It was generally presumed that he did and that therefore he would be offended if not offered it. He was very critical of the actions of the Portuguese army and the conduct of their campaign. He felt that he had been ignored by Galway who had failed to communicate with him, a breach of manners which could not be excused entirely by the presumption that Peterborough would be with the King.* Before he reached Guadalajara, Peterborough told Stanhope: 'There is nothing that I apprehend more than a little army with many generals...I am sure I will be commanded by nobody, and have as little mind to command...' It is possible that he had more reliance than he was prepared to admit on the possibility that Das Minas would also have had enough and be anxious to return home, an option now no longer open to the Portuguese. However Peterborough had never lost interest in going to Savoy; at one time he had hoped to go on there after taking the King to Madrid. He had never entirely lost sight of the possibility of using the fleet against Cadiz. But with all the setbacks and problems, somehow the life had gone out of the expedition.[15]

*The first messenger who had been stopped on the road to Valencia was said to be carrying letters for Peterborough.

Twenty-three

With a commission to raise a loan of 100,000 pistoles at Genoa and carrying bills from both the Portuguese Ambassador and Das Minas, Peterborough took his formal leave of the King on 10 August, only four days after the armies had joined. Escorted by a slender guard of scarcely sixty of Killigrew's dragoons, he arrived the following evening at Pastrana where he learnt for the first time of the loss of his baggage and artillery at Huete. Anxious that enemy forces should not hear of his departure, he travelled on all night to Almonacid where the party rested until the following afternoon. He then moved on to Garcinara where he found that the Alcaide had imprisoned a messenger who had been sent ahead. In retaliation, Peterborough ordered the Alcaide's house to be set on fire. It turned out that all the supporters of Anjou had left the town; only the well-disposed were still in residence.

Once again the party marched in the cool of the night, reaching Huete at 3 am. News of their movements had preceded them and there was not a soul to be seen; everyone was concealed, expecting retribution. Peterborough arrested some of the leading citizens who offered to pay him 10,000 pistoles in compensation for the plunder of his baggage if he would spare their town and the neighbouring area from destruction. He declined the offer of money but instead ordered them to bring the same value in corn and provisions for the army.

On Peterborough's part, this was a generous gesture at a time of considerable need. He was not what would then have been regarded as a wealthy man and had made a considerable personal investment in the Spanish expedition. He calculated that the loss of his baggage cost him £6,000. Of the sixteen wagons, eight had contained 'good eatables and drink'. Both Galway and Stanhope had a share in this loss, as Peterborough had intended that the supplies should be partly for their enjoyment. His ADC, Lieutenant de Roman, having rejoined the convoy, had also been taken prisoner. In addition the Duke of Berwick had acquired Peterborough's papers and correspondence which he later courteously returned.[1]

In the meantime General Wyndham and his troops had successfully captured and garrisoned Cuenca, a place of natural defensive strength, and were now on their way northwards. Peterborough was very much aware that it was by no means impossible for the country to rise against the Allies and cut off their retreat, as had happened behind the Portuguese advance. If the army was to act defensively even for a short time, it was crucial that communications with Valencia be maintained. His departure from Guadalajara was in that respect fortuitous as, by acting strongly in disaffected areas, he ensured that the way back remained open. Leaving Huete on the evening of his arrival, he made another night march, to Villar del Horno, 'to hasten Wyndham', who arrived the next morning.

On the day Peterborough left the camp, it had been decided to move the Allied army nearer to Madrid. They marched on 11 August, taking up a position three days later behind the Tajuna at Chinchón. The French army had followed on the other side of the Jarama and now faced them between Ciempozuelos and Aranjuez. Peterborough, in the capacity of 'a poor volunteer', advised Wyndham now to call a council of war to decide whether to continue towards the main army or remain at Huete until further information was received. The latter course was chosen. Wyndham was thus able to receive the provisions which were being gathered for the army; also enemy parties were dissuaded from being active in the area.[2]

Peterborough remained at Huete until 19 August. There were still other wrongs to be avenged. Many soldiers had been left behind on the march northwards because of sickness. Some were massacred by the local people while others were attacked and murdered on their way to rejoin their units. About 200 men were lost in this way.

Travelling by Torrejoncillo and Parilla to Valverde, Peterborough then went to Olmeda. Here the people of the place had murdered twenty guards and their officer and so he ordered their village to be set on fire. From Valverde, the earl moved on by Buenache to Almodóvar and Campillo. The only opposition encountered on this journey came from a party of country people under arms at a crossing on the River Cabriel. To avoid them, Peterborough went by a different route to cross near Pesquera and so reach Camporrobles.

The earl paused long enough here to write letters to both Admiral Wassenaer and Sir John Leake. Leake's letter accompanying the Queen's instructions had been rather gloomy in tone. The arrival of the commission binding Peterborough and himself as joint admirals only increased the malaise with which he had always viewed dealings with the earl. He believed that in some way Peterborough was now acting against him at home and threatening to blight his career. He seemed unaware that the earl actually had a high regard for him and considered him a more competent commander than Shovell. Although they had differences of opinion from time to time, there is no evidence that Peterborough was plotting against Leake. There was certainly an element of inter-service rivalry in their relationship and Peterborough sometimes thought he detected a degree of insubordination towards himself among Leake's officers. He was often irritated by what he considered to be the Navy's inflexible attitude towards orders and instructions. At the present time, his main complaint against the service was an incident of plundering at Cartagena which apparently had been permitted by Sir John Jennings. Peterborough found this infuriating; having succeeded in eradicating plunder in the land forces, in his view it was an outrage that the Navy should still play by other rules.

Two days after leaving Camporrobles, Peterborough was back in Valencia. Not everything was quite so well as he had left it. For one thing the heat was so intense that he thought of embarking on a frigate in the bay. There were various kinds of trouble afoot, very much as he had feared there might be. He discovered and prevented a conspiracy in the city which had intended to surrender the place into the hands of the French. There was a plot to murder both himself and the Viceroy. The mob was being particularly troublesome because its favourite, Basset, was still in prison. At his house in the Plaza de los Domenicos, Peterborough was not only obliged to double the guard but also place cannon at the gates. Then, to provide a diversion for himself and for anyone else in need of one, he organised a bullfight. To hide any disappointment, he intended to enjoy himself and provide entertainment for others. In the view of a contemporary Valencian historian, 'this man was in the first place polite, circumspect, and assiduous, enjoying leisure without abandoning himself to excess.'³

Peterborough found waiting at Valencia some cheering letters from home. The City of London had complimented him in conjunction with the Duke of Marlborough. Also his long-awaited commission as a vice-admiral of England had passed the seals but Godolphin had refrained from sending it to him 'for fear of tempting me from the land service'. The Queen had appointed the Countess of Peterborough a Lady of the Bedchamber; the recipient had made no mention of the honour in her own letter but left her husband to find out from others. Lord Barrymore had complained to the Queen that Peterborough had spoiled his regiment by removing his best officers to Pearce's Dragoons. The Queen had dismissed the complaint, claiming that she had every reason to believe that everything that Peterborough did was well done 'and would change nothing'. The Count Lescheraine arrived from Italy, bringing complimentary letters from the Duke of Marlborough.

For all that, the opinion at home had changed since these letters had been penned. This was due to the arrival of Major-General Richards and Mitford Crowe. Richards and Crowe had met up with each other on the journey home and had both arrived at Helchin on 13 August to visit Marlborough. The duke granted them both long private audiences and gained the decided impression from their conversations that the King took the wrong road to Madrid because of his animosity to Peterborough. Richards explained the reasons behind the journey and also the confused financial situation in Peterborough's command.

Soon after his visitors' departure, Marlborough received a letter from Wratislaw in Vienna which would have confirmed his earlier impression. Although a personal friend of Peterborough, Wratislaw was nonetheless convinced that the earl was unsuited to this command. He had his own informants in Spain. He was even aware that Peterborough and Leake were not always on the best of terms, a fact to which he attached much importance. It seems that Peterborough's views on the situation never reached him. About this time, the earl claimed to Hedges that he had proof that more than thirty of his letters to Wratislaw and others to Stepney, the British Ambassador in Vienna, had been stopped by the Court.[4]

When Richards reached London on 23 August, he handed to Hedges one of the lengthiest of Peterborough's letters. Written on 17 June OS, it consisted largely of complaints about the Austrian Court and also about the government at home, particularly regarding money and supply for the forces. Peterborough also complained that he lacked particular instructions in almost every sphere. This prompted a rapid reply from Hedges that it was quite impossible to give exact instructions for every case at such a distance when circumstances changed so quickly. The earl's basic instructions were quite wide enough.

Godolphin considered Peterborough's letter 'a two-edged sword'. Both he and Marlborough thought that the earl wanted it made public in Parliament so that he could make trouble with it. His complaints about the payment of the troops were not unjustified; the difficulty was that the two armies were on different establishments. The Portuguese army received four times as much for their baggage train as did

Peterborough's troops because the latter were on the Flanders foot. 'It were as just to offer a London labourer Yorkshire pay,' wrote the earl.

In his disappointment at the way the Spanish campaign had gone, Marlborough was quick to lay the blame on Peterborough. It may have been the experience of bygone years which coloured his comments. He implied that the earl's conduct was neither unexpected nor unfamiliar. 'It is a misfortune to have to do with so ill a man,' he wrote. Referring to Peterborough and his wife, he replied to his duchess, 'There is no villany that may not be expected from them. I have always observed since I have been in the world, that the next misfortune to that of having friendshipe with such people, is that of having any disput with them, so that care should be taken to have as little as is possible to doe with them...'

Godolphin took a calmer view and minimised the problems which Peterborough could cause in Parliament. He took care to point out that the earl's 'extravagance alone could not have hurt us, if those Germans had not outdone him both in folly and everything that is worse'. He had just answered a letter from the King of Spain; in writing it, he 'had not been able to forbear complaining of his inexcusable delays in not advancing sooner towards Madrid'. He knew, as did Marlborough, that the Austrian ministers were not above utilising Peterborough's ill humours in order to manipulate the King into complying with their own plans 'for squeezing the people of Aragon'.[5]

Peterborough did not make a long stay in Valencia. He was well aware that this was a most inopportune moment to remove any troops from Spain. Soon after his arrival a council of war decided that it was not even feasible to detach a sufficient escort to transport much-needed money to Galway's army. There was too great a danger of insurrection and the cutting of vital lines of communication.

A courier from Savoy had brought news of the raising of the siege of Turin. This was a little discredited by the simultaneous arrival from the same direction of Count Lescheraine, who had heard nothing. However there was a strong probability that the news was true. Peterborough continued to hope that he would be able to take part of the fleet to Italy. A show of force could still be effective and it was of vital importance to leave a winter squadron in the Mediterranean.

On 6 September the *Medway*, commanded by Captain Henry Mordaunt, Peterborough's younger son, arrived from Alicante, bringing the news that the castle there had at last surrendered. Captain Mordaunt also had a copy of the latest instructions, received on 31 August, to detach a squadron of thirteen ships for the West Indies. Peterborough went on board at once and two days later sailed for Alicante where he arrived on 9 September. He then moved on board Leake's flagship, the *Prince George*, and hoisted the Union flag. A subsequent council of war had no qualms in deciding that, with news of the raising of the siege of Turin, the Queen's instructions for Italy could be set aside as no longer applicable. This was precisely the decision that Peterborough had hoped for. He noted that the King had written to the admirals quite unnecessarily, asking them to prevent him from taking any troops away. That evening, to a gun salute, he went ashore to visit the town.

The following day another council was held. Prior to Peterborough's arrival, the admirals had already decided which ships should go to the West Indies with Jennings and which should remain with Byng and Leake. The instructions for the West Indies had been compiled on the presumption that King Charles was now in power in Madrid and would wish to send out Spanish ministers to take charge there. The council agreed that circumstances had changed but no persuasion on Peterborough's part could move them from their determination to carry out the instructions as sent. The earl's only resource was to send an urgent letter home to try to get the instructions altered, hoping that new orders might reach Jennings at Lisbon where the squadron would go first for supplies.

A further council on 12 September resolved that the part of the fleet not designated for the West Indies should attempt the islands of Mallorca and Menorca before returning to Lisbon where a winter squadron would be left. Leake would then return to England with those ships in most need of repair. Six ships were left on coastal duty with Peterborough who resigned himself to undertaking his Italian voyage with only two of them, despite the fact that a French squadron was said to be cruising off Genoa.[6]

On 13 September the fleet weighed anchor and departed; Sir John Jennings and his squadron left for Lisbon and the West Indies, Sir John Leake and the remainder to water at Altea and then proceed to the islands. The ships in need of repair and the transports sailed for England. Captain Henry Mordaunt took command of the *Resolution* in an exchange with Captain Owen. Mordaunt had taken a fancy to the *Resolution* and the arrangement was made by 'joynt consent'. His father saw the incident in a different light. 'I was forced to buy a ship for my son at sea rather than show him any the least partiality, giving two hundred pounds to an other Capt. to change with him...' The

Resolution, accompanied by the *Revenge*, was given the responsibility of conveying Peterborough to Italy.

Stanhope had warned Peterborough that the King was taking steps to justify his route to Madrid to the Queen. Charles had sent Count Gallas to London with a memorial setting out his reasons, together with the relevant extracts from Peterborough's letters which had affected his decisions. As it had been a great joy to the Court when Peterborough's papers had been captured, so it was an equal joy to the earl when they were returned unharmed from the Duke of Berwick. After the departure of the fleet, Peterborough took time to ensure that his case would be fairly represented at home. He sent another lengthy epistle to Secretary Hedges giving a complete account of events to date, supported by documentary evidence, letters, minutes of councils of war and other papers. He gave his reasons for not taking troops with him to Savoy and expressed the hope that on his return by the end of October he would be able to bring some German soldiers. All these papers were put into the care of Colonel Hamilton who sailed for Italy and reached London by 11 October.

On 17 September a council of land officers approved Peterborough's voyage to Italy, recognising the necessity of obtaining money. Also the season of rain and inactivity was about to begin when his presence was not so necessary. On 17 September the *Resolution* with Peterborough on board and the *Revenge* as escort set sail from Alicante. Leaving Altea the following afternoon, they met the *Mary* galley whose officers were able to give definite confirmation that the siege of Turin had been raised. The voyage to Italy was uneventful; they joined four other British ships on the way and reached Genoa on 29 September.⁷

The Allied army near Madrid remained at Chinchón until 9 September when it was decided to cross the Tagus and find quarters in Castile, nearer to Cuenca and behind the Júcar. Here they were joined by General Wyndham and around 900 foot. This reinforcement brought with it the much-needed supplies of bread and biscuit, the results of Peterborough's penal foray to Huete. Meanwhile Berwick's army moved from Colmenar on a parallel route. The Allies found it impossible to obtain tenable quarters over the Júcar. Afraid that the enemy force might get between them and Valencia, they pushed on south. Only once did it appear that the French might seek a battle; they made a rapid march to catch up near Villanueva de la Jara. The Allies expected an attack after they had camped near Iniesta but the French made no attempt, despite a decided advantage, so the Allies managed to decamp and cross the Cabriel in safety. By 5 October, except for the garrisons left at Cuenca and Requena, the entire Allied force had returned to Valencia.[8]

Peterborough remained some time in Genoa, giving out to interested parties that he hoped to raise money there. It was his intention to return to Spain at the end of the month after visiting the Duke of Savoy. Diplomatic circles stirred at the prospect of this visit. John Chetwynd, the British envoy in Turin, wrote home for information as to whether Peterborough was travelling incognito or on a particular mission. He knew that the earl had written to the Duke of Savoy 'as if he had some business of great consequence to negotiate'.

Godolphin considered that Peterborough's pretext of acquiring some dismounted German troopers a pretty slim one for a general; and he also wished to know as much as possible about the matters discussed with the Duke of Savoy. He was a little disturbed by the papers that Peterborough had sent home with Colonel Hamilton, particularly as copies of these were to be distributed to certain of the earl's friends as ammunition for trouble-making. He now suggested to Marlborough that it might be prudent to acquire from the Duke of Savoy the original, or an authentic copy, of the letter in which Peterborough had offered to put the Duke in King Charles's place. In government circles, thought was being given to some means of preventing the earl from returning to Spain while he was thus conveniently out of the country.

Leaving Genoa on 15 October, Peterborough travelled first to Novi and then on to Prince Eugène's camp near Alessandria. There he stayed only one night before moving on to Pavia, crossing the Po and reaching the Duke of Savoy's camp outside Pizzighettone on 19 October.

As the siege of this town was not expected to last many days longer, Peterborough decided to remain until it was over. He had several conversations with the Duke, always in the presence of the envoy, John Chetwynd. The topics chiefly covered were the King of Spain's journey to Madrid and the failure of any English troops to reach the Duke of Savoy. Regarding both incidents, Peterborough refuted any suggestions that he might have been personally at fault. However he did indicate his intention to press a scheme for next year's campaign on the coast of Provence. Anxious to discuss this also with Prince Eugène, Peterborough accompanied the Duke when he left for Pavia where he had planned to meet the Prince. Unfortunately in the meantime the rivers had risen and it was impossible for Prince Eugène to make the journey to meet them.

Having dined with the Duke at the Certosa of Pavia on 1 November, Peterborough set out for Turin accompanied by Chetwynd in order to pay his respects to the Duchess and the Duchess Dowager, Madame Royale. That night he was 'very handsomely received and lodged' in Milan at the house of the Marchese Cesare Visconti, Conte di Galerati.

On 6 November Peterborough left Turin for Casale, where the Duke had gone to meet Prince Eugène. Four days later he was in a position to convey to the Secretary of State and the Duke of Marlborough the plans which the two Princes proposed for the next campaign. They hoped to enter Provence with an army of 30,000 men with the prime intention of capturing Toulon. They expected England and Holland to send a fleet of thirty ships to the Mediterranean immediately, then gradually build up this number into the summer months and bring by sea an additional force of 5,000 men. They foresaw a problem of subsistence for the troops. To ease this, the Princes undertook to provide wheat, oats and barley if the Allies would cooperate by taking either Naples or Sicily in the spring. They thought that Peterborough should go at once to Lisbon to supervise the equipment of a strong squadron. The earl was cautious about undertaking such a project because of criticism from the home front. He acknowledged that it was a pity to be obliged to be on the defensive at home at a time when one's thoughts should be focused solely on how best to defeat the enemy.

Having put these thoughts on paper, Peterborough entrusted his letters to Colonel Pepper, who left from Alessandria on 16 November on his way home. His time spent with the Duke of Savoy had been most congenial. 'No Prince could be treated with yt respect and friendship by the way I have been two dayes and a half,' he wrote to Colonel Southwell, 'besides the happiness of having been so long out of Spain...'9

That autumn in England rumours abounded that Peterborough would be recalled summarily to account for his conduct. However, November arrived with still no action taken and, when it became known that he was in Turin, it was presumed that he was to remain at his post. While staying with Lord Wharton, William Walsh, the politician and literary critic, had been shown a letter from 'a certain great General in Spain'. He was so impressed by it that he told Lord Wharton: 'I wou'd by all means have that General recall'd, and set to writing here at home, for it was impossible that a Man with so much wit as he shew'd, cou'd be fit to command an Army or do any other Business.'

As far as the officers at Valencia were concerned, Peterborough had resigned his command and they were under Galway's orders. To the government at home, he had abandoned his army at a time of need and ignored his more recent commission as ambassador to the King of Spain. He may have been able to claim orders to go to Savoy but it was not envisaged that he would do so without troops. Above all, he had no orders at all to consult with the Duke of Savoy.

Peterborough had already taken active steps to defend himself at home. Stanhope's secretary, Horace Walpole, reached England at the end of October, ostensibly the bearer of an account of the state of the army but appearing also to be reporting the King's complaints against Peterborough. Anxious to avoid a dispute with any member of Stanhope's household, Peterborough had interviewed the young man before his departure and endeavoured to correct certain 'mistakes' in his account. Nevertheless the end result was considered rather unfriendly to Peterborough, who wrote a little aggrievedly to Stanhope: 'I have had a long account from England of the great favours I have received from your secretary, and cannot conceive how a person to whom I was so much a stranger should be so extremely busy upon my account.'

Sir Charles Hedges knew that Peterborough's memoirs were in the process of being printed in mid-November. He considered suppressing publication but took the reasonable view that to do so would cause more notice and excitement than to allow the printing to go forward.* Peterborough kept up the pressure from Genoa, where he had returned on 17 November, and *A Letter from an English Gentleman at Genoa to His Friend in Holland in Justification of the Earl of Peterborow's Conduct*, dated 21 November, was soon in print also. Godolphin suspected that Peterborough might suddenly appear for the sitting of Parliament; in fact the earl remained abroad, only expressing an anxiety to return if anyone felt he had faults to answer.[10]

On this visit to Genoa Peterborough discovered an enjoyment of Italy, the Italians and their way of life which he never lost. Italy became a country to which he would happily return for as long as travelling was physically possible. With the company of Colonel Breton, a likeminded individual, Peterborough planned to raise Stanhope's envy on their return 'with the account of our happy days in Italy – of the nights we will say nothing...' He was bringing back with him some good French wine 'sent me by Monsieur Pontchartrain' which would last

*This may have been an early edition of *An Account of the Earl of Peterborow's Conduct in Spain*, compiled by Dr John Freind, Peterborough's personal physician, who had accompanied him throughout his Spanish campaign. The book was widely available in 1707.

them for ten or twelve days, and laying up fifty hogsheads of it at Genoa 'for the campaign in Italy' in which he felt sure he would have a part.*

Peterborough had managed to acquire the money he had come for at rather a steep rate of interest, some from English merchants at Genoa and some from Turin. As soon as the latter had arrived, he set sail the next day for Barcelona with four ships, the *Resolution*, the *Antelope*, the *Revenge* and the *Garland*, which had all been cruising off the coast after cleaning. While cruising, they had been damaged in an encounter with some enemy ships, which partly accounted for the delay in leaving Genoa. Having anchored at Barcelona on 27 December 1706, Peterborough began an overland journey to Valencia three days later.[11]

Early in December Queen Anne had yielded to public pressure and appointed the Whig Earl of Sunderland as Secretary of State in the place of Sir Charles Hedges. It fell to Sunderland to answer Peterborough's letter to Hedges of 10 November. His response to the plans hatched with the Duke of Savoy and Prince Eugène was cool and discouraging. As the Duke of Savoy would know, he explained, it had always been the Queen's opinion that the most effectual action against the French would be to take the war into their own country, and that this could be done most advantageously in Provence or the Dauphiné. The Queen was already pursuing these matters with the States General. As for ships required in the Mediterranean, 'Her Majesty has long ago ordered the ships that are at Lisbon to be in a readiness to go into the Mediterranean.' Others would follow from England as needed. As for the plans regarding Naples, the Queen thought it impossible, in the King of Spain's present circumstances, that he could spare 5,000 men. Any attempt to do so would prejudice the priority of entering France.

While Peterborough was on his way back to Valencia, the winter season in London was in full swing. Whatever views they may have held of Peterborough and his lady, the Duke and Duchess of Marlborough put little of their isolationist policy into practice. Throughout the winter, the duke was a regular caller at Lady Peterborough's town house and listened while she expounded her political views on the wider European scene. The duchess came less often but before Christmas she extended an invitation to the countess to dine and 'name her

---

*Since Pontchartrain was Louis XIV's Navy Minister, presumably this wine was acquired by the capture of a French vessel. It would compensate for the inroads Peterborough had made on Stanhope's cellar. 'Your Hermitage is good,' he wrote on 30 August, 'the rest indifferent.' *Peterborough's Letters to Stanhope*, pp. 40, 48.

company'. Lady Peterborough chose as her fellow guests four Whigs, Dr Samuel Garth, the physician and wit and a crony of her husband's, and three Junto lords, Wharton, Halifax and Sunderland.

Within a few days of this event the Queen had ordered Sunderland to send Peterborough his letters of recall. '[The Queen] now thinks it is not necessary for her service that your Lordship continue any longer in Spain nor indeed that it would be agreeable to you to do so.'[12]

Twenty-four

On his return to Valencia on 10 January 1707, Peterborough was given a much warmer welcome than might have been expected. His journey from Barcelona had been slow, particularly in the latter stages, because of a severe foot injury. This impediment obliged him to 'travel the pace of a Spaniard, I mean of one that is not going to rob, or flying from the enemy'.

At the Court now established there the earl was in high good humour, enthusing about the plans agreed with the Duke of Savoy and Prince Eugène. He confidently expected to be returning soon to Italy, certain that the Queen would send instructions shortly. The King showed both interest and approval of the Savoy plan. More surprisingly, he showed great cordiality towards Peterborough, Galway having proved a counter-irritant.

Peterborough was now admitted to the twice-weekly consultations on the form of the spring campaign. Decisions had to be reached on how to utilise the reinforcements of 8,000 men under the command of Earl Rivers now known to be on their way, although originally intended for the coast of France. At a council on 15 January it was decided by a small majority to adopt an offensive strategy, marching as one body in the direction of Madrid and seeking to engage the enemy. So many members of the council had been of an opposite view that, at Peterborough's suggestion, the King asked that all members should state their opinions in writing. All the British and Portuguese generals supported the offensive but the King, Peterborough, Comte de Noyelles, the Austrians and the Spaniards opposed it.

Peterborough maintained that it had been agreed in the Savoy plan that offensive action should be taken in Italy and not in Spain. In the light of the experience of the previous year, the journey to Madrid could destroy the infantry; also it would have to be undertaken in the face of an army greatly superior in cavalry. Offensive action could risk the loss of everything. It was more important to garrison the towns in Catalonia and Valencia and make sure of keeping what they had already gained. It was known that enemy reinforcements were gathering in Roussillon and that a force under the Duke of Orleans was due to join Berwick in the spring, so any offensive would have to be undertaken before then.

Both Stanhope and Galway were keen supporters of an offensive campaign. 'Her Majesty', Stanhope argued, 'did not spend such vast sums, and send such number of forces, to garrison towns in Catalonia and Valencia, but to make King Charles master of the Spanish monarchy.' This, he had later to concede, might have been overstepping the mark: he had protested in the Queen's name in the presence of Peterborough, who – both Stanhope and Galway acknowledged – was of superior diplomatic rank and held an opposing view.[1]

The decision of the council of war was later confirmed by orders received from the Queen. Rivers's troops were to join with Galway's to act 'as one corps' for the march to Madrid. They were not to divide themselves or be distracted by side issues such as 'amusing themselves in taking inconsiderable places and such little Projects'.

The King took his own line. He refused to conform to the decision taken and announced his intention to take some troops to Catalonia 'to redress some disorders'. Throughout February the councils tried to dissuade him from this move but in March he left, promising to return for the campaign. All the King's ministers had been against this journey; only the Comte de Noyelles remained silent, thus raising the suspicion that he had been the author of the scheme. De Noyelles, Stanhope discovered, had been behind the move to go to Madrid by Saragossa, in the hope of getting a military command. He had built up an extraordinary hold over the King who now appeared to consult no one else. For reasons of his own advancement, he had been an advocate of a division of the forces since the previous autumn.

At the time of the despatch of Peterborough's letters of recall on 23 December/3 January 1706/7, Sunderland also informed both Galway and Rivers of the decision that had been taken. He sent another letter on 28 December/8 January as a precautionary measure. In Gibraltar on 13 January, Rivers had heard that Peterborough was still carrying himself in his accustomed manner, apparently unaware of any change in his position. On 24 January letters from England arrived at Valencia. Lady Peterborough had taken the opportunity to send an express to her husband, urging him to set out for England immediately as only his return could quash the stories and rumours being spread about him in London.

On the arrival of the Fleet on 7 February, Peterborough's recall became generally known. The former commander-in-chief took no formal leave of the King but gave out that he would soon leave for Italy. He sent a polite and cheerful letter of welcome to Rivers. On 27 February he wrote to Sunderland congratulating him on his appointment as a Secretary of State and giving him his views on the position in Spain; but he made no reference to his recall. He did refer to receiving the first public letters for five months, those of 11 and 31 November. It seems probable that Sunderland's December letters had not yet reached him.

It was noticed that during this period Peterborough no longer exercised his military command, apart from making one brief and unsuccessful expedition into Murcia with a detachment of troops. He was more actively involved in his naval command, particularly with the ships he had been left with over the winter. The King found this useful. His relationship with Peterborough was in a harmonious phase, whereas he was finding Galway and the other generals frustrating – they appeared to exclude him from their plans and councils. The fleet had made a successful visit to the islands at the end of the year and the King wished to send troops to Mallorca. He was unable to obtain any from the generals; instead he sent some of his own from Tortosa on board the ships still under Peterborough's orders.*

Out of the money he had acquired at such expense in Genoa, Peterborough allowed the King 13,000 pistoles. After consultation with Galway and Stanhope, the money was lodged with the abbot of the monastery of Poblet in Catalonia and earmarked 'for fortifications and the service of the troops towards the defence of Catalonia'. It could only be issued on Stanhope's guarantee that it would be employed for those uses.

As a result of his sunny relations with the King, Peterborough eventually set out for Italy armed with a letter stating that his journey was undertaken with the King's approval and permission. Experience had taught him that it was useful to have written evidence to produce in defence of one's conduct. The King seemed confident that Peterborough's journey would be of benefit to all and he confirmed his appointment as head of his forces.

Before he left, Peterborough was in possession of the letter from

---

*When Sir Cloudesley Shovell arrived at Alicante with the Fleet, none of these ships was there; they were all off on errands somewhere. Shovell was convinced that some must be in dire straits. 'Cavendish [the *Antelope*] tells me it will not be long before I shall see Elwes [the *Revenge*] or hear that he is starving or starved, for my Lord sends him up and down and never took care to provide or supply him with provisions which is very near quite at an end by this time.' Shovell to Byng 11 February OS, *Byng Papers*, vol. i, p. 147.[2]

Sunderland enclosing his letters of recall. On 6 March he returned the letters unopened. 'I believe the Queen will not be displeased yt these letters I send back to your Lordship are uselesse. I never offered my credentialls to the King...' On 14 March he set sail for Barcelona where he boarded his son's ship, the *Resolution*, and left for Genoa escorted by the *Enterprise* and the *Milford*.

Before leaving Barcelona, Peterborough had been made aware of the reaction of the government at home to his fund-raising activities in Italy. He had paid 'a most extravagant price' and the Queen had ordered that the bills should not be accepted. Moreover he was expected to return to England at once to explain his reasons for leaving Spain and treating with other princes without orders to do so. 'All objections are now reduced to my having taken up without order and with such losse such considerable summes att Genoa,' he told Stanhope. No one at home seemed able to appreciate the difficulties which had to be met in order to maintain an army in Spain. 'Surely if ever extraordinary measures were to be taken it was when an Army was in such extraordinary necessity, and fower or five thousand pounds more or lesse ought to be brought in ballance with the losse or safety of an Army.' After all, the Portuguese had been prepared to pay the price for this badly needed money.[3]

On this voyage to Italy the French were on the lookout. The reason for their vigilance was not only because Peterborough was on board but because they believed the ships also carried 40,000 pistoles for the Duke of Savoy. The English ships came up with six French men-of-war on the fifth day of the voyage, 30 March, between Corsica and the French coast. It was evident that an interception was intended. As nightfall was approaching, Peterborough requested that he and the Spanish envoy should be put on board the *Enterprise* so that they might get away under cover of darkness and make for the coast. During the night the *Enterprise* was still surrounded by enemy lights; by daybreak she was alone and made the best of her way towards Leghorn. The *Milford* had also stood off to the northwards but she was not followed and on the afternoon of 31 March came up with the *Enterprise* again. However, the incidents of the journey were not over. Late that night the *Enterprise* was attacked by a French privateer off Leghorn. There followed 'a little dispute' in which the privateer found the *Enterprise* well able to defend herself and eventually left her. Peterborough had been injured in the action; much bruised and suffering from a 'violent cold', he landed at Leghorn the next morning.

Meanwhile the *Resolution* had been left to face six French men-of-war in squally conditions. Action commenced and she fought back bravely. When she sustained damage to her mainmast, Captain Mordaunt decided to run for the shore rather than risk capture. Every approach by a French ship was met with spirited gunfire. Eventually the *Resolution* ran ashore in a sandy bay under the castle of Ventimiglia. Attempts by the French to make a capture by sending in boats were beaten back by gunfire. On the morning of 1 April Mordaunt ordered the crew and most of the cargo ashore and had the ship set alight. By early afternoon she had 'burnt to the water's edge'.

During the action Captain Mordaunt had been severely wounded by a cannon-ball in the right thigh. Although he had to be carried ashore, he remained in command throughout. He had acted courageously during the engagement and with decision and calmness. Later a state galley was sent from Genoa to collect him. His wound caused some weeks of illness which gave his parents much anxiety. He was a great favourite with them and by all accounts an able and attractive young man.[4]

Whatever plan had been concocted by the Duke of Savoy and Prince Eugène for the spring campaign of 1707, a more careful and efficient model had been prepared by the Duke of Marlborough. The Allies had agreed to a proposal to move into France by way of the Southern Alps and along the coast and to strike at the naval base of Toulon with the assistance of the fleet. In March this plan was thwarted by the Emperor who made a secret treaty with France whereby Italy was declared neutral territory. Consequently the French garrisons in the Milanese were released for duty elsewhere; many of them were directed to Roussillon to reinforce Berwick in Spain. It had been one of the aims of the Toulon plan to attract some of the French forces out of Spain and thus ease the pressure on Galway in Valencia.

Plans were further complicated by the Emperor's decision to march troops through Italy in order to take Naples, a separate kingdom and poorly defended. He seemed anxious to lay claim to this part of the Spanish Empire, fearing he might lose it in a peace settlement. Forces which might have been used for the Toulon expedition were thus diverted, postponing the descent until the summer.

It was some days before Peterborough was well enough to travel on from Leghorn and the news about his son did not improve his low spirits. He planned to 'make all haste for England', passing by way of Turin. By 14 April he had reached Genoa and his son's bedside. Writing to Stanhope, he was anxious over Harry's condition but his mind was still occupied with his concern that the government at home might misunderstand, or fail to appreciate, the urgency of the need for money which had caused his expensive transactions in Genoa that winter. Stanhope might be able to impress on them the reality of the situation. Peterborough had also heard news that a small army had left Paris for Murcia in early April under the command of the Duke of Orleans and was expected to join Berwick's forces in May. In fact this force made much quicker progress, although its commander moved at a more leisurely pace.

Moving on to Turin, Peterborough continued to correspond with the King and the Portuguese ambassador, fearing for the offensive policy which had been adopted and was now confirmed by orders from England. He still believed in the division of troops; the only way success could be achieved in the circumstances was to leave half the force to guard the Valencian border and move the rest rapidly by a 'stolen march' to the head of the Tagus. With the help of the Aragonese, this force could reach Madrid and interpose themselves between the Duke of Berwick's army and the expected reinforcements. This manoeuvre would cause Berwick to move towards Madrid, or even Burgos, and the defensive troops could then advance behind the retreating enemy. This plan could only be put in operation while Berwick still lacked reinforcements. Peterborough also feared that the commanders might underestimate the effect of the superior numbers of the enemy horse. The Allied foot, although strong regiments, were no match for horse in that country or any other. In a letter to the King of 27 April, Peterborough expressed his fears that the offensive policy would bring on a disaster; 'ils... courront risque de la perte entière de leur Infanterie par une bataille.' At the time of writing, he was unaware that the disaster had already taken place two days previously outside the walls of Almanza.

The Allied commanders had planned to start the spring offensive in April. They had moved their forces into Murcia in order to take one or two places where the enemy had made magazines. They also intended to strengthen their lines of communication before marching to the head of the Tagus and Madrid. While engaged on these tasks near the town of Almanza, the Duke of Berwick's army approached. Galway and Das Minas decided to attack. Because of the hostility of the surrounding countryside, Galway did not know that Berwick had recently received a reinforcement of 8,000 men from Roussillon. The French army now numbered 25,000 men. Galway and Das Minas were in command of 15–16,000.

It was a long and hard-fought battle but the superiority in numbers carried the day. There were heavy Allied losses, calculated as 4–5,000 men. French losses were also considerable, more than they cared to admit. The Allied command in the end offered their surrender to Berwick which surprised the French general – he appeared to consider the battle too close run for either side to be counted the victor.

This defeat was the final blow to the Austrian cause in Spain. The Allies retained several bases along the coast, including Barcelona, which they maintained with the assistance of the fleet and at considerable cost to the French, but they lost their territorial gains and Madrid became a faded dream.

As the news travelled and the reverberations were felt all over Europe, people tried to determine the reasons for the defeat and allot the blame. The King, who had not been present and had deprived the command of Stanhope's advice by taking him to Catalonia, was inclined to blame Galway but Marlborough would hear no ill of him. Events had turned out as Peterborough feared they would; that his advice had been right was realised in some quarters with chagrin and not a little indignation. As Godolphin wrote to Marlborough, 'what vexes mee most is to think how Lord Peterborow will tryumph...'

In May 1707 the tragedy was too close; there was no mood for triumph. 'The public misfortune touches me almost as much as if I had had a hand in itt,' wrote Peterborough, 'however having had some presentiment of itt, and foreseeing the terrible consequences such a defeat would bring to our affairs in every place, I did all in my power to prevent measures that might prove so fatall, as I shall doe the like to seek the remedies if they are to be compassed.' In retrospect, Peterborough believed that Providence had assisted him in his endeavours to secure the crown of Spain for King Charles; 'att least I may comfort myself in this, that I was not the man designed by Providence to loose itt...'[5]

Soon after his arrival in Turin, Peterborough had obtained an audience of the Duke of Savoy in order to present a 'sort of credential' from the King of Spain. When he explained some plans for entering Roussillon, the Duke stopped him, saying that he had already made plans with the Queen and would adhere to these. The Duke had heard that accusations had been made in England about Peterborough's conduct and that he no longer held the same credentials from the Queen as formerly.

In a friendly way, he urged the earl to lose no time in returning home so that these matters might be cleared up. Having given various explanations to the Duke which 'tended to his Lordship's justification' he left his presence intending to follow his advice.

In early May Peterborough was back in Genoa. He no longer held any naval command and so he had to wait for a ship which might take him to England. The particular ships which he might have expected to be available were retained by the King of Spain for the conveyance of his envoy to the Duke of Savoy. Peterborough was also so incommoded by the bruise he had received in the encounter at sea that he was unable to ride a horse (he was still complaining of this injury three months later). The presence of his son Harry, who was not yet recovered from his wound, was another reason for delay. The final hindrance was the fact that some of the English merchants in Genoa would not release any of Peterborough's money until their bills had been met in England.

When the news of Almanza reached him, the earl went back once more to Turin. At Genoa, Sir John Norris, 'the governing coxcomb', had arrived as an emissary from Sir Cloudesley Shovell to the Duke of Savoy. Peterborough accompanied him on his journey and showed himself to be 'as inquisitive as anybody else' about the subject of his visit.

At Turin Peterborough received some advice by letter from his wife. Lady Peterborough had learned of her husband's recall only towards the end of the parliamentary session. However she had noticed that Briançon, the Duke of Savoy's envoy in London, was not treating her with the particular degree of civility to which she had become accustomed. She therefore warned her husband that his recall would not be met with the honours which he might have been expecting and which might have been an inducement to his rapid return. Having urged him in December to come home as quickly as possible, she now changed her tune and wrote of joining him on the Continent, particularly in view of Harry's wound. 'Consider your curcumstancs,' she wrote, 'doe nott be deceaved thay have nothing to propose as a compensation.' She thought that her husband had been treated unjustly and insulted by the government. She believed that the ministry was afraid that he might take up some employment at a foreign court.

In her letter of 29 April/10 May Lady Peterborough was able to report one small success in her relentless campaign on her husband's behalf: a warrant to pay his equipage money for his embassy in Spain had been passed. Letters had come from Spain, she wrote, 'i doe nott doubt from ouer great politisian stanope', describing the council of war at Valencia. Peterborough's opposing view was being represented in London as 'hindering and contraditing thayr measures'. Writing to Stanhope from Turin on 24 May, Peterborough echoed the view. 'A messenger a purpose has come from England to presse my return home,' he wrote, 'as a person that interrupts my lord Galloway's great and prudent councils with contradictory and imprudent advice.'

A messenger now arrived in Turin bringing Peterborough's letters of recall a second time. The covering letter from Sunderland expressed the Queen's great surprise at the earl's action in returning his letters without also including his credentials. The Queen now sent positive orders to return at once to England 'as she is willing to believe your Lordship intends to do by the way of Italy'. The letter also stressed that the earl was now travelling in the capacity of a private person and the English envoy was asked to ensure that the Duke of Savoy was aware of his change of status.

Peterborough's immediate response to this letter was a sharp reply to Sunderland:

It is a fate I think I have not deserved by any of my actions to have it concluded I want Common Sense. Sure, my Ld, I could not be thought capable of a design of acting with her majesty's commission against her commands and intentions, and your Lords has very wrong Ideas of Spaine, if you think anybody would stay in itt, that has a pretence to come out of itt.

I thought I could not formally Give the King the trouble of an Audience to let him know I was no Ambassadour, unlesse I could formally show him I was one, or was designed for that Caracter; neither could I send back my Credentialls with the Recredentialls, since they were taken with all my other commissions by the Ennemy, when I lost all my baggage, att Guete nere Madrid.

You are pleased to tell me the Queen Lookes upon me as a private person. Your Lords will find I have great reason to Thank Heaven that I am soe; but your giving me now to understand that I have not Her Maty's allowance to act by commission from an other Prince, that is new, and all her majesty's Intentions as soon as communicated shall be complyed with to the uttmost of my power.

I confesse, my Lord, I did not know before that a Peer of England was a private person, and am yett to know how much of

English Liberty we have lost by our New Name, and as a private person I was apt to think I might serve a Prince Engag'd in the same interest. Att least I believe it was never refused afore and am not sensible I had served so ill as to deserve a particular and extraordinary restraint.

But, my Lord, the public misfortune hinders me from thinking of particular concerns. I wish it were as easy to recover the last fatall blow, as it will be to satisfy your Lordsp and the world that I have done all I could to prevent itt as a private person; and nobody can pretend to doubt that, had I been in the same public caracters, I should have avoided a fate I so plainly Foresaw, and did all I could to prevent others from falling into.

My Lord, it is plain there has been an impatience in some to have me return for England, but I am sure they cannot with more Earnestnesse desire my return home then I doe to assist att the meeting of the Brittish parliament.

This broadside was concluded with a postscript which suggested that any reply could be sent to the Duke of Marlborough's camp. On 20 May Peterborough wrote again, this time in a gentler manner, explaining his problems with travel and his intention to leave Milan for Germany. He also offered an explanation:

My lord, about the recredentialls sent back, I gave an order to my secretary which he executed in part when he could not doe it entirely. I had forgott that the Credentialls were lost and taken with my baggage by the enemy; that matter being quite out of my thoughts I gave no second consideration to itt. But the recredentialls could not be offered without the foundation, and what was not in my power could not be sent by me. I am concerned however least the Queen might have aprehended as if there had been some want of respect. I think it was accident more than anything else brought them home, looking upon them as uselesse papers and the King otherwise informed of the substance.

He then gave the same explanation to Marlborough. He was looking forward to telling everything to the duke, confidently expecting a just and fair hearing.[6]

In early June Peterborough had progressed as far as Milan. Here he found Prince Eugène who had been appointed Governor of the Milanese in April and he took the opportunity to talk to him. He also wrote to Marlborough that he proposed to visit Vienna before coming on to the camp. He was not going 'to treat as I have been tould with Princes without Credentialls'; instead, he confidently stated 'I believe I can putt some stop to the animosityes arising betwixt the Emperor and the Duke of Savoy, which may prove of ill consequence...' By the time Prince Eugène began his march into Southern France from Cuneo on 15 June, Peterborough was on his way to Vienna. On hearing of the earl's intention to travel overland to England, Marlborough had extended him a warm invitation to visit his camp in Belgium. To make things easier, he despatched a pass to await him at Cologne.[7]

At the court in Vienna Peterborough was accorded a much more civil welcome than would normally be given to a 'private person'. He claimed to some that he was hoping to persuade the Emperor to send more troops to assist King Charles. To Marlborough he had deplored the reduction of troops in North Italy which had resulted from the attempt on Naples by Imperial forces. He was not slow to point out that, had his advice been taken, the British fleet would have taken the place the previous year. It was presumed that Peterborough would be welcome at the Austrian court as someone who shared its opinion; he had previously encouraged an attack on Naples at a time when differences were upsetting harmonious relations between the Allies.

Peterborough was able to furnish Wratislaw with a complete account of events in Spain since he left as he saw them. There was also opportunity to inform his friend of the matters which the intercepted letters would have covered. After his visit, Wratislaw told Marlborough that the earl had 'shown himself sufficiently humble, although his ardour has occasionally transported him beyond the limits of moderation'. Wratislaw had tried to offer him advice and had urged him not to 'publish his manifesto' until he had spoken to the duke. He counselled caution to Marlborough in his dealings with Peterborough. 'I believe it will be dangerous to offend him,' he wrote, 'as he is an Englishman, and has been supplanted by a Frenchman who has been the cause of this irreparable loss. When you have spoken to him, you will probably be more satisfied with him than you imagine; for Prince Eugène has written to me that his Lordship thinks like a general, although he does not always express himself with propriety; and it is likewise true, that he predicted the misfortunes which have come to pass...' Wratislaw seemed sure of his ground. Marlborough took care to warn anyone who might encounter the errant earl and hear his story to be very careful how they responded, 'puisqu'il serait capable d'élargir et de donner tout un autre tour a ce qu'on lui voudrait dire'.

Peterborough left Vienna in early July and travelled to Leipzig by way of Bohemia and Dresden. At Altranstädt King Charles XII of Sweden was encamped with his army. Wratislaw had told Peterborough that the king was not easily approached by statesmen and certainly not by members of the Emperor's entourage. He thought that a private person might have a better chance of gaining an audience. It was with this in view that Peterborough arrived in Leipzig.

Travelling at an uncharacteristically slow pace because of the discomfort still caused by his bruise, he was relishing his journey, 'enjoying the pleasure of liberty and idleness, going from court to court in Germany, seeing wonders'. He had heard 'on the road' that Earl Rivers and his force had been recalled from Spain, which he considered made any urgency for his own return unnecessary. On his travels, he hoped to pick up information both useful to Marlborough and as ammunition for the new parliamentary session at home.[8]

Twenty-five

As a military commander Charles XII of Sweden had been impressive. In 1700, still only eighteen years of age, he had taken part in the Swedish victory over the Russians at Narva. In 1702, for the first time as commander, he had defeated the army of Augustus King of Poland and Elector of Saxony at Kliszów. In the spring of 1706, he defeated the same army at Fraustadt and later in the year marched into Saxony and imposed terms on the defeated Augustus in the Treaty of Altranstädt. Wintering in Saxony, his presence there posed some threat to the Empire.

What concerned the Allies and much of Europe was the question whether Charles was about to take a side in the War of the Spanish Succession and, if so, which side. Through his envoy Besenval, Louis XIV had already tried to persuade him to attack the Emperor's territory and thus help France regain lost ground. But if Charles could be described as having any kind of mission, he saw himself as a Protestant champion. His enmity towards Louis XIV, who was a persecutor of Protestants, was quite sufficient to make him oppose any suggestions the French might make.

Marlborough visited Charles XII in the spring of 1707 in response to Allied unease about his possible movements. He was also concerned that Charles's wish to form a League of Protestant Princes might seriously undermine the Grand Alliance.

The Swedish king had been the subject of drawing-room discussion with Lady Peterborough.

Whee have often discoursed this winter uppone that prince's subject [she told her husband], and i told his grace that all the ille i aprehended for the inseuing campangne was from his mighty arming; that itt was to compelle eather use or the frenche to except of indiferent termes, but the probabilite was of the frenche side… and that i feard him more than all the ceasars or Antony being so hardened against ouer sex, wich his grace did not accept was a raison for being a Herow to bee feared; but i am convinct he has thought him so, and worth out bidding france by his going to him…

Marlborough had indeed taken this view. Having conducted the interview with Charles XII with considerable skill and diplomacy, he had contrived to dissuade him from forming his League. He had also gained the clear impression that the Charles's real aim was against the Czar, that he would reserve his forces for this and would therefore make no intervention in Allied affairs.

Over the last winter Charles XII had equipped his army for a new campaign. In Peterborough's view, 'the King of Sweden gives more fears by his silence than ever any other monarch gave by his threats. It is undecided whether he is very wise or foolhardy; all we know is, he has fifty thousand men mad enough to obey with pleasure all he can command.'

By the time Peterborough had reached Altranstädt, Charles XII was believed to have accepted British mediation in his disputes with the Emperor, but he was still not prepared to receive Count Wratislaw. The English envoy to Sweden, the Revd John Robinson, told Peterborough that the King was unlikely to spend much time in Silesia before engaging in a war with the Czar. Peterborough managed to obtain an audience; his method of doing so was described in an intercepted letter from the French envoy, Besenval. The interview must have been achieved at great personal discomfort as the earl was still 'incommoded and not able to travel'.

Some days after his [Peterborough's] arrival, having come to Leipsic in a carriage, to the quarters of the Chancery, to pay his respects to the King of Sweden, they would not suffer him to enter the apartment where the Prince had shut himself up with Count Piper [his chief minister]. He did not conceal his chagrin at this disappointment; and while he amused himself with conversing in a parlour, he was informed that the King of Sweden was going out. He ran to present himself to that Prince, but found him gone; and mounting the horse of a groom, he made so much diligence, that joining him as he was going out of the village, he told him he was come to have the honour of paying his respects to him, and that his design had been to follow him for that purpose to his headquarters at Alt Ranstadt. 'The weakness of my horse', he added, 'obliged me to take the liberty of requesting your majesty not to go so fast; a liberty I would not have taken if I were mounted on the smallest of the horses with which your Majesty's stables are filled.' The King laughed, and listened to him afterwards all the way to Alt Ranstadt, as he understood enough of French to comprehend what his Lordship said.

When Peterborough recorded his views in writing and presented them at the Chancery, it was noticed that they did not appear to agree with those of the English and Dutch ministers. He had urged the King to act as arbiter in the affairs of Europe as he felt that the English would soon be obliged to sue for peace, being unable to support the war much longer if France kept the advantages she had gained this year. 'This Lord,' Besenval continued, 'who is bold, and has been treated as a madman by those among the Swedish ministers who are suspected of being pensioners of England, has sought opportunities of speaking to the King, their master, and has found one, as you may have seen by what goes above; and I hope he has not failed to profit by it. I do not know, however, whether his too great vivacity, and the ill offices of some Swedish ministers, may not have discredited his opinions.'

This intercepted letter must have caused some fluttering in diplomatic circles. Had the ideas taken the King's fancy, they would have undone much of the careful work already achieved by the Allies. Fortunately for them, the King seemed unimpressed by the earl's views.[1]

On 30 July 1707 Peterborough reached Hanover where he received a warm welcome from the Dowager Electress Sophia, who had been a girlhood friend of his mother. The Elector, on the other hand, took less pleasure in the earl's company. Nevertheless, conveyed there in a carriage and six sent by the Dowager, Peterborough dined and supped at Herrenhausen every day.

Under the Act of Settlement, the Electress Sophia was heiress presumptive to the British throne. In 1706 she had indicated to friends in England her great anxiety to pay a visit or even to spend the remainder of her declining years there. This idea proved anathema to Queen Anne. Surprisingly the Tories had wanted an invitation passed through Parliament but the Whigs produced the Regency Bill as a countermotion and this duly became law. This Act provided a mechanism whereby, on the death of Queen Anne, the government would continue under a system of lords justices until the arrival of the Hanoverian successor. Earlier that summer Lord Halifax had visited the Electoral court and had taken with him for the Elector a copy of the Act as well as the insignia of the Order of the Garter. The Electress Sophia was understood to be not entirely satisfied. It was thought in England that

Peterborough would 'make mischief there' by encouraging her claims and joining with those anxious to support her.

Like everyone else, the Electress heard all about Peterborough's own concerns. It was said that the earl had told the Elector that there were only two things for which he would have to ask pardon on his return, the taking of Barcelona and visiting his court. Apart from that, he appeared 'extravagantly Swedish, and an enemy of the Emperor'.[2]

From Hanover, Peterborough made his way towards Marlborough's camp at Meldert. As his route no longer took him by way of Cologne, he was obliged to ask for another pass. Marlborough sent a convoy to escort him from Maastricht to the camp. The Allied army had been encamped at Meldert since early May. The French army under Vendôme lay about ten miles to the south. Both commanders were under orders not to seek a battle. It was Marlborough's opinion that, once the Toulon expedition was under way, sooner or later Louis XIV would order Vendôme to release some of his troops for southern France. Such a reduction in numbers would bring the two armies towards an equal strength. Under those circumstances, it might be possible to persuade the Dutch authorities to alter their orders. By early August the expected orders had reached Vendôme and the force was weakened. However a plea from Marlborough that he might now attack was not accepted. The only remaining expedient was a night march which could alarm the French into withdrawing their camp; also an attack on the rear of the retreating army might provoke an engagement.

On the evening of 10 August this march set out; Peterborough joined it as it moved south-west. In increasingly appalling weather, the French retired ahead of the Allies until Soignies was reached on 14 August. An attempt to make a night attack on the tail of the French army proved abortive and there was no engagement.

For Marlborough it had been a difficult and frustrating summer. He was still waiting anxiously for news from Toulon; he had depended on this expedition as the major exercise of that year's campaign. Depressed by the defeat of Almanza, he received another check when the French army under Marshal Villars successfully forced the Lines of Stollhofen on the Rhine.

While Marlborough awaited Peterborough's visit, he tried to find out from the government in England what action they were likely to take on the earl's return and what attitude he should therefore adopt towards him. Godolphin advised caution and prudence in dealing with a man whose strong feelings could cause him to lose his judgement and who should be prevented if possible from taking actions which could injure himself. He appeared rather tired of being consulted by Marlborough: 'You seem to desire my advice that you may answer to his proposalls. I can't imagine first what he will propose...' The government had not decided on any definite course of action. It was believed that Harley and some of the Whigs thought that Peterborough should be asked to give an account of his conduct and that an investigation should be held into whether or not he had carried out his orders. Undoubtedly he was in possession of a certain amount of political ammunition. He had foretold the disaster of Almanza and his opinion, advising different action, had been recorded in writing. This might gain him the support of the Tories, who had become very critical of Galway.

Aware of the possible political storm ahead, Godolphin thought that Peterborough was relatively harmless as long as he stayed abroad and held no commissions there. Marlborough hoped to be able to persuade the earl to postpone any printing of a justification. Apart from that, the duke knew that he must be guarded in what he said as 'sooner or latter it will be in print'.[3]

As the army waited in the incessant rain, Marlborough shivered in the unseasonable chills of a wet August. 'I have at this time my winter cloaths and a fire in my chamber, but what is worse the ill weather hinders me from going abroad, so that 30 [Peterborough] has the opertunitys of very long conversation. What is said on[e] day the next destroyes...' Finding his verbal accounts long and confusing, Marlborough asked the earl to commit his thoughts to paper.

From the conversations, however, certain facts did emerge. Peterborough was clearly concerned about the nature of the charges which he had heard were being made against him in England. Marlborough was careful to say nothing about the authenticity of these but noted that the earl had numerous papers and minutes of councils of war with which to justify his conduct. Peterborough was also able to produce 'obliging letters' from the King of Spain – which seemed rather surprising, considering what that monarch had written about him in the past. The Duke of Savoy appeared to be very much his friend. Marlborough accepted Peterborough's sincerity and had some sympathy for him when he revealed that he was very much out of pocket by the expedition, having lost two equipages. He believed that making Peterborough's financial position easier might prevent him from making trouble in the future. Besides that, the earl was still anxious to serve the Queen and happy to do so abroad.

To judge from the tone of Marlborough's letters, Peterborough was a guest who had outstayed his welcome. '30 has said all that is possible to me, but nothing of leaving the army,' Marlborough wrote on 18 August. However, two days later the guest did leave, carrying a letter from the duke to Godolphin, a letter of recommendation which was non-committal to a nicety. As well as letters and papers in his justification, Peterborough had shown the duke a paper containing five charges made against him and his answers to them. 'My having been so constantly abroad', Marlborough wrote to Godolphin, 'makes me ignorant not only as to the paper, but also what other facts may be laid to his charge. But as he is resolved to acquaint you and lord Sunderland with everything, in order the Queen may have a treu information, I shal say no more, but that as far as I am capable of judging, I veryly think he has acted with great zeal.'

When Marlborough looked back on it, Peterborough's visit did not seem quite so bad after all. On 15 September the duke could write to his wife: 'It is most certain that I had the happyness of very long audiences from 30, but it was generally after my business was done, and I must own to you he was very diverting.'⁴

From Soignies, Peterborough intimated to Sunderland his imminent return and asked for a convoy across the Channel 'that I may not att last goe to Paris'. He was still pleading slow progress on the grounds of the 'ill-placed contusion' and planned next to visit his old friend Benjamin Furly in Rotterdam. On 12/23 August he had reached The Hague and obtained an audience of the Pensionary Heinsius to whom he gave a complete account of the Spanish campaign. On 17/28 August he was at Helvoetsluys where he found no sign of the expected convoy. Anxious to be home, he took the packet boat for England, leaving his valuable papers in safe custody to await a more secure mode of transport.⁵

Peterborough had outlined to Marlborough in July 1707 the attitude he intended to take when he reached England. 'If I have not done my duty, I desire no favour; if I have served well, I hope I may meet with a suitable protection, at least justification, as to all absurdities raised to my prejudice. I should be glad to have it from the Queen, and I have waited with great patience to that end. If not, my Lord, I can give it myself at any time, and cannot doubt but that the Queen will permit me to employ myself elsewhere, if her Majesty has no occasion for my services.'

On his return to Parsons Green, Peterborough received a letter, dated

21 August OS, from the Clerk to the Privy Council, Mr Povey, informing him that his name was not on the list of members summoned to the Council, 'whether upon acct of your absence or no I know not...' The Queen had instructed the Cabinet Council to decide in advance how they would treat Peterborough on his arrival. In Sunderland's absence, Harley was told that Peterborough should be called before the Queen and Cabinet Council and asked to give his reasons for leaving the army in Spain and going to visit the Duke of Savoy 'without order or leave upon that occasion, though in case any forces had been sent thither he had indeed leave to command those forces'.

On receipt of the clerk's letter Peterborough at once wrote to Harley asking him to inform the Queen of his arrival. He had intended to go at once to Windsor but, since his name had been 'struck out of the Council books', he wished to avoid the embarrassment of appearing for an audience and then being denied admittance. Normally it was the custom for a returning ambassador or other commissioner to seek an audience in order to give an account of his embassy. Harley was cautious about offering any advice, suggesting that the earl must decide for himself what action he should take, but he promised to lay his letter before the Queen.[6]

Eventually Peterborough was told that the Queen wished him to submit to her in the Cabinet Council in person a written account of his transactions. He was offered access to any papers in the Secretary's office which he might require, as it was known that most of his were still in Holland. To outsiders, it looked very odd that the earl had still not paid his respects at court; Marlborough feared he might injure himself by 'pushing his animosities so far as to hurt himself'.

Peterborough had been aware of charges against him for some time; he had told Marlborough of them and also of how he proposed to defend himself. The charges were five in number. The first objected that he neglected to assist Galway by not marching towards Madrid with the forces which he had in Valencia. Secondly, he did not give enough encouragement to the King to march to Valencia. Thirdly, he left the army, as he said, 'unseasonably and without orders, to goe disgusted to Italy where he had nothing to doe'. Fourthly, it was objected that he took up money at Genoa at twenty per cent, without orders or government advice. The fifth charge regarded the dispersal of five regiments of foot and one of dragoons around Valencia, when Galway was in need of them as reinforcements. To this list was added the final complaint regarding the disrespectful return of the unopened recredentials. In each case Peterborough had given reasons, backed by decisions of councils of war and other papers, why he had acted in such a way.

The earl busied himself over the preparation of his report and let it be known amongst his friends that he intended to be active when Parliament reassembled. At the end of September, as his report neared completion, he was told that the Queen also wished clarification on six particular heads. First, she wished to know why Peterborough had failed to march to Madrid on hearing of Galway's arrival; secondly, why he had discouraged the King from marching by way of Valencia; thirdly, his reason for declining to serve with Galway; fourthly, his departure for Italy, leaving his commissions and claiming orders from the Queen to do so; fifthly, his negotiation of matters with the Duke of Savoy without authority; and finally his reason for drawing bills for large sums of money on the Treasury when almost £50,000 of it never reached the Deputy Paymaster.

In due course Peterborough provided answers to all the heads and supported them by relevant documents. In response to the first head, he explained that it was initially a physical impossibility to move the troops from Valencia because of the absence of mules. His first information about Galway was unreliable and he believed him to be in command of sufficient troops. He was under orders to escort the King to Madrid and to keep troops in readiness to send to Italy. To the second head, the earl claimed that he had used all means to encourage the King to travel by Valencia, desiring the honour of escorting him to Madrid. His troops had captured Requena and secured an open passage. To the third head, Peterborough answered that Galway had offered the command of the English forces to him in the knowledge of his previous commission as 'general to the West Indies'. To avoid difficulties, Peterborough had offered to serve as a volunteer but he claimed to have instructions from the Queen, of a later date than 3 May, which allowed him to decline to serve under another general and to come home whenever he thought fit. To the fourth head, Peterborough believed this misunderstanding arose over the confusion attending his role as ambassador which he had not adopted. Councils of war had considered his orders to go to Italy both positive and clear, and had thought his going there necessary. There had been no definite news of the raising of the siege of Turin until he was actually at sea.

Regarding the fifth point, Peterborough claimed that he did act within his instructions; he had powers given him previously to negotiate with the Duke of Savoy but in fact he negotiated nothing. The transactions he undertook did not in any way prejudice the major services. Fate had settled the argument in any case and the papers written before contained 'rather prophecies than arguments'. Had the plans been carried out, the situation in Spain and elsewhere might have been very much better than in fact it was at present.

The tone of Peterborough's reply to the accusation that he had drawn large sums of money on the Treasury, of which £50,000 never reached the Paymaster, indicated that the whole question of finance was a sore point. He claimed that the entire sum raised at Genoa was transmitted into the hands of the paymasters of the Queen and the King of Portugal. Considerable sums were sent to England and these all went through the Lord Treasurer's office except for about £300 in presents. Against this, he pointed out how much he had lost in the public service, having taken to Spain £30,000 of his own money which he had raised by the sale of a manor, the taking up of two years' income from his estate and by loans from the government. He had borne the expense of transporting the King of Spain and his entourage and had lost two equipages, one on land and one at sea, in addition to the cost of his preparations for the West Indies. He had twice lost his vouchers for sums chargeable on the general account; they had been recovered from the enemy only to be lost on board the *Resolution* 'where the violence and inhumanity of the sailors were most incredible, breaking open all my scriptores and trunks and forcing from anybody the least thing he endeavoured to secure...' Finally, he was prepared to give the Queen a complete account.[7]

The first Parliament of Great Britain assembled on 23 October 1707 and the House of Lords commenced regular sittings in early November. Observers noted that Peterborough appeared to be on reasonable terms with the administration. He spoke to everybody in the House and was not rebuffed, although no one seemed to seek his company.

The Queen's speech on 6 November referred to the war in Spain and so a debate on the subject became inevitable. The Lords, however, preferred to discuss the state of the nation and, in an unprecedented manner, declined to reply to the Queen's speech for another six weeks. On 12 December they decided that all matters regarding Spain should be remitted to a Committee of the Whole House.

Despite the apparent good terms, the administration was meanwhile keeping Peterborough under observation and was not above intercepting his mail. It was not until the arrival of Arent Furly on 9 November that he received all his papers. In early December two brothers were employed to make copies of a trunkload of them in preparation for the possibility of proceedings in Parliament.[8]

Of the many concerns awaiting Peterborough's attention this autumn, not all of them were connected with Spain. He had been anxious for some time to litigate against Sir John Germaine, the widower of the Duchess of Norfolk, over the ownership of Drayton. In his present financial state he could not afford to miss the opportunity of acquiring this valuable property. A case concerning part of the estate was heard in the Queen's Bench Division on 21 November but the jury found for Sir John.*

Despite Marlborough's advice to the contrary, the autumn of 1707 saw the publication of a narrative somewhat laudatory in style but a fairly accurate account of the Spanish campaign in Catalonia and Valencia. Written by Doctor John Freind, Peterborough's personal physician during that period, *An Account of the Earl of Peterborow's Conduct in Spain* reached a wide public. In printing letters, minutes of councils of war and other relevant documents, it aimed to provide proof of Peterborough's conduct in face of the allegations which had been made, as well as providing a lively story. It was at least a named claim for authenticity, rather than the various pamphlets by anonymous gentlemen which appeared subsequently in the same year. *Impartial Remarks on the Earl of Peterborow's Conduct in Spain* and *The Earl of Peterborow's Vindication anent the bad Success in Spain* were part of a developing pamphlet war. These all provoked the great counterblast of *Remarks upon Dr Freind's Account of the Earl of Peterborow's Conduct in Spain* which was published the following year after the long debate in the House of Lords. *Freind's Account* has been criticised for bias, claiming all the credit for Peterborough to the exclusion of others. It was written to state a case rather than provide a record but nonetheless it is interesting to note how frequently Freind's high-flown description of the colourful campaign of Valencia is verified in fact by the unvarnished account in Arent Furly's journal or the letters written in the field by Colonel de St Pierre.[9]

The Committee of the Whole House appointed to discuss the affairs of Spain met first on 15 December. The subject of the Earl of Peterborough was brought up first by the Earl of Rochester, who remarked that

---

*Sir John Germaine had recently married Lady Elizabeth Berkeley. As Lady Betty Germaine, she reigned as mistress of Drayton for over forty years.

it was rare for a person who had been sent abroad with as many commissions as the earl had not to be thanked or taken notice of in some way on his return. It was a measure of anti-government feeling that the Tory opposition, in the form of Rochester, should have espoused the cause of Peterborough, a commander-in-chief who had been recalled under censure but who was also a committed Whig previously suspected of holding dangerous republican views. Many present had become familiar with Peterborough's exploits through the work of Dr Freind, and Lord Halifax made mention of the book in his reply. He likened it to the account of Alexander the Great by Quintus Curtius, an author who was believed to have skilfully blended fact with fiction.* Halifax proposed that it would be inappropriate to return the thanks of the House before the investigations into the earl's conduct had been completed.

Peterborough assured the House that the inquiry was precisely what he had hoped for. The Lords asked that various papers might be laid before them. They wished to see orders and instructions sent to Peterborough as well as those sent to Galway and Rivers, an account of money sent to Spain since the taking of Barcelona, the number of men sent since that time and how many were present at Almanza. Further requests included orders sent to Galway since he became commander-in-chief and all transactions with him regarding the relief of Barcelona. It was to be an extensive inquiry.[10]

In the meantime Peterborough had been informed that the Queen was not satisfied with his replies to the heads of inquiry and required further information on certain points. She wished him to hand over his accounts and was still expecting a complete written narrative.

The next major debate in the Lords took place on 19 December. The Queen attended informally and listened to the speeches until five o'clock in the afternoon. She would have heard Peterborough speak for almost an hour, 'a very clever speech', in which he recounted the difficulties of supporting a war in Spain. Prince Eugène had told him that Spain was considered such an unpopular field by the Germans 'that were it proposed to his army to be shot to death or go thither, every fourth man would choose to die'. In recounting his own experiences, the earl spoke modestly but in his own justification. He concluded that

*It was said that Peterborough was sufficiently flattered to be likened to Alexander the Great as to overlook the aspersions cast on Dr Freind. A. Cunningham, *History of Great Britain*, vol. ii (1787), pp. 14–15.

a good army sent to Spain could still be successful and he would be prepared to support it, even if it were to be commanded by Galway.

Peterborough's latter remarks found some support in the House. The Earl of Rochester moved that the army in Flanders should be put on the defensive so that 18–20,000 men could be sent from there to Spain. The feeling seemed so strongly in favour of Rochester's proposal that Marlborough was moved to speak more warmly than usual. It was not in his plan, he explained, to move the centre of the war away from Flanders, but he revealed to the House that it was hoped that Prince Eugène might be persuaded to undertake the command in Spain. This revelation cut the ground from under the feet of his opposition. Although this plan was shortly quashed by the Emperor, the House was made to feel at the time that the management of the war was still in good hands.[11]

After Christmas Peterborough expressed to Sunderland his weariness of answering heads of inquiry; if any further questions required to be put, he would prefer to be heard in person on oath before the Council. He was still at work on the narrative for the Queen. In January 1707/08, both Sunderland and Peterborough laid bundle upon bundle of paper before the House of Lords. The House resumed work on these on 13 January. Peterborough was expected to satisfy the House on five heads. The chief concerns of the ministry seemed to be that he had diverted the King of Spain from going to Madrid, that he would not join Galway who had a superior commission, that he took up money at Genoa without authority, that he sent back his letters of revocation unopened and that he failed to wait on the Queen on his arrival.

Peterborough's replies to what he called the charge were declamatory and involved. Some peers wanted him to take each head in turn and produce proof. Others pointed out that he was not on trial and the House was obliged to him for the information he was prepared to offer.

That Peterborough appreciated the opportunity of having his case aired in public was apparent. Joseph Addison noted: 'His Lordship has been extremely long in his Speeches…and shows a more than ordinary Gaiety in his behaviour both in the House and out of it since this Affaire has been in Agitation.' The House continued to sit in committee on Spanish affairs well into February. Peterborough was rarely a disappointing public speaker. 'He bids open defiance, and fires very thick at the ministry and sometimes with a good deal of wit, that people often attend it as they do a play…'

Soon after the opening of the Committee's proceedings, it was brought to Peterborough's attention that a book was about to be published as an answer to Dr Freind's *Account*.* It reflected scandalously on his conduct, so the earl claimed, and he had the printer and bookseller called before the House on a charge of breach of privilege. The charge was upheld by the Lords and the author, Dr Richard Kingston, was prosecuted.

There was a story current that Peterborough had obtained a sight of this book by disguising himself as a French parson, a friend of Lord Galway and interested in his vindication. Hearing that this book might contribute to it, he approached the printer with an offer to make a gratuitous translation into French and was able to make a thorough examination of the work.[12]

At the conclusion of Peterborough's evidence, it was presumed that the House of Lords would make some sort of pronouncement. A parallel debate in the House of Commons was also long drawn out and, in the opinion of some, was taking up valuable time which could be better spent on other matters. Peterborough had been criticised in both Houses by supporters of the Ministry and commended by the Tories. To some observers it seemed that the Lords were dragging their feet over the Peterborough question so that the Commons would be obliged to come to a decision first. There was a general feeling that, although his conduct had been irregular, there was little that could not be justified or explained away. Some doubt remained over his discouragement of the King on the road to Madrid but it was felt that he could clear himself over the money matters. By the middle of February Peterborough had called the last of his witnesses, some of his officers in Spain, 'all stoutly for him'. Nothing further occurred during March. At the end of the session and before the prorogation in April, some letters were returned to the earl but no report was made and the matter was allowed to lapse.

The consequences for Peterborough's future were inconclusive. Jonathan Swift, not at this time the intimate that he would become, had watched the affair with interest. 'It is a perfect Jest to see my Lord Peterborough, reputed as great a Whig as any in England, abhorred by his own Party and caressed by the Tories.' To the Earl of Shaftesbury, it was not a matter for jest but for sadness. He was sorry that Peterborough should quarrel with 'old Whigs' and ally himself to Robert

---

*It was probably *Remarks upon Dr Freind's Account of the Earl of Peterborow's Conduct in Spain 1708*.

Harley, a man politically isolated and much opposed. Shaftesbury believed that any Tory support of Peterborough was not in his best interest. They would be merely serving their own ends and would certainly injure him, as they had done before. A breach with Sunderland was pushing Peterborough into the Tory camp. Shaftesbury wrote regretfully to Benjamin Furly: 'We are not likely to see your friend Lord Peterborow employed again, as I could heartily wish.'[13]

Twenty-six

With the Parliamentary inquiry over Spain behind him, Peterborough could look to the future. As far as the war was concerned, he would not be offered another command and in other ways his hands were tied for the present. The Queen had asked him to produce a statement of his accounts and in the meantime, as much in retaliation for criticism as for expediency, the ministry had attached his property in Bedfordshire and Northamptonshire until the accounts were cleared. Peterborough was kept busy for many months; it was not until April 1709 that he asked for an audit and obtained a discharge.[1]

It may have been this occupation and the attachment which clipped the wings of another project. In March 1707 the French had made an abortive attempt to land the Pretender and some troops on the coast of Scotland. Afterwards Peterborough wrote to the Elector and his mother urging them to take steps to protect their interests in Britain by sending some member of their family to reside there. He hoped to revisit Hanover at the earliest opportunity and visit the Elector's army on the summer campaign.

In his reply the Elector stated that on principle he always acted in concert with the Queen and her ministers regarding the affairs of Great Britain. As for the projected journey, he felt that it might 'give umbrage and be a subject of sinister interpretations'. Robethon, who had drafted this reply, felt motivated to tell Marlborough of the correspondence, 'as I know what embarrassment this master firebrand would occasion...I thought proper to communicate the intelligence to your highness, who may perhaps find some means to frustrate this hopeful journey.' He added that he was unaware of the tone of the Electress's reply.[2]

On 30 July 1708, at Windsor, Peterborough was introduced into the Queen's presence by Godolphin. This apparent restoration to grace produced speculation; a rumour began to circulate that Peterborough was to become once again the governor of Jamaica. What was said at the audience is not recorded but as for the governorship, it was understood that the earl could not get the powers and conditions he would have liked and nothing more was heard of it. Now that Peterborough had access to the Queen again, it was thought that he would not hesitate to speak freely to her.[3]

That autumn Peterborough found another opportunity to speak freely, in a letter to one of his brothers who had written to remonstrate with him over his treatment of his son, Lord Mordaunt. There had been no reconciliation between the parents and the son after Mordaunt's disastrous marriage in 1705. As things stood at present, Mordaunt would receive no benefit under the terms of his father's will as he had married without parental consent. The main estate was due to pass to the second son, Harry, who his parents still hoped would contract a brilliant marriage.

Lord Mordaunt's circumstances were indeed straitened; at least, he found them so. After a bright beginning, his career in the Army was not prospering and he had difficulty in supporting his regiment financially. Since the autumn of 1707 he had been living in 'a small house in Yorkshire where Bread is cheap and where everything squares with my slender circumstances'. The house was at Middlethorpe, near his wife's family estates. He was himself on furlough; he had begged the government not to send him back to Spain just at the time his father was expected to come home, as he still hoped for a reconciliation.

That winter Mordaunt contracted smallpox quite severely but was much heartened to hear that his mother contacted a mutual friend in London every post for news of his welfare. Lady Peterborough had actively discouraged any meeting between Mordaunt and his father. In 1706 her violent opposition had effectively blocked the proposal to send Mordaunt with the Queen's compliments to the King of Spain.

Peterborough's 'very sincere' letter to his brother showed little sympathy with his son. Mordaunt's 'little spirit' in his situation seemed to upset his father more than anything. He appeared to be too fond of staying at home with his wife, 'that cursed cause of his misfortunes'. On 12 October 1708 the Viscountess Mordaunt gave birth to a son. 'Getting of Children' did pass muster as a reasonable way of employing the time, but the news of the forthcoming event made the earl unusually displeased, 'the worst news I have heard a great while'. He continued: 'It's very indifferent to me wt name he has, and I should never recomend my own, if I were upon good terms with my Ld Mordaunt.'[4] On 19 October the baby was christened Charles at the church of St Mary's Bishophill Senior, York. (In 1735 he succeeded his grandfather as fourth Earl of Peterborough.)

Charles Mordaunt, third Earl of Peterborough and Earl of Monmouth
(Sir G. Kneller, private collection)

Carey, Countess of Peterborough (Christian Richter, courtesy Bonhams)

LEFT John, Viscount Mordaunt, Peterborough's eldest son (painting destroyed)
RIGHT Captain Henry Mordaunt, second son (private collection). Artists unknown.

A view of San Mateo (author's photograph)

Anastasia, Countess of Peterborough (John Vanderbank, private collection)

Peterborough blamed his own difficult financial circumstances on the backlog of debt with which his estates were encumbered. The position could have been resolved by parting with some of his patrimony but he was reluctant to do this, hoping that matters would improve if his younger son made an advantageous marriage.

In the autumn of 1708 Lady Peterborough remained in the country while the earl was in London. Her health was not good and her husband thought that 'gentle and proper courses might procure a perfect recovery...I will send you a Friday some admirable clarrett, I have gott itt very cheap...a glasse of wine is good physick for Sept if you except against any other.'⁵

During the following winter Peterborough's activity was limited, with occasional attendance in Parliament. Weary and disillusioned, he contemplated asking leave of the Queen to go abroad for the benefit of his wife's health and because of 'the little satisfaction he found in this country'. He was still trying to find a way to put a stop to 'discourses...spread to his prejudice'. He had found an interested buyer for part of his estate in Bedfordshire and Northamptonshire and wished to strike a bargain but was unable to do so until the restraints had been lifted from his lands. He petitioned the Lord Treasurer for a statement of the accounts of the Spanish expedition and for details of all amounts chargeable against him. Subsequently his lands were relieved of encumbrances and the sale went forward.⁶

The proposed journey abroad never took place. Lady Peterborough's health did not improve and she died 'of a squinzy' during the night of Friday, 13 May 1709. Her body was placed in the Mordaunt family vault at Turvey on 28 May. Described by Abel Boyer as 'a Lady of admirable Wit and Judgement', Carey, Countess of Peterborough had a deep interest in the political scene both at home and abroad and her opinions were shrewd. As an ambitious and loyal wife, she represented her husband's interests with determination during his absences abroad as well as shouldering responsibility for his property and the arrangements for their daughter's marriage. Having borne five children, her relationships with the surviving three are not easy to assess. She claimed to have idolised her eldest son, John Lord Mordaunt, yet he was clearly in awe of her. Neither she nor her husband ever spoke a hard word of their second son, Harry. As for their daughter, Henrietta, whom they generally referred to as Harriet, her mother found her at times a most unsympathetic companion and professed that her marriage to the Marquess of Huntly in February 1707 was a relief. Relations improved after the marriage and the two were in correspondence in the year before Carey's death.

Lady Peterborough had very much concerned herself with the education of her children, particularly that of her daughter. 'Her education was my pleasur and my care', she wrote, 'out of the common road of inglish breeding.' Lord Shaftesbury commended her for these interests which he considered 'extraordinary, and almost without example in those of your rank'. As far as her own education was concerned, her letters were almost unique for phonetic spelling and quite irrational punctuation. They provide the modern reader with a constant puzzle and an interesting sidelight on eighteenth-century pronunciation. The Duke of Marlborough commented on her bad handwriting and the duchess wrote waspishly on the back of a letter: 'The lady that writ this letter pretended to be mighty learn'd and talked much of all the great Authors but they did not improve her so much as to make her writ good English...'

Her husband sincerely mourned her passing, and she was considered to have held a great influence over him. There is a brief letter written on black-edged paper among the correspondence of Robert Harley, Earl of Oxford, received on 21 June. Peterborough was lodging temporarily at the house of Mrs Grimes in Stratton Street and was about to leave town. He thanked his friend for inquiring after him. 'I find that being alone is most easy to mee in my circumstances and have seen no body... if you will doe mee the favour to call...I shall be glad to see you...'[7]

A family bereavement of this kind can act as a catalyst to draw the members together. At the end of June Peterborough left for the country. In September he was staying at Lord Mordaunt's house in Yorkshire. Here Lord Huntly had brought his wife from Scotland to see her father. In Yorkshire, news of the victory of Malplaquet reached the party. This hard-fought battle saw much loss of life. Included among the dead was Brigadier Lalo with whom Mordaunt had a contract over the disposal of their regiments at the conclusion of hostilities. Peterborough urged his son to visit the Duke of Marlborough and ensure that he regained Lalo's regiment (the Royal Scots Fusiliers). Mordaunt took the advice, carrying a letter from his father with him, and – after some lapse of time – successfully regained the regiment.[8]

In the winter of 1709 Peterborough renewed his litigation against Sir John Germaine and appealed against a former decision of the House of Lords. The case was heard on 21 February 1710 and lasted three days but the earl was unable to be present because of illness. The appeal was dismissed on the grounds that it had been heard before.

Peterborough also had other concerns on his mind. On the final day of the case his son Harry died from smallpox and was buried at Turvey on 1 March. On his return to England after his wound in 1707, Captain Henry Mordaunt had been court-martialled for the loss of his ship and exonerated. His recovery from his wound had been slow. At the time of his death it was rumoured that he had planned to go back to sea. He had been elected a member of Parliament for Malmesbury on two occasions, in 1705 and again in the spring of 1708. In the autumn of 1708 he had been at Dauntsey with his mother. He never married, advantageously or otherwise.[9]

The outbreak of smallpox that spring was of a particularly virulent strain. Despite his previous attack, Lord Mordaunt also contracted the disease and this time it proved fatal. He died at Winchester on 6 April. Mordaunt had by now reached the rank of brigadier-general in the army. At his death he left two sons, the younger, John, being less than one year old. The records are silent on how this double bereavement affected Peterborough who was left with responsibility for the care of his widowed daughter-in-law and his two grandsons.[10]

Despite personal grief and ill-health, Peterborough could not have failed to be aware of the gradual change of ministry which took place over the summer months of 1710. His friendship with Robert Harley, the Secretary of State, may have meant that he was aware of what was going on behind the scenes. Certainly Hoffman, the Imperial envoy, appeared to think that he was part of a cabal led by Harley.

The changes began almost as soon as the Parliament had gone into recess for the summer. The Queen then appointed the Duke of Shrewsbury as her Lord Chamberlain in place of the Earl of Kent. Shrewsbury was a moderate Whig and did not have strong party affiliations. His appointment, and the subsequent ministerial changes, were made on the advice of Harley in consultation with Shrewsbury and others. Harley's now notorious influence over the Queen was popularly considered to have been gained via the backstairs with the assistance of one of the Queen's Women of the Bedchamber, Mrs Abigail Masham.

It was the aim of Shrewsbury and Harley to achieve a moderate ministry by degrees. This inevitably developed into a group composed mainly of Tories, of whom Shrewsbury himself was the chief exception. Another moderate Whig, the Duke of Somerset, gave some assistance to Harley, clandestinely at his own request. In June the Earl of Sunderland was replaced as Secretary of State by the Earl of Dartmouth. In August Godolphin was replaced as Chancellor of the Exchequer by Harley; the office of Lord Treasurer remained vacant until the following year when it also fell into Harley's lap. As autumn approached, dissolution of the last Whig Parliament of Anne's reign became inevitable.

During the same summer Peterborough concluded a sale of property in Stagsden, Bedfordshire, to Sir Thomas Trevor, who later purchased further Mordaunt land at Chellington. The earl then spent some time at Bath and returned to town in the late summer. Rumours had circulated since August that he might receive appointments to the posts left vacant since the death of the Prince Consort in October 1708, the Chief Commissioner of the Admiralty and Captain General of the Marines.[11]

On 14 October 1710 the Queen ordered a commission to be prepared appointing the Earl of Peterborough Captain General of the Marines. Shrewsbury suggested to Harley that if he met the earl 'it would not be improper to let him know it, and that as to the other pretension there remain yet some difficulties'. The commission was not passed and made public until 2 November. The post was a sinecure with a salary of £5 per diem. As for the 'other pretension', nothing further was heard of it. Peterborough gave out that the Admiralty post was of little importance; his main desire was to go to sea once again. Some thought that he did not care to be joined in commission with Lord Haversham, while others believed his relationship with Harley still bore the marks of his treatment on return from Spain.

There is little evidence of strain in Peterborough's dealings with Harley, who had been one of the few friends that the earl was prepared to see while in mourning for his wife. In October Jonathan Swift gave the first of many animated descriptions of Peterborough in Harley's company in his *Journal to Stella*. Swift had been dining with Harley in the company of Matthew Prior and Sir Hugh Dalrymple, the Lord President of the Court of Session in Scotland. Later Peterborough joined the party; the acquaintance which already existed between the earl and Swift was renewed, to develop later into friendship. It was a cheerful evening during which the company amused themselves by making fun of a poem entitled 'Sid Hamet' which Harley produced from his pocket and Peterborough read aloud. The poem had been circulated anonymously but was in fact written by Swift. Peterborough is shown as relaxed and convivial, not dogged by disappointment or unhappiness.

It was part of Harley's Plan of Administration to attempt to 'secure' for the Tories members of the other party in the House of Lords before they should go too far the other way. It seemed that it was his intention to subject Peterborough to this treatment. While the Navy talked speculatively about a sea expedition, other sources in town were sending the earl 'several ways at once, to Vienna, West Indias and Spain...' The Admiralty idea having proved impossible, the administration were considering Peterborough for a diplomatic post at the courts of Vienna and Turin, places which Harley considered next in importance to The Hague.[12]

On 6 December 1710 Peterborough received his instructions. It was generally understood that his mission to the Emperor was to encourage him to prosecute the war in Spain with greater vigour: affairs there had reached a very low ebb. But Peterborough's main task was in fact to try to bring to a head negotiations to resolve the dispute between the Emperor and the Duke of Savoy which had already been in progress for some time. Peterborough's friendship and admiration for the Duke would naturally encourage him to do all he could but the matter would have to be handled with diplomacy.

The dispute had arisen through the reluctance of the Emperor to implement satisfactorily the conditions of the Treaty of 1703. Under this agreement the Duke of Savoy had been promised certain territorial concessions from the Empire in return for his support of the Alliance. It was not until after the Battle of Turin in 1707 that the Emperor agreed to hand over the stipulated territories; other concessions he would not make.

This awkward state of affairs led to the Duke of Savoy's refusal to command the Allied troops in the spring campaign of 1708. Eventually, after some diplomatic activity, it occurred to the Emperor that the Duke might prove a useful ally in another dispute between himself and the Pope. As a result the Emperor formally handed over the duchy of Monferrato and confirmed the Duke's hereditary suzerainty over the Imperial fiefs of Le Langhe. However in 1709 some of the fiefholders complained that the Duke had tried to exact oaths of fealty from them. To the Emperor, this action overstepped the mark and he withdrew his recognition of the right of suzerainty. Once again the Duke declined to lead the spring campaign. He appealed for arbitration to the Maritime Powers who were guarantors under the Treaty of 1703. As a result Brigadier Palmes was sent from London to Vienna to try to negotiate, with the assistance of an envoy from the States General. The Emperor was prepared to accept the mediation of the Maritime Powers but would not agree to any binding arbitration. Early in 1710 a settlement of a sort had been prepared by the guarantors. It was acceptable to the Duke of Savoy but the Emperor disliked it. This state of stalemate still obtained at the time of Peterborough's appointment.

The new envoy was instructed to call first at The Hague and consult with the British ministers there. He was ordered to make known his instructions to the Pensionary and the States General and to ask for the support of their ministers in Vienna. Having reached the Emperor's court, he was expected to cooperate with any envoy sent there by the Duke of Savoy and seek his advice. In assisting the Savoyard envoy to support his master's pretensions, Peterborough was to remain 'firm and steady in insisting upon the full Execution of the Treaty according to the plain intent and literal meaning of it, without deviating into Questions and Intricacys upon Points foreign to the genuine Explication of the Articles in dispute...' To the Emperor he was expected to underline the importance of the part played by the Duke of Savoy in the Alliance, the considerable sacrifices he had already made for it and the underlying fear that, were he not satisfied in his demands, he might accept offers from France which could ruin everything. Finally, he was to offer the Emperor a reasonable time limit for the acceptance or refusal of the terms of the settlement.[13]

The instructions having been issued, preparations for Peterborough's departure began almost immediately. Henry St John, now a Secretary of State, thought it politic that Peterborough should have left The Hague before the arrival of Sir James Wishart, one of the Commissioners of the Admiralty. Wishart had secret instructions to arrange with the Dutch an expedition to the West Indies with the purpose of attacking French trade there. St John wrote: 'Though my Lord might be a very proper man to command in such an expedition, yet we had rather commit the forming of the plan to another...'

Some difficulty then emerged over transport, as none of the yachts usually employed to convey ambassadors was available. At Christmas it was found that a 'convenient Frigat' could be ready in less than a week. Peterborough had a lot to accomplish in the time. He had recently conveyed the manor of Sudborough in Northamptonshire to trustees for sale. He had made a new will, making provision for payment of debts and leaving the main part of his property to his elder grandson, Charles Lord Mordaunt, on reaching the age of twenty-one.

Charles would forfeit the inheritance if in the meantime he married without his grandfather's consent.

Swift, whose friendship with Peterborough had developed into an agreement to correspond, was bidden to dine with the departing envoy at the Globe in the Strand on the day before he was due to leave. When he arrived to keep his appointment, he found the earl 'among half a dozen lawyers and attorneys and hangdogs, signing of deeds and stuff before his journey...I sat among that scurvy company till after four...' Peterborough had intended to expound to Swift his theories on the problem of Spain. After the disastrous outcome at Brihuega, when Stanhope was obliged to surrender and was taken prisoner along with 4,000 British troops, the matter had become a subject of common concern. Swift heard Peterborough forecast at the end of October that Stanhope would lose Spain by Christmas, explaining why this was sure to happen; and when Harley argued against him, he refused to shift his ground.[14]

After Brihuega the Allied army continued its withdrawal to Catalonia, the only part of Spain still loyal to the Austrian cause. It was the final chapter in the attempt to gain the crown of Spain for the Austrian claimant. Eventually even Catalonia was left to the Bourbons.

At home this major reverse in fortune gave rise to the call for a parliamentary examination into the cause of 'the late ill success in Spain'. In the event, the procedure developed into an exercise in denigrating Marlborough and the policies of the Whig government. Since fortunes in Spain had begun to fall at the time of the tragic Battle of Almanza, it was thought advisable to hear evidence from Peterborough on the events that preceded it. The House of Lords decided to ask the Queen that his departure might be delayed for a few days so that he could assist the House in its investigations.* The Queen having agreed, Peterborough had no reluctance in complying with the request.

On 5 January 1711 the earl was asked to reply to five questions. These covered Galway's proceedings at Madrid, the march to Guadalajara and then to Valencia, the contacts between himself at Valencia and Galway at Madrid, and the old chestnut of the reasons which induced the King to travel to Madrid by Aragon. Finally, he was questioned about the council of war at Valencia on 15 January 1707 and why the

---

*Peterborough's departure was so imminent that already (4 January) some of his servants and baggage had arrived at Greenwich.

King had left the army at that point to go to Barcelona. To all this, Peterborough made a verbatim reply which lasted for more than an hour and was later committed to paper. Bishop Nicolson considered the reply a repetition of 'Dr Freind's History of His Lordship's Wonders in Spain'. The earl naturally made the best use of the opportunity in his own interest; he stressed that the advice he had given latterly had been right and had not been followed. He made rather more than 'glancing reflections on the conduct of other generals', but at least the House allowed Galway to respond in writing to some of the statements made.

The following day it was the turn of Galway to give the House a narrative of the entire period of his service in Spain and the next Monday he submitted it in writing. Peterborough also handed in a written recapitulation of his answers.

On 9 January the Lords met again, a committee of the whole House was formed and heard readings of Galway's narrative and Peterborough's recapitulation. The Queen was present incognito and listened for four hours. Both Galway and Lord Tyrawley (formerly Sir Charles O'Hara) were called in to hear Peterborough's answers read. When Tyrawley was asked to give some information about the council of war at Valencia, he was reluctant to make a detailed reply as he wished to know if the Lords were making any accusation against him. There followed a debate on whether or not the House was in fact making accusations in its attempt to discover all the facts. There was a strong feeling that the matter had been taken too far. The Duke of Marlborough pointed out that 'if they designed to censure persons who had acted to the best of their understanding, they would have nobody to serve them', and Peterborough observed that 'no man can be accused for giving his opinion in a council of war'.

Tyrawley then gave evidence before the committee. The opinion which Peterborough had given at the council of war was read, as were some letters. Dr Freind gave evidence in corroboration of what Peterborough had said and vouched for the authenticity of the papers which had appeared in his book. At 9 pm the debate was further prolonged for another hour by a motion by Earl Ferrers who wished the committee to agree that 'the earl of Peterborough has given a very faithful, just, and honourable account of the Councils of War at Valencia'. The question was disputed on the grounds that such a statement reflected on the reputation of the other generals. Some peers were unhappy at the term 'just'. There was an attempt to stem discussion by a proposal to close the committee and resume the ordinary business of the House which was decided in the negative. The main question later passed unaltered and without a division.

A second debate, also in committee, took place on 11 January. The main subject of discussion was whether the policy of an offensive war, which had been favoured by Galway, Tyrawley and Stanhope, was the cause of the misfortunes in Spain, in particular the Battle of Almanza. Peterborough's assertion that the Duke of Savoy had been in favour of a defensive war in Spain led to some discussion over the plans for the descent on Toulon. A lighter moment occurred when Peterborough insisted on reading aloud a letter which he had sent to Secretary Hedges in 1706, describing the plans concerted with the Duke of Savoy and Prince Eugène. The letter was in French since both the Duke and the Prince spoke that language. Some lords called for a translation but Peterborough refused, saying that he was not a secretary. Eventually, the lengthy debate concluded with the resolution carried that the voting by Galway, Tyrawley and Stanhope for an offensive war was 'a great occasion' of the loss of the Battle of Almanza and other misfortunes.

On Friday 12 January it was the administration's turn to be examined, as letters from Sunderland to Galway had indicated ministerial approval of the offensive policy. The House was in committee and the Queen was again present. She was anxious for Peterborough's departure for Vienna as the Duke of Savoy's envoy was already there. As time was running short, she must have felt frustrated by some of the side issues which absorbed their lordships' attention. The question under discussion included the sentence: 'An offensive war in Spain was approved and directed by the Cabinet Council.' A long debate followed as to whether the term 'Cabinet Council' should be replaced by 'ministers'. In the course of discussion Peterborough amused them with an apt definition, 'that he thought the word Cabinet Council not so proper as Ministers. That he had heard a distinction between the Cabinet Council and the Privy Council; that the Privy Counsellors were such as were thought to know everything, and knew nothing, and those of the Cabinet Council thought nobody knew anything but themselves.' At the conclusion of the debate it was held that the ministers were 'justly to be blamed for contributing to all our misfortunes in Spain'.

Before the committee rose, the Duke of Argyll drew the attention of the House to Peterborough's imminent departure to Vienna. He expressed the hope that every peer was now convinced of the earl's 'great and eminent services to his country'. He put the question 'that the Earl of Peterborough, during the time he had the honour of commanding the army in Spain, did perform many great and eminent services, and if the opinion he gave in the Council of War at Valencia had been followed, it might, very probably, have prevented the misfortunes that have happened since in Spain'. The committee agreed without a division and the agreement was confirmed when the House resumed sitting. The Duke of Buckingham moved that Peterborough should be given the thanks of the House 'for his eminent and remarkable services'. On a general assent a speech of thanks was made by the Lord Keeper.

To be given the thanks of the House is always a signal honour. On this occasion it was offered after very minute inquiries, on more than one occasion, into Peterborough's conduct. It came unaccompanied by any more tangible and lasting tokens of appreciation; this fact was noted in the speech and contrasted with the honours heaped on the Duke of Marlborough. The Lord Keeper said: 'Such is your lordship's known generosity, and truly noble temper, that I assure myself the present I am now offering to your lordship is the more acceptable, as it comes pure and unmixt, and is unattended with any other reward which your lordship might justly think would be an alloy to it.'

Peterborough made a brief reply: 'I cannot reproach myself with any want of zeal for the public service, but your lordships' approbation of what I was able to do towards serving my Queen and country, gives me new life.' At this satisfactory conclusion of an old chapter, Peterborough left the House 'near Midnight' for Greenwich, the *Katharine* yacht and his journey to Vienna.[15]

Twenty-seven

In the eighteenth century a winter journey to Vienna was unlikely to lack incident. Peterborough's journey was no exception and was dogged by difficulties mostly caused by the weather. In his entourage there travelled a diplomat, Simon Clement, who appeared to be acting as the earl's secretary. Clement kept a diary, 'a Journal of what I found remarkable in my travailing with my Lord Peterborow to Vienna', in which he gives a vivid picture of the style in which a nobleman, bearing a character from his sovereign, moved about Europe in those days.

The journey did not begin well. On the evening of Saturday 13 January the *Katharine* yacht set out from Greenwich and anchored off the Hope for the night. She sailed next morning to meet her convoy off the Nore but found there only a message that the *Hector* awaited them off Harwich. The *Katharine* reached Harwich at 3 pm to find the *Hector* and three other men-of-war. The ship had been held back by the assembling of a fleet of eighty merchantmen which she had also been ordered to convoy, 'whereat my Lord was much offended'. Protest proved unavailing; the pilot refused to take the ship out at night.

The next day, 15 January, the entire fleet sailed. Off the coast of Holland they were struck by a violent storm and were forced to lie off shore all night. During the storm three of the fleet were lost, the *Hector* was missing and the merchantmen were badly damaged. Next morning the *Katharine* anchored safely off Helvoetsluys.[1]

Snow lay on the ground throughout the whole of the journey. In Holland they found it too deep on some roads for wheeled vehicles to pass easily and so they travelled to Rotterdam by boat. The next day Peterborough went on by canal to Delft, where he left the rest of the party and continued to The Hague. Here he remained for six days. He was well received by the States General, who gave ready agreement and support to the methods he was to follow in his negotiations in Vienna. He also visited the Pensionary Heinsius and the Queen's minister at The Hague, Lord Townshend.

He did not forget his friends at home. He wrote to both Harley and St John. Nine dozen bottles of champagne and burgundy were sent back with his returning transport for the benefit of the Secretary of State, Henry St John. 'The Capt of the yatch sayes he cannot cheat the Queen of more Customes att once with a safe conscience.' The wine was to be delivered into the custody of the Revd Dr Swift 'att Germain Street'. It would have been unsuitable to deposit smuggled goods on the doorstep of a Minister of the Crown, 'when I am satisfyed the church will give a compleat absolution, [and] it will encourage mee in my sins'.[2]

On 3 February 1711 NS the ambassadorial cortege set out from The Hague at night 'by moonshine'. It consisted of three vehicles, a berlin, a chaise and a baggage wagon. Peterborough regularly travelled late, having stopped for dinner in the early evening. He also habitually made early starts, often between 5 am and 7 am.

Passing by Utrecht and Arnhem, their route took them towards the Rhine. Reaching Düsseldorf on the evening of 7 February, they found it was carnival time and the inns were full. Fortunately their arrival was of enough consequence for the news to reach the Elector, who sent one of his officers, Count Frosini, to greet the earl and offer him accommodation in his house. On the next day, a Sunday, Peterborough had an audience of the Elector and later called on the Electress. He was present while the Elector dined and was later entertained lavishly in his own lodging. That evening he was invited to sit with their Highnesses at the opera, while his suite was 'placed in a convenient Gallery'.

Having been treated with all the marks of distinction, Peterborough took his leave and set out again at 2 am the next morning, without having any sleep. At the end of a long day of travel their accommodation that night was, in contrast to the luxury of Düsseldorf, 'a very bad Inn where we lay on straw'.

The party had its share of carriage accidents. On 10 February a long stop was made at Freilingen to mend the chaise. The next day it was the turn of the berlin, whose axletree broke. Clement had to walk nine miles through the forest to Königstein; fortunately the posthouse met with his approval. It was not far to Frankfurt and they put up that evening at a renowned hostelry called the Red House; it was 'fit for a nobleman's hous but very dear'.

Peterborough only remained in Frankfurt for one day before resuming his journey. Three days later the party arrived in Nuremberg. They were met by one of the principal gentlemen of the town who conveyed the magistrates' compliments and took them to see the Town House. The earl declined an invitation to dinner on account of his journey but the Master of Ceremonies sent him a present of five fish (including pike, carp and eel) 'and above 30 flagons...of several sorts of curious wines; My Ld not having conveniency of carriage, left it behind, but gave very generously to ye servants and ye poor.'

On 16 February another snowfall impeded their progress but they still made a 5.30 am start. At Ratisbon (Regensburg) they found the Danube frozen. A passage by water at this stage would have brought them to Vienna in three days. From Ratisbon Peterborough wrote to Harley:

> You must accept of a very indifferent letter from one going to Vienna in this season, a cruell one as ever was known; my hands are frozen, and I am hardly awake; my comfort is ye Princes of Germany better bred than we are (who) provide me with meat enough, and Tockai in abundance, and are so well interested in our affairs that they Drink your health to mee in most unreasonable Brimmers; I doe my best on that occasion as I will in all others where you have a concern.
>
> I have only Time to lett some one of my Friends know where I am...I would give Twenty pistolls for the least paper perfumed with Tabacco out of an English coffee house...I had rather have three lines from Dr Swift this moment att Ratisbonne, then all that ever was publish'd in the Louve print.
>
> But by the bye, if you doe not imediately make a Rich Dean or a poor Bishop of the Reverend aforesaid, send him to mee that he may be a Cardinall.

Reaching Passau, Peterborough found that a thaw had set in and the river was open. He decided to shorten the journey by going by water. As they approached Linz, they found it impossible to land because of the amount of ice and so they were obliged to put up at an inn in a suburb. In addition the roads had become impassable because of the thaw.

Resigned to a delay, Peterborough set out to visit the town and included the Jesuit College. After he had returned to his inn, he received an invitation to lodge in the College or at least dine with them there the following day. He felt able to accept the invitation to dine and was subsequently treated to a lavish and incredible meal which consisted mainly of fish, it being the season of Lent. One dish contained 'a Carp of two foot long in a Pye'. The dinner was stylishly presented and the company was entertained during the meal by 'a fine consort of Music with Trumpets and kettle drums'. Before dinner Peterborough and his entourage had been shown a very impressive collection of clockwork instruments owned by the Jesuits. In return for this generous hospitality, the earl made a disbursement to the poor and presented the Father Rector with a repeating gold watch valued at fifty pounds.

The same day, 21 February, saw a return of the freezing temperatures which made the roads once again passable. Hearing good reports, Peterborough set out that evening for Vienna, which he reached two days later, leaving Clement, his suite and the baggage to follow.[3]

Since it was Carnival time in Vienna, the conferences which Peterborough was expected to hold with the Duke of Savoy's envoy, Mellarède, were postponed for several days. Secretary St John administered a diplomatic rap over the knuckles from a distance, annoyed that 'such a trifling boyish consideration should retard a matter of this importance even a moment'.

From Vienna Peterborough told the Pensionary Heinsius that he found it difficult to work with the Imperial Court as they appeared suspicious of his motives. They doubted the sincerity of the interest of the new government in England in continuing the war; they believed that he was more likely to try to make difficulties in order to find an excuse to make peace with France than to encourage a more lively prosecution of the hostilities. To persuade them otherwise, the earl parted with some money for their troops who were very short. He had no orders to take such action, but this gesture and his arguments seemed to convince the Court of his goodwill.

The methods outlined in Peterborough's instructions could not hasten the painfully slow progress of the negotiations but he improved matters considerably by suggesting a compromise arrangement which would be acceptable to both the Emperor and the Duke. By this the Emperor would allow the Duke the possession of the fiefs of the Montferrat and a decision about rights and titles would be left for another occasion. At last light seemed to show at the end of the tunnel. However, by early April no progress had been made on any of the other points. Having given his approval to the arrangement, the Emperor then contracted an illness which led to his death on 17 April. For the time being all negotiations and discussions came to a conclusion.

Peterborough, whose agile mind could never remain fixed on one subject for long, was not the only one to turn his attention to questions of the succession and the affairs of Spain as soon as the probable outcome of the Emperor's illness brought these issues into focus. He had hoped to leave Vienna by mid-March and travel on to Turin. The government at home wasted some paper on persuading him to stay, but the uncertainty over the Emperor's health was enough to detain him at the hub of affairs. In addition, the Duke of Savoy wished him to remain until all the treaty conditions had been fulfilled.[4]

Before leaving Vienna, Peterborough sent Brigadier Palmes home with letters and a scheme worked out with the Austrian ministers for the future conduct of the war. He had already informed the British government of the plans. Among the proposals made was the sending of a force to reduce Sicily. At home this was considered too grandiose as there were no troops available for such a venture. It was also proposed to bring the forces in Spain up to their full quota. This was also considered impracticable, as it was known that the Austrians were in fact longing to leave Spain. Peterborough had made some sort of arrangement with the Austrians for the supply of 8,000 of their troops for the campaign in Italy. Ultimately these troops would be under the command of the Duke of Savoy but the arrangement appeared to include a proviso that the troops would be maintained at the Queen's expense. This idea did not find favour with a government already hard pressed for funds. To the Queen's ministers, the matter was clear: since the Hungarian rebels had laid down their arms, there was no reason, other than Austrian dilatoriness, why 8,000 men from the Hungarian border could not now be marched to Italy. By the time Palmes reached England, much hindered on his way by severe attacks of gout, Peterborough's plans had already 'grown dusty on the office shelves'.[5]

In the event of the Emperor's death various directions had been given to Prince Eugène. The Austrian Court was anxious that the election of the Archduke Charles as Emperor should go forward as smoothly as possible. Peterborough and his Dutch counterpart, Hamel Bruynincx, were summoned to the presence of the Empress Dowager, acting as Regent, to be told how much she was relying on the Maritime Powers to assist in achieving this aim. At a much earlier date Peterborough had taken the opportunity to speak to Count Wratislaw and Count Schönborn on a more complicated problem. Some of the Allies, he felt, would find it very hard to accept the fact of so much power being consolidated in one person, as would occur should King Charles of Spain hold the Austro-Hungarian Hapsburg inheritance as well as the crowns of Germany and Rome. The solution to the problem would surely be to offer the crown of Spain to the Duke of Savoy who, the earl believed, would not be unwelcome to the Spaniards. To cement relations between the House of Savoy and the House of Hapsburg, he suggested that a marriage might be arranged between the Duke's heir, the Prince of Piedmont, and the eldest daughter of the late Emperor Joseph. Later the Austrian ministers would deny giving any agreement to this scheme but they did at least listen. Wratislaw advised King Charles on how to react to the suggestions and encouraged Peterborough to go at once to Turin to ensure the Duke's cooperation with the plan.

In Vienna it had seemed that Peterborough wished to go on to Spain after Turin, probably with the intention of extracting promises from King Charles regarding the rest of the points in dispute between Savoy and the Empire. The Austrian Court saw a way of utilising Peterborough's enthusiasms in their own interest. When he left Vienna on 18 April, a courier was sent after him with a letter written on the Empress's orders, asking him to go to Spain and assist the King to return to Vienna as soon as possible. If he could not do so, he was asked to encourage the admirals of the Allied fleet in the Mediterranean to bring the King home with the utmost urgency. He was also asked to raise funds on Austrian credit in Italy to pay the troops in Spain.[6]

Peterborough reached Turin before the end of April 1711. The Duke of Savoy housed him at his hunting lodge, the Venerie, outside the city and spent much time in consultation with him, keeping him away from other company, even that of the British Resident, 'for fear of his bable'. In Vienna Peterborough had been rather indiscreet in speaking to other envoys about his theories on the succession and his views seemed well known in Italy. The Duke responded to his proposals about the crown of Spain by treating them as an 'agreeable chimera', but he was genuinely interested in the suggestion that his son should marry the eldest Josephine archduchess, and he did not forget it.

Since he had no instructions from England, Peterborough consulted the Duke on the advisability of his visit to Spain. The Duke was much in favour of it, as he felt it would serve his interests in gaining concessions and undertakings from the new Hapsburg heir. The assurances Peterborough felt able to make on the King's behalf were sufficiently persuasive to make the Duke state his intention of attending the coming campaign in person.

However, the financial situation was far from simple. There was no money to pay the Imperial troops in Italy, let alone those in Catalonia. Because of the known financial habits of the House of Austria, the merchants in Milan would not make loans on the reliable land tax raised in that area without counter-security from England. The funds normally used for the troops' supply could not be drawn because of the Emperor's death. In plain terms, the troops in Italy could not take the field at all unless £6,000 was procured for their pay. It seemed the ultimate irony that, having gone to so much trouble to persuade the Duke of Savoy to command the troops, there were now no troops to command. That such a situation could arise at all was an example of the inefficient financial arrangements of the Austrian Court.

In a long letter to the Earl of Dartmouth, Secretary of State for the Southern Department, Peterborough explained the intricacies of the situation to the best of his ability. To take up money in the Queen's name without orders was familiar ground, painfully trodden five years earlier, 'and tho the urgency of the occasion was almost equall to this, what a storm I was forced to stand upon that occasion...and yett we are undone if I doe not committ the same Folly.'[7]

With this problem still unresolved, Peterborough learnt that his friend the Duke of Argyll, now replacing Stanhope as Commander-in-Chief of the Forces in Spain, had reached Genoa on his way to that country. Loaded with commissions from the Duke of Savoy but probably none from the Queen, he set off to visit him.

Before leaving Turin, Peterborough had written a letter of twenty sheets to St John, 'wherein', reported the recipient, 'the whole world is parcelled out, as if with a fiat and the breath of his mouth it could be accomplished.' St John's reaction to the earl's ideas on the succession was strong. In a firm letter to an agent at The Hague, Mr Drummond, he stated: 'Lord Peterborough has had no orders to offer the Spanish Monarchy to the Duke of Savoy.' In the government's opinion Peterborough had left Vienna prematurely and against both the Queen's intentions and his instructions. When this opinion was passed on to him by Dartmouth, it produced a curt response from Genoa: 'This is to assure your Lordship that I shall ever obey the Queen with the outmost exactnesse, and that I did comply exactly with her Instructions when I left the Imperial Court.'

St John had also complained that Peterborough had left Vienna having only settled the question of the fiefs of the Montferrat, 'about half of one article out of four'. Later he apologised for the unease which Dartmouth's letter had caused Peterborough. In London they believed that this concession would be far from satisfactory to the Duke of Savoy; but in fact the Duke accepted it in order to facilitate a complete accommodation, and committed himself to the new campaign. Such a commitment was the crux of the entire negotiation.[8]

In the event of Peterborough's arrival in Spain, Wratislaw had advised King Charles to give a neutral response to the earl's ideas regarding the succession and to be too busy to consider the matter at present. Charles hoped that Peterborough's journey could be stopped, as he could do no good in Spain and no one there could get on with him. He was unhappy at surrendering his family's hereditary right to the throne of Spain but realised that such a move would be popular in places such as Savoy and Italy. He was reluctant to leave Spain without giving an assurance that he would return. Leaving Spain at all was no simple matter; the Admirals could not transport him without orders to do so.

Charles did not appreciate the interest the Austrian Court had in removing him from Spain. At The Hague in early May, Prince Eugène had incautiously let fall to Lord Raby 'that at any rate the Court at Vienna would have King Charles out of Spain'. Should they succeed, it was felt that they would also contrive to extricate themselves from the war there. St John outlined to Marlborough the attitude the government should adopt. 'We cannot be too open nor too zealous in promoting the election of King Charles to the Empire, nor, on the other hand, too silent on the subject of the Spanish succession, nor too industrious to evade entering on that argument.' Unknown to Marlborough, St John had recently taken over from the Earl of Jersey secret negotiations for a peace. This undercover operation had just produced a document, prepared by the French but agreed by the negotiators, by which Philip of Anjou would receive Spain.[9]

Peterborough's meeting at Genoa with the Duke of Argyll was referred to by Lord Raby as 'the junction of the two Mars'. They had certainly been friends; Argyll had given Peterborough strong support during the inquiry in the last Parliament. It was now believed, however, that there was a mutual distrust between them. Argyll was said to lack enthusiasm for Peterborough's presence in Spain. Despite appearing on the point of embarkation, the earl left Genoa on 27 May to return to Turin. On his arrival he informed the curious that he had found that the Admirals had received orders to convey King Charles and that the Duke of Argyll had everything well in hand; also so many of his friends seemed to know of his journey and be inquisitive about its purpose that it was no longer possible for him to go. That he had quarrelled with Argyll was firmly denied.

Peterborough had succeeded in taking up around £18,600 in bills for the payment of the Austrian troops in Italy. Dartmouth's letter, with the

Queen's disapproval of his 'engaging in any money concerns', came too late for the purpose. He remained only a short time at the Venerie before leaving again for Vienna. Mr Chetwynd had little contact with him but noted that the Duke of Savoy seemed disappointed that he did not go to Spain.[10]

Since the Duke of Savoy had now committed himself to the autumn campaign, it was important to press for the reinforcements of 8–9,000 troops promised by the Emperor under treaty. Since Peterborough's movements were uncertain, Charles Whitworth, at present in Berlin but previously the English ambassador in Moscow, was sent to Vienna to push the matter as its urgency allowed no delay. In fact Peterborough reached Vienna on 9 June in time to receive St John's communication about the troops. Before leaving for home five days later, he was able to present a memorandum to the Empress Dowager urging the sending of forces from Hungary in fulfilment of the Convention. On this occasion his reception by the Austrian ministers was noticeably cool; they too were disappointed that he had not gone to Spain.

Peterborough's homeward journey took him by way of Dresden and Hanover where he intended to visit Lord Raby. From Hanover on 21 June he wrote to Swift, telling him to direct his reply to Parsons Green. By 27 June he had reached The Hague, where he rested for three days. Criticisms of his conduct and his premature overtures to the Duke of Savoy had followed him across Europe. When he found that Counts Wratislaw and Schönborn had strongly denied the conversation with him which had been relayed by Mr Hamel-Bruynincx in April, Peterborough took care to deny it as well. It was noticed that he was a keen supporter of the Duke of Savoy as a candidate for the Spanish throne; his enthusiasm led him to expound his theories to the Portuguese envoy, who could scarcely be expected to endorse them.[11]

Peterborough landed near Yarmouth on 23 June/4 July and reached London the following day. He drove straight to the house of Count Maffei, the Savoyard minister, where he rested after his journey. That evening he presented himself at Kensington and was received very graciously by the Queen. The return journey from Vienna had been taken with 'great celerity'. The express messenger despatched by Peterborough in advance from Vienna in fact reached England after the earl. Servants, unable to keep up, had been abandoned at various points across Europe. Swift was astonished by the speed of the journey and recorded the episode in spirit if not fact in his lines to 'Mordanto' published in 1726.

Peterborough himself liked to boast, and others noticed, that he had returned without being recalled. In truth he had carried with him from the outset his letter of revocation for the Court at Turin, with instructions to use it whenever he saw fit. He was pleased with his reception at home and happy about what he had achieved abroad. The Duke of Savoy had been satisfied on a sufficient number of points to make his cooperation with the Allies assured. Peterborough felt that his own efforts had made it possible for the war to be continued. Despite Swift's warnings, he was dismayed to find on his return that the government now favoured a peace.

At this time Swift found the earl amazingly active both mentally and physically. He thought his vigour more that of a man of twenty-five years than of someone over fifty (he was fifty-three.) He noticed that Peterborough argued soundly with strong opinions but did not win over his hearer. 'He is a Person of great Talent,' wrote Swift, 'but dashed with something restless and capricious in his Nature...I doubt he will not have Credit enough with the Ministry to make them follow his Plans, and he is such a Sort of Person as may give good Advice, which wise Men may reasonably refuse to follow...'[12]

During long absences Peterborough's home thoughts from abroad frequently turned to his garden. Horticulture had always been an enthusiasm for which Parsons Green provided much scope. Like all gardens, attention had to be maintained and this was not always done. In 1705 Bowack described Peterborough's garden at Fulham as covering twenty acres but in a state of decay. 'Large cypress shades and pleasant wildernesses with fountains, statues, etc.' were to be found there. In the summer of 1711 Swift described it as 'the finest garden I have ever seen about this town, and abundance of hot walls for grapes, where they are in great plenty and ripening fast'. Peterborough liked his friends to use his garden while he was away. St John entertained Swift to dinner there in September of this year and again the following May, 'under a canopy in an Arbour...I never saw anything so fine and Romantick'.[13]

Still on good terms with the administration, Peterborough was not offered any work to do at home and was in England only briefly. In August he was appointed the Queen's special envoy to the election of the new Emperor at Frankfurt. It was expected that the Archduke Charles would be elected without trouble but Peterborough received credentials to visit every elector, expressing the Queen's views and encouraging their support of the Archduke. On his way he was expected to visit the Elector Palatine and also, if possible in the time, to meet King Augustus of Poland, another Vicar of the Empire, who was capable of making 'moves which may be disadvantageous to the common cause at the present juncture'. Passing through Holland en route, Peterborough had to make the Pensionary aware of his instructions and was expected to act in conjunction with the envoy from the States General.

Before his departure Peterborough talked about his task with his usual freedom. The Austrian ambassador, Count Gallas, expressed concern to St John about the purpose of this visit, and whether some of the topics the earl had mentioned were indeed included in the agenda. St John found he had to mollify the envoy by taking him step by step through the earl's instructions so that he could be satisfied that they contained nothing to which his government could make any objection. Along with much of the Austrian Court, Count Gallas shared a complete distrust and suspicion of Peterborough's actions. On his last embassy to Vienna, the Austrians had shadowed the earl's movements. The British Court considered this an unacceptable way in which to treat an ambassador.

By 17 August OS 1711 Peterborough had left London for Frankfurt. On the way to the coast his carriage overturned but he was able to continue his journey. However, having arrived in Holland he was found to be suffering from severe internal bleeding and was rumoured to be dying. A doctor summoned from Leyden diagnosed an internal injury caused by the carriage accident. After some delay to allow time for recovery, Peterborough resumed his journey and reached Frankfurt by 21 September NS.[14]

The arrival of the British ambassador in Frankfurt was eagerly awaited by the representatives of the Protestant States of the Empire. They hoped that he and his Dutch counterpart would be able to assist them in their efforts to have the fourth article of the Treaty of Ryswick abolished. This article had laid down that the religion of each state should remain what it was at the time of the Treaty. During the Nine Years War some Protestant states had been forcibly converted to Catholicism and they now wished to have their rights to worship recognised as had been done in the previous Treaty of Westphalia (1648). A clause in Peterborough's instructions directed him, together with the Dutch ambassador, to endeavour to have 'beneficial clauses' inserted in the Capitulation in favour of the Protestant Religion. To push this matter in particular was not productive in the circumstances of the

Election, so Peterborough and Count Rechteren felt they should restrict themselves to presenting a Memorial to the Electoral College in support of the Protestants, asking that they might have 'the liberty of building churches in this city'.

The climate was not optimistic. Peterborough was made to feel that 'nothing could be redressed, or so much as to be taken into consideration about the Protestants, notwithstanding infinite complaints and violations against the most plain and settled points in their favour by the constitution of the Empire'. Their requests could only be made in order to obstruct the election.

It was perhaps to underline the fact that he represented a strongly Protestant monarch that, in addition to the usual issue of ambassadorial plate from the Jewel House, there was included in Peterborough's equipage some rich and impressive furnishings for his private chapel.*

The election took place on 12 October and King Charles III of Spain became the Emperor Charles VI. He was now on his way home, having left his wife to govern Spain in his absence, and reached Frankfurt on 19 December 1711.

During an election it was the custom for all foreigners to leave the city. Peterborough took the opportunity to visit the Imperial army encamped near Speyer. Returning to Frankfurt after the election, both he and other envoys met with incomprehensible delays in being readmitted. Both the Papal Nuncio, present in a semi-official capacity, and the Dutch ambassador, Count Rechteren, were kept waiting. Peterborough himself was held up outside the gates for three hours. Whether this was the custom, or whether he had arrived too early, this treatment was not likely to impress a normally impatient diplomat in poor health.

This embassy was fraught with minor difficulties. Having asked for an audience with one of the Austrian ministers, Peterborough was informed he was not there, although the comings and goings to his room suggested the contrary. The Memorial presented jointly to the Diet by himself and Count Rechteren was not acknowledged. The impression given by the Electoral College was that its members were engaged on a matter of considerable domestic importance, as indeed they were, and that foreign representatives must bide their time. As for

*The list included 'a cloth of State of crimson damask with gold and silver fringe, a chair, two stools, two cushions, a foot stool and foot carpet, one large Bible of Imperial paper richly bound in two volumes, four Common Prayer books in quarto, one altar cloth of tissue and panned with velvet, 20 ells of fine diaper for towels, two large surplices of Holland (linen)'. *CTB* 1711, p. 552.

the Austrian ministers, when they 'once perceived that every body was resolved to yield rather than stop the Election, the barking of a dog was as much reguarded as any thing offered in the name of the Queen or States...'

This atmosphere, and perhaps too his state of health, encouraged Peterborough to leave the busy city and go to Augsburg later in October. Rumours reaching London suggested that his illness had recurred. The bruising which he suffered in the accident still caused him to spit blood from time to time as late as May 1713. His friends at home believed that the Queen intended to send him to Italy, where his health might improve in a warmer climate.[15]

Twenty-eight

During the early summer of 1711 Secretary St John and the Marquis de Torcy were conducting secret peace negotiations between Britain and France; then in July Matthew Prior was sent to Paris on behalf of the British government. By the time Prior returned in mid-August, Peterborough had already left for the Continent. He was known to be opposed to a peace and he may not have been told of the negotiations. Nevertheless he was very much aware of the Tory enthusiasm for it and many people suspected that something was afoot. St John believed that Peterborough's travels in Europe would bring him round to the idea that peace was the only way out of the present situation. If he was not 'in the secret', he must at least have had a shrewd idea of what was going on. A letter to him from St John of 18/29 September suggests that this was the case.

> The rumour of Mr Prior's journey into France, and of several other particulars concerning a negociation of peace, has been everywhere propagated with great industry. Your lordship thinks it neither proper nor possible to disown the fact. I confess my opinion is, that to take any pains either to deny or to own it, is below the character of the Queen; and certainly the best answer that any minister of hers can give, is to say, that her Majesty, on whom they have all leaned during the whole course of the war, may very well be trusted in preparing the way for peace, if any such treaty be on foot.

On 8 October NS the seven Preliminaries for Peace were signed by Mesnager on behalf of France and by the two Secretaries of State, St John and Dartmouth, on behalf of Britain. They were presented to the Queen and to the Allied Courts as proposals made by France as a foundation for peace. On 19/30 October St John wrote to Peterborough enclosing a copy of the 'offers made by France' which the Queen considered 'a sufficient inducement' to begin to consider conferences about a treaty.[1]

In one of his first letters to Oxford after leaving England on this embassy, Peterborough had said: 'Whenever I draw bills again for the House of Austria, I will be content to pay them myself.' The money he had taken up at Genoa in order to put the Austrian troops in the field had not been repaid. In leaving Germany for Italy, he thought he would pay his respects to the new Emperor in an attempt to regain his money. By 11 November he was in Milan, a little embarrassed by the interest he caused and the questions everyone wanted to ask regarding the movement for peace. Alexander Cunningham noted that the earl 'invented ingenious apologies and made such answers as he thought fit'.

While in Milan Peterborough was visited by Wratislaw but there is no record of an audience from the Emperor. Later he claimed that he had taken this opportunity to urge the Emperor to send Prince Eugène to England 'to obstruct the peace'. He then urged the same action on the Prince himself and believed that it would have been effective had his proposal been carried out promptly.

Having heard of the Preliminaries for Peace, the Emperor moved from Milan to Innsbruck where he met his Council of Regency. He heard also that Count Gallas had been dismissed from the British Court at the instigation of St John. Aware of the way that the wind was blowing, Gallas had been asking for some time that someone influential should be sent to represent Austrian interests. The Emperor decided to send Prince Eugène. Travelling by the Rhine and then to The Hague, the Prince eventually reached England in early January 1712, too late to influence the course of affairs. His friend and comrade in arms, the Duke of Marlborough, had just been dismissed from all his employments and succeeded in his command by the Duke of Ormonde.

In the meantime Peterborough made his way back to Frankfurt. He had hoped to go to Turin but he learnt that the Duke of Savoy, another unhappy ally, 'did not care for his company, and that he was resolved if he had come, to avoid talking to him about any business'.[2] This would include Peterborough's proposal of the marriage of his son with an Archduchess, about which the Duke seemed unenthusiastic. It was not clear whether his reluctance was an attempt to extract more territory in the Milanese as some form of recompense for the reversion of the Spanish Crown or whether, by appearing less keen on the marriage, he might thus encourage a greater dowry with the bride.

From London Peterborough was regularly promised further instructions. Dartmouth told the Queen that he was afraid that the earl 'would do more hurt than good at Turin' and proposed instead that he should be sent to Venice. 'I think he should be sent somewhere,' the Queen wrote to Lord Oxford, 'for I fear if he comes home while the Parliament is sitting, he will be very troublesome.'

The government had put off the sitting of Parliament for as long as possible because of the peace negotiations. In December the Preliminaries were presented to both Houses. No trouble was envisaged in the House of Commons because of the strong Tory majority. In the Lords there was more opposition, consolidated around the Duke of Marlborough and the unlikely figure of the High Tory Earl of Nottingham. Many people had misgivings over the mental attitude of those in power; France now appeared to be the friend, whereas the Allies were now the enemy. Peterborough was at heart a Whig, although employed by a Tory government. He had moved away from his party because he considered that they had become motivated by self-interest rather than the public good and would beggar the country with the war. Like the Duke of Shrewsbury, he was expected to have doubts about the conditions for peace and he was adept at causing trouble. He wrote to Dartmouth: 'A good Peace just att this Time must be the effect of good Fortune, or a great good Management.'[3]

In December 1711 Peterborough was in Augsburg. He sent formal intimation to Dartmouth that he was about to leave for Milan. He was chafing at the absence of instructions and, particularly, information. By Christmas he had still not been told the details of the peace negotiations, although on 15 December OS St John promised to send him a full history in cypher. Peterborough complained to the Earl of Oxford:

> My lord, I know my own infirmities…and shall allways be found most willing to quitt public employments, but I expect countenance and support whilst I am in them, and, above all things, to be made usefull, or to be returned to my garden and my Books.
>
> I have been two entire months without any letter, have not had the least hint by which I was enabled to make any reply to the enquisitive world, and this when I am sure that I have not been wanting in word, thought or deed, towards promoting the public interest, and making way for what I might guesse to be the views and intentions of our Ministers, but that word guesse explains all I would say.

Because of the expenses of two equipages in one year, Peterborough was once again 'out of a considerable summe of Ready Money'. Travelling post was an extravagant method of progress. He must therefore, he told Oxford, be able to rely on the punctual payment of his allowance every six months. 'I am sure you are too much my Friend to expose me to inconveniences abroad, and that you will restore mee to York Buildings, my bottle of clarrett and Dr Swift; I take it for an ill omen, and a sign I am insignificant, that I have not had a letter from him this journey, but I believe all sort of writting is forbid in England, but impudent libells against and scurrilous reflexions upon the Government.'

In early January 1712 Peterborough arrived in Venice amid much speculation as to what could have brought him. It was noted that he had talks with the Duke of Guastalla. He told Christian Cole, the British Resident, that he expected his stay to be short and that he had no business in Venice. Rumours abounded. The Venetians believed that the earl had been commissioned by the Queen to ask the Republic to send ambassadors to mediate in the peace process at Utrecht. In Turin the Imperial ministers told various people that Peterborough was trying to negotiate a treaty with the Venetians in order to limit the Emperor's power in Italy and he would shortly come to Turin to do the same thing there.

In the absence of instructions the earl had in fact settled down to enjoy Venice in the season approaching the Carnival. Alexander Cunningham, another British observer, renewed his acquaintance with him; they had met in Milan the previous autumn. He thought that Peterborough had fallen into very expensive company and tried unsuccessfully to introduce him to the circle of 'the virtuosi' who would cost him far less. Unfortunately, the earl was mentioned in connection with 'other strangers' who frequented social gatherings called *conversazione* and apparently lowered the tone by 'making amours' there. Whatever the extent of this conduct, it was enough to cause the authorities to investigate and, later in the year, prohibit such gatherings.[4]

The social diversions of the city did not prevent Peterborough from considering more serious matters in the company of Christian Cole. Arriving masked in the Venetian fashion at the Resident's lodgings, he discussed trade, finance and current affairs. From these conversations, Peterborough became well-informed about trade in the Mediterranean and developed his own ideas for the improvement of commerce between Britain and Venice in a Europe at peace. Cole had his own scheme for a Treaty of Commerce between Britain and Venice; the earl undertook to support this and persuade the government at home of its advantages.

On 19 February long-awaited instructions with credentials to the

Court of Savoy reached Peterborough who made plans at once to leave for Turin. His departure was delayed first by an attack of illness and then the news that his friend the Duke of Argyll had landed at Leghorn from Spain on his way to Utrecht. They met briefly in Venice before going their separate ways.[5]

Since the peace negotiations had opened at Utrecht in January 1712, Peterborough's instructions for his embassy to Savoy were mainly concerned with matters to be arranged there on behalf of Victor Amadeus. The Duke of Savoy was to be assured that the Queen's plenipotentiary would support, and insist on, the Alpine barrier which the Duke had requested and which accorded with his own plan. However, regarding the 'aggrandizing of his family in order to preserve a Ballance of Power in Italy', Peterborough was to tread warily; he was to stress that the Queen was of the same sentiment regarding the Duke's interests but thought such a scheme impracticable. It was suggested that the Duke should use the proposed marriage between the Prince of Piedmont and an Austrian archduchess as a foundation for other requests. What Victor Amadeus really required out of such a marriage was the gift of Milan as a dowry, a request unlikely to be granted.

On 5 March, while Peterborough was on his way to Turin, the Duke of Savoy's plenipotentiaries were putting forward claims for the barrier at Utrecht. News then reached Milan of the series of tragic deaths from smallpox in the French royal family. The Duke of Savoy's daughter, Marie Adelaide Duchess of Burgundy, was the first to contract the disease.

Peterborough's progress from Milan was again delayed by illness and he was still in poor health after reaching Turin. Nevertheless, by 16 March he was able to report the outcome of 'two or three long conversations' arising from visits by the Duke of Savoy. The Duke took a gloomy view of the peace negotiations, particularly if Britain was prepared to support a settlement which left France with Spain and the West Indies. British support for his barrier seemed of little value in the face of a power against whose 'exorbitant greatness' no guarantee could be found. At this time the younger Burgundian prince, heir to the French throne, was considered unlikely to survive. In the event of his death, the next heir was Philip of Anjou. In the Duke's view, the only way in which France could be restrained was by the 'union of those powers in peace, which had been able to reduce them in warr'.

Among the representatives of the Allies Peterborough detected alarm at the reports of secret negotiations. Some believed that a deal had already been signed and sealed. 'I have taken ye liberty with great confidence', wrote Peterborough, 'to affirm this must be false, all the intimations from the office give me authority for so doing, besides the conviction I have the thing is impossible…but I cannot say I have much successe in gaining belief.'[6]

Chetwynd, the British Resident, noted that Peterborough was not granted audiences so frequently or of such length as on his last visit. He was still treated with the respect due to his position but it seemed as if he lacked credit with the Duke, or power to convince him of the sincerity of his government's motives, particularly with regard to the prosecution of the war should the peace negotiations fail.

There was little Peterborough could do in Turin. The interest of everyone was focused on Utrecht. On 25 March, pending the outcome of events, he set off to Genoa to attend to financial affairs, intending perhaps to continue to Florence or Rome. In Genoa, however, a Queen's messenger caught up with him with instructions of a different nature.[7]

When Peterborough set out on his embassy to the Imperial Election at Frankfurt, he had carried with him a letter from Queen Anne to the Electress Dowager of Saxony, the mother of the Elector Augustus. In 1697 Augustus had converted to Catholicism in order to obtain the crown of Poland, although Saxony was one of the Protestant states of the Empire. In order to ensure that his family succeeded to the throne of Poland, Augustus now wished his son to change his religion. Queen Anne, a staunch upholder of the reformed faith, wrote to the Electress Dowager to express her grief at this news and her concern for the young Prince. Augustus had replaced the Prince's governor, Millintz, with a Jesuit and the Queen wished in some way to convey her support to the Prince to enable him to stand firm against his teachings. As the Prince was at Frankfurt for the election, the Queen had thought that it might be possible for Peterborough to consult with Millintz on how to proceed. In fact the earl managed to have a friendly conversation with the young Prince who apparently 'opened himself' to the British ambassador's sympathetic ear.[8]

The Electoral Prince of Saxony had arrived in Venice in February 1712 while Peterborough was in residence and was still there when the earl left for Turin. Queen Anne was afraid that the Prince's journey to Italy, and ultimately Rome, was another step in the process of his conversion. Peterborough, already known to the Prince and in the right place, was chosen as the emissary who would interrupt this journey.

[337]

Soon after his arrival in Genoa, Peterborough received instructions which amazed him.

It was intended that he should try to join the Prince on the road before he reached Rome in such a way as to make it appear a purely accidental encounter. The earl, a 'staunch Protestant', was then to get on sufficiently friendly terms with the Prince as to be able to argue strongly against any conversion to Rome. He was provided with a letter from Queen Anne inviting the Prince to accept the hospitality of the English Court, should he find that convenient. If the earl found that the Prince was being taken to Rome under some kind of restraint, he was to assist him to escape with the help of the replaced governor, Millintz, who was still in his entourage.

Peterborough was instructed to conduct the whole affair in strict secrecy. The instructions were in cypher and any subsequent communication with the Secretary of State was to be in cypher too. If he was in Turin when the instructions arrived, he must explain to the Duke of Savoy that, at his own request, the Queen had given him 'leave to see the city of Rome'. He was to return to Turin when he could be of no further use but the duration of the task was left to his own discretion.

Leaving Turin for Venice where he had left the Prince, Peterborough took care that his arrival was unexpected. Surprising Christian Cole at his dinner, he was informed that the Prince had left for Milan and that another visitor had already departed in pursuit of him. Because of his knowledge of the Prince and his affairs, a Mr George Mackenzie had been sent to assist Peterborough in his task, at the request of the Queen of Poland and the Electress Dowager. Mackenzie had held a diplomatic post in the British service in Poland and Saxony, where he had earned the trust and esteem of the Queen and her mother-in-law. He did not, however, appear to have been charged with the degree of secrecy which had been impressed upon Peterborough. Having asked Cole for a passport under an assumed name, Mackenzie had revealed in confidence to one person the purpose of his journey. When Peterborough arrived in Venice, at least three people were able to tell him that Mackenzie had gone to look for him and the Electoral Prince and why. By taking different routes, they had missed each other on the road. This state of affairs left the earl with no obvious plan of action. It seemed that the Prince meant to visit Turin after Milan but Peterborough could hardly return there, having made his excuses to the Duke of Savoy.[9]

While Peterborough was pondering on what to do next, a servant whom Cole had hired for Mackenzie reappeared in Venice with what proved subsequently to be a completely fabricated story of irrational and violent behaviour by Mackenzie near Brescia. As the servant had given evidence under oath, it was understandable that Peterborough and Cole should now consider Mackenzie unreliable as well as indiscreet. Anxious to stay out of the picture, Peterborough sent Cole with his own secretary, Stanyon, to Milan to find Mackenzie and bring him for a meeting in Verona. But in Milan the true purpose of Mackenzie's journey appeared to be common knowledge and rumours had also reached the Prince's entourage. However, on their way, Cole and Stanyon had found evidence to clear Mackenzie of any improper conduct.

When Peterborough reached Verona on 29 April, he thought it prudent not to receive the envoy so as to avoid having their names linked. Mackenzie, an obstinate and peppery character, was not unnaturally resentful at the suggestion that he had spoilt the game through a friend he believed he could trust and retired to Genoa until the dust had settled.[10]

On 25 April/6 May Dartmouth wrote to Peterborough to tell him how much the Queen regretted that his mission to the Electoral Prince had become public, as she thought it of such importance. It had been intended that Mackenzie should take his orders from Peterborough. The mission should now be abandoned but Peterborough should remain in Venice for further orders which might take him back to Turin where the Queen felt he could still be useful in connection with the treaty of peace.

Before this letter could reach him, the earl had already left Venice with the ultimate intention of going to Vienna. Meanwhile he went to Milan to see if he could salvage anything from the task originally entrusted to him which appeared to have gone so badly wrong. In conversation with Christian Cole, Prince Hercolani described Peterborough's attempt as an 'Apostolical journey'. Cole, obviously one of the earl's admirers, hoped it might still succeed 'by the great dexterity so natural to my lord Peterborow'.

It is clear that Peterborough had managed to build up some sort of correspondence with the Electoral Prince, probably through Millintz. He discovered that the Prince, a reluctant convert to Catholicism, believed that Queen Anne might be able to intercede with his father on his behalf and hoped that Peterborough, as the Queen's representative, might now attempt this. The earl agreed to help, intending to travel to Dresden by way of Vienna, thinking that at least it would postpone the Prince's departure for Rome.

[339]

On 2 June Peterborough wrote to Dartmouth to tell him of his plans. He hoped to impress on the King of Poland how unwise it would be to antagonise his Protestant subjects at this time, when the French had designs against him. There were great attractions in a piece of diplomacy of this nature after the frustrations of Milan and the awkwardness of the mission to the Electoral Prince. Having waited for five days in the hope of instructions, Peterborough left Milan. 'To be useless and insignificant att such a time as this, is what any person in my circumstances will avoid if he can,' he told Dartmouth. Besides it might move him to an area where it was possible to receive more news, rather than always living in 'those unfortunate places dedicated to ignorance'.[11]

Peterborough did not reappear in Turin until 16 August. His travels took him to see the King of Poland at Dresden, as well as other German princes among whom he found a general distaste for British policy. He also went to Vienna. The King of Poland had told him that he considered himself in disgrace with Queen Anne since he had recalled his troops from the Duke of Ormonde's command, and he was not impressed with her attempt to interfere in his family's religious affairs. Peterborough was made aware that he could make little headway here.

Having returned from Vienna, a visit to Milan showed the earl that the Prince's reluctant journey to Rome was about to continue and that at best his endeavours had only contrived to delay it. The Queen's response to his dispirited report was that she had decided on a different course of action and would write to the King of Poland herself. Peterborough made one final attempt in November. He thought that he had found a way of stopping the Prince to which the King could not object and followed him to Bologna. In the end this also proved unsuccessful and was his last move in this ineffectual business.[12]

Twenty-nine

At intervals during the summer of 1712 Viscount Bolingbroke, as St John had now become, hoped that he would soon be able to send Peterborough instructions more to his liking. In May he had expected that Philip of Anjou, King of Spain, would give up his throne in order to prepare to inherit the French crown. In that event, he had agreed with Torcy that the Spanish throne should be offered to the Duke of Savoy. To the surprise of many, Philip decided to retain what he had, rather than serve a long apprenticeship on an expectation.

Subsequently it was decided to propose that the Duke of Savoy should be offered Sicily at the Peace with the expectation of the crown of Spain should Philip's line fail. This arrangement was of importance for Britain as it would lessen the influence of Austria in Italy. Savoy and Sicily had no navy of their own, so the Duke would look to the British for naval support. Britain would thus gain the use of harbours and a sphere of influence in those seas in addition to the British bargaining counters at the Peace, the possession of Gibraltar and Port Mahon.

When Peterborough returned to Turin in August, he had several audiences of the Duke and his chief minister, the Marquis de St Thomas, and then left for Milan. He had still no instructions from home so he left behind couriers who could be sent at once to find him. On 30 August he had written despondently to Dartmouth from Milan where the Electoral Prince was about to set out on the road to Rome. He felt both useless and restless and, for the first time, wrote of a desire to come home, perhaps by way of Paris 'instead of passing thoro Countrys where I shall be so little wellcome'. There he might find Bolingbroke finalising the negotiations and be of some use to him.

He had other reasons too. Bolingbroke, who had been enjoying the 'shady walks and cool retreats' of Parsons Green in the owner's absence, had warned him that a Bill had been brought in the Commons with the intention of challenging some of the grants of land made by William III. Peterborough's property of Dauntsey could be affected by this, although the Bill was aimed at the acquisitions of the Earl of Portland. The Bill had been allowed to fall but it might reappear. Peterborough was anxious, although his friends at home assured him that they had his interests at heart.[1]

In early September Philip of Spain agreed to the cession of Sicily to the Duke of Savoy. The courier from Paris carrying the news reached Turin on 14 September. Peterborough's secretary collected his despatches and sent off another courier to find the earl who was at Lucca. Peterborough had the foresight to make a memorandum of the main points of the agreement which he sent at once to the Duke of Savoy in case he should be delayed on his journey. He was aware, and later embarrassed the Savoyard First Minister with his knowledge, that the Duke had been secretly negotiating with the Emperor while the diplomats were at work at Utrecht. For this reason speed was a necessity. Peterborough then rode day and night to Turin. The ways through the mountains to Bologna were very bad: at Modena he was obliged to stop for a day and a half by 'a violent fitt of the stone'. Despite these drawbacks he still managed to reach Turin on the morning of 22 September, after a journey of some 300 miles, and went immediately to a long audience with the Duke.

Peterborough's memorandum had reached Victor Amadeus two days before his arrival. The news of the cession of Sicily was a surprise for the Duke, who had not been consulted. The idea had emanated from Britain, and he was not slow to note the advantages for the British Navy and for British trade. Queen Anne herself had always professed a great affection for the Duke and his family, and wished to see him compensated for the loss of his expectations in Spain. She was also aware that he had been cut out of the succession to the British throne because of his Catholicism.*

If the Duke of Savoy had been asked what he would have liked to receive at the Peace, he would have chosen Milan. This was an unrealisable hope, as the Imperial Court were to look on it as their most important gain from the war. However, the cession of Sicily to Savoy was not popular with the Emperor. Such a move would act as a counterpoise to Imperial power in Italy. Austria still laid claim to Sicily, which had once been part of the double kingdom of the Two Sicilies. The other kingdom, Naples, was still part of the Austro-Spanish dominions.

Peterborough found the Duke less than enthusiastic about accepting

---

*His right was derived from his wife, Anne of Orleans, through her mother, Henrietta Anne, the youngest daughter of Charles I.

the British proposals. To persuade him of their value took all his powers of explanation. He felt himself on surer footing when urging the Duke to consider how little one could rely on Austrian promises.

Anxious for further discussion and information, the Duke wanted Peterborough to leave at once for England to consult with the government and was prepared to undertake not to enter into any agreement contrary to the Queen's interest in his absence. Peterborough himself was surprisingly reluctant to leave without orders to do so. He was sympathetic to the Duke's viewpoint and also aware that the Imperial attitude to Savoy was now friendly and very different from 'the haughty measures which they used to practise'. However the temperature could change. There were already numerous German troops in Italy and it would be a simple operation to exert Imperial pressure on Savoy.[2]

In face of these difficulties Peterborough felt it reasonable to make certain offers, but in 'terms of the outmost caution', to ease the situation. A fleet provided jointly by France and Britain or by either individually would enable the Duke to take possession of his new kingdom and would afford protection. Peterborough believed that a guarantee of protection could fix the Duke in the British interest as he respected his genuine unease about the Austrians and the future greatness of France.

During the diplomacy there was time for the earl to accept an invitation which was in itself a mark of respect to the British government. Peterborough and the envoy, Chetwynd, were invited by some of the Duke's generals to view the cavalry encamped at Carmagnola. Afterwards they attended a dinner given by the Comte de Prélat.

By 8 October 1712 both Peterborough and Chetwynd noticed that the Duke was warming to the British proposals. Peterborough attributed this development to a change in the Austrian attitude; the Imperial envoys had begun to use threats. A visit to court a few days later revealed the Duke upset and uneasy at words spoken to his envoys by the Imperial Ministers at Utrecht. He seemed afraid that the Austrians might get wind of his current negotiations with Britain and felt they might be misled if Peterborough absented himself for a while. As a result, the earl set out for Milan on 16 October and then on to Parma.[3]

Before leaving Turin, Peterborough told Dartmouth of another concern of the Duke's, namely his – Alpine – barrier. He had done his best to argue against the Duke's expectations of Monaco, Fort Barraux on the Isère and Briançon. The Duke was now claiming 'nothing but topps and sides of miserable barren mountaines, the whole, all the little scatterd houses and villages would not yield a particular man three thousand pounds a yeare'. It seemed an unobjectionable claim, as all it would afford him was a little security against the approach of an enemy.

In his letter the earl also took the opportunity to air his views on British trade with Italy. His reflections give evidence of much thought and research. His information had been gleaned in long conversations with Christian Cole, whose plans for trade he had promised to put forward to the government. At Venice he had noted the disadvantages to which British merchants were exposed. They had to accept the prices laid down by the Venetians and were unable to take their goods to another market if they were dissatisfied. In Savoy Peterborough noticed that French goods received preferential treatment. A higher duty was paid on English cloth than on that from a French source. This might be a good time to ensure that some equality was established. He visualised a huge advantage to British trade if the Duke of Savoy were in control of Sicily and the trade protected in his dominions. His border on the Mediterranean meant a journey of only fifteen miles overland to the River Po and then access to the whole of Italy. In this country there could be a ready market for Irish linen; at present Silesian linen reached Italy by way of the Danube and then through the mountains of Tyrol. There could also be a market for other goods from Britain such as fish, salt, cloth, tin, lead and iron. In return, Italian hemp and raw silk were among the best; beef and pork could be supplied for the Navy as well as oil and wine. Later the Duke of Savoy was urged to give preferential treatment to British merchants in Sicily but in the end they only received the same terms as had existed when the island was under Spanish government.

The British government considered that the Duke's claims about his barrier were reasonable. The plenipotentiaries at Utrecht had been instructed to propose 'an absolute neutrality for Italy', which should help to remove the Duke's fears about the Imperial troops. The Navy had been ordered to postpone the repatriation of German troops in Spain until the conclusion of the present negotiations, a command which also postponed the departure of the Empress from Barcelona.[4]

In November Peterborough returned to Turin to a difficult waiting game. The Duke still wished him to go home to state his case and the earl was equally anxious to return to attend to his private affairs. 'I wish with all my heart', he told Dartmouth, 'I might eat mince pies with you this winter.' However he was aware of the necessity for caution and waited for a formal recall. There was a feeling in Turin that the great affair was practically reaching its conclusion. The Duke was still uneasy about the Emperor and wanted Peterborough to stay away until the spring. The urgings to leave became so constant that the earl set out for Munich, where he remained incognito waiting for his recall.

Five years later, at a time when he was warned by the government that he was so much *persona non grata* with the Emperor that it would be wise to avoid the Imperial dominions while travelling, Peterborough revealed a strange footnote to the story of this period. He believed that one of the main reasons for Imperial antagonism to him was an understanding in the Austrian Court that he had been 'instrumentall in procuring the kingdome of Sicily for the Duke of Savoy'. The idea of Sicily had emanated from the British government and not the earl's fertile brain; it was Peterborough's role as envoy to support it. He carried out this commission officially, but he claimed later that, before leaving Turin, he had written in a private capacity to the Duke of Savoy giving reasons why he should not accept the offer of Sicily and that 'his true interest was never to depart from that of the court of Austria'. This amazing confession was made in 1717 to Joseph Addison as Secretary of State in order to demonstrate the injustice of the Imperial view.

The Austrian Empire was not included in the Peace of Utrecht and the Treaty in 1713 was signed by Britain and France. The Emperor continued the war against France until 1714 when peace was accepted by the Treaty of Rastatt. At this point the Emperor was awarded Sardinia while Max Emmanuel was restored to the Electorate of Bavaria. For Savoy, provided that the barrier against France was both tenable and practical in its agreed form, there was probably more to be feared from Austrian influence in Italy, which remained great and was centred on the Milanese. In the long run, Peterborough's advice to the Duke of Savoy, however improper, may have been right. In practice, the Duke kept his own counsel and rarely accepted any advice.[5]

On 22 December OS Peterborough was sent permission to return home. In his usual manner he lost no time on the road, and appeared unexpectedly at the Earl of Oxford's house on 10 January 1713 during a dinner-party. Jonathan Swift was among the company and described his arrival.

At 7 this Evening as we sate after dinner at Ld Treasrs. a servant sd Lord Peterborow was at the door. Ld Tr. and Ld Bol. went out to meet him, and brought him in. He was just returnd from abroad, where he has been above a year. Soon as he saw me, he left the D.Ormd. and other lds. and ran and kissd me before he spoke to them, but chid me terribly for not writing to him; which I never did the last time he was abroad, not knowing where he was; and he changed places so often, it was impossible a Lettr should overtake him. He left Engd with a Bruise by his Coach overturning, that made him spitt Blood, and was so ill we expected any Post to hear of his Death: But he outrode it, or outdrunk it, or something: and is come home lustyer than ever; he is at least 60 and has more Spirits than any young fellow I know in Engld: He has got the old Oxford Regimt of horse, and I believe will have a Garter, I love the hangdog dearly...

The earl was in fact only fifty-four years of age but undoubtedly vigorous. In August of the previous year he had been appointed Colonel of the Royal Regiment of Horse Guards after the death of its then Colonel, Earl Rivers. The regiment had been founded by Aubrey de Vere, Earl of Oxford. Swift was over-optimistic about the earl's health. The trouble caused by the carriage accident recurred soon after his return. On 10 March Peterborough was unable to dine with the Lord Treasurer on the grounds of illness, but Swift ascribed his indisposition to the presence of an Italian lady whom the earl had brought back in his entourage. In the later years of this decade, the earl kept as his mistress a lady from Bologna known as Catina. This may have been her first appearance in England.*6

Peterborough had looked forward to being of use to the government in the House of Lords after his return but there were few opportunities, as Parliament was continually prorogued until after the Treaty of Utrecht had been signed on 31 March OS. By the end of March he was once again dining with the Lord Treasurer, apparently in good spirits and 'making long Harangues'.

On 9 April, in the House of Lords, Peterborough took part in the debate on the Queen's speech. In May it was rumoured that he was likely to receive an elevation in the peerage but nothing was forthcoming. However his social life was active: a fellow-guest at the Duke of Ormonde's dinner, Lord Berkeley of Stratton, found him 'extreamly entertaining'.7

*Among the Peterborough family portraits was listed 'An Italian Lady by Kneller'. It is possible that the earl, in his secretive way in such matters, had considered her for a more distinguished role.

Peterborough enjoyed taking part in debates in the House of Lords. His speeches were often memorable to his contemporaries for their content, polish and wit rather than their effect in the debate. His style may appear laboured to a modern reader but it was much appreciated at the time. On 1 June 1713 a debate followed on a motion that the Union between England and Scotland should be dissolved. This motion resulted from economic grievances in Scotland brought to a head by the reimposition of a Malt Tax in the spring of this year. Malt was taxed at the same rate in England and Scotland despite the fact that Scottish malt was of an inferior quality and fetched a lower price. Scotland had received an exemption from the tax during the war and its reimposition, when the fighting had stopped but no peace treaty had been signed, was felt to be unfair. The Earl of Seafield moved for a dissolution of the Union. Peterborough spoke against the motion. He was recorded as being 'very pleasant in comparing the union to a marriage, and own'd we had been a little rough to our spouse'. He continued that

> since it was made, it could not be broke, being made by the great-est power on earth. That, though sometimes there happened a difference between man and wife, yet it did not presently break the marriage: so in the like manner, though England, who in this national marriage must be supposed to be the husband, might in some instances have been unkind to the lady, yet she ought not presently to sue for a divorce, the rather because she had very much mended her fortune by this match. [He added] that the union was a contract, than which nothing could be more binding.

The Earl of Islay remarked that he saw great differences between the union and a marriage, as the latter was an ordinance of God. Peterborough replied that 'he could not tell how it could be more solemn than it was, except they expected it should have come down from Heaven, like the Ten Commandments'. In conclusion, he was unsympathetic towards the Scottish people; he thought that they wanted all the advantages without giving anything back and would always be dissatisfied. In the end the motion was defeated.[8]

Peterborough was installed as a Knight of the Garter at Windsor on 4 August 1713. Also receiving this honour were the Duke of Beaufort, the Duke of Kent, the Earl of Oxford (the Lord Treasurer), Earl Poulett (the Lord Steward) and the Earl of Strafford, who had been one of the plenipotentiaries at The Hague. Strafford had invited his kinsman Peter

Wentworth to attend the ceremonies as his guest but he himself was installed by proxy.

Later Wentworth sent a description of the occasion to Strafford. The chapel had been crowded with people. Subsequently a very splendid dinner had been held in the Guard-chamber. When it came to the time for the toasts, each knight rose in turn to drink the Queen's health; as they did so, a herald read out their titles.

The expense of this entertainment was shared equally among the knights; each was expected to pay £228. 1s. Wentworth related that 'the town will have my Lord Peterborough had like not to have been installed at all, for he had not payed his fees that amount to near £300, which is by the statutes first to be paid, but of this I saw nothing, tho' I am creditably inform'd they were forc't to take his note.' On a previous occasion the Duke of Argyll had refused to pay until the ceremony was over, so the situation was not without precedent. The receipt of such an honour was a costly exercise, with the additional expense of the purchase of the elaborate robes.[9]

At the end of August Peterborough was appointed ambassador to the new King of Sicily. In informing Count Maffei of this event, Bolingbroke stressed that it was important that Peterborough should be well versed and informed in all matters connected with Savoy and Sicily. Soon after the appointment, and in view of the uncertainty surrounding the health of the Queen, Peterborough wrote a politic letter to the Elector of Hanover expressing his regret that he would be unable to call in the course of his journey to Sicily. Such a deprivation would not have caused the Elector a moment's distress, although the same might not be said for his aged mother.

The instructions issued on 2 October gave Peterborough full ambassadorial powers to the courts of the King of Sicily, to the Princes and States of Italy and to the Republic of Venice. His first task was to proceed to the court of Sicily to make appropriate compliments; subsequently he was expected to report to the Secretary of State on the condition of the island, its people and its trade. Typically of instructions from Queen Anne, he was to assist the Vaudois as far as possible and also other Protestant subjects in the King's dominions and to use the Queen's name to redress any hardships that they might be suffering. Peterborough's embassies to the Italian states were on a more flexible timetable, as and when directed. Basically he was expected to promote the observation of the convention of the neutrality of Italy, to prevent troubles breaking out which might threaten the Peace and to report meticulously any contravention of the agreement. He was also expected to obtain the release of any British slaves still remaining on Venetian or Italian ships and to communicate information to the British admiral in the Mediterranean when present.

On 5 October Peterborough was given further credentials to the French court *en passant* but as the Queen's Ambassador to the King of Sicily. He was expected to pass on communications from Her Majesty to the French King regarding treaty obligations in connection with Savoy, and to try to determine from the French ministers how far Louis would support the cause of the Catalans, a matter which was giving concern. The people of Catalonia had decided to resort to arms in defence of their hereditary rights and were refusing to submit peacefully to Bourbon government from Madrid.[10]

Practical steps were being taken to improve Peterborough's financial position. For this embassy his allowance of £1,500 for an equipage and £10 *per diem* as ordinary passed the Privy Seal on 15 October. Two days later he received a money warrant for most of the equipage money and a quarter's ordinary in advance. As General of the Marines, a sum of £6,000 was now owing to him. To accommodate the earl on his travels, the Treasurer of the Navy agreed to make an interim payment of £2,000, pending the preparation of warrants for the remainder of the money.

Peterborough engaged as his chaplain for the embassy the philosopher George Berkeley, whom Swift had busily introduced to all his influential friends the previous spring. Berkeley was a Fellow of Trinity College, Dublin, and Swift considered him 'a very ingenious man, and a great Philosopher'.

Bolingbroke compiled the final instructions, to be issued on 23 October, evidently with some misgivings over the possible conduct of the ambassador. As he explained to Secretary Bromley, it would be more for the Queen's service 'to tie his Lordship down by instructions, to the points he shall meddle with in his passage through France, than to leave him at liberty to entertain the French ministers and himself, with a variety of schemes which at best would make them imagine our councils here very uncertain, and which might perhaps start some new proposition, not agreeable to the Queen, and not easy to evade'. At this time the French were negotiating in secret with the Emperor the agreement formulated in the Treaty of Rastatt. Aware of this, Britain was anxious that France should put pressure on the Emperor, on Britain's behalf, to complete the guarantees promised to Victor Amadeus by the Treaty of 1703.

Bolingbroke asked Bromley to point out to the Queen that no mention had been made of consultations with the French regarding the future of the island of Sardinia. The Elector of Bavaria had laid claim to this island but it was now believed that he might be persuaded to abandon his claim. 'I avoided touching this point,' wrote Bolingbroke, '...not knowing how far the pleasure of giving kingdoms might transport his Lordship.' However he briefed Matthew Prior in Paris on Sardinia and told him that Peterborough knew nothing about it.[11]

Ultimately delayed by repairs necessary to the *Fubbs* yacht, which had been detailed to transport his baggage if not also himself, Peterborough left London on his embassy on 4 November. He reached Paris eleven days later, on 15/26 November. The next day he had consultations with the Sicilian ambassador who had expressed concern over the current negotiations between Prince Eugène and Marshal Villars.[12]

Soon after Peterborough's arrival in Paris, suggestions were made that some mystery surrounded his journey there. Schütz, the Hanoverian envoy in London, reported home that Peterborough was said to have been seen in Dunkirk and on the English coast incognito and going under the name of Smith or Thompson. He had been noticed at Dover wearing old clothes and with a patch over one eye. A servant had addressed him as 'my Lord' and he had thrashed the fellow. Later he was heard to say that 'ce coquin luy avait fait manquer un grand coup'. The rumoured explanation for this behaviour was that the government had asked Peterborough to go incognito to Bar-le-Duc to visit the Pretender. It was claimed that he had taken such a long time to reach Paris, three weeks, that he must have been somewhere else en route. All the stories claimed a reliable source which could not be named. In exile in Europe, the Duchess of Marlborough heard a version. Peterborough had reached Bar-le-Duc, she reported, and had been given a long conference with the Pretender and Lord Middleton. He had gone by the name of Smith at Calais and had sent most of his servants to Paris by a different route from his own.

From the facts available it is hard to see when such a visit could have taken place. Schütz himself provides the evidence for Peterborough's departure from London on 4/15 November; the earl seemed to put off his departure from day to day but eventually left after the conclusion of meetings which the ministers held with a Catalonian deputation. Peterborough's entourage, including George Berkeley, had set out earlier, on 25 October/5 November. They had arrived in Paris by 24 November NS, two days before the earl. Berkeley and Peterborough's aide-de-camp, Colonel Duhamel, had left London travelling in the earl's chariot which was left at Calais for his use. Duhamel rode fast to Paris to arrange accommodation while Berkeley waited for the stage coach.

According to Dangeau, Peterborough was accompanied on his journey to Paris by the French Ambassador in London, the Duc d'Aumont. He enjoyed secrecy, disguise and adventure. It may well be that some sort of enterprise was frustrated but, whatever he did or tried to do, he did not meet the Pretender. Two years later, while working for the Jacobites in Paris, Bolingbroke wrote to James suggesting people who might be approached and brought over to that party. Peterborough's name was mentioned. James replied: 'Tho' I never saw Ld Peterborow, yet his conversation with Iberville seems to answer perfectly the character I have had of him. Your intimacy with him makes you the most proper judge of what may most contribute to dipp him and of what he may be capable of being usefull in...'

With the uncertainties over the Queen's health, many people in public life were keeping a line open to Bar-le-Duc as a personal insurance policy. Both Oxford and Bolingbroke were certainly in touch. In later years Peterborough would hotly deny that the Queen, Oxford or Bolingbroke ever sought to bring in the Pretender in contravention of the Act of Settlement. As long as the Pretender remained a Catholic, Peterborough was most likely right; but it was the pipe-dream of every English Jacobite that James might change his religion to gain his crown. However James was made of sterner stuff and believed that his restoration must be quite unconditional.[13]

In Paris Peterborough took up residence at the Hôtel Modène. Without delay, Matthew Prior arranged a meeting at Versailles to deal with the Catalan question. On 4 December Peterborough was received in audience there by Louis XIV. Escorted from his lodgings by the Duc d'Aumont, he took with him Prior and also Admiral Jennings who was well versed on the Catalan problem. On their arrival they all had a meeting with the Marquis de Torcy, who later entertained them to dinner. Two of the guests had been carefully chosen, the Maréchal de Tessé, Peterborough's old opponent, and the Maréchal Tallard, once French Ambassador in London, who had spent a long but by no means uncomfortable imprisonment in England during the late war.

At about 5 pm the King received Peterborough in his closet 'with a great deal of respect'. Both Torcy and Prior were present at the audience. The King made it clear to the ambassador that he had already given 'very positive orders' to the Maréchal de Villars to give consideration to the

King of Sicily's claims in his negotiations with the Emperor. He was prepared to take 'equal measures' with Britain to ensure the performance of the guarantee. Should the Emperor fail to perform his obligations, it would then be the role of France and Britain to enforce them jointly. However, little progress was made on the Catalan question as Louis claimed that his influence over the King of Spain was slight. He considered it natural for a sovereign to have a priority for his own interests and thought that British interests at Madrid were stronger than those of the French. Prior wondered if this was a hint that Britain should try to build and strengthen those interests directly with Spain.

Before leaving for Sicily, Peterborough had two more meetings with ministers at Versailles. With the King's permission, Torcy gave both British ambassadors an account of the first conference at Rastatt and showed them the proposals made by Prince Eugène and the answers which Villars had been instructed to give. They received the impression that France sincerely wished for peace but that the Emperor's demands were excessive.[14]

Peterborough and his entourage left Paris on 14 December 1713 and travelled south through France, stopping at Lyons for eight days. While they were there, a fête was held to celebrate the erection of a statue of the King. A member of Peterborough's suite, Theophilus Oglethorpe, managed to lose 50 guineas at play at the Intendant's reception.*

After Lyons Peterborough took a different route from part of his suite, travelling to Marseilles and Toulon and then sailing to Genoa where the party was reunited. Berkeley was finding him 'a man of excellent parts and frank cheerful conversation'.

At Genoa there was no sign of the expected man-of-war or the yacht with the equipage. The latter was stormbound in England and did not leave until 8 March. Disliking delays, Peterborough decided to set out for Sicily, if necessary putting off his formal entry until his equipage arrived. He took this decision at the earnest request of the King of Sicily who was 'sufficiently embarrassed with his new subjects and his uncertain circumstances'. He transported himself and his household by sea to Leghorn where he left most of his suite. With two or three servants, he then sailed on board a Maltese vessel for Sicily, arriving on 17 February.[15]

---

*Oglethorpe belonged to a Jacobite family and his sisters lived in Paris. He had been an aide-de-camp to the Duke of Ormonde in Flanders and was now attached to Peterborough. He was hoping for some sort of employment in Sicily or Italy in a diplomatic capacity. See Peterborough to Oxford 5 March, BL Add. MSS 70,249.

In October 1713 Victor Amadeus, Duke of Savoy and King of Sicily, had been transported to his new kingdom by a British squadron and crowned in Palermo on 24 December. His acceptance of this monarchy, however, was acknowledged by neither the Emperor nor the Pope. For many centuries the Kings of Sicily had exercised considerable control over episcopal appointments and church affairs by virtue of the Monarchia Sicula or the Tribunal of the Monarchy. This power passed to Victor Amadeus and only served to exacerbate his already poor relations with the Vatican. In order to avoid unnecessary trouble with the Church, the King sent two Sicilian envoys to the Pope to attempt to work out some sort of settlement. Under Spanish rule one archbishop and two bishops had already exiled themselves from the island under protest and two of them had left interdicts on their spheres of influence.

Peterborough described life at the Palermitan court to Swift. 'One of your acquaintance found himself att a great table, the only unexcommunicated person by His Holinesse, the rest of the company Eating and Toasting under anathemas, with the Courage of a Hardened Heretick...' To the earl Sicily was 'the Extremity of the Earth' where he spent his time longing for news, particularly of the outcome of the negotiations which culminated in the Treaty of Rastatt.*

As so often on his travels, Peterborough found the lack of communication from home irksome. He had written regularly to Bolingbroke but was receiving none of his replies; presumably they were held up by the bad weather which had delayed the arrival of the equipage. One of Peterborough's sayings was in circulation. While abroad, he had been asked about the 'state and disposition of our Court'. He had replied that he could not tell, as he had been out of the country a fortnight.

Peterborough was able to tell the King of Sicily that the French had made stipulations on his behalf to the Emperor in precisely the terms that his ministers had wished; this had been done at the Queen's insistence. The outcome of the Treaty of Rastatt was unsatisfactory for Savoy. The Emperor had refused to acknowledge the Treaty of Utrecht, on which Victor Amadeus's sovereignty was founded. The Treaty of Rastatt was silent on the concerns of Savoy. The British government had been unsuccessful in pushing for the fulfilment of the final clauses of the Treaty of 1703. Other methods would have to be found if Britain and France wished to guarantee that the kingdom of Sicily should remain with Savoy.

*The Treaty was signed by France and Austria on 6 March 1714.

At home the Queen's health had caused alarm but she had made a good recovery and was expected to open the new session of Parliament on 16 February OS. It had been intimated to Peterborough that it was the Queen's wish that he should feel free to return whenever the ceremonial part of his visit was over, 'if you shall judge that yr attendance on the home and on the foreign service may be reconciled'. A warrant had at last been issued for the payment of the £6,000 due to him as General of the Marines. In April his appointment as Governor of Menorca was announced.[16]

Leaving Sicily on 21 April, Peterborough sailed for Naples on board HMS *Greyhound* with an escort of other British ships. Contrary winds lengthened the journey to four days. After three days in Naples, the earl moved on to Rome where he was received in audience by the Pope. The visit was cordial and ceremonial; the Pope invited him to tour the Vatican and ordered refreshments to be laid out in the gallery.

In fulfilment of his embassy to the Italian Princes, Peterborough left Rome on 5 May and travelled to Florence. From here he rejoined the rest of his suite at Leghorn. With his whole party he sailed to Genoa, where they arrived on 8 June to find the *Fubbs* yacht, refitted for Peterborough's embassy, at last arrived from England. In the warmth of the June weather, the earl used the yacht to entertain 'persons of quality', who were sometimes taken for a short cruise at sea.

Peterborough seemed in no hurry to conclude his embassy. Bolingbroke expected to find him back in Paris in May but instead he left Genoa at the end of June and moved on to Modena and Parma. He had been instructed to apply himself to 'promote a strict observation of the Convention for preserving the neutrality of Italy, and to do all to prevent troubles from arising which may threaten general peace'. He appeared to have spent some time in Parma discussing with the Duke the formation of a League of Italian Princes which might eventually succeed in removing Austrian power from Italy.* From Parma he travelled to Turin and then Lyons, reaching Paris again in early August.[17]

In the eighteenth century an ambassador was treated with the respect due to the sovereign whom he represented. On an official visit salutes were fired and guards turned out to greet him. In Paris Peterborough received the courtesies although he was not primarily accredited to that court. Louis XIV was at Marly, a favourite summer palace whose gardens contained a spectacular range of fountains and cascades. On 6

*Vienna claimed Parma as an Imperial fief.

August Peterborough went there and was entertained to dinner by the Marquis de Torcy. At the King's direction, he was taken later on a tour of the gardens by two friends, the Duc d'Aumont and M. d'Antin, and the fountains were turned on for his benefit. He was able to join the King on his promenade and was very courteously received. As an enthusiastic gardener, Peterborough noted the magnificence of the grounds, and as a reluctant courtier the extreme ceremony surrounding the movements of Louis XIV. Voltaire recorded the earl's comment: 'Il faut avouer que les hommes et les arbres plient ici à merveille.' While on this visit, Peterborough passed before the interested and critical eyes of Liselotte, Duchesse d'Orléans, Madame de France. A Princess Palatine by birth, she described Peterborough to a friend: 'He talked very amusingly. He is as witty as the devil, but is very eccentric, and he speaks in a peculiar manner.'

The French court had moved from Marly to Versailles when a courier reached it on 12 August with the news that Queen Anne was seriously ill and not likely to recover. She had taken ill on 29 July/9 August. The following day her condition had worsened and it became clear that indeed the illness might this time prove fatal. On 13 August, because of the state of the Queen's health, Peterborough requested, and received, a farewell audience of Louis XIV. The King gave him assurances that he would be faithful in adhering punctually to the Treaty made with Britain and that there need be no fears on that ground. Maréchal de Villars had arranged a supper and fête for Peterborough in the Cours but the earl left early.

Peterborough set out for London the next morning. Near Calais he encountered the courier bringing the news of the Queen's death. In 1715 the Earl of Stair, then ambassador to the French King, heard a story from Matthew Prior that Peterborough knew of the Queen's death before he went to take leave of the King and concealed the matter so that he could still be received as an ambassador. The evidence for the date of Peterborough's farewell audience comes from Dangeau's Journal, where it is given as 13 August NS. The Queen had died on the morning of 12 August NS. Dangeau also records that a courier bringing the news reached Versailles on 18 August; Matthew Prior received an audience of the King on 20 August at which he announced the news officially. Given the normal speed of communication, it seems extremely unlikely that Peterborough could have received the news of the Queen's death twenty-four hours after the event had occurred.[18]

Thirty

In some respects London was now a changed world. Peterborough had been away when the rivalry between Bolingbroke and Oxford had reached its peak. On 27 July 1714 the Queen had dismissed Oxford but could not be prevailed upon to appoint Bolingbroke as Treasurer in his place. At a regular meeting of the Privy Council the Duke of Argyll and the Duke of Somerset attended unexpectedly. Their moderating influence led to the Council's proposal to the Queen that the Treasurership should be given to Shrewsbury. With failing strength, the Queen was just able to hand the duke the white staff and sign the warrant for his appointment.

All matters concerning the Queen's death and the proclamation of her successor were directed and controlled by the Privy Council with Shrewsbury at its head. There was no difficulty or opposition, even although some members were known Jacobite sympathisers. Louis XIV had assured Peterborough that the French would extend no support to the Pretender and they were aware of the damage James had done to his own chances by declining to change or dissemble his religion.

The proclamation of the new monarch had been carried through smoothly and calmly. The Privy Council had sent respectful messages to Hanover urging his early arrival in the kingdom. Meanwhile the country was governed by regents, already chosen by George before the Queen's death, until the new king's arrival at Greenwich on 18 September.

Unlike his mother, George I never had much time for Peterborough and it was not in his character to pretend that he had. For the earl, there were to be no more splendid appointments, despite his spirited attempt 'to make up to the King and talk to him'. In view of enforced idleness, a winter in Italy with the prospect of the Carnival at Venice seemed attractive. In December Peterborough set out, this time in the character of a private person.[1]

Victor Amadeus had returned to Turin from Sicily at the end of September and it was natural that Peterborough should wish to visit him on his way to Venice. The earl had more than one reason for this visit: he was a suitor for the hand of Vittoria di Susa, the legitimised daughter of Victor Amadeus and his mistress, Madame de Verrue. The King was said to favour the match but the young lady considered the earl ugly and probably also old; her betrothal to Principe Carignano was announced at the end of October.[2]

Having spent the winter quietly and virtually incognito in Venice, Peterborough set off for home again in March 1715 to attend the session of the new Parliament. The Whigs had gained a reasonable majority in the recent election and were beginning investigations into the actions of the previous government, particularly in regard to the Peace negotiations. They had ordered the seizure of Matthew Prior's papers from Paris, an action which alarmed Bolingbroke, who knew that the Dutch and Austrians were questioning his conduct. When his own papers were requested, Bolingbroke lost his nerve and made rapid preparations to escape to France. He left on 27 March disguised as a servant in the suite of one of the French ministers. There is a story that he encountered Peterborough homeward bound on the road between Paris and Calais and the earl ignored him. In later years, however, the friendship was resumed.

After his return Peterborough received a frosty reception at Court. Later he was sent a letter telling him that he need not trouble himself to attend again. 'My lord Peterborough, I hear, is banished the Court,' wrote Alexander Pope to John Caryll, 'but I do not know the occasion.' The Duchesse d'Orléans had less trouble in looking for a reason. 'If Lord Peterborow talks about his King and the Prince of Wales in England in the same way as he does here, then he certainly deserves to be exiled from Court.' Her disapproval did not prevent her from passing on with relish some of the stories about the King which Peterborough had circulated that winter. She thought the earl a most unsuitable person to be Colonel of the Royal Horse Guards, and that he should write 'indigne' after his rank as the nuns did. In June Peterborough lost this appointment to the Duke of Argyll.[3]

The summer of 1715 was a period of active plotting and preparation among the Jacobites in France. James was desperate to reach Britain but every scheme foundered on the rock of the extreme efficiency of the spies employed by the British Ambassador in Paris, the Earl of Stair. James remained at Bar-le-Duc. In July Bolingbroke officially became his secretary of state in Paris. In England the Duke of Ormonde attempted to organise a rising in the West Country but the plans were discovered. Several shiploads of arms bound for Britain were noticed at French ports; Stair made representations to the French government and their passage was stopped.

In August Peterborough was granted a pass to travel abroad. A conversation which he had with d'Iberville, the French Ambassador in London, gave Bolingbroke the idea that the earl might be in a mood to be persuaded to join the Jacobite cause, provided one took care to use 'un certain degré de précaution'. The conversation was probably based on Peterborough's disgust at his treatment by the Court. However it moved Bolingbroke to ask for James's permission to approach the earl when he passed through Paris. Bolingbroke proposed that Peterborough might be sent to Sweden, where negotiations were under way for the supply of troops to support a rising; he knew that it would be difficult to satisfy the earl's pretensions in a military capacity. In the event Peterborough's departure was delayed and nothing more was heard of the project. On 30 July the Viscountess Mordaunt had died, leaving the earl with the charge of his two grandsons, now aged nine and eight respectively.[4]

The death of Louis XIV on 1 September 1715 removed a valuable support from the Pretender to the British throne and the Jacobite cause. Soon afterwards events took an unexpected turn. A disgruntled peer left the Court of George I, travelled north to his estates in Aberdeenshire and there at Braemar raised the standard which launched the rebellion of 1715. The Earl of Mar was not the best of military commanders. Among those who joined his standard was Peterborough's son-in-law, the Marquess of Huntly, as his father, the Duke of Gordon, was in poor health. The Duchess of Gordon was a keen Jacobite but the Marchioness of Huntly was of a different persuasion. Brought up in a Whig household, Lady Huntly had her own political views and was of sufficient spirit to be determined to rear her numerous children in the Protestant tradition, although the Gordons were a Catholic family. Huntly's involvement in the rebellion was cautious and much of his advice was overruled by greater enthusiasts. Lady Huntly prudently withdrew south and spent a year in England. Later, having been present at Sheriffmuir, her husband surrendered himself to government forces and was imprisoned in Edinburgh Castle. He received his remission and was released in November 1716.[5]

In the meantime Peterborough had uncovered a Jacobite conspiracy led by one George Flint, who at the time thought the earl 'an honest man'. This plot aimed to set fire to the palace, rob the bank of England, seize the Tower and proclaim the Pretender as James III. King George was alarmed by this and sent the Earl of Stair to make a protest to the Regent of France.

Whatever had delayed his departure, Peterborough had arrived in Paris by 3 December NS. He visited Stair and treated him to a long dissertation on current affairs. He talked in an extravagant manner for three hours, full of disgust with the Court and contempt for the conduct of the rebels. George Berkeley recorded that Peterborough always believed that after a time the rising of 1715 would dwindle and disappear.[6]

During the rest of the winter and early spring of 1716 Peterborough found something to interest him in Paris. Following the death of Louis XIV, the Duke of Orléans had assumed the regency on behalf of the five-year-old ailing child who was Louis XV. Orléans himself lay next in succession to the throne should the child king die. The Regent felt obliged to protect his own rights, as it was known that Philip V of Spain was still interested in his lineal inheritance despite having renounced it. Orléans had opened negotiations with Britain, asking that his Treaty rights should be guaranteed in exchange for his support of the Protestant Succession. Negotiations had moved smoothly until it was felt in London that the Regent was giving too much help to the Jacobites. Orléans was obliged to steer a difficult course. Aware that French public opinion favoured the Jacobites, he did not wish to find that he had supported the losing side.

The negotiations came to a standstill until the outcome of the rebellion became clear. At this point the French wished to reopen discussions. Having many friends at the French Court, Peterborough became aware of the situation and felt that he could act as an unofficial go-between. First he gave a lecture to Stair on the great advantages of friendship with France and then seemed to be 'upon the wing to go into England to promote this good design', but a month later he was still in Paris. It seemed that the French Court was using him to pump Stair on whether the British intended a rupture or a friendship with France. The French filled him with information on the terms they were prepared to offer; they were happy to accommodate British requests concerning the Pretender and wished to be on good terms with the ambassador. Stair confirmed that he had been instructed to maintain a 'good correspondence' with the French Court but he thought its intentions could be judged best by its response to the memorial he had submitted in January. This quelling reply was made to Peterborough when the earl seemed on the point of leaving for England, taking his friend the Duc d'Aumont with him. Some people thought that the earl had interfered in the negotiations and had spoiled what he had hoped to promote. Stair recorded in his journal: 'If I am mighty complaisant, I may have the honour of making this treaty; if I happen to be rusty, it will go into other hands.'

After many delays a treaty with the French was eventually signed in November 1716, although the draft had been completed in August. It was also signed by the Dutch and became known as the Triple Alliance. Under it, all the powers reaffirmed the terms of the Treaty of Utrecht and France confirmed its agreement to the engagements made therein regarding the succession in England and France. The Pretender was obliged to leave Avignon and move to Italy.[7]

In April 1716 Peterborough was back in London but not for long. He attended the House of Lords and took part in the debate on the second reading of the Septennial Bill. It was proposed in the bill that the Triennial Act should be repealed and the life of the parliament extended for another four years because of the unrest caused by the recent rebellion. The upheaval of an election might only increase the unrest. Peterborough's contributions to the debate have been recorded at least in part. Lord Islay commented that 'what was urged for the keeping of the Triennial Act was a matter of jest, and one might be very witty upon it'. Peterborough, who was against the bill, then remarked that he 'could not think that a matter which so much concerned the foundation of the Government and the liberties of England was a proper subject of jest, and as to being witty, it is not every man can be witty when he would'. Lord Islay had ascribed the increase of unrest since the King's accession chiefly to the fact that 'some persons, who had a great opinion of their own merit, were not in office'. Peterborough rose to speak next and said that 'whether he was in employment or no, he had still an entire affection for the King, and wish'd he could give his vote for this Bill; but that he would not be for a remedy which might cause a greater evil.' He was not sure how one could describe the manner of existence of a parliament which continued beyond the time for which it had been chosen unless, begging leave of the bench of Bishops, 'they had recourse to the distinction used in the Athanasian creed, for they would neither be made nor created, but proceeding...' The Septennial Bill became law in May.[8]

Jacobite agents in London, Paris and elsewhere kept a close watch on the movements of public figures and all sorts of small and unimportant details were recorded. When Peterborough left London for Italy on

6 May OS 1716, reports of his progress were sent regularly to the Earl of Mar, who was now the Pretender's secretary of state. The Jacobites supposed that Peterborough might have been sent by King George on a mission to the Italian princes although his own claim was that he 'wished to live quietly in Italy, being tired of the fatigues of this world'.

Although Peterborough spent only one night in Paris, the Jacobites believed he had a private audience with the Regent. Reaching Turin only eleven days after leaving London and travelling incognito as Mr Mordaunt, the earl entered the city on horseback with a bruised face partly concealed by a green silk patch, as his chaise had earlier overturned. The governor of the city refused to grant him a pass to continue as he was not prepared to state his destination. Peterborough was obliged to reveal his identity and send a message to his old friend the Marquis de St Thomas. However he avoided waiting on the King at the Venerie, pleading his bruise as his excuse.

Peterborough visited his banker, collected the repaired chaise and left the city in the afternoon. Before leaving he sent kind messages to Mar's correspondent, Theophilus Oglethorpe, and also to the French and Spanish ambassadors. Oglethorpe, who had received several visits from Peterborough since he had travelled in his suite in 1714, was trying to establish himself as a Jacobite envoy at the court of Turin. In his view, there was some offence taken at court because the earl had failed to pay his respects.

Peterborough was followed as he left the city for Genoa and it was noted that he discarded his mask at the first stage. At Genoa he took ship for Leghorn and from there made his way to Venice where he had arrived by 5 June. A few days after he had left Turin, more of his entourage passed through the city: his Venetian secretary, his mistress and the rest of his servants were travelling to Venice by Milan at a more leisurely pace.

In Venice Peterborough gave out that he intended to 'live by himself' but might visit Rome and Naples later. Oglethorpe pondered the purpose of the earl's journey but was not surprised by its manner 'as his actions are incomprehensible'. Peterborough had obviously made polite remarks to Jacobites, as Oglethorpe wrote to Mar: 'I wish his designs may be either really to assist our master, or to live quietly in Italy…for you know him a dangerous enemy.'[9]

As Peterborough gave no official intimation of his presence in Venice to the British Resident, Alexander Cunningham, no one called. He made no contact with any other British people staying there, with the exception of his banker. However his presence, and the fact that he kept up a correspondence with Turin, did not meet with approval in Vienna.

During the summer Peterborough heard that the Duke of Argyll had been relieved of his colonelcy of the Royal Horse Guards and so he hoped that he might get his old regiment back. Cunningham reluctantly granted a pass for 'Mr Charles Mordaunt' and a companion to go to Hanover.

The resident then entertained the secretary of state's office at home with a tale of the trouble that Peterborough had been put to, on account of the 'elopement' of his mistress. The lady, known as the Catina Bolognese, had apparently run away rather than face the journey to Hanover. She was in an advanced state of pregnancy and fled at the prospect of a fast and bumpy journey at the pace favoured by his lordship. It took Peterborough some time to find her and the search involved methods which resembled his campaigns in Spain. Eventually a priest gave him some information and Catina was traced to Verona. When Peterborough set off for Hanover on 17 August, the lady remained in Venice.[10]

After a nine days' journey, Peterborough found the court at Herrenhausen. The secretary of state in attendance was now his old friend and comrade in arms James Stanhope, with whom he enjoyed daily conversations; but he was unsuccessful in regaining his regiment. He dined with the King and irritated the courtiers, 'for he would always elbow his way in to be near the prince, and force him by it to speak to him'. He remarked to Mr Clavering 'that the King lived so happily here, that he believed he had forgot the Accident that happened to him and his Family the 1st of August 1714'.

While in Hanover Peterborough negotiated the sale of part of his estate; his steward and the purchaser had come out to meet him there.* By 18 September he was back in Venice. This time his journey took him ten days as he experienced nine falls on the way, 'without hurting himself in ye least'.[11]

Continuing to live quietly, Peterborough appeared to be taking up a more permanent residence in Venice. He sent to England for his plate, which reached him at the very end of the year. Bringing it into town, the earl and his mistress were almost lost in a fog which had settled on the city. In November Peterborough received a visit from the Hanoverian

---

*This was probably the sale of the manor of Chellington to Sir Thomas Trevor. *V.C.H.* Bedfordshire, vol. iii, p. 55.

Resident and in December he gave a dinner for General Schulenburg's brother, who had arrived from Hanover.

British society in Venice numbered about thirty noblemen and gentlemen during this winter. Some later moved on to Rome in January. Peterborough thought of doing so too but wanted to return to England for the parliamentary session. In the event, he remained in Venice for the Carnival during which he gave a ball. The occasion was noted for the quantity of wine and delicious refreshments offered. Catina was Queen of the Ball, 'richement habillée', but her presence made it impossible for Venetian ladies of quality to attend.[12]

Peterborough left for Rome at the end of February 1717, spending some time in Bologna on the way and reaching Rome late in March. He remained there for almost a month. His departure was precipitated by an order from the Pope to leave the city within twenty-four hours as his conduct, in taking his mistress with him wherever he went, had given offence. The Pope considered that the earl profaned the churches by taking this woman to the 'holy public functions', and the ladies of quality were scandalised to meet her driving with him in the Corso. The earl obeyed promptly and left his nephew, Mr Hamilton, to escort his retinue.*

Back in Venice by 7 May, Peterborough left for England within two weeks. Meanwhile Joseph Addison, the recently appointed secretary of state for the Southern Department, had written to him to administer a royal reproof. The King had received a complaint from the imperial court that Peterborough, while in Italy, had 'talked very much against the interests of the Emperor, and [had] spoken of his person in a reflecting manner'. Addison underlined the good terms which the King maintained with the Emperor and pointed out that it was inadvisable to speak in such a way so close to the imperial dominions. Under the circumstances, the King thought it would be prudent for Peterborough to postpone any plan for visiting the kingdom of Naples, or any other part of the Emperor's territory, 'lest any misfortune should befall you upon this account, or any occasion be given for a new complaint'.[13]

This timely advice caught up with the earl when he reached Paris on 2 July and he lost no time in replying. He had been made aware in Rome by a relative who had recently visited Vienna (his nephew Hamilton?) that there was ill-feeling towards him there. He explained that the

*This nephew was probably the son of Peterborough's youngest sister, Anne Mordaunt, who had married James Hamilton of Tollymore. Her son had been at Oxford in 1713 and was now travelling in Europe.

Austrians wrongly ascribed to him a reponsibility for the 'last peace' and also believed him to have been instrumental in acquiring the kingdom of Sicily for the Duke of Savoy. He could not recall having spoken with disrespect of the person of the Emperor and if any criticism was implied in general discourse he would be glad to be told of the occasion. Considering the service he had given to the Emperor previously, the large sum of £20,000 which he had lent him for the campaign in the last year of the war and which it had cost him £1,000 to recover, he thought it a little hard that he should not have free passage through the imperial dominions. To comply with the King's order would cause him no hardship and in a few days he would be in London where he could answer any particular charges.[14]

During this summer Peterborough seemed more welcome at court than he had been for many years. He was at supper twice with the King and regularly attended the Princess of Wales's drawing room. Later he claimed that he had been offered employment at the change of ministry in the spring but had declined it. The Jacobites noticed that government ministers were again visiting Parsons Green and that Peterborough was 'remarkably carest at Court for his intelligence while abroad'. The earl left for the Continent again at the end of July, taking his two young grandsons with him.[15]

Thirty-one

Arriving at Calais on 11 August NS 1717, Peterborough was received with a salute from the Guards who turned out on the orders of the French Court. Jacobite observers thought this compliment unusual unless the earl was on official business. He reached Paris two days later, almost simultaneously with information from an English Jacobite source that he was on his way to Italy to murder the Pretender by means of hired assassins.

The story came first by messenger to Madame de Mézières, a member of the Jacobite Oglethorpe family, who sent him on to St Germains. Here the widowed Queen, Mary of Modena, was understandably concerned and Lieutenant General Dillon warned the Pretender immediately by letter. James, who had taken up residence in the papal palace of Urbino in July, found the news hard to believe, although he accepted the necessity for precautions. Meanwhile Peterborough called on Madame de Mézières and talked away cheerfully about his journey to Bologna, saying he was off 'to make the little war at Naples'. As was his way, he was facetious about the British government and appeared unaware of the story about him; this, to Mme de Mézières's sister, Fanny, was 'the secret of the comedy'.[1]

When Peterborough set out from Paris on 21 August, every detail of his journey was noted by Jacobite spies. Travelling as Lord Mordaunt, he first stopped in Lyons where he visited a banker called Philibert with a letter of credit for £1,400. Then he moved through the mountains to Turin where he arrived on 27 August and put up at a 'poor tavern'. The following day he set out to dine with the Governor of Turin and make an afternoon call on Madame Royale. Unknown to the Jacobites, he also had a private audience with the King of Sicily, who assured him that he had not taken, and did not intend to take, any part in 'ye Spanish business'. That month the island of Sardinia had been overrun by a Spanish force.

Leaving Turin on 29 August, Peterborough informed the Governor and the French Ambassador that his route lay by Alessandria and Piacenza to Reggio Emilia where he had a house. Mindful of Addison's warning about the imperial dominions, he rode fast from Alessandria to Novi and took a post chaise to Genoa, where he embarked for Sestri. By 5 September he had reached Parma where he visited the Duke, a nobleman he had come to know well as a result of his previous embassy. Having visited the famous gardens at Colorno, he travelled to Modena and joined his mistress at Bologna on 6 September. For the next few days he rarely went out but if he did he disguised himself as a woman. A Venetian gentleman, Signor Sante, came on a visit.[2]

Without consulting the Pope, the Pretender wrote on 10 September to Cardinal Origo, the Archbishop of Bologna, asking that Peterborough and his servants be put under arrest and the earl's papers examined. James had received information from so many quarters that he felt that Peterborough must be arrested at least for his own safety but treated in the style suited to a nobleman. It was not the first time that he had been faced with assassination threats; there had been other rumours while he was at Avignon.

Cardinal Origo granted James's request. Armed with a papal warrant from the Cardinal and accompanied by a number of soldiers and *sbirri* in the papal service, two Irish officers in the Pretender's suite arrived at Peterborough's house at Bologna around noon on 11 September. They examined the earl's papers and those of his mistress but nothing incriminating could be found. There was no sign of any large sum of money in the house; in fact the earl was typically vague as to the amount of money he had with him.*

Peterborough and his servants were taken under arrest to the castle of Forte Urbano near Modena on the River Panaro. On the journey the earl tried to persuade Colonel O'Brien of his innocence; he felt that the charge against him had been trumped up as the result of some imperial interest. He also thought that the possibility that he might be given a command in the Spanish invasion could be causing resentment in some Italian quarters. He had received an anonymous letter before leaving England saying that he was discovered, but ignored it, assuming it was just some attempt to prevent his journey. All the earl's remarks were carefully recorded and sent to the Cardinal.

At Forte Urbano Peterborough was treated respectfully enough. He was allowed to write, which he made full use of, and was free to walk

---

*The Duke of Gordon had a story that once he came across the sum of £4,000 in Peterborough's house which the earl seemed quite unaware of possessing. J. Menzies to L. Inese, 17/28 October 1717, HMC *Stuart Papers Windsor*, vol. v, p. 166.

around within the Forte on his parole. He asked to speak to a member of the Pretender's court, Colonel Dominic Sheldon (they had friends in common), but he hoped that no one would expect him to meet the Pretender himself, as this would be open to misinterpretation in England.[3]

The Pretender sent Sir John O'Brien to assist with the interrogation. Peterborough requested the attendance of Auditor Michelli to whom he dictated 'reflections on his arrest' for the benefit of Cardinal Origo. In these Peterborough explained the purpose of his visit to Italy, his proposed itinerary (from Bologna he had intended to go to Venice for three weeks before returning to Paris) and the reason for his method of travel. He also expounded at length on the unlikelihood of his participation in the undertaking of which he was suspected. When the Pretender saw this document, he did not believe the reasons given and considered most of them implausible. Peterborough later published a manifesto proclaiming his innocence based on the 'reflections'.*

Meanwhile the earl used much of his time in captivity in writing to his friends. He assured them that he was in no hurry to be released but only to have his innocence established. Among his correspondents were the Dukes of Modena and Parma as well as a friend in Venice. O'Brien managed to intercept a visit from the Marchese Rangoni, a friend of the Duke of Modena; he was afraid that the Duke might contact King George before James and his Court had finalised their investigations.

Peterborough himself seemed to bear no personal grudge against the Pretender for his imprisonment. He wrote to a British diplomat, possibly Davenant at Genoa, anxious that no violent action should be taken on his behalf but that all endeavours should be centred on discovering the basis of the accusation and from whence it came. He wished it to be known in diplomatic circles that he had been warned not to travel in imperial dominions and that there had been absolutely no secrecy attached to his journey to Italy. He also requested that 'you will be pleased on this occasion, for my security, not to reflect too much upon the young spark, but upon those who could give him such malicious informations, excusing the tenderness of a mother when the safety of a son is concerned, and the fears of a young prince to whom they represent his life in danger...'[4]

At the beginning of October James sent Dominic Sheldon to interview Peterborough. Sheldon was told to return the earl's papers and

---

*A copy of the Reflections, annotated by James, is among the Stuart Papers. HMC *Stuart Papers Windsor*, vol. v, pp. 74–9.

stress that it was now his business to justify himself. Peterborough again protested his innocence, signing a paper to that effect and another which gave details of an underlying motive for his visit to Italy based on a letter in the form of a memorandum to the Regent of France which had been found among his papers.

Peterborough appeared to have become a sort of self-appointed ambassador to further the peace of Europe. Before he left Italy as the Queen's ambassador, he had discussed with the Duke of Parma the possibility of forming a league of Italian Princes to counteract the Emperor's power in Italy. He had become friendly with the Parmesan minister in London, Count Giovanni-Angelo Gazzola, who had recently been appointed Governor of Parma and had invited him to visit him there.

It was Peterborough's view that the way towards a stable future for Europe was to form an alliance between France, Spain, the King of Sicily and the Italian Princes in order to balance imperial power. In this alliance a key figure was the Duke of Parma whose niece and step-daughter, Elizabeth, had become the second wife of Philip V of Spain. Basically the King of Spain and the Emperor did not acknowledge each other's titles and had conflicting interests in Italy. The alliance would be an attempt to prevent a fresh war from erupting, as Philip of Spain hoped to regain the two Sicilies and the Emperor wished to add Sicily to Naples and keep Spain out of Italy.

In his letter to the Regent Peterborough outlined his plan, which explained his visits to Turin and Parma. He added that he had kept himself out of employments at home in order to work for a better understanding between France and Britain. To the Jacobites, all this information was of little real interest: as far as they were concerned it neither proved nor disproved anything. In the meantime the British government, and James Stanhope in particular, were working towards persuading the Emperor to join the Triple Alliance in order to resolve the crisis with Spain following on its acquisition of Sardinia.[5]

News of Peterborough's plight reached Joseph Addison in London from both Cunningham in Venice and Davenant in Genoa. To Davenant Addison's reply was prompt: Peterborough was not 'invested with any power or character from His Majesty'. In Venice Cunningham, meeting the Papal Nuncio at the house of the Imperial Ambassador, took the opportunity to give him a verbal trouncing regarding the manner of the arrest. 'I told him one might have expected that ye pope would have made a better use of St Peter's keys than to give them to ye pretender...yt ye pretender should exert ane act of jurisdiction where he is, was a manifest usurpation upon ye right of St Peter, of wch ye Church might feel ye effects, and yt ye keys were poluted thereby...' Such comments would have only added to the Pope's alarm at the noise made by the whole affair. His nervousness was noted and encouraged by Count Gallas, now the Imperial Ambassador in Rome. By early October the Jacobites were fully aware of the Pope's impatience to have Peterborough set at liberty.

In Paris a Jacobite envoy informed the Regent of the arrest and the reasons for it. He was a little disconcerted to find that the Regent was not only well informed of the matter but asked him rather pointedly whether the arrest had been made on the Pope's order.

The Regent had also heard that in England many people had laughed off Peterborough's predicament but some thought this was no way in which to treat a peer of the realm. This view was officially expressed by Addison in reply to Stair; the King had voiced 'a great indignation both as to the fact itself of seizing an English Peer in that manner, and likewise as to the pretences which have been made use of for the doing of it, which seem to carry a high reflection upon His Majesty himself...'⁶

On 14 October Peterborough was released on parole to remain at Bologna. Soon afterwards he was visited on James's orders by Sir John O'Brien. There is a description of the visit left by Sir John in the Stuart Papers. Peterborough, wrapped in a cloak and escorted by Auditeur Michelli and two servants, met O'Brien under the arcades. They walked on until they found an open place where there was light. The discussion began around matters mentioned in Sheldon's report and O'Brien urged Peterborough to clear himself of the suspicions which had still not evaporated even though he was now at liberty. The earl stated that he had already written to the Regent who would have taken steps to persuade Queen Mary of the true reasons of his visit to Italy. He clearly found O'Brien's questions distasteful and terminated the interview abruptly.⁷

At home in England diplomatic wheels were beginning to turn on Peterborough's behalf. On 17 October NS Addison wrote to the earl that the King had heard of his arrest, and 'would lose no time in procuring your Liberty, and demanding Satisfaction for the great Injury which has been done your lordship'. Since there was no diplomatic envoy in Rome, Davenant in Genoa had offered to negotiate; but the British government took another route. Focusing on King George's friendship with the Emperor, Addison asked Count Gallas, the Imperial envoy at

Rome, to obtain reparation from the Pope for having arrested a peer of the realm on a pretext which reflected on the King himself. Gallas, who ironically had been speaking already in Peterborough's favour, was asked to request that the earl be set free at once and his servants and papers restored to him. He was instructed to state that the Pope must disown the action in writing and declare that it was not done on his orders. He must promise never again to meddle in matters concerning England or interest himself in the Pretender's cause. He was expected to punish the Cardinal Legate at Bologna for the part he had played and undertake that for the future he would never molest a subject of the King within the Papal States for any reason connected with the Pretender. Should the Pope be hesitant about concurring in these matters, orders had already been sent to a squadron of the British Navy to sail to Civita Vecchia 'where it will find occasion to give marks of the King's just resentment'. The instructions to Gallas were sent in secret. There was little secrecy about the order to the Fleet; it was talked about openly and was precisely the sort of reparation which all along the Pope had nervously anticipated.

On 17 November Sheldon sent Peterborough a stiff letter informing him that James was releasing him from his parole. This was being done at the Pope's request, despite the fact that the earl had still not given satisfaction of his innocence. The communication bore all the marks of an attempt to get out of an awkward situation without loss of face. Many Jacobites, believing that Peterborough had been arrested too quickly, would have preferred that James had released him on his own initiative. No concrete evidence against him had ever appeared and the position was untenable. Others stuck firmly to their views, believing that James's action had won much support and that those who had acted in friendship towards Peterborough, such as the Duke of Parma, would find themselves isolated. James wrote ruefully to Cardinal Gualterio that he supposed that for his honour he must now scoff at the whole matter.[8]

In Bologna Peterborough had been leading a relatively unrestricted life. He visited the Duke of Modena and entertained rather more lavishly than before. He even dined with Cardinal Origo, an action criticised in England as inappropriate and premature. He had issued a total of three manifestos proclaiming his innocence, which were circulating well beyond the Italian states. Addison told Davenant that the attitude to be taken towards the story of Peterborough's supposed conspiracy was that 'the Point should by no means be treated as a matter of a disputable nature, but with all that scorn and contempt which it deserves...'[9]

Among the maelstrom of evidence and allegations, it becomes clear that Peterborough never gave active support to the Jacobite cause. Suggestions by the earl that he had never born any ill-will to the Pretender, indeed quite the contrary, were greeted with scorn and disbelief in Jacobite circles. On 17 November he went to Modena to meet his son-in-law, the Duke of Gordon, whose travels had brought him to Italy. They returned to Bologna together and later went to Florence to visit the Grand Duke of Tuscany. On 2 December Peterborough left Bologna for Venice where he planned to stay for the Carnival unless home affairs called him.[10]

Peterborough had left Bologna firmly resolved to discover the root of the matter, which he believed was an English plot against him. Mar wrote to Paris to warn the Oglethorpes, and particularly Fanny, that the earl was bound to make trouble for them when he arrived there. As far as can be ascertained from the Stuart Papers, the original story of the assassination plot emanated from information received by the Earl of Oxford. He told Anne Oglethorpe, who passed the news on to her sister, Mme de Mézières, from whom it reached Queen Mary. After this original communication, similar stories came from England by various hands. James wrote to the Earl of Oxford on 16 December 1717: 'A commendable zeal in you and a reasonable prudence in me occasioned what I wish now had never happened, but I hope no ill effect will come from it.' Fanny Oglethorpe thought it would be extremely difficult to keep the truth from Peterborough. Far too many people already knew who sent the message; Lord Oxford and his party were bound to be exposed. She had heard that Peterborough was furious, 'besides it's disagreeable to have a man like him for an enemy, who, you may be sure, will sit on our skirts.'[11]

They had a little time to wait before the expected invasion. Peterborough left Venice on 1 January 1718 and had reached Paris by 22 February. He sent a message to the Oglethorpes that he would be with them in four days' time. 'That day', wrote Fanny, 'I'll have the headache.' Later she wrote to Mar 'from the country' with the news that Peterborough had taken a house in Paris for six months. 'He goes to the fair without his Garter, with a great cloak in which he wraps up his 2 grandchildren, only their heads appear, and 2 Venice ladies support him, which he calls his guards.' He had just celebrated his sixtieth birthday.[12]

Peterborough had maintained no contact with Bolingbroke since his disgrace and had told Dominic Sheldon that he distrusted him. Soon after the earl reached Paris, Bolingbroke tried to contact him through a mutual friend, Madame de Ferriol, and was a little surprised to learn that he thought a meeting both necessary and important. It had not taken the earl long to find out the English source of the stories about him. He wanted to meet Bolingbroke because of his former close friendship with Oxford.

By 13 April a meeting had taken place. Much of the time was taken up by Peterborough recounting his adventure at Bologna which he claimed had cost him £10,000, but he also indicated that he intended to publish something about Oxford on his return to England and in this connection asked if he might have access to some letters in Bolingbroke's possession of which he only had the minutes. Bolingbroke agreed to hand these over as he no longer had any contact with Oxford. The meeting lasted for six hours and, apart from the agreement about the letters, was otherwise inconclusive. However the conversation was long and intense and even arrangements for the conveyance of the letters were forgotten 'in the heat of discourse'. At this time, having abandoned the Jacobite interest, Bolingbroke was only interested in his own restitution – in which he did not think Peterborough could do much to assist – but he did send the letters. Peterborough seems to have intended the meeting solely as a means of obtaining ammunition against the Earl of Oxford.[13]

The Oglethorpe family were kept waiting for the earl's visit. In early May 'he bolted in upon us and began very high,' wrote Fanny, 'saying we were the authors of his misfortune, by my eldest sister's means, that he would follow the source of that affair and it should not end so.' Mme de Mézières remained very calm and claimed ignorance of his insinuations; if he thought them guilty of something, then he should not visit. The earl seemed to accept her assurances that she had learnt the story from a public source and the subject passed. He then 'spoke only in general terms and, talking a great deal, found the way to say ill of nobody'. Soon after this visit Peterborough and his family returned to England.[14]

Thirty-two

At home in the winter of 1718–19, Peterborough busied himself with attendance at the House of Lords. His lasting friendship with the poet Alexander Pope probably also began in this season – one of Pope's earliest recorded visits to Parsons Green took place in the spring of 1719. Pope belonged to a circle of friends who were mainly interested in literature and the arts but who also indulged in political argument and even gossip. Jonathan Swift, who still retained Peterborough's friendship, also moved in this circle when he was in England. Into this society Peterborough fitted with ease and increasing pleasure.[1]

On 28 February 1719 a Bill was introduced in the Lords 'for settling the Peerage of Great Britain'. It proposed to fix for all time the number of peers who could sit in the House of Lords and limited the royal prerogative to the creation of only six new English peers. The Scottish nobility would be represented by twenty-five hereditary peers instead of the sixteen at present elected.

The underlying reason for this legislation was the insecurity felt by the Whig government. The Whigs had brought in George I but did not command the huge popular goodwill accorded to their predecessors who had supported William III. In addition, the unfortunate hostility which existed between George and his heir, the Prince of Wales, was taken advantage of by the Tory opposition who courted and supported the Prince. Because of this state of affairs, the King made no complaint about parting with his prerogative in the creation of peers. Ostensibly, the Bill sought to prevent any further creations en bloc, such as had occurred in 1714 when Queen Anne had created twelve new Tory peers in order to push the Treaty of Utrecht through the House of Lords. The Whigs were afraid that the Prince of Wales on his accession might use his prerogative to create a permanent Tory majority and so were trying to ensure the continuation of their own majority in the Lords.

The present sixteen Scottish representative peers were sympathetic to the Whig government; an additional nine would be chosen from reliable supporters. Thereafter, if a hereditary Scottish peerage became extinct, a replacement would be chosen from the Scottish nobility. In

England, a new creation would only be made when an existing peerage became extinct. The Bill would create an oligarchy of the Lords, outside the influence of the King or the House of Commons.

The Bill was introduced so late in the session that a recess supervened before it could be taken any further. During the recess a pamphlet war broke out over the contentious issue. The Bill was greeted with much opposition by members of the House of Commons and by a degree of amazement by the Scots. The first pamphlet against it was published on 14 March; it was entitled *The Plebeian* and was believed to come from the pen of Sir Richard Steele. Another salvo was fired very soon afterwards (17 March) by Sir Robert Walpole, with the issue of *The Thoughts of a Member of the Lower House in Relation to a Project for Restraining and Limiting the Power of the Crown in the Future Creation of Peers*. These pamphlets were answered on the part of the government by Joseph Addison in *The Old Whig* and by Lord Molesworth in *The Patrician*. The fight continued with another pamphlet from Walpole and also from Molesworth.

On 30 March 1719 Lord Peterborough entered the lists on behalf of the government interest with *Remarks on a Pamphlet Entitled 'The Thoughts of a Member of the Lower House'*. Whatever the merits of the argument, the pamphlet gives some idea of the command of language and imagery which made Peterborough's public speeches so attractive and entertaining to his contemporaries. It proved popular and ran to three editions.

Those who wrote in defence of the Bill generally dealt with four main points: the assertion that the Bill was in breach of the Union, that it removed a Crown prerogative, that it altered the constitution and finally that it would result in an over-powerful House of Lords. In the main, Peterborough's pamphlet concerned itself with the first and last of these points.

With regard to the Union, Peterborough wrote that disaster would occur if the original Act was considered so sacrosanct as to be incapable of amendment. Flaws had appeared early. 'If we consider seriously, there will appear the highest absurdities in our present frame: we are like a ship built of old and green timber, so ill patch'd together that we must founder in the first storm. And there is nothing more ridiculous than to say the legislature ought not, cannot, shall not save two nations in the extremest danger, by proper alterations in the known and usual methods of the constitution...' The dangers would manifest themselves in continual unrest.

Men of spirit, subjected to national and perpetual injuries, will never cease to resent them, and never lose any opportunity to ease or revenge themselves. When there is a prospect of a remedy...there is a room for patience...there is imprinted in human nature a necessary tenderness for posterity, but NEVER is a very disagreeable word... Whoever is for adhering strictly to the present terms of Union, whoever is of opinion that the visible Mistakes in those injudicious laws are not to be amended by the legislature, I declare him a damn'd Papist in politicks; for he is placing an infallibility in the makers of those laws, more prejudicial to the state, than the infallibility of the Pope to true religion; he is also securing to all pretenders whatsoever, whether supported by Spaniards, Swedes, Muscovites or Turks, the nation of Scotland ready to take arms upon all occasions and to all ages.

A permanent injustice had been done to the nobility of Scotland by the invention of the electoral peerage, he claimed. If a stranger were to ask by whom the elected peers were chosen, he might be surprised to be informed 'that their immediate generation is from the King and ministers; that they are lords at pleasure only, and upon their good behaviour; that they die in a short time like insects, and can revive no more, but by the sunshine of the Court'. This injustice would be remedied by the twenty-five Scottish hereditary peers who would sit in a position of equality with English peers in the Lords. At present, the elected peers 'are received with disgust by the English peerage and so they sit amongst them with indignation'.

Next Peterborough turned his attention to the supposed omnipotence to be gained by the House of Lords should this Bill become law. This he scorned as a chimera. 'One would think by the general turn of these pamphlets that all Kings and Ministers had been lately prepared to sing in concerts...but lords (Heaven protect us!) are such terrible creatures that, one grain more added in their ballance, makes them omnipotent and irresistible, and capable to toss the King and Commons in a blanket; as they serve a scoundrel who cannot pay his bett in a cock-pit.' As for the dangers of the establishment of an aristocracy, 'the degrees of evil between an aristocracy and a democracy are little to the purpose; natural things are often improved by a mixture of different ingredients, and a lover of the English constitution should remember that the drams of aristocracy and democracy which are flung into our composition are the antidotes to that poison of tyranny, with which at present almost the whole world is infected.'

As for the so-called 'terror of the Lords',

> they must labour against wind and tide who endeavour to persuade that the peers of England, in or out of Parliament, are dangerous to the constitution of England, or in the least condition to insult or impose upon the Crown, or House of Commons... What are the Lords? a few in number, only possest (as one author has it) of an *imaginary Dignity*; they represent nothing but themselves, and so can have no addition of strength but from themselves; they are in no circumstances which can make them popular, but rather remain a mark for envy; the greatest part of them are poor, and none of them are possest of a dangerous wealth; they have no holdings which procure them dependencies; they are possest of no castles or strong places, nor have they any being as to action, but at the power of another, that is, when considered as a body, they are dissolvable at pleasure: and can there be a description of more harmless creatures?...

It is the Commons who have 20,000 disciplined men at their disposal, and receive and dispense the nation's income. 'The Lords in their greatest splendor and authority, with their Speaker at their head, what have they to contend with against all these supposed enemies? They have an empty embroider'd purse and a black rod.'

Peterborough concluded this section:

> I hope by this time, taking the whole into consideration, we may lay aside our fears of the Lords being capable to insult the Crown, or subvert the government, even when aggrandized and fortified with all this Act can give them.
>
> Which, give me leave to say, will be just nothing. Just what they were before the passing of this law, the same they will be afterwards. All that can be pretended is a little defensive armour.

No other writer in this controversy attempted to prove that the Lords were basically a harmless and powerless lot. There was so much uncertainty, and so much genuine concern that their powers could become too great. Nonetheless, Peterborough's views contributed trenchantly to the debate.

The Peerage Bill passed its second reading and committee stage in the Lords but, at Stanhope's request, the third reading was postponed because of the opposition to it in the Commons. In the meantime Parliament was prorogued and the Bill lost. In the next Parliament, the following winter, the measure reappeared; it passed through the Lords but was defeated in the Commons.[2]

In the summer of 1718 the Emperor was finally persuaded to join the Triple Alliance and the Quadruple Alliance so formed was intended to prevent war between Spain and Austria, a possibility which appeared increasingly likely. In addition to the dispute between Spain and Austria over the ownership of the Two Sicilies, there was now the wish of the Queen of Spain, Elizabeth Farnese, to add Tuscany to her own inheritance of Parma for the benefit of her son, Don Carlos. The Emperor opposed this wish.

Elizabeth was ably assisted and encouraged in her ambitions by another Parmesan, the Cardinal Alberoni. Coming from humble stock, Giulio Alberoni rose through his own natural ability and skill to become First Minister of Spain. In 1714 he was merely an agent of the Duke of Parma at the Court of Spain and helped to arrange the marriage of the recently bereaved Philip V to Elizabeth Farnese. He guided the new Queen's steps on her arrival in Spain, particularly in the summary dismissal and return to France of the Princesse des Ursins, who had been the power behind the Spanish throne. Through Alberoni, Parmesan politics began to have some influence on the Spanish outlook. The Duke of Parma held the opinion that a Spanish interest in Parma and Tuscany was the key to the diminution of Austrian power in Italy.

In the Quadruple Alliance an attempt was made to find a solution to the problem of the conflicting interests. A scheme was worked out by the Regent of France and James Stanhope whereby the Spanish prince, Don Carlos, would receive the reversion of Tuscany and Parma while the Emperor relinquished Sardinia to Victor Amadeus and received Sicily in exchange. The Emperor, who was contending with various other problems, was prepared to agree to this arrangement and it was decided that Spain should be coerced into agreement, if necessary by force. Spain found the plan totally abhorrent as leaning too much to the Emperor's advantage.

Before Stanhope's attempted diplomacy could have any chance of success, a newly refurbished Spanish fleet was despatched to regain Naples and Sicily. A British fleet commanded by Admiral Byng had already been deployed to watch Spanish movements in the Mediterranean and it destroyed the Spanish fleet in an engagement off Cape

Pássero. In retaliation for this action, Spain decided to support the Jacobite cause. She arranged to supply the Duke of Ormonde with a squadron to assist in an invasion of England and some forces for a descent in Scotland. Britain declared war on Spain in December 1718. After the discovery of a plot organised by the Spanish Ambassador to France, the Prince of Cellamare, to replace Orléans with Philip V as Regent, France followed suit in January 1719.

The Jacobite projects were not successful. A storm dispersed the squadron bound for England; the small expeditionary force which landed in Scotland was defeated by government troops at Glenshiel in March. In the meantime a French army had marched into the north of Spain.[3]

By the summer of 1719 both Stanhope and the Regent's favourite, the Abbé Dubois, had become convinced that the main obstacle to peace lay in the person of the Cardinal Alberoni. The cardinal's power over the Spanish Queen was paramount and she in turn influenced her husband.

Since leaving Italy, Peterborough had kept up a correspondence with the Duke of Parma, whose interest he believed could be used to good effect to obtain a peace between France and Spain. He was unstinting in his advice to the Duke. He claimed, and it may be believed, that it was partly as a result of his encouragement that the Duke decided to send an envoy, the Marquis Scotti, to Spain to promote the cause of peace. Unfortunately Alberoni construed the Duke's action as an attempt to 'sacrifice the interests of the King of Spain to get rid of his [the Duke's] present pressures by the German contributions', and represented it as such to the King and Queen.

Peterborough himself crossed to Paris in June 1719 and soon became infected with the French view that Alberoni was the obstacle in the peace initiatives. The Marquis Scotti had reached Spain in July but Alberoni soon found a means of dispensing with his presence near the Court and sent him to Paris, where the Regent offered him a gift of 50,000 francs to promote the downfall of Alberoni. Scotti was also seen much in the company of Peterborough. The earl spent the rest of the summer travelling and was believed to be consulting Parmesan envoys at different courts. The British government took pains to make clear that he was doing so in an unofficial capacity.

At the end of September Peterborough was in Cassel, paying court to the Landgrave; in November, he was back in Paris. Here he received an urgent message from the Duke of Parma that he should go to meet one of his ministers 'on the confines of Lombardy'. Under an assumed name the earl posted off immediately to Novi where he had a series of meetings with his old friend Gazzola, the Governor of Parma.

In an audience with the Regent, Peterborough had already discussed the best methods for getting rid of Alberoni and it had been decided that some definite action must be taken by the Duke of Parma. Peterborough had already won round both Sunderland and Stanhope to this way of thinking. As a result of the conversations at Novi, the Duke of Parma indicated that he was prepared to act, provided that the Regent could give him 'a letter he can show, in which it may be declared that, seeing the Cardinal has made so ill a use of the confidence of his master in prolonging a war…the courts of France and England will take the resolution not to enter into any negotiation of peace until the Cardinal shall be driven from the ministry.' Peterborough wrote to Stanhope: 'Italian princes are great lovers of negociations, but seldome disposed to take ye proper methods to bring matters to a conclusion; but ye Duke of Parma will and must exert himself, and sees the necessity of getting rid of Alberoni att any rate, or reducing him without losse of Time to reason.'

Although the negotiations with Parma were supposedly secret, neither they nor the actions of Marquis Scotti had bypassed Alberoni. Scotti now returned to Spain to take part in the final dénouement. Alberoni seemed ready for resignation, saying he found the burden of office too great. With reference to Peterborough's negotiations, he told the Duke of Parma that the earl was 'regarded in Spain as a most pretentious fool and a consummate blackguard and his very name was sufficient to make his terms disliked'.

The Duke of Parma sent a letter to his niece the Queen, giving the Allies' terms. He also wrote to Alberoni, urging him to resign. On 15 December the King and Queen left the city, having handed to a minister a decree giving Alberoni eight days to leave Madrid and three weeks to leave the country. After this, it was only a short time before Spain agreed to the Allies' terms.[4]

After Novi, Peterborough spent some time at Genoa but he changed his mind about going on to Venice. By Christmas he was in Paris and before leaving for England at the end of January, he told Madame de Ferriol of his satisfaction at hearing the news that Spain had agreed to the terms laid down by the Quadruple Alliance. He felt that he had worked towards this outcome for a number of years and that there would now be a lasting union between the courts of Paris and Madrid.[5]

In February 1720 Peterborough celebrated his sixty-second birthday. For the remaining fifteen years of his life there was a certain slowing down of activity. The visits to Europe still took place but the epic journeys became things of the past. He still remained a vigorous correspondent and continued to take an interest in politics, literature and horticulture. In 1721 he wrote to Madame de Ferriol, lamenting that he had not visited her for many months. Later that year he told her that the government had given orders for letters to be opened; his had received particular attention. A letter he had written to a French lady under the cover of Madame de Caylus had been carefully examined. It had been flowery and gallant, and Peterborough had been highly entertained to be told that spies had read into it a hidden meaning, believing it an elaborate code for matters political.[6]

Letter-writing was an art which Peterborough always took seriously. When the days of sitting up all night to write despatches were over, he took pride in sending his friends polished epistles, carefully thought out, elegantly centred on the page and often with an exactly kept margin in which he might add a tidy postscript. To the researcher, his characteristic handwriting, close to italic script, is of a welcome legibility; it hardly faltered in illness or old age.

Around 1720 Peterborough began a series of letters to a new female correspondent. Not only did she preserve them but she kept copies of her replies as well. The earl owed his introduction to Mrs Henrietta Howard to Lady Mohun, who had married his nephew, Colonel Charles Mordaunt.

Mrs Howard was the daughter of Sir Henry Hobart, Bt of Blickling Hall, Norfolk. In 1706 she had married the Hon. Charles Howard, the youngest son of the 5th Earl of Suffolk. Financial problems soon loomed. It seemed a good way to get rid of their creditors to move to the Electress's court at Hanover and this proved a sound future investment. The Howards returned to England around the time of the arrival of King George.

While her husband became a Groom of the Bedchamber to the King, Mrs Howard received the position of Woman of the Bedchamber in the household of the anglophile Princess of Wales, Caroline of Anspach. The Howard marriage itself had foundered. In 1717, when the quarrel between the King and the Prince of Wales had become so acute that the Prince was banished from the Court at St James, Mrs Howard followed her mistress to the new establishment at Leicester House and became permanently estranged from her husband. In summer it became a custom for the Prince and Princess to stay at Richmond Lodge and it was at Richmond that Mrs Howard made the acquaintance of Alexander Pope and John Gay. The Prince of Wales was devoted to his wife whom he considered the epitome of womanly beauty but he believed that he owed it to his consequence and position to keep a mistress. He pursued Mary Bellenden unsuccessfully for some time and made Mrs Howard his confidante. Mary Bellenden left the court on her marriage in 1720 and it was then that Mrs Howard became the Prince's mistress.

Henrietta Howard was a woman of considerable charm who kept the attachment of her friends to the end of her life. A contemporary description of her states: 'Her face was not beautiful but pleasing. Her hair was extremely fair and remarkably fine. Her arms were square and lean, that is, ugly. Her countenance was an undecided one.' Thus she was seen through the eyes of her friend, Philip Dormer Stanhope. The undecided countenance may have remained so as a mask to what she really thought. She had a reputation for tact and discretion: because of this, she was nicknamed 'the Swiss' and her house 'the Swiss Cantons'. Her demeanour may have been a contributing factor to her long enjoyment of royal favour.

She was however a little deaf, an affliction which increased with age. Alexander Pope wrote a poem about her, entitled 'On a Certain Lady at Court'.

> I know the thing that's most uncommon;
> (Envy, be silent and attend!)
> I know a Reasonable Woman,
> Handsome and witty, yet a Friend.
>
> Not warp'd by Passion, aw'd by Rumour,
> Not grave thro' Pride, or gay thro' Folly,
> An equal Mixture of good Humour,
> And sensible soft Melancholy.
>
> Has she no Faults then (Envy says) Sir?
> Yes she has one, I must aver:
> When all the World conspires to praise her,
> The Woman's deaf, and does not hear.

These lines were written in 1732, when Pope's friendship with Mrs Howard had already lasted fifteen years.

On the face of it, the correspondence between Lord Peterborough and Mrs Howard appeared on his part a series of impassioned love letters and on hers cool rejoinders. It was based on an agreement between them. In one of the earlier letters, having received no answer for some time, the earl writes: 'Permit me to give you an account of my last duet without my partner; and as by the original articles of our scribbling treaty, you were sincerely to tell me your opinion, so remember your long silence, and give me an answer to this.' Mrs Howard entered into the spirit of the enterprise and engaged the assistance of her friend, the poet John Gay, in drafting her replies.* Few of the letters are dated and only occasionally refer to current events, thus giving some clue to chronology. Most seem to have been exchanged between 1720 and 1725 but Peterborough continued the correspondence at intervals until shortly before his death.

These letters make tedious reading to the modern eye. Flowery compliments and sentimental utterances, as if every day was St Valentine's, seem only pathetic when sent by an elderly admirer to a woman young enough to be his daughter. It is possible that Peterborough thought that Mrs Howard's coolness and air of inconsequence, and also her wry humour and ability to gently mock at herself, would protect her from any emotional involvement. Her position at Court and as the Prince's mistress was one of influence, although there is little evidence that she used this influence as much as might have been expected. She appeared to accept Peterborough's courtship as an amusing diversion; at one time she did seem to wonder if, on his side, it might be serious.

Lady Mohun described Peterborough to her friend at a time when he was also paying court to another lady.

Our gallant Gardiner has ever been lucky enough to be distinguished for somthing in the world, but I cannot comprehend that it can satisfie his vanity to be received as a lover by one who confesses herself a grandmother, and to be as plain with my dear H. tis no such mighty proof of your philosophy and quallity of mind as you would infer, that you are not mortified at the inconstancy of a superannuated gallant; however I dare answer so much for his Justice and understanding, that he must be sensible of your worth above others, and of consequence will esteem it preferably to the rest; I think him good-natured, and generous, which are two valuable quallitys, but I know at the same time he is in an

---

*Mrs Howard's correspondence is now in the British Library. The letters from Lord Peterborough are in BL Add. MSS 22,625. Some of her correspondence was edited by J. W. Croker and printed in 1824.

error as to his application. He has somthing in his head which he often mistakes for love, but I doubt it will prove a Don Quixott passion which he must subsist with an imaginary Dulcinea.[7]

In considering Peterborough's part in this correspondence, it must be remembered that the letters span the period when the earl made the acquaintance of Anastasia Robinson, the singer, whom he secretly married in 1722. As for Mrs Howard, she referred to her correspondent as her knight-errant. Many of the letters take the form of philosophical essays on the nature of love and although finely expressed make tedious and lengthy reading.

Two letters later in the correspondence give an example of their style. Mrs Howard challenges her knight-errant on his claim of faithfulness and devotion.

Consider, my Lord, you have but one heart; and then consider whether you have a right to dispose of it. Is there not a lady at Paris who is convinced that nobody has it but herself? Did you not bequeath it to another lady at Turin? At Venice, you disposed of it to six or seven: and you again parted with it at Naples and in Sicily.

I am, therefore, obliged, my Lord, to believe that one who disposes of his heart in so profuse a manner is like a juggler who seems to fling away a piece of money, but still has it in his own keeping.

This provoked a reply of which the following is a part.

Give me leave to tell you your intelligence is very imperfect, and in many cases false; I have no knoledge of the Lady you begin with, I was ever too good an Englishman to submitt to a french Ennemy, and were I to offer anything to a Lady att Paris, it should be three bottles of chaimpagne, and not one heart.

Att Turin I was so busied in making Kings that I had not time to think of Ladies, and was so far from making a conveighance yt I know no person there ever had the least pretence to me or I to them.

Venice indeed was an idle place, and proper enough for an idle engagement, but alas Madame, hate does not differ more from Love, then a Venetian amusement from an English Passion, or such a one as I feel for you.

In truth you never had in any countrey, or could have but one

Rivall, for in no place I ever found any to compare to you but one, and that was an English Lady and a wife, so yt after all this vagabond heart never went out of its own countrey, and the first, and Last, True and warm passion seised me in this cold Climate, and the deep and lasting wounds were given me att home...

In another letter Peterborough makes a delicate reference to Mrs Howard's physical complaint. 'I conclude with a melancholy comparison where we are both concerned, to those who are a little deaf one ought to raise the voice; I never was quick-sighted in my own behalf; if you will speak with your eyes any thing obliging you must Look Loudly, or I shall never hear or aprehend...'

Not all the letters are of continuous sentimental content. There are glimpses of a leisured life at Twickenham, Fulham and further afield as well as the occasional mention of current affairs. It is pleasant to know that Peterborough sent ladies bouquets of orange flowers from his gardens at Parsons Green; the same place yielded a 'baskett of pears' which the earl kindly left with Mrs Howard's servant, 'our uncle Harry being to entertain Ladies'. The mood of Peterborough's letters could change rapidly from passionate outpourings on the one hand to wit and humour on the other, or a subtle blend of both.

An early letter obviously came from Bath. 'Give me leave to tell you all the Phytisians agree in this, that there is something so nice and refined in Dr Sloan's idea about the Bath watters in your case, that the notion is only fitt for ye head of a member of the Royall Society, and for one whose closett is filled with triffling curiosities; we therefore hope that you will not think it is for self interest alone that wee wish you here...'[8]

In 1723 the Prince of Wales made a gift of stock valued at £11,500 to his mistress and also the contents of her apartments at Court. Mrs Howard decided without hesitation that the money should be used to build a house in which she could live on her retirement from Court. A site was selected on the Thames near Richmond and Twickenham and the purchase was completed in March 1724.

The original land consisted of 11.5 acres of Twickenham East Field known as Marble Hill. Later in the same year an adjoining fourteen acres were added. Plans for the house were begun almost immediately and were drawn up by the architect Colen Campbell.

From the beginning Alexander Pope was closely involved with the plans for the grounds. As a keen gardener, Peterborough was also interested but he had a competitor in Lord Bathurst who, along with Pope, is generally given credit for the landscaping. In the summer of 1723 Peterborough invited Pope to dine at Parsons Green in the company of Lord Bolingbroke and Lord Harcourt. 'Pray doe me the favour', he wrote, 'to send me the breadth, and depth of the marble Field; you may have itt measured by moonlight by a Ten foot Rod, or anybody used to grounds will make a neer guesse by pushing itt over.'*

Peterborough paid a brief visit to France later in the summer. On his return he was unable to visit Mrs Howard because of an indisposition. He wrote to Pope for news of the work. 'I was impatient to know the issue of the affaire, and what she intended for the autumn, for no time is to be Lost either if she intends to build outhouses or prepare for planting...'⁹

There is no record of whether Peterborough's advice and plans were followed or not. In 1724 he wrote to congratulate Mrs Howard on her acquisition.

> ...Fair Lady, I dislike my Rivalls amongst the living, more then those amongst the dead, must I yield to Lord Herbert and Ld Ily; if I had built the castle of Blenheim, and filled the Land with Domes and Towers, I had deserved my fate, for I hear I am to be layed aside as an extravagant person fitt to build nothing but palaces...I can even wish well to the house and garden under all these mortifications; may every Tree prosper planted by whatever hand, may you ever be pleased and happy, whatever happens to your unfortunate Gardiner and architect, degraded and turned of.

It is likely that the assistance Peterborough gave was of a purely practical nature. He was a working as well as a supervising gardener and may have actually taken part in the planting. In the *Imitations of Horace*, Book II Satire I, Pope recalled him:

> And He, whose light'ning pierc'd th'Iberian Lines,
> Now forms my Quincunx, and now ranks my Vines,
> Or tames the Genius of the stubborn plain,
> Almost as quickly as he conquer'd Spain.

It took some time for Marble Hill House to be completed and the final payment for the work was not made until 1729. In 1731 Charles Howard succeeded his brother as 7th Earl of Suffolk. As a peeress the

---

*Pope used the back of this brief note to translate part of Book V of the *Odyssey*.

Countess of Suffolk was obliged to relinquish her position as a Woman of the Bedchamber to the Queen; instead she was offered that of Groom of the Stole, a greater honour with far fewer duties. This enabled her to spend a little more time at Marble Hill. The Earl of Suffolk died in 1733 and the following year Lady Suffolk retired from Court.[10]

On 28 December 1723 there appeared in *The British Journal* some lines of poetry entitled 'Song', with Mrs Howard's name in the last verse. No author was given; the verses were merely described as 'By a Person of Quality'. Later these verses were included in the last volume of the Pope-Swift *Miscellany* of 1727. They appeared in *The Universal Magazine* of January 1777, identified as the work of the Earl of Peterborough. Collected in his *Catalogue of Royal and Noble Authors*, vol. iv, Horace Walpole described the poet as 'one of those men of careless wit and negligent grace, who scatter a thousand bon-mots and idle verses, which we painful compilers gather and hoard, till the owners stare to find themselves authors'. This is the version which appeared in 1727:*

> I said to my heart, between sleeping and waking,
> Thou wild thing, that always art leaping or aching,
> What Black, Brown or Fair; in what Clime, in what nation,
> By turns has not taught thee a pit-a-pat-ation?
>
> Thus accused, the wild thing gave this sober reply,
> See the heart without motion, though Celia pass by:
> Not the beauty she has, nor the wit that she borrows,
> Gives the eye any joys, or the heart any sorrows.
>
> When our Sappho appears, she whose wit so refined,
> I'm forced to applaud with the rest of mankind:
> Whatever she says is with spirit and fire;
> Every word I attend, but I only admire.
>
> Prudentia, as vainly, would put in her Claim,
> Ever gazing on Heaven, tho' Man is her Aim,
> Tis Love, not Devotion, that turns up her Eyes:
> Those Stars of this World are too good for the Skies.
>
> But Chloe so lively, so easy, so fair,
> Her wit so genteel, without art, without care;
> When she comes in my way, the motion, the pain,
> The leapings, the achings, return all again.

---

*Pope's poem on the same subject, written in 1732, echoes the sentiment of the last verse.

O, wonderful Creature! a Woman of reason!
Never grave out of Pride, never gay out of Season:
When so easy to guess who this Angel should be,
Wou'd one think Mrs H...d ne'er dreamt it was she?[11]

In old age the Countess of Suffolk had long conversations with
Horace Walpole, who kept notes of what she said and the dates of the
conversations. Walpole was an inveterate collector of anecdotes and he
gathered up a heap of memories, some of which showed a chronologi-
cal inexactitude which might be expected in a lady of advanced years.
Lady Suffolk had various stories of Lord Peterborough and said that he
often wrote sermons 'particularly a very fine one on the death of his
first wife, of whom he was very fond'. She claimed to have seen at various times three different manuscript volumes of Peterborough's
memoirs. In his latter years the earl was certainly engaged in such a
work. In Hawkins's *History of Music* there is a story about him which
the author received from Lady Suffolk. Some time before the Revolution of 1688, Lord Mordaunt, as Peterborough then was, greatly
admired a lady who was very fond of birds. She had seen a fine canary
with a very beautiful voice in a coffee house near Charing Cross.
Mordaunt was determined to acquire the bird for her and entered into
negotiations with its owner, a widow, offering a handsome sum for it.
The widow declined to sell. Mordaunt then resorted to a different solution. He managed to find another bird almost identical in plumage but
a hen with no voice. Unnoticed by the widow, he exchanged the birds.
He continued to frequent the coffee house from time to time to avoid
suspicion but there was none. At a much later date, he reminded the
widow of his generous offer to buy the bird, and asked her if she had
not regretted her decision. This she emphatically denied, 'nor would I
now take any sum for him, for, would you believe it? from the time that
our good King was forced to go abroad and leave us, the dear creature
has not sung a note.'[12]

Thirty-three

The Royal Academy of Music was formed by public subscription in 1719 for 'the encouragement of musick'. The encouragement was to take the form of a continual supply of operas composed and directed by Georg Friederich Handel. In the event, Handel was not the only composer to be employed by the Academy but in the summer of 1719 he made a trip to Europe specifically for the purpose of finding singers for it. All the singers then engaged were Italian except for one. The exception was the popular and established English singer, Anastasia Robinson, who was approached by Dr John Arbuthnot, one of the Academy's directors. Anastasia spoke Italian and in the Academy's first season in 1720 she sang the role of Zenobia in Handel's opera *Radamisto*, a part written for her.

The Robinsons came from an established Catholic family in Leicestershire but were of slender means. A portrait-painter by profession, Thomas Robinson, Anastasia's father, had been studying in Italy at the time of her birth and her early years were spent there. His wife had some personal fortune but she died during Anastasia's infancy. Robinson later married a Miss Lane from the family who had sheltered Charles II.

Early in her life Anastasia developed a gift for music and a fine natural voice and was in due course given lessons by Dr Croft. Her friend and contemporary Mrs Pendarves (later Mrs Delany) has left this description of her:

> Mrs Anastasia Robinson was of middling stature, not handsome, but of a pleasing modest countenance with large blue eyes; her deportment easy, unaffected, and graceful; her manner and address very engaging, and her behaviour, on all occasions, that of a gentlewoman, with perfect propriety. She was not only liked by her acquaintance, but loved and caressed by persons of the highest rank, with whom she appeared always equal without assuming.

Anastasia's attraction and popularity as a singer were as much due to her stage presence as to her voice. By all accounts she had great charm. She was a well-educated woman and wrote in a clear and legible hand.

Thomas Robinson's failing eyesight gradually forced him to give up his profession and it was financial difficulties which caused Anastasia to turn her considerable musical gifts into a means of earning an income. She began by giving small London recitals, at which she accompanied herself, at their home in York Buildings. Later the family moved to the more fashionable quarter of Golden Square where her recitals attracted a large audience and the house 'was frequented by all the men of genius and refined taste of the time'.

In 1713 Handel wrote his first part for Mrs Robinson in his 'Birthday Ode for Queen Anne' and in June of that year she had a benefit concert at the opera house. Her introduction to the operatic stage took place in February 1714 when she appeared in the opera *Creso*. The following season she had a principal part in *Arminio*, and in June 1715 she sang in Handel's opera *Amadigi*, and also the part of Almirena in a revival of another Handel opera, *Rinaldo*.[1]

In the next few years Mrs Robinson was regularly employed on the operatic stage. After her benefit concert in Drury Lane in January 1720, she sang in Handel's *Radamisto*, which had a run of ten performances from 27 April, and in June she appeared in Scarlatti's opera *Narciso*. This was the first season of the Royal Academy opera. However, in a revival of *Radamisto* in December the title role, previously performed by the soprano Margarita Durastanti, was taken by the castrato alto, Francesco Bernardi, known as 'Il Senesino'. As a result, Durastanti was given the part originally sung by Mrs Robinson, who was not employed.

The period of unemployment did not last long. In the spring of 1721 Mrs Robinson appeared in a composite opera, *Muzio Scevola*, to which three composers had contributed: the music for the first act was composed by Filippo Amadei, for the second by Giovanni Bononcini and for the third by Handel. In the winter season she appeared in another Handel opera, *Floridante*.

In 1722 there was a change in the singer's fortunes. Having had a part in Bononcini's opera *Crispo* in January, she was given the title role in his new opera, *Griselda*, which opened in February. Giovanni Bononcini was at the height of his popularity and already had a wide reputation in Europe for his operas and cantatas. Mrs Robinson was said to haunt the composer; it is very likely that she found his music suited her voice, as Handel's compositions were becoming increasingly challenging.

It is traditionally believed that it was Mrs Robinson's portrayal of the heroine, Griselda, which made a conquest of Peterborough. Mrs Delany recalled that he and General H—* were the most attentive of her many admirers. The general's attentions were so marked, and of such long standing, that it was presumed he would make a proposal of marriage. However this was apparently not his intention; 'a declaration of a very contrary nature was treated with the contempt it deserved, though Mrs A. Robinson was very much prepossessed in his favour.'

After this setback, it is not surprising that Mrs Robinson believed it unlikely that Peterborough would do any better. She greeted his courtship with a coolness and caution which only increased his admiration. Eventually he made his declaration in honourable terms. 'He found it would be vain to make proposals on any other, and as he omitted no circumstance that could engage her esteem and gratitude, she accepted them, as she was sincerely attached to him.' However Peterborough did insist, and Anastasia agreed, that the marriage should remain a secret 'till a more convenient time'.

It is difficult to imagine a greater contrast between the character of Peterborough and that of Anastasia Robinson. It was perhaps precisely this contrast which made her so attractive. Her calm good breeding and peaceful presence, derived from an inner strength rather than mere passivity, may have been the anchor and shelter needed by this mercurial personality in his later years. Peterborough had little piety in his make-up, despite the efforts of a devout mother and his fondness for preaching. Anastasia was a sincere and practising Catholic and eventually introduced into the earl's household her step-uncle, a Jesuit priest, as her personal chaplain. Together with strength of character, she also had understanding and good humour, assets much needed in her professional life. She would also require them in her marriage to a man whom Mrs Delany described as one 'whose uncontrollable temper and high opinion of his own actions made him a very awful husband'. Anastasia explained to the Modenese Ambassador in 1723: 'Nature design'd me a peaceable Creature, and it is true as strange, that I am a Woman and cannot scold.'

The marriage of Lord Peterborough and Anastasia Robinson is generally believed to have taken place in 1722. Her friend the Countess of Oxford was a witness. Anastasia continued her operatic career for

*This may have been General Hamilton.

another two years. In 1723 the Robinson family moved from Twickenham to a house at Parsons Green, Fulham, very near to Peterborough's own.*

In 1723 Anastasia sat to the portrait painter Vanderbank, who depicted her at a double manual harpsichord. She was also celebrated in verse. John Gay wrote:

> O soothe me with some soft Italian air,
> Let harmony compose my tortured ear;
> When Anastasia's voice commands the strain
> The melting warble thrills through every vein,
> Thought stands suspended, silence pleased attends,
> While in her notes the heavenly choir descends.

Mrs Robinson's stage career continued but after the arrival of another Italian singer of great powers, Francesca Cuzzoni, she received less prominent parts. This new singer made her debut in Handel's *Ottone* in the spring of 1723. There were difficulties during rehearsals. Cuzzoni objected to her opening aria and argued with the composer. Handel picked her up by the waist and swore that he would throw her out of the window if she gave any further trouble. Mrs Robinson was also unhappy about her part but made a diplomatic approach to the librettist through an intermediary. Her original aria was replaced with 'a short melancholy song' as she had requested. Handel also altered her last song, retaining its style but making it easier to sing. *Ottone* ran to fourteen performances and was followed in May by another Handel opera, *Flavio*, in which Mrs Robinson also appeared.[2]

In February 1724 Handel brought out a new opera, *Giulio Cesare*, in which Mrs Robinson was engaged to sing. At a public rehearsal an incident occurred which caused quite a considerable stir in society. Il Senesino behaved offensively towards Mrs Robinson and Lord Peterborough caned him for it. The happening caused much talk and not a little amusement as the earl was of slight stature and thin, whereas Senesino was large, solid and majestic. Lady Mary Wortley Montagu recounted the story in her usual sharp manner to her sister, the Countess of Mar:

*Traditionally supposed to have been Vine Cottage in the Fulham Road, but rate books show that Mrs Robinson lived at or near Parsons Green 1724–9 – in a fairly large house judging by the assessment, but the position cannot be ascertained. Feret, *Fulham Old and New*, vol. ii, p. 147.

Could one believe that Lady Holdernesse is a Beauty and in Love? and that Mrs Robinson is at the same time a prude and a kept Mistriss? and these things in spite of Nature and Fortune...The 2nd Heroine has engag'd halfe the Town in Arms from the Nicety of her virtue, which was not able to bear the too near approach of Senesino in the Opera, and her Condescention in accepting of Lord Peterborrough for a Champion, who has signaliz'd both his Love and Courage upon this occasion in as many instances as ever D[on] Quixote did for Dulcinea. Poor Senesino like a vanquish'd Giant was forc'd to confess upon his knees that Anastasia was a non pareil of virtue and of Beauty. Lord Stanhope, as dwarf to the said Giant, jok'd of his side, and was challeng'd for his pains. Lord Delawar was lord Peterborrough's second; my Lady miscarry'd.* The Whole Town divided into partys on this important point. Innumerable have been the disorders between the 2 sexes on so great an Account, besides halfe the House of Peers being put under Arrest. By the Providence of Heaven and the wise cares of his Majesty no bloodshed ensu'd. However, things are now tolerably accommodated, and the Fair Lady rides through the Town in Triumph in the shineing Berlin of her Hero, not to reckon the Essential advantage of £100 per month which (tis said) he allows her...

It was hard for Anastasia to be presumed a kept mistress when she was in fact a wife, and typical of Peterborough to go unthinking to her defence, thereby drawing attention to her position. Jonathan Swift commented sourly on the story to Charles Ford: 'Ld Peterborows Gallantry is exactly of a Size with the whole Tenor of his Life, onely in complyance to his Age he seeks to make a Noise without the Fatigues of travelling, though he will be less able to perform his present Journy than any of his past. He neither moves my Joy, Pity, nor Sorrow...'

At the conclusion of the season on 13 June Mrs Robinson left the theatre permanently. Residing quietly in Fulham with her stepmother and half-sister Margaret, she did not take up residence under Peterborough's roof until later in the decade, when the earl's health began to give trouble and he had acquired a property in Southampton. Sir John Hawkins claimed that Anastasia held a kind of musical academy at Parsons Green. Certainly the earl gave numerous dinners, suppers and

*Philip Stanhope, later Earl of Chesterfield, 1694–1773; Lord Delawar was John West, 7th Baron and later 1st Earl De La Warr, 1693–1766.

musical evenings at which the leading musicians of the day performed. At the suppers, it was not uncommon for some of the dishes to have been prepared by the earl himself, wearing a costume similar to that of a tavern cook to do so. He said that he had been obliged to learn to cook on his campaigns in Spain.[3]

During this decade Peterborough still retained his interest in politics and the European scene. In May 1721 he took part in a debate in the House of Lords on the second reading of a Bill against 'Blasphemy and Profaneness'. Despite the laudable appearance of the title, in fact the Bill was directed against Nonconformists and was strongly supported by the bishops. Cobbett recorded part of Peterborough's contribution: 'Though he was for a parliamentary King, yet he did not desire to have a parliamentary God, or a parliamentary religion; and if the House were for such a one, he would go to Rome and endeavour to be chosen a cardinal; for he had rather sit in a conclave than with their lordships upon those terms.' The Bill was eventually thrown out.

Later that summer the earl was again on the Continent. 'Les marches de Peterborough sont toujours mystérieuses,' wrote Bolingbroke to Mme de Ferriol. Peterborough was in touch with his old friend the Duke of Parma, encouraging him against the Emperor. The previous year Charles VI had handed over Sardinia to Victor Amadeus of Savoy in exchange for Sicily.[4]

In May 1722 Peterborough was appointed General of all the Marine Forces of Great Britain, a post he had held in the later part of Queen Anne's reign. It was a useful sinecure bringing in a salary of £3,600 per annum, provided it was paid. His commission ran until the Marines were disbanded or no longer employed as such. Bolingbroke was quick to point out that there had been no Marine forces in England for nine years.[5]

On 16 June 1722 the Duke of Marlborough died and Peterborough attended his funeral as one of the ten assistants to the chief mourner, the Duke of Montagu. He was honouring an association which had lasted for many years. The Duchess Sarah, however, had never forgiven the earl for speaking against her husband in Parliament. Her fierce loyalty painted Peterborough completely black. In her memoirs, she linked him with Earl Rivers; they were two lords, she wrote, 'who, being discontented that favours and rewards were not heaped upon them by the ministry, became mere tools to promote the designs of their enemies'. Peterborough was 'a man who to the same vileness of soul had joined a sort of knight-errantry, that made up a very odd sort of composition. One who had wasted his fortune and worn out his credit, and had nothing left but so much resolution and so little honour as made him capable of any thing they had to put upon him.'⁶

One of the officiating clergymen at the Duke of Marlborough's funeral had been Francis Atterbury, Bishop of Rochester. In August he was arrested and imprisoned for alleged complicity in a Jacobite plot. In April 1723 a Bill of Pains and Penalties was brought against him in the Commons, where it was carried with large majorities; in May it appeared in the Lords. Alexander Pope was one of those called to give evidence on the bishop's behalf; this may have been one of the several occasions that year when the poet lodged in Peterborough's house in Bolton Street. Peterborough himself attended the House and voted in favour of the Bill. The measure was carried by a majority of 83 votes to 43. Atterbury was sentenced to banishment for life.

As it happened, it was the turn of another exile to come home. After much political engineering, Bolingbroke received a pardon on 25 May 1723: he could now return to England without fear of arrest. Although he did not shake off the penalties imposed by Act of Attainder, his return gave pleasure to his friends. In Pope's case it was one friend regained and another lost. He wrote to Swift:

> Tis sure my particular ill fate, that all those I have most lov'd and with whom I have most liv'd must be banish'd. After both of you [meaning Swift and Bolingbroke] left England, my constant Host was the Bishop of Rochester. Sure this is a Nation that is cursedly afraid of being overrun with too much politeness, and cannot regain one Great Genius but at the expense of another. I tremble for my Lord Peterborow (whom I now lodge with); he has too much wit, as well as Courage to make a solid General, and if he escapes being banish'd by others, I fear he will banish himself...⁷

When Bolingbroke returned to England on 23 June for a visit lasting almost two months, Peterborough was one of those ready to entertain him and planned a supper for him at Parsons Green in the company of Lord Harcourt and Alexander Pope. In this summer of 1723 the earl was also very interested in the landscape plans for Marble Hill. Later in the season he visited Paris and presented a memorial from Dr John Arbuthnot to the Regent. He also made the acquaintance of Arbuthnot's brother, Robert, a banker in Rouen, who apparently possessed some of the 'knight-errant' qualities shared by Peterborough.

Soon after his return from Paris in early September, Peterborough was actively involved in helping the Robinsons move house from Twickenham to Fulham. He contributed some organisational skill and joined them all later for a cheerful supper at the conclusion of their labours. That autumn he was concerned about the plantings at Marble Hill and discussed them with Pope. December saw the first anonymous publication of his poem about Mrs Howard.[8]

In February 1724 the incident with Senesino was not the only occasion on which Peterborough's name was linked with the opera. In the same month Hogarth published a print entitled *The Bad Taste of the Town*. It was intended to underline the way in which the traditional theatre had suffered because of the popularity of operas and masquerades. In the print a banner depicts the opera; it shows three singers with three peers kneeling before them, one of whom, said to be Peterborough, is pouring out a bag of money at the singers' feet, saying 'Pray accept £8,000.' In a letter written about this time Pope mentions Peterborough's unsuccessful attempts at 'reconciling and healing the wounds of the various and discordant Potentates and Parties of the Opera'.[9]

This year in Europe the Congress of Cambrai met at last in April. It had been summoned two years previously in order to work out the territorial arrangements agreed in the Quadruple Alliance. The agreement that Don Carlos of Spain should inherit Tuscany and Parma was proving difficult to implement. The Emperor was slow to allow his investiture and appeared to have no intention of facilitating the procedure. Also he was not allowing the Swiss garrisons to enter the two duchies. Irritated by the delay, the Queen of Spain sent a special emissary, the Marquis of Monteleone, secretly to London and Versailles with proposals to speed up the process. In trying to force the hands of France and Britain to take action to carry out the provisions of the Alliance, the Spanish proposals rather overshot the mark. Among them was a demand that Don Carlos be escorted immediately to his duchies by the Swiss garrisons. Such an undertaking would have been an overtly hostile action against the Emperor and unlikely to find favour with France. British support might have been assured had not another proposal included a promise to restore Gibraltar to Spain.

Monteleone's mission was not a success, nor was his visit kept a secret, although the proposals were. Monteleone, a Sicilian by birth, was a talented diplomat who had been Spanish Ambassador in London. Peterborough knew him well and, hearing that he was in Paris in May, asked to be allowed to go to meet him. The King thought that this friendship might be turned to good account and asked the Secretary of State, Lord Townshend, to give the earl a memorandum of matters which might or might not be discussed with Monteleone. The British Ambassador in Paris, Horatio Walpole, was sent a copy of the memorandum and asked to appear ignorant of the purpose of Peterborough's visit. The earl himself entered into the spirit of the mission with zeal. Townshend was able to assure Walpole that Peterborough would 'act in everything to your heart's content, provided he has care and caution enough not to let Monteleone suspect he is employed either by the King or your Exc. which my Lord tells me he will manage so, that he will defy either him or the Devil to find it out'.

The memorandum referred in the first place to the possibility that Monteleone might have a plan to alter the succession to the French throne. Since this had been established by Treaty, he must be warned of the dangers of such an attempt; any suggestion of a union of the crowns of France and Spain might give rise to jealousy and it would be impossible for Britain to support Spain in these circumstances, a fact which must be clearly spelled out. He was warned how to act if a scheme concocted by Marshal Tessé to form a new Quadruple Alliance against the Emperor should be mentioned. He was considered more suitable than the Ambassador to broach the subject of Northern affairs. He might ask Monteleone to use his influence at the Court of France to bring about a reconciliation between the King and the Czar. In addition, he might be able to use his prudence and dexterity to persuade Monteleone to help to bring about the removal of the current Spanish Ambassador from Paris, 'a most determined Jacobite', whose house was used as 'a sanctuary for rebels'.[10]

Although his memorandum was compiled in early May, Peterborough did not arrive in Paris until 14/25 August and he called immediately on the British Ambassador, Horatio Walpole. They had met before many years previously, when Walpole was Brigadier Stanhope's secretary in Spain. Peterborough briefly indicated his interest in meeting Monteleone and explained that he had been given some guidelines as to his conduct. Very soon afterwards he made contact with the Spanish emissary and next day was able to bring him to visit Walpole to assure him that the Spanish demands were entirely in accordance with the terms of the Quadruple Alliance and nothing more. Later Peterborough told Walpole that Monteleone had a project which he wished to propose to the French first, before informing the British Ambassador, as this would serve British interests better.

That evening Peterborough dined *en famille* with the Ambassador who described the scene in a letter to his brother, Robert. 'He [Peterborough] entertained the table with some of his old frolics in Spain; with my having been his enemy formerly; but having reconciled himself to the chief of the family, he believed all was now well again with us.' After dinner Peterborough and Walpole moved on to the residence of the Parmesan minister where Monteleone had dined. Here they remained some time until the indefatigable earl went on to visit some ladies.[11]

Filled with indignation at the lack of spirit in France against the Emperor's behaviour, Peterborough spent much time at Fontainebleau in the company of Monteleone and of his former adversary, the Maréchal Tessé, who was very much one of the Old Guard. He was incensed by the attitude of the Imperial envoys at the Congress to the 'Pretentions of Parma', in which he had concerned himself for so many years. Soon, wherever he went, his discourse was of the Congress and the Emperor whether in serious or in lighter vein. If this sort of talk could do anything to alarm the Emperor, Walpole thought it would do no harm. He noted that most people thought Peterborough had nothing to do with the diplomatic process, 'though one or two sensible persons have let fall to me that he comes by order, and instructed from, our court'.

Peterborough also worked out a plan of campaign. He believed that a good body of troops should be sent to Italy, namely to Placentia and Parma, without directly attacking the Emperor's forces; such a move would probably provoke the Emperor into war. The English Fleet might then capture Sicily and Naples. On another front, the Emperor could be expelled from Flanders. Having heard Peterborough explain this scheme, the Dutch Ambassador asked him what he proposed to do with Sicily and Naples; 'his lordship was at a loss, and had nothing to say but that it was too good a morsel to want an owner long.' Flanders he would give to the States General, for which the Ambassador thanked him.

Walpole believed that Peterborough would have done a real service if he had managed to divert Monteleone from some of his more extreme views and convince him of their danger. It would also have been beneficial if he could alter the views of Maréchal Tessé, who was often in his company. To the serious diplomat, this type of diplomacy appeared to be so much hot air. 'I do not see any remedy for it,' wrote Walpole, 'but to lett these extraordinary exhalations of such warm heads evaporate, and after we have gazed, wondered, and been amused a little, we may return to our old plain dull way of negotiating again and of keeping all things quiet.'[12]

On 2 September Peterborough left Fontainebleau ahead of most of the foreign ministers and went to visit the Court. At this time the young King, Louis XV, was assisted in government by the Duc de Bourbon and the Duc d'Orléans, the son of the late Regent. The earl was well received, 'as his quality deserves'; he was always an acceptable guest because of his wit but he was treated as merely the friend and supporter of Monteleone. It was noted, however, that he always spoke with respect and esteem of George I and the British government. The French Foreign Minister, de Morville, gave the earl an interview but his calm dry manner prevented Peterborough from trying to persuade him to take a more vigorous attitude towards the Emperor. Peterborough was also pleased at obtaining an hour's profitable conversation with the Duc de Bourbon; once again he had 'little encouragement to preach up vigour and resolution to him…the French nation, once so formidable, is of a sudden sunk into a Lethargy.'[13]

Before leaving France, Peterborough sent the Duke of Newcastle his views at some length. Monteleone had assured him that his intentions were merely to transport Don Carlos to Italy in accordance with the treaty provisions. The Spanish emissary had no wish to interfere with the established succession in France, neither had he any proposal to make that was not in line with the Quadruple Alliance. He was also most anxious to foster a friendship between the crowns of England and Spain and was sure to push for some sort of agreement to come out of the Congress.

Peterborough's reflections on the state of the French government were less optimistic.

If your Lop could but have a sight of the French Ministers, you would be surprised; the two at the head of the War and Marine are pretty young Gentlemen with little powder'd periwigs and patches upon their Faces to increase their Charms; they are just turned of Twenty, and such as I could wish, were we to have no Engagements with them.

This is the less to be wondered at since all those bred under the last King are laid aside, as [are] all those that may be thought partial to the duke of Orleans, so there remains no great Choice; neither am I surprised at their pacifick Discourses; the old

Marshals of France are rich and at their ease, and unwilling to be laid aside as useless, and the younger pretenders are against war lest they should be disappointed in their hopes of command; Luxury and Pleasure prevail, and the common Expression from the highest to the lowest is this, pourquoi la Guerre, nous n'avons rien a désirer, nous ne voudrions point un Colombier de plus.

Peterborough waited to hear the outcome of Monteleone's meeting with the French ministers but the Spanish envoy had failed to shake the French from their anxiety for peace. They had asked that his proposals be submitted in writing, a clear postponement of decision. George I told Newcastle that he was glad that the plans had come to nothing and that peace was maintained. Peterborough left for home on 10 September 1724 at the conclusion of his last venture into the world of diplomacy. He had entered into it with all the usual signs of vivacity and humour but from time to time he referred to what his health would permit him to do. There had been no difficulty in masking the purpose of his journey by claiming that his doctors had suggested he should try the waters of Bourbon. He travelled home at a pace suitable to a constitution which had seen sixty-six summers.[14]

Thirty-four

In June 1725 Peterborough made a prolonged visit to Bath. Lady Hervey sent a description of him to Mrs Howard.

> Lord Peterborough is here and has been so some time, though by his dress one would believe he had not designed to make any stay; for he wears boots all day, and, as I hear, must do so, having brought no shoes with him. It is a comical sight to see him with his blue ribbon and star, and a cabbage under each arm, or a chicken in his hand, which, after he himself has purchased at market, he carries home for his dinner...

The wearing of boots all day is certainly odd and so is – a contemporary reader might think – a peer of the realm doing his own market shopping. The Garter ribbon and star would have occasioned no remark; it was obligatory for knights to wear the insignia at all times, although there were certain modifications for travelling dress.

In September Peterborough was back at Parsons Green and taking a member of the Walpole family to see Marble Hill.[1] We next hear of him taking part in a debate in the Lords in early February 1726 on the subject of a treaty formed at Hanover in 1725 between Britain, Prussia and France against the Emperor and Spain. He spoke 'in his usual manner', with references to his Spanish experiences.

This year Peterborough was able to renew his acquaintance with Jonathan Swift, the Dean of St Patrick's. Little correspondence seemed to have passed between them in recent years, or little that has survived. Swift had won some acclaim the previous year for some pamphlets, which were published anonymously and known as 'Drapier's letters', reputed to be written by a humble tradesman as a protest against 'Wood's halfpence', a new coinage imposed on Ireland.* The opposition to the coinage was so general, and so successfully spread by 'Drapier's letters', that the patent was withdrawn.

---

*The patent for this coinage had been issued to one Wood, who had purchased it from the Duchess of Kendal, one of the King's German mistresses.

Swift had espoused some of the ills of Ireland as a personal cause. He had a deep concern for the plight of the peasantry, for the difficulty in finding a market for Irish goods and for the state of the Church. He arrived in England in April 1726 and through Peterborough's good offices obtained an interview with Sir Robert Walpole at 8 am on 27 April. The meeting lasted an hour and was entirely taken up with the affairs of Ireland. As Swift explained later to Peterborough, he felt that he had been able to make little impression. It was evident that Walpole had been briefed well by former administrations with ideas that were alien to Swift's; he proved so expansive on the subject that it seemed pointless to argue. Swift gave Peterborough in writing the heads of his own argument, asking that they might be sent to Sir Robert. Before the Dean returned to Ireland, Peterborough gave a farewell dinner for him at Parsons Green.[2]

While he was in England, Swift had made arrangements for the anonymous publication of *Gulliver's Travels* and the book appeared in print on 28 October. Only a few of his intimates, such as Pope and Arbuthnot, knew the author's identity. Peterborough was not in the secret but clearly had his suspicions. The book was an instant success. At the end of November Peterborough wrote to Swift:

I was endeavouring to give an answer to yours in a new dialect which most of us are very fond of. I depended much upon a Lady [Anastasia] who had a good Ear and a pliant Tongue, in hopes she might have taught me to draw sounds out of consonants, but she, being a profest friend to the Italian speech and vowels, would give me no assistance, and so I am forced to write to you in the yahoo language…Strange distempers rage in the nation which your friend the Doctor [Arbuthnot] takes no care of; in some, the imagination is struck with the apprehension of swelling to a Giant, or dwindling to a pigmee, others expect an Oration equall to any of Cicero's from an Eloquent Barb, and some take the braying of an Asse for the Emperor's speech in favour of the Viena Alliance. The knoledge of the antient world is of no use, men have lost their Tittles, continents and islands have gott new names just upon the appearance of a certain Book in the world; women bring forth Rabbetts, and Every man, whose wife has conceived, expects an heir with Four leggs. Itt was concluded not long agoe that such confusion could only be brought about by the black Art, and by the spells of a notorious scribbling Magitian, who was generally suspected, and was to be recommended to the mercy of the Inqui-sition...For they pretended to bring in Certain proofs of his appearing in severall shapes, att one time a Drappier, att another a Wapping Surgeon, sometimes a Nardac [the highest rank in Lilliput], sometimes a Reverend Divine. Nay more that he could raise the dead, that he had brought Philosophers, Heroes and poets in the same Caravan from the other World, and after a few questions, had sent them all to play at Quadrilles in a flying Island of his own...

Thus the Dean's leg was very firmly pulled. Swift wrote to Pope in December: 'This moment I am so happy to have a letter from my Lord Peterborow...tho' he all-to-be-Gullivers me by very strong insinua-tions...'[3]

When Swift next visited England, in April 1727, he found that Peter-borough was entertaining an interesting and congenial guest at Parsons Green. François Marie Arouet de Voltaire had arrived in England in May 1726. He had just been released from the Bastille where he had served a period of imprisonment for sending a challenge to the Cheva-lier de Rohan. His release was given on condition that he leave the country immediately and, having already made the acquaintance of several Englishmen of note, he decided that England would be a suit-able place of exile. He was also anxious to publish a work he had writ-ten on the life of Henry IV, 'La Henriade', which was considered unacceptable in France. Voltaire had met Bolingbroke in Paris in 1722 and he also knew a wealthy English merchant, Everard Falkener. It is very likely that he had also made Peterborough's acquaintance in Paris on one of the earl's many visits; they were both recorded as being part of the court of admirers who surrounded the French *comédie* actress, Adrienne Lecouvreur. Voltaire had also corresponded with Alexander Pope about 'La Henriade'.[4]

Early in 1727 Voltaire was seeking sponsors for the publication of his book. Peterborough and Bolingbroke each subscribed for twenty copies and the publication took place in March. In 1765 Voltaire told a visitor, Major Broome, that he had spent three months with Lord Peter-borough and had been much in the company of Swift for whom he developed a great admiration. He must also have heard repeatedly the stories of Peterborough's adventures in Spain, which the earl so loved to relate and which never failed to entertain. The combination of these influences bore fruit in a historical novel, *L'Histoire de Jenni*, which

Voltaire published in 1775. The book is the story of a fictitious son of Dr John Freind and it is set initially against the background of the capture of Barcelona. The narrative is interspersed with conversations on philosophical subjects. A modern writer, Charles Dédéyan, sees in this work a reflection of much of Swift's thought.[5]

In January 1728, as a distinguished former pupil, Peterborough was honoured to be invited by Westminster School to be the Steward at the Anniversary Dinner. Both his grandsons had received their education at Westminster. In February 1728 he celebrated his seventieth birthday. His health was not always good and he took care of it. This year he visited Bath on three occasions, in May, July and September, and he spent some time in the country in April. The previous autumn he had been very anxious to be well enough to attend the coronation of George II in October. 'Feeling some symtomes of the prevailing feavour,' he told Mrs Howard, 'I have lett blood and used all possible preventions.'

Dr Richard Towne had returned to England from Barbados in 1726 in order to publish *A Treatise of the Diseases Most Frequent in the West Indies*. He moved in the literary circle of Pope and Voltaire and became a friend of both Mrs Robinson and Peterborough; he also had horticultural interests. Before he returned to Barbados in the summer of 1728, Towne had begun a translation of Voltaire's *Henriade*. Having heard of Towne's safe arrival in Barbados, Peterborough wrote on 3 July: 'Mrs Robinson has desired me to make you a thousand compliments on her behalf... She sendes by this oportunity Mr Voltaire's book, and we all joyn in Encouraging you to goe on in what you have so well begun, and Mr Pope has promised to look over the Translation if ever you think fitt to publish it, with the Care and Sincerity of a Friend.'

It seems that Peterborough and Anastasia were still not living under the same roof. In a letter to Dr Towne in the spring of this year, Peterborough enclosed some fennel seed from Mrs Robinson, 'for I had none'. This suggests that at least they cultivated separate gardens.[6]

Voltaire left England rather suddenly, sometime in September or October 1728, and much to the surprise of his friends. He may have had a disagreement with his bookseller.* In 1732 a rather hostile notice appeared in *The Gentleman's Magazine* at the time of the publication of Voltaire's *History of Charles XII of Sweden*. The notice stated:

It is no wonder that a Frenchman should be partial in his Character of the English Nation, especially after having enriched himself

*See J. Churton Collins, *Voltaire, Montesquieu and Rousseau in England* (1908), p. 109.

with our Contributions he behaved so ill that he was refused Admittance into those Noblemen's and Gentlemen's Families, in which he had been received with great Marks of Favour and Distinction. He left England full of resentment, and wrote the K. of Sweden's life to abuse this Nation and the Hanover Family.

This notice appeared only four years after Voltaire's departure, and from the available evidence it seems that the claims made were overstated and not substantiated. But Voltaire did make some enemies. After another sixty-five years the same periodical printed another story. It aroused some interest by its great detail and the fact that the writer, described only by the abbreviation 'El. B.', claimed to be able to vouch for its authenticity. A few months later another contributor recognised the initials as those of a man 'whose writings must always be read with profit'. Whatever his reputation, 'El. B.' made it clear that the name of Voltaire always aroused his anger. The story he told was as follows.

While staying in Peterborough's house, Voltaire was employed by the earl to write an important book. He used a London bookseller to assist in its preparation and printing, and made an initial payment to the bookseller from the earl when the work commenced. As progress was made, Voltaire asked Peterborough for further instalments, which the earl promptly supplied. After the first instalment, none of the subsequent payments ever reached the bookseller. When Peterborough grew impatient over the delay in production, Voltaire blamed the dilatoriness of the bookseller. When the bookseller applied to Voltaire for further advances, he was told that the earl would pay no more until the work was completed but there was no hurry. Eventually the bookseller became suspicious and decided to approach Peterborough directly. He called at Parsons Green and was shown into the gardens where the earl was entertaining friends. On hearing from the bookseller that the work was held up for lack of funds, Peterborough assured him that he had forwarded money at every request. The bookseller replied that he had never received more than ten pounds. This news infuriated the earl and when Voltaire appeared at the end of one of the long walks, he drew his sword and had to be forcibly restrained from rushing forward to attack him. A Mr St André, who was struggling to control the angry peer, shouted to Voltaire 'fly for your life,' which he instantly did.* Hiding in a nearby village that night, the Frenchman went to London the next day

*There was surgeon named St André at this time who later operated on Peterborough in 1735.

and left for the Continent immediately, abandoning his papers and portmanteau in Peterborough's house. The narrator noted in particular that Voltaire left without his hat.[7]

In the preface to this story the narrator evinces very strong anger against Voltaire as an individual, even after such a long lapse of time. Peterborough's reaction, albeit exaggerated for dramatic effect, is nonetheless in keeping with his character. However the plausibility of the story is much diminished when one reads a letter from Peterborough to Dr Towne in Barbados, written within two months of Voltaire's departure.

> It is as hard to account for our politicks, as for Mr Voltaire's resolutions and conduct; the country and people of England are in disgrace at present, and (he) has taken his Leave of us, as of a foolish people who believe in God and Trust ministers, and he is gone to Constantinople in order to believe in the gospells, which he says it is impossible to doe, living amongst the Teachers of Christianity...

There is nothing here but amused tolerance and the dismay generally felt at Voltaire's departure. Peterborough seems to make it quite clear that it is the country of England that is in disgrace, not Voltaire. Had the scene in the garden been the trigger for Voltaire's departure, it would have been quite unlike Peterborough to be able to mention his name, so soon after the event, without an expletive.

Voltaire himself bore Peterborough no ill will. He once said that the earl had taught him the art of despising riches. In his *Histoire de Jenni*, published in 1775, he described him thus: 'Vous connaissez son coeur; il est aussi tendre pour ses amis que terrible à ses ennemis. Jamais homme ne fut plus compatissant avec une physionomie plus dure.'[8]

In December 1728 the Duke of Gordon, Peterborough's son-in-law, died after a brief illness, leaving a family of ten surviving children; his heir, Cosmo George, was only aged about seven. The duchess had reared her children in the Anglican tradition although the Gordons were a Catholic family. Soon after the duke's death, Peterborough visited his daughter in Scotland and consulted with the Earl of Aberdeen regarding the young duke's education.[9]

In May 1729 there appear the first letters sent from Padwell near Southampton, from the property known as Bevis Mount. Here Peterborough spent some of the happiest days of his later years. Significantly the letters are sent by Anastasia to her friend the Earl of Oxford, on one occasion urging him and his wife, at Peterborough's request, to use the gardens at Parsons Green in their absence. This year also marked the period of deterioration in the earl's health which brought Mrs Robinson to take up her residence with him. Anastasia's half-brother, the Revd William Lane, came to Padwell to act as her chaplain.[10]

Presumably the attractions of Bevis Mount were its size, which was modest, and its location on the South Coast with the benefits of climate and sea air. In an undated letter to Mrs Howard, the earl described his latest acquisition as

> the wild Romantick cottage where I pass my Time…My Blenheim would not afford Lodgings for two Maids of honour and their equipage, and yet I cannot forbear wishing that you might sometime or other, see my purchase of fowerscore pounds a yeare. Tho' you had seen the prodigies of Norfolk the day before I should depend upon your partiality to Bevismount, the noble Title of my Palace, which has putt the Publick to noe expence…

To the estate of Padwell Peterborough subsequently added the property of Bevis Hill which lay to the east between Padwell and the Itchen. In 1730 he added St Denys Abbey and the estate of Portswood. Bevis Hill gave the artificial appearance of a burial mound. In the opinion of Dr Speed, an eighteenth-century scholar, it had also been used as a scout watch for the Roman station Clausentum at Bitterne on the other side of the river. By an old tradition the hill was considered to have been the burial place of the legendary hero Sir Bevis. Peterborough had the top of the hill levelled in order to build a summer-house with good cellars underneath, later used as an ice-house. During the excavations a human skeleton was unearthed; it was at least seven feet long but lacked the skull. The bones were in good condition when found but eventually disintegrated due to too much handling. This discovery gave some credence to the legend.

Alexander Pope first visited Bevis Mount in 1731 and spent three weeks there in 1733. In August 1734 he described the summerhouse. 'I write this from the most beautiful Top of a Hill I ever saw, a little house that overlooks the Sea, Southampton, and the Isle of Wight, where I study, write, and have what leisure I please…' He told Mrs Knight: 'This place is beautiful beyond imagination, and as easy as it is beautiful.'[11]

By August 1734 it is obvious that Peterborough's plans for the gardens had produced results, at least in part. Pope's previous visits did not give rise to such praise for his surroundings. However, like many gardens, improvement was a continuing process; work was still being done at the time of the earl's death in 1735. In the years following, Pope himself gave much advice to Anastasia.

In later years Bevis Mount attracted much interest and accounts written by visitors give an idea of the layout of the grounds. The garden was largely a wilderness with gravel walks, ornamented by Italian marble statues. The landscaping was so arranged that the grounds felt larger than in fact they were. The walks culminated in the summer-house on the Mount with its view over Southampton and the Itchen. There was also a bowling-green and a ninepin alley. Until Peterborough added to it, the house had been little more than a farmhouse, and rarely attracted much comment from visitors. Lady Peterborough continued to make improvements and was considered to have better taste than her late husband.

'The difference in ye beauty of the gardens at high and low water is so great', wrote Jeremiah Miller in 1743, 'that the late earl would never carry any Gentleman into his garden, nor indeed suffer them to go in, if he could help it, unless the tide was full in.' Anastasia was not so particular. When the Earl of Oxford, accompanied by George Vertue, dined with her in 1738, she showed them the gardens. 'We walked over the garden which was still new to me and most delightful,' the earl recorded, 'but the cross-tide would not come up.' George Vertue was enchanted by the place and 'the beauty and contrivance of those Gardens'. The views and ornaments were 'so agreeably disposed...that the pleasure rises as you ascend the Hill'.[12]

Life at Bevis Mount was relaxed, healthy and even bucolic. The house had been a farmhouse and Peterborough liked to refer to Anastasia as 'the Farmeress at Bevis'. She certainly kept cows but references in the earl's correspondence to writing letters from haystacks were probably allegorical. Peterborough also liked to point out the contrast between his modest dwelling and the vast piles raised by the Duke of Marlborough at Blenheim and Viscount Cobham at Stowe. After visiting the latter, Peterborough reflected to Pope: 'I must confess that in going to Lord Cobham's, I was not led by curiosity. I went thither to see what I had seen, and what I was sure to like. I had the idea of those gardens so fixt in my imagination by many descriptions, that nothing surprized me; Immensity, and Van Brugh appear in the whole, and in every part...I confess the stately Sacharissa at Stow, but am content with my little Amoret.'[13]

It is generally considered that Pope is referring to Peterborough in his *Imitations of Horace*, Book I, Ep.1:

Our Gen'rals now, retir'd to their Estates,
Hang their old Trophies o'er the Garden gates,
In Life's cool evening satiate of applause,
Nor fond of bleeding, ev'n in Brunswick's cause.

It was indeed 'Life's cool evening'. Many of the fires had burned out.
Although still capable of bursts of energy and considerable physical
endurance, Peterborough was being weakened by illness. His attitude
to life is typified in a letter to Pope in May 1732 in which he expresses
the wish that Jonathan Swift might see Bevis Mount.

> But Sir, I must give you some good news in relation to myself,
> because I know you wish me well; I am cur'd of some diseases in
> my old age, which tormented me very much in my youth.
>
> I was possest with violent and uneasy passions, such as a
> peevish concern for Truth, and a saucy love for my Country.
>
> When a Christian Priest preached against the Spirit of the
> Gospel, when an English Judge determined against Magna Carta,
> when the Minister acted against common Sense, I used to fret.
>
> Now Sir, let what will happen, I keep myself in temper: As I
> have no flattering hopes, so I banish all useless fears; but as to the
> things of this world, I find myself in a condition beyond expecta-
> tion...
>
> If the Translator of Homer find fault with this unheroick dispo-
> sition, (or what I more fear) if the Draper of Ireland accuse the
> Englishman of want of spirit; I silence you both with one line out
> of your own Horace, Quid te exempta juvat spinis e pluribus una?
> For I take the whole to be so corrupted that a cure in any part
> would be of little avail...'[14]

Despite the attractions of Bevis Mount, Peterborough still liked to be
in town for at least part of the parliamentary sessions. His appearances
were far less frequent than of old and generally centred on some matter
which was of particular interest to him. In March 1730 he spoke twice
in the debate in the Lords on the Pensions Bill. This measure provided
that a member of the House of Commons, on taking his seat, should
subscribe an oath that he would not accept a pension from the Crown.
Peterborough opposed the measure and gave as his reason his belief
that the Bill would not have the effect intended, 'for the King would
only defer paying a member till the Parliament ended'. He continued
'that he was too good a Protestant to oblige anybody to confess, not

even to the reverend Bishops, much less to one another, but the Bill was to oblige the members to confess to each other whether they had a pension.' On 19 March the House of Lords threw out the Bill.

At the end of April 1730 Peterborough was said to be 'dangerously indisposed' at Parsons Green. There are no notices of him that summer. In October he wrote in a tired and despondent letter to Mrs Howard: 'The world has become so indifferent to me that I can even amuse myself with the thought of going out of it...'[15]

In a valetudinarian way, Peterborough began to consider compiling his memoirs. On more than one visit Pope had noticed papers and documents lying about. In old age Mrs Howard, then Countess of Suffolk, remembered seeing 'at least three volumes at different times'.

Peterborough had once used the services of Aaron Hill in selecting materials. Hill was a poet but he also had other means of employment. Peterborough's attention was drawn to him when he published a poem in 1709 entitled 'Camillus' which praised the earl's exploits in Spain and generally took the tone of crying shame on those who tried to denigrate his achievements. As a result the earl offered him a post as secretary in his household. Soon afterwards Hill married an heiress, who removed him from Peterborough's employment; she objected to her husband's leaving her for one of the earl's long embassies.

In 1731 Hill was once again in verse with his 'Advice to the Poets'. Pope saw the lines, thought them of merit and forwarded them to Peterborough, who had been mentioned in them. He told Hill: 'I this day have writ to Lord Peterborough a letter with your Poem. The Familiarity in which we have liv'd some Years makes it not unusual, in either him or me, to tell each other anything that pleases us...'[16]

Pope stayed with Peterborough at Parsons Green in the spring of 1731, and also went on one of his visits to Bevis Mount in September, 'where I have a Catholick friend [Anastasia] who will take care of my soul and shall dine with a Jesuit [William Lane] thrice a week...'

At the end of October Peterborough went to Bath. Through some mischance or other he had contrived to lose all his shirts on his way there, 'so that his lordship was obliged to some of his acquaintance for clean linen during his residence at the Bath...'[17]

Peterborough rarely appeared in Parliament during the first two months of 1732 but made six appearances in March. Away in the country in April, he was back in town in May and attending the debates in the Lords on the Bill to prevent the directors of the

Charitable Corporation from leaving the country.* The earl made a spirited speech in the debate. Viscount Percival noted in his diary: 'This Lord, though 80 years old, has his parts as quick as any man of 30.' Peterborough was in fact only seventy-four.

Percival also recorded a story that his wife had brought home from Court. A few days earlier Peterborough had attended the Queen's levée. The ladies had been discussing a Mr Spencer, a younger brother of the Earl of Sunderland. Apparently this gentleman was fond of taking frequent baths at home. One day a visitor was admitted in error to his room while he was still in the bathtub. The caller kept his visit short so that he would not unduly inconvenience his host and got up to take his leave 'but Mr Spencer, out of a sprightly and frolicsome humour, leaped out of the bath, naked as he was, and waited on him down to the very street door. The Queen...talking of the action as a very extraordinary one, my Lord Peterborough replied that Mr Spencer was a man of extraordinary breeding to acknowledge the favour of a common visit in his birthday clothes...'[18]

* The directors, including Sir Robert Sutton, had misappropriated the funds of the Corporation which had been set up to lend small sums to the 'industrious poor'.

Thirty-five

The last years of Peterborough's life were warmed and lit by the calm presence and devoted care of his second wife, Anastasia, and the easy intimacy of his friendship with the poet Alexander Pope. The letters exchanged between the two friends seem pedantic to modern eyes but were the well-honed products of correspondents who took time and pleasure in writing well, knowing that the recipient would be appreciative of their efforts.

In August 1732 Peterborough returned to Bevis Mount after his visit to Stowe and related his impressions to Pope. Later in the year he expressed his reluctance to come to town, although it was obligatory to do so for a royal birthday. In the end it was family matters as well as royal occasions which took Peterborough to town at the end of October. A marriage had been arranged between Peterborough's niece, Anna Maria Mordaunt, and Stephen Poyntz of Midgham, Berkshire, at present Governor to the Duke of Cumberland and later a diplomat. The bride had been for some years a maid of honour to Queen Caroline. The earl wrote to his daughter: 'I am always rejoyced when a young Lady gettes out of harms way...'

The Duchess of Gordon was in need of her father's assistance. Left a widow with a large family, she had been obliged to observe 'all decent frugality'. At this time some indigent peers received an allowance from the Civil List. The duchess hoped for such relief and enlisted the help of the Lord Advocate, Duncan Forbes of Culloden, in order to obtain it. Her trump card was that she had raised her children as Protestants in an otherwise Catholic family. Forbes had made numerous representations on her behalf, even the Queen had added her support, but he now thought that the duchess should ask her father to follow up the matter in person. The foundation had been well laid. When Peterborough called on Sir Robert Walpole on 4 November to press the matter, he was met with the news that the King had just given his approval to the grant of the duchess's pension.*[1]

---

*Peterborough's letters to his daughter reflect the formality of the times. He commenced 'Lady Dutchesse' and concluded 'Dear Lady your affectionate most ob. servt Peterborow.'

In January 1733 what was described as an 'epidemical cold' swept through London. It was probably a virulent type of influenza. Large numbers of people succumbed and many died. The newspapers regularly reported illness and deaths among members of the aristocracy. On 16 January Peterborough attended Parliament on 'the first day of ye Sessions'; it was in fact his last attendance. Later the same day he contracted the infection and became dangerously ill. On 23 January Lord Hervey wrote to Henry Fox: 'They say Lord Peterborough can not recover; so that of the veteran nobility there is now only his Grace (or rather Highness) of Somerset remaining.'

However, against all expectations, the earl did recover. At the end of February he was very much better and writing letters, although still confined to his room. He wrote twice to Swift and sent a courteous letter to the Lord Advocate thanking him for his efforts on behalf of the Duchess of Gordon.

Around this time Peterborough wrote a letter of a more unusual kind. It was addressed to Lady Mary Wortley Montagu and written at the request of Alexander Pope. Since early in the previous decade, the friendship which had existed between Pope and Lady Mary had soured to the point of active hostility. The reasons for this breach are not truly known although various stories have been told. It may be that Pope made a profession of love which was greeted with mockery. Certainly Pope came to believe that the attacks on his character appearing in verse from time to time emanated from Lady Mary or were motivated by her. Pope began to retaliate, sometimes quite openly, at other times by more veiled allusions. Pope's *First Satire on the Second Book of Horace Imitated* was published in 1733, and included the lines:

> Slander or Poison, dread from Delia's rage,
> Hard words or hanging, if your Judge be Page.
> From furious Sappho scarce a milder fate,
> P-x'd by her love, or libell'd by her hate.

Lady Mary identified herself (correctly) as Sappho. Instead of letting the matter pass or become a point of conjecture, she revealed that the dart had gone home by calling on Peterborough to try to discover what lay behind it. It appears that she received little assistance from the earl. The letter which he subsequently wrote to her, generally considered to have been at Pope's dictation, contains cutting sarcasm. However, it is phrased at outset and conclusion with a degree of hauteur which suggests that the whole subject was distasteful to the writer.

Madame, I was very unwilling to have my name Made use of in an affair in which I had noe concern, and therefore would not engage my self to speak to Mr Pope, but he coming to my house the moment you went away, I gave him as exact an account as I could of our conversation.

He said to me what I had taken the Liberty to say to you, that he wonder'd how the Town could apply those Lines to any but some noted common woeman, that he should yet be more surprised if you should take them to your Self. He named me fower remarkable poetesses and scribblers, Mrs Centlivre, Mrs Haywood, Mrs Manly, and Mrs Been [Behn], Ladies famous indeed in their generation, and some of them Esteemed to have given very unfortunate favours to their Friends, assuring me that Such only were the objects of his satire.

I hope this assurance will prevent your furthur mistake, and any ill consequences; upon so odd a Subject I have nothing more to add.

Your Ladys: most humble and obedient /servant / Peterborow.[2]

Later in the spring, as soon as he was well enough to travel, the earl went to Bath on the advice of his doctors. Swift sent an answer to his letters.

I never knew or heard of any Person so volatile and so fixed as your Lordship: You, while your Imagination is carrying you through every Corner of the World where you have or have not been, can at the same Time remember to do offices of Favour and Kindness to the meanest of your Friends...

I remember Lord Oxford's Ministry used to tell me, that not knowing where to write to you, they were forced to write at you. It is so with me; for you are in one Thing an Evangelical Man, that you know not where to lay your Head, and I think you have no House. Pray, my Lord, write to me, that I may have the Pleasure, in this enslaved Country, of going about, and showing my depending Parsons a Letter from the Earl of Peterborough...

In the autumn of 1733 Pope was again at Bevis Mount for three weeks, the guest of 'the Lord and Lady of Mount-Bevis' as he liked to call them. Peterborough was well enough to go on expeditions and on one occasion took the poet to visit Winchester College. He gave the school ten guineas, to be distributed to the boys as prizes. Pope set them an essay subject for the competition, and chose that of 'Peterborough'. Six boys, one of them William Whitehead, won a guinea prize. The remaining four guineas were used to subscribe for copies of Pine's *Horace*, which was about to be published.[3]

In the summer of 1734 Peterborough was in London briefly, having called on another keen gardener, Lord Bathurst, at Cirencester. At the end of July Pope joined the earl at Bevis Mount for a long holiday lasting well into September. He had arrived unwell, weary and out of sorts and here he found rest '(where you would least expect it) under my Lord Peterborow'. He was able to make use of the summer-house, where he could work or just look at the views of the Itchen and the Isle of Wight. The earl and his guest made various excursions in the neighbourhood. One such outing was to Beaulieu Palace House to call on the Duchess of Montagu. The Duchess had been Lady Mary Churchill, whom Peterborough had once hoped might marry his son, Lord Mordaunt. That summer the earl also entertained other guests such as Mr and Mrs Stephen Poyntz.

In a long and vivid letter to Martha Blount, Pope has left a description of one of their more ambitious expeditions. This took the form of an adventure by sea. About 7 August Peterborough and Pope sailed from Southampton on a yacht manned by three seamen and with the earl at the helm. The first ship that they encountered proved to be a merchantman from France with a cargo of wine. They relieved it of some brandy, Frontiniac and claret to add to their substantial picnic of cold pie, pigeon and turkey. The original plan, to anchor off the Isle of Wight, had to be abandoned because of the state of the tide; instead they cruised along the mainland coast and anchored near a promontory. As they approached the shore by boat, Peterborough and Pope were impressed by the beauty of their surroundings, a wooded hillside with a ruined castle at the water's edge. Although the castle looked like a suitable place for a picnic, the two friends agreed that first they should explore the area separately, keeping in touch by calling to one another. Pope wandered off and eventually came upon a ruined barn sitting in a natural grove of oak trees where there was good turf. Thinking this a more attractive place for a picnic than the castle which might harbour snakes and toads, he began to call for the earl but received no response. After about half an hour during which Pope hunted for him fruitlessly, Peterborough appeared, full of enthusiasm for a marvellous site further inland and refusing to consider anywhere else. Reluctant and hungry, Pope toiled off after his friend for half a mile into the woods, arriving in the end at ivy-covered ruins situated in a profusion of wild flowers and roses. They had found Netley Abbey. Here they ate their dinner, with a fallen pillar as their table and two ruined capitals as seats. Afterwards they took time to examine the church and Pope made many sketches. The idyllic experience was abruptly brought to an end by the arrival of a seaman to alert them to the state of the tide and they had to hurry back to the boat. Darkness was falling and a moon rising by the time they were on their return to Southampton.[4]

There is an eighteenth-century drawing of the view from Bevis Mount called Pope's View. It shows the Itchen as it flows into Southampton Water and is a totally rural prospect, quite unlike what may be seen today. In 1736 Pope described Bevis Mount as 'the quietest place I can go to, where I never yet pass'd a fortnight, but by a fatality, I think, I fall to writing verses'. In this summer of 1734, Pope had been at work on his third 'Imitation of Horace' (the Second Satire of the First Book), the 'Epistle to a Lady' for Martha Blount and probably also 'An Epistle to Dr Arbuthnot'. On his way home Pope planned to stay at Colonel Mordaunt's house at Freefolk, Hampshire, and go with Peterborough on some visits to neighbouring seats.[5]

Peterborough came up to London in January 1735 and attended the Court. Later in the spring he took lodgings in Kensington 'for the air', where Pope found him seriously ill and spent much of his time sitting with him. By May his health had much improved. However these troubles caused Peterborough to consider Anastasia's position should he die. In order to ensure that his family would accept her as his widow, and not merely as a dependent, he had to present her to them as his lawful wife. Mrs Delany recorded how this announcement was staged:

He [Peterborough] appointed a day for all his nearest relations to meet him at the apartment over the gateway of St James's Palace belonging to Mr Poyntz, who was married to Lord Peterborough's niece, and at that time preceptor of Prince William, afterwards Duke of Cumberland: he also appointed Lady Peterborough to be there at the same time. When they were all assembled, he began a most eloquent oration, enumerating all the virtues and perfections of Mrs A. Robinson, and the rectitude of her conduct during his long acquaintance with her, for which he acknowledged his great obligation and sincere attachment, declaring he was determined to do her that justice which he ought to have done long ago, which was, presenting her to all his family as his wife. He spoke this harangue with so much energy, and in parts so pathetically, that Lady Peterborough, not being apprised of his intentions, was so affected that she fainted away in the midst of the company...[6]

Satisfying the lawyers of this *fait accompli* was not such a simple matter. Peterborough later told Pope that he had been obliged to re-marry his wife in the church at Bristol, since the parson who had originally performed the ceremony had died. In late May or early June Peterborough was in Bristol to consult the surgeon Nathaniel St André, and it may have been on this occasion that the marriage took place. He wrote to Stephen Poyntz from the country this spring, sending apologies for being unable to attend Court as he was obliged to go to Bath.

The advice which Peterborough received from the surgeon was that an operation of 'cutting into the bladder for the suppression of urine' was necessary to alleviate his condition. Such a procedure had many attendant risks. There is no clear indication of when the operation took place but other evidence suggests a date in early July. On 13 June Peterborough wrote to Pope from Bath.

I have lead my self out of temptation, and brought my self into the ways of Pennance, which the Lady approves of, it has a good Catholick Sound. I have left the Mount to gett into the bottom, making Tryall of the Bath watters; hitherto I can make no judgement, if they prove nott too hott, for severall of my Complaints they are very proper... Some of my uneasy Symptomes are abated but I am weaker than I was, such long continuance of pains are scarse to be resisted, however I submitt to directions, tho sometimes opprest with too much care and Kind persecution...

Peterborough had been enjoying Mum, a beer from Brunswick, and he sent Pope a cask of it.

There is a story in Seward's *Anecdotes* about Peterborough's operation. In those days before the discovery of anaesthesia, surgeons preferred that the patients should be tied down to a bed or chair so that they would remain still. Peterborough refused to be tied down but the surgeon insisted. The earl eventually won the argument by stating 'that it should never be said that a Mordaunt was ever seen bound... He then ordered the surgeon to place him in the position most advantageous for the operation and in which he remained without flinching till it was over…'* In November Pope told Swift that the earl had taken coach for Southampton the day after the operation; 'this is a man that will neither live nor die like any other mortal.'

By the end of July the news that Peterborough had openly acknowledged his wife was being passed round in the social world. Sarah, Duchess of Marlborough wrote to her granddaughter.

> My Lord Peterborough has owned his marriage with Mrs Robinson. He had a dangerous operation that was to be made and a clergyman that was with him at Bristol told him that Mrs Robinson had suffered a great deal in her reputation upon his account, and if he was married to her he ought to own it. My Lord Peterborough said, that the King of France did not own Madame Maintenon, which in effect was owning it and putting himself in the place of the King of France. The clergyman pressed him on and said that was not the same case at all; and at last his Lordship declared to him that he had been married to her many years. After he was well enough to go into the public room, his manner of making this marriage so was to desire somebody to tell my Lady Peterborough that he would speak to her.[7]

At the advanced age (for those times) of seventy-seven, Peterborough had shown an amazing fortitude under the surgeon's knife and now an equal determination to recover. Back at Bevis Mount, he was able to reply to a kind letter of inquiry from Mrs Howard, now Countess of Suffolk, in almost his usual vein. He had been reading a book which had given him much comfort 'in my most uneasy moments', and was now sending her a copy. It was a life of Julian the Apostate.† He still hoped to see her at Bevis Mount one day.

> The Lady, the Book, or both together have brought me allmost in to a raving way, I want to make an apointment with you Mr Pope and a few Friends more to meet upon the Summitt of my Bevis Hill, from thence after a speech, and a tender farewell to take my leap towards the Clouds (as Julian expresses itt) to mix amongst the Starrs, but I make my bargain for a very fine day, that you may see my last amusements to advantage…

Pope was immensely depressed about his friend's condition; in

*The same information is given in Joseph Spence's *Anecdotes*. Spence claimed to have received his knowledge from Pope.
†Probably the life by the Abbé de la Bléterie published in this year.

mid-July he believed he was on the point of losing him. He wrote to Caryll: 'I am afraid you and I shall never meet again with Lord Peterborow...Every year takes away something or other, and when it takes away a friend, it hurts us indeed, especially those we have long known, who ought to know us best...'[8]

Despite his weak state, Peterborough thought that a warmer climate would aid his chance of recovery or at least add to his comfort. He decided to leave for France at the end of August. Various relatives gathered to take leave of him. The earl asked Pope to come and to ask Lord Bathurst too. These seem to have been the only friends to have received this invitation. Pope wrote to Bathurst as bidden, certain that this farewell would be their last. 'I hope this is not quite an Unreasonable Desire, that you would meet me there, after the 24 till the 30, which will be all the time I can stay: and to see the last of an old Hero, the last Sparks of such a Noble Flame, it will be a thing to dwell on our Memory, and to talk of in our old age...'

In his anxiety, Peterborough wrote another brief letter to Pope; the letter is poignant in its irregularity on the page and evidently written with great effort.

> Sir I have with me now a crowd of relations, they leave me on the sixth, I goe in a fortnight to France but hope I shall see you att Bevis Mount before I goe whenever you apoint I will send my coach for you to Farnham, I wish you could prevail with Ld Bathurst to return my visit
>
> Dear Friend your most affectionate servt Peterborow.
>
> Aug the 20th.

The letter was trouble enough; the direction was penned in Anastasia's hand.

Pope reached Southampton before 25 August and soon after sent Martha Blount a description of the scene.

> I found my Lord Peterborow on his couch, where he gave me an account of the excessive Sufferings he had past thro', with a weak voice, but spirited; he talked of nothing but the great amendment of his condition, and of finishing the Buildings and Gardens for his best friend to injoy after him; that he had one care more, when he went into France; which was, to give a true account to Posterity of some Parts of History in Queen Anne's reign, which Burnet had scandalously represented; and of some others, to justify Her

against the Imputation of intending to bring in the Pretender, which (to his knowledge) neither her Ministers Oxford and Bolingbroke, nor She, had any design to do... The warmth with which he spoke of these Subjects, made me think him much recover'd, as well as his talking of his present State as a Heaven to what was past. I lay in the next room to him, where I found he was awake, and call'd for help most hours of the night, sometimes crying out for pain: in the morning he got up at nine, and was carry'd into his Garden in a Chair; he fainted away twice there. He fell about 12 into a violent pang which made his limbs all shake and his teeth chatter, and for some time he lay cold as death. His Wound was drest (which is done constantly 4 times a day) and he grew gay, and Sate at dinner with ten people. After this he was again in torment for a quarter of an hour; and as soon as the Pang was over, was carried into the Garden to the Workmen, talk'd again of his History, and declaim'd with great Spirit against the Meanness of the present Great men and Ministers, and the decay of Public Spirit and Honour. It is impossible to conceive how much his Heart is above his Condition: he is dying every other hour, and obstinate to do whatever he has a mind to. He has concerted no measures beforehand for his Journey, but to get a Yatcht in which he will Set sail, but no place fixed on to reside at, nor has he determin'd what place to land at, or provided any Accomodations for his going on land. He talks of getting towards Lyons, but undoubtedly he can never travel but to the Seashore. I pity the poor Woman who is to share in all he suffers, and who can in no one thing persuade him to Spare himself. I think he must be lost in the attempt; and attempt it he will.

He has with him, day after day, not only all his Relations, but every creature of the Town of Southampton that pleases. He lies on his Couch and receives them: tho' he says little. When his Pains come, he desires them to walk out, but invites them to stay and dine or sup etc. Sir Wilfred Lawson and his Lady, Mrs Mordant and Col. Mordant are here;* Tomorrow come Mr Poyntz etc. for

*Lady Lawson was Peterborough's niece, the daughter of his late brother, Lieutenant General the Hon. Harry Mordaunt. Colonel Mordaunt was her brother; he lived at Freefolk, Hampshire, and had been elected recently as MP for Whitchurch. Latterly Peterborough's right hand man, he inherited Bevis Mount after Anastasia's death. The identity of Mrs Mordaunt is less certain; she may have been the widow of Peterborough's brother, the Hon. Lewis Mordaunt and the mother of Mrs Poyntz.

2 days only, and they all go away together. He says he will go at the months End, if he is alive... Nothing can be more affecting and melancholy to me than what I see here: yet he takes my Visit so kindly, that I should have lost One great pleasure had I not come. I have nothing more to say, as I have nothing in my mind but this present Object, which indeed is Extraordinary; This Man was never born to dye like other men, any more than to live like them...[9]

Writing to Lord Oxford two days later, Pope did not seem to think that Peterborough's condition was as bad as he had at first feared. Although his wound seemed to give him some discomfort and cause fever, the earl showed remarkable spirit and courage. Pope began to believe that the intended journey was in fact feasible. He was also greatly impressed by Anastasia's stamina. 'The Lady is indeed fully imploy'd, and has a thousand Cares to discharge; but I think Virtue can enable people to work miracles, above the natural Constitution, and surely God assists her, that she is so well as she is...' In a lighter vein he added: 'I suppose I need not tell you that Lord P. has ownd his Marriage to all his Relations here assembled, and that Lady Pet. desires my Lady Oxford's acceptance of her Sincere humble Services.'

Pope's letters are full of the sense of the finality of this visit. There cannot have been many people in the world who have had as many epitaphs written for them by a poet of Pope's standing than had Peterborough. They are all in prose but the sincerity is very real. 'I am taking my leave (a melancholy office) of a friend I have long had a true regard for, and one of the most obliging turn, and the finest talents to make others easy and pleased, of any that I ever knew. There will not be many finer gentlemen left in the world...' In a letter to Lord Bathurst in October, Pope wrote of Peterborough as one 'of those with whom my soul rested, and lean'd upon...'[10]

Pope saw his friend once more before his departure. By 2 September Peterborough had been transported to Portsmouth by horse litter. Here the *Fubbs* yacht lay at anchor in readiness to take him to France. However the departure did not take place as planned. The earl had a relapse and 'was at the point of death, having been speechless several hours'. His will was finalised on 9 September.

Joseph Spence, in his *Anecdotes*, recalled having seen Peterborough in his lodgings in Kensington after his operation. The earl kept to his bed most of the time but rose to join other company for dinner. Like

Pope, Spence was amazed at his determination. The earl told him that he was resolved to go abroad, and asked him whether he would recommend Lisbon or Naples. Spence did not think he could possibly live more than five or six days.[11]

According to the account given in the *London Evening Post*, Peterborough's health then improved so much after his relapse that, finding HMS *Gibraltar* was ready to leave for Lisbon, he decided to go there, 'in order to surprize Sir John Norris...with a visit', instead of sailing on the *Fubbs* to Bordeaux. Peterborough had known Norris before; he had once thought him 'a governing coxcomb' who had too much influence with Shovell. Norris had since enjoyed a distinguished naval career and was now in command of a squadron in the Tagus which was there to show solidarity with an old British ally, Portugal, now involved in a dispute with Spain.

The *Gibraltar* reached Lisbon after a voyage of ten days in almost continuous gales and rain. On Sunday 5 October she sailed into the mouth of the Tagus on the evening tide. The next day all the barges in the fleet towed her to her anchorage off Lisbon. To a salute of seventeen guns, the Earl of Peterborough, General of His Majesty's Marine Forces, went ashore; the countess disembarked a day later. The visitors took up residence in a villa near the Campo Grande belonging to Mr Carey.

There was a certain splendour in returning to scenes of former commands even in such a decayed state. There were others besides Norris who could remember old times. Don Diego de Mendonca, who had served as Secretary of State to the previous King of Portugal, vividly remembered Peterborough in his younger and more vigorous days. 'Alas,' he lamented, 'where now is all his martial ardour? Will he rouse me before the day, and not suffer me to rest a moment till his business be done? Those days are gone for ever...'[12]

Peterborough had only a few days left. Whether he had overindulged or whether he was affected by a change of diet, he became seriously ill of a flux said to be caused 'by Eating Grapes'. This illness proved a fight the old warrior could not win. As he lay dying, he gave instructions that his watch, which had been a present from Victor Amadeus whose arms it bore on its inner case, should be given to Alexander Pope.* It was a very personal bequest; the watch had accom-

---

*Pope had inscribed on the outer case of the watch the words: 'Victor Amadeus, Rex Siciliae, Dux Sabaudiae etc. etc. Carolo Mordaunt, Comiti de Peterborow, D.D. Car. Mor. Com. de Pet. Alexandro Pope moriens legavit 1735.'

panied Peterborough ever since he had received it. Pope felt that it was given 'that I might have something to put me every day in mind of him'. The earl died at 7 am on 15/26 October 1735, a morning of fair weather.[13]

The final scene had still to be played. On 16/27 October Lord Tyrawley the British Ambassador and Sir John Norris paid their respects to Lady Peterborough and agreed arrangements for conveying the earl's body home for burial. It was decided that the countess and her household should accompany the coffin on HMS *Berwick* which was due to leave for England at the end of the month. The Portuguese authorities stipulated that no public ceremonies should accompany the removal of the body, despite the rank which the earl had held, a stipulation normally made in the case of the death of a Protestant.

Peterborough's body was embalmed before being placed in the coffin. Under cover of darkness and escorted by horse guards, it was transported to the house of Sir John Norris where a room had been specially prepared to receive it. Sir John then invited all the commanding officers of the Fleet to attend the removal of the coffin to HMS *Berwick*.

At 3 pm on Monday 20 October OS, the body of the Earl of Peterborough was carried under a pall to the waterside, where a barge was waiting. The bearers were Lord Tyrawley, Admiral Sir John Norris, Vice Admiral Balchon and the senior captain, Captain Robinson. Four other captains followed. The coffin was then placed in the barge and a black mourning flag bearing the earl's arms was unfurled. At sight of the flag, the entire fleet fired three volleys of small arms at five-minute intervals. As the barge moved away towards the *Berwick*, the officers followed each in his own boat. As the flotilla passed, the *Britannia*, Norris's flagship, began the salute. Formerly Peterborough's own flagship whose gilded cabin was fitted to his specification, she gave her former joint-admiral fifteen guns at half-minute intervals. She was followed by the flagships of the vice admiral and the rear admiral who each gave thirteen guns in sequence. Then the rest of the fleet, firing in order of seniority, gave nine guns each.

On arrival at the *Berwick*, the coffin was received on board by the captain, the Hon. George Clinton. The escort completed, the officers returned to their own ships; the admiral was rowed to the waterside, took down his flag and went ashore. That night, Sir John recorded in his journal: 'My reason for yousing this ceremony was to show the Portuguese the respect we bore to a person that commanded our army and bore a joint Admiral of our Fleet, they not thinking it proper to afford the least notice of him tho' he had command [of] an Army in this countrey...' At the conclusion of the salute from the fleet there can have been few people in Lisbon and the surrounding countryside unaware of his passing.[14]

In an age when form and ceremony meant more than they do today, Peterborough would have appreciated the irony of the situation. Here full naval honours had been paid to a man who had held high naval rank for a comparatively brief period, although in possession of a military sinecure at the time of his death. He had considered himself a seaman but in the eyes of the Navy he was no tarpaulin. He had loved the sea and ships all his days but his naval command had been resented by some in the service who had risen through the ranks.

Had Peterborough died at Bevis Mount, a quiet cortege would have trundled slowly across country to the family vault at Turvey. Dying as he did among the scenes of the most colourful period in his life, where his subsequent adventures were already legendary, his passing became a focus for national pride and his achievements were honoured.

But there was still a long way to go. The coffin remained on board the *Berwick* for more than a week before the Countess of Peterborough and her entourage came on board and the ship sailed for home. Leaving on 30 October, the *Berwick* made a reasonable voyage and anchored at Spithead on 10 November. The following day Lady Peterborough disembarked and the coffin was removed on 12 November.

Three days later Colonel Mordaunt waited on the King and delivered up the insignia of the Order of the Garter worn by his late uncle. That weekend a suitably caparisoned hearse made its way from London to Southampton to transport Peterborough's body to its last resting place. The coffin was placed inside an outer coffin which was covered with crimson velvet 'adorn'd with Coronets etc'.

On 19 November, under the supervision of the late earl's steward, Mr Read, and attended by two coaches, the hearse reached Parsons Green. The following day it set out for Turvey. On 21 November, as an inscription tells us, what was mortal of Charles Earl of Peterborough was laid to rest beside six of his ancestors. The journey had ended.*[15]

---

*The Mordaunt vault is situated under the organ chamber in Turvey Parish Church. The inscription is on a plaque on the floor close to the organ chamber.

Notes

ABBREVIATIONS

BL	British Library
BIHR	*Bulletin of the Institute of Historical Research*
CTB	*Calendar of Treasury Books*
CTP	*Calendar of Treasury Papers*
DWL	Dr Williams's Library
EHR	*English Historical Review*
HMC	Historical Manuscripts Commission
LBJM	*Letter Book of John Mordaunt*
LJ	*Journals of the House of Lords*
NLS	National Library of Scotland
NRAS	National Register of Archives, Scotland
NRO	Northamptonshire Record Office
PRO	Public Record Office
SP	State Papers: CO Colonial Office; FO Foreign Office; WO War Office
VCH	*Victoria County History*

CHAPTER ONE

1 *Clarendon State Papers*, vol. iii, p. 388; *Calendar of the Clarendon State Papers*, vol. iii, p. 262; vol. iv, p. 29; 'T.W.', *The Trial of Mr Mordaunt* (1661), p. 2.

2 R. Halstead, *Succinct Genealogies* (1685), p. 411; Edward Hyde, Earl of Clarendon, *History of the Rebellion*, ed. W. D. Macray (Oxford, 1888), vol. vi, p. 58; *Calendar of State Papers Domestic Series 1648–9*, p. 178; M. A. E. Green, ed., *Calendar of the Proceedings of the Committee for Compounding 1643–60* (1889–92), vol. i, p. 769; *Cal. S. P. Dom. 1652*, pp. 423, 498 et seq.; E. S. de Beer, ed., *The Diary of John Evelyn* (Oxford, 1955), vol. iii, pp. 156, 189, 194; vol. iv, p.34; M. Coate, ed., *Letter Book of John Mordaunt 1658–60* (1945), no. 219, p. 161.

3 *Clar. S. P.*, vol. iii, p. 388; 'T.W.', *The Trial of Mr Mordaunt*, pp. 2, 7, 18–19, 40–2; Sir Ralph Freeman to the Lords Commissioners for Petitions re Alderman Foote, HMC *Seventh Report, House of Lords*

Calendar, p. 103; Earl of Roden, ed., *Private Diarie of Viscountess Mordaunt* (Duncairn, 1856), 1 and 2 June 1658.

4 *Cal. Clar. S. P.*, vol. iv, p. 113; HMC *Tenth Report*, appendix vi, pp. 189, 190, 191; *LBJM*, pp. 2, 4n, 5.

5 HMC *Tenth Report*, appendix vi, pp. 189, 190, 191; *LBJM*, pp. 2, 4n, 5, 50, 145, 146; *Private Diarie*, p. 28; R. Hutton, *The Restoration* (Oxford, 1985), pp. 55-8; *Cal. S. P. Dom. 1659-60*, p. 46; T. Carte, *Life of James Duke of Ormonde* (1735-6) vol. ii, p. 191; *Cal. Comm. Comp.*, vol. i, pp. 769-70, vol. v, pp. 32, 52; D. Underdown, *Royalist Conspiracy in England 1649-60* (Yale, 1960), pp. 249, 259, 266-7, 273-4, 279; G. Davies, *The Restoration of Charles II 1658-1660* (1955), pp. 134-9.

6 *Cal. Clar. S. P.*, vol. viii, p. 571; *Calendar of Treasury Books 1660-7*, p. 109; Thomas Weston's Accounts, BL Add. MSS 15,907; *Cal. S. P. Dom. 1660-1*, p. 139, *1663-4*, p. 340; John Evelyn, *A Philosophical Discourse of Earth* (1675), p. 145; C. J. Feret, *Fulham Old and New* (1900), vol. ii, pp. 134, 138, 141, 145.

7 E. W. Thibaudeau, ed., *Autograph Letters in the Collection of Alfred Morrison: Bulstrode Papers* (1897), pp. 51, 64, 66; *Private Diarie*, p. 153, 23 March 1674; G. F. R. Barker and A. H. Stenning, *The Record of Old Westminsters* (1928), vol. ii, p. 661; J. Foster, *Alumni Oxoniensis*, vol. iii (1892), p. 1026.

8 *Private Diarie*, pp. 175, 178; BL Egerton MSS 3,329, ff. 7, 9; Evelyn, *Diary*, vol. iv, 23 Feb. 1676; J. M. Wilson, ed., *Rochester-Savile Letters* (Columbus, Ohio, 1941), p. 42; HMC *Egmont* MSS, vol. ii, p. 51; J. R. Tanner, *Catalogue of the Pepysian Manuscripts* (Navy Records Society 1903-23), vol. ii, p. 396.

9 *Private Diarie*, p. 200; *CTB 1676-79*, p. 444; *Cal. S. P. Dom. 1677-8*, p. 271; *Pepysian MSS*, vol. i, p. 364; S. Martin-Leake, *Life of Admiral Sir John Leake*, ed., G. A. R. Callendar (Navy Records Society, 1920), vol. i, introduction; C. Ballard, *The Great Earl of Peterborough* (1930), p. 16; F. S. Russell, *The Earl of Peterborough* (1887), vol. i, p. 56; W. Stebbing, *Peterborough* (1890), p. 6; W. L. Clowes, *The Royal Navy* (1898), vol. ii, pp. 452, 454; *Cal. S. P. Dom. 1678*, pp. 186, 190, 195; G. Manwaring, ed., *The Diary of the Revd Henry Teonge 1675-79* (1927), pp. 222, 226-7, 229; BL Add. MSS 15,907; HMC *Ormonde* MSS, N.S. vol. iv, pp. 517-18, vol. v, p. 281; E. M. Thompson, ed., *Correspondence of the Family of Hatton 1601-1704* (Camden Society, 1878), vol. i, p. 222; HMC *Fourteenth Report 4, Kenyon* MSS, p. 116; Roger Morrice, Entering Book MS 31P, p. 251, Dr Williams's Library.

10 HMC *Seventh Report, Verney* MSS, p. 496; HMC *Ormonde* MSS, N.S. vol. v, p. 325; Henry Sidney, *Diary of the Times of Charles II*, ed., R. W. Blencowe (1843), vol. ii, p. 62; Russell, vol. i, pp. 57-8; Stebbing, p. 7; grant to Sir Alexander Fraser, *Cal. S. P. Dom. 1673*, p. 476; *Cal. S. P.*

Dom. 1665–6, p. 25, 1673–5, p. 246; HMC *Rutland* MSS, vol. ii, pp. 31, 32.

11 Lady Peterborough to her husband March 1707, NRAS 4155; N. Luttrell, *A Brief Relation of State Affairs 1678–1714* (Oxford, 1857), vol. v, p. 4; Henrietta, later Duchess of Gordon, date of birth from her tomb in Elgin Cathedral; Fulham parish register quoted in D. Lysons, *Environs of London* (1792–6), vol. ii, p. 380.

12 John Ross, *Tangers Rescue* (1681); G. G. van Prinsterer, *Archives de la Maison Orange Nassau* (The Hague, 1858–61), second series, vol. v 1650–88, pp. 401, 407; HMC *Ormonde* MSS, N. S., vol. v, p. 331; Lord Russell, ed., *An Account of the Life of Rachel Wriothesley, Lady Russell* (1819), p. 112; Sidney, *Diary*, vol. ii, p. 88; Fairborne to Jenkins 17 July 1680, CO 279/25, f. 269; Shere's account, 20 Sept. CO 279/26, f. 78; Fairborne's account 23 Sept. CO 279/26, ff. 86–9; log of the *Foresight*, Adm. 51/364; E. M. G. Routh, *Tangier 1680–84* (1912), pp. 184, 187–190; *Particular Relation of the Late Success of His Majesty's Forces at Tangier* (1680).

CHAPTER TWO

1 *The Journals of the House of Lords*, vol. xiii, p. 723; A. Morrison, *Catalogue of the Collection of Autograph Letters*, first series (1883–92), vol. iv, p. 163; Sir Richard Bulstrode, *Memoirs* (1721), p. 264; W. D. Christie, *A Life of Anthony Ashley Cooper, First Earl of Shaftesbury 1621–83* (1871), vol. ii, p. 200.

2 J. Oldmixon, *History of England* (1730), p. 657; HMC *Ormonde* MSS, N.S., vol. vi, p. 12; HMC *Fourth Report, Balliol College* MSS, p. 451; Morrison, *Catalogue* 1st series, vol. v, p. 133.

3 *Cal. S. P. Dom.* 1680–81, pp. 216, 328, 427; Sidney, *Diary*, pp. 180, 198.

4 Bulstrode, *Memoirs*, p. 142; *Cal. S. P. Dom.* 1680–81, p. 427; Luttrell, vol. i, p. 142; *Hatton Corr.* vol. ii, p. 9; HMC *Ormonde* MSS, N.S., vol. vi, pp. 222, 225.

5 *Cal. S. P. Dom.* 1680–81, p. 686; Tanner, *Catalogue of Pepysian MSS*, vol. i, p. 272; *CTB* 1681–85, p. 718.

6 HMC *Rutland* MSS, vol. ii, p. 62; *Cal. S. P. Dom.* 1680–81, pp. 256, 497.

7 Abstract of Lady Mordaunt's Will, BL Add. MSS 17,018, f. 129; Evelyn, *Diary*, vol. iv, pp. 202, 259, 273, 275; *Victoria County History of Surrey* (1903), vol. iii, pp. 236, 306; BL Add. MSS 15,892, f. 100.

8 E. Godfrey, *The Trial of Count Königsmarck* (1929), pp. 24–8, 32–47, 185; *Cal. S. P. Dom.* 1682, pp. 113–14, 116, 129, 138, 140; A. Browning, ed., *Memoirs of Sir John Reresby* (Glasgow, 1936), pp. 249–50,

255; Luttrell, vol. i, p. 174; HMC *Ormonde* MSS, N.S., vol. vi, p. 338; Morrice, Entering Book DWL MS31Q, pp. 326–7, 331.

9 E. d'Oyley, *James, Duke of Monmouth* (1938), p. 212; Stebbing, p. 12; *Cal. S. P. Dom.* 1683, vol. iii, pp. 137, 193; Luttrell, vol. i, p. 293; HMC *Seventh Report, Verney* MSS, p. 481; H. Walpole, *Reminiscences and Notes of Conversations with Lady Suffolk* (Oxford, 1924), pp. 124–6; M. Cranston, *John Locke* (Oxford, 1985), p. 230.

10 J. Miller, *James II, a Study in Kingship* (1991), pp. 136, 140–1; Lord Braybrooke, ed., *The Autobiography of Sir John Bramston* (Camden Society, 1845), pp. 216–17; Oldmixon, p. 707; G. Burnet, *History of His Own Time* (Oxford, 1823), vol. iii, p. 85; Timberland, ed., *History and Proceedings of the House of Lords* (1742), vol. i, p. 316; J. Ralph, *History of England* (1744), vol. i, p. 909; Leopold von Ranke, *A History of England* (Oxford, 1875), vol. iv, pp. 276–7.

11 J. S. Clarke, *The Life of James II* (1816), vol. ii, p. 204; *Cal. S. P. Dom.* 1686–87, no. 1862; N. Japikse, ed., *Correspondentie van Willem III en van Hans Willem Bentinck, Eersten Graaf van Portland* (The Hague, 1927–37, series I in two parts, series II in three parts), 1st series (1927–8) vol. ii, pp. 7, 9; T. Forster, *Original Letters of John Locke, Algernon Sydney and Anthony, Lord Shaftesbury* (1830), p. 138; Japikse, *Corr.*, second series, vol. ii, p. 742.

12 Burnet, *History*, vol. iii, p. 261; Japikse, first series, vol. ii, p. 7; G. A. E. Ellis, ed., *Ellis Correspondence* (1829), vol. i, p. 178; Morrice, DWL MS31Q, pp. 648–9.

13 Barillon's despatch quoted in Lord Macaulay, *History of England* (1889), vol. i, p. 344n.

14 Japikse, first series, vol. ii, p. 10; *Ellis Corr.*, vol. i, p. 289, also pp. 242, 246, 250; HMC *Eighth Report, Denbigh* MSS, p. 559.

15 HMC *Downshire Papers*, vol. i, pp. 260, 261; BL Add. Charter 73,991; J. R. Jones, *The Revolution of 1688 in England* (New York, 1972), p. 250; Sir John Dalrymple, *Memoirs of Great Britain and Ireland* (1771–88), vol. iii, pp. 202–3; Japikse, *Corr.*, first series, vol. ii, p. 597, second series, vol. i, p. 33, vol. ii, pp. 751, 768; HMC *Eighth Report, Denbigh* MSS, p. 558.

16 F. E. Dyer, *The Life of Admiral Sir John Narborough* (1931), p. 224; *Calendar of State Papers, America and West Indies* 1685–8, pp. 506, 529, 536; HMC *Montagu of Beaulieu* MSS, p. 200.

CHAPTER THREE

1 *Ellis Correspondence*, vol. ii, p. 52.
2 Dalrymple, *Memoirs*, vol. i, p. 147; *Ellis Corr.*, vol. ii, pp. 228, 276–7.

3 J. Miller, *The Glorious Revolution* (1983), pp. 11–13; G. Holmes, *The Making of a Great Power* (1993), p. 186; John Whittle, *An Exact Diary of the Late Expedition of the Prince of Orange* (1689), pp. 195–8.

4 Thomas Cropper to his wife, 6 Nov., Middleton Papers, BL Add. MSS 41,805, f. 135; J. Carswell, *The Descent on England* (1969), pp. 169–70; William III to Admiral Herbert, 6 November, BL Egerton MSS 2,621, f. 39.

5 R. Beddard, *A Kingdom without a King* (Oxford, 1988), introduction p. 21; 'List of those coming with the Prince', BL Add. MSS 41,822, ff. 230, 231; BL Add. MSS 41,805, f. 135; Morrice, Entering Book DWL MS 31Q, p. 308.

6 E. Green, *The March of William of Orange through Somerset* (1892), p. 56; Whittle, pp. 41–5; BL Egerton MSS 2,621, f. 41; von Ranke, *History of England*, vol. iv, p. 439; Clarke, *Life of James II*, vol. ii, p. 214.

7 *Journaal van Constantijn Huygens* (Utrecht, 1876–8), vol. i, p. 18; Bentinck to Herbert, 21 November/1 December 1688, N. Japikse, *Correspondentie*, second series (1937), vol. iii, p. 65; C. Dalton, *English Army Lists and Commission Registers 1661–1714*, vol. ii (1894), p. 243; Sir Philip Monckton, *The Monckton Papers*, ed. E. Peacock (1884), p. 6; Oldmixon, p. 755; HMC *Dartmouth* MSS, vol. i, p. 193; Huygens's *Journaal*, vol. i, p. 23; Beddard, pp. 21, 26–7, 200–3; *Ellis Corr.*, vol. ii, p. 297.

8 BL Egerton MSS 2,621, ff. 57, 60; J. Childs, *The Army, James II and the Glorious Revolution* (Manchester, 1980), p. 191; BL Add. MSS 41,805, f. 201; HMC *Seventh Report, Graham Papers*, p. 416.

9 Harrington Papers, BL Add. MSS 36,707, f. 48; Sir Patrick Hume, 'Diary of the March from Exeter to London', Sir G. H. Rose, ed., *The Marchmont Papers* (1831), vol. iii, p. 100; S. W. Singer, ed., *The Correspondence of Henry Hyde, Earl of Clarendon and his Brother, Laurence Hyde with the Diary* (1828), vol. i, pp. 207, 211–12, 213–14; BL Add. MSS 36,707, f. 49; Whittle, pp. 55–6; *Marchmont Papers*, vol. iii, p. 99.

10 Whittle, pp. 61–3, 64; *Marchmont Papers*, vol. ii, p. 100; *Clarendon Diary*, pp. 219–22; Beddard, p. 28.

11 S. Pepys to Lord Dartmouth, 10 December, HMC *Dartmouth* MSS, vol. i, p. 228; J. Miller, *James II*, p. 205; Morrice, DWL MS 31Q, p. 550.

12 *Clarendon Diary*, p. 223; Sir Patrick Hume's Diary, *Marchmont Papers*, vol. iii, p. 102; Beddard, pp. 71, 172; BL Add. MSS 36,707, f. 51; 'Journal of the Provisional Government', 14 December, printed in Beddard, pp. 98, 105, 116.

13 Beddard, p. 121; *Marchmont Papers*, vol. iii, p. 102; *Clarendon Diary*, pp. 224–5, 227.

14 *Clarendon Diary*, pp. 228–9, 230; letter of Halifax to the Prince, Beddard, p. 59.

15 Morrice, DWL MS 31 Q, p. 378; *Marchmont Papers*, vol. iii, p. 102; Evelyn, *Diary*, vol. iv, 18 December 1688; *Clarendon Diary*, p. 230; Childs, p. 198.

16 Beddard, pp. 123–52; Morrice DWL MS 31Q, p. 367.

17 BL Add. MSS 36,707, f. 52; Beddard, pp. 153–7; Miller, *James II*, p. 208.

CHAPTER FOUR

1 *Clarendon Diary*, vol. ii, p. 234; Beddard, pp. 159–62; BL Add. MSS 36,707, f. 53.

2 Lady Mordaunt to Locke 21/31 January (1689), E. S. de Beer, *Correspondence of John Locke* (Oxford, 1978), vol. iii, pp. 538–9, no. 1099; Locke to Clarke 18/28 January, p. 537, no. 1098; *Clarendon Diary*, vol. ii, p. 237; 31 December, Dalton, vol. ii, p. 243; BL Add. MSS 36,707, f. 52.

3 W. A. Speck, *Reluctant Revolutionaries* (Oxford, 1989), p. 24; W. Sachse, *Lord Somers* (Manchester, 1975), p. 29; Commons' Resolution of 28 January, printed in J. Miller, *The Glorious Revolution*, p. 21.

4 *LJ* vol. xiv, 31 January, 6 February; BL Add. MSS 40,621, f. 24; Speck, pp. 99–100; Morrice, DWL MS 31Q, pp. 453–4; E. Cruickshanks, D. Hayton and C. Jones, 'Divisions in the House of Lords 1689–94', *Bulletin of the Institution of Historical Research*, vol. liii (1980), pp. 63–5, 84; *Clarendon Diary*, vol. ii, p. 261; Huygens, *Journaal*, vol. ii, pp. 81, 82; A. Simpson, ed., 'Notes of a Noble Lord', *English Historical Review*, vol. lii (1937), pp. 94–5; Burnet, *History*, vol. iii (1833), pp. 395–6; Miller, *Glorious Revolution*, pp. 108–9.

5 *LJ* vol. xiv, 6 February; Locke to Philip van Limborch 26 January/5 February and 6/16 February, Locke, *Corr.*, vol. iii, pp. 539–40, 555; Lady Mordaunt to Dijkvelt 13 January, HMC *Eighth Report, Denbigh MSS*, pp. 558–9.

6 *LJ* vol. xiv, 6, 8 and 12 February; Sachse, p. 35.

7 Sir Edward Harley to Robert Harley 12 February, BL Add. MSS 40,621, f. 24; *Clarendon Diary*, vol. ii, 12 February, p. 262; Cranston, *John Locke*, p. 311 and note; *LJ* vol. xiv, 13 February; Huygens, *Journaal*, vol. i, p. 86; Speck, pp. 112–14; Holmes, p. 216.

8 Sir Edward Harley to R. Harley 16 February, HMC *Portland* MSS, vol. iii, p. 428; Morrice, DWL MS 31Q, p. 468; BL Add. MSS 36,707, f. 57; Luttrell, vol. i, pp. 502, 519; D. Ogg, *England in the Reigns of James II and William III* (Oxford, 1984), pp. 228–30; D. H. Somerville, *The King of Hearts, Charles Talbot, Duke of Shrewsbury* (1962), p. 56; *Cal. S. P. Dom.* 1689–90, p. 53; *CTB* 1689–92, p. 25; Burnet, vol. iv, p. 7; B. D.

Henning, *The House of Commons 1660–90* (1983), pp. 471–3; *Memoirs of Reresby*, p. 564.

9 *Memoirs of Reresby*, p. 565; Dalrymple, vol. i, p. 6; Chatsworth MSS, Devonshire House notebook sub 'Monmouth, Lord', quoted in H. G. Horwitz, *Parliament, Policy and Politics in the Reign of William III* (Manchester, 1977), p. 19; 'Spencer House Journals' printed in H. Foxcroft, *The Life and Letters of Sir George Savile, Marquis of Halifax* (1898), vol. ii, ch. 8, appendix; HMC *Portland* MSS, vol. iii, p. 431; Morrice, DWL MS 31R, p. 494; *Cal. S. P. Dom.* 1687–9, no. 2125; *CTB* 1689–92, pp. 26–78, 221.

10 BL Add. MSS 50,842; HMC *House of Lords* MSS 1689–90, pp. 27, 179; *LJ* vol. xiv, pp. 216, 237, 331, 356; *Cal. S. P. Col. Amer. and W. Indies* 1689–97, p. 6; Morrice, DWL MS 31R, pp. 482, 479; BL Add. MSS 40,621, f. 24; *CTB* 1689–92, p. 609; Luttrell, vol. i, p. 513; Macaulay, *History of England*, vol. i, p. 687n.

11 Lord King, *Life of John Locke* (1858), p. 172; *Locke Corr.*, vol. iii, p. 573; Cranston, pp. 312–13; *CTB* 1689–92, pp. 684, 110.

12 *Cal. S .P. Dom.*1689–90, pp. 45, 54, 56; Luttrell, vol. i, p. 519; Foxcroft, *Halifax*, vol. ii, p. 207; Lord Dartmouth's note, Burnet, vol. iv, p. 73.

13 *Clarendon Diary*, vol. ii, p. 273; *An Exact Account of the Ceremonial at the Coronation of King William and Queen Mary* (1689); L. E. Tanner, *History of the Coronation* (1952), pp. 18, 57; Speck, p. 165; Lady Rachel Russell to Dr Fitzwilliam 12 April, T. Sellwood, ed., *Letters of Lady Rachel Russell* (1801), p. 212.

CHAPTER FIVE

1 *LJ* vol. xiv, p. 174; *CTB* 1689–92, pp. 26–78.

2 BL Harleian MSS 7,018, ff. 253, 255; *Cal. S. P. Dom.* 1689–90, p. 97; *LJ* vol. xiv, p. 203; J. Childs, *The British Army of William III* (Manchester, 1987), pp. 22–6; Luttrell, vol. i, p. 512.

3 *LJ* vol. xiv, pp. 216, 253; *Clarendon Diary*, vol. ii, p. 278; Monmouth to Locke 9 June, King, *Life of Locke*, p. 237, and *Locke Corr.*, vol. iii, p. 637; 'Autobiography of Dr George Clarke', HMC *Leyborne-Popham* MSS, pp. 268–70; Childs, pp. 27–30.

4 *CTB* 1689–92, pp. 26–78; C. Clay, *Public Finance and Private Wealth: The Career of Sir Stephen Fox* (Oxford, 1978), pp. 219–20.

5 Foxcroft, *Halifax*, vol. ii, ch. 8, appendix, pp. 228, 231, 233; for John Hampden see Henning, *The Commons 1660–90*, vol. ii, p. 469; A. Pye to Abigail Harley 3 December 1689, HMC *Portland* MSS, vol. iii, p. 442; poem, 'Omnia Sponte' (1691), W. J. Cameron, ed., *Poems on*

Affairs of State (New Haven, 1971), vol. v (1688–97), p. 358; Huygens, *Journaal,* vol. i, p. 219.

6 Foxcroft, *Halifax,* vol. ii, pp. 222, 224, 226, 228, 229, 233, 236; Morrice, DWL MS 31R, p. 570; Luttrell, vol. i, p. 556.

7 *Cal. S. P. Dom.* 1689–90, p. 191; Luttrell, vol. i, p. 561.

8 HMC *Leyborne-Popham* MSS, p. 270; *Cal. S. P. Dom.* 1689–90, pp. 187, 217.

9 *LJ* vol. xiv, pp. 311–12; Morrice, DWL MS 31Q, p. 596; Luttrell, vol. i, pp. 568, 569; G. S. de Krey, *A Fractured Society; the Politics of London in the First Age of Party 1688–1719* (Oxford, 1985), pp. 57–8.

10 Morrice, DWL MS 31Q, pp. 633; F. W. Fairholt, *Lord Mayor's Pageants* (1843), part i, pp. 107–8; Luttrell, vol. i, p. 597; R. J. Kerr and I. C. Duncan, eds., *The Portledge Papers* (1928), p. 63; 29 October, Diary of Sir John Knatchbull, BL Add. MSS 33,923, ff. 430–81; De Krey, pp. 58–9; *LJ* vol. xiv, p. 329; HMC *Fifth Report, Sutherland* MSS, p. 207.

11 Morrice, DWL MS 31R, p. 1, 58; De Krey, p. 62; C. Clay, p. 233.

12 J. Halliday, 'The Club and the Revolution in Scotland', *Scottish Historical Review*, vol. xlv (1966), pp. 145–55; W. Fraser, ed., *The Annandale Family Book* (Edinburgh, 1894), vol. i, pp. cclxv–vi; David Nairn to the Earl of Melville 15 October 1689, W. Fraser, ed., *The Melvilles, Earls of Melville* (Edinburgh, 1890), vol. i, pp. 211–12; Morrice, DWL MS 31Q, p. 619.

13 Foxcroft, *Halifax,* vol. ii, pp. 74–5, 91–2, 114; *Clarendon Diary*, vol. ii, p. 295; *Memoirs of Reresby*, p. 564.

14 Foxcroft, *Halifax,* vol. ii, appendix, pp. 222 et seq., 247, 249; Morrice, DWL MS 31R, p. 115; Huygens, *Journaal,* vol. i, p. 248.

15 *CTB* 1689–92, p. 543; Morrice, DWL MS 31R, p. 25; Luttrell, vol. ii, p. 22.

CHAPTER SIX

1 HMC *House of Lords* MSS 1690–1, pp. 3–4, 34, 42–4; Morrice, DWL MS 31R, pp. 133, 141; HMC *Le Fleming* MSS, p. 269; HMC *House of Lords* MSS 1690–1, p. 48.

2 Fatio de Duillier to Newton 24 February 1689/90, H. W. Turnbull, ed., *Correspondence of Sir Isaac Newton* (Cambridge, 1959–77), vol. iii, p. 390; *Locke Corr.*, vol. iv, p. 15, no. 1252, p. 83, no. 1292n; King, *Life of Locke*, p. 4.

3 *CTB* 1689–92, pp. 516, 579, 685; *VCH Wiltshire* (1991), vol. xiv, pp. 65, 68; Burke, *Dormant and Extinct Peerage* (1883), pp. 379 et seq.; *Cal. S. P. Dom.* 1690–1, p. 29.

4 Foxcroft, *Halifax,* vol. ii, ch. 8, appendix, 'Spencer House Journal', 23

May; HMC *Downshire Papers*, vol. ii, p. 347; HMC *Finch* MSS, vol. iii, appendix 3, p. 378; Luttrell, vol. ii, p. 51.

5 J. Carter, 'Cabinet Records for the Reign of William III', *EHR*, vol. lxxviii (1963), pp. 98–9; W. A. Speck, 'William–and Mary?' in *The Revolution of 1688–9, Changing Perspectives* (Cambridge, 1992), p. 134; Horwitz, p. 60.

6 R. Doebner, ed., *Memoirs of Mary Queen of England* (1886), p. 30; D. Stewart, *Sir Godfrey Kneller and the English Baroque Portrait* (Oxford, 1983), pp. 44, 123.

7 *Poems on Affairs of State*, vol. v, pp. 196, 207, 213; R. Doebner, ed., *Memoirs of Mary*, p. 30; BL Harleian MSS, 6,584, f. 299; M. Ashley, *John Wildman, Postmaster and Plotter* (1947), pp. 292, 293; J. Halliday, pp. 155–9.

8 *Cal. S. P. Dom.* 1689–90, p. 450; Morrice, DWL MS 31Q, p. 630; Lord Carmarthen to King William 16 June, Dalrymple, vol. iv, p. 174, same to same 13 June, p. 107, Queen Mary to King William 26 June, p. 119; J. Ferguson, *Robert Ferguson the Plotter* (1887), p. 284.

9 Carmarthen to King William 16 June, Dalrymple, vol. iv, p. 174; *Clarendon Diary*, vol. ii, pp. 306, 318; HMC *Finch* MSS, vol. ii, p. 317; Morrice, DWL MS 31R, p. 164; Carmarthen to King 26 June, *Cal. S. P. Dom.* 1690–1, p. 41; *Leven and Melville Papers* (Bannatyne Club, 1843), pp. 447, 449, 451.

10 Ogg, pp. 352–7; G. Clark, *The Later Stuarts 1660–1714* (Oxford, 1955), pp. 164–6; Mary to William 26 June, Dalrymple, vol. iv, p. 119, same to same 7 July, p. 133.

11 Mary to William 28 June, Dalrymple, vol. iv, p. 123; Morrice, DWL MS 31R, p. 164; HMC *Finch* MSS, vol. ii, p. 319.

12 HMC *Finch* MSS, vol. iii, pp. 379, 440; Ogg, pp. 353–4; Mary to William 3 July, Dalrymple, vol. iv, p. 126, same to same 7 July, p. 133; Earl of Nottingham to King 3 July, HMC *Finch* MSS, vol. ii, pp. 335, 339; J. P. W. Ehrman, *The Navy in the War of William III* (Cambridge, 1953), pp. 350–2.

13 Mary to William 6 July, Dalrymple, vol. iv, p. 131, same to same 7 July, p. 133; Ehrman, pp. 346–7; HMC *Downshire Papers*, vol. i, pp. 353, 354, 365, 367.

CHAPTER SEVEN

1 Mary to William 15 July, Dalrymple, vol. iv, p. 141; Luttrell, vol. ii, p. 79; De Krey, pp. 68–9.

2 Mary to William 15 July, Dalrymple, vol. iv, p. 141, same to same 22 July, p. 144; same to same 24 July, p. 146; Ehrman, pp. 355–6.

3 HMC *Ninth Report, Manvers* MSS, p. 378; Ogg, p. 356; HMC *Le Fleming* MSS, p. 282.

4 The Earl of Melville to the Queen 2 July, *Leven and Melville Papers*, pp. 456–7, same to same 24 July, p. 476, Melville to Sir James Montgomery 26 July, p. 479, Melville to the Queen 29 July, pp. 479–80; Mary to William 16 August, Dalrymple, vol. iv, pp. 161–2.

5 Sir William Lockhart to the Earl of Melville 24 August, *Leven and Melville Papers*, pp. 499–500, narrative of Queen's interview 6 September, pp. 523–34; P. Hume Brown, *History of Scotland* (Cambridge, 1909), vol. iii, pp. 16–17.

6 Ogg, p. 256; W. S. Churchill, *Marlborough, His Life and Times* (1933), vol. i, pp. 277–83; *Cal. S. P. Dom.* 1690–1, p. 114; HMC *Finch* MSS, vol. iv, p. 1; Benjamin Furly to Locke 27 October, *Locke Corr.*, vol. iv, p. 154; Marquis d'Albeville to James II 6 November NS, HMC *Finch* MSS, vol. ii, p. 474.

7 Locke to Edward Clarke 1 September, *Locke Corr.*, vol. iv, p. 121, no. 1313; Morrice, DWL MS 31R, pp. 200, 207.

8 HMC *Le Fleming* MSS, p. 306; Edward Harley to Abigail Harley 16 December, HMC *Portland* MSS, vol. iii, p. 455.

9 J. Childs, *The Nine Years' War and the British Army* (Manchester, 1991), pp. 157–62; Churchill, *Marlborough*, vol. i, pp. 296–7; Locke to Furly 3 February OS, *Locke Corr.*, vol. iv, p. 196.

10 Furly to Locke 27 January/6 February, *Locke Corr.*, vol. iv, p. 192, Furly to Locke 10/20 March, p. 226; Childs, pp. 159–62; Luttrell, vol. ii, p. 196; HMC *Le Fleming* MSS, p. 320; Morrice, DWL MS 31R, p. 237.

11 Luttrell, vol. ii, p. 206; Robert Harley to Sir Edward Harley 11 April, HMC *Portland* MSS, vol. iii, p. 462; HMC *Le Fleming* MSS, p. 325; HMC *Fifth Report, Pine-Coffin* MSS, p. 381; Lady Elphinstone to Locke 14 April, *Locke Corr.*, vol. iv, pp. 250–1, no. 1383 (modernised spelling); *Portledge Papers*, p. 105; HMC *Eighth Report, Denbigh* MSS, p. 563.

12 Luttrell, vol. ii, pp. 215, 219, 238; Huygens, *Journaal*, vol. i, p. 425; *LJ* vol. xiv, p. 619.

13 Monmouth to Locke (30 July?), no. 1411 and note, *Locke Corr.*, vol. iv, p. 303, note to no. 1414, p. 308; Locke to Clarke 9 October, B. Rand, ed., *Correspondence of John Locke and Edward Clarke* (1927), p. 316.

14 Luttrell, vol. ii, p. 308; HMC *House of Lords* MSS 1690–1, pp. 261 et seq.; – to Dijkvelt 24 November/4 December, HMC *Seventh Report, Denbigh* MSS, p. 208, same to same 27 November/7 December and 1/11 December, p. 209, same to same 8/18 December, p. 210; Bonnet's report 1/11 December, von Ranke, vol. vi, appendix, pp. 171–2; Luttrell, vol. ii, p. 311; *LJ* vol. xiv, pp. 665–6; *VCH Wiltshire*, vol. xiv, p. 68; Foxcroft, *Halifax*, vol. ii, p. 146.

15 Warrant in Monmouth's favour, *Cal. S. P. Dom.* 1689–90, p. 350. The report of the Wallwyn case is in HMC *Thirteenth Report, House of Lords* MSS 1690–1, pp. 454–62.

16 Robert Pawling to Locke 31 (December) 1691, no. 1444, *Locke Corr.*, vol. iv, p. 352; *Cal. S. P. Dom.* 1689–90, p. 542; Mrs Wallwyn to the Earl of Nottingham, HMC *Finch* MSS, vol. ii, p. 267; HMC *House of Lords* MSS 1690–1, p. 456.

17 HMC *House of Lords* MSS 1690–1, pp. 456, 459–60, affidavit of Frances, wife of John Shepheard Gent., pp. 458–9, evidence of John Shepheard, p. 457; W. H. Cooke, *Collections towards the History and Antiquities of the County of Hereford* (1882), vol. iii, p. 22.

18 Locke to Clarke 27 January, *Correspondence of Locke and Clarke*, p. 331; draft agreement etc., HMC *House of Lords* MSS 1690–1, p. 462; Cooke, *County of Hereford*, vol. iii, pp. 19–22.

CHAPTER EIGHT

1 Luttrell, vol. ii, pp. 356–8, 376; Lady Monmouth to Locke 2 April, *Locke Corr.*, vol. iv, pp. 438–40, (spelling modernised).

2 Nottingham to Clarke 6 April, *Cal. S. P. Dom.* 1691–2, pp. 218, 224, 234; Nottingham to Blathwayt 8 April, HMC *Finch* MSS, vol. iv, p. 63, 12 April, p. 67.

3 Nottingham to Blathwayt 15 April, HMC *Finch* MSS, vol. iv, p. 74; Charles Lyttleton to Lord Hatton 8 April, *Hatton Corr.*, vol. ii, p. 174; *Cal. S. P. Dom.* 1691–2, pp. 233, 245.

4 Nottingham to Admiralty Commissioners 20 April, HMC *Finch* MSS, vol. iv, p. 83, and to Carter 23 April, p. 97, Monmouth to Nottingham [19 April] Tuesday, no. 145, p. 83, same to same 20 April, no. 154, p. 85, same to same 21 April, no. 160, p. 88.

5 Monmouth to [Nottingham] 23 April, HMC *Finch* MSS, vol. iv, no. 179, p. 97, Nottingham to Blathwayt 26 April, p. 100.

6 Col. Gibson to Nottingham 24 April, HMC *Finch* MSS, vol. iv, p. 100, Carter to – 30 April, p. 112; Lord Jermyn to – 30 April, *Cal. S. P. Dom.* 1691–2, p. 262.

7 Nottingham to Principal Officers of Ordnance 9 May, *Cal. S. P. Dom.* 1691–2, p. 276; Charles Lyttleton 21 May, *Hatton Corr.*, vol. ii, p. 178; Luttrell, vol. ii, p. 460; Ogg, pp. 368–9.

8 *Cal. S. P. Dom.* 1691–2, pp. 309, 360; CTB 1689–92, p. 1681.

9 Childs, *Nine Years' War,* pp. 187–96; Luttrell, vol. ii, pp. 478, 518; Furly to Locke 7/17 June, 31 August/10 September, *Locke Corr.*, vol. iv, pp. 461, 515; Huygens, *Journaal,* vol. ii, p. 79; *Cal. S. P. Dom.* 1691–2, p. 381.

10 Robert Pawling to Locke 25 August, *Locke Corr.*, vol. iv, p. 506,

Monmouth to Locke 10 September, pp. 518–9, and 10 October, p. 527; *Portledge Papers*, p. 146; Dr Kingston to Nottingham 17 September, HMC *Finch* MSS, vol. iv, p. 461.

11 Childs, *Nine Years' War*, pp. 199–210; Monmouth to Locke, 19 November, printed in King, p. 238; H. G. Horwitz, *Revolution Politicks, the Career of Daniel Finch, Second Earl of Nottingham 1647–1730* (Cambridge, 1968), p. 139.

12 N. Luttrell, *Parliamentary Diary*, ed. H. G. Horwitz (1972, pp. 243, 251, 272; Bonnet's report 22 November/2 December, von Ranke, vol. vi, p. 184; *LJ* vol. xv, pp. 136–7.

13 Cruickshanks, 'Division Lists', pp. 70–2, 84; Horwitz, *Parliament, Policy and Politics*, pp. 109–10; letters to Dijkvelt 3/13 January and 6/16 January, HMC *Seventh Report, Denbigh* MSS, p. 212; Bonnet's report, von Ranke, vol. vi, p. 199.

14 *LJ* vol. xv, pp. 207, 211, 212–13, 213–14; Luttrell, vol. iii, p. 30; Somerville, p. 73; HMC *House of Lords* MSS 1692–3, vol. xiv, p. 296; Sachse, pp. 65–6; *LJ* vol. xv, pp. 232, 244, 250.

15 Luttrell, vol. iii, pp. 62, 64, 70; King, *Life of Locke*, p. 239.

16 Childs, pp. 220–46; Ogg, pp. 384–5, 388–90.

17 *CTB* 1689–92, pp. 863, 1157, 1158, 1592, 1722, 1734, 1756, 1787, 1971; *CTB* 1693–6, pp. 253, 268, 737, 738.

18 HMC *Seventh Report, Denbigh* MSS, pp. 216, 218; Luttrell, vol. iii, pp. 14, 234; (The Bishop of St David's) to the Earl of Huntingdon 2, 5 and 7 December, HMC *Hastings* MSS, vol. ii, p. 233, and 9 December, p. 234; *LJ* vol. xv, pp. 185, 188–9, 311, 312, 315, 317.

19 HMC *Seventh Report, Denbigh* MSS, p. 218; E. M. Thompson, ed., *The Letters of Humphrey Prideaux to John Ellis* (1875), p. 165.

20 Luttrell, vol. iii, pp. 265, 301, 302; Charles Hatton to – 6 February, *Hatton Corr.*, vol. ii, p. 200; *Cal. S. P. Dom.* 1694–5, pp. 20, 115, 238; *CTB* 1693–6, p. 546.

21 *LJ* vol. xv, pp. 359, 361, 362, 366; Luttrell, vol. iii, p. 276; Master's log of HMS *Mordaunt*, Adm. 52/68; *Cal. Col. Papers, America and West Indies*, 1693–6, p. 248; BL Althorp Papers, C.11.2.

22 *LJ* vol. xv, pp. 392, 394; Somerville, pp. 87–8; Horwitz, p. 132.

CHAPTER NINE

1 Luttrell, vol. iii, p. 299; Bonnet 24 April/4 May, von Ranke, vol. vi, p. 247; *LJ* vol. xv, pp. 424, 425–6; Horwitz, *Parliament, Policy and Politics*, p. 131; A. S. Turberville, *The House of Lords in the Reign of William III* (Oxford, 1913), p. 192; G. M. Dickson, 'War Finance', *New Cambridge Modern History* (Cambridge, 1970), vol. vi, p. 289.

2 Luttrell, vol. iii, p. 306; Childs, p. 252; *Cal. S. P. Dom.* 1694–5, p. 204; W. Coxe, ed., *Private and Original Correspondence of Charles Talbot, Duke of Shrewsbury, with King William, Etc.* (1821), pp. 52–3; Churchill, *Marlborough,* vol. i, p. 318; T. Harris, *Politics under the later Stuarts* (1993), p. 209; Burnet, vol. vi, p. 222, Dartmouth's note.

3 *LJ* vol. xv, pp. 430, 443, 445, 446, 450; H. Manners Sutton, ed., *Lexington Papers* (1851), p. 23; Bonnet 18/28 December, von Ranke, vol. vi, p. 260; Somerville, p. 95.

4 Martha Lockhart to Locke, quoted in Cranston, p. 386; Horwitz, p. 143.

5 Luttrell, vol. iii, p. 432; *LJ* vol. xv, pp. 471, 509, 510; Horwitz, p. 145.

6 James Vernon to Lord Lexington 26 March, BL Add. MSS 46,527, f. 74; *Cal. S. P. Dom.* 1694–5, p. 320; RM to Frances, Countess of Huntingdon 4 April, HMC *Hastings* MSS, vol. ii, p. 244; L'Hermitage despatch 8 April, BL Add. MSS 17,677 PP, f. 209; Luttrell, vol. iii, p. 457; *CTB* 1693–6, p. 988.

7 *LJ* vol. xv, pp. 527, 528, 532, 536, 544, 547, 557–8, 564, 581, 592; L'Hermitage report 12, 15, 22, 26, 29 April NS, BL Add. MSS 17,677 PP, ff. 213–14, 219, 228, 232, 235–6; James Vernon to Lord Lexington 5 April, BL Add. MSS 46,527, f. 77; HMC *Hastings* MSS, vol. ii, p. 247; Horwitz, p. 151; *Cal. S. P. Dom.* 1694–5, p. 322.

8 (14 May), Luttrell, vol. iii, p. 471; Horwitz, p. 155; 9 May, Evelyn, *Diary,* vol. v, p. 210; Pawling to Locke 18 May, *Locke Corr.,* vol. v, p. 375; Ogg, p. 322.

9 Childs, *Nine Years' War,* pp. 275, 296–7; Monmouth to Trumbull 12 September, HMC *Downshire Papers,* vol. i, p. 548, Dr Wallis to Trumbull, p. 586; Luttrell, vol. iii, p. 536; *LJ* vol. xv, p. 596.

10 Notices in Luttrell, vol. iii, 17 October to 11 November, pp. 538, 547; James Vernon to – 30 October, *Cal. S. P. Dom.* 1694–5, p. 91; C. Jackson, ed., *The Diary of Abraham de la Pryme* (Surtees Society, 1870), pp. 73–4; Somerville, pp. 104–5.

11 *LJ* vol. xv, pp. 597, 598–9; Somerville, pp. 108–9; *LJ* vol. xv, pp. 603–4, 607–8, 610, 611; HMC *Hastings* MSS, vol. ii, p. 312.

12 Monmouth to Locke, King, *Life of Locke,* p. 240; Cranston, pp. 400–5; Somerville, p. 109.

13 Clark, *The Later Stuarts,* p. 184; *LJ* vol. xv, p. 647; Miller, *James II,* p. 238; Duque de Berwick y de Alba, *El Mariscal de Berwick* (Madrid, 1925), p. 22; Churchill, *Marlborough,* vol. i. pp. 383–6; Somerville, pp. 109–12; Ogg, pp. 426–7; Holmes, p. 198.

14 J. Verney to Lord Hatton, BL Add. MSS 29,566, f. 156; Bonnet's despatch 28 February/9 March, BL Add. MSS 30,000A, f. 19; *LJ* vol. xv, pp. 679, 683, 685; HMC *Hastings* MSS, vol. ii, p. 259; Luttrell, vol. iv, p. 22; A. Browning, *Thomas Osborne, Earl of Danby and Duke of*

Leeds 1637 –1712 (Glasgow, 1951), vol. i, p. 533, vol. iii, p. 191; Clarke, pp. 184–5; Holmes, p. 198; Horwitz, pp. 168–9,175–6.

15 *LJ* vol. xv, pp. 712, 732.

16 *LJ* vol. xv, p.747, 748; *Portledge Papers*, p. 229; Bonnet's despatches 3/13 March, 1/11 May, BL Add. MSS 30,000A, ff. 26, 122; G. P. R. James, ed., *Letters Illustrative of the Reign of William III Addressed to the Duke of Shrewsbury by James Vernon Esq.* (1841), vol. i, pp. 150, 165; BL Add. MSS 17,677 RR, f. 177; Horwitz, p. 178; Somerville, pp. 115–17.

CHAPTER TEN

1 *CTB* 1696–7, p. 224; Luttrell, vol. iv, p. 112, 15 September; *Cal. S. P. Dom.* 1696, pp. 394, 397; W. Courtney 3 March 1696/97, HMC *Downshire Papers*, vol. i, p. 635; Vernon to Shrewsbury 1 October 1696, *Vernon Corr.*, vol. i, p. 13, 29 December, p. 149, 2 January 1697, p. 154.

2 Vernon to Shrewsbury 28 January 1696/97, *Vernon Corr.*, vol. i, p. 191, 23 January, p. 180; see also Thomas Bruce, Earl of Ailesbury, *Memoirs*, ed., W. E. Buckley (Roxburghe Club, 1890), p. 407.

3 Clark, p. 185; Ogg, pp. 435–6; Luttrell, vol. iv, pp. 72, 74; *Cal. S. P. Dom.* 1696, pp. 223, 224, 234, 236, 257, 259–60, 270–1, 286, 306, 319, 337, 344, 351, 381, 492–5 (Sir John's confession); BL Add. MSS 33,251; Somerville, pp. 122–4; *LJ* vol. xvi, pp. 65–6; Vernon to Shrewsbury, *Vernon Corr.*, vol. i, pp. 12–13, 29, 33; Somers to Shrewsbury 19 October, *Shrewsbury Corr.*, pp. 411, 412, 414; Somerville, pp. 124–7; Horwitz, pp. 183–5.

4 *LJ* vol. xvi, p. 69; *Cal. S. P. Dom.* 1696, p. 429; Somerville, pp. 126–7, 128; Horwitz, p. 185.

5 *Vernon Corr.*, vol. i, pp. 2, 129; *Shrewsbury Corr.*, pp. 408 et seq., 427; HMC *Downshire Papers*, vol. i, p. 694; Somerville, pp. 110–11, 124; Horwitz, p. 186.

6 Horwitz, pp. 185–6; *Shrewsbury Corr.*, pp. 432, 435; *Vernon Corr.*, vol. i, p. 89.

7 *LJ* vol. xvi, p. 26; *Vernon Corr.*, vol. i, p. 95; Lord Wharton to Shrewsbury 1 December, *Shrewsbury Corr.*, p. 437.

8 HMC *Buccleuch (Montagu)* MSS, vol. ii, pp. 426, 429; *LJ* vol. xvi, p. 33.

9 *LJ* vol. xvi, pp. 39, 41, 43; *Vernon Corr.*, vol. i, pp. 133–4, 96–8 (wrongly placed under 2 Dec.); *LJ* vol. xvi, pp. 45–7; HMC *House of Lords* MSS NS 1695–7, pp. 283–5; *Shrewsbury Corr.*, p. 443.

10 *LJ* vol. xvi, pp. 52–3; *Vernon Corr.*, vol. i, pp. 138–9.

11 Wharton to Shrewsbury 24 December, *Shrewsbury Corr.*, p. 443; *LJ* vol. xvi, p. 48; HMC *House of Lords* MSS NS 1695–7, p. 286.

12 *Vernon Corr.*, vol. i, p. 149; HMC *Buccleuch (Montagu)* MSS, vol. ii, p. 434; *Shrewsbury Corr.*, pp. 454, 455.

13 *LJ* vol. xvi, pp. 60–1, 62.

14 *LJ* vol. xvi, pp. 61–3; HMC *House of Lords* MSS NS 1695–7, p. 288.

15 The various accounts of Monmouth's speech give aspects of his arguments and are mostly complementary as the writers try to search for the main points. The nearest to an official account is a set of notes of his speech in the House of Lords Manuscripts. Written in note form, the account becomes disjointed as if the writer was confused or thought the speaker was becoming repetitive. A more readable account, in the Middleton papers, follows closely the order of subjects in the House of Lords notes and does give an indication of the line of argument, despite many digressions. Other accounts, in Vernon's correspondence and L'Hermitage's reports, tend to stress the colourful points made but are useful for impressions and comments. *LJ* vol. xvi, pp. 51–4; HMC *House of Lords* MSS NS 1695–7, pp. 288–90; *Vernon Corr.*, vol. i, p. 162; BL Add. MSS 41,843; BL Add. MSS 17,677 RR, f. 177; Luttrell, vol. iv, pp. 166, 167.

16 *LJ* vol. xvi, pp. 63, 71; HMC *House of Lords* MSS NS 1695–7, p. 290; *Shrewsbury Corr.*, p. 457; HMC *Buccleuch (Montagu)* MSS, vol. ii, p. 438; BL Add. MSS 41,843; BL Add. MSS 17,677 RR, f. 186; notes of evidence are printed in *LJ* vol. xvi, pp. 65–72.

17 *LJ* vol. xvi, pp. 72, 73; BL Add. MSS 28,941, f. 197; *Vernon Corr.*, vol. i, p. 172; BL Add. MSS 41,843; BL Add. MSS 33,251, f. 190; *Shrewsbury Corr.*, p. 462; Burnet, *History*, vol. iv, p. 340; *Locke Corr.*, vol. v, p. 753.

CHAPTER ELEVEN

1 Somers to Shrewsbury 20 January, *Shrewsbury Corr.*, p. 465; BL Add. MSS 17,677 RR, ff. 189–90; *Vernon Corr.*, vol. i, p. 177, 185.

2 *Portledge Papers*, p. 250; *Memoirs of Ailesbury*, pp. 391 et seq., 416.

3 *Vernon Corr.*, vol. i, pp. 180, 185, 191, 196, 200, 205; BL Add. MSS 17,677 RR, ff. 221–2 .

4 HMC *Buccleuch (Montagu)* MSS, vol. ii, p. 462; *Vernon Corr.*, vol. i, pp. 200, 210, 287; *Shrewsbury Corr.*, p. 475.

5 L'Hermitage 9 April, BL Add. MSS 17,677 RR, ff. 270, 282, 283; Bonnet's despatch 30 March/9 April, BL Add. MSS 30,000A, ff. 287, 288; *LJ* vol. xvi, pp. 139–40; HMC *House of Lords* MSS 1695–70, p. 301; James Vernon to Matthew Prior 30 March, 2 April, HMC *Bath Longleat* MSS, vol. iii, p. 107; Luttrell, vol. iv, pp. 203, 205.

6 HMC *Hastings* MSS, vol. ii, pp. 289, 290; Vernon to Prior 2/12 April, HMC *Bath Longleat* MSS, vol. iii, p. 107.

7 *Locke Corr.*, vol. vi, p. 81; *LJ* vol. xvi, pp. 143; *Vernon Corr.*, vol. i, pp. 246, 261; *CTB* 1697, pp. 171.

8 Luttrell, vol. iv, p. 241; *Cal. S. P. Dom.* 1697, pp. 206, 207; HMC *House of Lords* MSS NS, vol. v, p. 173 et seq.; *Vernon Corr.*, vol. i, p. 274.

9 *Locke Corr.*, vol. vi, pp. 175, 185.

10 *Vernon Corr.*, vol. i, pp. 312, 326.

11 *Cal. S. P. Dom.* 1697, pp. 467, 468, 470, 474; Bonnet 12/22 November, BL Add. MSS 30,000A, f. 375; L'Hermitage, BL Add. MSS 17,677 RR, f. 507; *Memoirs of Ailesbury*, p. 407.

12 Horwitz, pp. 225–30; Somerville, pp. 145–6, 148; *Vernon Corr.*, vol. i, pp. 447, 448, 456, 459; BL Althorp Papers, C. 20, p. 17; Somers to Shrewsbury 6/16 January 1697/8, *Shrewsbury Corr.*, p. 524; HMC *House of Lords* MSS NS, vol. v, p. 175.

13 Tallard to Louis XIV 8 April 1698, P. Grimblot, ed., *The Letters of William III and Louis XIV* (1848), vol. i, p. 352; Montagu to Shrewsbury 1/11 February 1697/8, *Shrewsbury Corr.*, p. 531; *LJ* vol. xvi, pp. 225, 226, 227–8, 234; BL Add. MSS 30,000B, f. 71; HMC *House of Lords* MSS 1697–9, pp. 128, 129; *Cal. S. P. Dom.* 1698, pp. 129, 145; Luttrell, vol. iv, p. 351; Horwitz, pp. 230–1, 231, 235; Turberville, pp. 101–5.

14 *LJ* vol. xvi, p. 315; HMC *House of Lords* MSS, vol. x (1712–14), pp. 167–8; K. G. Davies, *The Royal African Company* (1957), pp. 132–3.

15 *LJ* vol. xvi, pp. 319, 325, 327, 329; HMC *House of Lords* MSS NS 1697–9, p. 228; *Vernon Corr.*, vol. ii, p. 106.

16 *LJ* vol. xvi, pp. 335, 342; Luttrell, vol. iv, p. 399; Horwitz, pp. 233–4; Macaulay, vol. ii, pp. 661–3; Holmes, p. 296; Ogg, p. 443; J. Keay, *The Honourable Company* (1993), p. 182.

17 11 January 1697/8, BL Add. MSS 30,000 B, f. 9; a contemporary analysis of the election result was found among Harley's papers and printed in Horwitz, p. 240; Sir G. Clark, 'From Nine Years' War to the War of the Spanish Succession', *New Cambridge Modern History*, vol. vi, pp. 381–94.

18 Sunderland to Shrewsbury 25 November/5 December [1698], *Shrewsbury Corr.*, p. 563; Grimblot, vol. ii, pp. 194, 195.

19 *LJ* vol. xvi, p. 377; Bonnet's report 14/24 February 1699, BL Add. MSS 30,000 C, f. 47.

20 *Vernon Corr.*, vol. ii, p. 267.

21 HMC *Buccleuch (Montagu)* MSS, vol. ii, pp. 623–6; *Vernon Corr.*, vol. ii, p. 342; Somerville, pp. 79–80; W. Cobbett, *Parliamentary History of England* (1810), vol. v, p. 237; *Cal. Treasury Papers* 1697–1701/2, pp. 318–19.

CHAPTER TWELVE

1   *LJ* vol. xvi, pp. 476, 482, 483, 484, 487; *Vernon Corr.*, vol. ii, pp. 368, 371, 377, 384, 440; *Shrewsbury Corr.*, p. 597; BL Add. MSS 30,000 C, ff. 279–82; BL Add. MSS 17,677 TT, f. 318, UU, ff. 103v –4.

2   *Vernon Corr.*, vol. ii, p. 404; HMC *Fifteenth Report, Johnstone* MSS, p. 115; *Hatton Corr.*, vol. ii, p. 246; *LJ* vol. xvi, p. 491.

3   *LJ* vol. xvi, pp. 508, 514, 515, 518, 519, 524, 526; Hume Brown, vol. iii, p. 39.

4   *LJ* vol. xvi, pp. 515–19, 521, 522, 526; Luttrell, vol. iv, pp. 613, 615; *Vernon Corr.*, vol. ii, pp. 438, 440, 445, 450.

5   *LJ* vol. xvi, pp. 540, 545, 562; J. R. Tanner, ed., *The Private Correspondence of Samuel Pepys* (1926), vol. i, p. 323.

6   *LJ* vol. xvi, pp. 567–80; Ogg, p. 451–2; Horwitz, pp. 266–8; Turberville, p. 206.

7   Ogg, pp. 453–6; Horwitz, pp. 270, 275–8; Luttrell, vol. v, p. 4.

8   *LJ* vol. xvi, pp. 593, 595, 596, 600; L'Hermitage Report, BL Add. MSS 17,677 WW, f. 157; Horwitz, pp. 281, 282.

9   *Cal. S. P. Dom.* 1700–2, pp. 248, 257; *LJ* vol. xvi, pp. 619, 622, 623, 628; Horwitz, pp. 284–5; Ogg, p. 462.

10   *LJ* vol. xvi, pp. 639, 652, 668, 677; Horwitz, pp. 286–7; Clark, pp. 194–5.

11   *LJ* vol. xvi, p. 689; Horwitz, p. 284.

12   *LJ* vol. xvi, pp. 726, 730–1, 737, 747, 762, 763.

13   *LJ* vol. xvi, pp. 765, 769; Holmes, p. 338; Horwitz, pp. 291–2; Ogg, pp. 464–6.

14   *LJ* vol. xvi, p. 770.

15   Horwitz, pp. 295–6; Churchill, *Marlborough,* vol. i, p. 447; Furly to Locke, 17/28 July, *Locke Corr.*, vol. vii, p. 379.

16   Horwitz, pp. 296–7; *The Journals of the House of Commons*, vol. xiii, pp. 679, 682, 711–12; W. Cobbett, *The Parliamentary History of England* (1806–19), vol. v, pp. 1337–8; Luttrell, vol. v, pp. 136–7; T. Forster, *Original letters of John Locke, et al.*, p. 147.

17   *LJ* vol. xvii, pp. 6, 7, 9–10, 11, 50–1, 59, 63; Luttrell, vol. v, p. 129; B. van T'Hoff, ed., *Marlborough-Heinsius Correspondence* (The Hague, 1951), no. 38, p. 19; H. Snyder, ed., *Marlborough-Godolphin Correspondence* (Oxford, 1975), vol. i, p. 95; Horwitz, pp. 302–4.

CHAPTER THIRTEEN

1   *Several Orations of Demosthenes translated by the Earl of Peterborough and others* (1744).

2   A. Boyer, *Annals of the Reign of Queen Anne* (1703), vol. i, p. 53; *Marlborough-Godolphin Corr.*, vol. i, p. 95, 101; Luttrell, vol. v, pp. 223, 225; 26 December 1702, King, *Life and Letters of John Locke*, p. 241.

3   King, p. 241; *Locke Corr.*, vol. vii, p. 337, 704, 717, 721, 723.

4   *Cal. Treasury Papers* 1702–7, p. 118; *Cal. S. P. Dom.* 1702–3, p. 530; *CTB* 1703, p. 30; *Cal. S. P. America and West Indies* 1702–3, p. 94; *Locke Corr.*, vol. vii, pp. 700, 706–7, 713.

5   *Cal. S. P. Am. and W. Ind.* 1702–3, pp. 89–90; for the life of Codrington see V. T. Harlow, *Christopher Codrington 1668–1710* (Oxford, 1928).

6   *Cal. S. P. Dom.* 1702–3, pp. 274, 276, 530; BL Add. MSS 61,164, f. 33; *Cal. S. P. Am. and W. Ind.* 1702–3, p. 94.

7   Rijksarchiev, The Hague, Archief Heinsius No. 858 (1); *Marlborough-Heinsius Corr.*, pp. 45, 46, 49; *Cal. S. P. Dom.* 1702–3, pp. 536–7, 538–9; *Locke Corr.*, vol. vii, pp. 740–1; *Marlborough-Godolphin Corr.*, vol. i, p. 75, n. 6; Peterborough to Sunderland 27 February 1706, BL Add. MSS 61,514, f. 27; *CTB* 1703, pp. 18, 117, 205; Luttrell, vol. v, p. 269.

8   C. Jones and G. Holmes, eds., *The London Diaries of William Nicolson 1702–18* (Oxford, 1985), p. 175; T. Forster, *Original Letters of Locke et al.*, p. 138; K. Feiling, *History of the Tory Party* (Oxford, 1924), pp. 368–9.

9   Luttrell, vol. v, pp. 259, 261; HMC *House of Lords* MSS NS, vol. v, pp. 173 et seq.; *LJ* vol. xvii, pp. 200, 204, 249, 252; *Nicolson Diaries*, pp. 179–80.

10 BL Add. MSS 61,458, ff. 193, 195, 199; *Marlborough-Godolphin Corr.*, vol. i, p. 219; BL Add. MSS 61,164, f. 35.

11 *LJ* vol. xvii, pp. 319, 331; *Cal. S. P. Dom.* 1703–4, p. 276.

12 H. Williams, ed., *The Correspondence of Jonathan Swift* (Oxford, 1963), vol. i, p. 39.

13 Locke to Furly, 12 October 1702 quoted in Cranston, *John Locke*, p. 455; Bodleian Library MSS Locke c. 12, ff. 212, 214 quoted in Cranston, pp. 462, 463; Cranston, p. 469.

14 Churchill, *Marlborough*, vol. ii, pp. 170–2; A. J. Veenendaal, 'The War of the Spanish Succession in Europe', *New Cambridge Modern History*, vol. vi, pp. 418–20; G. M. Trevelyan, *England under Queen Anne*, vol. i (1931), pp. 298–303; Holmes, pp. 238–9; B. Coward, *The Stuart Age* (1994), p. 410.

15 Trevelyan, vol. i, pp. 304–7; Churchill, vol. ii, pp. 166–9; G. Symcox, *Victor Amadeus II* (1983), pp. 135–43.

16 A. Parnell, *The War of the Succession in Spain* (1905), p. 42; Boyer, vol. ii, pp. 225–9; J. A. C. Hugill, *No Peace Without Spain* (Kensal Press, Oxford, 1991), pp. 55–60.

17 Trevelyan, vol. i, pp. 410–18; Parnell, pp. 43–67; J. H. Owen, *The War at Sea under Queen Anne* (1938), p. 129; Hugill, pp. 90–8, 99–111.

18 Peterborough to Marlborough 23 May, BL Add. MSS 61,164, f. 37; Sir George Murray, ed., *Letters and Dispatches of John Churchill, First Duke of Marlborough* (1845), vol. i, p. 344; Dalton, vol. v, p. 42; John Millner, *A Compendious Journal of All the Marches, Famous Battles, Sieges and Actions of the Triumphant Armies of the Confederate High Allies in the Late War against France 1701–12* (1733), pp. 99–100; Boyer, vol. iii, p. 60; F. W. Hamilton, *History of the First or Grenadier Guards* (1814), vol. i, p. 447.

19 Dalton, vol. v, p. 81, pt. ii, p. 29; *Marlborough Dispatches*, vol. i, p. 473; BL Add. MSS 61,164, f. 43.

20 Luttrell, vol. v, p. 498; Boyer, vol. iii, p. 158; *Nicolson Diaries*, pp. 253–4.

21 *Vernon Corr.*, vol. iii, p. 281; Gilbert Eliot, Earl of Minto, ed., *The Correspondence of George Baillie of Jerviswood 1702–8* (Bannatyne Club, 1842), pp. 16–17, 26; *Nicolson Diaries*, pp. 244–6.

CHAPTER FOURTEEN

1 H. Kuenzel, *Leben des Landgrafen Georg von Hessen-Darmstadt* (Friedberg and London, 1859), p. 548; Parnell, p. 106; A. D. Francis, *The Methuens and Portugal* (1966), p. 294.

2 A. D. Francis, 'Prince George of Hesse-Darmstadt and the Plans for the Expedition to Spain of 1702', *BIHR* vol. xlii (1969), p. 59; Sir George Clark, 'The Nine Years' War', *New Cambridge Modern History*, vol. vi, p. 249, A. J. Veenendaal, 'The War of the Spanish Succession in Europe', p. 423.

3 WO 25/8 f. 176; Luttrell, vol. v, pp. 534, 535; Boyer, vol. iv, p. 8; HMC *Tenth Report Bagot* MSS, p. 339; O. Klopp, *Der Fall des Hauses Stuart* (Vienna, 1881–5), vol. xi, p. 488; BL Add. MSS 61,164, f. 37; BL Add. MSS 61,458, ff. 205, 209, 211, 217; HMC *House of Lords* MSS, vol. vii, pp. 401, 407; *Memoirs of Ailesbury*, p. 629.

4 BL Stowe MSS 222 f. 287, 298; Hoffmann's despatch quoted in Klopp, vol. xi, p. 489; Kuenzel, pp. 558–9; J. J. G. Pelet, *Mémoires Militaires relatifs à la succession d'Espagne sous Louis XIV*, vol. v (Paris, 1850), p. 631.

5 Archiev Heinsius no. 1016 (1); *Letters from the Earl of Peterborough to General Stanhope in Spain* (1834), p. 1; R. D. Merriman, *Queen Anne's Navy 1702–1714* (Navy Record Society, 1961), p. 71.

6 Pelet, p. 630. The figure of 5,000 men was estimated by Parliament for the expedition and was the sum of the six regiments named, HMC

House of Lords MSS, vol. vii, p. 448; Dutch forces, *Marlborough-Godolphin Corr.*, vol. i, p. 418; reports of 8,000 men are given by Hedges, W. Blackley, ed., *The Diplomatic Correspondence of Richard Hill 1703–6* (1845), vol. i, p. 200 and HMC *House of Lords* MSS, vol. x, p. 250, and by Hoffmann in Kuenzel, p. 559. Maj. R. E. Scouller, *The Armies of Queen Anne* (Oxford, 1966), p. 353; F. Duncan, *History of the Royal Regiment of Artillery* (1872), vol. i, p. 67; Parnell, p. 109; *Marlborough Dispatches*, vol. ii, p. 28; *Marlborough-Godolphin Corr.*, vol. i, pp. 421, 422; *Cal. Treas. Papers 1702–7*, pp. 337–8; WO 47/22; Charles, Earl of Peterborough, Military Orders, Museo de Historia de la Ciudad, Barcelona, ff. 3, 7, 9, 10.

7 J. Burchett, *Transactions at Sea* (1720), p. 684; HMC *House of Lords* MSS, vol. vii, p. 364; BL Add. MSS 61,458, f. 211; Luttrell, vol. v, pp. 554–5; Peterborough to Hedges 22 and 25 May, SP 94/75; Stanhope of Chevening MSS O135/11; Boyer, vol. iv, p. 137.

8 Peterborough to Hedges 30 May, SP 94/75; *Life of Leake*, vol. i, p. 277; Peterborough to A. Stanhope 19 April, Stanhope of Chevening MSS 034, Furly's journal 28–30 May, 0135/11; BL Add. MSS 28,056, ff. 270–2; B. Tunstall, ed., *The Byng Papers* (1930–31), vol. i, pp. 72–4; log of the *Ranelagh* 28–31 May, Adm. 51/266.

9 Adm 51/266; Furly's journal 7 June; *Life of Leake*, vol. i, pp. 277–8; Burchett, p. 685; A. Furly to the Earl of Shaftesbury, 27 June/7 July 1705, PRO 30/24/45, no. 61.

10 *Hill Corr.*, vol. i, p. 214, vol. ii, p. 544; HMC *House of Lords* MSS, vol. vii, pp. 361, 363; Pelet, vol. v, pp. 629–31.

11 Peterborough's Military Orders, Barcelona, f. 18; HMC *House of Lords* MSS, vol. vii, p. 361, vol. x, p. 250; P. Voltes Bou, *La Guerra de Sucesion en Valencia* (Barcelona, 1964), p. 24; Kuenzel, p. 571.

12 HMC *House of Lords* MSS, vol. vii, pp. 501–6; Peterborough to Hill 28 October 1705, BL Add. MSS 28,057, f. 25; *Hill Corr.*, vol. i, p. 214; Archiev Heinsius No. 1016 (2); Kuenzel, pp. 570–2; Voltes Bou, p. 27; Parnell, pp. 110–11; *Life of Leake*, vol. i, p. 278; log of the *Leopard* 6 July, Adm 52/210; log of the *Ranelagh* 8 July, Adm 51/266; A. D. Francis, *The First Peninsular War* (1975), p. 173.

13 Council of war 28 June, SP 94/75; BL Stowe MSS 468, ff. 98, 101; BL Stowe MSS 467, f. 29v; BL Add. MSS 28,056, ff. 285, 293; HMC *Frankland-Russell-Astley* MSS, p. 180; A. Furly to the Earl of Shaftesbury 7 July OS 1705, PRO 30/24/45.

14 Parnell, pp. 40–1; log of the *Ranelagh*, Adm 51/266.

15 Furly's journal 20–24 July; log of the *Devonshire* 23–24 July, Adm 51/242; BL Add. MSS 5,441, f. 48; A. Morrison, *Catalogue of Autograph Letters*, first series, vol. v, (1883–92), p. 133; E. R. James, ed., *The Military Memoirs of Colonel de St Pierre* (1882), p. 27; *Life of Leake*,

vol. i, p. 279; R. E. Scouller, 'The Peninsula in the War of the Spanish Succession', *Journal of the Society for Army Historical Research*, vol. liv (1976), p. 237; Hamilton, vol. ii, p. 3; Parnell, p. 114; Peterborough to Hedges 22 July OS, SP 94/75; Paul Methuen to John Methuen 4 August NS, BL Add. MSS 28,056, f. 301.

CHAPTER FIFTEEN

1 Log of the *Ranelagh* 27–30 July, Adm 51/266; Furly's journal 26–30 July; Peterborough to Godolphin 1 August OS, Morrison, vol. v, pp. 133–4; BL Stowe MSS 467, f. 34; *Memoirs of St Pierre*, p. 27; *Life of Leake*, vol. i, p. 279; C. T. Atkinson, ed., 'A Royal Dragoon in the Spanish Succession War', *Journal of the Society for Army Historical Research* (1938), p. 13.

2 Log of the *Lyme* 31 July, Adm 51/4250; *Hill Corr.*, pp. 570, 579; HMC *House of Lords* MSS, vol. x, p. 251; Stowe MSS 471 f. 3v; M. Landau, *Geschichte Kaiser Karls VI* (Stuttgart, 1889), p. 266; BL Add. MSS 28,056, f. 351, 28,058, f. 1; Peterborough to Godolphin 1 August OS, Morrison, p. 134; Boyer, vol. iv, pp. 140–1.

3 Peterborough's Military Orders, Barcelona, ff. 18, 20; H. Kamen, *The War of the Succession in Spain 1700–1715* (1969), p. 278; *Memoirs of St Pierre*, p. 27; *Life of Leake*, vol. i, p. 280; log of the *Ranelagh* 6 August, Adm 51/266; Parnell, p. 114; G. Escolano, *Decadas de la Historia de la Ciudad de Valencia* ed. J. B. Perales (Madrid, 1880), vol. iii, p. 832.

4 Furly's journal 5 August; log of the *Devonshire* 5, 9, 11 August, Adm 51/242; *Life of Leake*, vol. i, p. 280; BL Add. MSS 28,056, f. 323 et seq.; HMC *House of Lords* MSS, vol. x, p. 251.

5 Log of the *Fubbs* 9 and 10 August, Adm 51/377; BL Stowe MSS 467, ff. 34v, 35; *Memoirs of St Pierre*, p. 28; *Life of Leake*, vol. i, p. 281; Boyer, vol. iv, pp. 141–2; Furly's journal 11 August; log of the *Lyme* 11 August, Adm 51/4250.

6 Log of the *Devonshire* 12 August, Adm 51/242; BL Add. MSS 28,056, f. 323 et seq.; *Memoirs of St Pierre*, p. 28; *Life of Leake*, vol. i, p. 281; Boyer, vol. iv, p. 143; BL Stowe MSS 471, ff. 3–4; Feliú de la Peña, *Anales de Cataluña* (Barcelona, 1709), vol. iii, p. 534; J. B. Targe, *Histoire de l'Avènement de la Maison de Bourbon* (Paris, 1772), vol. iv, pp. 106–7; HMC *House of Lords* MSS, vol. x, p. 251.

7 Log of the *Fubbs* 13 August, Adm 51/377; BL Add. MSS 28,056, ff. 323 et seq.; *Memoirs of St Pierre*, p. 29; log of the *Britannia* 13, 14 August, BL Add. MSS 28,126; BL Stowe MSS 467, f. 35; *Life of Leake*, vol. i, p. 281.

8 BL Stowe MSS 467, f. 35, 471 ff. 4v, 5; Dr J. Freind, *An Account of the Earl of Peterborow's Conduct in Spain* (1707), pp. 12–14; BL Add. MSS 28,056, f. 324.

9 BL Stowe MSS 467, ff. 35–6; *Memoirs of St Pierre*, p. 29; *Life of Leake*, vol. i, pp. 282–3; HMC *House of Lords* MSS, vol. vii, pp. 411, 412.

10 BL Add. MSS 28,056, ff. 323 et seq.; *Hill Corr.*, pp. 220–1; BL Stowe MSS, 471 ff. 5v, 6; BL Stowe MSS 467, f. 36v.

11 BL Stowe MSS 467, ff. 36v, 37; Furly's journal 22, 24 August; council of war 22 August OS, SP 94/75; HMC *House of Lords* MSS, vol. vii, pp. 494–5, 411–12; BL Add. MSS 28,056, ff. 323 et seq.; *Life of Leake*, vol. i, pp. 283–5; *Memoirs of St Pierre*, p. 31; *Impartial Inquiry into the Management of the War in Spain* (1712), p. 27.

12 BL Add. MSS 28,056, ff. 323 et seq.; BL Stowe MSS 468, ff. 107 and 109, 467, f. 37v; 26 August, SP 94/75; Furly's journal 25, 26 August; HMC *House of Lords* MSS, vol. vii, p. 413; *Impartial Inquiry*, p. 28; *Memoirs of St Pierre*, p. 31; Freind, pp. 22–3; BL Stowe MSS 471, f. 6v; Österreichisches Kriegsarchiv AFA 1705, Spanien und Portugal 243, ff. 8–9, this letter is a copy only.

13 BL Stowe MSS 471, f. 23, 468, f. 107; *Hill Corr.*, p. 220; Kuenzel, pp. 656–8.

14 HMC *House of Lords* MSS, vol. vii, pp. 414, 423; BL Add. MSS 28,056, ff. 323 et seq.; Burchett, pp. 686–7; *Life of Leake*, vol. i, pp. 285–6; Kuenzel, p. 659; Furly's journal 27 August; log of the *Britannia* 27 August, BL Add. MSS 28,126.

15 BL Add. MSS 28,056, ff. 323 et seq.; *Impartial Inquiry*, pp. 35, 40; 28 August, SP 94/75; Furly's journal 28 August.

16 Furly's journal 29 August; *Impartial Inquiry*, p. 41; BL Add. MSS 28,056, ff. 323 et seq.; Kuenzel, p. 665; log of the *Fubbs* 29 August, Adm 51/377.

17 Kuenzel, p. 660; Furly's journal 30 August, 1 September; HMC *House of Lords* MSS, vol. vii, pp. 424, 425, 416–17; *Impartial Inquiry*, pp. 36–7.

18 *Impartial Inquiry*, p. 42; BL Stowe MSS 467, f. 38, 468, ff. 109, 111, 111v, 471, f. 7; *Memoirs of St Pierre*, p. 34.

CHAPTER SIXTEEN

1 Freind, pp. 35–6; Boyer, vol. iv, introduction and p. 146; *Remarks upon Dr Freind's Account of the Earl of Peterborow's Conduct in Spain* (1708), pp. 19–20, 50; HMC *House of Lords* MSS, vol. vii, pp. 509–10; Paul Methuen to his father 10 October 1705, BL Add. MSS 28,056,

f. 327 et seq.; Castellví, Narraciones (Österreichisches Staatsarchiv W. 937), vol. ii, f. 348; *Memoirs of St Pierre*, p. 34; BL Stowe MSS 468, f. 38v.; Peterborough to Prince George of Hesse-Darmstadt 29 August/1 September, printed in Kuenzel, p. 662; Peterborough to Hill, copy in Furly's hand, BL Add. MSS. 28,057, f. 25, printed in *Hill Corr.*, vol. i, p. 230. The conversation with the officer is in *Memoirs of St Pierre*, pp. 32–4.

2 Feliú de la Peña, vol. iii, p. 537; P. Voltes Bou, *Barcelona durante el Gobierno del Archiduque Carlos de Austria* (Barcelona, 1963), p. 51; 2 September, Adm 51/377; Furly's journal 2 September; Kuenzel, pp. 663, 665; BL Stowe MSS 467, f. 38v; Norris's log 2 September, BL Add. MSS 28,126; *Impartial Inquiry*, p. 42.

3 Accounts of the action at Montjuich can be found in BL Add. MSS 28,056, f. 337 et seq.; BL Stowe MSS 467, ff. 38–9v; BL Stowe MSS 468, ff. 109–11; BL Stowe MSS 471, f. 7 et seq.; 'Royal Dragoon', p. 14; *Memoirs of St Pierre*, pp. 34–41; Furly's journal 3 September; A. Furly to Shaftesbury, PRO 30/24/45 no. 95; *Remarks*, pp. 51–2; Feliú de la Peña, vol. iii, pp. 537–8; Inquiry into the conduct of Lord Charlemont, WO 71/1, ff. 111, 113, 121; Morrison, first series, vol. v, p. 135; *Life of Leake*, vol. i, pp. 289–90 where the importance of Peterborough's action is noted in an account not normally favourable to him.

4 Furly's journal 3 September; 'Royal Dragoon', p. 14; BL Stowe MSS 468, f. 109v; HMC *House of Lords* MSS, vol. vii, p. 510; BL Add. MSS 61,164, f. 49, 61,458, f. 213, 28,056, f. 309 et seq.; evidence of Colonel Purcell, WO 71/1.

5 Letter from a naval officer quoted in Lord Mahon, *War of the Spanish Succession* (1836), p. 151; Hugill, p. 186.

CHAPTER SEVENTEEN

1 BL Stowe MSS 467, ff. 39v–40, 471, ff. 9v–10, 468, f. 10; Furly's journal 4–6 September; BL Add. MSS 28,056, f. 337 et seq.; log of the *Devonshire* 4–5 September, Adm 51/242; Allemonde to Fagel, G. de Lamberty, *Mémoires pour servir a l'histoire du XVIIIme siècle* (Paris, 1735), vol. iii, p. 531; *Life of Leake*, vol. i, p. 290; Furly to Shaftesbury 9 September OS, PRO 30/24/45.

2 Furly's journal 8, 12, 17, 18, 20 September; BL Add. MSS 28,056, f. 337 et seq.; Boyer, vol. iv, p. 151; Furly to Shaftesbury 9 September, PRO 30/24/45; BL Stowe MSS 467, ff. 40–1v; HMC *House of Lords* MSS NS, vol. vii, p. 418; *Life of Leake*, vol. i, pp. 290–1; BL Stowe MSS 468, ff. 110, 113v, 471, f. 10; S. Martin-Leake, *The Life of Captain Stephen Martin 1666–1740* ed. C. R. Markham (1895),

pp. 82–3; *Memoirs of St Pierre*, pp. 41–2; Peterborough's Military Orders, Barcelona, f. 11.

3 BL Stowe MSS 468, ff. 110, 113v; Feliú de la Peña, p. 540; BL Stowe MSS 467, ff. 40–40v; *Impartial Inquiry*, p. 52; HMC *House of Lords* MSS NS, vol. vii, pp. 419–20; BL Add. MSS 28,056, f. 337 et seq.; Furly's journal 26 September; Lamberty, vol. iii, p. 531.

4 BL Add. MSS 28,126, 8 September; Peterborough to Godolphin 9 September OS, Morrison, first series, vol. v, p. 135; Furly's journal 9 September; Luttrell, vol. v, p. 598; HMC *Buccleuch (Montagu)* MSS, p. 798.

5 HMC *House of Lords* MSS NS, vol. vii, p. 420; *Life of Leake*, vol. i, p. 291; Burchett, p. 687; BL Stowe MSS 467, ff. 41v–2; BL Add. MSS 28,056, f. 337 et seq.; Lamberty, vol. iii, p. 532; P. Voltes Bou, *Barcelona*, p. 55; Feliú de la Peña, vol. iii, p. 540; Furly's journal 22–3 September.

6 BL Add. MSS 28,056, f. 337 et seq.; BL Stowe MSS 471, ff. 10v, 18, 467, f. 42; council of war 27 September, SP 94/75; Furly's journal 27, 28 September, 2 October; *Memoirs of St Pierre*, p. 42; *Life of Leake*, vol. i, pp. 292–3; *Stephen Martin*, p. 83; Lamberty, vol. iii, p. 533; HMC *House of Lords* MSS NS, vol. vii, p. 418; *Hill Corr.*, pp. 641, 645.

7 BL Stowe MSS 467, ff. 42–42v; Lamberty, vol. iii, p. 534; BL Stowe MSS 471, ff. 18–19; log of the *Fubbs* 3 October, Adm 51/377; *Memoirs of St Pierre*, pp. 42–3; *Stephen Martin*, pp. 83–4; Burnet, vol. v, pp. 213–14; Targe, vol. iv, p. 125; King Charles to Queen Anne 23 October, Kriegsakten 249 (1705–08) Österreichisches Staatsarchiv; Furly's journal 3 October; Feliú de la Peña, vol. iii, pp. 541–2; HMC *House of Lords* MSS NS, vol. vii, p. 418; Boyer, vol. iv, pp. 152–3.

8 Furly's journal 4, 5, 6 October; HMC *House of Lords* MSS NS, vol. vii, p. 419; Lamberty, vol. iii, p. 534; Boyer, vol. iv, p. 153; Lady Peterborough to Lord Shaftesbury 6 September [actually 6 Oct], PRO 30/24/21; Luttrell, vol. v, p. 598.

9 Lamberty, vol. iii, pp. 534, 544–5; Furly's journal 7, 8, 12, 13 October; *Memoirs of St Pierre*, pp. 43–4; P. Voltes Bou, *Barcelona*, p. 57; BL Add. MSS 28,103, f. 91; BL Add. MSS 28,056, f. 329–33; log of the *Britannia*, Adm 51/138; *Life of Leake*, vol. i, pp. 294–5, 296–6; BL Add. MSS 5,442, f. 2; *Stephen Martin*, p. 85; log of the *Fubbs* 12, 14, 15 October, Adm 51/377; Norris's log of the *Britannia*, BL Add. MSS 28,126

CHAPTER EIGHTEEN

1 P. Voltes Bou, *Barcelona*, pp. 70–1; Furly's journal, 27, 28 October.

2 Peterborough to Harley 19 November 1705, BL Add. MSS 70,249;

Peterborough to Stanhope 18/29 November, *Peterborough's Letters to Stanhope*, p. 4; St Pierre, p. 45; P. Voltes Bou, *Barcelona*, p. 70; BL Add. MSS 28,056, f. 392; Furly to Shaftesbury 20 November/1 December, PRO 30/24/45; V. Bacallar y Sanna, Marquès de San Felipe, *Comentarios de la Guerra de Espana y Historia de Su Rey Felipe V* (Madrid, 1957), p. 99; Furly's journal.

3 BL Add. MSS 28,056, ff. 351, 392; 20 November/1 December, PRO 30/24/45; Peterborough to Hedges 23 October/3 November, SP 94/75; BL Add. MSS 28,057, f. 25.

4 Liechtenstein to Wratislaw 5 November 1705, *Feldzüge des Prinzen Eugen von Savoyen* (Vienna, 1881), Series I, band vii, pp. 553–4; Peterborough and Crowe to the Lord Treasurer, BL Add. MSS 28,056, f. 392; Peterborough to Stanhope 18 November, *Peterborough's Letters to Stanhope*, p. 5; Galway to the King, BL Add. MSS 28,056, ff. 377, 379; Furly's journal 1 November; Peterborough to Robert Harley 19 November, BL Add. MSS 70,249.

5 BL Add. MSS 28,056, ff. 369, 377, 392; Peterborough to Hedges 18 November OS, SP 94/75; Kamen, pp. 95, 253–4; Parnell, p. 137; Francis, *Peninsular War*, pp. 197–8; Luttrell, vol. v, p. 616; Hedges to Peterborough 18/29 December, SP 104/207; Furly to Shaftesbury 20 November OS, PRO 30/24/45.

6 BL Add. MSS 28,056, ff. 391, 392; 20 November OS, PRO 30/24/45; Peterborough to Harley 19 November OS, BL Add. MSS 70,249.

7 Luttrell, vol. v, pp. 613, 616; William, Lord Cowper, *Private Diary* (Roxburghe Club, 1833), pp. 19–20; *Nicolson Diaries*, p. 328; Peterborough to Stanhope 18/29 November, *Peterborough's Letters to Stanhope*, pp. 3, 4, 6; Lady Peterborough to the Earl of Shaftesbury, PRO 30/24/21, no. 233; Lady Peterborough to the Duchess of Marlborough 12 October, BL Add. MSS 61,458, f. 213; HMC *Cowper* MSS, vol. iii, p. 64.

8 BL Add. MSS 28,056, ff. 357, 379, 381, 383, 385, 387; Cowper, *Private Diary*, p. 27; Hedges to Peterborough 4/15 December, SP 104/129.

9 BL Add. MSS 28,056, f. 392; Peterborough to Hedges 18/29 November, SP 94/75; Peterborough to Stanhope, *Peterborough's Letters to Stanhope*, pp. 2–4; Furly to Shaftesbury 20 November/1 December, PRO 30/24 45; Furly's journal 14/25 December; Cowper, *Private Diary*, p. 27.

10 Kamen, pp. 280–4; Feliú de la Peña, vol. iii, p. 549; Petition of the City of Valencia to the King (1707), Milicia 1643–1757, f. 6857, Museo Historico, Valencia; J. M. de Miñana, 'De Bello Rustico Valentino', *Revue Hispanique,* vol. lv (Paris, 1922), p. 465; BL Add. MSS 28,056, f. 392.

11 *Memoirs of St Pierre*, pp. 45–6; Miñana, p. 473; Col. J. Jones, 'A Journal of the Siege of San Mateo 1707', *Accounts of Sieges 1680–1708*, no. 7, pp. 1–13; Parnell, p. 144.

12 Furly to Shaftesbury 6 February, PRO 30/24/45; Peterborough to Godolphin 11 January, Morrison, vol. v, pp. 136–9; Furly's journal; BL Add. MSS 28,058, f. 7 (translation in Russell, vol. i, pp. 259–60); Boyer, vol. iv, p. 160; St Pierre to Lord Raby, BL Add. MSS 31,134, f. 295; 'Royal Dragoon', p. 15; *Memoirs of St Pierre*, p. 51; Freind, pp. 205–15; 'Siege of San Mateo', pp. 13–21; Peterborough's letter to Major Jones printed in Freind, pp. 211–13; *Remarks upon Dr Freind's Account*, p. 294. For French accounts, see Hugill, pp. 195–7.

CHAPTER NINETEEN

1 'Siege of San Mateo', p. 21; *Memoirs of St Pierre*, p. 51; BL Add. MSS 31,134, f. 296; Miñana, p. 487.

2 Morrison, first series, vol. v, pp. 139–40; *Memoirs of St Pierre*, pp. 51–3; BL Add. MSS 31,134, f. 297; BL Add. MSS 28,058, f. 9; Crowe to Peterborough 14 January, printed in Freind, p. 219.

3 Morrison, first series, vol. v, p. 140; Freind, p. 254; Furly's journal 6 January; Hugill, pp. 198–9.

4 Morrison, first series, vol. v, pp. 137, 140; St Pierre to Lord Raby, BL Add. MSS 31,134, f. 297; Furly's journal 6–8 January; Freind, pp. 241–3; Furly to Shaftesbury 6 February, PRO 30/24/45.

5 Morrison, first series, vol. v, p. 140; King to Peterborough, BL Add. MSS 28,057, f. 15.

6 Freind, p. 232; Furly's journal 15 January.

7 Furly's journal 16–17 January; Peterborough to Godolphin 11 January OS, Morrison, first series, vol. v, pp. 136–43, the original manuscript of this letter is not available but the date, 11 January OS, is probably a misreading for 17 January OS as Peterborough arrived at Castellón on that date (on 11 January OS he was at Vinaros) and all the events to 17 January are described in the letter, including the arrival of Nebot's Horse. Miñana, p. 487.

8 Furly's journal 18, 21 January; Furly to Shaftesbury 6 February, PRO 30/24/45; Freind, pp. 249–52; *Memoirs of St Pierre*, pp. 53–8.

9 Account of Murviedro, Furly's journal 22 January; Freind, p. 256–70; *Memoirs of St Pierre*, pp. 55–7; Furly to Shaftesbury 6 February, PRO 30/24/45; O'Mahony to Arcos printed in Hugill, pp. 199–200.

10 Furly's journal 23 January; *Memoirs of St Pierre*, p. 58; 'Royal Dragoon', p. 16; Joseph Vicente Orti y Mayor, Diario de lo Sucedido en la Ciudad de Valencia 1700–15, vol. 1705–9, 3 February, Universidad de Valencia MS 460.

11 Furly's journal 24 January; Furly to Shaftesbury 6 February, PRO 30/24/45; *Memoirs of St Pierre*, p. 58; 'Royal Dragoon', p. 17; Fuster y

Menbrado, Dietario de Valencia February 1706, Biblioteca Municipal, Valencia, Folio 6424; Miñana, p. 492; Orti y Mayor, 4 February; St Pierre to Lord Raby, BL Add. MSS 31,134, f. 298.

12 St Pierre to Lord Raby, BL Add. MSS 31,134 f. 297; *Memoirs of St Pierre*, p. 59.

13 Miñana, p. 492; Fuster y Menbrado, 6, 21 February; *Memoirs of St Pierre*, pp. 48–9; P. Voltes Bou, *La Guerra en Valencia*, p. 33; Kamen, pp. 286–7; Furly to Shaftesbury 6 February, PRO 30/24/45; Orti y Mayor, 19 March.

14 Fuster y Menbrado, February; Furly's journal 27 January; Orti y Mayor, 7 February; *The Case of Colonel Burston with Respect to the Dispute between him and Lt. Gen. Wills* (1720), pp. 3–9; Crow to Lord Treasurer, BL Add. MSS 28,057, f. 22.

15 Lettres du Maréchal de Tessé 18 January, BL Add. MSS 9,776; log of the *Lyme*, 1, 2 February OS, Adm 51/4250; Furly's journal 3 February; Lamberty, vol. iv, p. 146.

16 Furly's journal 3, 8 February; *Mémoires et Lettres du Maréchal de Tessé* (Paris, 1806), vol. ii, pp. 213–16; Fuster y Menbrado 17 February; Miñana, p. 492.

17 Peterborough to Godolphin 9 April, BL Add. MSS 28,057, f. 91; Furly's journal, 20, 21, 26 February; Crowe to the Duke of Newcastle, HMC *Portland* MSS, vol. ii, pp. 191–2; Freind; Miñana, p. 494.

18 Hugill, pp. 200–2; Furly's journal, 16 February OS; Peterborough to the King 26 February, Öst. Kriegsarchiv, Afa 1705, MS 243, f. 208.

CHAPTER TWENTY

1 HMC *House of Lords* MSS NS, vol. vii, pp. 367, 448; BL Stowe MSS 471, f. 30 et seq.; Marlborough to Peterborough 5/16 February, *Marlborough's Dispatches*, vol. ii, p. 416; Hedges to Peterborough 7/18 February, SP 104/207; Wyndham to Lord Treasurer 21 February/4 March, BL Add. MSS 28,057 f. 53, Peterborough to same 26 May, f. 190.

2 Methuen to Hedges 22 March, BL Add. MSS 28,057, f. 77; *Mémoires du Maréchal de Berwick* (Paris, 1779), vol. i, p. 277; A. Baudrillart, *Philippe V et la Cour de France* (Paris, 1890), vol. i, p. 256; Peterborough to Leake 11 February OS, BL Add. MSS 5,442, f. 18; Peterborough to the King 13 March, printed in Russell, vol. i, p. 312 and referred to in Liechtenstein to Wratislaw 15 April, Öst. Staatsarchiv, Kriegsakten 249; Furly's journal 3, 5 March; Peterborough to Leake 10 March OS, BL Add. MSS 5,442, f. 24; Furly to Stanhope 10 March, Stanhope of Chevening MSS, O136/11; Crowe to Lord Treasurer 23 February, BL Add. MSS 28,057, f. 30, Peterborough to same 26 May, f. 190.

3 Boyer, vol. v, pp. 112–13; Peterborough to the Duke of Savoy, BL Add. MSS 28,057, f. 93; BL Add. MSS 5,438, f. 48v; HMC *House of Lords MSS NS*, vol. vii, p. 432; *Life of Leake*, vol. ii, pp. 5–7, 8.

4 Furly's journal 13, 14, 15, 16, 18 March; Orti y Mayor, 24 March; St Pierre to Lord Raby, BL Add. MSS 31,134, f. 298; Boyer, vol. v, p. 114; Cifuentes to Peterborough, BL Add. MSS 28,057, f. 97.

5 Peterborough to Leake, BL Add. MSS 5,442, f. 28; HMC *House of Lords MSS NS*, vol. vii, p. 427; Furly's journal 12, 16, 19 March; Peterborough to Lord Treasurer, BL Add. MSS 28,057, f. 91, Peterborough to Duke of Savoy, f. 93; *Marlborough-Godolphin Corr.*, vol. ii, p. 710.

6 'Royal Dragoon', p. 17; Furly's journal 21, 23 March, 1 April; Freind; BL Add. MSS 28,057, f. 91; Peterborough to Leake, BL Add. MSS 5,438, ff. 48v, 50; Miñana, p. 502.

7 *Life of Leake*, vol. i, p. 305; BL Add. MSS 5,438, f. 17; BL Add. MSS 28,057, f. 47; Burchett, p. 690; *Stephen Martin*, pp. 87–8.

8 BL Add. MSS 5,438, f. 24; BL Add. MSS 5,441, f. 106; Burchett, pp. 690, 692; *Life of Leake*, vol. i, p. 332, vol. ii, p. 2.

9 Stanhope to Hedges, SP 94/76 no. 7, no. 9; Methuen to Hedges, BL Add. MSS 28,057, f. 85; Stanhope to Peterborough 27 March, Chevening MSS O141/17; BL Add. MSS 9,115, f. 4v; HMC *House of Lords MSS NS*, vol. vii, pp. 430–1; BL Stowe MSS 471, f. 31.

10 BL Add. MSS 9,115, ff. 6–7; SP 94/76 no. 9; HMC *House of Lords MSS NS*, vol. vii, pp. 432–3; *Life of Leake*, vol. ii, pp. 10–11; Peterborough to the Lord Treasurer, BL Add. MSS 28,057, f. 150; BL Add. MSS 5,438, f. 29; Furly's journal 18 April.

11 BL Add. MSS 5,438, f. 29, 51v; N. Budiani to Lord Cutts 1 May OS, HMC *Frankland-Russell-Astley* MSS, pp. 191–2; HMC *House of Lords MSS NS*, vol. vii, pp. 435–6; BL Stowe MSS 471, ff. 31–2; *Life of Leake*, vol. ii, pp. 14–18.

12 Boyer, vol. v, pp. 113–15; Mahon, p. 180; *Mémoires de Tessé*, vol. ii, pp. 217–18, 221.

13 Boyer, vol. v, pp. 115–24; Targe, vol. iv, p. 381; Feliú de la Peña, vol. iii, pp. 559–60; Liechtenstein to Wratislaw 15 April, Öst. Staats. Kriegsakten 249.

14 Tessé to Chamillart, BL Add. MSS 9,776, ff. 199, 201v, 204; Feliú de la Peña, vol. iii, p. 562; *The Case of Colonel Burston*, pp. 12–14; 'Royal Dragoon', p. 17; *Memoirs of St Pierre*, p. 60; St Pierre to Lord Raby 22 May, BL Add. MSS 31,134, f. 314v; Boyer, vol. v, p. 125.

15 *Mémoires de Tessé*, vol. ii, p. 221; Boyer, vol. v, pp. 122–4, 24, 125.

16 San Felipe, p. 106; *Memoirs of St Pierre*, p. 60; BL Add. MSS 31,134, f. 314v; BL Add. MSS 9,776, f. 234; Boyer, vol. v, pp. 126–7; Peterborough to Leake, BL Add. MSS 5,438, f. 53; Feliú de la Peña, vol. iii, p.

566; *The Case of Colonel Burston*, pp. 13–14; Liechtenstein to Wratislaw (after the siege), Öst. Staats. Kriegsakten 249.

17 Boyer, vol. v, pp. 127–8; BL Add. MSS 9,115, f. 9; log of the *Fubbs*, Adm
51/377; log of the *Leopard*, Adm 52/210; *The Case of Colonel Burston*,
p. 14; BL Add. MSS 5,438, f. 54v; BL Add. MSS 28,057, f. 150; HMC
House of Lords MSS NS, vol. vii, p. 436; *Life of Leake*, vol. ii, pp.
19–22; HMC *Fourteenth Report, Hare* MSS, p. 209; BL Stowe MSS
471, f. 32.

18 *Life of Leake*, vol. ii, pp. 19–22, 23–4; Boyer, vol. v, pp. 128–9, 135;
Mémoires de Tessé, vol. ii, p. 222; 'Royal Dragoon', p. 18; log of the
Leopard, Adm 52/210; log of the *Fubbs*, Adm 51/377; HMC *Ormonde*
MSS NS, vol. viii, p. 233; log of the *Resolution*, Adm 52/269; log of the
Ranelagh, Adm 51/266; BL Stowe MSS 471, f. 32v; Burchett, p. 693.

CHAPTER TWENTY-ONE

1 BL Add. MSS 28,057, f. 150; Peterborough to Queen Anne 13 May,
Morrison, first series, vol. v, p. 143.

2 Boyer vol. v, pp. 128–9, 136–7; *Life of Leake*, vol. ii, p. 19; *Mémoires de
Tessé*, vol. ii, pp. 222–3; Stanhope to Hedges, SP 94/76 no. 15; St Pierre
to Lord Raby, BL Add. MSS 31,134, f. 315; HMC *Fourteenth Report,
Hare* MSS, p. 209; Burchett, p. 693; BL Stowe MSS 471, ff. 34–5; Furly's
journal, 1 May; 'Haddock Correspondence', *Camden Miscellany*, vol.
viii (1883), pp. 49–50; P. Methuen to Hedges 9 May, SP 89/19.

3 BL Add. MSS 9,776, f. 248; BL Stowe MSS 471, ff. 34–5; Stanhope to
Hedges, SP 94/76 no. 17; Boyer, vol. v, pp. 137–8; Burchett, p. 693;
Mémoires de Berwick, vol. i, p. 295.

4 *Mémoires de Berwick*, vol. i, pp. 280–94; Methuen to Galway, BL Add.
MSS 28,057, f. 131; Boyer, vol. v, p. 288; *An Account of the Earl of Galway's Conduct in Spain* (1711), pp. 42–4; 'The Comparison or Accounts
of both sides fairly stated' (1711), *Somers Tracts* (1965), p. 407.

5 SP 94/76 no. 15; Peterborough to the Queen 13 May, Morrison, first
series, vol. v, p. 143; Boyer, vol. v, pp. 116, 123; BL Stowe MSS 471, ff.
32v–3v; P. Methuen to J. Methuen 26 May, printed in *Marlborough's
Dispatches*, vol. ii, p. 571n.

6 P. Methuen to J. Methuen, *Marlborough's Dispatches*, vol. ii, p. 571n;
Peterborough to Leake 2 May, BL Add. MSS 5,438, f. 54v; Feliú de la
Peña, vol. iii, p. 566; 'Royal Dragoon', p. 17; St Pierre to Lord Raby 22
May, BL Add. MSS 31,134, ff. 314v–15; BL Add. MSS 28,057, f. 154;
Morrison, first series, vol. v, pp. 143–4; SP 94/76 no. 15; *Stephen
Martin*, pp. 94–5; log of the *Devonshire*, Adm 51/242; Liechtenstein to
Wratislaw 14 May, Öst. Staats. Kriegsakten 249.

7 SP 94/76 nos. 17, 20, 21, 24; *Life of Leake*, vol. ii, pp. 29, 44–5; Furly's journal 10 May; P. Methuen to Hedges 17 May, SP 89/19; P. Methuen to J. Methuen 26 May, Russell, vol. ii, appendix pp. 367–70; Peterborough to Hedges 6 September, SP 94/76.

8 St Pierre to Lord Raby 22 May, BL Add. MSS 31,134, f. 313; *Life of Leake*, vol. ii, p. 45; Peterborough to Hedges, SP 94/76 no. 27, the King to Peterborough 26 May, no. 22, Peterborough to the King 26 May, no. 23, Stanhope to Hedges 31 May, no. 28; *Col. Burston*, p. 15; Furly's journal 18 May; P. Methuen to J. Methuen 26 May, Russell, vol. ii, appendix p. 369; HMC *House of Lords* MSS NS, vol. vii, pp. 467–8, 469–70; BL Stowe MSS 471, f. 35.

9 HMC *House of Lords* MSS NS, vol. vii, p. 469; Peterborough to Lord Treasurer 29 May, Morrison, first series, vol. v, p. 144; P. Methuen to J. Methuen, Russell, vol. ii, appendix p. 369; Peterborough to Lord Treasurer 12 and 26 May, BL Add. MSS 28,057, ff. 154, 190; Furly's journal 18 May; Peterborough to Lord Halifax, BL Add. MSS 7,121, f. 41.

10 'Royal Dragoon' p. 18; *Life of Leake*, vol. ii, p. 48; Furly's journal 22 May, 24 May; BL Stowe MSS 471, f. 35v; Peterborough to Hedges 6/17 June, 3 September, SP 94/76; list of troops, 5 June, SP 94/76 no. 31; HMC *House of Lords* MSS NS, vol. vii, p. 512.

11 Stanhope to Peterborough 14 June, no. 35, Peterborough to Hedges 17 June, SP 94/76; Peterborough to Stanhope, Russell, vol. ii, appendix pp. 343–4; HMC *House of Lords* MSS NS, vol. vii, Peterborough to the King 1 July, p. 484, depositions of Colonel Pitt and Arent Furly, pp. 512–14.

12 HMC *House of Lords* MSS NS, vol. vii, Stanhope to Peterborough 11 June, pp. 476–7, the King to Peterborough 7 June p. 486, 9 June p. 471, 11 June p. 486, Peterborough to the King 13 June pp. 472–4.

13 HMC *House of Lords* MSS NS, vol. vii, p. 454, evidence of Colonel Andrew Bisset pp. 508–9; Furly's journal 3 June; BL Add. MSS 5,441, ff. 136, 138; BL Stowe MSS 471, ff. 36v–7; Peterborough to Godolphin 23 June, BL Add. MSS 28,057, ff. 247, 251.

14 HMC *House of Lords* MSS NS, vol. vii, pp. 455, 482, 483, 487; Furly's journal 8 June; Stanhope to Peterborough, Mahon, appendix p. xvii.

15 W. Coxe, ed., *Memoirs of Horatio Lord Walpole* (1802), pp. 5–6; Targe p. 396; Feliú de la Peña, vol. iii, p. 577; Stanhope to Peterborough 29 June, HMC *House of Lords* MSS NS, vol. vii, pp. 478–9, the King to Peterborough pp. 487–8; Conde de Assumar to Peterborough 29 June, BL Add. MSS 28,057, f. 264.

16 Stanhope to Peterborough 1 July, Mahon, appendix pp. xvii–ix; the King to Peterborough 2 July, BL Add. MSS 28,057, f. 278, 3 July f. 276, Peterborough to the King 5 July, f. 282, the King to Peterborough 7 July, f. 288; Liechtenstein to Wratislaw 6 July, Öst. Staats. Kriegsakten 249.

17 Stanhope to Godolphin 10 July, Mahon, appendix pp. xxii–iii; Stanhope to Godolphin 3 July, BL Add. MSS 9,115, f. 143; Furly to Shaftesbury 4 September, PRO 30/24/45; Galway's Answers, BL Add. MSS 15,916, f. 21

1 Furly's journal 25 June; Freind p. 104; Peterborough to the King, BL Add. MSS 28,057, f. 284, Galway to Methuen 21 June, f. 239, Galway to Godolphin 27 June, f. 258; *Mémoires de Berwick*, vol. i, pp. 298–311; *Galway's Conduct in Spain*, p. 48.

2 Orti y Mayor 29 June; Furly's journal 25, 26 June; BL Add. MSS 28,058, f. 23; Peterborough to Hedges 3 September, SP 94/76; BL Add. MSS 9,115, f. 10v; Galway to Leake 3 July, BL Add. MSS 5,441, f. 150.

3 Hedges to Peterborough 23 May OS, SP 104/207; Peterborough to Stanhope 8 July, Russell, vol. ii, appendix pp. 353–5; Peterborough to Godolphin 11 January, Morrison, first series, vol. v, p. 141; Stanhope to Peterborough 8 July, Mahon, appendix p. xxii; *Marlborough-Godolphin Corr.*, 13 June OS, pp. 583–4, 27 June/8 July p. 602; Luttrell, vol. vi, p. 61.

4 *Life of Leake*, vol. ii, pp. 44, 51, 53–4, 84; HMC *House of Lords* MSS NS, vol. vii, pp. 511–12; BL Add. MSS 5,438, Peterborough to Leake 19 June f. 55v, Leake to Peterborough 5 June f. 34v, Peterborough to Leake 20 June f. 57; Peterborough to Leake, BL Add. MSS 5,441, ff. 141, 195; Fuster y Menbrado 12 June; Peterborough to Hedges 14 July, SP 94/76; *Stephen Martin*, p. 95; Peterborough to Stanhope 20 June, Russell, vol. ii, appendix p. 347; Furly's journal 10 June.

5 BL Add. MSS 5,438, Leake to Peterborough 17 June OS f. 36, Leake to Peterborough 21 June f. 40v, Peterborough to Leake 26 July f. 63, Leake to Peterborough 22 July ff. 81, 92; *Stephen Martin*, pp. 95–7; BL Add. MSS 5,441, ff. 152, 148; *Life of Leake*, vol. ii, pp. 69, 78, 82–3; BL Add. MSS 5,442, ff. 136, 142, 144, 146; Furly's journal 2 July; log of the *Devonshire*, Adm 51/242; Burchett p. 695.

6 *Life of Leake*, vol. ii, p. 48; Peterborough to Leake 26 June, BL Add. MSS 5,438, f. 57v, Leake to Jennings 26 June f. 41v, Peterborough to Leake 13 July ff. 60–3; HMC *Fifth Report, Cholmondeley* MSS, p. 349; Peterborough to Hedges 14 July, SP 94/76; Stanhope to Peterborough 19 July, BL Add. MSS 5,441, f. 172.

7 Instructions to Peterborough 2/13 April, HMC *House of Lords* MSS NS, vol. vii, p. 367; Leake to Peterborough 27 May, BL Add. MSS 5,438, ff. 32v, 33v, Peterborough to Leake 9 June f. 55v; *Life of Leake*, vol. ii, p. 51; King to Peterborough 14 June, BL Add. MSS 5,441, ff. 136,

138; Stanhope to Peterborough 14 June, SP 94/76 no. 35, Peterborough to Hedges 17 June.

8   Peterborough to Hedges 17 June SP 94/76; Furly to Shaftesbury 20 June OS, PRO 30/24/45; Peterborough to the King, HMC *House of Lords* MSS NS, vol. vii, pp. 481–2; Peterborough to Leake 26 June, BL Add. MSS 5,441, f. 146; *Marlborough-Godolphin Corr.*, vol. i, p. 547; Hedges to Peterborough 19 June, BL Add. MSS 5,442, ff. 48, 50; extract of Hedges's letter, HMC *House of Lords* MSS, vol. vii, p. 369, and SP 94/76 no. 36.

9   Stanhope to Hedges 24 July, Mahon, appendix pp. xxiv–v; 'The Comparison', *Somers Tracts*, p. 408; *Mémoires de Berwick*, vol. i, p. 311; Stanhope to Peterborough 17 July, BL Add. MSS 5,441, f. 174, 19 July f. 172, 20 July f. 176, the King to Peterborough 20 July f. 176; Stanhope to Galway 20 July, Stanhope of Chevening MSS O141/17; Peterborough to Stanhope printed in Russell, vol. ii, pp. 357–8; *Peterborough's Letters to Stanhope*, pp. 26, 27–8; BL Add. MSS 9,115, ff. 10v–11; Peterborough to Hedges 3 September, SP 94/76.

10 Peterborough to Wyndham 17 July, HMC *House of Lords* MSS NS, vol. vii, p. 499, Wyndham to Peterborough pp. 497, 498, evidence of officers pp. 508–11, Stanhope to Peterborough 29 July pp. 489–90; Furly's journal 13, 15, 16 July; Miñana p. 514; Peterborough to Hedges 3 September, SP 94/76; St Pierre to Raby 3 July OS, BL Add. MSS 31,134, f. 328; Fuster y Menbrado 20 July; *Peterborough's Letters to Stanhope*, 20 July pp. 26, 27–8, 24 July pp. 28–30; Russell, vol. ii, appendix p. 359.

11 Peterborough to Stanhope 1, 16 August, Russell, vol. ii, appendix pp. 360–2; Furly's journal 17–18, 21, 24, 27 July; *Mémoires de Berwick*, vol. i, pp. 324–5; Peterborough to Hedges 3 September, Stanhope to Hedges 10 August, SP 94/76; BL Add. MSS 9,115, f. 11v.

12 *Mémoires de Berwick*, vol. i, pp. 311–12, 314–15; Stanhope to Peterborough 31 July, HMC *House of Lords* MSS NS, vol. vii, p. 494; Furly to Shaftesbury 4 September, PRO 30/24/45; Stanhope to Hedges 10 August, SP 94/76; Galway's Answers, BL Add. MSS 15,916, f. 21; Stanhope to Godolphin 27 July, Mahon, appendix p. xxvii; Peterborough to Hedges 3 September, SP 94/76.

13 Stanhope to Hedges 10 August, SP 94/76 and Mahon, appendix pp. xxviii–x; Peterborough to Hedges 3 September, SP 94/76; Furly's journal 29 July; Peterborough to Wassenaer 25 August, BL Add. MSS 5,438, f. 65v; Pepper's account, BL Add. MSS 9,115, f. 12; Furly to Shaftesbury 4 September, PRO 30/24/45.

14 Leake to Peterborough 22 July, BL Add. MSS 5,438, f. 81; Peterborough to Hedges 3 September, SP 94/76; *Mémoires de Berwick*, vol. i, p. 315; Freind pp. 137–9; Pepper's account, BL Add. MSS 9,115, f. 12v; St Pierre to Raby 28 September, BL Add. MSS 31,134, f. 343.

15 Galway to Methuen 10/21 June, BL Add. MSS 28,057, f. 243, King Charles to Godolphin 24 July f. 307; (Galway's Narrative, Cobbett, *Parliamentary History*, vol. vi, p. 945); Stanhope to Godolphin 24 July, Mahon, appendix pp. xxvi–vii; Godolphin to Marlborough, W. Coxe, *Memoirs of the Duke of Marlborough* (1847–8), vol. i, p. 470; Hedges to Peterborough 23 July, HMC *House of Lords* MSS NS, vol. vii, p. 370; Peterborough to Hedges 3 September, SP 94/76; Freind p. 104; Peterborough to Stanhope 1 August, Russell, vol. ii, p. 361; Furly to Shaftesbury 20 June OS, PRO 30/24/45.

CHAPTER TWENTY-THREE

1 Furly's journal 27 July, 2 August; Freind pp. 141–4; Peterborough to Hedges 3 September, SP 94/76; Pepper's account, BL Add. MSS 9,115, ff. 12, 13, 13v; Furly to Shaftesbury 4 September, PRO 30/24/45; Peterborough to Stanhope 16 August, Russell, vol. ii, pp. 362–3, 18 August, pp. 363–4, 30 August, p. 366; *Peterborough's Letters to Stanhope* pp. 34–5, 37; *Mémoires de Berwick*, vol. i, pp. 324–5.

2 Peterborough to Stanhope 16 August, Russell, vol. ii, pp. 362–3; Furly's journal 2, 3 August; *Mémoires de Berwick*, vol. i, pp. 323, 325; Pepper's account, BL Add. MSS 9,115, f. 13; Stanhope to Hedges 22 August, SP 94/76.

3 *Account of Galway's Conduct in Spain*, p. 73; Furly's journal 5–16 August; Peterborough to Stanhope 20 July, Russell, vol. ii, p. 358, 24 July p. 359; Peterborough to Leake 25 August, BL Add. MSS 5,438, f. 65, and to Wassenaer f. 65v, Leake to Prince George's secretary 19 August, f. 89; Fuster y Menbrado 27 August; Peterborough to Hedges 3 September, SP 94/76; Miñana p. 522.

4 Peterborough to Stanhope 30 August, Russell, vol. ii, p. 365; BL Stowe MSS 471, f. 46; Marlborough to Godolphin 16 August, 3 September, *Marlborough-Godolphin Corr.*, vol. i, pp. 644, 657; Wratislaw to Marlborough 25 August, BL Add. MSS 9,115, f. 160; Peterborough to Hedges 3 September, SP 94/76.

5 BL Stowe MSS 471, ff. 36v, 37, 46; Peterborough to Hedges 17 June, BL Add. MSS 61,164, f. 64, copy in SP 94/76; Godolphin to Marlborough 26 August, *Marlborough-Godolphin Corr.*, vol. i, p. 651, 3 September, p. 657, 2/13 September, p. 663, Marlborough to his duchess p. 674.

6 BL Add. MSS 28,058, f. 25; Furly's evidence, HMC *House of Lords* MSS NS, vol. vii, p. 511; Furly's journal 26, 29, 30 August, 1 September; Leake to Peterborough 26 August, BL Add. MSS 5,438, f. 90v, Leake to Stanhope 28 August, f. 91, council of war 1 September, f. 69; Fuster y Menbrado 8 September; BL Add. MSS 5,442, ff. 56, 64, 171, 175;

Luttrell, vol. vi, pp. 91–2; log of the *Ranelagh*, Adm 51/266; Peterborough to Stanhope 10 September, *Peterborough's Letters to Stanhope*, pp. 41–3; Leake's letter 26 September, HMC *Eighth Report, Marlborough* MSS p. 17.

7 Log of the *Ranelagh*, Adm 51/266; log of the *Resolution*, Adm 52/269; Peterborough to Marlborough 7 February 1706/7, BL Add. MSS 61,164, f. 86; Leake to Prince George's secretary 4 September, BL Add. MSS 5,438, f. 95; Peterborough to Stanhope 7 September, *Peterborough's Letters to Stanhope*, pp. 40–1; Gallas's Memorial 31 August, HMC *House of Lords* MSS NS, vol. vii, pp. 450–5; Peterborough to Hedges 3 September, SP 94/76; Furly's journal 6, 11, 12, 18 September; Freind p. 160; Godolphin to Marlborough 30 September/11 October, Coxe, vol. i, p. 471.

8 *Mémoires de Berwick*, vol. i, p. 325 et seq.; BL Add. MSS 15,916, f. 21; 'The Comparison', *Somers Tracts* p. 409; *Account of Galway's Conduct*, p. 73; Stanhope to Hedges 5 October, Mahon, appendix p. xxxiii.

9 Paul Methuen to Hedges 2 October, SP 89/19; Chetwynd to Hedges 9 October, SP 92/27 no. 382, 22 October no. 386, 28 October no. 389, 5 November no. 393; Godolphin to Marlborough 30 September OS, *Marlborough-Godolphin Corr.*, vol. ii, p. 697, 13 October p. 710; Furly's journal 4, 5, 6, 8, 19, 21, 22, 27 October, 5 November; Halifax to Somers 3 October, Philip Yorke, 2nd Earl of Hardwicke, ed., *Miscellaneous State Papers, from 1501 to 1726* (1778), vol. ii, p. 472; Peterborough to Godolphin 6 November, BL Add. MSS 28,057, f. 324; Peterborough to Hedges 10 November, *Impartial Inquiry* pp. 210–18; Peterborough to Colonel Southwell 10 November, BL Add. MSS 61,515, f. 90; Peterborough to Marlborough 10 November, BL Add. MSS 61,164, f. 78.

10 Walsh to Pope 9 September, G. Sherburn, ed., *The Correspondence of Alexander Pope* (Oxford, 1956), vol. i, pp. 21–2; Godolphin to Marlborough 22 October, *Marlborough-Godolphin Corr.*, vol. ii, p. 721; Benjamin Furly to Shaftesbury 2 November, PRO 30/24/45; R. Palmer to Lord Fermanagh 19 November, HMC *Seventh Report, Verney* MSS, p. 506; Luttrell vol. vi, p. 97; Peterborough to Stanhope 10 September, *Peterborough's Letters to Stanhope*, p. 43, no date p. 47; Erasmus Lewis to Robert Harley 31 October, HMC *Portland* MSS, vol. iv, p. 343; Boyer, vol. v, appendix pp. 82 et seq.; Peterborough to Godolphin 6 November, BL Add. MSS 28,057, f. 324.

11 Peterborough to Stanhope 10 January, *Peterborough's Letters to Stanhope*, p. 49, 6 January p. 48, no date p. 47; *CTB* 1706–7 pp. 131, 132; *Impartial Inquiry*, appendix iii, p. 46; Furly's journal 4, 5, 6 November, 5, 16, 19 December.

12 Sunderland to Peterborough 10, 23 December, SP 104/208; Lady Peterborough to her husband 21 March and 22 April OS, NRAS 4155; J.

Addison to G. Stepney 17 December, W. Graham, ed., *Letters of Joseph Addison* (1941), p. 66.

CHAPTER TWENTY-FOUR

1 Peterborough to Stanhope 6 and 10 January, *Peterborough's Letters to Stanhope*, pp. 48–9; *Account of Galway's Conduct in Spain*, pp. 75, 76–8; Stanhope to Rivers 16 January, HMC *Bath Longleat* MSS, vol. i, p. 152; Furly's journal 4 January; 'Questions to the Earl of Peterborow,' BL Add. MSS 22,200; Stanhope to Hedges 15 January, Mahon, appendix, p. xliv; 'Earl of Galway's Answer,' 18 January 1710 OS, BL Add. MSS 15,916, f. 21.

2 Sunderland to Galway 23 December, SP 89/19; Stanhope to Lord Treasurer 8 March and 24 October 1706, Mahon, appendix, pp. xlvi–vii, xxxix; Sunderland to Rivers 23 December, HMC *Bath Longleat* MSS, vol. i, p. 141, Rivers to Sunderland 13 January, p. 151, Rivers to Lord Treasurer January, p. 159; Lady Peterborough to Lord Peterborough n. d., NRAS 4155; Peterborough to Rivers 1 February OS, BL Add. MSS 70,249, f. g; Peterborough to Sunderland 27 February, BL Add. MSS 61,514, f. 27 et seq.; Godolphin to Marlborough 10 April OS, *Marlborough-Godolphin Corr.*, p. 749; 'Galway's Answer,' BL Add. MSS 15,916; Furly's journal 8 January OS; Shovell to Byng 31 January OS, *Byng Papers*, vol. i, p. 144.

3 Stanhope to Sunderland 23 February, Mahon, appendix, p. xlvi; Peterborough to Stanhope 10 March, *Peterborough's Letters to Stanhope*, p. 50; orders to Peterborough from King Charles, BL Add. MSS 28,057, ff. 330, 332, translation in Stanhope of Chevening MSS O137/22, no. 4; Sunderland to Peterborough 14 January OS, SP 104/208, and HMC *House of Lords* MSS NS, vol. vii, pp. 370–1; Peterborough to Stanhope 25 March, Stanhope of Chevening MSS O137/11.

4 Peterborough to Sunderland 6 April, BL Add. MSS 61,514, f. 43; Furly's journal 19–21 March OS; Burchett, pp. 691–2; Boyer, vol. vi, pp. 220–1; Lady Peterborough to Lord Peterborough (18) and 22 April OS, NRAS 4155; Peterborough to Stanhope 14 April, Stanhope of Chevening MSS O137/11; Marshal Tessé to Prince Antoine de Monaco 17 April, *Lettres du Maréchal de Tessé au Prince Antoine de Monaco* (Paris, 1917), p. 5.

5 Peterborough to Stanhope 14 April, 24 May, Stanhope of Chevening MSS O137/11; Peterborough to Portuguese Ambassador 21 April, Freind, pp. 182–7; Peterborough to King Charles 27 April, Lamberty, vol. iv, p. 576; Godolphin to Marlborough 3 May OS, *Marlborough-Godolphin Corr.*, p. 766. Account of Almanza based on Churchill,

Marlborough, vol. iii, pp. 216–22; more detail is given in Hugill, pp. 250–62.

6 Chetwynd to Sunderland 4 May, printed in Russell, vol. ii, pp. 146–7; Marlborough to Godolphin 19 and 25 May, *Marlborough-Godolphin Corr.*, pp. 771, 792; Chetwynd to Marlborough 24 May, printed in Churchill, *Marlborough*, vol. iii, p. 231; Peterborough to Marlborough (20 May), BL Add. MSS 61,164, f. 114; Peterborough to Harley 8 May, BL Add. MSS 70,249, no. 45; Lady Peterborough to Lord Peterborough 29 April OS, NRAS 4155; Peterborough to Stanhope 24 May, Stanhope of Chevening MSS O137/11; *CTB* 1706–7, p. 282; Sunderland to Peterborough 15 April OS, Sunderland to Chetwynd 15 April OS, SP 104/208; Luttrell, vol. vi, p. 181; Peterborough to Sunderland n. d. and 20 May, BL Add. MSS 61,514, ff. 49, 53.

7 Sir George MacMunn, *Prince Eugene* (1953), pp. 168–9; Peterborough to Marlborough 7 June, BL Add. MSS 61,164, f. 118; Marlborough to Peterborough 15 May, *Marlborough's Dispatches*, vol. iii, p. 365.

8 Lord Raby to the Earl of Manchester 26 July, Christian Cole, *Memoirs of Affairs of State* (1733), p. 463; Marlborough to the Duchess of Marlborough 27 June, *Marlborough-Godolphin Corr.*, pp. 821–2, Godolphin to Marlborough 10/21 July, p. 811; Peterborough to Marlborough 22 July, BL Add. MSS 61,164, f. 124; Wratislaw to Marlborough 2 July, printed in Russell, vol. ii, pp. 148–9, and Marlborough to Count Maffey 19 May, p. 154; Peterborough to Stanhope 18 July, *Peterborough's Letters to Stanhope*, p. 50.

CHAPTER TWENTY-FIVE

1 Lady Peterborough to her husband (18 April?), NRAS 4155; Peterborough to Marlborough 22 July, BL Add. MSS 61,164, f. 24; Besenval's intercepted letter is in Coxe, vol. ii, p. 80 and also printed in Russell, vol. ii, pp. 150–1.

2 Queen of Bohemia to Lady Mordaunt 20/30 October 1659, *LBJM*, no. 59, p. 35; Robethon to Cardonnel 2 August, Coxe, vol. ii, p. 124, Godolphin to Marlborough 4/15 and 5/16 August, p. 126; Johnston to Sir W. T., 30 October OS, HMC *Downshire Papers*, vol. i, p. 853.

3 Marlborough to Peterborough 5 August, *Marlborough's Dispatches*, vol. iii, p. 501; Godolphin to Marlborough 10/21 July, *Marlborough-Godolphin Corr.*, p. 811, Marlborough to his duchess 14/25 August, p. 881.

4 Marlborough to his duchess 7/18 August, *Marlborough-Godolphin Corr.*, p. 876, Marlborough to Godolphin 18 August, p. 875, 9/20 August, p. 877, Marlborough to his duchess 4/15 September, p. 905;

Peterborough's paper of charges and answers, BL Add. MSS 61,110, f. 77.

5 Peterborough to Sunderland 16 August, BL Add. MSS 61,514, f. 55; Heinsius to Marlborough 24 August, *Marlborough-Heinsius Corr.*, p. 338; Marlborough to Peterborough 15 September, *Marlborough's Dispatches*, vol. iii, p. 560; Godolphin to Harley 14 August OS, HMC *Bath Longleat* MSS, vol. i, p. 178; Peterborough to Harley 23 August OS, BL Add. MSS 61,514, f. 65.

6 Peterborough to Marlborough 22 July, BL Add. MSS 61,164, f. 124; Peterborough to Harley 22 August, BL Add. MSS 61,514, f. 59; Godolphin to Harley 14 and 21 August, HMC *Bath Longleat* MSS, vol. i, p. 178.

7 Harley to Peterborough 25 August OS, HMC *House of Lords* MSS NS, vol. vii, p. 396, Sunderland to Peterborough 28 September, p. 398, 'Answers to Heads,' pp. 400–6; Marlborough to Godolphin 12 September, printed in Russell, vol. ii, p. 159; Addison to the Earl of Manchester 29 August, *Addison's Letters*, p. 75; Peterborough to Marlborough August, BL Add. MSS 61,110, f. 77; Peterborough to Sunderland 16 September, BL Add. MSS 61,514, f. 101.

8 *LJ* vol. xviii, p. 333; James Johnston to Sir W. T. 30 October, HMC *Downshire Papers*, vol. i, p. 853; HMC *House of Lords* MSS NS, vol. vii, p. 357; E. Lewis to Harley 25 September, HMC *Portland* MSS, vol. iv, p. 450; account books of Arent Furly, Stanhope of Chevening MSS O133/1.

9 Luttrell, vol. vi, p. 237.

10 *LJ* vol. xviii, p. 362; Vernon to Shrewsbury 16 December, *Vernon Corr.*, vol. iii, p. 297; Boyer, vol. vi, p. 296.

11 HMC *House of Lords* MSS NS, vol. vii, pp. 406–7; Vernon to Shrewsbury 18 December, *Vernon Corr.*, vol. iii, p. 298; Lord Raby to Leibnitz 17 January, printed in J. M. Kemble, *State Papers and Correspondence* (1857), p. 464; Sir John Percival to Dr. Percival 27 December, HMC *Egmont* MSS, vol. ii, p. 221; Addison to Manchester 23 December, *Addison's Letters*, p. 84.

12 Peterborough to Sunderland 30 December, BL Add. MSS 61,514, f. 202; Vernon to Shrewsbury 13 January, *Vernon Corr.*, vol. iii, p. 303 and 17 January, p. 312 et seq.; Addison to Manchester 16/27 January, *Addison's Letters*, p. 86; Edwin to Manchester 6 February, printed in William Montagu, Duke of Manchester, *Court and Society from Elizabeth to Anne* (1864), vol. ii, p. 277; *Nicolson Diaries*, pp. 441–2, 443–4.

13 Vernon to Shrewsbury 29 January, *Vernon Corr.*, vol. iii, p. 328, 31 January, p. 333, 5 February, p. 339; Boyer, vol. vi, p. 313; H. T. Dickinson, *Bolingbroke* (1970), p. 56; *Nicolson Diaries*, pp. 448–51, 453;

Swift to Archbishop King 5 February, *Swift Corr.*, vol. i, p. 68; Shaftesbury to B. Furly 15 January, Forster, *Letters of Locke et al.*, p. 189.

CHAPTER TWENTY-SIX

1 *CTP* 1708–14, p. 94, Peterborough to the Lord Treasurer c. 26 March 1709, p. 106; *CTB* 1709, p. 132.
2 Peterborough to the Elector of Hanover 3 April 1708, BL Stowe MSS 223, f. 144, Elector to Peterborough, f. 149 (translations in J. Macpherson, *Original Papers* (1775), vol. ii, p. 110); Marlborough to Godolphin 24 May, enclosing a letter from Robethon, *Marlborough-Godolphin Corr.*, pp. 980–1.
3 Godolphin to Marlborough 30 July, *Marlborough-Godolphin Corr.*, p. 1056 and note; Luttrell, vol. vi, p. 333; newsletter 26 August, HMC *Portland* MSS, vol. iv, p. 503.
4 MS copy of Peterborough to his brother 10 August 1708, NRAS 4155; Lord Mordaunt to Marlborough 9 June and 4 July 1707, 12 January 1708, BL Add. MSS 61,292, ff. 22, 24, 26; Godolphin to Marlborough 13 June 1706, Marlborough to Godolphin 27 June/8 July 1706, *Marlborough-Godolphin Corr.*, pp. 583, 602; Parish Register of St Mary's Bishophill Senior, York, BL Add. MSS 29,764, f. 39.
5 *CTB* 1702, pp. 190, 351; Vernon to Shrewsbury 15 January 1707/1708, *Vernon Corr.*, vol. iii, p. 307; Peterborough to his wife 19 September 1708, NRAS 4155.
6 Earl of Mar to Lord Grange 13 January, HMC *Mar and Kellie* MSS, vol. i, p. 479; *CTP* 1708–14, pp. 106, 109; *CTB* 1709, pp. 128, 130, 131, 132.
7 Boyer, vol. viii, p. 384; Turvey Parish Register quoted in W. M. Harvey, *History and Antiquity of the Hundred of Willey, Beds* (1872–8), p. 186 et seq.; Lady Seafield to Lord Deskford 11 May 1708, J. Grant, ed., *Correspondence of James 1st Earl of Seafield*, Scottish History Society (Edinburgh, 1912), p. 475; Peterborough to Harley (rec. 1 June), BL Add. MSS 70,249; Duchess of Marlborough's note on a letter from Lady Peterborough, BL Add. MSS 61,458, f. 197; Lady Peterborough to the Earl of Shaftesbury 6 September 1705, PRO 30/24/21, no. 233; Lord Shaftesbury to Lady Peterborough October 1705, printed in B. Rand, ed., *The Life and Unpublished Letters of Anthony, Earl of Shaftesbury* (1900), p. 341.
8 Peterborough to Marlborough 12/23 September, BL Add. MSS 61,164, f. 139; Dalton, *Army List*, vol. vi, p. 98; Marlborough to Godolphin 7 October NS, *Marlborough-Godolphin Corr.*, p. 1393; Luttrell, vol. vi, p. 510.

9 HMC *House of Lords* MSS NS, vol. viii, pp. 348–51; Boyer, vol. ix, p. 406; Luttrell, vol. vi, p. 549; Harvey, p. 186 et seq.
10 Boyer, vol. ix, p. 413; Harvey, p. 186 et seq.
11 *VCH Bedfordshire*, vol. iii, pp. 55, 96; Luttrell, vol. vi, p. 618; Mr Maynwaring to Duchess of Marlborough, Lord John Russell, ed., *The Private Correspondence of Sarah, Duchess of Marlborough* (1838), vol. i, p. 362; J. Cartwright, ed., *The Wentworth Papers 1705–39* (1883), pp. 137, 138; HMC *Tenth Report, Bagot* MSS, p. 342; Hoffmann's despatch – July, quoted in Churchill, *Marlborough*, vol. iv, p. 237.
12 HMC *Bath Longleat* MSS, vol. i, p. 199; Mr Maynwaring to Duchess of Marlborough, *Private Corr.*, vol. i, p. 390; *Wentworth Papers*, pp. 138, 154; J. Swift, *Journal to Stella*, ed. H. Williams (Oxford, 1948), vol. i, p. 59; Hardwicke, *State Papers*, vol. ii, p. 487; R. Molesworth to Hon. Mrs Molesworth 6 November, HMC *Various Collections, Clements* MSS, p. 248.
13 Instructions to Peterborough 6 December 1711 (1710), SP 92/29; Symcox, pp. 157–9.
14 St John to Drummond 1 December 1710, G. Parke, ed., *The Letters and Correspondence of Henry St John, Lord Viscount Bolingbroke* (1798), vol. i, p. 33, 20 December, p. 49; St John to Peterborough 25 December, SP 104/40; NRO MSS Y2 1464, 1468; *Journal to Stella*, pp. 140, 151.
15 *Journal to Stella*, p. 155; Galway's answers, BL Add. MSS 15,916, f. 21; questions to Peterborough and his answers, BL Add. MSS 27,200; Peterborough's MS notes of answers, NRAS 4155; *Nicolson Diaries*, p. 529–30, 531, 532, 533; Cowper, *Diary*, p. 52; Boyer, vol. ix, pp. 288, 289, 290, 292; St John to Palmes 9 January, SP 104/40; Cobbett, *Parliamentary History*, vol. vi, pp. 936–82; *The Rt. Hon. the Lord Keeper's Speech to the Rt. Hon. the Earl of Peterborough 12 January 1710/11* (Edinburgh 1710/11); for the Battle of Brihuega, see Churchill, *Marlborough*, vol. iv, pp. 294–5, Hugill, pp. 326–30.

CHAPTER TWENTY-SEVEN

1 St John to Palmes 12 January, SP 104/40; Simon Clement's Journal, BL Egerton MSS 2,167.
2 Peterborough to (St John or Harley) 3 February NS 1711, NRAS 4155.
3 Clement's Journal, BL Egerton MSS 2,167; Peterborough to Harley 15 February NS 1710/11, BL Add. MSS 70,249; Peterborough to Lord Townshend 19 February, BL Add. MSS 38,501 f. 248; Cockburne to Warre 3/14 March, SP 92/27; Boyer, vol. ix, p. 120.
4 St John to Peterborough 6 February, St John to Palmes 13 March, SP

104/40; Palmes to Walpole 7 March, BL Add. MSS 38,501 f. 271; Cockburne to Warre 14/25 April, SP 92/27; Peterborough to Heinsius 6 April, Archief Heinsius, Rijksarchief, The Hague, no. 1620 (2).

5 Peterborough to Harley 8 April, 8 May OS, BL Add. MSS 70,249; St John to Peterborough 24 April OS, 8 May, SP 104/40; memorial of Prince Eugène to the Duke of Marlborough, translation in BL Add. MSS 37,358, f. 243, St John to Peterborough 22 May OS, f. 247; St John to Marlborough 15 May OS, *Bolingbroke Corr.*, vol. i, p. 209.

6 Lamberty, vol. vi, pp. 637–40, 642; Wratislaw to Charles III 22 April 1711, printed in A. von Arneth, *Eigenhändige Correspondenz des Königs Karl III von Spanien* (Vienna, 1856), p. 148; Wratislaw to Peterborough 21 April, Empress Dowager to Peterborough 25 April, SP 92/29.

7 Chetwynd to Lord Raby 3 July, SP 92/27 no. 460; Symcox, p. 162; Lamberty, vol. iv, p. 642; Chetwynd to Dartmouth 9/20 May, SP 92/28; Peterborough to Dartmouth 8 May, SP 92/29.

8 St John to Lord Raby 18 May OS, *Bolingbroke Corr.*, vol.i, p. 214, St John to Drummond 27 April OS, p. 170; Dartmouth to Peterborough 10 April OS, FO 90/37; Peterborough to Dartmouth 14 May, SP 92/29; St John to Peterborough 29 May OS, SP 104/40.

9 Wratislaw to Charles 22 April, Charles to Wratislaw 25 April, 27 May and 31 July, printed in von Arneth, pp. 148–9, 152, 157–63, 202; Lord Raby to Harley 5 May, HMC *Portland* MSS vol. ix, p. 292; Lord Raby to St John 26 May, (BL Add. MSS 31,135) printed in H. N. Fieldhouse, 'St John and Savoy,' appendix iii, *EHR*, vol. l (1935), pp. 278–84; St John to Marlborough, *Bolingbroke Corr.*, vol. i, p. 202.

10 Peterborough to Dartmouth 14 May, SP 92/29; Chetwynd to Lord Raby 23 May, SP 92/27, no. 450, 3 July, no. 460; Lamberty, vol. vi, p. 642; Marlborough to Heinsius 28 May, *Marlborough-Heinsius Corr.*, p. 546, no. 953; *CTB* 1711, p. 85; Bridges's memorial 14 August 1711, SP 92/29; Dartmouth to Peterborough 18 May, FO 90/37. The bills were presumably accepted although a memorial concerning them appeared as late as 10 October and referred to a letter from the Savoyard envoy.

11 St John to Whitworth 29 May OS, BL Add. MSS 37,358, f. 239, St John to Peterborough 22 May OS, f. 247, Peterborough's memorial, f. 249; Chetwynd to Lord Raby 3 July, SP 92/27, no. 460; Peterborough to Swift 21 June NS, *Swift Corr.*, vol. i, p. 235; Lamberty, vol. vi, p. 645.

12 Boyer, vol. x, pp. 89, 216; Swift, *Journal to Stella*, vol. i, pp. 297, 306; 'Additional Instructions to the Earl of Peterborow,' FO 90/37 f. 78; Swift to Archbishop King 12 July, *Swift Corr.*, vol. i, p. 237.

13 J. Bowack, *Antiquities of Middlesex* (1705–6), p. 37 (quoted in Feret, vol. i, p. 145); Swift, *Journal to Stella*, vol. i, pp. 349, 535.

14 St John to Drummond 3/14 August, *Bolingbroke Corr.*, vol. i, p. 297;

H. Davenant to St John 13 September, SP 81/90, f. 187, 17 September, f. 191; Peterborough's instructions printed in B. Curtis Brown, *Letters of Queen Anne* (1968), pp. 334–7; St John to Whitworth 17/28 August, BL Add. MSS 37,358, f. 399; Swift, *Journal to Stella*, vol. i, p. 599; Lamberty, vol. vi, p. 656; Peterborough to Oxford 4 October, BL Add. MSS 70,249.

15 Curtis Brown, pp. 336–7; H. Davenant to St John 6 September, SP 81/90, f. 183, 17 September, f. 191, 1 October, f. 193; Peterborough to Oxford 4 October, BL Add. MSS 70,249; Boyer, vol. x, p. 70; Lamberty, vol. vi, p. 659; I. Behaghel to Hill 29 October, *Hill's Corr.*, p. 838; Swift, *Journal to Stella*, vol. i, p. 386.

CHAPTER TWENTY-EIGHT

1 St John to Oxford 4 September, HMC *Portland* MSS., vol. v, p. 84; G. M. Trevelyan, *England under Queen Anne* (1934), vol. iii, pp. 182–3; St John to Peterborough 18 September, *Bolingbroke Corr.*, vol. i, p. 361, 19 October, p. 423.

2 Peterborough to Oxford 4 October 1711, BL Add. MSS 70,249; Chetwynd to Dartmouth 11 November, 14/25 November, 2 December, SP 92/28; A. Cunningham, *A History of Great Britain from 1688 to the Accession of George I* (1787), vol. ii, pp. 389–90; Peterborough to J. Addison 4 July 1717, *Addison's Letters*, appendix ii, p. 502; Churchill, *Marlborough*, vol. iv, p. 427; Dickinson, pp. 86–92.

3 St John to Strafford 30 November OS, *Bolingbroke Corr.*, vol. ii, p. 28, St John to Peterborough 15 December OS, p. 78; Queen to Oxford 16 November OS, Curtis Brown, p. 357; Peterborough to Dartmouth 19 December, SP 92/29.

4 Peterborough to Oxford 26 December 1711, BL Add. MSS 70,249; I. Behaghel to Hill 24 September, *Hill Corr.*, p. 833, 24 December, p. 839; Cole to Dartmouth 8, 15 January, H. Broughton to Lord Strafford 5 August, SP 99/59; Chetwynd to Dartmouth 20 February, SP 92/28; A. Cunningham to Lord Treasurer 13 March 1712, HMC *Portland* MSS, vol. v, p. 147.

5 Cole to Dartmouth 19, 26, 28 February, 4 March, 28 October, SP 99/59; Chetwynd to Strafford 26 February, SP 92/27, no. 472.

6 Instructions to Peterborough 8 January OS, FO 90/37; Chetwynd to Strafford 12 March, SP 92/27; Chetwynd to Dartmouth 16 March, SP 92/28; Peterborough to Dartmouth 16 March, SP 92/29.

7 Chetwynd to Dartmouth 24, 26 March, SP 92/28; Peterborough to Dartmouth 26 March, SP 92/29.

8 Draft of Queen Anne's letter 8 August 1711 OS, *Bolingbroke Corr.*, vol.

i, p. 310; C. Cole to Dartmouth 11 September 1711, SP 99/59; St John to Oxford 4 September 1711 OS, HMC *Portland* MSS, vol. v, p. 84; Dartmouth to Peterborough 22 February 1711/12 OS, FO 90/37.

9 Cole to Dartmouth 19 February, 8, 15 April, SP 99/59; instructions to Peterborough 22 February OS, Dartmouth to Peterborough 7 March OS, FO 90/37; letter of 22 February in cypher, BL Add. MSS 4,107; Peterborough to Dartmouth 11 April, SP 92/29.

10 Peterborough to Dartmouth 11 April and 13 May, Stanyan to Peterborough 4 May OS, SP 92/29; Cole to Dartmouth 15, 22, 26 April, 6, 20 May, SP 99/59.

11 Dartmouth to Peterborough 25 April OS, FO 90/37; Cole to Dartmouth 27 May, SP 99/59; Peterborough to Dartmouth 27 May, 2, 7 June, SP 92/29.

12 Chetwynd to Dartmouth 13 July, SP 92/28; Chetwynd to Warr 17 August, SP 92/27, no. 495; Peterborough to Dartmouth 30 August, 11 November, SP 92/29; N. Davies, *God's Playground: A History of Poland* (Oxford, 1981), vol. i, p. 496; Dartmouth to Peterborough 22 September OS, FO 90/37.

CHAPTER TWENTY-NINE

1 St John to Peterborough 27 May OS, *Bolingbroke Corr.*, vol. ii, p. 347, St John to Torcy 17 July, p. 446, St John to Peterborough 18 July OS, p. 456; Chetwynd to Warr 17 August, SP 92/27, no. 495, Chetwynd to Ayers 20 August, Payne to Ayers 27 August, no. 499; Peterborough to Dartmouth 30 August, SP 92/29.

2 Prior to Bolingbroke 9 and 29 September, *Bolingbroke Corr.*, vol. iii, p. 54; Chetwynd to Dartmouth 17 September, SP 92/28; Peterborough to Dartmouth 17, 24 and 27 September, SP 92/29; *Memoirs of the Marquis de Torcy* (1757), vol. ii, p. 336.

3 Peterborough's memorandum and letter to Dartmouth 3 October, letter of 8 October, SP 92/29; Payne to Ayers 5 October, SP 92/27; Chetwynd to Dartmouth 8, 12, 16 and 19 October, SP 92/28.

4 Memorandum from Peterborough to Dartmouth 16 October, SP 92/29; Dartmouth to Peterborough 13 November OS, FO 90/37.

5 Peterborough to Dartmouth 16, 19 and 23 November, SP 92/29; Peterborough to Addison 4 July 1717, *Addison's Letters*, appendix ii, p. 501.

6 Swift, *Journal to Stella*, vol. ii, pp. 599, 638; Dalton, *Army List*, vol. vi, pp. 2, 25; *Wentworth Papers*, pp. 307, 318.

7 *LJ*, vol. xix, pp. 503, 511; Swift, *Journal to Stella*, vol. ii, pp. 647, 657; *Wentworth Papers*, pp. 328, 334; Macpherson, *Original Papers*, vol. ii, p. 401.

8 *LJ*, vol. xix, p. 555; *Wentworth Papers*, p. 331 (wrongly dated); Cobbett, *Parliamentary History*, vol. vi (1810), p. 1217.

9 Peter Wentworth to Earl Strafford 7 and 17 August, *Wentworth Papers*, pp. 347, 348.

10 Bolingbroke to Count Maffei 28 August, *Bolingbroke Corr.*, vol. iv, p. 248; Peterborough to the Elector of Hanover 3 September OS, BL Stowe MSS 225, f. 179; Peterborough's credentials and instructions 2 October 1713, FO 90/38A, 5 October, FO 90/13; additional instructions 13 October, SP 105/268.

11 *CTB* 1713, pp. 56, 57, 385, 390, 408; George Berkeley to Sir John Percival 15 October, HMC *Seventh Report, Egmont* MSS, p. 239; Swift, *Journal to Stella*, vol. ii, p. 659; instructions 23 October, FO 90/38A; Bolingbroke to Bromley 21 October, *Bolingbroke Corr.*, vol. iv, pp. 330, 332; Bolingbroke's office to Prior 23 October, SP 78/157, f. 325.

12 *CTB* 1713, p. 414; Schütz to Elector of Hanover 6/17 November, BL Stowe MSS 225, f. 270; M. Prior, *History of His Own Time* (1740), p. 399; Peterborough to Marquis de St Thomas 27 November NS, Morrison, first series, vol. v, p. 144.

13 Schütz to Elector 3/14, 6/17, 24 November/6 December, BL Stowe MSS 225, ff. 268, 270, 303, 305; Sarah to Mr Jennens 5 December OS, Sarah, Duchess of Marlborough, *Letters (at Madresfield Court)* (1875); *Journal du Marquis de Dangeau* (Paris, 1858), vol. xv, p. 38; George Berkeley to Sir John Percival 24 November NS, B. Rand, ed., *Berkeley and Percival: the Correspondence of George Berkeley and Sir John Percival* (Cambridge, 1914), p. 128; James III to Lord Bolingbroke 23 August 1715, HMC *Stuart Papers Windsor*, vol. i, p. 400; Alexander Pope to Martha Blount 25 August 1735, *Pope Corr.*, vol. iii, p. 486.

14 Prior, *History*, pp. 399–400; Prior to Bolingbroke 29 November, 6 and 14 December, SP 78/157, ff. 371, 376, 384; *Journal de Dangeau*, vol. xv, p. 40.

15 George Berkeley to Sir John Percival 28 December 1713, 4 and 19 February 1714, *Berkeley and Percival*, pp. 130, 132, 134; Bolingbroke to Peterborough 4 February OS, SP 104/94; *CTB* 1714, p. 266; Peterborough to Oxford 17 February, BL Add. MSS 70,249.

16 Peterborough to Swift 5 March, *Swift Corr.*, vol. ii, p. 13, Swift to Peterborough 18 May, p. 20; Bolingbroke to Peterborough 4 February and 15 April, SP 104/94; *CTB* 1714, p. 116; Dalton, *Army List*, vol. vi, p. 185; Symcox, pp. 171–3.

17 News letter 18 May, HMC *Portland* MSS, vol. v, p. 442; John Fleetwood to Bolingbroke 27 April, SP 93/4, no. 23; log of *Fubbs*, Adm 51/377; *CTB* 1716, p. 216; George Berkeley to Sir John Percival 13 July, *Berkeley and Percival*, p. 138; FO 90/38A; S. Harcourt-Smith, *Alberoni and the Spanish Conspiracy* (1943), p. 160.

18 Journal de Dangeau, vol. xv, pp. 205, 207, 208, 210; T. Besterman, ed., *Voltaire's Notebooks* (Geneva, 1952), vol. ii, p. 368; Madame to the Raugravine Louisa 22 September NS, G. Scott Stevenson, ed., *The Letters of Madame* (1925), p. 79; Louis XIV to Iberville 22 August, Baudrillart, vol. i, p. 587; Prior, *History*, p. 411; 'Journal of the Earl of Stair' 25 January 1715, Hardwicke, *State Papers*, vol. ii, p. 528.

CHAPTER THIRTY

1 HMC *Portland* MSS, vol. v, pp. 485, 503; John Arbuthnot to Swift 19 October, *Swift Corr.*, vol. ii, p. 137; Duke of Berwick to James III 18 December 1714, HMC *Stuart Papers Windsor*, vol. i, p. 339.

2 Marchesa Vitelleschi, *Romance of Savoy* (1905), vol. ii, p. 450; Symcox, p. 75.

3 H. Broughton to General Stanhope 18 January, 8, 15 March, SP 99/61; story in Russell, vol. ii, pp. 229–30; Dickinson, p. 135; *Pope Corr.*, vol. i, p. 289; Madame to Raugravine Louisa 12 March, 15 April, *Letters of Madame*, vol. ii, pp. 85, 87; letter of 18 January, O. Amiel, ed., *Lettres de la Princesse Palatine* (1982), p. 348; C. Dalton, *George I's Army* (1910), p. 187.

4 G. Berkeley to Lord Percival 9 August OS, *Berkeley and Percival*, p. 142; Bolingbroke to Torcy 20 August, HMC *Stuart Papers Windsor*, vol. i, p. 396, James III to Bolingbroke 23 August, p. 400, Bolingbroke to James III 23 and 26 August, pp. 404–5.

5 For the Jacobite Rebellion of 1715 see P. Miller, *James* (1980), pp. 152–95; B. Lenman, *The Jacobite Risings in Britain 1689–1746* (1980), pp. 107–54. For the Huntlys' activities during this time see HMC *Stuart Papers Windsor*, vols. ii and iii.

6 L. Norton, ed., *The Historical Memoirs of the Duc de St Simon* (1972), vol. iii, p. 39; G. Flint to Mar 18 June 1718, HMC *Stuart Papers Windsor*, vol. vi, p. 551; 'Lord Stair's Journal' 3 December 1715, Hardwicke, *State Papers*, vol. ii, p. 550; G. Berkeley to Lord Percival 3 November OS, *Berkeley and Percival*, p. 153.

7 'Stair's Journal' 23 January, 17 February and 11 March 1716, Hardwicke, *State Papers*, vol. ii, pp. 550–3; W. Sichel, *Bolingbroke and His Times* (1901–2), vol. ii, p. 103.

8 J. Menzies to L. Inese 16/27 April, HMC *Stuart Papers Windsor*, vol. ii, p. 123; Cobbett, *Parliamentary History*, vol. vii, p. 303; Timberland, vol. iii, pp. 35–9.

9 Lt. Gen. Dillon to the Duke of Mar 23 May NS, HMC *Stuart Papers Windsor*, vol. ii, p. 177, T. Oglethorpe to Mar 29 May and 9 June, pp. 194–5, 211; A. Cunningham to Pringle 5 and 12 June, SP 99/61.

10 Cunningham to Secretary of State 14 August, SP 99/61; J. Robethon to Lord Polwarth 17/28 August, HMC *Lord Polwarth* MSS, vol. i, p. 65.

11 T. Oglethorpe to Mar 14 October, HMC *Stuart Papers Windsor*, vol. iii, p. 78, G. Hooker to Mar 11 September, vol. ii, p. 423; J. Clavering to Lady Cowper, Hon. S. Cowper, ed., *The Diary of Mary Countess Cowper 1714 –20* (1865), appendix e; Cunningham to Pringle 28 September, SP 99/61.

12 Cunningham to Methuen 13 November, Cunningham to Pringle 11 December and 1 January 1717, Cunningham to Methuen 29 January, Cunningham to Stanhope 5 February, SP 99/61.

13 Cunningham to Methuen 26 February, 19 March, 2 and 29 April, 7 May, Cunningham to Addison 21 May, SP 99/61; Addison to Peterborough 6 May OS, *Addison's Letters*, pp. 358–9.

14 Peterborough to Addison 4 July, *Addison's Letters*, appendix ii, pp. 501–3.

15 Dillon to James III 18 August, HMC *Stuart Papers Windsor*, vol. iv, p. 525, J. Menzies to L. Inese 17/28 October, vol. v, p. 166, Sheldon's account, p. 586; Peterborough to (a British envoy) 9 October, J. M. Graham, ed., *Annals and Correspondence of the Viscount and First and Second Earls of Stair* (Edinburgh, 1875), vol. ii, p. 335; J. Wilson to L. M. 29 August, HMC *Hodgkin* MSS, p. 230.

CHAPTER THIRTY-ONE

1 Graeme to Mar 12 August, HMC *Stuart Papers Windsor*, vol. iv, p. 510, Dillon to James III 14 and 18 August, pp. 519, 525, Mar to Queen Mary 13 August, p. 517, F. Oglethorpe to Mar 27 August, p. 534, 14 October, vol. v, p. 102.

2 Sir John O'Brien, 'Remarks on Lord Peterborough's Journey' and a letter from a private person at Parma, HMC *Stuart Papers Windsor*, vol. v, appendix p. 573, Sir J. O'Brien's account, p. 580; Cunningham to Addison 17 September, SP 99/61.

3 James III to Cardinal Origo 10 September, BL Add. MSS 20,292, f. 140, memorandum from James III, f. 149; James III to Cardinal Origo 10 September, HMC *Stuart Papers Windsor*, vol. v, p. 27, account of Peterborough's conversation with O'Brien, appendix pp. 574–6; Cunningham to Addison 17 and 24 September, SP 99/61; British Minister at Genoa to Stair 1717, *Stair Annals*, vol. ii, p. 9.

4 Letter from Sir John O'Brien 25 September, HMC *Stuart Papers Windsor*, vol. v, p. 73; Cunningham to Addison 1 October, SP 99/61; Peterborough to (a British envoy) 9 October, *Stair Annals*, vol. ii, p. 334.

5 HMC *Stuart Papers Windsor*, vol. v, appendix pp. 577, 586–92; S. Harcourt-Smith, *Alberoni*, p. 160.

6 J. Addison to Davenant 19 September OS, SP 104/96; Cunningham to Addison 24 September, SP 99/61; Sheldon to O'Brien 27 September, HMC *Stuart Papers Windsor*, vol. v, appendix p. 584, Dillon to James III 2 October, p. 94, Queen Mary to Mar 11 October, p. 133; Lord Bathurst to Lord Strafford 9 October OS, *Wentworth Papers*, p. 444; J. Addison to the Earl of Stair 3 October OS, *Addison's Letters*, p. 379.

7 James III to Cardinal Origo 12 October, HMC *Stuart Papers Windsor*, vol. v, p. 136, James III to Pope 12 October, appendix p. 596, O'Brien's account, p. 600; James III to Cardinal Origo 17 October, BL Add. MSS 20,292, f. 164; letter to Count Gazzola 17 October, BL Add. MSS 20,312, f. 91.

8 Addison to Peterborough 6 October OS, *Addison's Letters*, p. 380; Addison to Count Gallas 14 October OS, SP 104/96, translation in *Addison's Letters*, p. 383; Sheldon to Peterborough 14 November, HMC *Stuart Papers Windsor*, vol. v, p. 206, L. Inese to Mar 15 November, p. 209; letter to Count Gazzola 11 November, BL Add. MSS 20,312, f. 94; James III to Cardinal Gualterio, BL Add. MSS 20,292, f. 168.

9 Letter to Mr Belloni 14 November, BL Add. MSS 20,312, f. 123, Bianchini to James III 13 November, f. 114; news letters, HMC *Portland MSS*, vol. v, pp. 535, 537; Addison to Davenant 28 October OS, SP 104/96.

10 Mar to James III 17 November, HMC *Stuart Papers Windsor*, vol. v, p. 213, Cockburne to Mar 4 and 8 December, pp. 253, 262; news letter 26 November OS, HMC *Portland MSS*, vol. v, p. 540; Cunningham to Addison, and Cunningham to Stanyon 10 December, SP 99/61.

11 Mar to F. Oglethorpe 26 November, HMC *Stuart Papers Windsor*, vol. v, p. 241, James III to Earl of Oxford 16 December, p. 281, F. Oglethorpe to Mar 25 December, p. 325.

12 Cunningham to Stanyon, and Cunningham to Addison 31 December, SP 99/61; O'Brien to J. Paterson 2 January 1718, HMC *Stuart Papers Windsor*, vol. v, p. 353, F. Oglethorpe to Mar 22 and 28 February, pp. 466, 517.

13 Bolingbroke to Mme de Ferriol 27 February, P.H. Grimoard, ed., *Lettres Historiques, Politiques, Philosophique ... de Bolingbroke* (Paris, 1808), vol. ii, p. 461; Bolingbroke to Stair 25 March and 13 April, P. Baratier, ed., *Lettres Inédites de Bolingbroke à Lord Stair 1716–20* (Trévoux, 1939), pp. 67, 69 and note.

14 F. Oglethorpe to Mar 7 May, HMC *Stuart Papers Windsor*, vol. vi, p. 411.

CHAPTER THIRTY-TWO

1 A. Pope to Teresa and Martha Blount, *Pope Corr.*, vol. ii, p. 1.

2 *The Thoughts of a Member of the Lower House* (1719); *Remarks on the Thoughts of a Member of the Lower House* (1719), pp. 10, 11, 13, 14, 18, 19, 29, 33, 36; E. R. Turner, 'The Peerage Bill of 1719,' *EHR*, vol. xxviii (1913), pp. 243–57; 'The Peerage Bill in 1719,' *Retrospective Review*, second series, vol. ii (1828), pp. 121–2; A. S. Turberville, *The House of Lords in the Eighteenth Century* (Oxford, 1927), pp. 169–77.

3 For the history of Cardinal Alberoni see E. Armstrong, *Elisabeth Farnese* (1892), pp. 50–63, and S. Harcourt-Smith, *Alberoni*.

4 Peterborough to Stanhope 20 November 1719, Stanhope of Chevening MSS, O145/18; Craggs to Stair 24 September, *Stair Annals*, vol. ii, pp. 402–3, Peterborough to the Regent 20 November, translation printed on pp. 122–3; J. Haldane to Lord Polwarth 28 September, HMC *Lord Polwarth* MSS, vol. ii, p. 313; Alberoni to Duke of Parma 29 November, quoted in E. Armstrong, p. 123.

5 Burgess to Craggs 15 and 22 December, SP 99/62; Peterborough to Mme de Ferriol January 1720, *Lettres Historiques de Bolingbroke*, vol. iii, p. 43.

6 Peterborough to Mme de Ferriol (January 1721) and 8/19 February 1721, *Lettres Historiques de Bolingbroke*, vol. iii, pp. 66, 70–2.

7 Pope's poem is printed in M. Mack, *Alexander Pope* (1985), p. 378, and Pope, *Poetical Works*, ed. H. Davis (Oxford 1967), p. 642; Peterborough to Mrs Howard, J. Croker, ed., *Letters to and from Henrietta Countess of Suffolk 1712–1767* (1824), vol. i, p. 127; Lady Mohun to Mrs Howard 18 August, BL Add. MSS 22,625, f. 125.

8 Mrs Howard to Peterborough, printed in Russell, vol. ii, p. 304; Peterborough to Mrs Howard, BL Add. MSS 22,625, ff. 37, 38, 62, 89.

9 Details of Marble Hill can be found in L. Melville, *Lady Suffolk and her Circle* (1924), J. Bryant, *Marble Hill House* (1988) with designs by Colen Campbell on p. 27, J. Bryant, *Mrs Howard: A Woman of Reason*, Exhibition Catalogue (1988); Peterborough to Pope (July) 1723 and autumn, *Pope Corr.*, vol. ii, pp. 183, 196.

10 Peterborough to Mrs Howard, BL Add. MSS 22,625, ff. 107; 'Imitations of Horace' book ii, satire i, Pope, *Poetical Works*, p. 344.

11 The original version of the poem printed in 1723 appears in N. Ault, ed., *A Treasury of Unfamiliar Lyrics* (1938), pp. 284–5. In the 1727 version, one or two subtle alterations were made to the text, tightening the metre, Swift, *Miscellanies* (1727), vol. iv, pp. 166–7; H. Walpole, *A Catalogue of Royal and Noble Authors of England, Scotland and Ireland* ed. T. Park (1806), vol. iv, pp. 162, 168.

12 5 September 1762, H. Walpole, *Notes of Conversations with Lady*

Suffolk, pp. 131–2; Sir J. Hawkins, *History of the Science and Practice of Music* (1776), vol. v, pp. 304–5 and note.

CHAPTER THIRTY-THREE

1 *Autobiography and Correspondence of Mary Granville, Mrs Delany* (1861), vol. i, p. 72. There are long notices about Anastasia Robinson in Hawkins, vol. v, pp. 301–5 and Charles Burney, *A General History of Music* (1789), vol. iv, pp. 244–86. Further information is given in J. Simon, ed., *Handel: A Celebration of his Life and Times*, exhibition catalogue, National Portrait Gallery (1985).
2 Alexander Pope to (Martha?) Blount (January 1720), *Pope Corr.*, vol. ii, p. 30, Atterbury to Pope 1722, p. 123; *Delany Corr.*, pp. 72–3; Anastasia Robinson to Giuseppe Riva 1722, quoted in J. Simon, *Handel*, no. 100, p. 129.
3 Lady Mary Wortley Montagu to the Countess of Mar 6 Sept 1721, R. Halsband, ed., *The Complete Letters of Lady Mary Wortley Montagu* (Oxford, 1965), vol. ii, p. 13, March 1724, vol. iii, p. 36; J. Swift to Charles Ford 13 February 1713/14, *Swift Corr.*, vol. iii, p. 7; Hawkins, p. 305.
4 Cobbett, *Parliamentary History*, vol. vii, p. 894; Bolingbroke to Mme de Ferriol 30 July, Sichel, vol. ii, appendix p. 498; Baudrillart, vol. ii, p. 433.
5 C. Dalton, *George I's Army*, vol. ii, p. 332; Bolingbroke to Mme de Ferriol June 1722, *Lettres Historiques*, vol. iii, p. 177.
6 Dalton, p. 114; W. King, ed., *Memoirs of Sarah Duchess of Marlborough* (1930), pp. 246–7.
7 A. Pope to J. Swift (August 1723) and note, *Pope Corr.*, vol. ii, p. 183.
8 Peterborough to Pope (1723), *Pope Corr.*, vol. ii, p. 183, Arbuthnot to Pope September 1723, and Peterborough to Pope, p. 196.
9 For the Hogarth print, see J. Simon, *Handel*, no. 106, p. 135; Pope to Peterborough (August 1723), *Pope Corr.*, vol. ii, p. 190.
10 Townshend to H. Walpole 3 May, Newcastle Papers, vol. lv, BL Add. MSS 32,740, ff. 41, 43.
11 H. Walpole to R. Walpole 28 August 1724, Lord Mahon, *History of England* (1713–83), vol. ii, appendix p. 107; Baudrillart, vol. iii, p. 121.
12 H. Walpole to Newcastle 2 September NS, BL Add. MSS 32,740, f. 171.
13 H. Walpole to Newcastle 8 September NS, BL Add. MSS 32,740, ff. 208–13, Peterborough to Newcastle 9 September, ff. 216–18.
14 Peterborough to Newcastle 9 September NS, BL Add. MSS 32,740, ff. 216–18, H. Walpole to Newcastle 7 September, f. 275, Newcastle to Walpole 7 September OS, f. 320; Peterborough to the Spanish Ambassador 29 August NS, SP 94/77; Baudrillart, vol. iii, p. 122.

[471]

CHAPTER THIRTY-FOUR

1 Gay and Pope to Fortescue 23 September, *Pope Corr.*, vol. ii, p. 322, Pope to Jacob Tonson January 1724/25, p. 285; Lady Hervey to Mrs Howard 7 June 1725, *Letters to Henrietta, Countess of Suffolk*, vol. i, p. 181.

2 E. Harley to Earl of Oxford 1 February 1726, HMC *Portland Papers*, vol. vi, p. 11; Peterborough to Swift 23 April 1726, *Swift Corr.*, vol. iii, p. 131, Swift to Peterborough 28 April, pp. 131–5; W. D. Taylor, *Jonathan Swift* (1933), pp. 150–8; V. Glendinning, *Jonathan Swift* (1998), pp. 166–72.

3 Peterborough to Swift 29 November 1726, *Swift Corr.*, vol. iii, pp. 191–2; Swift to Pope 5 December, *Pope Corr.*, vol. ii, p. 420.

4 For Voltaire's visit to England see J. Churton Collins, *Voltaire, Montesquieu and Rousseau in England* (1908), pp. 7–33; C. B. Chase, *The Young Voltaire* (1926), pp. 75 et seq.; C. Dédéyan, *Le retour de Salente ou Voltaire et l'Angleterre* (Paris 1988); E. F. G. Barbier, *Chronique de la Régence* (Paris 1885), vol. ii, p. 94.

5 Extract from 'The Journal of Major W. Broome,' printed in *Notes and Queries*, first series, vol. x (1854), p. 403; Voltaire, *Histoire de Jenni*, ed. J. H. Brumfitt and M. I. G. Davis (1960); Dédéyan, p. 85.

6 Barker and Stenning, *Record of old Westminsters*, p. 661; Voltaire to Rolland Puchot des Alleurs 11 April 1728, T. Besterman, ed., *Voltaire's Correspondence* (Geneva, 1953), vol. ii, p. 66, Voltaire to Dr R. Towne 23 July/3 August, p. 80; Peterborough to Townshend 20 May, HMC *Townshend* MSS, p. 120; the letters of Peterborough to Dr Richard Towne, (spring) and 3 July 1728, are printed in M. Mack, *Collected in Himself* (Yale, 1982), appendix B, pp. 476, 477; Peterborough to Mrs Howard, BL Add. MSS 22,625, f. 114.

7 *Gentleman's Magazine* May 1732, vol. ii, p. 739; the story of Voltaire and Peterborough, *Gentleman's Magazine* 1797, vol. lxviii, part ii, pp. 820–1, 1009.

8 Peterborough to Dr R. Towne 14 November 1728, printed in Mack, op. cit., pp. 477–8; A. Friedmann, ed., *Mémoires de Voltaire* (1966), vol. iii, p. 252; *Histoire de Jenni*, p. 80.

9 Cosmo, Marquess of Huntly to Earl of Marchmont 25 December 1728, HMC *Lord Polwarth* MSS, vol. v, no. 36; Duchess of Gordon to Duncan Forbes of Culloden, n. d., NLS 2,970, f. 206.

10 Mrs Robinson to the Earl of Oxford 24 and 31 May 1729, HMC *Portland Papers*, vol. i, p. 24; J. E. Power, 'Pope's Jesuit,' *Notes and Queries*, vol. ccxiv (1969), pp. 184–6.

11 Peterborough to Mrs Howard BL Add. MSS 22,625, f. 119; Dr Speed quoted in J. S. Davies, *A History of Southampton* (1883), p. 2; *Journal*

of the British Archaeological Association, vol. xv (1859), p. 279; G.
Vertue, *Notebooks*, vol. vi (Walpole Society, vol. xxx, 1955); Pope to Dr
Arbuthnot 2 August 1734, *Pope Corr.*, vol. iii, p. 423, Pope to Mrs
Knight 5 August, p. 425.

12 'An Account of a Tour in Hampshire and Sussex' (1743), BL Add. MSS
15,776; Pope to the Earl of Oxford 1 September 1734, *Pope Corr.*, vol.
iii, p. 429; Earl of Oxford, 'A Journey through Hampshire, Wiltshire,
and Berkshire to Oxford 1738,' 25 October, HMC *Portland Papers*, vol.
vi, p. 175; Vertue, p. 91.

13 Peterborough to Pope (August 1732), *Pope Corr.*, vol. iii, pp. 281, 310.

14 'Imitations of Horace' Book i, epistle i, Pope, *Poetical Works*, p. 351;
Peterborough to Pope (early May 1732), *Pope Corr.*, vol. iii, p. 282.

15 A. S. Turberville, *The House of Lords in the Eighteenth Century*, p. 198;
Whitehall Evening Post, 25 April 1730, quoted in *Pope Corr.*, vol. iii, p.
105n; Peterborough to Mrs Howard October 1730, BL Add. MSS
22,625, f. 115 as printed in Russell, vol. ii, pp. 308–9.

16 Pope to Hill 14 March and 4 April 1731, *Pope Corr.*, vol. iii, pp. 182,
188; H. Walpole, *Notes of Conversations with Lady Suffolk*, p. 124. For
details of Aaron Hill's life, see the article in *DNB*, also D. Brewster,
Aaron Hill, Poet, Dramatist and Projector (New York, 1966).

17 Pope to J. Knight 23 August, *Pope Corr.*, vol. iii, p. 217; Earl of Orrery
to Lady Kaye 3 November, HMC *Dartmouth* MSS, vol. i, p. 327.

18 *LJ* vol. xxiv, pp. 69, 78, 149; HMC *Egmont Diary*, vol. i, p. 279.

CHAPTER THIRTY-FIVE

1 Peterborough to Pope (August 1732), *Pope Corr.*, vol. iii, p. 310, Peterborough to Pope (October 1732), p. 317; Peterborough to the Duchess
of Gordon 5 November, NLS 2967, f. 190; Duchess of Gordon to
Duncan Forbes of Culloden n. d., NLS 2970, f. 206.

2 Lord Hervey to Henry Fox 18 and 23 January, Earl of Ilchester, ed.,
Lord Hervey and His Friends (1950), pp. 154, 155; Peterborough to
Duncan Forbes of Culloden n. d. (1733), NLS 2970, f. 207; Pope to
Swift 27 February, *Pope Corr.*, vol. iii, p. 349, Peterborough to Lady
Mary Wortley Montagu, p. 349; 'First Satire of the Second Book of
Horace Imitated,' Pope, *Poetical Works*, p. 343.

3 Swift to Peterborough (1733), *Swift Corr.*, vol. iv, p. 167; Pope to Caryll
24 September 1733, *Pope Corr.*, vol. iii, p. 387, Pope to Earl of Oxford
20 October, p. 389; the visit to Winchester is described in 'A Memorial
of William Whitehead,' Earl of Harcourt, ed., *Harcourt Papers* (Oxford,
1880–90), vol. vii, p. 206.

4 Pope to Mrs Knight 5 August 1734, *Pope Corr.*, vol. iii, p. 425, Pope to

the Earl of Oxford 1 September, p. 429; Pope to Martha Blount 11 August, printed in G. S. Rousseau, 'A new Pope Letter,' *Philological Quarterly*, vol. xlv (1966), pp. 410–18.

5 Pope's View is reproduced in F. J. C. Hearnshaw, *A Short History of Southampton* (1910), p. 109; Pope to Fortescue 21 September 1736, *Pope Corr.*, vol. iv, p. 33.

6 Pope to Caryll 12 May, *Pope Corr.*, vol. iii, p. 455, Pope to Fortescue, given as 1732/33 p. 342, is more likely to refer to this illness; *London Evening Post* 11–13 March 1735; Mrs Delany, *Autobiography and Correspondence*, vol. i, pp. 73 et seq.

7 Pope to Martha Blount 25 August, *Pope Corr.*, vol. iii, p. 487, Peterborough to Pope 13 June, p. 468, Pope to Swift (November), p. 508; S. W. Singer, ed., *Anecdotes, Observations and Characters of Books and Men Collected from the Conversation of Mr Pope and Other Eminent Persons of His Time by the Reverend Joseph Spence* (1964), p. 107; S. Seward, *Anecdotes of Some Distinguished Persons* (1796), vol. ii, p. 325; Sarah Duchess of Marlborough to Diana Duchess of Bedford 30 July, printed in G. Scott Thomson, ed., *Letters of a Grandmother* (1944), p. 161.

8 Peterborough to the Countess of Suffolk July 1735, BL Add. MSS 22,625, f. 121; Pope to the Earl of Orrery 12 July, *Pope Corr.*, vol. iii, p. 469, Pope to Caryll 17 July, p. 474.

9 Pope to Lord Bathurst 19 August, *Pope Corr.*, vol. iii, p. 483, Pope to Martha Blount, p. 487; Peterborough to Pope 20 August, NLS 582, no. 668.

10 Pope to the Earl of Oxford 27 August, *Pope Corr.*, vol. iii, p. 489, Pope to Mrs Knight 29 August, p. 490, Pope to Lord Bathurst 8 October, p. 499.

11 *London Evening Post* 30 August–2 September, 4–6 September 1735; log of HMS *Gibraltar* 20–5 September, Adm 51/390; *Spence's Anecdotes*, section iv, pp. 107–8; Feret, *Fulham Old and New*, vol. ii, pp. 145 et seq.

12 Log of HMS *Gibraltar* 25 September–5 October, Adm 51/390; 'Journal of Sir John Norris' 5 and 6 October, BL Add. MSS 28,130; Peterborough to Stanhope 18 November 1705, *Peterborough's Letters to Stanhope*, p. 7; J. Hanway, *A Journal of 8 Days Journey* (1757), vol. i, p. 29.

13 *Gentleman's Magazine* 1735, p. 681; Pope to Swift November 1735, *Pope Corr.*, vol. iii, p. 508; Norris's Journal 15 October, BL Add. MSS 28,130; Pope in his turn left the watch to George Arbuthnot.

14 Norris's Journal 16, 19 and 20 October, BL Add. MSS 28, 130; log of HMS *Britannia* 15 and 21 October, Adm 51/138; log of HMS *Berwick* 21 October, Adm 51/105.

15 Log of HMS *Berwick* 29, 30 October, 10, 11, 12 November, Adm 51/105; *London Evening Post* 15–18, 20–2 November; Turvey Parish Register quoted in Harvey, *Hundred of Willey Beds.*, pp. 186 et seq.

Bibliography

MANUSCRIPT SOURCES

British Library
Add. Ch. 73,991; Add. MSS 4,107 (letter of Peterborough in cipher 1712); 4,743 (Davenant correspondence); 5,438 (Leake's letterbook 1705–6); 5,441 (Peterborough's letters to Leake); 5,442 (notes of councils of war etc.); 7,121 (Peterborough to Halifax 1706); 9,115 (Col. Pepper's account etc.); 9,776 (lettres du Maréchal de Tessé); 15,776 (tour in Hampshire and Sussex 1743); 15,892 (Hyde correspondence); 15,907 (Thomas Weston's accounts); 15,916 (Galway's answers); 17,018, f. 129 (Lady Mordaunt's will); 17,677 PP, RR, TT, UU, WW (L'Hermitage Dispatches); 20,292, 20,312 (Peterborough's arrest at Bologna); 22,200 (questions to the Earl of Peterborow); 22,625 (Peterborough to Mrs Howard); 27,200 (questions to Peterborough and his answers); 28,056, 28057 (letters to Godolphin 1705–6); 28,058 (notes of councils of war etc.); 28,103 (Peterborough's letters to Queen Anne); 28,126 (Norris's log of the *Britannia*); 28,130 (journal of Sir John Norris); 28,941; 29,566 (Hatton-Finch Papers); 29,764 (extracts from Parish Registers); 30,000 A, B, C (Bonnet's Dispatches); 31,134 (St Pierre to Lord Raby 1706–7); 32,740 (Newcastle Papers lv); 33,251; 33,923, ff.430–81 (Diary of Sir John Knatchbull); 34,515 (Somers MSS); 36,707 (Harrington Papers); 37,358 (Whitworth Papers); 38,501 (Townshend correspondence); 40,621; 41,805, 41,822, 41,843 (Middleton Papers); 46,527 (Lexington Papers, vol. iii); 50,842 (Book of Instruction for the Conduct of the Bedchamber of William III); 61,110 (Peterborough's paper of charges and answers, Blenheim Papers), 61,164, 61,292, 61,458, 61,514, 61,515 (Blenheim Papers); 70,249 (Portland Papers)
Althorp MSS c. 11. 2, 20
Egerton MSS 2167, 2537, 2621, 3329
Harleian MSS 6,210, 6,684, 7,018
Stowe MSS 222, 223, 225 (Hanover State Papers); 467 (John Richards's diary); 468 (John Richards's letter book); 471 (Richards's Memorial of Expedition to Barcelona)
Biblioteca Municipal, Valencia
Fuster y Menbrado, Dietario de Valencia, Folio 6424

Dr Williams's Library
  Roger Morrice, Entering Book, vols. i, ii, iii
Kent Archives Office
  Stanhope of Chevening MSS
  O34 (letter to A. Stanhope); O133/1 (Arent Furly's account books);
  O135/11 (Arent Furly's Journal); O136/11 (Furly's letters to Stanhope);
  O137/11 (Peterborough to Stanhope); O141/17 (letters from Stanhope
    1706);
  O145/18 (Peterborough to Stanhope 1719)
Museo de Historia de la Ciudad, Barcelona
  Charles Earl of Peterborough, Military Orders
Museo Historico Valencia
  Milicia 1643–1757
National Library of Scotland
  MSS 582 (Peterborough to Pope 1735); 2970, 2967 (Gordon Correspon-
    dence)
National Register of Archives, Scotland
  4155 Peterborough family letters
Northamptonshire Record Office
  MSS Y2 (Peterborough's will 1710)
Österreichisches Kriegsarchiv, Vienna
  AFA 1705 Spanien und Portugal 243
Österreichisches Staatsarchiv, Vienna
  W 937 Castellvi, Narraciones; Kriegsakten 249
Public Record Office
  Adm 51/105 (log of HMS *Berwick*); 51/138, (log of HMS *Britannia*);
    51/242, (log of HMS *Devonshire*); 51/266 (log of HMS *Ranelagh*);
    51/364 (log of HMS *Foresight*); 51/377 (log of HMY *Fubbs*); 51/390
    (log of HMS *Gibraltar*); 51/4250 (log of HMS *Lyme*); 52/68 (master's
    log of HMS *Mordaunt*); 52/210 (log of HMS *Leopard*); 52/269 (log of
    HMS *Resolution*)
  CO 279/25, 26 (Tangier 1681)
  FO 90/13 (credentials to King of France 1713); 90/37 (Dartmouth to
    Peterborough 1710–12); 90/38A (instructions to Peterborough 1713)
  PRO 30/24/21, 45 (Shaftesbury correspondence)
  SP 78/157 (Bolingbroke and Prior); 81/90 (Davenant to St John); 89/19
    (letters from Milner and Methuen to Hedges); 92/27, 92/28
    (Chetwynd's reports from Turin); 92/29 (Savoy, letters and instruc-
    tions); 93/4 (Naples, letters); 94/75 (Peterborough's letters to Hedges);
    94/76 (Peterborough and Stanhope to Hedges); 94/77 (Peterborough
    to Spanish Ambassador); 99/59 (Cole's reports from Venice); 99/61
    (letters from Venice 1715–17); 99/62 (letters from Venice 1719);
    104/40 St John's letter book 1710–12); 104/94 (Bolingbroke's letter

book 1713–14); 104/96 (Addison to Davenant and Gallas); 104/129 (Secretary's letter book, Spain, 1705–6); 104/207 Hedges's letters to Peterborough); 104/208 (Sunderland's letters to Peterborough); 105/268 (additional instructions October 1713)

WO 25/8 (Commission Book 1704–7); 47/22; 71/1 (Inquiry into the conduct of Lord Charlemont)

Rijksarchief, The Hague
    Archief Heinsius
Universitad de Valencia
    Josef Vicente Orti y Mayor, Diario de lo Sucedido en la Ciudad de Valencia 1700–15, vol. 1705–9, MS 460

PRINTED SOURCES

[Addison, Joseph] *The Letters of Joseph Addison*, ed. W. Graham (Oxford 1941)

Annandale Family Book, The, ed. W. Fraser, 2 vols. (Edinburgh 1894)

Arneth, A. von, ed., *Eigenhandige Correspondenz des Konigs Karl III von Spanien* (Vienna 1856)

Atkinson, C. D., ed., 'A Royal Dragoon in the Spanish Succession War', *Journal of the Society for Army Historical Research* (1938)

[Baillie, George] *The Correspondence of George Baillie of Jerviswood*, ed. Gilbert Eliot, Earl of Minto (Bannatyne Club, Edinburgh 1842)

Baker, L. M., ed., *Letters of Elizabeth of Bohemia* (1953)

Beddard, R., *A Kingdom without a King: The Journal of the Provisional Government in the Revolution of 1688* (Oxford 1988)

Berkeley and Percival: The Correspondence of George Berkeley and Sir John Percival, ed. B. Rand (Cambridge 1914)

Berwick, Marshal Duke of, *Mémoires du Maréchal de Berwick*, 2 vols. (Paris 1779)

[Bolingbroke] *Letters and Correspondence of Henry St John, Lord Viscount Bolingbroke*, ed. G. Parke, 4 vols. (1798)

[Bolingbroke] *Lettres Historiques, Politiques, Philosophiques de Bolingbroke*, ed. P. H. Grimoard, 3 vols. (Paris 1808)

[Bolingbroke] *Lettres Inédites de Bolingbroke à Lord Stair 1716–1720*, ed. P. Baratier (Trévoux 1939)

Boyer, A., *History of the Reign of Queen Anne Digested into Annals*, 11 vols. (1703–13)

Braybrooke, Lord, ed., *Autobiography of Sir John Bramston* (Camden Society 1845)

[Broome, Major] 'Extract from the Journal of Major Broome', *Notes and Queries*, first series, vol. x (1854)

Brown, B. Curtis, *Letters of Queen Anne* (1968)

Browning, A., ed., *Memoirs of Sir John Reresby* (Glasgow 1936)

Bruce, Thomas, Earl of Ailesbury, *Memoirs*, ed. W. E. Buckley (Roxburghe Club, Edinburgh, 1890), 2 vols.

Bulstrode, Sir Richard, *Memoirs* (1721)

Burchett, J., *Transactions at Sea* (1720)

Burnet, Gilbert, *History of His Own Time*, 6 vols. (Oxford 1833)

[Burston, Colonel] *The Case of Colonel Burston with Respect to the Dispute between Him and Lt. Gen. Wills* (1720)

Byng Papers, The, ed. B. Tunstall, 3 vols., (1930–1)

Calendar of Clarendon State Papers, 14 vols. (1869–1932)

Calendar of the Proceedings of the Committee for Compounding, ed. M. A. E. Green, 5 vols. (1889–92)

Calendar of State Papers Domestic Series 1648–9, 1652, 1659–60, 1660–1, 1665–6, 1673, 1677–8, 1678, 1680–1, 1682, 1686–7, 1687–9, 1689–90, 1690–1, 1691–2, 1694–5, 1696, 1697, 1698, 1700–2, 1702–3, 1703–4

Calendar of State Papers Colonial Series, America and West Indies 1685–8, 1689–97, 1702–3

Calendar of Treasury Books 1660–7, 1676–9, 1681–5, 1689–92, 1693–6, 1696–7, 1697, 1702, 1703, 1706–7, 1709, 1711, 1713, 1714, 1716

Calendar of Treasury Papers, ed. E. J. Redington, 4 vols. (1868–79)

Carte, T., *Life of James Duke of Ormonde*, 3 vols. (1735–6)

Clarendon, Earl of, *History of the Rebellion*, ed. Macray, 6 vols. (1888)

——, *The Life* and *The Continuation of the Life*, 2 vols. (1857)

Clarendon State Papers, 3 vols. (1767–96)

[Clarendon] *Correspondence of Henry Hyde, Earl of Clarendon, and His Brother, Laurence Hyde, The*, ed. S. W. Singer, 2 vols. (1828)

Clarke, J. S., *Life of James II*, 2 vols. (1816)

Cobbett, W., *Parliamentary History of England*, 36 vols. (1806–20)

Cole, Christian, *Memoirs of Affairs of State* (1733)

[Commons, House of] *Journal of the House of Commons*, vol. xiii

Cowper, Mary Countess: *Diary of Mary Countess Cowper 1714–1720*, ed. S. Cowper (1865)

Cowper, W., Lord Cowper, *Private Diary* (Roxburghe Club 1833)

Cunningham, A., *History of Great Britain from 1688 to the accession of George I*, 2 vols. (1787)

Dalrymple, Sir John, *Memoirs of Great Britain and Ireland*, 4 vols. (1771–88)

Dalton, C., *English Army Lists and Commission Registers 1661–1714*, 6 vols. (1892–4)

Dangeau, Marquis de, *Journal*, vol. xv (Paris 1858)

[Delany] *Autobiography and Correspondence of Mary Granville, Mrs Delany*, ed. Lady Llanover, 3 vols. (1861)

[Demosthenes] *Several Orations of Demosthenes Translated by the Earl of Peterborough and Others* (1744)

Ellis Correspondence, ed. G. A. E. Ellis, 2 vols. (1829)

[Eugen, Prince] *Feldzüge des Prinzen Eugen von Savoyen*, I Series, band vii (Wien 1881)

[Evelyn, John] *Diary of John Evelyn*, ed. E. S. de Beer, 6 vols. (Oxford 1955)

Evelyn, John, *A Philosophical Discourse on Earth* (1675)

Exact Account of the Ceremonial at the Coronation of King William and Queen Mary, An (1689)

Feliú de la Peña y Farell, N., *Anales de Cataluña*, vol. iii (Barcelona 1709)

Freind, Dr John, *An Account of the Earl of Peterborow's Conduct in Spain* (1707)

[Galway, Earl of] *An Account of the Earl of Galway's Conduct in Spain* (1711)

Gentleman's Magazine, vol. ii (1732), vol. v (1735), vol. lxviii (1797)

'Haddock Correspondence', *Camden Miscellany*, vol. viii (1883)

Halstead, R., *Succinct Genealogies* (1685)

Hanway, J., *A Journal of Eight Days' Journey from Portsmouth to Kingston-upon-Thames*, 2 vols. (1757)

Harcourt Papers, ed. E. W. Harcourt, 7 vols. (Oxford 1880–90)

Hardwicke's State Papers, 2 vols. (1778)

Hartmann, C. H., ed., *Memoirs of Captain Carleton* (1929)

[Hatton Family] *The Correspondence of the Family of Hatton*, 2 vols. (Camden Society 1878)

Hawkins, Sir John, *History of the Science and Practice of Music*, 5 vols. (1776)

[Hervey, Lord] *Lord Hervey and His Friends 1726–1738*, ed. Earl of Ilchester (1950)

[Hill, Richard] *The Diplomatic Correspondence of Richard Hill 1703–1706*, ed. W. Blackley, 2 vols. (1845)

Historical Manuscripts Commission

Fourth Report, Balliol College MSS (1874); *Fifth Report, Sutherland* MSS, *Pine-Coffin* MSS, *Cholmondeley* MSS (1876); *Seventh Report, House of Lords Calendar, Verney* MSS, *Graham* MSS, *Denbigh* MSS (1879); *Eighth Report, Denbigh* MSS, *Marlborough* MSS (1881); *Ninth Report, Manvers* MSS (1884); *Tenth Report, appendix vi, Bagot* MSS (1885); *Fourteenth Report*, vol. iv, *Kenyon* MSS, *Hare* MSS (1895); *Fifteenth Report, Johnstone* MSS (1897); *Bath Longleat* MSS, 3 vols. (1904–8); Buccleuch (Montagu) MSS (1903); *Cowper* MSS, 3 vols. (1888–9); *Dartmouth* MSS (1887); *Downshire Papers* (1924); *Egmont* MSS, *Egmont Diary*, 3 vols. (1920–3); *Finch* MSS (1924); *Frankland-Russell-Astley* MSS (1900); *Hastings* MSS (1928–47); *Hodgkin* MSS (1897); *House of Lords* MSS, New Series, 12 vols. (1900–53); *Le Fleming*

MSS (1890); *Montagu of Beaulieu* MSS (1900); *Leyborne-Popham* MSS, *Autobiography of Dr George Clarke* (1899); *Lord Polwarth* MSS, 5 vols. (1911–61); *Mar and Kellie* MSS (1904); *Ormonde* MSS, New Series, 8 vols. (1902–20); *Portland* MSS, 10 vols. (1891–1931); *Portland Papers* (1893); *Rutland* MSS 4 vols. (1888–1905); *Stuart Papers, Windsor Castle*, 7 vols. (1902–23); *Townshend* MSS (1887); *Various Collections, Clements* MSS

Huygens, C., *Journaal van Constantijn Huygens* (Utrecht 1876)

Impartial Inquiry into the Management of the War in Spain (1712)

Japikse, N., *Correspondentie van Willem III en van Hans Willem Bentinck, Eersten Graaf van Portland* (The Hague 1927–37), first series in two parts, second series in three parts

Jones, Col. J., 'A Journal of the Siege of San Mateo 1707', *Accounts of Sieges 1680–1708*, no. 7

[Keeper, The Lord]*The Rt. Hon. the Lord Keeper's Speech to the Rt. Hon. the Earl of Peterborough 12 January 1710/1711* (Edinburgh 1710/11)

Kemble, J. M., *State Papers and Correspondence* (1857)

Lamberty, G. de, *Mémoires pour servir à l'Histoire du XVIIIme Siecle*, 6 vols. (Paris 1735)

Leven and Melville Papers (Bannatyne Club 1843)

Lexington Papers, ed. H. Manners Sutton (1851)

[Locke, John] *The Correspondence of John Locke*, ed. E. S. de Beer, 8 vols. (Oxford 1978); *The Correspondence of John Locke and Edward Clarke*, ed. B. Rand (1927); *Original Letters of John Locke, Algernon Sidney et al.*, ed. T. Forster (1830)

London Evening Post 11–13 March, 30 August–2 September, 4–6 September, 15–18, 20–2 November 1735

[Lords, House of] *Journal of the House of Lords*, vols. xiii, xiv, xv, xvi, xvii, xix, xxiv

Luttrell, N., *Brief Relation of State Affairs 1678–1714*, 6 vols.(Oxford 1857)

Luttrell, N., *Parliamentary Diary*, ed. H. Horwitz (1972)

Macpherson, J., *Original Papers*, 2 vols. (1775)

[Marchmont, Earl of] *A Selection from the Papers of the Earls of Marchmont*, ed. Sir G. H. Rose, 3 vols. (1831)

[Marlborough, Duke of] *The Letters and Dispatches of John Churchill, First Duke of Marlborough*, ed. Sir G. Murray, 5 vols. (1845)

[Marlborough, Duke of] *The Marlborough–Godolphin Correspondence*, ed. H. Snyder, 3 vols. (Oxford 1975)

[Marlborough, Duke of] *The Marlborough–Heinsius Correspondence*, ed. B. van T'Hoff (The Hague 1951)

Marlborough, Sarah, Duchess of, *Letters* (*at Madresfield Court*) (1875)

——, *Memoirs*, ed. W. King (1930)

[Marlborough, Sarah, Duchess of] *Letters of a Grandmother 1732–1735*

(*Sarah, Duchess of Marlborough to Diana, Duchess of Bedford*), ed. G. S. Thomson (1944)

[Marlborough, Sarah, Duchess of] *The Private Correspondence of Sarah Duchess of Marlborough*, ed. Lord John Russell, 2 vols. (1838)

[Mary, Queen] *Memoirs of Mary Queen of England*, ed. R. Doebner (1886)

Melvilles, Earls of Melville, The, ed. W. Fraser, 2 vols. (Edinburgh 1890)

Millner, J., *A Compendious Journal of all the Marches, Famous Battles, Sieges and Actions of the Triumphant Armies of the Confederate High Allies in the Late War against France, 1701–1712* (1733)

Monckton, Sir Philip, *The Monckton Papers*, ed. E. Peacock (1884)

[Mordaunt, John] *Letter Book of John Mordaunt 1658–1660*, ed. M. Coate (Camden Society 1945)

[Mordaunt, Viscountess] *Private Diarie of Viscountess Mordaunt*, ed. Earl of Roden (1856)

[Morrison, Alfred] *Catalogue of the Collection of Autograph Letters and Historical Documents Formed by Alfred Morrison*, ed. E. W. Thibaudeau, 6 vols. (1883–92)

[Morrison, Alfred] *Autograph Letters in the Collection of Alfred Morrison: Bulstrode Papers* (1897)

[Newton, Sir Isaac] *The Correspondence of Sir Isaac Newton*, ed. H. W. Turnbull, 7 vols. (Cambridge 1959–77)

[Nicolson, William] *The London Diaries of William Nicolson 1702–1718*, ed. C. Jones and G. Holmes (Oxford 1985)

Oldmixon, J., *History of England* (1730)

[Palatine, Princess] *Lettres de la Princesse Palatine*, ed. O. Amiel (1982)

Particular Relation of the Late Success of His Majesty's Forces at Tangier (1680)

[Pepys, Samuel] *Catalogue of Pepysian MSS in Magdalen College*, ed. J. R. Tanner, 4 vols. (Navy Records Society 1903–23)

[Pepys, Samuel] *The Private Correspondence of Samuel Pepys*, ed. J. R. Tanner, 2 vols. (1926)

[Peterborough, Earl of] *Letters of the Earl of Peterborough to General Stanhope in Spain* (1834)

Poems on Affairs of State, ed. W. J. Cameron, vol. v (New Haven, Connecticut 1971)

Pope, Alexander, *Poetical Works*, ed. H. Davis (Oxford 1967)

[Pope, Alexander] *The Correspondence of Alexander Pope*, ed. G. Sherburn, 5 vols., (Oxford 1956)

Portledge Papers, The, eds. R. J. Kerr and I. C. Duncan (1928)

[Prideaux, Humphrey] *Letters of Humphrey Prideaux to John Ellis*, ed. E. M. Thompson (1875)

Prinsterer, G. G. van, *Archives de la Maison Orange-Nassau*, second series, vol. v (The Hague, 1861)

Prior, Matthew, *History of His Own Time* (1740)

[Pryme, Abraham de la] *The Diary of Abraham de la Pryme*, ed. C. Jackson (Surtees Society 1870)

Ralph, J., *History of England during the Reigns of King William, Queen Anne, and George I* (1744)

Remarks on the Thoughts of a Member of the Lower House (1719)

Remarks upon Dr Freind's Account of the Earl of Peterborow's Conduct in Spain (1708)

Rochester Savile Letters, ed. J. H. Wilson (Columbus, Ohio 1941)

Ross, John, *Tangiers Rescue* (1681)

[Russell, Lady Rachel] *Letters of Lady Rachel Russell*, ed. T. Sellwood (1801)

[St Pierre, Colonel de] *The Military Memoirs of Colonel de St Pierre*, ed. E. R. James (1882)

[St Simon, Duc de] *Historical Memoirs of the Duc de St Simon*, ed. L. Norton (1972)

Stevenson, G., ed., *Letters of Madame* (1925)

[Seafield, Earl of] *The Correspondence of James First Earl of Seafield*, ed. J. Grant (Scottish History Society, Edinburgh 1912)

Seward, S., *Anecdotes of Some Distinguished Persons* (1796)

[Shaftesbury, Earl of] *Life and Unpublished Letters of Anthony Earl of Shaftesbury*, ed. B. Rand (1900)

[Shrewsbury, Duke of] *The Private and Original Correspondence of Charles Talbot, Duke of Shrewsbury, with King William, Etc.*, ed. W. Coxe (1821)

Sidney, Henry, *Diary of the Times of Charles II*, ed. R. W. Blencowe, 2 vols. (1843)

Simpson, A., 'Notes of a Noble Lord', *English Historical Review*, vol. lii (1937)

[Somers, Lord] 'The Comparison or Accounts of Both Sides Fairly Stated (1711)', *Somers Tracts* (1965)

Spence, J., *Anecdotes, Observations of Books and Men Collected from the Conversations of Mr Pope and Other Eminent Persons of His Time by the Reverend Joseph Spence*, ed. S. W. Singer (1964)

[Stair, 1st and 2nd Earls of] Graham, J. M., ed., *Annals and Correspondence of the Viscount and First and Second Earls of Stair* (Edinburgh 1875)

[Suffolk, Henrietta, Countess of] *Letters to and from Henrietta Countess of Suffolk 1712–1767*, ed. J. Croker, 2 vols. (1824)

[Swift, Jonathan] *The Correspondence of Jonathan Swift*, ed. H. Williams, 5 vols. (Oxford 1963–5)

Swift, Jonathan, *Journal to Stella*, ed. H. Williams, 2 vols. (Oxford 1974)

——, *Miscellanies* (1727)

[Teonge, Revd Henry]*Diary of the Revd Henry Teonge 1675–79*, ed. G. E. Manwaring (1927)

[Tessé, Maréchal de] *Lettres du Maréchal de Tessé au Prince Antoine de Monaco* (Paris 1917)

[Tessé, Maréchal de] *Mémoires et Lettres du Maréchal de Tessé*, 2 vols. (Paris 1806)

Thoughts of a Member of the Lower House, The (1719)

Timberland, E., ed., *History and Proceedings of the House of Lords*, 3 vols. (1742)

[Torcy, Marquis de] *Memoirs of the Marquis de Torcy*, 2 vols. (1757)

T. W., *The Trial of Mr Mordaunt at the Pretended High Court of Justice in Westminster Hall, 1 and 2 June 1658* (1661).

[Vernon, James] *Letters Illustrative of the Reign of William III Addressed to the Duke of Shrewsbury by James Vernon Esq.*, ed. G. P. R. James, 3 vols. (1841)

Vertue, G., *Notebooks*, vol. vi (Walpole Society, Oxford, vol. xxx, 1955)

[Voltaire] *The Correspondence of Voltaire*, ed. T Besterman, 107 vols. (Geneva 1953–65)

[Voltaire]*Mémoires de Voltaire*, ed. A. Friedmann (1966), vol. iii

[Voltaire] *Voltaire's Notebooks*, ed. T. Besterman, 2 vols. (Geneva 1952)

Walpole, H[oratio], *Reminiscences and Notes of Conversations with Lady Suffolk* (Oxford 1924)

[Walpole, Horatio Lord] *Memoirs of Horatio Lord Walpole*, ed. W. Coxe (1802)

Wentworth Papers, ed. J. Cartwright (1883)

Whittle, J., *An Exact Diary of the late Expedition of the Prince of Orange* (1689)

[William III, King] *Letters of William III and Louis XIV*, ed. P. Grimblot, 2 vols. (1848)

[Wortley Montagu, Mary] *Letters of Lady Mary Wortley Montagu*, ed. R. Halsband, (Oxford 1965–7)

SELECT BIBLIOGRAPHY

Books

Armstrong, E., *Elizabeth Farnese* (1892)

Ashley, M., *John Wildman, Postmaster and Plotter* (1947)

Ault, N., *A Treasury of Unfamiliar Lyrics* (1938)

Bacallar y Sana, V., Marques de San Felipe, *Commentarios de la Guerra de Espana y Historia de su Rey Felipe V* (Madrid 1957)

Ballard, C., *The Great Earl of Peterborough* (1930)

Barbier, E. F. G., *Chronique de la Régence*, 8 vols. (Paris 1885)

Barker, G. F. R., and Stenning, A. H., *The Record of Old Westminsters*, 2 vols. (1928)

Baudrillart, A., *Philippe V et la Cour de France*, 5 vols. (Paris 1890–1900)

Berwick y Alba, Duque de, *El Mariscal de Berwick* (Madrid 1925)

Bowack, J., *Antiquities of Middlesex* (1705–6)

Brewster, D., *Aaron Hill, Poet, Dramatist and Projector* (New York 1966)

Brown, P. Hume, *History of Scotland*, 3 vols. (Cambridge 1909)

Browning, A., *Thomas Osborne, Earl of Danby and Duke of Leeds 1632–1712*, 3 vols. (Glasgow 1951)

Bryant, J., *Marble Hill House* (1988)

Bryant, J., *Mrs Howard: A Woman of Reason* (1988), Exhibition Catalogue

Burke, *Dormant and Extinct Peerage* (1883)

Burney, C., *General History of Music*, 4 vols. (1789)

Carswell, J., *The Descent on England* (1969)

Chase, C. B., *The Young Voltaire* (1926)

Childs, J., *The Army, James II and the Glorious Revolution* (Manchester 1980)

——, *The British Army of William III* (Manchester 1987)

——, *The Nine Years' War and the British Army* (Manchester 1991)

Christie, W. D., *A Life of Anthony Ashley Cooper, First Earl of Shaftesbury*, 2 vols. (1871)

Churchill, W. S., *Marlborough, His Life and Times*, 4 vols. (1933)

Clark, G., *The Later Stuarts 1660–1714* (Oxford 1955)

Clay, C., *Public Finance and Private Wealth: The Career of Sir Stephen Fox* (Oxford 1978)

Clowes, W. L., *The Royal Navy*, 7 vols. (1898)

Cockayne, G. E., *The Complete Peerage*, 8 vols. (1887–98)

Collins, J. Churton, *Voltaire, Montesquieu and Rousseau in England* (1908)

Cooke, W. H., *Collections towards the History and Antiquities of the County of Hereford*, vol. iii (1882)

Coward, B., *The Stuart Age* (1994)

Coxe, W., *Memoirs of the Duke of Marlborough*, 3 vols. (1847–8)

Cranston, M., *John Locke* (Oxford 1985)

Dalton, C., *George I's Army* (1910)

Davies, G., *The Restoration of Charles II 1658–1660* (1955)

Davies, J. S., *A History of Southampton* (1883)

Davies, K. G., *The Royal African Company* (1957)

Davies, N., *God's Playground: A History of Poland*, 2 vols. (Oxford 1981)

Dédéyan, C., *Le Retour de Salente ou Voltaire et Angleterre* (Paris 1988)

Dickinson, H. T., *Bolingbroke* (1970)

Duncan, F., *History of the Royal Regiment of Artillery*, 2 vols. (1872)

Dyer, F. E., *Life of Admiral Sir John Narborough* (1931)

Ehrman, J. P. W., *The Navy in the War of William III* (Cambridge 1953)

Escolano, G., *Decadas de la Historia de la Ciudad de Valencia*, ed. J. B. Perales, vol. iii (Madrid 1880)

Fairholt, F. W., *Lord Mayor's Pageants*, part i (1843)

Feret, C. J., *Fulham Old and New*, 2 vols. (1900)

Ferguson, J., *Robert Ferguson the Plotter* (1887)

Foster, J., *Alumni Oxoniensis*, vol. iii (1892)

Foxcroft, H. C., *Life and Letters of the First Marquess of Halifax* (1898)

Francis, A. D., *The First Peninsular War* (1975)

Francis, A. D., *The Methuens and Portugal* (1966)

Glendinning, V., *Jonathan Swift* (1998)

Godber, J., *History of Bedfordshire* (1969)

Godfrey, E., *The Trial of Count Königsmarck* (1929)

Green, E., *The March of William of Orange through Somerset* (1892)

Hamilton, F. W., *History of the First or Grenadier Guards*, 3 vols. (1874)

Handel: A Celebration of His Life and Times, ed. J. Simon, Exhibition Catalogue, National Portrait Gallery (1985)

Harcourt-Smith, S., *Alberoni and the Spanish Conspiracy* (1943)

Harlow, V. T., *Christopher Codrington 1668–1710* (Oxford 1928)

Harris, T., *Politics under the Later Stuarts* (1993)

Harvey, W. M., *History and Antiquity of the Hundred of Willey, Bedfordshire* (1872–8)

Hearnshaw, F. J. C., *A Short History of Southampton* (1910)

Henning, B. D., ed., *The History of Parliament: The House of Commons 1660–1690*, 3 vols. (1983)

Hill, C. P., *Who's Who in Stuart Britain* (1988)

Holmes, G., *The Making of a Great Power* (1993)

Horwitz, H. G., *Parliament, Policy and Politics in the Reign of William III* (Manchester 1977)

——, *Revolution Politicks: The Career of Daniel Finch, Second Earl of Nottingham 1647–1730* (1968)

Hugill, J. A. C., *No Peace Without Spain*, (Oxford, Kensal Press 1991)

Hutton, R., *The Restoration* (Oxford 1985)

Jones, J. R., *The Revolution of 1688 in England* (New York 1972)

Kamen, H., *The War of the Succession in Spain 1700–1715* (1969)

Keay, J., *The Honourable Company* (1993)

Kenyon, J. P., *Revolution Principles* (Cambridge 1977)

King, Lord, *The Life of John Locke* (1858)

Klopp, O., *Der Fall des Hauses Stuart und die Sukzession des Hauses Hannover in Gross-Britannien und Irland*, 14 vols. (Wien 1875–88)

Krey, G. S. de, *A Fractured Society: The Politics of London in the First Age of Party 1688–1715* (Oxford 1985)

Kuenzel, H., *Leben des Landgrafen Georg von Hessen-Darmstadt* (Freidburg 1859)

Landau, M., *Geschichte Kaiser Karls VI* (Stuttgart 1889)

Lenman, B., *The Jacobite Risings in Britain 1689–1746* (1980)

Lysons, D., *Environs of London*, 4 vols. (1792–6)

Macaulay, Lord, *History of England*, 2 vols. (1889)

Mack, M., *Alexander Pope* (1985)

——, *Collected in Himself* (Yale 1982)

MacMunn, Sir George, *Prince Eugene* (1953)

Mahon, Lord, *History of England 1713–1783*, 7 vols. (1853)

——, *War of the Spanish Succession* (1836)

Manchester, Duke of, *Court and Society from Elizabeth to Anne*, 2 vols. (1864)

Martin-Leake, S., *Life of Admiral Sir John Leake*, ed. G. A. R. Callender, 2 vols. (Navy Records Society 1920)

——, *Life of Captain Stephen Martin 1666–1740*, ed. C. R. Markham (1895)

Melville, L., *Lady Suffolk and Her Circle* (1924)

Merriman, R. D., *Queen Anne's Navy 1702–1714* (Navy Records Society 1961)

Miller, J., *The Glorious Revolution* (1983)

——, *James II, A Study in Kingship* (1991)

Miller, P., *James* (1980)

Ogg, D., *England in the Reigns of James II and William III* (Oxford 1984)

Owen, J. H., *The War at Sea under Queen Anne* (1938)

Oyley, E. d', *James Duke of Monmouth* (1938)

Parnell, A., *The War of the Succession in Spain 1702–1711* (1905)

Pelet, J. J. G., *Mémoires Militaires rélatifs à la succession d'Espagne sous Louis XIV*, 11 vols. (Paris 1836–62)

Ranke, L. von, *A History of England Principally in the Seventeenth Century*, 6 vols. (Oxford 1875)

Routh, E. M. G., *Tangier 1680–84* (1912)

Russell, F. S., *The Earl of Peterborough and Monmouth*, 2 vols. (1887)

Russell, Lord, *Life of Rachel Wriothesley Lady Russell* (1819)

Sachse, W., *Lord Somers* (Manchester 1975)

Scouller, R. E., *The Armies of Queen Anne* (Oxford 1966)

Sichel, W., *Bolingbroke and His Times*, 2 vols. (1901–2)

Somerville, D., *The King of Hearts* (1962)

Speck, W. A., *Reluctant Revolutionaries* (Oxford 1989)

Stebbing, W., *Peterborough* (1890)

Stewart, D., *Sir Godfrey Kneller and the English Baroque Portrait* (Oxford 1983)

Symcox, G., *Victor Amadeus* (1983)

Tanner, L. E., *History of the Coronation* (1952)

Targe, J. B., *L'Avènement de la Maison de Bourbon*, 6 vols. (Paris 1772)

Taylor, W. D., *Jonathan Swift* (1933)

Tighe R. R. and Davies, J. E., *Annals of Windsor*, 2 vols. (1858)

Trevelyan, G. M., *England under Queen Anne*, 3 vols. (1931–4)
Turberville, A. S., *The House of Lords in the Eighteenth Century* (Oxford 1927)
——, *The House of Lords in the Reign of William III* (Oxford 1913)
Underdown, D., *Royalist Conspiracy in England 1649–1660* (Yale 1960)
Victoria History of the Counties of England: Bedfordshire, vol. iii (1912); *Surrey*, vols. ii (1905) and iii (1911); *Wiltshire*, vol. xiv (1992)
Vitelleschi, Marchesa, *Romance of Savoy*, 2 vols. (1905)
Voltes Bou, P., *Barcelona durante el Gobierno del Archiduque Carlos de Austria* (Barcelona 1963)
——, *La Guerra de Succesion en Valencia* (Barcelona 1964)
Voltaire, *Histoire de Jenni*, ed. J. H. Brumfitt and M. I. G. Davis (1960)
Walpole, H., *A Catalogue of Royal and Noble Authors of England, Scotland and Ireland*, ed. T. Park, 5 vols. (1806)
Warburton, G. E., *A Memoir of Charles Mordaunt, Earl of Peterborough* (1853)

Articles
Carter, J., 'Cabinet Records for the Reign of William III', *English Historical Review*, vol. lxxviii (1963)
Clark, Sir G., 'The Nine Years' War', and 'From Nine Years' War to the War of the Spanish Succession', *New Cambridge Modern History*, vol. vi (Cambridge 1970)
Cruickshanks, E., and others, 'Divisions in the House of Lords 1689–1694', *Bulletin of the Institute of Historical Research*, vol. liii (1980)
Dickson, G. M., 'War Finance', *New Cambridge Modern History*, vol. vi (Cambridge 1970)
Fieldhouse, H. N., 'St John and Savoy', appendix iii, *English Historical Review*, vol. l (1935)
Francis, A. D., 'Prince George of Hesse-Darmstadt and the Plans for the Expedition to Spain of 1702', *Bulletin of the Institute of Historical Research*, vol. xlii (1969)
Gierowski, J. and Kaminski, A., 'The Eclipse of Poland', *New Cambridge Modern History*, vol. vi (Cambridge 1970)
Haley, K. H. D., 'A List of the English Peers c. May 1687', *English Historical Review*, vol. lxix (1954)
Halliday, J., 'The Club and the Revolution in Scotland', *Scottish History Review*, vol. xlv (1966)
Journal of the British Archaeological Association, vol. xv (1859)
Miñana, J. M. de, 'De La Guerra Rustica Valenciana (De Bello Rustico Valentino)', *Revue Hispanique*, vol. lv (Paris 1922)
'The Peerage Bill in 1719', *Retrospective Review*, second series, vol. ii (1828)
Power, J. E., 'Pope's Jesuit', *Notes and Queries*, vol. ccxiv (1969)

Rousseau, G. S., 'A New Pope Letter', *Philological Quarterly*, vol. xlv (1966)

Scouller, R. E., 'The Peninsula in the War of the Spanish Succession', *Journal of the Society for Army Historical Research*, vol. liv (1976)

Speck, W. A., 'William – and Mary?', *The Revolution of 1688–89* (Cambridge 1992)

Trevelyan, G. M., 'Peterborough and Barcelona 1705', *Cambridge Historical Journal*, vol. iii (1929–31)

Turner, E. R., 'The Peerage Bill of 1719', *English Historical Review*, vol. xxviii (1913)

Veenendaal, A. J., 'The War of the Spanish Succession in Europe', *New Cambridge Modern History*, vol. vi (Cambridge 1970)

Index

234, 243; character 160–1, 251;
expedition to Barcelona 164–9,
182; at Barcelona 168, 169–76,
196, 206, 225, 228, 234, 237, 238,
243, 244, 255, 256; his Austrian
court 169, 170, 172, 175, 188,
200, 201, 202, 203, 204, 207, 216,
226, 236, 247, 248, 249, 251, 252,
253, 254, 256, 260, 262, 263, 264,
272, 273, 275, 281; his troops
172, 220, 246, 247, 248, 249, 252,
254, 260, 279, 283; and
Montjuich 179, 180, 181, 188;
proclaimed King in Barcelona 197,
199; his supporters in Valencia
207, 208, 213, 223; his letters to
Leake 233, 239, 274; his attitude
to Peterborough 236, 253, 254,
272, 278, 281, 283, 326, 363; on
the road to Madrid 245, 249, 251,
252, 254, 256, 261, 263, 264, 268,
272, 273, 275, 276, 299, 300, 304,
305, 315; letters to Peterborough
246, 249–54, 297; his expenses
247, 248, 253, 254, 258, 265;
leaves Barcelona 251; at
Guadalajara 267, 269; sends
Count Gallas to London 253, 275;
and Comte de Noyelles 282; and
Battle of Almanza 287; election as
Emperor 323, 328, 330, 331; and
the Duke of Savoy 324, 342–3,
352, 353, 363, 393; his return
from Spain 324, 326, 330, 333;
sends Prince Eugène to England
333; as Emperor 335, 349, 368,
400; does not acknowledge Treaty
of Utrecht 353; in Quadruple
Alliance 377, 395, 396, 397, 398
Charles XII, King of Sweden 292; his
career 293; his League of
Protestant Princes 293–4; and
Peterborough's visit 294–5
Châteaurenault, François Louis

Rousselet de, Vice Admiral and
Marshal of France 137
Chaworth, Lady 8
Chellington, manor of 112n., 312,
362n.
Chelsea College 95, 96, 102
Chesshyre, John 143
Chesterfield, Earl of, *see* Stanhope
Chetwynd, John, British envoy at
Turin 276, 277, 289, 324, 327,
337, 343
Chiari, Battle of (1701) 147
Chichester, Arthur, third Earl of
Donegal 163, 172, 235
Chichester, earldom of 37
Chinchón 270, 275
Chiva 224, 225
Christ Church, Oxford 4, 138
Churchill, John, first Baron, later
Earl then Duke of Marlborough
67, 121, 132n., 149, 265n., 287,
291, 292, 310, 318, 326, 407;
defected to William of Orange 24;
opposed the lodging of James II in
the Tower 27; Privy Councillor 51,
56; at Cork and Kinsale 62; at the
trial of Sir John Fenwick 97, 100,
124; and Monmouth's censure
107; as a Tory 114; lays treaties
before House of Lords 134; on
accession of Queen Anne 136; and
Peterborough's West Indian
appointment 136, 139, 140;
dukedom 144; his 'great design'
(1703) 145; calls for his
resignation 145; and William's
military plans 148; as a military
commander 150; and
Peterborough's command in Spain
154, 155, 156, 230, 271, 272, 273,
276; and Toulon 155, 157–8, 277,
285, 296; visits Lady Peterborough
279, 293; his camp 290, 291, 296;
and Peterborough's recall 291,

convoy, Irish 232, 234
Conyngham, Major General Henry 172, 206, 223
Cook, Sir Thomas, Governor of East India Company 89
Cork, siege of, 62
Cornbury, Lord, *see* Hyde
Cornwallis, Charles, third Baron 99
coronation; of William and Mary 37–8, 39; of James II 38; of Elizabeth II 38n.
Corsica 284
Corzana, Conde de 157, 160
Cosimo III, Grand Duke of Tuscany 371
Council of Nine 50–1, 54, 59, 62
Councils: Grand Councils at Lisbon 160; councils of war of land officers 167, 168, 171, 172, 173, 174, 175, 180, 213–4, 221, 224, 225, 229, 230, 256, 262, 263, 270, 273, 275, 300; councils of war of flag officers 169, 171, 173–4, 175, 232, 233, 274; councils held by King Charles 170, 180, 251; Grand Council at Barcelona 245, 257; council of war at Guadalajara 265, 266; council at Valencia (January 1707) 281, 282, 289, 315, 316, 318
Courteen, Sir William 11
Courts: of Chancery 112, 143; of King's Bench 66, 110; of Exchequer 66; of general officers 95; of Requests 98, 202
Coutenay, Mr, of Amsterdam 54
Cowper, William, later lord Chancellor 143
Craggs, Joseph 178
Crew, Dr Nathaniel, Bishop of Durham 33
Croft, Dr William 388
Croix Couvert 168, 186, 199
Croker, J.W. 382n.

Cromwell, Oliver, Lord Protector 1, 3, 149
Crone, Mr, a Jacobite 54
Crowe, Mitford 159, 164, 165, 168, 200, 203, 204, 210, 217, 227, 239, 272
Cuenca 261, 263, 270, 275, 276
Cullera 225
Cumberland, William, Duke of 411, 415
Cuneo 291
Cunningham, Alexander 333, 335, 361, 362, 368
Curtius, Quintus 303
Customs Commissioners 95
Cutts, John, Baron Cutts of Gowran 95
Cuzzoni, Francesca 391

Dalrymple, Sir Hugh, Lord President of the Court of Session 312
Dalrymple, John, second Earl of Stair 355, 357–8, 359, 369; negotiations with French Court 359–60
Dalrymple of Stair, Sir John 46
Danby, Earl of, *see* Osborne
Dangeau, Marquis de 351; his Journal 355
Danube, River 321, 344
Danvers, Elizabeth née Mordaunt 50n.
Danvers, Silvester 50n.
Danvers, Sir John 50, 66
Danvers, John (son of preceding) 50, 66, 67
Danvers family 50, 66
Darien, Panama 124, 151; *see also* Company of Scotland
Darmstadt 189
Daroca 261
Dartmouth, Baron and Earl of, *see* Legge
Dauntsey, Wiltshire 50, 65, 119, 132, 341; case of Browne v. Wayte

Gloucester, William Henry, Duke of 64, 125, 128

Godolphin, Mrs Margaret, *née* Blagge 5

Godolphin, Sidney, first Baron 67; a commissioner from the King to William 24; Treasury Commissioner 35, 41, 48; member of Council of Nine 62; and the trial of Sir John Fenwick 97, 101, 124; and Monmouth's censure 107; as a Tory 114; First Lord of the Treasury 128; in the Cockpit circle 136; and Peterborough's West Indian appointment 136; calls for his resignation 145; his ministry 151; and War of Spanish Succession 161, 171, 172, 174, 181, 191, 192, 218, 230, 244, 247, 249, 260, 267, 271, 272; and Peterborough 273, 276, 278, 287, 296–7, 298, 307; replaced as Chancellor of the Exchequer 312

Golden Square 389

Gordon, Alexander, Marquess of Huntly, later second Duke of Gordon 310, 358, 366n., 371, 405

Gordon, Cosmo George, third Duke of Gordon 405

Gordon, Duchess of, wife of first Duke 358

Gordon, George, first Duke of 358

Gordon, Henrietta (Harriet), *née* Mordaunt, Marchioness of Huntly and Duchess of Gordon, birth 8, 13; her portrait at Drayton 112; rumour of marriage to Duke of Norfolk 126; marriage 309; and her mother 309–10; raised her children as Protestants 358, 405, 411; her political views 358; visited by her father in Scotland 405; pension from the Crown 411, 412

Gordon, William, second Earl of Aberdeen 405

Gorges, Brigadier 155, 172, 184, 186, 210, 218, 234, 258; his regiment 257, 258

Goudet, John 118

Gould, schoolmaster at Dauntsey 132

Gracia, convent of 184

Grafton, Duke of, *see* Fitzroy

Grand Alliance, the 129, 131, 134, 293

Granville, Charles, Viscount Lansdowne 136

Great Trust 3

Greenwich 89, 315n., 318, 319; Royal Naval Hospital 89; Painted Hall 89n.; Queen's House 89

Grey, Henry, Earl and later Duke of Kent 311, 347

Grey, Thomas, second Earl of Stamford 27, 107

Grey of Warke, Forde, third Baron, first Earl of Tankerville 15, 92n., 93, 98, 99, 131

Grimes, Mrs 310

Guadalajara 260, 261, 264, 268, 270, 315

Guadarama 255

Gualterio, Cardinal 370

Guastalla, Duke of 335

Guernsey 73, 74, 75, 76

Guipuzcoa 118

Guise, Sir John 23

Gunpowder Plot, anniversary of 22

Gwynne, Sir Rowland 14, 154

Haddock, Sir Richard 61

Hales, Sir Edward, 17, 26

Halifax, first Baron later Earl of, *see* Montagu

Halifax, Marquess of, *see* Savile

Ham House 27

Lowther, Sir John 48, 51, 62
Lucca 342
Lumley, Richard, first Baron and Viscount, first Earl of Scarbrough 131; signed invitation to William 21; as an Army Commissioner 39
Luxembourg, François-Henri de Montmorency, Duc de 77
Lyons 352, 354, 365, 419

Maastricht 296
Macclesfield, Earl of, see Gerard
Mackenzie, George 338–9
Madrid 164, 165
Maffei, Count Annibale 327, 348
magazines 246, 250
Maintenon, Françoise d'Aubigné, Madame de 417
Málaga, 197; Battle of (1704) 149, 150
Mallorca 201, 253, 256, 266, 274, 283
Mallory, Captain, witness against John Mordaunt 2
Malmesbury, elections at 132–3
Malmesbury Abbey 50
Malplaquet, Battle of (1709) 310
Malt Tax 347
Malta, knights of 172
Manchester, Earl of, see Montagu
Manley, Mrs Delarivière 413
Mar, Earl of, see Erskine
Marble Hill 51n., 384, 385, 394, 400
Marchamalo 264
Marie-Adelaide of Savoy, Duchess of Burgundy 146, 336
Marie-Jeanne-Baptiste of Savoy-Carignan, Madame Royale 277, 365
Marie-Louise of Savoy, Duchess of Anjou, Queen of Spain 146, 147, 242–3, 251, 252
marines 163, 174, 179, 184, 188, 200, 223, 238, 240, 246, 258

Marlborough, Earl and Duke of, see Churchill
Marly 354
Marseilles 352
Marshall, Hezekiah, Commissary of Provisions 139
Martorell 228, 237
Mary, Princess of Orange, later Mary II 11, 75; declared joint sovereign with William 33; arrived at Whitehall 34; coronation 38; and the Council of Nine 50–1, 54, 55, 56; her opinion of Monmouth 51, 62; and Sir James Montgomery 61; death 87; and Greenwich Palace as a hospital for seamen 89
Mary Beatrice, Queen of James II 26, 101; her jointure trustees 50; and Peterborough's supposed attempt to murder the Pretender 365, 367, 369, 371
Masham, Mrs Abigail 311
Masham, Damaris, Lady 65, 73
Mataró 166, 174, 183, 228, 237, 238; the Jurados of 167
Maurice, Mr, Member of Parliament 88
Max Emmanuel, Elector of Bavaria 345
Mead, Mr, Paymaster 247, 248
Meadows, Sir Philip 92n.
Meldert 296
Melfort, Earl of, see Drummond
Mellarède, Pierre, comte de Bettonet 322
Melville, George, first Earl of Melville, Secretary of State for Scotland 46, 61
Mendonca, Don Diego de 421
Menorca 201, 253, 256, 266, 274, 354
merchants: English 256, 279, 288; French 222, 344; in Milan 324; in Venice 344; British in Sicily 344

394, 409, 412; member of
William's Privy Council 34, 83, 88,
102, 109, 116; First Lord of the
Treasury 34, 39, 41, 42, 45, 48,
81; his City regiment of horse 36,
42, 44, 61; on Lords' Committees
36, 80, 111, 118, 128, 129, 131,
133; investigates death of Earl of
Essex 36; Gentleman of the
Bedchamber to the King 37, 38,
64, 79, 81, 83, 88, 109, 111, 112;
Lord Lieutenant of
Northamptonshire 37, 86, 128,
136; created Earl of Monmouth
37, 39; as an Army Commissioner
39, 40, 41; letters to Locke 40, 65,
78, 80, 91–2, 113, 141;
investigation of plots 43, 53; and
Jacobites 43, 53, 54, 86–7, 358–9,
361, 371; and Scottish affairs 45,
46, 47, 52, 53, 347; contact with
Sir James Montgomery 47, 52–3,
61, 82; in opposition to Halifax
47; grant of Dauntsey, Wiltshire
49–50, 66, 67, 341; one of 'the
Nine' 51, 62; and the 'lemon
letters' 54, 56, 58, 59, 63; and the
Navy 55, 56, 57, 58, 59, 60–1;
conversations with Queen Mary
59, 60; at sea with William 63; fire
in his lodgings at Whitehall 64–5;
as a gardener 65, 66, 138–9, 201,
328, 334, 355, 382, 384–5, 403,
406, 407, 418; and the case of
Fulke Wallwyn 68–72; in
command in Guernsey (1692) 74,
75, 76; Triennial Parliaments Bill
81–2, 83, 87, 88, 89;
Commissioner for Prizes 85;
grudge against Lord Normanby
88, 89; Commissioner for
Greenwich Hospital 89; on
progress with the King 90;
proposed Association in Lords

(1696) 93; declined post of First
Admiralty Commissioner 94;
Ulysses Brown and the hold-up at
Chelsea 95, 96, 102, 120; and Sir
John Fenwick 97, 98, 99, 100,
101–2, 103, 104–5, 105–6, 107,
108, 116, 120; sent to the Tower
108; his release 111; illnesses 111,
191, 262, 281, 284, 285, 288, 292,
298, 311, 329, 331, 336, 342, 346,
403, 406, 408, 409, 412, 415, 416,
419–20, 421; and Matthew Smith
112, 120, 123–4; inherited
earldom of Peterborough 112;
court actions against the Duchess
of Norfolk 112, 116, 126, 143;
mistaken for Duke of Berwick
113–14; support of Sunderland
115; in cabals against the Court
116, 119; and matters between
Lords and Commons 117, 130–1;
and Royal African Company 117;
in debates in the House of Lords
119, 125, 127, 128, 144, 150, 151,
152, 304, 346, 347, 360, 393, 400,
408–9, 409–10; in conversation
with Vernon 120–1, 121–2, 126;
and his brother Harry 122, 128;
financial matters 122, 142, 200,
205, 229, 246–7, 249, 250, 253,
257, 263, 265, 269, 279, 284, 286,
288, 297, 299, 300–1, 305, 307,
309, 312, 322, 324, 325, 326–7,
333, 334–5, 337, 348, 349, 354,
364, 365, 366, 366n., 372, 393;
and the Duke of Shrewsbury 124;
and Union between England and
Scotland 125, 131, 152, 347,
374–5; and the case of Colonel
Park 132–3; Captain-General of all
the forces in the West Indies 134,
136, 138, 139–40, 141, 142, 267,
300; translates *First Olynthiac* of
Demosthenes 136; as Governor of

385, 408; his poem on Mrs
Howard 386–7, 395; the Senesino
incident 391–2, 395; Continental
visits 393, 394–5, 395–6, 396–7,
398, 399; at Marlborough's
funeral 393; and the Opera 395;
and Monteleone in Paris 396–9; in
Bath 400, 403, 409, 413, 416; and
Voltaire 402–3, 404–5;
correspondence with Dr Towne
403, 405; at Bevis Mount 405–8,
411, 417; and his daughter's
pension 411, 412; letter to Lady
Mary Wortley Montagu 412; his
operation 416–17, 420;
acknowledges his marriage
415–16, 417, 420; his last journey
418, 420; at Lisbon 421; his death
407, 422

Mordaunt, Charles, later Viscount
Mordaunt, fourth earl of
Peterborough 308, 314–15, 358,
364, 371, 403

Mordaunt, Colonel Charles, nephew
of third Earl of Peterborough 380

Mordaunt, Elizabeth, née Carey,
Viscountess Mordaunt, 7; birth of
first son, 1; shares husband's
imprisonment 1; friendship with
Queen of Bohemia 2; her bankrupt
estate 13; friendship with Princess
Sophia Palatine 295

Mordaunt, Elizabeth, née Howard,
Dowager Countess of
Peterborough, widow of John, first
earl 1, 4, 6; support of younger son
2; care of grandchildren 3; estates
sequestered 3

Mordaunt, Frances, née Poulett,
Viscountess Mordaunt 205, 308,
311, 358

Mordaunt, George, fourth son of
third Earl of Peterborough 8

Mordaunt, Henrietta (Harriet),

daughter of third Earl of
Peterborough, later Marchioness
of Huntly and Duchess of Gordon,
see Gordon

Mordaunt, Henry, second Earl of
Peterborough 37, 38, 86; in Lord
Holland's rising (1648) 1; illnesses
111; death 112

Mordaunt, Henry, Captain, second
son of third Earl of Peterborough,
birth 8; naval career 144, 273,
274, 284; loss of the Resolution
285, 311; his wound 285, 286,
288, 311; and his father's estate
308; and his parents 309; his death
311; Member of Parliament for
Malmesbury 311

Mordaunt, Henry, third son of John
Viscount Mordaunt 4; King's
Scholar at Westminster School 4;
Member of Parliament for
Brackley 79, 90; and foreign
commanders of British troops 79;
Captain in Lumley's regiment 82,
83; Colonel of Monmouth's
regiment 83; Treasurer of the
Ordnance 122; Deputy Lord
Lieutenant of Northamptonshire
128; his children 419n.

Mordaunt, John, Colonel, later
General Sir John 415, 419, 419n.,
423

Mordaunt, John, first Earl of
Peterborough 1, 112

Mordaunt, John, later Viscount
Mordaunt, in touch with Ormond
and recruiting forces (1658) 1;
marriage to Elizabeth Carey (May
1657) 2; trial for treason and
acquittal 2– 3; escaped to France
(1659) 3; links with City of
London 3, 44; appointed Governor
of Windsor Castle 4; appointed
Lord Lieutenant of Surrey 4; death

crown to William and Mary 34; and the War in Spain 226; of Great Britain 301

Quakers 93

the Spanish West Indies 134; in the
West Indies 142; Portuguese 145;
in Second Methuen Treaty 146
traders, free 117
Traguera 208, 210, 212
Treasons Act 97
Treasury Board 35, 41, 44, 48, 77;
raising loans for public funding
44–5
Trelawney, Charles, Colonel 39
Trenchard, Sir John, Secretary of
State 80, 85, 88
Trevelyan, George M. 178
Trevor, Thomas later Sir, 78, 312,
362n.
Trials for Treasons Bill, *see* Bills
Triennial Parliaments Act 81, 83, 84,
87, 88, 89, 118, 360
Triple Alliance, the 360, 368, 377
Trumbull, Sir William, Secretary of
State 95, 98, 102, 112
T'Serclaes Tilly, Albert-Octave,
Prince de 210
Turin 277, 279, 285, 286, 287, 288,
289, 313, 322, 324, 325, 328, 333,
335, 336, 337, 338, 339, 341, 342,
344, 354, 361, 362, 365, 368, 383;
siege of 194, 200, 259, 260, 261,
273, 274, 275, 300; the Venaria
324, 327; Governor of 365
Turks 166
Turvey, Beds, 112n., 311, 423; Old
Hall 119; Parish Church 423n.
Tuscany 127, 377, 395; Tuscan
presidii 118; Grand Duke of, *see*
Cosimo III
Twickenham 384, 391, 395
Tyrol, mountains of 344

Uhlfeldt, Count 163, 244
uniforms 201
Union between England and Scotland
125, 126, 131, 347, 374–5
United Provinces 131, 134

Universal Magazine, The 386
Urbino 365
Urgel 194
Ursins, Anne Marie de la Trémoîlle-
Noirmoutier, Princesse des 377
Utrecht 320, 335, 336, 337; Peace
negotiations 336, 342, 343, 344,
357; Peace or Treaty of 345, 346,
348, 353, 360, 373

Val de Robres 223
Valencia 164, 166, 169, 170, 171,
173, 180, 201, 203, 206, 208, 219,
210, 214, 227, 228, 232, 234, 236,
245, 246, 251, 252, 253, 256, 258,
261, 276, 281, 282, 285, 286, 299,
300, 302; Viceroy of 204, 208,
218, 221, 223; campaign of 207,
212, 213–15, 217, 245, 302; rising
of (1693) 207
Valencia, city of 215, 216, 218, 219,
220, 221, 222, 227, 229, 230, 231,
234, 244, 245, 247, 249, 254, 255,
256, 257, 261, 262, 263, 266, 270,
271, 275, 277, 279, 281, 315;
magistrates of 208, 228–9; Jurats
of 218; Deputies of the States 221;
French merchants 222; Audiencia
223; church of San Felipe 223;
Plaza de los Domenicos 271; Plaza
de Santo Domingo 223; Convent
of Santo Domingo 262; defences of
224; the Grau 231, 248
Valencians 204, 223, 245; militia
208; writers 223, 271; regiment
229; noblemen 263
Vallivana 209, 210
Valverde 270
Vanbrugh, Sir John 407
Vanderbank, John, portrait painter
391
Vatican, The 354
Vaudois 348
Velasco, Don Francisco de, Governor

[526]

of Barcelona 167, 183, 194, 195, 196, 198, 213

Vendôme, Louis Joseph, Duc de, Marshal of France 147, 148, 195, 259, 296; his army 296

Venerie (Venaria Reale) the 324, 327, 361

Venice 333, 335, 338, 339, 361, 367, 379, 383; the Carnival 335, 356, 363, 371; republic of 348

Ventimiglia 285

Vere, Aubrey de, twentieth Earl of Oxford 25, 107, 346

Vernon, Captain 256

Vernon, James, Shrewsbury's secretary, and the incident near Chelsea College 95; on Monmouth 106, 111; and the revelations of Ulysses Brown 110, 120; Secretary of State 115; conversations with Peterborough 120–1, 121–2, 126; and Smith's second book 123; describes Peterborough 126; questioned about Second Partition Treaty 129

Vernon, Mary (Moll) née Kirke, Lady 5

Vernon, Sir Thomas 5n.

Verona 339, 362

Verrue, Comtesse de 357

Versailles 351–2, 355

Vertue, George 407

Vich 159, 165, 166, 168, 203

Victor Amadeus II, Duke of Savoy 127, 164, 168, 193, 194, 200, 253, 279, 281, 284, 288, 289, 291, 338, 356–7, 421, 421n.; his aims 146; and Second Partition Treaty 147; treaty with Emperor 147, 148, 349, 352, 353; his Alpine barrier 148, 336, 343–4, 345; and action against Toulon 155, 157–8, 159, 193, 317; orders to assist him 168, 171, 172, 173, 174, 182, 257, 259,

260, 266; correspondence with Peterborough 191, 192, 229, 230, 260; reinforcements for 253, 254, 256, 257, 258, 259, 263, 276; conversations with Peterborough 276, 277, 287, 297, 299, 301, 336, 341, 345, 365; plans for spring campaign (1707) 285, 287, 317; dispute with Emperor 313–14, 322, 323, 325, 345; and the crown of Spain 323–4, 325, 327, 341; agrees to command troops 324, 325, 327, 328; an unhappy ally 333; and peace negotiations 336, 337, 339, 341, 342–3; as King of Sicily 341, 342, 344, 345, 348, 352, 353, 361, 363, 368; marriage of his daughter 357; exchange of Sicily for Sardinia 377, 393

Victor Amadeus, Prince of Piedmont, son of preceding 324, 333, 336

Vigo bay 137, 145

Vilanova 166

Villa Carey, see Parsons Green

Villafames 218

Villafranca 251

Villanueva 218, 264

Villanueva de la Jara 275

Villar del Horno 270

Villareal 215, 216

Villars, Claude Louis Hector, Duc de, Marshal of France 296, 350, 351, 352, 355

Villatorcas, Marqués de 223

Villefranche 148, 158n., 165

Villiers, Edward, first Earl of Jersey 123, 126, 127, 326

Vinaros 208, 211, 213, 214, 216, 227, 232, 234; militia 210

Voltaire, François Marie Arouet de 355; Siècle de Louis XIV 196n.; at Parsons Green 402, 405; 'La Henriade' 402, 403; and Swift 402; L'Histoire de Jenni 402–3,